The International Critical Commentary

A CRITICAL AND EXEGETICAL COMMENTARY

ON

THE REVELATION OF ST. JOHN

BY

R. H. CHARLES, D.Litt., D.D.

VOLUME II

ISBN: 9781314304251

Published by:
HardPress Publishing
8345 NW 66TH ST #2561
MIAMI FL 33166-2626

Email: info@hardpress.net
Web: http://www.hardpress.net

A CRITICAL AND EXEGETICAL COMMENTARY

ON

THE REVELATION OF ST. JOHN

WITH INTRODUCTION, NOTES, AND INDICES

ALSO

THE GREEK TEXT AND ENGLISH TRANSLATION

BY

R. H. CHARLES, D.Litt., D.D.
ARCHDEACON OF WESTMINSTER
FELLOW OF THE BRITISH ACADEMY

(IN TWO VOLUMES)

VOL. II

EDINBURGH
T. & T. CLARK, 38 GEORGE STREET

PRINTED BY
MORRISON AND GIBB LIMITED
FOR
T. & T. CLARK, EDINBURGH
NEW YORK: CHARLES SCRIBNER'S SONS

FIRST EDITION 1920
Reprinted 1959

CONTENTS.

VOLUME II.

ADDENDA ET CORRIGENDA.

VOLUME II.

Page 10, line 1. See Abbott, *Notes on N.T. Criticism*, p. 104, for passages in Origen and Clement of Alex. in which παρθένοι are applied to men, and in Ignatius (*Smyrn.* 13) to widows. But nothing that he says can explain the application of οἳ μετὰ γυναικῶν οὐκ ἐμολύνθησαν to women.

Page 27, line 9. *For* "Only the faithful . . . fifth seal" *read* "The faithful suffer physical martyrdom, but their prayers become an instrument of wrath in the hands of God." See vol. ii. 403, note 2.

Page 49, line 7 *ab imo*. Transpose the subject-matter of the fifth and sixth beatitudes. See vol. ii. 445, note 1.

Page 72, line 3 *ab imo*. *Delete* "Again we should expect καθίζει . . . iii. 21." Our author only uses the participle of καθῆσθαι, but his sources (xvii. 9, 15, xviii. 7) use the pres. ind. In the LXX the pres. and imperf. forms of καθίζω have disappeared, their place being taken by κάθημαι, ἐκαθήμην. See Thackeray, *Gram.* 271 sq.

Page 75, line 8. *After* "first" *add* "either in Dan. iv. 34 (LXX), θεὸς τ. θεῶν καὶ κύριος τ. κυρίων καὶ βασιλεὺς τ. βασιλέων, or (rather in the pre-Maccabean section of 1 Enoch—see my second edition, p. lii sq.)."

Page 90, lines 25–27. *Delete* "κάθημαι . . . iii. 21; and." See note above on p. 72, l. 3.

Page 168. On the twelve precious stones see British Museum *Guide to . . . Minerals mentioned in the Bible*, 1911.

Page 203, line 4 *ab imo*. The line "[καὶ λέγει . . . εἰσιν] should *not* be bracketed, but read immediately before xxi. 6^b–8. See vol. ii. 379, 444, where it is restored to its right place.

Page 219, line 3 *ab imo.* *After* "world" *add* "of the living." Christ judges the living: God Himself judges the dead according to our author's view.

Page 234, line 18. *Add* "Where no reading of Tyc is quoted, Tyc agrees with vg."

Page 234, line 20. *Add* "From 20^1 to 21^5 (nova facio omnia) Pr in his comm. has copied verbatim the work of Augustine (*de Civ. Dei,* xx. 7–17), retaining Augustine's Italian text. In the *App. Crit.* these verses are quoted without any mark of distinction.

Page 240, ver. 11, line 2. *After* 2020: *add* *ηχουσησ* 181:

" " " 11, " 11. *For* post Θυατειρ. pon *read* tr after Θυατειρ. Similarly elsewhere.

Page 256, ver. 7, line 30. *Delete* (+*και ουδεισ ανοιξει* Or^8), and Or^8 in next line. Or^8 conflates A 025 and 046 here. See vol. i. p. clxxvi.

Page 279, ver. 2, lines 5, 8, 9. *Delete* et $ℵ^c$. Similarly elsewhere.

Page 288, ver. 12, line 11. *Delete* Or^8. Or^8 conflates 046 al and Aℵ 025: and reads *και το τριτον αυτησ μη φανη ημερα* (so 046 al) *και η ημερα μη φανη το τριτον* (*τεταρτον* A) *αυτησ* (so Aℵ 025).

THE REVELATION
OF ST. JOHN.

CHAPTER XIV.

Introduction.

§ 1. *Character and Object of this Chapter.*

The entire chapter is *proleptic* in character. That is, the orderly development of future events as set forth in the successive visions is here, as in two sections heretofore, abandoned, and all the coming judgments from xvi. 17 to xx. 7–10, are summarized in xiv. 6–11, 14, 18–20. To this summary is prefixed a short description of the blessed (who are identical with the 144,000 in vii. 4–8) in the Millennial Kingdom established on the earth with Mount Zion as its centre, xiv. 1–5. Thus we have in this chapter a general introduction to xvi. 17–xx. 1–10. It is therefore of the nature of an *intermezzo.*

The object of xiv. is to encourage the faithful to endurance in the face of impending universal martyrdom. Hence in xiv. 1–5 the veil is lifted for a moment from the future and to the Seer is disclosed a vision of the martyrs enjoying the blessedness of the Millennial Kingdom on Mount Zion in attendance on their Lord. We have here a later stage of their blessedness than that depicted in vii. 9–17, where the martyrs are represented as having arrived or arriving in heaven straight from the scene of martyrdom. See Chapter vii., Introduction, § 10.

But the faithful are further encouraged to endurance and loyalty by the proclamation of the doom of the proud antichristian power, xiv. 8–11, and of all the heathen powers whether confederate with it or not, xiv. 14, 18–20.

This chapter[1] thus contains three visions, which are all proleptic.

[1] xiv. 12–13 belong to xiii., and are read immediately after xiii. 18 in this edition. They are from the hand of our author.

1. xiv. 1–5. Vision of the glorified martyrs with the Lamb on Mount Zion during the Millennial reign. Cf. xx. 4. The greater part of xiv. 4–5 is interpolated.

2. xiv. 6–11. Vision of the judgment on the antichristian Roman Empire and its adherents and their everlasting torment. Cf. xvi. 17–xviii.

3. xiv. 14, 18–20. Vision of the judgment executed by the Son of Man on the heathen nations. Cf. xix. 11–21 and xx. 7–10(?). The paragraph xiv. 15–17 is an interpolation. See pp. 19–21.

§ 2. *This chapter, with the exception of certain interpolations* (cf. xiv. 4–5, 15–17), *is from the hand of our author;* for (1) the order of the words is Hebraic: (2) the diction and style are decidedly his.

The first question needs no discussion: the fact is so obvious. Hence we shall limit our consideration to (2).

(2) The diction is that of our author except in xiv. 15–17, which in the first place is a doublet of xiv. 14, 18–20 and in the next exhibits three constructions, which are against the usage of our author (see notes on *τῷ καθημένῳ ἐπὶ τῆς νεφέλης* in xiv. 15, *ὁ καθήμενος ἐπὶ τῆς νεφέλης* and *ἔβαλεν . . . ἐπὶ τὴν γῆν* in xiv. 16). Of xiv. 3^{c}–5 only *οἱ ἠγορασμένοι ἀπὸ τῶν ἀνθρώπων ἀπαρχὴ τῷ θεῷ· ἄμωμοί εἰσιν* seems to be original. The interpolations in those verses are, however, in the style of our author, except, perhaps, *ὅπου ἂν ὑπάγει* in xiv. 4, but the thought conveyed is wholly against the context.

I will now enumerate some of the phrases characteristic of our author, though not, except in a few cases, peculiar to him.

1. καὶ εἶδον καὶ ἰδού. See iv. 1, note. γεγραμμένον ἐπὶ τῶν μετώπων αὐτῶν. See vii. 3, note. **2.** φωνὴν ἐκ τοῦ οὐρανοῦ, x. 4, 8, xi. 12, xiv. 13. ὡς φωνὴν ὑδάτων πολλῶν; cf. i. 15, xix. 6. φωνὴν κιθαρῳδῶν. Cf. xviii. 22. **2–3.** In καθαριζόντων . . . καὶ ᾄδουσιν we have the familiar Hebrew idiom reproduced already in i. 5–6, ii. 2, 9, etc. (see note *in loc.*). ᾄδουσιν ὡς ᾠδὴν καινήν; cf. v. 9. ἐνώπιον τοῦ θρόνου; cf. iv. 5, 6, etc. **4.** The use of *ἀπαρχὴ* = "sacrifice," though not found elsewhere in our author, is in keeping with his frequent use of Greek words in the same sense as in the LXX. **5.** The asyndetic addition of the clause *ἄμωμοί εἰσιν* (cf. xvi. 6) **6.** πετόμενον ἐν μεσουρανήματι. Already in viii. 13. With εὐαγγελίσαι ἐπὶ τοὺς κατοικοῦντας (A., καθημένους, ℵCPQ); cf. x. 7. The enumeration πᾶν ἔθνος καὶ φυλὴν κτλ. (see note on v. 9) and the grammatical irregularity λέγων in 7 instead of *λέγοντα* are both characteristic of his style. **7.** λέγων ἐν φωνῇ μεγάλῃ. Cf. xiv. 9. ἐν is used also before *φωνῇ μεγ.* after *κηρύσσειν* (v. 2), but after *κράζειν* only in passages from another hand (xiv. 15, xviii. 2). On the other hand it is absent after λέγειν in this phrase (v. 12, viii. 13), after *κράζειν* (vi. 10, vii. 2, 10, x. 3), after *φωνεῖν* (xiv. 18). Hence our author varies in his use of this phrase in connection with *λέγειν*. See note on x. 2. **φοβήθητε τὸν θεόν.** So xv. 4, xix. 5 (cf. xi 18, *φοβουμένους τὸ ὄνομά σου*). **δότε αὐτῷ δόξαν.** Cf. xvi. 9, xix. 7—also in the incorporated source, xi. 13. **ἦλθεν ἡ ὥρα τῆς κρίσεως.** Cf. similar phrases: vi. 17, *ἦλθεν ἡ ἡμέρα . . . τῆς ὀργῆς αὐτῶν*; xi. 18, *ἦλθεν . . . ὁ καιρὸς τῶν νεκρῶν κριθῆναι*; xviii. 10, *ἦλθεν ἡ κρίσις σου*: also in interpolated section, xiv. 15. **προσκυνήσατε**, c. dat. of God: cf. iv. 10, vii. 11, note, xi. 16, xix. 10, xxii. 9, whereas it takes the acc. of *τὸ θηρίον* in 9—in both respects exhibiting our author's usage. **πηγὰς ὑδάτων**: cf. viii. 10, xvi. 4.

8. **οἴνου τοῦ θυμοῦ τῆς πορνείας.** So xviii. 3. See note *in loc.* **9.** **προσκυνεῖ τὸ θηρίον.** See note on 7. **λαμβάνει χάραγμα.** Cf. xiv. 11, xix. 20, xx. 4. But we should probably read *τὸ χάραγμα*. See note *in loc.* **ἐπὶ τοῦ μετώπου.** We should most probably read *ἐπὶ τὸ μέτωπον*, since the context clearly comes from our author's hand. See note on vii. 3. ℵ reads the dative. **ἐπὶ τὴν χεῖρα.** Cf. xx. 1, 4. See note on xiii. 16. **10.** **καὶ αὐτὸς πίεται.** For the use of *καί* see note on xiv. 10. **βασανισθήσεται ἐν πυρὶ καὶ θείῳ.** *βασανίζω* is found four times elsewhere in our author, while *βασανισμός* (see next verse), which occurs four times, is not attested elsewhere in the N.T. With *πυρὶ καὶ θείῳ* cf. xx. 10, xxi. 8, xix. 20. **11.** **ὁ καπνὸς . . . ἀναβαίνει.** Cf. viii. 4, ix. 2, xix. 3. **οὐχ ἔχουσιν ἀνάπαυσιν κτλ.** Already in iv. 8. **οἱ προσκυνοῦντες τὸ θηρίον.** Characteristic of our author both as to grammar and diction. **12.** **ὧδε ἡ ὑπομονὴ κτλ.** Cf. xiii. 10. **τῶν ἁγίων . . . οἱ τηροῦντες τὰς ἐντολας.** For the phrase cf. xii. 17. The irregularity is characteristic of our author. **13.** **λέγει τὸ πνεῦμα.** Cf. ii. 7, etc., xxii. 17. **14.** **καὶ εἶδον καὶ ἰδού.** See iv. 1, note. **ἐπὶ τὴν νεφέλην καθήμενον.** Characteristic of our author: see note on iv. 2, and contrast the non-Johannine constructions of this phrase in 15, 16. **ὅμοιον υἱὸν ἀνθρώπου.** This unique construction is found only in our author. It has already occurred in i. 13, and, as we have seen in the Additional Note on i. 13, vol. i. p. 36, might be regarded as a further development of other linguistic constructions, to which attention is called in that note.

Interpolation—15–17. In this short section there are four constructions which are foreign to our author's use. These are given in the note on 15–17, p. 21. Other grounds for regarding 15–17 as interpolated are given in the note on 14–20, p. 18 sq.

18–20. These verses are in keeping with the diction and style of our author. They contain, it is true, several words not found elsewhere in our author *φωνεῖν, τρυγᾶν, βότρυς, ἄμπελος, ἀκμάζειν, σταφυλή, χαλινός*, but these help to delineate his subject.

18. ἐφώνησεν φωνῇ μεγάλῃ. Though *φωνεῖν* is not found elsewhere in our author the construction is always that which he uses with *κράζειν*, and in two cases out of four with λέγειν. πέμψον σου τὸ δρέπανον. The vernacular use of the pronoun here is elsewhere in our author not infrequent. **19.** ἔβαλεν . . . εἰς τὴν γῆν. See note *in loc.* ληνὸν τοῦ θυμοῦ τοῦ θεοῦ. Cf. xix. 15. ἐπατήθη ὁ ληνός. Cf. xix. 15. ἄχρι τῶν χαλινῶν. *ἄχρι* occurs six times in our author as a preposition and five times as a conjunction, but not once in the other Johannine writings in the N.T.

§ 3. *Interpolated passages*, 3^c–4^c (*ἀπὸ τῆς γῆς . . . ἠγοράσθησαν*), 4^c, *καὶ τῷ ἀρνίῳ*, and probably 5, *καὶ ἐν τῷ στόματι αὐτῶν οὐχ εὑρέθη ψεῦδος*. See the grounds for this conclusion *in loc.* 15–17. That these verses are an intrusion is manifest on many grounds. See the general grounds in the note on 14–20, p. 18 sq., and the grammatical grounds in the note on 15–17, p. 21.

XIV. 1–5. A proleptic vision of the 144,000 with the Lamb on Mount Zion—*i.e.* of the risen martyrs with Christ during the Millennial reign. That these are the same as the 144,000 in vii. 4–8, *i.e.* the spiritual Israel, the entire Christian community, alike Jewish and Gentile, which were sealed to protect them from the demonic woes, that are to follow speedily, we hope to prove in the course of our criticism of verses 1–5 (see also vol. i. p. 199 sqq.). In vii. 9–17 this same body of the faithful is represented as arriving in heaven during the great final tribulation, or as already assembled there at its close. Here they are represented as having at a later stage come down to earth for the Millennial reign (cf. xx. 4). The vision is therefore proleptic. There is a progressive note in each vision.

1. καὶ εἶδον καὶ ἰδού. See note in iv. 1.

τὸ ἀρνίον. The Lamb is here set over against the Beast in xiii., and the followers of the Lamb with His name and that of His Father over against the followers of the Beast with his mark on their forehead.

From O.T. times Mount Zion was associated in the minds of the faithful with divine deliverance. Thus Joel ii. 32 (iii. 5) writes: "And it shall come to pass, that whosoever shall call on the name of the Lord shall be delivered; for in Mount Zion and Jerusalem shall be those that escape, as the Lord hath said." In the 8th cent. B.C. there existed for a time the belief that Jerusalem could not be destroyed. In later times it was held that a special blessing attached to residence in Palestine. It alone was to escape the woes that would befall the rest of the earth: cf. 2 Bar. xxix. 2 (where see my note), xl. 2, lxxi. 1; 4 Ezra xiii. 48, 49, vi. 25. This idea was revived in Talmudic literature.

This appearance of the Messiah with a mighty multitude on

Mount Zion was a Jewish expectation, as we see in 4 Ezra xiii. 35, 39, 40, "But he shall stand upon the summit of Mount Zion. . . . And whereas thou didst see that he summoned and gathered to himself another multitude which was peaceable, these are the ten tribes." In 4 Ezra ii. 42 (Christian or Christian recast of Jewish material) we have a close parallel to our text: "I Esdras saw upon *Mount Zion a great multitude which I could not* (*dst. c*, 'no man could') *number, and they all praised the Lord with songs.* 43. *And in the midst of them there was a young man of high stature*, taller than all the rest, and upon every one of their heads he set crowns . . . 44. So I asked the angel and said: Who are these, my Lord? 45. He answered and said unto me: *These be they that have put off the mortal clothing and put on the immortal*, and have confessed the name of God."

This last work was probably written about 200–250 A.D., and therefore forms an early testimony to the right interpretation of the 144,000 on Mount Zion in our text; for it appears to identify the multitude described in vii. 9–17 and that in our text. In accordance with vii. 9–17 the writer of 4 Ezra ii. 42–47 represents them as having confessed and stood out stoutly for the name of God, and so as now clad in the garments of immortality, and in accordance with xiv. 1–5 of our text they stand on Mount Zion with the Messiah.

ἑκατον τεσσεράκοντα κτλ. The answer to the question as to the identity of the 144,000 that accompany the Lamb has in part been given in the Introduction to Chap. vii. where we have found them to be the same as the 144,000 in vii. 4–8 and the great multitude in vii. 9–17. But, though the constituents of the multitude are the same, the circumstances are different. In the vision before us the scene is upon earth (cf. ver. 2). The blessed faithful follow the Lamb on Mount Zion. And yet they have already passed through the gates of death, and have been presented as an offering (ἀπαρχή) to God (xiv. 4). Hence we have here a momentary vision of the saints, who have returned to earth to share in the Millennial reign. (Cf. xx. 4–6.)

But the above identification of the 144,000 in vii. 4–8 and xiv. 1–5 is apparently rejected by every modern scholar, save Alford, who has clung fast to it, although unable to surmount the chief difficulty that stands in its way. A minor difficulty, *i.e.* the absence of the defining article to identify these 144,000 with those spoken of in vii. 4, he treats as negligible on the ground that the reader was meant to identify the two hosts, seeing that they consist of the same number and are both marked on the forehead as God's own possession.

Alford may be right in ignoring the absence of the article (cf. xv. 2, where the expected article is missing, ὡς θάλασσαν instead of τὴν θάλασσαν, and xiv. 9, where τό is wanting before χάραγμα), but the present writer is of opinion that the real explanation is that it was excised by the interpolator of the introductory sentences in xiv. 4–5, who sought by his manipulation of the text to destroy the identity of the 144,000 in vii. 4–8 and the 144,000 in the present passage, and to transform them into a body of monkish celibates. Having thus explained the absence of the article, there is another and greater difficulty, which stands in the way of this identification, and this is that the 144,000 are described as "first-fruits" to God and to the Lamb. If these 144,000, as the present writer holds, are identical with the entire body of Christians living in the last days, who have been sealed with a view to their protection against the demonic woes, how is it that they are designated as "first fruits"? It is the interpretation set on this word ἀπαρχή by all scholars in the past that has misled them into differentiating the 144,000 in vii. 4–8 and in xiv. 1–5. This word has hitherto been taken universally to mean "first fruits" in this passage. That in the Pauline Epistles and in St. James it bears this meaning is indubitable. But this is by no means the case in the LXX, although Grimm's Lexicon and Thayer's enlarged edition of Grimm state that ἀπαρχή is generally the equivalent of ראשית. So far is this from being the case that it is generally *not* the equivalent of this word. Thus whereas ἀπαρχή occurs about 66 times in the LXX, it is a rendering of ראשית only 19 times. In the remaining 47 times, it is once a rendering for the Hebrew word for "tithe," 4 times of חלב (= "fat," in which case it means "the best of"), and 40 times a rendering of תרומה (= "offering" or "oblation"), and once of תנופה (= "offering"). Thus we see that in the LXX oftener than twice out of three times it means "an offering." In Sirach it occurs four times, but only once with the meaning of "first fruits," while in the other three passages it signifies either an "offering" or "gift." Hesychius also notes that one of its Greek meanings is προσφορά. It is clear, then, that in the Greek Bible of Judaism ἀπαρχή meant "offering," "sacrifice," or "gift" nearly 3 times out of 4.[1] Now

[1] The above note was written before the publication of Moulton and Milligan's *Vocabulary of the Greek Testament*. Though these editors have not corrected the misstatements in Grimm's and Thayer's lexicons, to which they give their *imprimatur* in their preface, they have shown from the Magnesian inscriptions (ed. Kern. 1900), that ἀπαρχή is very commonly used as = a "gift" to a deity, and that this use occurred as early as the 6th cent. B.C. in Athens (*Syll. Inscr. Graec.*², Dittenberger, 1898–1901). They conclude that in the N.T. "we are perhaps at liberty to render 'sacrifice' or 'gift' where it improves the sense," though they do not specify any individual passage save Rom. viii. 23. The Magnesia above referred to was in the neighbourhood of Ephesus. Hence the local and κοινή use of ἀπαρχή confirms the conclusions arrived at above.

it is just this meaning that our text requires. The faithful, whether as martyrs or confessors, are sacrifices to God. As such they are offered on the heavenly altar, vi. 9. A further sacrificial reference is discoverable in the epithet in xiv. 5, where they are said to be *ἄμωμοι*, that is, "unblemished," sacrificially perfect.

ἔχουσαι τὸ ὄνομα αὐτοῦ καὶ τὸ ὄνομα τοῦ πατρὸς αὐτοῦ κτλ. With this clause we might compare iii. 12, where a threefold inscription on the foreheads of the faithful is mentioned. But, if we compare xxii. 4, where the name is simply said to be that of God, and 4 of the present chapter, where *καὶ τῷ ἀρνίῳ* appears to be an interpolation, it is possible that *αὐτοῦ καὶ τὸ ὄνομα* is also an interpolation. The seal consists in the name of God inscribed on the brow. This inscription declares that the person so inscribed is God's own possession: it is at the same time evidence that his character is such as befits a servant of God.

2. φωνὴν ἐκ τοῦ οὐρανοῦ κτλ. The singers are the angel choirs in heaven and not the 144,000 in Mt. Zion, but the new song is intelligible to the 144,000 and to them alone owing to their fellowship with Christ.

Most of the phrases of this verse occur elsewhere in our author, see p. 2.

κιθαρῳδῶν κιθαριζόντων . . . 3. καὶ ᾄδουσιν. These words should be rendered: "harpers harping . . . and singing." It is another instance of the literal reproduction in Greek of a familiar Hebrew idiom, which we have found already in i. 5–6, ii. 2, 9, 20, vii. 14, xv. 3. Thus the style is very characteristic of our author. Here the new song is at first sung not by the redeemed (as in xv. 3; 4 Ezra ii. 42), but by angelic choirs before the throne.

3. καὶ ᾄδουσιν = *καὶ ᾀδόντων*. See preceding note.

ὡς ᾠδὴν καινήν. See note on v. 9.

ἐνώπιον τοῦ θρόνου. See Introd. to Chap. xiv. § 2.

οὐδεὶς ἐδύνατο κτλ. Only those who are redeemed from the earth can learn the song: for the soul apprehends only that for which it has an affinity. Their spiritual experience won through travail and tears is the mother of understanding. The song is the expression of the inner life, and so in the measure of their spiritual growth is likewise the measure of their spiritual apprehension.

οἱ ἠγορασμένοι ἀπὸ τῆς γῆς. The diction and thought here have already occurred in v. 9, 10. That passage is of supreme importance in dealing with the text immediately before us. Now the leading thought in v. 9, 10 is that the faithful are bought by Christ for God, and consecrated to His service as kings and priests. Here also, whether we retain or omit the disturbing clauses *ἀπὸ τῆς γῆς· οὗτοί εἰσιν οἳ . . . ἠγοράσθησαν*, the idea is of a like nature. The 144,000 have been bought to be an offering or sacrifice (ἀπαρχή, xiv. 4: see note on 1) unto God: cf. vi. 9.

This verse, with the exception of the words ἀπὸ τῶν ἀνθρώπων ἀπαρχὴ τῷ θεῷ or ἠγοράσθησαν ἀπὸ τῶν ἀνθρώπων ἀπαρχὴ τῷ θεῷ, seems to be a later addition due to the incorporation of a marginal explanatory gloss. In support of the aorist we might adduce our author's usage elsewhere: see v. 9, ἠγόρασας τῷ θεῷ . . . ἐκ πάσης φυλῆς κτλ. If, on the other hand, we adopt the former view, then in οἱ ἠγορασμένοι . . . καὶ . . . οὐχ εὑρέθη we have, if the latter clause is original, another instance of our author's reproduction in Greek of a Hebrew idiom: see ii. 2, 9, 20, vii. 14, xiv. 2–3. This combination of the perfect and aorist is found often in our author: cf. ii. 3, 5, iii. 2, 3, 17, xvi. 6. That καὶ τῷ ἀρνίῳ is an addition appears to be clear from the fact that the 144,000 have been bought by the Son for the Father; and not by the Son for the Father and for Himself: cf. v. 9. The Church is the *bride* of the Lamb: cf. xix. 7, 8; Eph. v. 27, not an *offering* presented to Him. If the above clauses are interpolated, the original of 3^c–4 may have run as follows: οἱ ἠγορασμένοι ἀπὸ τῶν ἀνθρώπων ἀπαρχὴ τῷ θεῷ. We shall now deal with the clauses, which for the time being we have assumed to be interpolations.

But let us waive for the moment the question of the authenticity of these clauses and study them in themselves and with regard to their immediate context. Now, first of all, it is admitted, so far as I am aware, on all hands that *the 144,000*, whether identical with the 144,000 in vii. 4–8, or representing the élite of the saints composed of Christian ascetics (Bousset, Moffatt), *must embrace both men and women.* That παρθένοι can be used of men is of course acknowledged. So far all is clear. But when we start from these premises and try to explain οὗτοί εἰσιν οἳ μετὰ γυναικῶν οὐκ ἐμολύνθησαν we are plunged into hopeless difficulties. For, if we take these words literally, it is obvious that *they cannot be used of women. Nor indeed can they be applied to women in any intelligible sense, whatever the metaphorical meaning may be that we attach to the words.* Had the writer wished, he could easily have found a phrase applicable literally and metaphorically alike to men and women, such as οἳ ἐν τῇ πορνείᾳ οὐκ ἐμολύνθησαν. πορνεία is used metaphorically in xiv. 8, xvii. 2, 4, xviii. 3, xix. 2, and πορνεύω in xvii. 2, xviii. 3, 9 in the sense of idolatrous worship. Such a clause could be used both of men and women, in a literal or metaphorical sense, and the same idea could have been expressed in other ways. Hence we conclude either that men alone are referred to in the text, or that this passage is interpolated. Since we cannot accept the former alternative, we are forced to adopt the latter, and the task devolves upon us to settle, so far as we may, the ground of the interpolation, its extent and meaning.

Now the chief *ground* for this interpolation is most naturally to be discovered in the misunderstanding of the word ἀπαρχή as "first fruits." The monkish interpolator, convinced that the highest type of the Christian life was the celibate, naturally identified the 144,000, who form the "first fruits" (or best portion of the Christian Church), with the celibates. The superiority of the celibate life, though un-Jewish and un-Christian, was early adopted from the Gnostics and other Christian heretics. Thus Saturninus and Basilides declared that "marriage and generation are from Satan" (Iren. *Adv. Haer.* i. 24), while Tatian (Eus. *H.E.* IV. xxix. 3) pronounced marriage to be "corruption and fornication." Marcion (Hipp. *Phil.* vii. 17–19) established churches of celibates, while the Encratites claimed a self-restraint in advance of that of the Christians. Similarly the religions of Isis and Mithra had their celibates throughout the Roman Empire, as Buddhism in the far East, certain orders of the Aztec priesthood in Mexico, the Vestal Virgins in Rome, and the "Virgins of the Sun" in Peru. The pressure of such ideas *from without* early made itself felt, not in the N.T. but in early Christianity, as we see from Polycarp, *Ad Phil.* ii. iv. v.; Hermas, *Vis.* ii. 2, 3, *Sim.* ix. 11 (see Hastings, *Encyc. of Ethics and Religion*, iii. 271–273, from which the above facts are drawn). The interpolation was probably made by John's editor.

It is, of course, possible that the interpolated passage appeared first as a marginal gloss on the passage, and that it was subsequently incorporated into the text with a necessary change or two.

As regards the *extent*, it appears to begin with ἀπὸ τῆς γῆς and end with ἠγοράσθησαν. The repetition of the ἀγοράζω with two different adverbial phrases is remarkable. That ἀπὸ τῶν ἀνθρώπων is to be preferred to ἀπὸ τῆς γῆς seems clear from v. 9, where we have ἠγόρασας . . . ἐκ πάσης φυλῆς.

The *meaning* of the interpolation we have already gathered from the foregoing criticism of the passage. The glosser or interpolator, as the case may be, took the passage to refer to celibates, and, as the peculiar clause (οἳ μετὰ γυναικῶν οὐκ ἐμολύνθησαν) proves, made it refer to male celibates. They were the "first fruits" of the entire Christian Church (for such, of course, he conceived the meaning of ἀπαρχή).

This word as used by the interpolator carries with it the degradation of marriage—an idea inadmissible in the N.T. The use of the aorist here shows that their life on earth regarded as a discipline belongs to the past.

4. παρθένοι. The word *παρθένος* was applied to men also: cf. *Life of Asenath*, 3. *ἐστὶν δὲ οὗτος ὁ Ἰωσὴφ ἀνὴρ θεοσεβὴς . . . καὶ παρθένος.* 6. *διότι καὶ αὐτὸς παρθένος.* In Suidas it is applied to Abel: *Ἀβὲλ οὗτος παρθένος καὶ δίκαιος ὑπῆρχε.* Cf. also Epiph. i. 385 C. *παρθενεύω* is used of males in Just. *Frag.* 1577 A.

οὗτοι οἱ ἀκολουθοῦντες κτλ. These words can hardly fail to be an echo of our Lord's: cf. Mk. ii. 14, x. 21; Luke ix. 59; John i. 43, xxi. 19. For another echo cf. 1 Pet. ii. 21, *ἵνα ἐπακολουθήσητε τοῖς ἴχνεσιν αὐτοῦ.* In vii. 17 it is said that the Lamb will be the shepherd of the blessed described in vii. 14–15. This means according to oriental conceptions that the blessed follow Him. Thus to follow Christ is characteristic of the faithful, whether on earth, on which they were called to follow Him even unto death (Matt. x. 38, xvi. 24, 25), or in the Millennial kingdom, or in heaven. But it would be possible to take *ἀκολουθοῦντες* as referring to the past, and the subsequent words as implying that in such following of the Lamb they underwent martyrdom. Cf. vii. 14, xii. 11. But the context does not favour this interpretation. **ὅπου ἂν ὑπάγει.** *ὅπου* elsewhere in the Apocalypse means "where," but with verbs of motion it was used as the equivalent of *ὅποι*. Cf. John viii. 21, 22, xiii. 33, 36. The *ἂν* in this connection is impossible in classical Greek. In viii. 1 we have *ὅταν ἤνοιξεν*, and in Mk. vi. 56 *ἂν* occurs after *ὅπου* with the past imperfect indicative. The construction seems to imply an action of indefinite frequency: cf. Robertson, *Gram.* 958.

ἀπὸ τῶν ἀνθρώπων. This phrase summarizes the full enumeration given in v. 9. **ἀπαρχή** = "sacrifice" or "offering." See note on 1. [**καὶ τῷ ἀρνίῳ.**] An addition. See note on 4.

5. καὶ ἐν τῷ στόματι αὐτῶν οὐχ εὑρέθη ψεῦδος. This clause recalls most nearly Zeph. iii. 13, *καὶ οὐ μὴ εὑρεθῇ ἐν τῷ στόματι αὐτῶν γλῶσσα δολία*, and Isa. liii. 9. In 1 Pet. ii. 22 we have the latter reproduced: *οὐδὲ εὑρέθη δόλος ἐν τῷ στόματι αὐτοῦ.* Cf. John i. 47. It must, however, be confessed that this clause follows weakly after *οἱ ἠγορασμένοι . . . ἀπαρχὴ τῷ θεῷ.*

ἄμωμοί εἰσιν. This sentence introduced asyndetically is in the style of our author: cf. xvi. 6. *ἄμωμος* [= תמים] describes best the character of the *ἀπαρχή*; in the LXX it has three times out of four a sacrificial reference, and affirms the flawlessness of the victim. It is that which is unblemished, sacrificially perfect. In 1 Pet. i. 19 Christ Himself is described as *ἀμνοῦ ἀμώμου*, and in Heb. ix. 14 as offering Himself as an unblemished sacrifice unto God (*ἑαυτὸν προσήνεγκεν ἄμωμον τῷ θεῷ*). In the present context the 144,000 who had been offered in sacrifice to God (*ἀπαρχὴ τῷ θεῷ*) are likewise described as *ἄμωμοι*. In the five other passages, where it occurs in the Pauline Epistles and Jude, the clause has an ethical meaning and connotes "blamelessness."

Note on xiv. 1–5.—This section has been an occasion of great difficulty to scholars. I have sought to show that much of this difficulty arose from misconception of the word ἀπαρχή. But, as we have seen, there are other difficulties, which cannot be got rid of save by the excision of certain clauses. Völter (iv. 38 sq., 139 sq.) excises xiv. 4–5 and a phrase in xiv. 1, and then identifies the 144,000 here with the 144,000 in vii. 4–8. Weyland excises xiv. 1, 4–5, Erbes xiv. 4^{ab}, and a phrase in 4^{d}. Spitta is the most drastic of all. He changes τὸ ὄνομα . . . πατρὸς αὐτοῦ into τὸ ὄνομα τοῦ θεοῦ ζῶντος: excises 2^{c}–3 and reduces 4–5 to the following form: οὗτοι ἠγοράσθησαν ἀπὸ τῶν ἀνθρώπων ἀπαρχὴ τῷ θεῷ. (See pp. 144 sq., 147 sq., 536.) Wellhausen recognizes the fact that the text shows undoubted signs of interpolation. Bousset admits the possibility of a source underlying xiv. 1–5, but he thinks it impossible to recover it. He therefore takes the text as it stands and interprets the 144,000 to be a body of Christian ascetics and, therefore, different from the 144,000 in vii. 4–8. He thinks, however, that there are signs in the Apocalypse that these two bodies were originally identical.

In the above study of xiv. 1–5 I have attempted to show that xiv. 1–3 comes from the hand of our author (see also Introd. p. 2) save probably one phrase (τὸ ὄνομα αὐτοῦ καί) in xiv. 1. As regards xiv. 4–5 the case is different. Here the diction is not much of a guide to us, but the ideas and the irregularity of the order of the sentences are. Thus of the various descriptions of the 144,000 in 4–5 it is clear from the earlier chapters that the essential one is, without doubt, that which describes them as a sacrifice to God.

At the close of 5 this idea recurs in the words, ἄμωμοί εἰσιν, but a purely ethical description intervenes—καὶ ἐν τῷ στόματι . . . ψεῦδος. This appears irregular, but greater difficulties have already emerged in connection with 4^{a}, where the un-Jewish and un-Christian idea is presented, that the very élite of the blessed consists of ascetics, and that, too, male ascetics. On these and other grounds we have excised certain clauses and concluded that, before the monkish glosser went to work, our author's text read as follows in xiv. 3^{c}–5, οἱ ἠγορασμένοι ἀπὸ τῶν ἀνθρώπων ἀπαρχὴ τῷ θεῷ· ἄμωμοί εἰσιν. But καὶ ἐν τῷ στόματι . . . ψεῦδος may be original. To the interpolator of the above clauses we may owe also the removal of the article before the 144,000, which identified this 144,000 with the 144,000 in vii. 4–8.

6–11. Vision of the judgment to be executed on the Roman Empire and its worshippers, in which three angels make proclamation. The first proclaimed to all men an eternal Gospel, the burden of which was that all men should worship the one God who had created heaven and earth, for that the hour of judgment had come (6–7). The second announced, as though already accomplished, the fall of Rome, which had made all the nations to drink of the wine of her fornication (8). The third proclaimed that those who submitted to the mandates of Rome would share in the everlasting torment that awaited her (9–11).

6. ἄλλον ἄγγελον. The presence of the ἄλλον occasions some difficulty. It is supported by the best textual authorities. If it is original, we might, perhaps, with Düsterdieck explain the word as used in contradistinction to the angels that had appeared in earlier scenes. He compares x. 1 where ἄλλον ἄγγελον has already been mentioned, who, as in the present instance, proclaims the impending end of the world. Erbes and J. Weiss suppose we have here a reference to viii. 13, where the phraseology is certainly similar: *ἑνὸς ἀετοῦ πετομένου ἐν μεσουρανήματι λέγοντος φωνῇ μεγάλῃ*. Bousset suggests that in ἄλλον ἄγγελον we have a dittography, and J. Weiss that it is a corruption of ἄλλον αἴετον. Cf. viii. 13. It seems best to explain ἄλλ. ἄγγ. as = "another, an angel." See note on 15 below. The difficulty recurs in 8, 9.

πετόμενον ἐν μεσουρανήματι. Cf. viii. 13, xix. 17. In the O.T. the angels are not represented with wings save in its latest books: cf. Dan. ix. 21.

εὐαγγέλιον αἰώνιον. This phrase is found here only in the Johannine writings, whereas the cognate verb occurs here and in x. 7. εὐαγγέλιον here is not to be translated as if it were τὸ εὐαγγέλιον. Its character is defined by its present context and x. 7. It is a proclamation of the impending end of the world and of the final judgment, which, while it is a message of good tidings to the faithful, constitutes for all nations a last summons to repentance.

In x. 7 it was made known to His servants the prophets, here it is proclaimed to all the world. This gospel is termed αἰώνιον because possibly our author wishes to emphasize its unchangeable validity for all eternity.

τοὺς κατοικοῦντας ἐπὶ τῆς γῆς (A and some cursives). ℵCPQ read τ. καθημένους ἐπὶ τ. γῆς. The textual evidence is here indecisive. Difficulties beset both readings. The second reading is against the normal usage of our author. We should expect ἐπὶ τ. γῆν = after the καθημένους. But ἐπὶ τ. γῆς is the universal construction in our author after κατοικεῖν. Hence if we could discover any good ground for the change of κατοικοῦντας into καθημένους, we shall have little hesitation in recognizing A as right. Now, though the scribes of ℵCPQ were occasionally doubtful as to our author's constructions after ὁ καθήμενος, τοῦ καθημένου, τῷ *καθημένῳ*, they could have had no doubt as to the meaning of the phrase *οἱ κατοικοῦντες ἐπὶ τῆς γῆς* (always so except in xiii. 12, xvii. 1, 2, where these constructions are found in sources) elsewhere in our author, *i.e.* iii. 10, vi. 10, viii. 13, etc. And since this meaning was always bad in all other passages, and since it could not bear such a meaning here, some early scribe may have been led to substitute *καθημένους* for *κατοικοῦντας* and thus give the phrase the neutral colour it required here. But, if this hypothesis of the origin of *καθημένους* is right, its presence here can only call for condemnation. It is against our author's usage wholly in this construction: indeed, according to his usage it could only mean "those who sat on the earth."[1]

If, then, we accept the reading of A, we must in this one passage attach a purely neutral or geographical sense to the phrase, such as it bears not infrequently in 1 Enoch (see xxxviii. 5, note). See note on xi. 10.

πᾶν ἔθνος καὶ φυλὴν κτλ. See note on v. 9.

λέγων. The grammatical irregularity is characteristic of our author. See iv. 1, xi. 1.

7. λέγων ἐν φωνῇ μεγάλῃ. See Introduction to this Chapter, § 2: also note on x. 2.

φοβήθητε τὸν θεὸν κτλ. This gospel is based on a purely theistic foundation. But, when the last hour has come, a man's chief concern is not dogmatic fullness or correctness of creed, but only self-humiliation before and self-surrender to the Lord of all. With this announcement we might compare the gospel as preached by our Lord in Mark i. 15, *μετανοεῖτε καὶ πιστεύετε ἐν εὐαγγελίῳ*.

But a really excellent parallel is to be found in St. Paul's speech at Lystra, Acts xiv. 15: *εὐαγγελιζόμενοι ὑμᾶς ἀπὸ τούτων τῶν ματαίων ἐπιστρέφειν ἐπὶ θεὸν ζῶντα ὃς ἐποίησεν τὸν οὐρανὸν καὶ τὴν γῆν καὶ τὴν θάλασσαν κτλ.* On the creation idea, cf. x. 6 of our text.

The clause *φοβ. τ. θεόν* is found in Eccles. xii. 13, and *δότε αὐτῷ δόξαν* in Josh. vii. 19; 1 Sam. vi. 5; Isa. xlii. 12; Jer. xiii. 16, but they both belong to our author's phraseology: see Introd. to Chap. xiv., p. 3.

ἦλθεν ἡ ὥρα τῆς κρίσεως αὐτοῦ. The diction and form of this sentence are characteristic of our author, but are of still more frequent occurrence in the Fourth Gospel. Cf. ii. 4, iv. 21, 23,

[1] *οἱ κατοικοῦντες ἐπὶ τ. γῆς* is a rendering of ישבים על הארץ, and this is the normal rendering of it in the LXX. In a few cases in the LXX of Jeremiah only do we find *οἱ καθήμενοι ἐπὶ τ. γῆς* or *τ. γῆν*: cf. xxxii. (xxv.) 29, 30. With definite localities it occurs more frequently: cf. Dan. ix. 7, where we have *καθημένοις ἐν Ἰερουσαλήμ* (LXX *κατοικοῦσιν ἐν Ἰερο.*, Theod. (A)). See note on this phrase in xiii., Introd. § 4.

v. 25, 28, vii. 30, viii. 20, xii. 23, xiii. 1, xvi. 2, 4, 21, 25, 32, xvii. 1.

προσκυνήσατε τῷ ποιήσαντι. This is the usage of our author: contrast 9 where this verb takes the acc. of *τὸ θηρίον*—also the usage of our author. See note on vii. 11.

προσκυνήσατε τῷ ποιήσαντι τὸν οὐρανὸν κτλ. Since God has created the world, man's allegiance is due to God. The fact of God as creator has already been brought forward in iv. 11, x. 6, but in both these passages *κτίζειν* and not *ποιεῖν* has been used. References to the creative activity of God are rare in the N.T. but frequent in the O.T. See note on iv. 11.

πηγὰς ὑδάτων. The absence of the article is noteworthy, contrast xvi. 4, viii. 10. The phrase is a familiar O.T. one: cf. 1 Kings xviii. 5; 2 Kings iii. 19 (מעיני מים), 25; Ex. xv. 27; Num. xxxiii. 9.

8. The second angel proclaims the fall of Rome.

ἄλλος δεύτερος ἄγγελος. So the best MSS. But we should rather expect simply *ἄγγελος δεύτερος* or *ἄλλος ἄγγ. δεύτ.*; for when our author uses another adjective in addition to *ἄλλος* it is added after the noun: cf. vi. 4, x. 1, xiv. 9, xv. 1: *i.e.* "another angel, a second one."

ἔπεσεν, ἔπεσεν Βαβυλών. These words are already found in Isa. xxi. 9. נפלה נפלה בבל, LXX, *πέπτωκεν πέπτωκεν Βαβυλών.* Cf. Jer. li. 8. But the two clauses *ἔπεσεν . . . τὰ ἔθνη* seem to be derived by our author immediately from xviii. 2–3 (a source). To *Βαβυλών* our author always attaches the epithet *ἡ μεγάλη*, an epithet which goes back to Dan. iv. 27 (בבל רבתא); cf. xvi. 19, xvii. 5, xviii. 2, 10, 21. That Babylon was already a synonym for Rome in the first century A.D. is clear from 2 Bar. xi. 1; Sibyl. Or. v. 143, 159; 1 Pet. v. 13 (?). Cf. also xvi. 19, xvii. 5, xviii. 2, 10, 21.

ἣ ἐκ τοῦ οἴνου [τοῦ θυμοῦ] τῆς πορνείας αὐτῆς πεπότικεν πάντα τὰ ἔθνη. This very extraordinary form of speech, which recurs in xviii. 3, can hardly be original. The text as it stands combines two wholly disparate ideas. The first is *ἐκ τοῦ οἴνου τῆς πορνείας αὐτῆς*—a phrase which occurs in xvii. 2—*i.e.* "the wine of her fornication," which Babylon has made all the nations to drink. This wine symbolizes the intoxicating power, the corrupting influence of Rome. The second is *ἐκ τοῦ οἴνου τοῦ θυμοῦ (τοῦ θεοῦ)*—a phrase which occurs in xiv. 10—*i.e.* "the wine of the wrath of God," which He will give Babylon to drink. This latter phrase recurs in a fuller form in xvi. 19, xix. 15, *τοῦ οἴνου τοῦ θυμοῦ τῆς ὀργῆς αὐτοῦ.* But in the O.T. it is God Himself that presents through His prophet this wine of wrath to the nations: cf. Jer. xxv. 15, which seems to have been in the mind of our author, *λάβε τὸ ποτήριον τοῦ οἴνου τοῦ ἀκράτου τούτου ἐκ χειρός μου* *καὶ ποτιεῖς πάντα τὰ ἔθνη.* In xxviii. (li.) 7 Babylon is said to be a cup in the hand of the Lord whereof the nations have drunk and become mad: *ποτήριον χρυσοῦν Βαβυλὼν ἐν χειρὶ κυρίου μεθύσκον πᾶσαν τὴν γῆν. Ἀπὸ τοῦ οἴνου αὐτῆς ἐπίοσαν ἔθνη. διὰ τοῦτο ἐσαλεύθησαν* (יִתְהֹלְלוּ).

As we study the above facts two ways of dealing with the text appear to be open to us. 1. Excise *τοῦ θυμοῦ* as an interpolation due to the occurrence of the phrase *τοῦ οἴνου τοῦ θυμοῦ* in 10. The extraordinary divergence of the MSS in xviii. 3, where the phrase recurs, points either to an interpolated or a very difficult text. 2. Since our author appears to have had Jer. xxv. 15 sq. in his mind, and since the text there has הַיַּיִן הַחֵמָה (= "the wine which is wrath," *i.e.* wine of wrath), it is possible that he took חֵמָה in the sense of "poison," which it sometimes bears (cf. Deut. xxxii. 24, 33; Ps. lviii. 5, cxl. 4). The fact that it maddens the nations (Jer. xxv. 16, li. 7; Hab. ii. 15) might be taken to favour this meaning. If this be right, then our text would mean "the wine of the poison of her fornication." But it seems best to regard *τοῦ θυμοῦ* as an interpolation. The nations, having drunk of the wine of the fornication of Babylon, have really therein drunk the wine of the wrath of God.

9. The third angel proclaims a doom of everlasting torment for adherents of the Imperial cult. This forms a counter proclamation to that in xiii. 15, 17.

ἐν φωνῇ μεγάλῃ. See note on x. 2.

προσκυνεῖ τὸ θηρίον. See note on 7.

† λαμβάνει χάραγμα †. Cf. xii. 11, xix. 20, xx. 4. On *χάραγμα*, see xiii. 16, note. The absence of the article before *χάραγμα* is suspicious. The context leads us to expect it. First it immediately follows the definite mention of the Beast (*τὸ θηρίον*), whose mark it is. Next this mark has already been twice mentioned in xiii.—in the first instance in xiii. 16, without the article because mentioned for the first time, and again in xiii. 17 with the article. Finally the angel would not speak in this indefinite way of this brand of hell. Contrast xx. 4. All mankind knew "the mark." We must suppose the angel knew so also. Hence we should read *τὸ χάραγμα* or excise *καὶ λαμβάνει . . . χεῖρα αὐτοῦ* as an interpolation.

† ἐπὶ τοῦ μετώπου †. This construction of *ἐπὶ* with *μετώπου* is against our author's usage We should expect *ἐπὶ τὸ μέτωπον*. See notes on vii. 3, xiii. 16. When we combine these two irregularities just dealt with, we are forced, it seems, to infer either that the text is corrupt or that we have in *καὶ λαμβάνει . . . χεῖρα αὐτοῦ* a marginal gloss. The closing words of 11 support the former conclusion. Hence we should probably read καὶ λαμβάνει τὸ χάραγμα ἐπὶ τὸ μέτωπον αὐτοῦ ἢ ἐπὶ τὴν χεῖρα αὐτοῦ.

10. καὶ αὐτὸς πίεται, "he too (the man who has received the mark) shall drink." To Rome herself finally this cup is given in xvi. 17. The καί introduces the apodosis as in x. 17 (iii. 20 אQ)

ἐκ τοῦ οἴνου τοῦ θυμοῦ τοῦ θεοῦ τοῦ κεκερασμένου ἀκράτου ἐν τῷ ποτηρίῳ τῆς ὀργῆς. Parallel expressions to ποτήριον τῆς ὀργῆς αὐτοῦ are found in Isa. li. 17, 22; Jer. xxv. 15, and in xviii. 6 in our text. The subject has in part been discussed under ver. 8 above. The only real difficulty lies in the words τοῦ οἴνου τοῦ θυμοῦ . . . τοῦ κεκερασμένου ἀκράτου. The source of the expression appears to be Ps. lxxv. 9, ὅτι ποτήριον ἐν χειρὶ κυρίου, οἴνου ἀκράτου πλῆρες κεράσματος. Here the Mass. has יין חמר מלא מסך for the last four words. We should also compare Jer. xxxii. 1 (xxv. 15) τὸ ποτήριον τοῦ οἴνου τοῦ ἀκράτου = כוס היין החמה הזאת. We have still another parallel in Pss. Sol. viii. 15, διὰ τοῦτο ἐκέρασεν αὐτοῖς ὁ θεὸς πνεῦμα πλανήσεως· ἐπότισεν αὐτοὺς ποτήριον οἴνου ἀκράτου εἰς μέθην. From the last passage it follows that there can be no inconsistency between ἐκέρασεν and ἀκράτου. The verb refers to the mingling of this wine with elements (as the literal wine with spices) that will not weaken it but render it noxious or poisonous, whereas the adjective (ἀκράτου) states that it is unmixed with water. For this use of ἄκρατος cf. 3 Macc. v. 2; Galen (in Wetstein): οἶνον ἄκρατον εἶναι λέγομεν, ᾧ μὴ μέμικται τὸ ὕδωρ ἢ . . . ὀλίγον μέμικται. In Ps. lxxv. 9 the same explanation of the LXX would hold good, though in that case we have to read יין חֶמֶר. In Jer. xxxii. 1 (xxv. 15) ἀκράτου therefore implies יין החמר, and not the Massoretic reading given above. On the other hand, it must be stated that modern scholars, though they accept החמר as the reading in Jer. xxv. 15, do not attribute to it the same meaning either here or in Ps. lxxv. 9 as the LXX.

From the above authorities we conclude that the passage is to be explained "the wine of the wrath of God which is mingled sheer in the cup," etc. But for the close parallels given above we might accept the proposal of Ewald, Alford and others that from the almost universal custom of mixing wine with water the common term for preparing wine came to be κεράννυμι. Thus Eustathius says on Od. v. 93 that in κέρασσε δὲ νέκταρ ἐρυθρόν the verb κέρασσε = ἐνέχει. A further suggestion may be offered. Our author, we know, was better acquainted with Hebrew than with Greek. It is possible, therefore, that judging from the LXX he took ἄκρατος to be a right rendering of חמר just as the author of Pss. Sol. xvi. 11 took ὀλιγοψυχία (which really means "faintheartedness") to be a right rendering of קצר רוח (= "impatience"), a misrendering that is also found in the LXX. If this be so, then we might assign to ἄκρατος the meaning of חמר, and render "the wine of the wrath of God which is mingled foaming in the cup." The "foaming" or "fermentation" is still going on; for God has just mingled this cup of judgment for the nations.

βασανισθήσεται ἐν πυρὶ καὶ θείῳ. The imagery goes back to the torments to be inflicted on Edom: Isa. xxxiv. 8–10. The punishment of brimstone and fire appears first in connection with Sodom and Gomorrah (Gen. xix. 24). As Anderson Scott writes *in loc.*, "it is instructive to trace the development of the symbolism springing from the circumstances of an event in history, providing the traditional features, first of any great judgment, then of the day of the Lord, and, finally, of the judgment of Christ." Our author uses this symbolism again in xix. 20, xx. 10, xxi. 8.

ἐνώπιον τῶν ἀγγέλων. The idea has occurred already in 1 Enoch xlviii. 9 in another form:

> "And I will give them over into the hands of Mine elect:
> As straw in fire, so shall they burn before the face of the holy:
> As lead in water, so shall they sink before the face of the righteous,
> And no trace of them shall any more be found."

In 1 Enoch xxvii. 2, 3, xc. 26, 27, 4 Ezra vii. 36, as in the passage before us, the sufferings of the wicked form an ever-present spectacle to the righteous; but not so in the Parables of 1 Enoch. There Gehenna and its victims form only a temporary spectacle. Then they vanish from the presence of the righteous for ever, as in the later sections of the Apocalypse. See 1 Enoch xlviii. 9, note, lxii. 12, 13. This is not due to any moralisation of the idea but to the conception of a new heaven and a new earth, which exclude the possibility of the Gehenna conception. In Luke xii. 9 the wicked are to be disowned by Christ in the presence of His angels. This idea of Gehenna as an ever-present spectacle over against Paradise arose through a mistaken etymology of the phrase דראון עולם in Isa. lxvi. 24 and Dan. xii. 2. In the 1st cent. B.C. or as early as the close of the 2nd cent. B.C. Jewish scholars regarded דראין as derived from ראה. Thus the LXX of Isa. lxvi. 24 renders this word ἔσονται εἰς ὅρασιν.

καὶ ἐνώπιον τοῦ ἀρνίου. Many critics remove this phrase as a gloss owing to the position after τῶν ἀγγέλων. If it is original it is best to render the phrase: "even before the Lamb." Bousset suggests that the phrase "before the angels" is a late Jewish periphrasis for "before God." Cf. Luke xv. 10, xii. 8, 9;

and Bousset's *Rel. des Judentums*, 308, but in the present context this is unlikely.

11. καὶ ὁ καπνὸς τοῦ βασανισμοῦ αὐτῶν . . . ἀναβαίνει. Cf. xviii. 9, xix. 3, xx. 10; Isa. xxxiv. 10, ἔσται ἡ γῆ αὐτῆς ὡς πίσσα καιομένη νυκτὸς καὶ ἡμέρας, καὶ οὐ σβεσθήσεται εἰς τὸν αἰῶνα χρόνον, καὶ ἀναβήσεται ὁ καπνὸς αὐτῆς ἄνω. The word *βασανισμός* is used here as denoting the condition of those in torment, and similarly in xviii. 7, 10, 15, whereas in the gloss (?) in ix. 5 it has an active meaning. In Luke xvi. 23, 28 (Wisd. iii. 1; 4 Macc. xiii. 15) *βάσανος* is used to denote passive suffering.

οὐχ ἔχουσιν ἀνάπαυσιν κτλ. Cf. iv. 8, where the same Greek clause occurs, but there it means the deliberate and willing surrender on the part of the Cherubim of their entire time to the praise of God, whereas here it denotes the involuntary endurance of ceaseless torment on the part of those who worship the Beast: cf. 1 Enoch lxiii. 6.

> "And now we long for a little rest but find it not:
> We follow hard upon and obtain it not."

εἴ τις λαμβάνει = οἱ λαμβάνοντες.

XIV. 12-13. These verses do not belong here but have in this edition been restored to their original position after xiii. 15. Just as at the close of xiii. 10 our author enforced the need of patience and faithfulness under the persecutions described in xiii. 10^abc^, so after he has foretold universal persecution and martyrdom for the saints in xiii 15, and in xiv. 12 has enforced the need of patience on the part of the saints, a voice from heaven is heard declaring the blessedness of those who die in the Lord. For a full treatment of these verses see the section that follows immediately after xiii. 15, vol. i. pp. 368-373.

14, 18-20. A proleptic vision of the preliminary Messianic judgment executed by the Son of Man on the heathen nations, which is described in detail in xix. 11-16, and further apparently in xx. 7-10, and under another form in xvii. 14. Although nearly all scholars have taken 14-20 to be the work of one hand, it is clear, as Wellhausen has already recognized, that in 14-20 there are doublets. Wellhausen takes these to be 14-16 and 17-20, but a study of the text and context shows that this analysis of the passage cannot be sustained. No more can that of Bousset, who regards xiv. 14-20 as originally from a foreign source, like xi. 1-13, and considers xiv. 17-18 as the addition of a reviser. For (1) since in xiv. 15-17 there are constructions (see notes on 15-17, p. 21) which are against our author's use, we conclude that these verses are an intrusion here, and that xiv. 14, 18-20 represent the original text. (2) Again the phrase ἄλλος ἄγγελος (15) is noteworthy. It shows that the interpolator failed to recognize the "One like a Son of Man" in 14 as Christ, and took Him to be simply an angel, and hence assigned a mightier rôle to this second and unnamed angel. But to place beside the Son of Man a second figure, and that merely an angelic one as the judge of the earth, is hardly intelligible from any point of view.

(3) When 15–17 are removed, the text describes the Son of Man reaping the *vintage of the earth* just as in xix. 11–16, where He treads the *winepress of the wrath of God.* This fact is also against Wellhausen's analysis which would connect the Son of Man with the harvesting of the earth and an angel with the gathering in of the vintage of the earth. (4) Again, neither θερίζω (Matt. xxv. 24, etc.) nor any of its derivatives (Matt. ix. 37 sq., xiii. 30, xxv. 24; Mark iv. 29; John iv. 35 sqq.) is used elsewhere in the Apocalypse in regard to divine judgment, whereas in xix. vintage terms are applied metaphorically as in xiv. 18–20 to this judgment. (5) Again, instead of τὸ δρέπανόν σου in 15 we should expect σου τὸ δρέπανον τὸ ὀξύ, as rightly in 18, seeing that the δρέπανον is already described as ὀξύ in 14. (6) Finally, when the intrusive doublet (15–17) is removed, we understand why it is that the angel from the altar conveys the command to the Son of Man to gather in the vintage of the earth. The angel of the altar has had to do with the souls of those who had been martyred, and whose souls had cried in vi. 9 from beneath the altar to God for judgment on the inhabitants of the earth. This act of Messianic judgment is thus connected with the prayers of the martyrs: cf. Luke xviii. 7, 8.

14. There can be no question as to the identity of the divine figure seated on the cloud. He is described as "One like a Son of Man." The phrase ὅμοιον υἱὸν ἀνθρώπου is a solecism so far as regards form, and is found only in our author here and in i. 13. The O.T. source of this expression is undoubtedly Dan. vii. 13. "I saw in the night visions, and behold, there came with the clouds of heaven one like unto a son of man (LXX, ὡς υἱὸς ἀνθώπου)." But the expression, though identical in both works, so far as language goes, is dissimilar in meaning. According to the interpretation of the angel in Dan. vii. 18, 22, 27, the phrase denotes the saints of the Most High. But this is not all. In apocalyptic visions, where men or bodies of men are symbolized by beasts (as in Daniel, 1 Enoch, Testaments of the XII Patriarchs, etc.), angels and supernatural beings are symbolized by men. If, therefore, the expression "Son of Man" is to be taken strictly in Daniel, it undoubtedly suggests a supernatural being or body of such beings—supernatural beings but not angels; for the form of the phrase excludes this possibility. In the apocalyptic vision an angel is simply designated "a man." Hence the words "like a man" = "like an angel," *i.e.* a being who is of a supernatural character but not an angel. Thus in Daniel we are to infer that the faithful remnant in Israel are to be transformed into supernatural beings as in 1 Enoch xc. 38 (161 B.C.). That this is the meaning of the text is proved by the adjoining clause, "there came with the clouds of heaven." This clause implies beyond question supernatural authority.

Thus in Daniel the phrase is a collective designation of the righteous Israelites after they have undergone a heavenly transformation.

But a further development was necessary before we arrive at the conception conveyed by this phrase in our author, and this development was reached first, so far as existing literature goes, in 1 Enoch xxxvii.–lxxi., the author of which interpreted "one like a son of man" of an individual, *i.e.* the Messiah, and by so doing rose to the conception of a supernatural Messiah. Thus the way was prepared for the N.T. designation "the Son of Man" (ὁ υἱὸς τοῦ ἀνθρώπου) which in the Gospels has thrown off its distinctive apocalyptic form—"*like* unto a Son of Man" (ὡς υἱὸς ἀνθρώπου), a form, however, which has been retained in the Apocalypse. On this use of ὡς in apocalyptic see additional note on i. 10, vol. i. p. 35 sq For a like transition inside our author, cf. xv. 2, where we have first ὡς θάλασσαν ὑαλίνην and then τὴν θάλασσαν τὴν ὑαλίνην.

In 4 Ezra xiii. 3 (before 70 A.D.?) we find the very same expression. The Latin here is wanting, but the Syriac = ὡς ὁμοίωμα υἱοῦ ἀνθρώπου, where, however, the Syriac is only a paraphrastic rendering of ὅμοιον as in the Peshitto of Ezek. i. 5, 22, 26, x. 1; and of Rev. i. 13, xiv. 14. See Gwynn, *Apocalypse of St. John*, i. 13, note. Thus the Syriac of the Peshitto in Rev. i. 13, xiv. 14, and 4 Ezra xiii. 3 is exactly the same, and both presuppose ὅμοιον υἱὸν (*i.e.* υἱῷ) ἀνθρώπου. Hence 4 Ezra xiii. 3 should be rendered as follows:

"And I beheld and lo! the wind caused to come up out of the heart of the seas one like a son of man. And I beheld and lo! this son of man flew with the clouds of heaven." The Ethiopic version supports this rendering.

ὅμοιον υἱόν. See the last note but one.

ἐπὶ τὴν νεφέλην καθήμενον. Cf. Dan. vii. 13. See note on i. 7.

στέφανον χρυσοῦν. We have here the golden wreath but not the διαδήματα, which he wears in xix. 12. Even in the Apocalypse the στέφανος has many associations. Probably it carries with it here the idea of victory as in ii. 10, iii. 11, vi. 2.

[15–17. We have seen already in note on p. 18 that these

verses are a doublet of 14, 18–20. We have found that 14, 18–20 come from the hand of our author and form a uniform picture, the unity of which is broken up by the interpolated verses 15–17. This doublet was probably suggested by the poetic parallelism in Joel iii. 13.

> "Put ye in the sickle, for the harvest is ripe:
> Come, tread ye, for the winepress is full."

In 15–17 the judgment is represented as a harvesting of the earth. This figure is used both in the O.T. and in the Gospels in relation to the last judgment: cf. Matt. xiii. 30, 39, but not in the Apocalypse, save in the present interpolated passage, where the figure is worked out fully and vividly. The interpolator of 15–17 has, of course, imitated the phrasing and diction of the Apocalypse, but he betrays his ignorance in four constructions, *i.e.* in 15, *κράζων ἐν φωνῇ μεγάλῃ*, whereas our author would have written *κράζων φωνῇ μεγάλῃ* (see Introd. to this Chap. § 2); *τῷ καθημένῳ ἐπὶ τῆς νεφέλης* (whereas our author would have written *ἐπὶ τῇ νεφέλῃ*: see vol. i. p. 112 sq.): in 16, *ὁ καθήμενος ἐπὶ τῆς νεφέλης* (whereas our author would have used *ἐπὶ τὴν νεφέλην*); and *ἔβαλεν . . . ἐπὶ τὴν γῆν* (whereas our author would have written *ἔβαλεν . . . εἰς τὴν γῆν*).

15. ἄλλος ἄγγελος. The attempt to explain the *ἄλλος* here as looking back to 6 or 9 can hardly be justified, since 6–11 and 14–20 are quite distinct visions. Even the use of *καὶ εἶδον καὶ ἰδού* in xiv. 14 (see note on iv. 1) is sufficient to prove that this is so.

It is most important to distinguish the different meanings of *ἄλλος* in xiv. 8, 9, 15, 17, 18. In xiv. 8, 9 there is no difficulty. *ἄλλος* is used idiomatically as in classical Greek, and the phrase = "another, the second angel," etc. But in xiv. 15, 17, 18 there is this use and another. In 15, 17 we have the ordinary use, where the phrase = "another angel." For the interpolator of xiv. 15–17 regarded the Son of Man in xiv. 14 merely as an angel, since in xiv. 17 he makes an angel hold joint authority with Him in the Messianic Judgment and discharge in xiv. 19–20 the duty assigned to the Messiah in xix. 11–16. Hence in xiv. 15 *ἄλλος ἄγγελος* = "another angel." But in xiv. 18 the phrase is to be rendered differently. There, on the excision of xiv. 15–17 as an interpolation, the *ἄλλος* in *ἄλλ. ἄγγ.* refers back indeed to the Son of Man in xiv. 14, but at the same time it distinguishes this angel from the Son of Man, as a different kind of being; for nowhere throughout our author is the Son of Man conceived of as an angel. Hence *ἄλλ. ἄγγ.* = "another, an angel." Cf. the use of *ἕτερος* in Luke xxiii. 32.

ἐκ τοῦ ναοῦ. *I.e.* the heavenly temple. See note in vol. i. p. 111 sq.

κράζων ἐν φωνῇ μεγάλῃ. Our author does not insert the *ἐν*: cf. vi. 10, vii. 2, 10, x. 3, xix. 17, where we have *κράζειν φωνῇ μεγάλῃ*. It is true that in xviii. 2 we have *κράζειν ἐν ἰσχυρᾷ φωνῇ*. But this latter passage is from another source.

τῷ καθημένῳ ἐπὶ τῆς νεφέλης. Here and in the next verse the construction is against the usage of our author, though it is the more usual in classical Greek. See note on iv. 2.

In the three lines beginning with *πέμψον τὸ δρέπανόν σου* we have apparently a paraphrase of Joel iv. 13, שִׁלְחוּ מַגָּל כִּי בָשַׁל קָצִיר, the first line being an expanded translation of the first two words in Joel, and the second and third lines being probably duplicate paraphrastic renderings of the last three words, though, like the LXX and the Targum, they presuppose a text differing from the Massoretic. Thus line two, *ὅτι ἦλθεν ἡ ὥρα θερίσαι*, presupposes by *ἦλθεν* some Hebrew verb = "has come" as also does the LXX by *παρέστηκεν* (cf. Mark iv. 29, *ἀποστέλλει τὸ δρέπανον, ὅτι παρέστηκεν ὁ θερισμός*) and the Targum by מטא. In line three, *ὅτι † ἐξηράνθη † ὁ θερισμὸς τῆς γῆς, ἐξηράνθη* presupposes יבשׁ. Is this a corruption of בשׁל? *ξηραίνω* is unexampled in the sense of "to ripen," so far as I am aware, but might be explained as a rendering of a corrupt text. *ξηραίνω* means "to dry up," as in xvi. 12, or "to wither" when used of plants (cf. Matt. xiii. 6, etc.) or of crops (cf. Joel i. 17, *ἐξηράνθη σῖτος*), but not "to ripen." It will be observed that the writer of 15–17 uses some form of the Hebrew text and not the LXX.

τὸ δρέπανόν σου. We should observe two things here. First, we should expect the addition of *τὸ ὀξύ* here, since the epithet is already attached to *δρέπανον* in 14. In 18, which we hold to be the original sequel to 14, we find, as we should expect, *πέμψον σου τὸ δρέπανον τὸ ὀξύ*. Next, in 15 we note the position of the *σου* after its noun, in which case the emphasis is laid on the pronoun, whereas in 18 the *σου* stands before its noun, in which case the emphasis is laid on *τὸ δρέπανον τὸ ὀξύ*—a fact which points to the thoroughness with which the vintage is carried out in 19–20.

ὥρα θερίσαι. For the construction cf. v. 5, ix. 10, xi. 6, xvi. 9.

16. This verse is modelled on 19, the judgment being referred to under the figure of a harvest instead of a vintage. But, as I have already pointed out on 15, the construction *ὁ καθήμενος ἐπὶ τῆς νεφέλης* is against the usage of our author. *ἔβαλεν . . . ἐπὶ τὴν γῆν* is unexampled in our author. In such a construction *εἰς* not *ἐπί* is always used by him. See note on 19.

17. τοῦ ναοῦ ἐν τῷ οὐρανῷ. See note in vol. i. p. 111 sq.]

18. We here resume the original vision into which 15–17 were interpolated. In this verse *ἄλλος ἄγγελος* is to be rendered "another, an angel." See note on 15 above. The phrase ὁ ἔχων ἐξουσίαν ἐπὶ τοῦ πυρός appears to be interpolated. At all events it makes no contribution to the context. If it had any right to a place in our text it might have been in viii. 3, but even there it would have been meaningless. Lists of angels who were set over the natural elements will be found in 1 Enoch lx. 11–21; Jub. ii. 2. See Bousset, *Religion des Judentums*[1], 317; *Encyc. Bib.* ii. 1258 sqq.; *Jewish Encyc.* i. 589 sqq.

ἄγγελος . . . ἐκ τοῦ θυσιαστηρίου. When the disturbing interpolation, 15–17, is removed, the rôle of the angel, who came forth from the altar, is at once intelligible. The number of the martyrs is at last complete, and now their prayer (vi. 10) from beneath the altar can be fulfilled, and so the angel, who has to do with the souls of the martyrs beneath the altar, is entrusted by God with the task of carrying to the Son of Man the command to undertake the judgment of the earth—to thrust in the sickle and reap the vintage and tread the winepress of the wrath of God (cf. xix. 15). This judgment is the Messianic judgment that precedes the Millennial reign of the Messiah. In xvi. 7 the altar itself proclaims the truth and righteousness of God's judgments. In ix. 13 a voice from the altar commands the letting loose of the first demonic woe against those who had not the seal of God in their foreheads. On this—the one heavenly altar—see note in vol. i. p. 224 sq. Only one angel is mentioned here in connection with the righteous martyrs beneath the altar. But in contemporary and earlier apocalyptic many angels were said to keep guard over the souls of the departed righteous: cf. 1 Enoch c. 5; 4 Ezra vii. 85, 95.

ὁ ἔχων ἐξουσίαν κτλ. See note at the beginning of this verse.

ἐφώνησεν φωνῇ μεγάλῃ. φωνεῖν is found only here in our author. For the entire phrase cf. Mark i. 26; Acts xvi. 28.

τὸ δρέπανον τὸ ὀξύ, *i.e.* the sharp sickle mentioned in 14.

πέμψον σου τὸ δρέπανον. Here (cf. 15) we have a tristich, of which the first and third lines are largely a reproduction of Joel iv. 13. The first line consists simply of the words in Joel, with the addition of the epithet "sharp," which the context requires (cf. 14 *ad fin.*), while the third line is in part a translation and in part a transformation of the clause in Joel, כי בשל קציר; for ἤκμασαν is a good rendering of בשל, whereas αἱ σταφυλαὶ αὐτῆς is simply substituted instead of θερισμός = קציר. And yet this tristich gives the impression of the master hand, and drives home in each line with ever-increasing force the thought of the Seer, who does not quote but simply transforms an O.T. couplet to serve his present purpose. What a contrast it presents to the feebleness of the tristich in 15! It should perhaps be mentioned here that some scholars have taken 15–16 to refer to the ingathering of the saints, and 17–20 to the judgment that befalls the wicked, and thought that there is a delicate propriety in the fact that the former is assigned to the Son of Man, and the latter to a nameless angel. But there is no support for this view in our author; for in xix. 11–16 it is this very treading of the winepress of the wrath of God that is especially the rôle of the Son of God. Moreover, in the rest of the N.T. the words θερίζειν and θερισμός are used of reaping harvests good or bad, alike as regards man (cf. Matt. xxv. 24, 26; Gal. vi. 7, 8; 1 Cor. ix. 11) and the angels, who are termed the θεριστάς (see Matt. xiii. 30, 39: cf. Mark iv. 29). As a man sows good or evil, he reaps accordingly. Similarly in the judgment, the angels gather alike the tares and the wheat in the last great harvesting (Matt. xiii. 30, 39). The word σῖτος, "wheat," as a symbol of the righteous is not found in our author. Finally—to resume once more—in xiv. 6–20 we have a proleptic summary from the divine standpoint of the Messianic judgments which are represented on a larger canvas in xvi. 18–xviii. and xix. 11–21, xx. 7–10. Thus there is no ground for the attempt to differentiate and justify the occurrence side by side of what are really doublets. 15–17 are, from whatever standpoint we regard them, a disturbing element in the text.

19. ἔβαλεν . . . εἰς τὴν γῆν. Our author uses either ἐπὶ τῆς γῆς, v. 3, 10, 13, vii. 1, x. 2, 5, 8, xvi. 18, xviii. 24, or εἰς τὴν γῆν, v. 6, vi. 13, viii. 5, 7, ix. 1, 3, xii. 4, 9, 13, xiii. 13, xvi. 1, 2. ἔβαλεν . . . ἐπὶ τὴν γῆν is found only in the interpolated passage, xiv. 15–17. ἔβαλεν is here another rendering of שלח in Joel iv. 13.

[ὁ ἄγγελος]. An interpolation due to the hand that inserted 15–18. The Son of Man is never described as an angel. See note on 15.

τὴν ληνὸν . . . τὸν μέγαν. This irregularity is probably to be explained by the fact that ληνός in classical Greek is sometimes masculine (Winer, § lix. 4, p. 661; cf. Kautzsch's Gesenius' *Heb. Gram.* for similar anomalies in Heb.: § 110 *k*, 135 *o*, 144*a*, 145 *p*, *t*, *u*). Analogous solecisms are characteristic of our author: cf. xxi. 14, τὸ τεῖχος . . . ἔχων.

ληνὸν τοῦ θυμοῦ τοῦ θεοῦ. Here and in xix. 15 only in the N.T. The phrase τοῦ θυμοῦ τοῦ θεοῦ is rather frequent: cf. xv. 1, 7, xvi. 1, 19, xix. 15.

20. Though the Messianic judgment as executed by the Son of Man is here described in awful terms, it is not the final judgment, which is regarded by our author as the prerogative of the Father: cf. xx. 11 sqq. The diction appears to be influenced by Isa. lxiii. 3, where Yahweh declares, "I have trodden the winepress alone," and in 1 Enoch c. 3, "And the horses shall walk up to the breast in the blood of sinners, And the chariot shall be submerged to its height." This phraseology reappears in Talmudic writings in connection with the carnage at Bether in the time of Hadrian: see my note in 1 Enoch c. 3: also 4 Ezra xv. 35, erit sanguis a gladio usque ad ventrem equi; 36, et femur hominis et poplites cameli.

ἔξωθεν τῆς πόλεως. There can be no question as to the identity of "the city." It is not Rome (for its destruction has already been announced in the hearing of the Seer in 9), but Jerusalem. It is, moreover, most probably not the earthly Jerusalem but the heavenly Jerusalem which is to descend from heaven to be the centre of the Kingdom of Christ for the 1000 years. For in the notes on xx. 1–6 we shall see that the heavenly Jerusalem described in xxi. 9–xxii. 2 is in reality the city that is to come down from heaven to take the place of the old Jerusalem and become the capital of Christ's kingdom for the 1000 years. If xiv. 14, 18–20 is a proleptic summary of xix. 11–21 only, then the city referred to might be the historic Jerusalem, or rather its ruined site: but if this is a summary of xix. 11–21 and also xx. 7–10, then the city can be none other than the city that came down from heaven—the seat of the Messianic Kingdom.

Jewish tradition had long associated the neighbourhood of Jerusalem with the scene of the judgment of the Gentiles. According to Joel iii. 2, 12, God was to assemble and judge the Gentiles in "the valley of Jehoshaphat," a phrase which Theodotion renders by τὴν χώραν τῆς κρίσεως. According to the Midrash Mishle, 68[d], God was to judge the whole world in this valley. It is referred to in 1 Enoch liii. 1 (where see my note). Zechariah speaks also of the judgment of the Gentiles, who laid Jerusalem desolate, being executed on the Mount of Olives (xiv. 2 sqq., 12 sq.). In our author it is all the heathen nations that are to be similarly judged.

ἐξῆλθεν αἷμα κτλ. See preceding notes.

ἀπὸ σταδίων κτλ. = "to a distance of 1600 furlongs." This peculiar use of ἀπό is found also in John xi. 18, xxi. 8 (ἀπὸ πηχῶν διακοσίων). Abbott (*Gram.* p. 227) describes it as "a natural transposition arising from the desire to give prominence to the notion 'distant,' as in our 'distant two hundred cubits,' and then illogically allowing the preposition that signifies distance to govern 'cubits.'" Similar transpositions occur in the case of πρό, as in John xii. 1, πρὸ ἓξ ἡμερῶν τοῦ πάσχα; LXX of Amos i. 1, iv. 7, Hippocrates, πρὸ τριῶν ἡμερῶν τῆς τελευτῆς (this last is quoted from Moulton, *Gram.* 101, note): and also in the case of μετά: cf. Test. Reub. i. 2; Test. Zeb. i. 1; Plut. *Coriol.* 11. These idioms are not Latinisms but of Greek origin.

As regards the number itself various explanations have been offered, but none is absolutely convincing. Some have found in 1600 the idea of completeness, and therefore inferred that the deluge of blood swept over the whole earth (as Victorinus—per omnes mundi quattuor partes), the holy city alone being exempt. Others have conceived that Palestine only was designed by the number, since according to Jerome (Ep. 129, *Ad Dard.*) the length of Palestine from Dan to Beersheba was 160 miles. But 160 miles = only 1280 stades. A nearer approach to the number in our text is to be found in the *Itinerarium* of Antoninus, according to which Palestine was said to be 1664 stades from Tyre to El-Arish.

Of the two above interpretations I am inclined to adopt the former. The more we study xiv. 14, 18–20 the more clear it becomes that it deals with the same subject as xix. 11–21, for xiv. 18–19 clearly state that the judgment is of the whole earth. Hence it is not merely the heathen nations that had submitted to the antichristian empire of Rome that are destroyed in xix. 11–21, but likewise all the remaining heathen nations that rebel against the kingdom of Christ (xx. 7–10) after the lapse of the 1000 years. Hence the slaughter is commensurate with the inhabited world.

ἄχρι τῶν χαλινῶν τῶν ἵππων. These words apparently refer to the heavenly horsemen who are mentioned definitely (xix. 14[a]) in another vision dealing with the same events, *i.e.* xix. 11–21.

CHAPTER XV.

§ 1. *Character and object of this Chapter.*

The chronological order of events in the Seer's visions of the future is here resumed. In other words, this chapter, so far as chronological order goes, follows immediately on xiii.; for, as we have seen (see p. 1: cf. 32), xiv. broke away from this order and was wholly proleptic, passing over as it did the first six Bowls and summarizing the divine judgments from the seventh Bowl (xvi. 17) to xx. 7–10. In order, therefore, to recognize the connection between xiii. and the present chapter, we have only to remember that in xiii. 15 the second Beast caused all that refused to worship the first Beast to be put to death. Thus all the faithful were put to death and the roll of the martyrs was complete with the close of xiii.; and when we come to xv. we find that xv. 2–4 looks upon the destruction of the entire body of the faithful as already an event of the past (see note on xv. 2–4), and represents the entire martyr host as standing on the sea of glass before God and singing a song of praise to the Lord God of Hosts. xv. 1 is an interpolation (see § 7). In xv. 5–xvi. 1 the Seer has a vision of the appointment of seven angels with seven

Bowls to execute the last series of cosmic woes upon the earth. It is to be observed that in these three series—the Seals, the Trumpets, and the Bowls—there is a distinct development and not a mere recapitulation as has hitherto either wholly or in part been assumed by students of the Apocalypse. This will be clear as we advance.

For *to the first four Seals and the sixth all men*—saints and sinners, Christians and heathen alike—*are subject.* Only the faithful are the victims of the fifth Seal. The sixth Seal describes in hyperbolic language the signs which precede the end, which, however, is not so near as the unbelievers apprehend. But there are worse things to come, the fifth, sixth and seventh, or rather the first, second, and third, Trumpets,[1] that is, the three demonic Woes, viii.–ix., xi. 14^b, 15, xii.–xiii. In vii. the faithful are sealed in order to secure them from these Woes. *Hence these Woes did not affect the faithful, but only those that were without the seal of God.* When we come to the Bowls we have arrived at a fresh stage of development. Since the martyrdom of the faithful is complete in xiii. and all the martyrs are represented as already in heaven in xv. 2–4, it is clear that only the heathen nations, that form the Roman Empire or hold aloof from it, survive.

On this heathen world, limited in the fifth Bowl to the empire of the Beast, are poured down the plagues of the seven Bowls. Whilst the Seals and the Trumpets or Woes could be regarded as having a disciplining effect on the faithful, however they might affect the unbelievers, the Bowls cannot be regarded in any other light than that of punishments, though such expressions as those in xvi. 9, 11, which refer to the refusal of men to repent notwithstanding these plagues, point to the fact that repentance was still possible for them. That the plagues, which are universal and not local (except the fifth), do not annihilate the heathen nations is clear from the fact that the eternal gospel (xiv. 6) is to be preached to the surviving nations after the close of the seven Bowls and the Messianic judgment (xix. 11–21).

§ 2. *Relation of xv. to xiv. and xvi.–xx.* In xiv. our author has given three proleptic visions—the first portraying the blessedness awaiting the martyrs in the Millennial kingdom, while the second and third describe the judgments about to befall Rome and the heathen nations. Thus xiv. summarized the outstanding events from the close of the universal martyrdom of the faithful to the final judgment. From this prelude the Seer now returns to describe in detail the events thus briefly foreshadowed, and first of all the blessedness into which the martyred faithful enter immediately on death, xv. 2–4, and the subsequent

[1] We have seen that the first four Trumpets are an interpolation in the text (see p. 219 sqq.).

Millennial reign on earth, xx. 4-6 (cf. xiv. 1-5). Next we have the vision of the seven last Plagues, which are to descend on the heathen world, from which all the faithful had already been removed, xv. 5-xviii. (cf. xiv. 6-11). The doom of antichristian Rome, which does not come to pass till the seventh Plague, is portrayed with great fullness in xvii.-xviii. On the destruction of Rome there follow thanksgivings in heaven, xix. 1-8. The next act of judgment is that executed by the Son of Man on the heathen nations, xix. 11-21 (cf. xiv. 14, 18-20).

§ 3. *This chapter consists of two visions.* The first, xv. 2-4, deals with the triumphal song sung by the martyrs as they stand round the sea of glass in heaven. It is a song of unmixed praise and thanksgiving; for the last martyrdom on earth is over and the ranks of the martyrs in heaven are now complete. The second vision relates to the Seven Angels who come forth from the heavenly Temple and are thereupon furnished with the seven Bowls which are full of the wrath of God.

§ 4. *The diction of xv. 2-8 is, except in the case of one phrase in 6, that of our author.* This will be apparent as we proceed.

1. This verse could be assigned to him in point of diction but not the phrase **ἀγγέλους ἑπτὰ ἔχοντας πληγὰς ἑπτά**, because of the context. As I shall show in § 7 *ad fin.*, our author could not use this expression here or in 6. Otherwise the language recalls that of our author, but yet in certain respects with a difference. **καὶ εἶδον** is, of course, attested throughout the book. **σημεῖον.** This word has already been used in a like (and yet not altogether like) connection in xii. 1, 3. A perfect parallel to its present usage would have led us to expect it in viii. 13. **μέγα καὶ θαυμαστόν**: cf. xv. 3. **ἀγγέλους ἑπτά.** This is the right order for the numeral in our author. **τὰς ἐσχάτας** seems borrowed from xxi. 9. **ὅτι ἐν αὐταῖς ἐτελέσθη κτλ.**: cf. 8. But the subject-matter is open to objection (see note *in loc.*).

2. **νικῶντας ἐκ.** A pregnant construction. Though *νικᾶν* is a favourite verb with our author the construction here is unique in Greek. **τοῦ θηρίου καὶ . . . τῆς εἰκόνος αὐτοῦ καὶ . . . τοῦ ἀριθμοῦ τ. ὀνόματος.** Cf. xiii. 17, xiv. 11. **ἑστῶτας ἐπὶ τ. θάλασσαν.** Our author in x. 5, 8 writes *ἐπί* with the gen. in this phrase. But his usage is not fixed. See note on xv. 2. **κιθάρας τοῦ θεοῦ**—a Hebraism.

3. **καὶ ᾄδουσιν.** Here, as in xiv. 3, *καὶ ᾄδουσιν* is to be taken as *καὶ ᾄδοντας.* In fact this is the reading of ℵ Prim. Vg. and S^1. See note on xiv. 3. **κύριε ὁ θεὸς ὁ παντοκράτωρ.** A familiar title of God in our author: cf. i. 8, iv. 8, xi. 17, xvi. 7, xix. 6, xxi. 22. **δίκαιαι καὶ ἀληθιναί** recurs in converse order in xvi. 7, xix. 2.

4. ὅσιος. Used only in xvi. 5, as here of God, but not in the rest of the N.T. πάντα τὰ ἔθνη . . . προσκυνήσουσιν. Cf. xiv. 7, where all the nations are bidden προσκυνήσατε τῷ ποιήσαντι. ἐφανερώθησαν. Cf. iii. 18. 5. καὶ μετὰ ταῦτα εἶδον. A clause used in our author introducing a new vision: cf. iv. 1 *n*. Hence 1 cannot be right, since it has already introduced the vision. ἠνοίγη ὁ ναός . . . ἐν τῷ οὐρανῷ. Cf. xi. 19.

6. ἔχοντες τὰς ἑπτὰ πληγάς. This phrase descriptive of the seven angels, as also in xv. 1, is against the usage of our author as well as against the context. See below, § 7. ἐνδεδυμένοι λίθον . . . καὶ περιεζωσμένοι . . . ζώνας χρυσᾶς. Cf. i. 13, xix. 14. 7. γεμούσας. Cf. iv. 6, 8, etc. τοῦ ζῶντος εἰς τοὺς αἰῶνας τῶν αἰώνων. Cf. iv. 9 *n*., x. 6. 8. ἄχρι τελεσθῶσι. Cf. xvii. 17, xx. 3, for the same clause.

§ 5. *Strongly Hebraic character of xv.*

This chapter is Hebraic in character. 1. The writer translates in xv. 4 the Hebrew of Jer. x 7, where the LXX is lacking: ὁ βασιλεὺς . . . τίς οὐ μὴ φοβηθῇ; Here Theodotion and Aquila render τίς οὐ μὴ φοβηθήσεταί σε βασιλεῦ τῶν ἐθνῶν; It is true that the words πάντα τὰ ἔθνη . . . ἐνώπιόν σου in 4 agree *verbatim* with the LXX of Ps. lxxxvi. 9, save that it omits ὅσα ἐποίησας after ἔθνη. But there is nothing distinctive in the LXX rendering.

2. As regards the order this is also Hebraic. The verb nearly always begins the clause or follows immediately on the subject as in 4, 7, 8. In 4 the position of ἐφανερώθησαν serves to gives emphasis.

3. There are some Hebraisms. Thus in 2–3 we have τοὺς νικῶντας = τ. νενικηκότας . . . after the model of the Hebrew participle: ἑστῶτας καὶ ᾄδουσιν = ἑστῶτας . . . καὶ ᾄδοντας (see *in loc.*): and κιθάρας τοῦ θεοῦ = כנרות האלהים. Possibly νικῶντας ἐκ may be due to a Hebraism.

4. In 5, 6 there are two phrases which apparently cannot be satisfactorily explained except on the hypothesis that ὁ ναὸς τῆς σκηνῆς τοῦ μαρτυρίου in 5 is a translation from a Hebrew text, and that a corrupt one, and that the second phrase in 6 is due to the translator taking שֵׁשׁ to mean λίθον, whereas in this context it could only = βύσσινον. See text *in locis*.

§ 6. *xv. 2–8 appears to be a translation by our author from a Hebrew source.*

Since xv. 2–8 is from the hand of our author (§ 4), and since, according to § 5, xv. 2–8 is not only strongly Hebraistic but appears to imply a Hebrew source; and, finally, since in xv. 5, 6 the text can be best explained on the hypothesis of a corrupt

Hebrew source, this section appears to be a translation by our author from a Hebrew source.

§ 7. *xv. 1 appears to be an interpolation, the chapter having originally begun with xv. 2: further, for* οἱ ἑπτὰ ἄγγελοι οἱ ἔχοντες τὰς ἑπτὰ πληγάς *in 6 we should read simply* ἄγγελοι ἑπτά. (Cf. xv. 7, xvi. 1.) The question has naturally been asked, how can the Seer have seen the angels in xv. 1, before they came forth from the Temple, which was not opened till xv. 5? This fact has caused much difficulty, and, as we should expect, a variety of explanations has been offered. Völter in his last works assigns xv. 5-6 to the Apocalypse of Cerinthus and xv. 1-4, 7 to an editor in Trajan's time. Weyland ascribes xv. 1, 6-8 to an editor and the remaining verses to two different sources. Spitta traces xv. 1 and fragments of 2, 3, 5 and 7 to an editor: Erbes, xv. 1, 5-8 to an editor of the year 80 A.D., and J. Weiss, xv. 1-4, 6-7 to an editor of the year 95 A.D.

None of these solutions of the difficulty has gained acceptance, and so Bousset thinks there is no need to excise any part of the text, and that xv. 1 is simply to be regarded as a superscription. But this explanation is, if anything, less satisfactory than the preceding. For (1) a superscription should not be introduced by the words καὶ εἶδον, but rather be something of the nature of ἡ ὅρασις τῶν ἑπτὰ ἀγγέλων κτλ. (2) If it were a superscription it ought to have been inserted immediately after 4 and not before 2, seeing that 2-4 constitute an independent and absolutely different vision. (3) That a new and important vision is introduced by xv. 5 is shown by the use of the clause μετὰ ταῦτα εἶδον. See iv. 1 *n.* (4) Again, as I have shown below, the Seven Angels are wrongly described in this verse as "seven angels having seven plagues—the last." Their right description would be "seven angels having seven bowls." (5) The clause ὅτι ἐν αὐταῖς ἐτελέσθη ὁ θυμὸς τοῦ θεοῦ is unjustifiable. The wrath of God cannot be conceived as coming to an end till sin is at an end or adequately punished. And this does not take place till the final judgment. (6) The scene of the Seer's vision is wrongly represented as having been experienced on the earth—εἶδον ἄλλο σημεῖον ἐν τῷ οὐρανῷ (cf. xii. 1, 3)—whereas it was undoubtedly in heaven: cf. xv. 5 sqq. Accordingly there appears to be no other way of solving the difficulty than to suppose either that xv. 1 is due to a marginal gloss subsequently incorporated in the text, or that it was an early interpolation by a scribe. Hence the chapter really begins with the vision of the triumphant martyrs in heaven, xv. 2-4, while xv. 5 introduces the vision of seven angels coming forth from the Temple in heaven. In xv. 6 instead of οἱ ἑπτὰ ἄγγελοι οἱ ἔχοντες τὰς ἑπτὰ πληγάς we should simply read ἄγγελοι ἑπτά. The change was made when xv. 1 was incorporated in the text. The interpolator, moreover, made a very inept addition. He did not know his text. For, as is clear from xv. 7, the Seven Angels did not receive "the bowls full of the wrath of God" till after they had left the Temple, whereas in 6 they are represented as having the plagues before doing so. Again, these Seven Angels, when they are mentioned subsequently, as they are four times, are never described as "the seven angels having the seven plagues," but simply as "the seven angels," xv. 7, xvi. 1, or "the seven angels which had the seven bowls," in xvii. 1, xxi. 9. Each bowl contains a plague, and so the seven plagues, xv. 8, result respectively from the pouring forth in succession of the seven Bowls.

1. This verse cannot be original, as we have already seen in the Introd. to this Chapter, § 7. It is true that the style resembles that of our author, but there are strong grounds against its being from his hand. The first is that the Seer cannot have seen the angels in 1, seeing that the Temple is closed till 5, and the angels do not emerge from it till then. But there are other and more radical grounds for the rejection of this verse. (1) First, as we are aware (see note on iv. 1) the clause *καὶ μετὰ ταῦτα εἶδον* (xv. 5) always introduces a new and important section in the Apocalypse; but, if it had already been introduced in xv. 1, then this clause would be out of place. Moreover, in xv. 1 the clause *καὶ εἶδον* is used by our Seer to introduce the less important sections. The interpolator of xv. 1 does not seem to have been aware of this usage. If we excise xv. 1 and remember that xiv. is wholly proleptic in character, referring as it does to events subsequent to xvi. 17 (see p. 2), then the blessedness of the martyred faithful is set forth in contrast to their terrible plight in xiii. (2) The expression *ἀγγέλους ἑπτὰ ἔχοντας πληγὰς ἑπτά* is not that used by our author elsewhere, save in 6 where it appears also to be an interpolation, though it may have been suggested by the last clause in xv. 8. For the last three words we should have *ἔχοντας φιάλας ἑπτά*: cf. xv. 7, xvii. 1, xxi. 9. See also 8. The phraseology throughout xvi. also supports this objection. (3) The words *τὰς ἐσχάτας* (probably derived from xxi. 9) are generally explained as the last plagues in contrast to the plagues mentioned in ix. 20; but that this is not the meaning of *the writer of this verse* is clear from the clause which follows, with which we shall now deal. (4) The clause just referred to—*ὅτι ἐν αὐταῖς ἐτελέσθη ὁ θυμὸς τοῦ θεοῦ*—cannot be given any satisfactory explanation. It manifestly states that the wrath of God will be consummated in these seven Bowls, whereas the last and most terrible of the divine judgments do not take place till after their close. The right expression is found in xv. 8, ἄχρι τελεσθῶσιν αἱ ἑπτὰ πληγαί, which is probably the source of the interpolator's phrase. These seven Plagues can be described as wholly consummated in xvi.–xviii., but not so the wrath of God.

On the above grounds we cannot but regard xv. 1 as an interpolation. When this interpolation was once effected, ἄγγελοι ἑπτά in 6 was changed into οἱ ἑπτὰ ἄγγελοι οἱ ἔχοντες τὰς ἑπτὰ πληγάς in order to adapt the context to the text thus interpolated. The incongruity of the addition οἱ ἔχοντες τ. ἑπτὰ πληγάς is very glaring, seeing that the seven angels do not receive the plague-bearing Bowls till the next verse.

καὶ εἶδον. See notes on iv. 1.

καὶ εἶδον . . . ἐν τῷ οὐρανῷ. This clause seems to have been suggested by xii. 1.

ἄλλο σημεῖον ἐν τῷ οὐρανῷ. Cf. xii. 1, 3, where this phrase implies that the Seer is on earth. But clearly in the vision of the Seven Angels he is in heaven: see xv. 5, xvi. 1. This fact the interpolator failed to recognize.

μέγα καὶ θαυμαστόν. Suggested (?) by the phrase μεγάλα καὶ θαυμαστά in 3. **ἀγγέλους ἑπτὰ . . . τοῦ θεοῦ.** This passage has already been dealt with above. See also note on 7.

2–4. With this vision the march in the development of future events is resumed. The line of advance was abandoned for the time being in xiv., which, as we have seen, is wholly proleptic, and summarized all the coming judgments from the seventh Bowl to the immediate advent of the final judgment. Hence xv. 2–4 is to be taken in close connection with xiii. In xiii. 15 the second Beast is represented as exterminating the entire body of the faithful, and xv. 2–4 looks upon that extermination as already an event of the past. The roll of the martyrs is at last complete, and no longer are any of the faithful to be found on the earth, but only the heathen nations, which are either devoted followers of the Antichrist or occupy a neutral position. xv. 2–4 thus forms a companion picture to vii. 9–16. In both these the roll of the martyrs has just been completed or is on the eve of completion in heaven. The final judgment is still in the distance; for the conversion of the nations (cf. the announcement of the glad tidings in xiv. 6) is foretold (xv. 4) as an event of the future. In xiv. 1–5 and xx. 4, which depict a later stage, the martyrs have descended with Christ to the earth to share with Him the Millennial reign.

2. ὡς (see Additional Note, i. p. 35 sq.) **θάλασσαν ὑαλίνην** (= כַּיָּם זְכוֹכִית). This sea has already been referred to in iv. 6. The absence of the article is what we expect in this Hebraistic expression, which = "the likeness of a sea of glass."

μεμιγμένην πυρί. This description is not attached to the heavenly sea when it is mentioned in iv. 6. But the difference of context is a sufficient explanation. In iv. 6 the vision is one of peace, whereas here it is one of judgment. This phrase, therefore, may refer either to the sea as glowing with the wrath of God, or as reflecting the lightnings that proceeded from the throne of God, though there is here, it is true, no mention of these lightnings. In 2 Enoch xxix. 1–2 there is a passage that may be quoted, though it does not throw any real light on the text. "From the gleam of My eye the lightning received its wonderful nature, which is both fire in water, and water in fire."

τοὺς νικῶντας ἐκ τοῦ θηρίου. This is a very difficult phrase. There is no difficulty with the participle. Here *νικῶντας* = *νενικηκότας*. The great tribulation is over, and the martyrs have triumphed over the Beast by proving faithful unto death. As our author thinks in Hebrew, his use of the Greek participle reflects that of the Hebrew participle, which, as we are aware, can = *νικῶντας*, *νενικηκότας* or *νικησομένους* according to the context. Here *νικῶντας* is to be taken as a perfect participle. The roll of the martyrs is at last complete, but it has only just been completed. The Antichristian powers have not yet been judged, nor has the Millennial Kingdom been as yet established. When this kingdom is established the martyrs shall descend and reign (v. 10) with Christ for 1000 years (xiv. 1–5, xx. 4), and all the nations of the earth, which had not been leagued with Rome, shall come and worship before God (xv. 4, xxi. 24–26).

νικῶντας ἐκ. The use of *ἐκ* after *νικῶντας* is very difficult. Winer (p. 460) quotes this passage in connection with a number of other passages where *ἐκ* is found, but not one of them has the same source as *ἐκ* here. He compares the Latin expression "victoriam ferre ex aliquo," Livy, viii. 8, etc. But it would be difficult to justify the occurrence of a Latinism in our text. There is just the possibility that our author was here reproducing the Hebrew idiom הגברים מן־החיה (cf. 2 Sam. i. 23; Ps. lxv. 3) = "those who had been stronger than the beast." But no adequate explanation has as yet been offered.

As Swete (*in loc.*) has pointed out, the martyrs show themselves as conquerors up to the moment of death: cf. *Ep. Smyrn.* 19, *διὰ τῆς ὑπομονῆς καταγωνισάμενος τὸν ἄδικον ἄρχοντα καὶ οὕτως τὸν τῆς ἀφθαρσίας στέφανον ἀπολαβών.* *Passio S. Perpetuae*, 18, "illuxit dies victoriae illorum, et processerunt de carcere in amphitheatrum quasi in caelum, hilares et vultu decori." But our Seer follows them into the life beyond and sees the exultant host celebrating not their own victory but the praises of God.

ἐκ τοῦ θηρίου καὶ ἐκ τῆς εἰκόνος κτλ. Cf. xiii. 1, 14, 17. xiv. 9, 11, xix. 20, xx. 4.

ἑστῶτας ἐπὶ τὴν θάλασσαν. This phrase could mean "standing on" (cf. x. 5, 8, xii. 18, xiv. 1) or "standing by" (cf. iii. 20). This scene of the victors standing on the heavenly sea with harps in their hands and praising God recalls Israel's song of triumph over Egypt on the shore of the Red Sea. The phraseology is unusual. In x. 5, 8 *ἵστημι* is used with *ἐπὶ τῆς θαλάσσης*. Further, our author prefers generally the phrase *ἐπὶ τῆς θαλάσσης* to *ἐπὶ τὴν θάλασσαν*: cf. vii. 1[b], x. 2, 5, 8. But the fact that *ἵστημι ἐπί* is in the case of all other nouns followed by the accusative (iii. 20, vii. 1[a], viii. 3, xi. 11, xii. 18, xiv. 1) may have led to the use of the accusative (instead of the gen.) of *θάλασσα* in the present instance after *ἑστῶτας ἐπί*.

κιθάρας τοῦ θεοῦ = "harps belonging to the service of God." The omission of the article before *κιθάρας* is a Hebraism. On this idea cf. v. 8, xiv. 2. With this phrase we might compare 1 Thess. iv. 16, *ἐν σάλπιγγι θεοῦ*, and 1 Chron. xvi. 42; 2 Chron. vii. 6, כלי שיר האלהים = "instruments to accompany the songs of God."

3. καὶ ᾄδουσιν. These words are to be taken as = *καὶ ᾄδοντας* and the passage to be rendered: "I saw . . . standing on the sea . . . and singing." This Hebraism has occurred several times already: see note on xiv. 2–3.

[τὴν ᾠδὴν Μωυσέως τοῦ δούλου τοῦ θεοῦ καὶ] τὴν ᾠδὴν τοῦ ἀρνίου. Now that the martyr host is completed, and are already standing before God, they sing a song of praise to God, but not one of triumph over their enemies—a fact which differentiates this song from that in Ex. xv. The first words, "the song of Moses the servant of God," recall Ex. xiv. 31, xv. 1, where Moses and the children of Israel sang a song of thanksgiving to God, but still more a paean of triumph over the Egyptians and of joy at their destruction (Ex. xv. 2–19).

As that song was sung on earth, on the shore of the Red Sea by Israel after the flesh, so this song is sung in heaven by the Sea of Glass before God by the spiritual Israel.

The expression *τὴν ᾠδὴν Μωυσέως . . . καὶ τ. ᾠδὴν τοῦ ἀρνίου* creates insuperable difficulties. To excise (as most editors have done) *καὶ τ. ᾠδὴν τοῦ ἀρνίου* as an interpolation would only aggravate the difficulty in the present context. For, since it was through the Lamb that the Christian martyrs triumphed, if the song that followed was associated with any name, that name must have been that of the Lamb. Hence the difficulty does not originate in connection with this phrase, but rather with *τ. ᾠδὴν Μωυσέως*. How then are we to explain the collocation of the two phrases? Bousset is of opinion that the repetition of the phrase suggests that the victors sang first the old Song of Moses (Ex. xv. 2–19) and then a new song—that of the Lamb, which is then given. This apparently is the view of Swete.

"St. John does not write τ. ᾠδὴν Μωυσέως καὶ τοῦ ἀρνίου, for the notes are distinct though they form a harmony." This view can hardly be regarded as satisfactory. That the old dispensation is superseded is the *essential* belief of our author, and it can no less have been his conviction that in heaven the faithful members of the old dispensation would accept the teaching of the new. Moreover, if our author deliberately omits all reference to the Law throughout the Apocalypse, it would be surprising if he referred here to its author Moses, and placed him before the Lamb. This being so, we can hardly suppose that our author implies that the song of Moses, given in Ex. xv. 2–19, was actually sung by a body of Christian martyrs before the throne. We, therefore, expect that, *if the text is original*, the song given in our text, which makes no definite mention of either Moses or of the Lamb, was sung alike by the martyred faithful of Judaism and Christianity, and that too led by the Lamb, as the song in Ex. xv. was led by Moses. But the form of the text is against this conclusion, and implies that the song or songs are led by Moses and the Lamb.

Thus there seems to be no way out of the difficulty save by assuming that the words τ. ᾠδὴν Μωυσέως τοῦ δούλου τοῦ θεοῦ originated in a marginal gloss, which was subsequently incorporated in the text. Moreover, the nature of the song supports this assumption, since it is not a song of triumph, but simply a paean of thanksgiving, which the martyrs sing, when in the first perfect unclouded vision of God they wholly forget themselves and burst forth into praise of the Lord God of Hosts, who alone is holy, whose works are great and marvellous, whose ways are righteousness and truth, and to whom all the nations shall do homage, because of the coming manifestation of God's righteous judgments.

Not until this stage does the Seer behold the complete spiritual transformation of the faithful in heaven. At the same time by its mention of divine judgments to come, it prepares the way for the advent of the Seven Angels with their plagues. This song, therefore, though sung by the victorious Christian host of martyrs, could not be more fittingly conceived. Its sole theme is God; for, in the perfect vision of God, self is wholly forgotten, and so far as there is a reference to the earth from which they have been delivered, it is one of hopefulness: "the nations shall come and worship before Thee."

The gloss τ. ᾠδὴν Μωυσέως κτλ. in this context is probably due to the fact that the triumph of the actual Israel over the Egyptians at the Red Sea was certainly regarded by the Christians of the first century as prefiguring the triumphs of the spiritual Israel, as we see from the Pauline Epistles.

This song of Moses in Ex. xv. had already been incorporated in the Temple Services. Thus it was sung at the evening sacrifice on the Sabbath (Edersheim, *The Temple*, p. 188), and in the benediction that followed the Shema there is a reference to it: "A new song did they that were delivered sing to Thy name by the seashore" (*Encyc. Bib.* iv. 4954). According to Philo (*De Vita Contempl.* xi.) this song was sung by the Therapeutae, the men forming one chorus and the women the other, while in the *De Agricultura*, xvii., he writes: "the chorus of men will have Moses for their leader and that of the women will be under the guidance of Miriam. . . . Accordingly all the men sing the song on the seashore. . . . Moses being the leader of their song; and the women sing—Miriam being their leader."

The Martyrs' Song is formed almost wholly of O.T. expressions.

μεγάλα καὶ θαυμαστὰ τὰ ἔργα σου. The first epithet as describing the works of God is found in Ps. xcii. 5, cxi. 2, and the second in Ps. xcviii. 1, cxxxix. 14; 1 Chron. xvi. 9.

κύριε, ὁ θεὸς ὁ παντοκράτωρ. See Amos iv. 13, but the phrase occurs several times elsewhere in our text (see note on i. 8).

δίκαιαι καὶ ἀληθιναὶ αἱ ὁδοί σου. Cf. xvi. 7, xix. 2; Ps. cxlv. 17, *δίκαιος κύριος ἐν πάσαις ταῖς ὁδοῖς αὐτοῦ*: Deut. xxxii. 4, *ἀληθινὰ τὰ ἔργα αὐτοῦ*.

ὁ βασιλεὺς τῶν ἐθνῶν. **4. τίς οὐ μὴ φοβηθῇ.** These clauses are a rendering of Jer. x. 7, which, though present in Aquila and Theodotion, are wanting in the LXX. The title "king of the nations" is here peculiarly appropriate, since it is God's dealings with the nations alike in the way of condemnation and of mercy that is the theme of this song and of the chapters that follow.

καὶ δοξάσει τὸ ὄνομά σου. Cf. Ps. lxxxvi. 9, *δοξάσουσιν τὸ ὄνομά σου*; see also 12; Mal. i. 11, *τὸ ὄνομά σου δεδόξασται ἐν τοῖς ἔθνεσιν*. **μόνος ὅσιος.** Cf. 1 Sam. ii. 2, *ὅτι οὐκ ἔστιν ἅγιος ὡς κύριος*. With the expression *μόνος ὅσιος* cf. Rom. xvi. 27, *μόνῳ σοφῷ*.

ὅτι πάντα τὰ ἔθνη ἥξουσιν . . . ἐνώπιόν σου. From Ps. lxxxvi. 9.

τὰ δικαιώματα κτλ. Cf. Ps. xcviii. 2. *δικαιώματα* here means the judicial sentences of God in relation to the nations either in the way of mercy or condemnation. On Rome and all the adherents of the Empire will be manifested the judgments of God; whereas during the Millennial period the rest of the nations will experience His mercy. Cf. xiv. 6–7, which refer to the Millennial period. On the other hand, some scholars take *δικαιώματα* in the sense of "righteous deeds"—a meaning which it undoubtedly possesses in the gloss in xix. 9 But xvi. 1, *φιάλας τοῦ θυμοῦ τοῦ θεοῦ*, xvi. 7, *δίκαιαι αἱ κρίσεις σου*, and other analogous expressions are in favour of the interpretation given above.

πάντα τὰ ἔθνη ἥξουσιν κτλ. These words point forward to the conversion of the nations during the Millennial reign: cf. xxi. 24 sq., xxii. 2. In xiv. 7 the nations are exhorted to repent and worship God. Of course it is only the nations that survive the judgments in xvi.–xix. that are so converted.

ὅτι . . . ἐφανερώθησαν. This clause gives the ground for the clause that immediately precedes: "for Thy righteous judgments shall have been made manifest."

XV. 5–XVI. 1. The commission of the Seven Angels with the Bowls.

5. καὶ μετὰ ταῦτα εἶδον. As has been shown on iv. 1, this phrase is never used except at the beginning of an important section. Thus the insertion of xv. 1, which already deals with this subject, is wholly against the usage of our author. See also above on 1.

ἠνοίγη ὁ ναὸς . . . ἐν τῷ οὐρανῷ. So in xi. 19.

ὁ ναὸς † τῆς σκηνῆς τοῦ μαρτυρίου †.

This designation of the heavenly Temple is certainly strange —"the temple of the tabernacle of the testimony." It appears either to be an interpolation or the rendering of a corrupt Hebrew source. If we translate the phrase into Hebrew it is clear that *ναός* must be rendered by הֵיכָל, *σκηνή* generally by אֹהֶל (occasionally by מִשְׁכָּן), and *μαρτύριον* by מוֹעֵד (or possibly by עֵדוּת). But it must certainly be confessed that היכל אהל מועד is an absolutely unexampled designation, and difficult to justify.

The phrase in the text cannot be a rendering of משכן אהל מועד (cf. Ex. xl. 2, 6, 29, since *ναός* is never used to translate משכן).

Züllig thinks that this expression is used in order to recall the fact that, when the Tabernacle with all its holy vessels was brought up to Jerusalem by the order of Solomon, the Ark was removed from it and set up in the most holy place in the Temple (2 Chron. v. 5; 1 Kings viii. 4), and that from that time forward the temple could also bear the name of the Tabernacle, and that in fact it is called *mishhkan* (משכן) in Ps. lxxxiv. 2, cxxxii. 5, and *ohel* (אהל) in Ezek. xli. 1. Hence he would, as Bousset, render the entire phrase as "the temple, that is, the tabernacle of the testimony." The genitive would in this case be one of apposition. But against the identification of the *ναός* and *σκηνή* in our text there is the very great objection, that in Apocalyptic, from the vision in Isa. vi. to the latest times, it is *the Temple*, whether in heaven or on earth, *and not the Tabernacle*, that is referred to as the scene of apocalyptic vision. See note on viii. 3. Hence, since throughout the rest of the Apocalypse this usage is followed, the natural inference is that it is followed here. If this be so, then it is to be concluded that *τῆς σκηνῆς τοῦ μαρτυρίου* is an addition. If we might here assume a Hebrew original, we could dispose of the difficulty. Thus *ὁ ναὸς τῆς σκηνῆς τοῦ μαρτυρίου ἐν τῷ οὐρανῷ* = היכל אהל מועד בשמים, which might easily be a corruption of היכל אלהים שבשמים = *ὁ ναὸς τοῦ θεοῦ ὁ ἐν τῷ οὐρανῷ*—the very phrase that is found in xi. 19, with the same verb in both cases, *i.e.* *ἠνοίγη*.

6. οἱ ἑπτὰ ἄγγ. οἱ ἐχ. τ. ἑπτὰ πληγάς. As we have already seen on 1, we should excise *οἱ ἔχ. τ. ἑπτὰ πληγάς* as an addition from the hand that added 1 and read simply *ἄγγελοι ἑπτά*.

ἐνδεδυμένοι † λίθον † . . . περιεζωσμένοι . . . ζώνας χρυσᾶς. See note on the diction in i. 13.

ἐνδεδυμένοι † λίθον † καθαρὸν λαμπρόν. AC, a few Cursives, and the MSS of the Vulg. read *λίθον* for *λίνον*, which is found in the lesser authorities. That *λίθον* would more readily be changed into *λίνον* and not *vice versa* is evident in itself. Besides, though the best Codd. of the Vulg. have *lapide* the official text has *linteo*. WH adduce Ezek. xxviii. 13, *πάντα λίθον χρηστὸν ἐνδέδεσαι* in support of *λίθον*. Further, *λίνον* (= flax) is not used as the equivalent of *λινοῦν* (= a garment made of *flax*) except in a few passages throughout Greek literature: cf. Homer, *Il.* ix. 661, *Od.* xiii. 73, 118; Aesch. *Suppl.* 120, 132, Etym. Magn. The evidence, therefore, is strongly in favour of *λίθον*. But, notwithstanding the advocacy of WH, *λίθον* cannot be right. We must, therefore, assume either that, despite the very great improbability, *λίθον* is a primitive corruption of the all but unexampled word *λίνον* (= "linen garment"—a most unusual meaning), or that we have here a mistranslation from the Hebrew. *ἐνδεδυμένοι λίθον* = לבושים שֵׁשׁ. But שֵׁשׁ, as we know, means either *βύσσινος*, Gen. xli. 42; Ex. xxviii. 35 (39), or *λίθος* (cf. Esth. i. 6) or *μάρμαρος* (Cant. v. 15). In fact, in later Hebrew it generally means "alabaster" or "marble." In the Epistle of Jeremy 71 the same mistranslation, as Ball has shown, occurs: "Ye shall know them to be no gods by the purple and the marble (*τῆς μαρμάρου*) which rotteth upon them." Here *μάρμαρος* = שֵׁשׁ, which should have been rendered by *τοῦ βυσσίνου* = "fine linen." "Marble doesn't rot," as Ball remarks. Now returning to our text, if we may assume a Hebrew original, then instead of *ἐνδεδυμένοι λίθον καθαρὸν λαμπρόν* we should read **ἐνδεδυμένοι βύσσινον καθαρὸν λαμπρόν**. To confirm this conclusion we have only to turn to xix. 8, where we find *περιβάληται βύσσινον λαμπρὸν καθαρόν*, or to xix. 14, where we have the clause that should be in our text, *ἐνδεδυμένοι* *βύσσινον λευκὸν καθαρόν.* Hence we render "clothed in fine linen pure bright." On the significance of this expression see note on iii. 5.

περιεζωσμένοι κτλ. Cf. i. 13.

7. *ἓν ἐκ τῶν τεσσάρων ζῴων, i.e.* one of the Cherubim. See note on iv. 6. The Cherubim in the Apocalyptic of the 1st cent. A.D. have come to be the chief order of angels. It is fitting therefore that one of them should act as an intermediary between God and the Seven Angels of the Bowls. Even in Ezek. x. 7 it is one of the Cherubim that hands over to one of the seven angels of judgment coals of fire to be sprinkled on the earth.

ἑπτὰ φιάλας χρυσᾶς. On the position of *ἑπτά* before its noun see note on viii. 2.

φιάλας . . . γεμούσας τοῦ θυμοῦ τοῦ θεοῦ. It is highly probable that the Greek word *φιάλη* was adopted into both Hebrew and Aramaic as early as the beginning of the Christian era: see Levi's two Lexicons *in loc.* It is noteworthy that it is used in connection with the same idea as in our text in the Targum on Isa. li. 17, where the Hebrew כוס חמתו (= "the cup of His wrath") is explained by פילי כסא דלוטא and in 22 כוס חמתי by פילי כסא דחמתי. Again in the Targum of Jon. on Gen. xl. 12 we have פיילא דרגזא = "the bowl of wrath" (*i.e.* of the divine wrath). The word thus appears to have had the same idea associated with it as in our text. With the present passage cf. xiv. 8, 10.

τοῦ ζῶντος εἰς τοὺς αἰῶνας. See note on iv. 9.

8. **ἐγεμίσθη ὁ ναὸς καπνοῦ ἐκ τῆς δόξης τοῦ θεοῦ.** *γεμίζω* belongs to the vocabulary of our author but is not used in this connection in the LXX. The first four words recall the statement in Isa. vi. 4, where in connection with the great vision of Isaiah it is said that "the house (*i.e.* the Temple) was filled with smoke" (*ὁ οἶκος ἐνεπλήσθη καπνοῦ*—LXX). The combined ideas of the Temple being filled with smoke and with the glory of the Lord are found in Ezek. x. 4, "The house (*i.e.* the Temple) was filled with the cloud, and the court was full of the brightness of the Lord's glory": Ex. xl. 35, "Moses was not able to enter into the tent of meeting because the cloud abode thereon, and the glory of the Lord filled the tabernacle." See also 1 Kings viii. 10. The glory of God is spoken of as filling the temple in Ezek. xliv. 4; 2 Chron. vii. 2–3. During such manifestations of God's presence no one could enter the earthly temple. In all the O.T. passages above cited the presence of God is a mark of His gracious purposes. Hence the inability of humanity to approach God in these passages was due to the infinite transcendence of God and His unapproachableness by merely finite creatures. But that cannot be the meaning of the clause in our text.

ἐκ τῆς δυνάμεως. This attribute of God is here set parallel with His glory. It is to be manifested in the plagues that follow.

οὐδεὶς ἐδύνατο εἰσελθεῖν κτλ. As we have seen in the first note on this verse, none could enter the earthly Temple in the O.T. during special manifestations of God's presence therein. But, since this cannot hold of the heavenly Temple, inasmuch as in heaven the heavenly hosts are constantly represented as standing in God's immediate presence, it seems necessary to attach a figurative meaning to the clause *οὐδεὶς ἐδύνατο εἰσελθεῖν κτλ.*, and to interpret these words as meaning that, until the plagues were accomplished, none could avert by prayer the doom about to befall the earth through these plagues. At the close of these judgments God's gracious purposes with regard to the nations would take effect: see xiv. 6, xxi. 24, 26.

CHAPTER XVI.

§ 1. *The object of this Chapter.*

The object of this chapter is to set forth the last series of plagues that are to befall the earth. These plagues are symbolized under the seven Bowls which are poured forth by Seven Angels.

In these seven Bowls we have no mere repetition of the divine visitations in the Seals and Woes. Not only are they different in themselves from the Seals and Woes, but they differ further in respect of time and the people affected by them. Although these facts have been brought forward in the Introduction to xv., it is necessary here to emphasize them anew, since the prevailing view is that in the Bowls we have not advanced chronologically, but that in the Seals, Trumpets (Woes), and Bowls the same great principles of God's government are displayed under different aspects. Even scholars, like Bousset, who are opposed to the Recapitulation Theory, are disposed to acknowledge in some degree its validity in regard to the Seals, Trumpets, and Bowls. Though the reader should consult the Introduction to xv., I will here repeat the two chief *differentiae* between the Bowls and the Seals and Woes. These are that the people affected in each series is different and that their order is alike logical and chronological. Under the Seals (save the fifth to which only the Christians were subject) Christian and heathen alike suffer. Then after the sealing of the faithful takes place, all those who had not been so sealed are exposed to the three demonic Woes. In the course of the third Woe the last of the faithful are martyred, and at its close the world is inhabited only by the heathen nations. Then follows the last series of cosmic and other plagues, which are all embracing in their incidence with the exception of the fifth Bowl, which is confined to the kingdom of the Beast, just as the fifth Seal affected only the faithful.

§ 2. *State of the Text.*

The text of this chapter has suffered much through faulty transcription and deliberate alteration. xvi. 1 has *μεγάλης φωνῆς* —an abnormal order of words in our author. Both the context and the diction of xvi. 2[c], and certain clauses in 13–14 are against their authenticity, as is shown in the notes on these passages. The apparently meaningless interchange of *εἰς* and *ἐπί* after *ἐκχέω* is strange. xvi. 10 has sustained the loss of several clauses. xvi. 5[b]–7, which belongs to xix., has been restored in this edition to its original position after xix. 4; xvi. 15, which belongs to iii., has been restored after iii. 3[a].

§ 3. *Diction and Idiom.*

When the interpolated clauses in xvi. 2, 13–14 are removed, the entire phraseology and constructions are those of our author, with the exception of xvi. 1. There are, as was to be expected, phrases not found elsewhere in our author, but these are not against any established usage on his part.

(*a*) *Diction.*

1. ἤκουσα . . . φωνῆς ἐκ: cf. iii. 20, xiv. 13, xxi. 3. Elsewhere in our author *φωνήν* after *ἠκούειν*. τοῖς ἑπτὰ ἀγγέλοις: cf. xv. 6, 8, xvii. 1, xxi. 9. ὑπάγετε κ. ἐκχέετε: cf. x. 8, *ὕπαγε λάβε*. ἐκχέετε . . . εἰς: cf. 2, 3, 4, but *ἐκχ*. . . . *ἐπί* in 8, 10, 12, 17. τοῦ θυμοῦ τοῦ θεοῦ: cf. xiv. 10, 19, xv. 7.

2. ἀπῆλθεν . . . καὶ ἐξέχεεν: cf. v. 7, *ἦλθεν καὶ εἴληφεν*: xvii. 1, xxi. 9 (a Hebraism). Cf. John v. 15, ix. 7, 11, xii. 36. ἐγένετο ἕλκος . . . ἐπί. Here only in our author. On the interpolation *τοὺς ἔχοντας . . . αὐτοῦ*, see note *in loc.*

5[b]–7. See Introd. to xvi. 5[b]–7 on p. 120 sqq.

9. καῦμα: cf. vii. 16. ἐβλασφήμησαν τὸ ὄνομα: cf. xiii. 6. δοῦναι αὐτῷ δόξαν: cf. iv. 9, xi. 13, xiv. 7, xix. 7.

10. τὸν θρόνον τοῦ θηρίου: cf. xiii. 2. ἐσκοτωμένη: cf. ix. 2, where the word refers to the same phenomenon. ἐκ τοῦ πόνου: cf. 11, xxi. 4. Only once elsewhere in N.T., *i.e.* Col. iv. 13.

11. τὸν θεὸν τοῦ οὐρανοῦ: cf. xi. 13 (a source). οὐ μετενόησαν ἐκ τ. ἔργων αὐτῶν: cf. ii. 21, 22, ix. 20, 21.

12. ἑτοιμασθῇ. A frequent word in our author. ἀπὸ ἀνατολῶν ἡλίου: cf. vii. 2.

13. τοῦ δράκοντος . . . τοῦ θηρίου: cf. xiii. 4. τοῦ ψευδοπροφήτου: cf. xix. 20, xx. 10. πνεύματα τρία: such is our author's order: see note on viii. 2.

14. τῆς οἰκουμένης ὅλης: cf. iii. 10, xii. 9. συναγαγεῖν αὐτοὺς εἰς τ. πόλεμον: cf. xx. 8, where the same words recur: see also xix. 19. τῆς ἡμέρας τ. μεγάλης: cf. vi. 17. τοῦ θεοῦ τοῦ παντοκράτορος: cf. i. 8, iv. 8 *n.*, xi. 17, xv. 3, etc.

15. This verse should be read after iii. 3[a]. Every phrase of it has its parallel in iii. See notes *in loc.*

16. τὸν καλούμενον: cf. i. 9, xi. 8, xii. 9, xix. 11. Ἑβραϊστί: cf. ix. 11.

17. φωνὴ . . . ἐκ τοῦ ναοῦ ἀπὸ τοῦ θρόνου: cf. xx. 2, 10 for this combination of prepositions. Elsewhere we have *φωνὴ ἀπὸ τ. θρόνου* in xix. 5 and *φ. ἐκ τ. θρ.* in xxi. 3 and *ἐκ τ. θρ.* with other nouns iv. 5, xxii. 1. γέγονεν: cf. xxi. 6.

18. ἀστραπαὶ καὶ φωναὶ καὶ βρονταί: cf. viii. 5, xi. 19. σεισμὸς . . . μέγας. Cf. vi. 12, viii. 5, xi. 19, xvi. 18.

19. τὸ ποτήριον τοῦ οἴνου τοῦ θυμοῦ τῆς ὀργῆς: cf. xiv. 8, 10, xix. 15.

20. ἔφυγεν, καὶ . . . οὐχ εὑρέθησαν: cf. xx. 11.

21. χαλάζα μεγάλη: cf. xi. 19. ἐβλασφήμησαν: see above on 9.

(*b*) *Idiom.*

1. μεγάλης φωνῆς: the order of the words in this phrase is unique in our author. It is certainly abnormal and is corrected in אP into *φωνῆς μεγάλης*. But there are a few instances where the adjective precedes its noun in our author: cf. i. 10, iii. 12 (in both passages, however, between art. and noun), and *ὀλίγος* in three cases.

2. ἐγένετο . . . ἐπί: unique in our author.

3. αἷμα ὡς νεκροῦ, *i.e.* *αἷμα ὡς αἷμα νεκροῦ*: see Additional Note in vol. i. p. 35.

8. ἐδόθη αὐτῷ *cum inf.*: cf. vi. 4, vii. 2, etc.

9. ἔχοντος τὴν ἐξουσίαν ἐπί: cf. note on ii. 26 on this idiomatic use of art. with *ἐξουσίαν*. οὐ μετενόησαν . . . δοῦναι: cf. xi. 18, *ἦλθεν . . . ὁ καιρὸς . . . δοῦναι*, xvi. 19, *ἐμνήσθη . . . δοῦναι*.

1. μεγάλης φωνῆς. In every other instance of this phrase, in the Apocalypse, i. 10, v. 2, 12, vi. 10, vii. 2, 10, viii. 13, x. 3, xi. 12, 15, xii. 10, xiv. 7, 9, 15, 18, xvi. 17, xix. 1, 17, xxi. 3, the noun *φωνή* precedes the adjective. This "great voice," as that in 17, seems to be that of God Himself and not of an angel. According to xv. 8 none could enter the Temple till the plagues were accomplished. But it is possible that it is the voice of the angel of the altar, as in xiv. 18.

ἐκχέετε τὰς ἑπτὰ φιάλας κτλ. Cf. Dan. ix. 11, Jer. x. 25, xlii. 18, xliv. 6, on this Semitic use of the verb נתך or שָׁפַךְ. *ἐκχέω* occurs repeatedly in this chapter and not elsewhere in the Apocalypse.

ἐκχέετε (see Winer, § 13, 23. Blass, p. 41, would read *ἐκχέατε*) . . . **εἰς τ. γῆν.** So also in 2. Cf. *ἐξέχεεν εἰς τ. θάλασσαν* in 3, and the same verb with *εἰς τοὺς ποταμούς* in 4. On the other hand, we have the same verb with *ἐπὶ τ. ποταμόν* in 12, and with *ἐπὶ τ. ἥλιον* (8), *ἐπὶ τ. θρόνον* (10), and *ἐπὶ τ. ἀέρα* (17).

τὰς ἑπτὰ φιάλας τοῦ θυμοῦ. On the first four Trumpets, which can hardly on any hypothesis be regarded as the work of our author, see Introd. to viii., vol. i. p. 219 sq.

2. This plague recalls the sixth Egyptian plague: Ex. ix. 10–11; Deut. xxviii. 35.

ἐγένετο ἕλκος . . . πονηρόν. The first two words we have in Ex. ix. 10, וַיְהִי שְׁחִין, and the two latter in Deut. xxviii. 35 and Job ii. 7, בִּשְׁחִין רָע. In the last two passages the LXX renders *ἕλκει πονηρῷ.*

ἐγένετο . . . ἐπὶ τοὺς ἀνθρώπους. In Ex. ix. 10 we have *ἐγένετο . . . ἐν τοῖς ἀνθρώποις* (*i.e.* באדם). Thus our author is independent of the LXX. For the construction, Luke i. 65, iii. 2 are generally quoted. *ἐπὶ τοὺς ἀνθρώπους*, "upon men," *i.e.* on all mankind: cf. xvi. 8, 21.

[**τ. ἔχοντας τὸ χάραγμα τοῦ θηρίου καὶ τοὺς προσκυνοῦντας τῇ εἰκόνι αὐτοῦ.**] Cf. xiii. 17, xiv. 9, 11, xix. 20.

This clause has been assigned by Spitta (p. 163) to the final editor of the Book, though he does not specify the grounds. There are, however, good reasons for regarding them as a gloss. 1. The fourth Plague is universal in its incidence as regards the sun, and also the second so far as those on the sea are concerned. That the third is so likewise as regards all fresh waters is clear. Such also is the sixth and the seventh as regards the Euphrates and the air. Hence it is natural to expect that the first Plague is of the same character as in the second, third, and fourth, *i.e.* universal in its incidence. 2. The construction *τοὺς προσκυνοῦντας τῇ εἰκόνι αὐτοῦ* is against our author's usage. See note on vii. 11.

If the above conclusion is not valid, then we must assume that only the adherents of the Roman Empire, and not the rest of the heathen, are affected by the first Plague. In this respect the first and fifth Plagues would have the same incidence. But not only are the followers of the Beast subject to certain physical evils, but they alone are susceptible to the deceitful signs wrought by the false prophet (xix. 20). With this susceptibility to evil influence we should contrast the security against demonic influences enjoyed by those who were sealed by God in vii. 4–8, ix. 4. But all the faithful have already been removed from the earth (see Introd. to xv. p. 26).

3. This Plague recalls the first Egyptian plague, Ex. vii. 17–21, though in the latter the Nile alone is smitten.

ἐγένετο αἷμα. Cf. Ex. vii. 19, היה דם.

πᾶσα ψυχὴ ζωῆς. (Cf. כל־נפש החיה, Gen. i. 21, or נפש חיה, i. 30.) τὰ ἐν τῇ θαλάσσῃ. In viii. 9 only a third of the things in the sea perished. Here the destruction is complete.

4. εἰς τ. ποταμοὺς καὶ τ. πηγὰς τῶν ὑδάτων. See note on viii. 10.

ἐγένετο αἷμα, *i.e.* the fresh waters became blood.

5a. [καὶ ἤκουσα τοῦ ἀγγέλου τῶν ὑδάτων λέγοντος.] An interpolation to introduce xvi. 5b–7, which originally followed after xix. 4, and to which context it is restored in this edition. Cf. 1 Enoch lxvi. 2. "Those angels were over the powers of the waters." In vii. 1 of our text the angels who had control of the winds are referred to, and in xiv. 18 the angel over fire, though the latter appears to be a gloss. On the various classes of angels see the Index to Charles' *The Apocr. and Pseudep.* vol. ii.; Bousset, *Rel. des Judenthums*, 317, also *Jewish Encyc.*, art. "Angelology."

5b–7. This passage has been restored after xix. 4, where the grounds are fully stated for this restoration.

8. The fourth Bowl takes effect on the sun, and causes a plague of excessive heat.

ἐξέχεεν . . . ἐπὶ τὸν ἥλιον. On the use of ἐπί here instead of εἰς as in the preceding verses, see note on 1. The construction ἐδόθη αὐτῷ is a frequent one in our author: see Introd. to Chap. vii., vol. i. p. 191.

9. ἐκαυματίσθησαν . . . καῦμα. (See Blass, *Gr.* p. 91 sq.) Contrast vii. 16, οὐδὲ μὴ παίσῃ ἔτι (emended) αὐτοὺς ὁ ἥλιος οὐδὲ πᾶν καῦμα.

ἐβλασφήμησαν τὸ ὄνομα τοῦ θεοῦ. Cf. xiii. 6; Isa. lii. 5; Rom. ii. 24; 1 Tim. vi. 1; Jas. ii. 7.

ἔχοντος τὴν ἐξουσίαν. See note on ii. 26 on the significance of the article with ἐξουσίαν. Bousset brackets here with the inferior MSS the article. This is strange, since he is aware that when ἐξουσία is accompanied by the art. it connotes full authority or power, and this is certainly the meaning in the present passage.

οὐ μετενόησαν. Cf. ix. 20, 21, xvi. 11. In xi. 13 the Jews repent owing to the earthquake.

δοῦναι αὐτῷ δόξαν. Cf. xi. 13, xiv. 7, xix. 7.

10–11. The fifth Bowl. If we compare this Bowl with the first Woe it is clear that they are developments of the same tradition, though they refer to different periods, the Christians being still upon the earth during the Woes, but not during the Bowls. Thus both affect only the adherents of the beast (xvi. 10: cf. ix. 4). In xvi. 10 the kingdom of the beast is darkened; in ix. 2 the sun is darkened by the smoke issuing from the pit, and from this smoke issued the demonic locusts. In xvi. 10–11 men gnawed their tongues through pain and blasphemed the God of heaven; in ix. 5–6 men were tormented by the locusts and sought death but could not find it.

Similarly we shall find that the sixth Bowl agrees closely with the second Woe (see note on xvi. 12–16), and the seventh Bowl with the third Woe (see note on xvi. 17–21). These facts will help us in the elucidation of the difficulties affecting the fifth Bowl.

But there is another point worthy of consideration. If we compare the seven Bowls with the Seven Seals, we find that, whereas only the faithful were the victims of the fifth Seal, only the followers of the beast are affected by the fifth Bowl.

10. The visitation on the kingdom of the Antichrist.

τὸν θρόνον τοῦ θηρίου, *i.e.* Rome. Cf. xiii. 2, *ἔδωκεν αὐτῷ* (*i.e.* *τῷ θηρίῳ*) *ὁ δράκων . . . τὸν θρόνον αὐτοῦ*. The first four Bowls had affected the world at large; the fifth assails only the kingdom of the Beast.

ἡ βασιλεία αὐτοῦ ἐσκοτωμένη. Owing to this clause the fifth Plague has been taken to be one of darkness recalling the Egyptian one, Ex. x. 21 sqq. But this interpretation cannot be upheld. A plague of darkness would be wholly insufficient to explain the agony experienced by the adherents of the Beast after the pouring out of the fifth Bowl. Hence something else than the darkness that ensued on the pouring out of the fifth Bowl must be presupposed as the cause of this agony. Now, if we turn to the first Woe of which the fifth Bowl is in some sense an abbreviation, we can explain both these statements. There we find that the sun was *darkened* by the smoke that issued from the pit (ix. 2). There is every reason for supposing that we have here the true explanation of the darkening of the kingdom of the Beast. Further, the cause of the torments endured by the adherents of the Beast (xvi. 10, *ἐμασῶντο τὰς γλώσσας αὐτῶν ἐκ τοῦ πόνου*) is to be traced to the demonic locusts which issued from the smoke that ascended from the pit. Men were so tortured by the scorpion-like stings of these locusts (ix. 10) that they longed for death to end their agony (ix. 5–6). Hence we infer that after *ἐσκοτωμένη* several clauses have been lost, in which the causes of the darkness and the sufferings of mankind were given. The hypothesis that certain clauses of the nature suggested originally stood after *ἐσκοτωμένη* is established by a clause in 11, *i.e.* *καὶ ἐκ τῶν ἑλκῶν αὐτῶν*. These sores could not have been caused by the darkness. Spitta and, so far as I am aware, Spitta alone (p. 171) has recognized this fact that the fifth Bowl originally treated of demonic locusts as the first Woe does. But he rejects (171, 576) *τὸν θρόνον τοῦ θηρίου· καὶ ἐγένετο ἡ βασιλεία αὐτοῦ ἐσκοτωμένη* as an addition from the hand of the final editor on the ground that the throne of the beast is not to be identified with Rome but with the abyss as in ix. 11, and that accordingly the place on which the fifth Bowl is to be poured should be named, where the plague in question is to be developed, analogously with the rest of the plagues (xvi. 2, 3, 4, 8, 12, 17). He also excises the clause καὶ ἐκ τῶν ἑλκῶν αὐτῶν to the weakening of his own hypothesis. But I have already shown above that ἡ βασιλεία αὐτοῦ ἐσκοτωμένη can be fully justified. Nor can any valid objection be taken to τὸν θρόνον τοῦ θηρίου, seeing that already in xiii. 2 the Dragon had given his throne to the Beast. Thus it is only necessary here to suppose a lacuna in the text.

ἐμασῶντο κτλ. In the LXX only in Job xxx. 5.

11. Their sufferings drove the followers of the beast to fresh blasphemy instead of to repentance.

τὸν θεὸν τοῦ οὐρανοῦ. See xi. 13.

καὶ ἐκ τῶν ἑλκῶν αὐτῶν. This phrase proves that the sufferings of the subjects of the Beast are not intelligible from the text as it stands after the loss of the clauses referred to in the note on 10. Some scholars explain it as referring to the phrase ἕλκος κακόν in 2.

οὐ μετενόησαν ἐκ τῶν ἔργων. So already in ii. 21, ix. 20.

12-16. The sixth Bowl—at all events xvi. 12—is related to the second Woe, ix. 13-21. In the latter passage we have an account of the demonic horsemen from the Euphrates, whose objective is the heathen unbelieving world. In the present context the river Euphrates is dried up in order that the way may be prepared for the kings coming from the East under Nero *redivivus*, and their objective is Rome, the throne of the Beast. This forecast reappears in xvii. 12-13, 17, 16. The powers of the Beast are therefore at variance. On the other hand, the gathering together of the kings of the earth to Armageddon is a distant echo of the onslaught of the forces of Gog in Ezekiel on Jerusalem. This expectation has undergone many developments in the interval, and reappears in a duplicated form under the actual designation of Gog and Magog in xx. 7-10, where it represents the last uprising of the powers of evil before their final destruction by fire from heaven. But the present context (xvi. 13-16) reproduces an earlier form of this expectation, and this form of it is referred to twice elsewhere in the book—in xiv. 14, 18-20, and xix. 11-21. In these three passages, which refer to a universal insurrection of the heathen nations at the instigation of the demons and the Beast and the False Prophet, *before the Messianic Kingdom*, the forces of evil are destroyed by the Messiah, and the Beast and the False Prophet cast into the lake of fire, whereas in the final insurrection of the heathen nations due to the direct instigation of Satan *at the close of the Messianic Kingdom* they are annihilated by fire from heaven, and Satan himself cast into the lake of fire, where already were the Beast and the False Prophet.

Further, it is to be observed that the uprising of the kings of the East against Rome is only the preparatory step to their conflict with the Lamb, as we see in xvii. 12–17. Hence their combination here (xvi. 12) with the kings of the whole earth (xvii. 14) to resist the Lamb.

12. The march of the kings of the East against Rome, which is described more fully in xvii. 12–13, 17, 16.

τὸν ποταμὸν . . . Εὐφράτην. Cf. ix. 14.

ἐξηράνθη τὸ ὕδωρ αὐτοῦ. For the idea cf. Ex. xiv. 21; Josh. iii. 13–17; Isa. xi. 15 sq., xliv. 27, li. 10; Jer. xxviii. (li.) 36; Zech. x. 11; 4 Ezra xiii. 43–47.

ἑτοιμασθῇ. Cf. Isa. xl. 3, ἑτοιμάσατε τὴν ὁδόν. For the use of this verb in the second Woe, cf. ix. 15. It is a favourite with our author: cf. viii. 6, ix. 7, xii. 6, xix. 7, xxi. 2.

13, 14^bc, 16. The gathering together of all the kings of the earth to war against God and Christ. Cf. Ps. ii. 2. See note above on 12–16.

13. Three unclean spirits from the Dragon (*i.e.* Satan: cf. xii. 3, 9), the Beast, and the False Prophet (*i.e.* the second Beast) go forth to call together the kings of the earth. Cf. 1 Kings xxii. 22. Contrast the three angels in xiv. 6 sqq.

τοῦ ψευδοπροφήτου. Here for the first time the second Beast (xiii. 11 sqq) is so designated.

πνεύματα . . . ἀκάθαρτα. Cf. Matt. x. 1; Mark i. 23, etc.

[ὡς βάτραχοι.] First we observe that the construction is *unique* in the Apocalypse. According to the universal usage outside the present passage we should here have ὡς βατράχους, as indeed ℵ* and many cursives actually do read. But the best authorities support the abnormal text. However, as we shall see on the next verse, the context requires the excision of ὡς βάτραχοι . . . σημεῖα as a marginal gloss subsequently incorporated in the text. As regards the use of the phrase, it may be observed that frogs were regarded in the Zend religion (see *S.B.E.* iv. 171, note) as the source of plagues and death. In Hermas, *Vis.* iv. 1. 6, locusts of a fiery colour are seen by the Seer coming forth from the mouth of a great monster: ἰδοὺ βλέπω θηρίον μέγιστον . . . καὶ ἐκ τοῦ στόματος αὐτοῦ ἀκρίδες πύριναι ἐξεπορεύοντο. This conception combines the ideas under lying ix. 3 and xvi. 13. Frogs were regarded as the agents of Ahriman: cf. *Plut. de Iside*, 46 (Moffatt).

14. [εἰσὶν γὰρ πνεύματα δαιμονίων ποιοῦντα σημεῖα.] There are difficulties attaching to this clause. 1. It has been taken parenthetically by Bousset and Holtzmann as an explanatory remark of our author: "there are, to wit, demonic spirits, sign workers" (as their masters, xiii. 13, 14). The phrase πνεύματα δαιμονίων should be rendered "spirits, that is, demons," *i.e.* "demonic spirits," as in Luke iv. 33, πνεῦμα δαιμονίου ἀκαθάρτου = "a spirit, that is, an unclean demon." The genitive is one of apposition or definition: cf. ii. 10, ὁ στέφανος τῆς ζωῆς. Demons have no spirits, but are themselves spirits. According to 1 Enoch xv. 8, 9, 11, xvi. 1, xix., xcix. 7, the demons were the spirits which went forth from the antediluvian giants on their destruction, these giants being the children of the fallen angels and the daughters of men (cf. Gen. vi. 1). These demons were not to incur punishment till the final judgment: cf. Matt. viii. 29; 1 Enoch xvi. 1; Jubilees x. 5–11. They were subject to Satan as in our text: cf. Matt. xii. 24–28. 2. Or it may be rendered: "they are, to wit, demonic spirits, sign workers." But however we take this clause it is of the nature of a gloss.

† ἃ ἐκπορεύεται †.—This—the best attested text—is wholly unsatisfactory. ℵ* and several cursives read ἐκπορεύεσθαι. Though this is less unsatisfactory it is against our author's usage as well as against Greek idiom. The context undoubtedly requires ἐκπορευόμενα, since without this participle the construction and meaning are both defective. For the preceding words εἶδον ἐκ τοῦ στόματος τοῦ δράκοντος . . . πνεύματα τρία are incomplete in both respects without the participle ἐκπορευόμενα. The phrase ἐκ τ. στόματος . . . ἐκπορεύεσθαι is of frequent occurrence in our text: cf. i. 16, ix. 17, 18, xi. 5, xix. 15, 21. Thus we should read εἶδον ἐκ τ. στόματος τ. δράκοντος . . . πνεύματα τρία . . . ἐκπορευόμενα (cf. i. 16 for the same separation of ἐκ τ. στόματος and the verb), and translate: "and I saw from the mouth of the dragon . . . three unclean spirits going forth." The present text εἶδον ἐκ τ. στόματος . . . πνεύματα τρία without a participle, which at once explains the ἐκ and completes the sentence, is, so far as I am aware, unexampled, and yet it has been thoughtlessly accepted by every grammarian and student of the Apocalypse, perhaps in many cases from the idea that any construction is possible in this Book.

Hence, since for ἃ ἐκπορεύεται we must read ἐκπορευόμενα and connect it with εἶδον ἐκ κτλ., we conclude that εἰσὶν γὰρ . . . σημεῖα is a marginal gloss, and likewise ὡς βάτραχοι if this is the earliest form of this phrase. Thus ὡς βάτραχοι . . . σημεῖα was originally a marginal gloss which on its incorporation into the text brought about the change of ἐκπορευόμενα into ἃ ἐκπορεύεται.

τῆς οἰκουμένης ὅλης. Cf. iii. 10, xii. 9, for the same phrase and the same thought connection.

συναγαγεῖν αὐτοὺς κτλ Cf. xx. 8.

τῆς ἡμέρας τῆς μεγάλης τοῦ θεοῦ. This is the great day of Yahweh's reckoning with the ungodly nations. Cf. 2 Pet. iii. 12.

ἡ τοῦ θεοῦ ἡμέρα. See Charles' *Eschatology*² (see Index), also the authorities quoted in the note of vi. 17 of our text.

τοῦ θεοῦ τοῦ παντοκράτορος. A divine title frequently found in our author: cf. i. 8, iv. 8 (note), xi. 17, xv. 3, xvi. 7, xix. 6, 15, xxi. 22.

15. With Könnecke (*Emendationen zu Stellen NT.* 35–37, whose work I have not seen; the reference I owe to Moffatt) this verse is to be taken as an intrusion here. Originally either it stood between iii. 3^a and 3^b, where it would complete the *ἰδού* series of ii. 22, iii. 9, 20, or it should with Beza be transposed before iii. 18. I therefore bracket it with most modern critics in its present context.

What Könnecke's arguments are I do not know, but the cogency of his suggestion manifests itself on a comparison of 15 with iii. 2–4. To see how fitly it comes in after iii. 3^a we have only to compare *ἰδοὺ ἔρχομαι* with the series of verbs so introduced in ii. 22, iii. 9, 20: *ὡς κλέπτης· μακάριος ὁ γρηγορῶν καὶ τηρῶν τὰ ἡμάτια αὐτοῦ* (xvi. 15^{ab}) with *γίνου γρηγορῶν* in iii. 2 and *ἐὰν οὖν μὴ γρηγορήσῃς, ἥξω ὡς κλέπτης* in iii. 3^b (observe also the use of *τηρεῖν* though without an expressed object in iii. 3^a and *οὐκ ἐμόλυναν τὰ ἱμάτια αὐτῶν* in iii. 4): *ἵνα μὴ γυμνὸς περιπατῇ* (xvi. 15) with *περιπατήσουσιν μετ' ἐμοῦ ἐν λευκοῖς* in iii. 4, and the remaining words *καὶ βλέπωσιν τὴν ἀσχημοσύνην αὐτοῦ* with *ἵνα . . . μὴ φανερωθῇ ἡ αἰσχύνη τῆς γυμνότητός σου*, iii. 18. *κλέπτης* and *γρηγορεῖν* occur only in xvi. 15 and iii. 2–3 in our author.

This verse implies that the sixth Bowl will take the world by surprise. But it is hard to see how the elaborate preparations of the kings of the East followed by those of all the kings of the world could do so. Finally, the utter inappropriateness of 15 in its present context is further evident from the fact that all the faithful have already been removed from the earth.

This verse forms one of the seven beatitudes in the Apocalypse: i. 3 (iii. 3) (xiv. 13), xix. 9, xx. 6, xxii. 14, 7. When xvi. 15 is restored to its original context, we find a special appositeness in their order: first beatitude (i. 3) deals with those who read the prophecy; the second (iii. 3, *i.e.* xvi. 15) with those who watch and keep their garments clean: the third, xiv. 12–13 (to be read after xiii. 15), with those who die in the Lord in the last persecution: the fourth, xix. 9, with those who are invited to the marriage supper of the Lamb: the fifth, xx. 6, with those who share in the first resurrection: the sixth, xxii. 14, with those who had washed their garments and had permission to eat of the tree of life during the Millennial Kingdom: the seventh, xxii. 7, with those who keep the words of this Book.

16. This verse should follow immediately on 14, and 15 be transferred to its original context between iii. 3^a and iii. 3^b.

συνήγαγεν. Neuter nouns in the plural are followed either by the singular (viii. 3, xiii. 14, xiv. 13, xvi. 14, etc.) or plural verb in the Apocalypse, but mostly by the latter.

τὸν καλούμενον. Cf. i. 9, xi. 8, xii. 9.

Ἑβραϊστί. See ix. 11.

Ἅρ Μαγεδών. No convincing interpretation has as yet been given of this phrase, which should probably be translated "the mountains of Megiddo." The city Megiddo was notable as the scene where Barak and Deborah overthrew the forces of Sisera by "the waters of Megiddo" (Judg. v. 19–21), and Pharaoh Necho defeated and slew Josiah, *i.e.*, in "the plain of Megiddo" (2 Kings xxiii. 29, 30; 2 Chron. xxxv. 22; Herod. ii. 159). But the phrase "mountains of Megiddo" is not found elsewhere. Owing to this fact it has been proposed by Hilgenfeld to take *Ἅρ Μαγεδών* as = עַר מגדון, where, עַר = עִיר = "city of Megiddo." Völter regards *Ἅρ* as = אֶרֶץ, "land." But both these conjectures have failed to meet with acceptance. It is best at present to regard the first element in the phrase as = "mountains"; for the final conflict in Ezek. xxxviii. 8, 21, xxxix. 2, 4, 17—a passage which influenced our author in xx. 8–11—was to take place on "the mountains of Israel." In Dan. xi. 45 the writer expected that Antiochus would meet his end "between the sea and the glorious holy mountain." Since Megiddo is not associated with any eschatological expectation, it is possible some corruption underlies this word. Hence the phrase in Daniel, "glorious holy mountain" (= Mt. Zion), as well as the expression in Ezekiel, "mountains of Israel," may give some support to the conjecture cited by Cheyne (*Encyc. Bib.* i. 311) that *Ἅρ Μαγεδών* = הַר מִגְדּוֹ, his "fruitful mountain." This would associate the battle scene with Jerusalem as in Joel iii. 2; Zech. xiv. 2 sqq.; 1 Enoch lvi. 7, xc. 13–19. As Rome was to be laid desolate by the kings of the East, xvi. 12, xvii. 16–17, so (after the destruction of the kings of the East—see xix. 13 *n.*) the kings of the whole earth were to be destroyed in the neighbourhood of Zion. Now, since xvi. 14, 16 and xx. 8–10 are both ultimately derived from Ezek. xxxviii.–xxxxix., and since in xx. 8–10 the scene of the last great struggle at the close of the Millennial Kingdom is placed in the neighbourhood of the Heavenly Jerusalem (which has taken the place of the Old), it is possible that *Ἅρ Μαγεδών* may be a corruption either for הַר מִגְדּוֹ = "his fruitful mountain," as above suggested, or for עִר־חֶמְדָּה, "the desirable city" (*i.e.* Jerusalem: cf. ארץ חמדה, "the desirable land," *i.e.* Palestine, Jer. iii. 19; Zech. vii. 14). The latter suggestion derives some countenance from xx. 9, *τὴν πόλιν τὴν ἠγαπημένον*, which is there surrounded by the hostile armies of Gog and Magog. But everything connected with the text and meaning of the phrase is uncertain. Hence Gunkel, followed by Cheyne and Bousset, conjectures in his *Schöpfung und Chaos*, 263–266, that we have in this mysterious phrase a survival of some ancient myth—no longer intelligible to our author—which associated the final conflict of the gods with some ancient mountain. Hommel's suggestion that the phrase goes back to הר מועד (Isa. xiv. 13) = "the mountain in the north where the gods meet," springs from the same view of the passage. Hence Bousset concludes that the context here goes back to an ancient myth which described the assault on the holy mountain of the gods by an army of demons mustered by certain evil spirits. To this myth our author in Bousset's opinion gave an historical character by connecting it with the Parthians. See Nestle's art. in Hastings' *D.B.* ii. 304 sq.

17–21. The seventh Bowl. Just as the fifth and sixth Bowls showed undeniable affinities with the first and second Woes, so the seventh Bowl appears to be slightly related to the third Woe, xi. 14–19. In xvi. 17 a voice from heaven declares that the punishment of the heathen and of the great city of Rome is now completed in the pouring out of the seventh Bowl with the results about to be recounted. In xi. 18^h it is said that the time has come for "destroying those who destroy the earth": cf. xix. 2. This connection is indeed slight in itself, but there are others, for the "earthquake and great hail" in xi. 19 are described at som length in xvi. 18–21.

ἐξέχεεν . . . ἐπὶ τὸν ἀέρα. On this visitation on the air cf. ix. 2. The construction with *ἐπί* here is extraordinary: see note on 1.

ἐκ τοῦ ναοῦ ἀπὸ τοῦ θρόνου. A divine voice was heard coming from the Temple in xvi. 1. Here the place whence it comes is more nearly defined. Throughout the Apocalypse the throne is connected with the Temple, though at times it is impossible to visualize the vision. But, as we have seen in the note on iv. 2, the combination of the Temple and throne scenery goes far back into Judaism.

φωνὴ . . . ἀπὸ τοῦ θρόνου. So also in xix. 5. It is noteworthy that in exactly a similar connection our author uses *ἐκ τοῦ θρόνου* in xxi. 3.

γέγονεν. Cf. xxi. 6. The great voice from the throne, which had commanded these plagues, xvi. 1, now proclaims that they are at an end.

18. ἀστραπαὶ καὶ φωναὶ καὶ βρονταί. See notes on iv. 5, viii. 5.

σεισμὸς . . . μέγας. Cf. viii. 5, xi. 19.

οἷος οὐκ ἐγένετο ἀφ' οὗ ἄνθρωποι ἐγένοντο ἐπὶ τῆς γῆς. The phraseology is borrowed from Dan. xii. 1. Cf. Theod. θλίψις, οἵα οὐ γέγονεν ἀφ' ἧς γεγένηται ἔθνος ἐν τῇ γῇ (ἐπὶ τῆς γῆς, AQ), and the LXX οἵα οὐκ ἐγενήθη ἀφ' οὗ ἐγενήθησαν. Here the ἐπὶ τῆς γῆς is found both in our text and Theod.—a fact which may point to the presence of בארין in the text of Daniel in the 1st cent. A.D. Our text is clearly an independent rendering of Dan. xii. 1. Cf. Ass. Mos. viii. 1, "ira quae talis non fuit in illis."

19. [**καὶ ἐγένετο . . . εἰς τρία μέρη**] **καὶ οἱ πόλεις τῶν ἐθνῶν ἔπεσαν.** I have bracketed the first clause; for εἰς τρία μέρη is against the usage of our author, who would have written εἰς μέρη τρία: cf. xvi. 13, xxi. 13 (four times). Moreover, there is no hint in xvii.–xviii. that Rome had suffered from a violent earthquake. Rome is dealt with in the words which follow—καὶ Βαβυλῶν κτλ. These words prepare the reader for xvii.–xviii.

ἐγένετο . . . εἰς. Cf. Acts v. 36. In viii. 11 of our author the text is corrupt.

ἡ πόλις ἡ μεγάλη. Here as in xiv. 8 (see note) it is Rome, not Jerusalem, that is designated as "Babylon the Great." Jerusalem had already been in part overthrown by an earthquake in xi. 13: 7000 of its inhabitants had been thereby destroyed and the rest had repented. Here, according to the interpolator, it is Rome that is visited by an earthquake, and that an earthquake such as had never yet been experienced on earth, and yet in xvii. 3–4 Rome appears not to have suffered in this earthquake in the least degree. Its final overthrow and destruction are yet to come in xvii.–xviii. This judgment and that of the great hail do not lead men to repent: rather they blaspheme the more: cf. ver. 21. To identify Babylon here with Jerusalem, as is done by J. Weiss, Moffatt, and some other scholars, is against the whole context and the right conception of xvii.–xviii.

ἐμνήσθη δοῦναι. The passive use of μνησθῆναι is found in Ezek. iii. 20 (οὐ μὴ μνησθῶσιν αἱ δικαιοσύναι αὐτοῦ), xviii. 22, 24. It is found also in Acts x. 31 and elsewhere. As regards the construction we should compare xi. 18, ἦλθεν ὁ καιρὸς . . . δοῦναι, xvi. 9, οὐ μετενόησαν δοῦναι. In Ps. cix. 16 and ciii. 18 we find the infinitive in Hebrew after זכר.

τὸ ποτήριον τοῦ οἴνου τοῦ θυμοῦ τῆς ὀργῆς αὐτοῦ. See notes on xiv. 8, 10. The expression τοῦ θυμοῦ τῆς ὀργῆς recurs in xix. 15. In Isa. vii. 4; Jer. iv. 26, xxv. 16 (xlix. 37). xxxii. 23 (xxv. 37); Lam. i. 12, ii. 3, iv. 11; Ezek. xxiii. 25; Hos. xi. 9; Nah. i. 6, we find the combination ὀργὴ θυμοῦ (=חרין אף). The order θυμὸς ὀργῆς is infrequent in the LXX but it is found: cf. Isa. ix. 18.

20. πᾶσα νῆσος ἔφυγεν. Cf. vi. 14. πᾶν ὄρος καὶ νῆσος . . . ἐκινήθησαν.

οὐχ εὑρέθησαν. Cf. v. 4, xii. 8, xiv. 5, xviii. 21, xx. 11 (ἔφυγεν ἡ γῆ . . . καὶ τόπος οὐχ εὑρέθη)—a familiar Hebrew expression (לא נמצאו): cf. Ps. xxxvi. (xxxvii.) 36.

ὄρη οὐχ εὑρέθησαν. This disappearance of the mountains is one of the signs of the end of the world: cf. vi. 14; also Ass. Mos. x. 4, "And the high mountains shall be made low, and the hills shall be shaken and fall," also 1 Enoch i. 6. In later Christian Apocalyptic this idea is found not unfrequently: cf. Sibyl. Or. viii. 234, 236, ὑψώσει δὲ φάραγγας, ὀλεῖ δ' ὑψώματα βουνῶν, ὕψος δ' οὐκέτι λοιπὸν (so Hase) ἐν ἀνθρώποισι φανεῖται. ἶσα δ' ὄρη πεδίοις ἔσται καὶ πᾶσα θάλασσα οὐκέτι πλοῦν ἕξει.

A Latin translation of viii. 217–250 is given in Augustine, *De Civitate Dei*, xviii. 23:

> "Dejiciet colles, valles extollet ab imo.
> Non erit in rebus hominum sublime vel altum.
> Tam aequantur campis montes et coerula ponti
> Omnia cessabunt."

Lactantius, *Div. Instit.* vii. 16, 11, "Montes quoque altissimi decident et planis aequabuntur, mare innavigabile constituetur."

The idea underlying these passages is to be carefully distinguished from that which appears in the Zend religion to the effect that the mountains, being the work of the evil spirit Ahriman, would disappear with him, and the new earth would be "an iceless, slopeless plain; even the mountain whose summit is the support of the Kinvat bridge they keep down, and it will not exist," Bund. xxx. 33 (*S.B.E.* v. 129 sq.). The object of the earth being made a smooth plain was, as Böklen states (*Eschatologie*, p. 133), to make intercourse easy for the renewed humanity. In this connection, cf. Sib. Or. iii. 776 sqq.

Yet another idea underlies the use of analogous phrases in Isa. xl. 4; 1 Bar. v. 5–9; Pss. Sol. xi. 5.

21. χάλαζα μεγάλη. So also in xi. 19. Probably the בָּרָד כָּבֵד of Ex. ix. 24—the seventh of the Egyptian plagues.

ὡς ταλαντιαία. A talent (τάλαντον = כִּכָּר) weighed something between 108 and 130 lbs. The word ταλαντιαῖος is found in Polybius and Josephus, as Swete points out.

ἐβλασφήμησαν . . . τὸν θεόν. As in xvi. 9, 11 so here the effect of the judgment is only to harden the hearts of the heathen nations. This attitude of theirs stands in contrast with that of the Jews in xi. 13.

σφόδρα. Here only in our author. It stands last like מְאֹד in Hebrew, not only here but elsewhere in the N.T. Cf. Matt. ii. 10, xxvi. 22; Mark xvi. 4, etc. But in all such cases σφόδρα follows immediately after the adjective it qualifies, whereas here, as occasionally in the case of the Hebrew מְאֹד, the adjective and adverb are sundered.

CHAPTER XVII.

§ 1. *Contents and Authorship.*

This chapter begins with a promise on the part of an angel to the Seer to show him "the judgment of the Great Harlot," but throughout the chapter this subject is not referred to save once (in xvii. 16), and alike the vision in xvii. 3^{b}–6 and its interpretation by the angel are concerned with the Beast, which according to the present form of the text symbolizes the demonic Nero, or Nero returning from the abyss to lead the Parthian powers against Rome. The judgment of the Great Harlot is given at length in xviii.

But if we are to give the subject the fuller treatment it demands, we soon recognize that xvii. cannot be treated apart from xviii. Thus in xvii. 1 an angel summoned the Seer to show him "the judgment of the Great Harlot," and transported him in the spirit (xvii. 3) to the wilderness, where he had a vision of the woman and of the scarlet Beast, whereon she sat, with its seven heads and ten horns. Now the woman was magnificently arrayed in purple and scarlet and adorned with gold and precious stones, and on her forehead she bore the name of Babylon, the mother of fornication and abomination, and she was drunken with the blood of Christian martyrs (xvii. 4–6). And when the Seer was filled with amazement at what he saw, the angel turned aside from his original purpose of showing him the judgment of the Great Harlot, and proceeded to explain the hidden meaning of the woman and the Beast with the seven heads and ten horns. The Beast, said the angel, "was and is not and is about to come up out of the abyss and goeth to destruction," and all the faithless upon earth shall marvel at his return after his death (xvii. 7–8), but they that are wise will not do so; for they will see that the seven heads are seven kings, of whom the sixth is at present reigning. This sixth would in due course be succeeded by the seventh, who would reign but a short time. And on the death of the seventh king would follow an eighth, who was in reality the Beast—and yet he would not be the eighth king, since he was actually one of the seven (xvii. 9–11). (The Beast is clearly here the demonic Nero returning to earth from the abyss.)

So much for the seven heads. As for the ten horns, these are ten subordinate kings who will shortly come into their royal authority, and with one accord will, through the ordinance of

God, place all their power at the disposal of the Beast, and the Beast and these kings will hate the Harlot, and destroy her by fire (xvii. 12–13, 17, 16). And having destroyed the Harlot they will go to war with the Lamb, but they will be overcome by the Lamb and His followers (xvii. 14, a conquest implied by xix. 13). Now the Harlot is none other than the city Rome (xvii. 18), whose doom is described in the vision that follows.

So much for the thought of the chapter as it stands. But the order of events is strange and unexpected. Though the Seer has promised in xvii. 1 a vision of the judgment of the Great Harlot, in all the verses that follow there is not a reference to this subject save in xvii. 16. The promise, in fact, is not redeemed till xviii., for the single mention of this judgment in xvii. 16 cannot be regarded as a fulfilment of it. xviii. is necessarily introduced by the technical phrase μετὰ ταῦτα εἶδον, since other weighty subjects have intervened between xvii. 1 and its fulfilment in xviii.

The irregular character of this chapter prepares us for the conclusion which a detailed study of it makes manifest, *i.e.* that our author is here using sources which for convenience' sake are here designated as A and B. A = 1^c–2, 3^b–6^a, 7, 18, and some clauses in 8–10. B is fragmentary: 11–13, 17, 16 (see § 5). The order of the words in A is Semitic, but not in B, and whereas the diction and idiom in both show indubitable traces of our author's hand, they just as indubitably contain idioms which are against his usage (§ 3). Again, though the thought underlying the *present* form of the chapter is that of our author, even the most superficial criticism makes it clear that this thought is superinduced, and that the meaning of the symbol "the Beast" has been transformed by additions to the text. Thus in A the Beast symbolized the Roman Empire, a meaning which still survives in xvii. 3, whereas in B it symbolized the living Nero returning from the East at the head of the Parthian kings in order to destroy Rome (§ 4). By certain additions in xvii. 8, 11 the Beast has come to symbolize Nero *redivivus* or the demonic Nero coming up from the abyss—an expectation prevalent from 90 A.D. onwards in many Christian communities.

There are certain dislocations of the text. Thus xvii. 17 should be transposed before xvii. 16, and xvii. 14—an addition of our author—should be placed after xvii. 16, since it deals with the destruction of the Beast and his Parthian allies, who in xvii. 17, 16 have already destroyed Rome. There are two glosses, one in xvii. 9, which gives an alternative and wrong interpretation of the seven heads in xvii. 9, and another in xvii. 15, which was originally a marginal gloss on ἐπὶ ὑδάτων in xvii. 1 and has got wrongly thrust into its present position (§ 4).

In the Introd. to xviii. we shall find grounds for regarding A and xviii. as derived from one and the same source.

§ 2. *The order of the Words.*

So far as the order of the words goes, this chapter falls into two parts. xvii. 1–10 is Hebraic as to order. Thus the verb precedes the object three times in xvii. 7, twice in xvii. 3, and once in xvii. 1, 6. In xvii. 8 the verb precedes the subject twice, and once in xvii. 1 and 2. In xvii. 4–5 there are only substantive sentences.

In xvii. 11–17 the order is decidedly non-Semitic. Only once, *i.e.* in xvii. 17, does the verb precede the subject, whereas the object, and also the subject where expressed, precede the verb twice in each of the verses xvii. 12, 13, 16 (*i.e.* six times in three verses). Again, in each of xvii. 14, 16, 17 the order subj. vb. obj. occurs once, and in each of xvii. 14, 15 the order subj. and vb. It is true that in some of these cases the order is quite good Semitic, inasmuch as its unusualness serves to mark emphasis, opposition, or the like: but in respect of order xvii. 11–17 is, as a whole, non-Semitic and differs in this respect from xvii. 1–10. Such a fact can hardly be accidental, and must be accounted for. The linguistic character of xvii. 11–17 is almost without parallel in the rest of the book save in xi. 1–13, which on these and other grounds we were obliged to attribute to a Greek or Aramaic source (see i. p. 270 sqq.). *Any theory as to the authorship of xvii. should account for these facts.* So far as these facts go we are predisposed to assign xvii. 1–10 and xvii. 11–17 (or the original forms of these; for they exhibit undoubted marks of revision, as we shall see presently) *to different sources, the latter apparently to a Greek source.*

§ 3. *The diction and idiom of this Chapter show manifest traces of the hand of our author (in the way of revision, as we shall see later), but they are frequently against his usage.*

(*a*) *Traces of the hand of our author, especially in xvii. 1–9, 14 (which verse is wholly from his hand).*—καὶ ἦλθεν . . . δείξω in xvii. 1, recurs in xxi. 9: indeed every word and phrase of xvii. 1 are from our author. Thus εἷς ἐκ is his universal usage. On ἐλάλησεν . . . λέγων and δείξω σοι see iv. 1 *n.* In xvii. 3, ἀπήνεγκεν . . . ἐν πνεύματι recurs in xxi. 10. The constructions καθημένης ἐπὶ ὑδάτων, xvii. 1[1] and καθημένην ἐπὶ θηρίον in xvii. 3

[1] If, as we shall seek to prove, part of xvii. 1 has come from a source, then the form of the phrase *καθημένης ἐπὶ ὑδάτων πολλῶν* seems to come from our author; for the phrase is clearly derived from Jer. li. (xxviii.) 13, and since *καθῆσθαι* is never used as a translation of שכן which is in the original here,

are also his idiom (see iv. 2, note). περιβεβλημένη c. acc. xvii. 4 (see iii. 5, note); also ἐπὶ τὸ μέτωπον αὐτῆς, xvii. 5 (see vii. 3 *n.*); also οἱ κατοικοῦντες ἐπὶ τῆς γῆς, xvii. 8 [1] (see i. p. 336, and contrast οἱ κατοικοῦντες τὴν γῆν, xvii. 2); also ἦν καὶ οὐκ ἔστιν καὶ μέλλει ἀναβαίνειν . . . ὑπάγει and ὅτι ἦν . . . πάρεσται in xvii. 8; ὧδε . . . σοφίαν (cf. xiii. 18) in xvii. 9; ὃ ἦν . . . ἔστιν and καὶ εἰς ἀπώλειαν ὑπάγει in xvii. 11, and οἵτινες (= οἵ) in xvii. 12. xvii. 14 is wholly from his hand: with οὗτοι . . . νικήσει αὐτούς cf. xiii. 7, which is his; with κύριος . . . βασιλέων cf. xix. 16—while πιστός is often used by him. In xvii. 16 we have an instance of an idiom used by our author; *i.e.* ἠρημωμένην ποιήσουσιν αὐτήν: cf. xii. 15, xxi. 5. In xvii. 17 with τελεσθήσονται cf. x. 7, xv. 8, xx. 3, 5, 7.

(*b*) *Idiom and diction against his usage.*—In xvii. 2, οἱ κατοικοῦντες τὴν γῆν conflicts with the universal usage of our author: see vol. i. p. 336, and note on xi. 10. γέμοντα ὀνόματα, xvii. 3 (3^b) —elsewhere c. gen. See n. on xvii. 3. In xvii. 8 γέγραπται ἐπὶ τὸ βιβλίον is against his usage; for in this phrase we have always γράφεσθαι ἐν τῷ βιβλίῳ elsewhere: cf. (i. 3) xiii. 8, xx. 12, xxi. 27 [xxii. 18, 19]. In different phrases γράφειν ἐπί *cum acc.* is found: cf. ii. 17, ἐπὶ τὴν ψῆφον . . . γεγραμμένον: iii. 12, γράψω ἐπ' αὐτὸν τὸ ὄνομα: cf. also xix. 16. The order in αὐτὸν δεῖ is against his usage, xvii. 10—elsewhere δεῖ precedes: cf. x. 11, xx. 3, xi. 5: ἐκ τῶν ἑπτά, xvii. 11—elsewhere in Apoc. always εἷς ἐκ: cf. v. 5, vi. 1 (*bis*), vii. 13, ix. 13, xiii. 3, xv. 7, xvii. 1, xxi. 9.

In xvii. 8, which like xiii. 8 is a rendering of the same Hebrew source, the split relative is not reproduced in the Greek, though it is in xiii. 8. In xvii. 15 οὗ is used, though our author uses ὅπου always elsewhere (but this verse is a gloss on xvii. 1). γνώμη in xvii. 13, 17 is not found elsewhere in the Apoc., and the form of the enumeration in xvii. 15 is not that of our author. Here ὄχλοι is substituted for λαοί: see note *in loc.* Finally, in xvii. 17 ἄχρι is followed by the indicative (by the subjunctive in inferior MSS) but elsewhere in our author by the subjunctive: see ii. 25, note.

From (*b*) we see that this chapter exhibits many constructions, which are against our author's usage elsewhere in the Apocalypse.

On the other hand, (*a*) just as decidedly exhibits his handiwork. Since the thought underlying the *present* form of the text is that of our author, the obvious hypothesis is that he is making use of sources, which he revises and recasts to suit his

κατασκηνούσης (as in the LXX) would be the natural rendering. But our author could not use this latter participle, since it is reserved by him for dwellers in heaven; see note on xvii. 1. Hence we have καθημένης ἐπὶ ὑδάτων instead possibly of κατασκηνούσης ἐπὶ ὑδάτων.

[1] Since this verse has been recast by our author, this form of this phrase instead of that in xvii. 2 may be due to him.

own purpose. In other words, *the evidence of this section tends to prove that not only is xvii. 11–17 based on a source, as we inferred in* § *2, but also xvii. 1–10, 18.*

Further research will define more closely the extent and character of these sources. But first of all we must show that the conclusions provisionally arrived at from the form of the text are confirmed by the subject-matter. Hence we shall now proceed to prove that the chapter as it stands is of a composite nature.

§ 4. *The text is deranged and composite—being based on two Sources.*

The text is deranged, however we may account for it. For whereas in xvii. 7 the angel promises to disclose the mystery of the woman and the Beast (which the Seer had already seen in xvii. 3) and in this order, he at once proceeds to tell the mystery of the Beast, and there is no mention of the woman till xvii. 18. Hence the natural position of xvii. 18 is immediately after xvii. 7. Again, xvii. 17, which gives the explanation of xvii. 13, can hardly have been read unless in immediate connection with xvii. 13: *i.e.* 13, "These have one mind, and they give their power and authority unto the beast. 17. For God did put into their hearts to do His mind [and to come to one mind], and to give their kingdom unto the beast," etc.

The chapter is also composite. We have already seen in § 3 that whereas certain parts of the chapter show clear traces of the hand of John, the phraseology of certain other parts is decidedly against his usage. We have also seen in § 2 that the order of the words in xvii. 1–10 is Semitic, whereas that in xvii. 11–17 is not so. Now, if with these facts we combine the further one that, whereas xvii. 1–10 culminates in a prediction of the death of Titus (xvii. 10), the other (xvii. 11–17) culminates in a prediction of the destruction of the Harlot City (xvii. 16), we can hardly evade the conclusion that behind these two sections there were two independent sources.[1] But there is another indication of the independence of these two sections. In xvii. 3, 7 the Beast can only be the Roman Empire, whereas originally in xvii. 11–13, 17, 16 the Beast was not the Roman Empire (as originally in xvii. 3–10), but the living Nero returning from the East at the head of the Parthian kings.

That our author, therefore, has laid two sources under contribution is to be concluded from the above phenomena, in the first of which the Beast represented the Roman Empire,

[1] I have thus on largely independent grounds arrived at the same conclusions as Wellhausen (*Analyse*, 26–29) on the original sources of this chapter.

whereas in the second it represented the living Nero returning from the East at the head of the Parthian hosts (cf. xvi. 12).

To the above evidence of the compositeness of this chapter we might add the twofold explanation of the seven heads in xvii. 9–10 as symbolizing seven hills and seven kings: the glaring contradiction between xvii. 16, where the ten horns are represented as God's agents in destroying Rome, although they had themselves been *already* destroyed by the Lamb and His followers in xvii. 14,[1] and the belated gloss in xvii. 15, which has no *raison d'être* in its present position but was obviously added by a stupid scribe originally in the margin opposite xvii. 1 as an explanation of τῆς πόρνης . . . τῆς καθημένης ἐπὶ ὑδάτων.

§ 5. *The two Sources A and B, and their dates.*

In the determination of these two sources I agree on the whole with Wellhausen.[2] A consists, according to this scholar, of 3 (with the exception of the phrase "and ten horns")–4, 6^b–7 (with the exception of "and the ten horns"), 9 (excluding all but the words "the seven heads"), 10 (omitting the initial "and"). He thinks that 18 may have originally stood after 7 but was omitted by the redactor, who, however, out of a feeling of conscientiousness added it at the close of B! B consists, he holds, of 11–13, 16 (omitting "and the ten horns which thou sawest and the beast"), 17. A and B were bound together by a redactor and revised. In A, 6 is a Christian addition, and in B 14. xvii. 1–3 may, with the exception of xvii. 1^a, have belonged either to A or B.

I am unable to accept Wellhausen's hypothesis in all its details, but, as we have already seen (§§ 2, 3), the evidence of the order of the words and to some extent the idioms point to two sources, and these, like Wellhausen, I designate as A and B.

(*a*) A consisted originally of 1^c (beginning with τὸ κρίμα τῆς πόρνης . . .)–2, 3^b (καὶ εἶδον . . .)–6 (om. καὶ ἐκ. . . . Ἰησοῦ), 7, 18, 8 (om. ἦν καὶ οὐκ . . . ὑπάγει which addition has displaced a clause: om. also ὅτι ἦν . . . πάρεσται), 9 (om. ὧδε . . . σοφίαν and ἑπτὰ . . . αὐτῶν), 10 (om. the first καί).

In this oracle the beast is the Roman Empire, its seven heads are the Roman emperors, five of whom belong to the past, one is, *i.e.*, Vespasian, whereas the seventh, Titus, as the

[1] This, however, is no doubt due to an accidental displacement. When it is read after 11–13, 17, 16 this contradiction disappears. In the text as it stands the demonic Nero returning from the abyss is the Antichrist, and therefore must be destroyed by the Christ.

[2] Bousset regards xvii. 1–7, 9–11, 15–18 as an original Jewish source of Vespasian's time, while he assigns xvii. 8, 12–14 and certain clauses in 6, 9, 11 to the last editor of the Apocalypse.

destroyer of Jerusalem, would speedily perish. The date is thus fixed and the authorship may have been Jewish-Christian.

(*b*) B = 11 (om. ὃ ἦν καὶ οὐκ ἔστιν καὶ and καὶ εἰς ἀπώλειαν ὑπάγει), 12–13, 17, 16. In this second oracle the Beast is Nero returning from the East, and not the Roman Empire as in A. The order of the words, as we have shown (§ 2), differs in B from that in A. This source is fragmentary. Preceding ver. 11 there must have been some account of the seven heads, but not that in A, since it identified the Beast with the Roman Empire and not with Nero.[1] Since the eighth is spoken of, *i.e.* Nero returning from the East, we may conclude with great probability that it was written during the reign of Titus. The oracle may be regarded as written by a Jew; for whereas the hatred of the Jews was fierce against Rome in the time of Vespasian and Titus, it was not so on the part of the Christians. The Christians, moreover, could not have had any sympathy with Nero. Their expectation is best expressed in the addition of John, *i.e.* ver. 14, where Nero and his allies attack the Lamb.

We have already observed that 15 was originally a marginal gloss on ver. 1, τῆς πόρνης . . . ἐπὶ ὑδάτων. Ver. 14 is clearly from the hand of John, 16 manifestly stood originally after 17.

§ 6. *Our author's editing of A and B and the new meaning given thereby to the whole.*

Now that we have determined the extent of A and B, we have next to show the use our author made of them. First of all, the introductory words in xvii. 1, καὶ ἦλθεν εἷς ἐκ . . . Δεῦρο δείξω σοι, are clearly from his hand. Then follow the words from A, τὸ κρίμα . . . τῆς πορνείας αὐτῆς, which form the title of xviii. But though πόρνης is preceded by the article—another fact pointing to a source—the Harlot has not been mentioned as yet. The original vision of the Harlot consisted of the source A, in which the Beast was the Roman Empire on which the woman (Rome) was seated. This source our author introduces by 3^a καὶ ἀπήνεγκέν με εἰς ἔρημον ἐν πνεύματι. In 3^b–7 he makes no change save by the insertion (?) of καὶ κέρατα δέκα in 3, in order to prepare for B (*i.e.* 11–13, 17, 16), and by the addition of the clause 6^b καὶ ἐκ τοῦ αἵματος . . . Ἰησοῦ. In 8–10 he has recast the text. For the original form of 8 see the note *in loc.* (p. 67 sq.). His additions, ἦν καὶ οὐκ ἔστιν . . . ὑπάγει and ὅτι ἦν . . . πάρεσται, transform the meaning of the verse, which, though it originally identified the Beast with the Roman Empire, signifies in its present form the demonic Nero returning from the abyss.

[1] The Beast is the supporter of the woman, *i.e.* Rome (xvii. 3), in A, whereas in B the Beast is the destroyer of Rome, xvii. 12, 16.

In 9, ὧδε ὁ νοῦς . . . σοφίαν is from his hand, while ἑπτὰ ὄρη . . . ἐπ' αὐτῶν καί is clearly the gloss of an ignorant scribe. Ver. 18, which originally stood in A after 7, was transposed to its present position in order to introduce the great chapter xviii. on the doom of Rome.

Having utilized A our author now proceeds to incorporate B of which only 11–13, 17, 16 survives in our author's work. The introduction, as we have already pointed out (§ 5 (*b*)), has been omitted and its place is now taken by 10, which belongs to A. Two clauses have been introduced by our author into 11, *i.e.* ὃ ἦν καὶ οὐκ ἔστιν and καὶ εἰς ἀπώλειαν ὑπάγει. By their introduction the expectation of a living Nero returning from the East at the head of the Parthians is transformed into an expectation of a demonic Nero, as in xvii. 8. 12–13 are apparently as they stood in the original oracle, but 14–15 had no place there. 15 is, as we have elsewhere observed, a gloss, which stood originally in the margin opposite ver. 1 (τῆς πορνῆς . . . ἐπὶ ὑδάτων), while 14 comes from our author's hand; but, since it could only properly follow 16, as it deals with the destruction of the Beast and his Parthian allies, who in 16 destroy Rome, it has most probably got displaced. Thus 11–17 should be read in the following order: 11–13, 17, 16, 14.

Thus by his editorial changes and additions our author has transformed the original meaning of his sources except in ver. 3, where the Beast is still the Roman Empire. Throughout the rest of the chapter, however, the Beast has become none other than the demonic Nero.

§ 7. *A* (=xvii. 1^c–2, 3^b–6^a, 7, 18, and certain clauses in 8–10) *was probably derived from the same source as xviii.*

See Introd. to xviii. § 7.

§ 8. *A, though found by our author in a Greek form, was most probably translated from a Hebrew source.*

In §§ 6, 3 I have shown that, although there are indubitable signs of our author's revision of A, yet some idioms and constructions survive, which are contrary to his usage—such as οἱ κατοικοῦντες τὴν γῆν (xvii. 2), γέμοντα ὀνόματα (xvii. 3), γέγραπται ἐπὶ τὸ βιβλίον (xvii. 8). It thus appears that the Greek form of A is not due to our author.

But, further, there are signs that A was originally written in Hebrew. Thus, if πορνῶν is the original text in xvii. 5, the context (βδελυγμάτων) suggests that we should here have not "harlots" but "harlotry." This, as I have shown in the note *in loc.*, could have arisen from a misreading of זְנוּת (=harlotry) as זֹנוֹת = "harlots."

But the strongest evidence is that found in ver. 8, which is a doublet of xiii. 3^c, 8. These two passages cannot, so far as I can discover, be explained except as independent Greek renderings of one and the same Hebrew original, the Greek rendering of xiii. 3^c, 8 being that of our author and the Greek of xviii. 8 being that of some unknown scholar. This question is fully dealt with in the Introd. to xiii. § 4, vol. i. p. 337.

1. καὶ ἦλθεν εἷς ἐκ τῶν ἑπτὰ ἀγγέλων τῶν ἐχόντων τὰς ἑπτὰ φιάλας, καὶ ἐλάλησεν μετ' ἐμοῦ λέγων· Δεῦρο, δείξω σοι τὸ κρίμα τῆς πόρνης τῆς μεγάλης τῆς καθημένης ἐπὶ ὑδάτων πολλῶν,

2. μεθ' ἧς ἐπόρνευσαν οἱ βασιλεῖς τῆς γῆς, καὶ ἐμεθύσθησαν οἱ κατοικοῦντες τὴν γῆν ἐκ τοῦ οἴνου τῆς πορνείας αὐτῆς.

1. εἷς . . . ἀγγέλων. One of the angels of the Bowls acts as the angel of interpretation. The words *καὶ ἦλθεν εἷς . . . δείξω σοι* recur in xxi. 9. On *ἐλάλησε μετ' ἐμοῦ λέγων* see iv. 1 *n.* *δείξω σοι* has already occurred in iv. 1; *δεῦρο*, as we have seen, recurs in xxi. 9.

τὸ κρίμα τῆς πόρνης . . . πορνείας αὐτῆς. These words form the title that should be prefixed to chap. xviii. They prepare us for a *vision* of the judgment of the Great Harlot, but there is none such in xvii. 3–18: only a prediction of it in xvii. 16. But in xviii. we have an elaborate vision of this judgment, and it is therefore to this chapter that these words form a title. And lest there should be any doubt on this head we find that the greater part of the title xvii. 2 is repeated in xviii. 3, though the order of the clauses is reversed and the diction slightly changed, and that the words *τὸ κρίμα* reappear as *ἡ κρίσις* in reference to her in xviii. 10. Cf. also xviii. 8, 20. But since the Great Harlot has not hitherto been mentioned, another vision is necessary to her identification. In this vision (xvii. 3–6) she appears riding the Beast with seven heads and ten horns—elements which are duly interpreted in xvii. 9, 12.

τὸ κρίμα τῆς πόρνης. The Harlot is the city of Rome. This word is applied to Nineveh by Nahum (iii. 4), and to Tyre by Isaiah (xxiii. 16, 17). In 5 it is named Babylon. The doom of Babylon has already been pronounced twice, xiv. 8, xvi. 19. Rome is already known by this name in 1 Pet. v. 13; 2 Bar. lxvii. 7, "The King of Babylon will arise who has now destroyed Zion"; and the Sibylline Oracles, v. 143, 159.

τῆς καθημένης ἐπὶ ὑδάτων πολλῶν. This is an independent translation of Jer. li. (LXX—xxviii.) 13, שכנתי על מים רבים. The LXX has here *κατασκηνοῦντας* (*κατασκηνοῦσα*, Q) *ἐφ' ὕδασι πολλοῖς*. *κατασκηνοῦν* or *σκηνοῦν* is the natural rendering of שָׁכַן here, but our author reserves this word for dwellers in heaven: cf. vii. 15, xii. 12,

xiii. 6. Rome cannot be rightly described as "sitting on many waters," but the description of Babylon, which stood for the personification of wickedness in the O.T., is here simply taken over. The idea of security may underlie the phrase: Babylon felt safe owing to the many waters on which it was situated—the Euphrates which flowed through it and the morasses and canals by which it was surrounded (see Cornill on Jer. li. 13). Yet this fact that Rome did not sit on many waters was a difficulty to a later writer and led to the gloss in xvii. 15, that the many waters are many peoples. Bousset thinks that a still older tradition lies behind this figure of a woman seated on many waters, and compares Sibyll. Or. iii. 75–77, v. 18, viii. 200. Gunkel (*Schöpfung*, 361) finds in the "many waters" a reference to the abyss which was the dwelling of Tiamat. But, however this may be, there was no consciousness of the Babylonian myth in the mind of the writer.

2. ἐπόρνευσαν οἱ βασιλεῖς τῆς γῆς. Cf. xviii. 3, 9 for the recurrence of this diction. The *πορνεία* of which the kings of the earth are guilty is set down to the account of all the nations in xiv. 8. They have all shared in the vices and idolatries of Rome. With **ἐμεθύσθησαν** cf. Jer. xxviii. (li.) 7, *ποτήριον χρυσοῦν Βαβυλὼν ἐν χειρὶ κυρίου, μεθύσκον πᾶσαν τὴν γῆν.* It points to the result of *πεπότικεν* in xiv. 8: cf. also xviii. 3. **οἱ κατοικοῦντες τὴν γῆν.** On this construction, found here only, see note on xi. 10, and § 4 of the Introd. to xiii., vol. i. p. 336. On **οἴνου πορνείας** cf. xiv. 8, xviii. 3. We should observe that the relative construction is broken off in the sentence, *καὶ ἐμεθύσθησαν . . . αὐτῆς.* This is good Hebrew. It is also good Greek: see W.–M. sect. xxii. p. 186.

It is noteworthy that in the two clauses *μεθ' ἧς ἐπόρνευσαν . . γῆς* and *καὶ ἐμεθύσθησαν . . . αὐτῆς* of this verse and in xviii. 3, the same thought and largely the same language recur, but in the reverse order.

3. καὶ ἀπήνεγκέν με εἰς ἔρημον ἐν πνεύματι. καὶ εἶδον γυναῖκα καθημένην ἐπὶ θηρίον κόκκινον, γέμοντα ὀνόματα βλασφημίας, ἔχων κεφαλὰς ἑπτὰ καὶ κέρατα δέκα.

This clause introduces a new vision. See note on iv. 2. The Seer has the vision of Babylon in the wilderness: of the Heavenly Jerusalem from a lofty mountain top, xxi. 10, where see note. The contrast is significant. Many scholars think that the wilderness as the scene of the vision was suggested by Isa. xxi. 1, where to the vision of the fall of Babylon is affixed the heading, "The oracle of the wilderness of the sea" (מַשָּׂא מִדְבַּר־יָם). Here the LXX has simply *τὸ ὅραμα τῆς ἐρήμου.*

γυναῖκα . . . ἐπὶ θηρίον κόκκινον. The omission of the article before *θηρίον* points to an independent vision here. The Beast is undoubtedly the Roman Empire. On its power the Harlot reposes. The scarlet colour indicates the luxury and ostentatious magnificence of the empire, and refers probably not to the Beast itself but to its covering. Swete quotes Juv. iii. 283 sq., "Cavet hunc, quem coccina laena Vitari iubet et comitum longissimus ordo." The word is a rendering in the LXX of תּוֹלָע, תּוֹלֵעָה, שָׁנִי, כַּרְמִיל, תולעת שני or שני תולעה.

In this vision of the Harlot we may have an indirect contrast to the woman clothed with the sun in xii. 1–6. There is no real contradiction between the description of the woman in 1 as sitting on many waters and here sitting on the beast. The former is a traditional epithet of Babylon used descriptively by the angel, the latter represents the actual appearance in the vision.

γέμοντα ὀνόματα βλασφημιάς. The construction is *κατὰ σύνεσιν*. In xiii. 1 names of blasphemy are only on the seven heads, *i.e.* the seven deified emperors. Here they cover the entire body, and may refer to the innumerable deities of her own and subject countries which Rome recognized. *γέμειν* c. acc. once in xvii. 4[d], but always elsewhere in Apoc. c. gen. iv. 6, 8, v. 8, xv. 7, xvii. 4[d], xxi. 9.

ἔχων κεφαλὰς ἑπτά. Probably the original text. On the *κεφαλὰς ἑπτά* see note on xiii. 1.

4. περιβεβλημένη . . . μαργαρίταις. Almost the same phrase recurs in xviii. 16.

πορφυροῦν καὶ κόκκινον. "Purple and scarlet." These colours symbolize the luxury and splendour of imperial Rome. The two colours are nearly allied, for the *χλαμύδα κοκκίνην* of Matt. xxvii. 28 is called *πορφύρα* in Mark xv. 17, 20, and *ἱμάτιον πορφυροῦν* in John xix. 2, 5. But the colours are distinct. See Ex. xxv. 4, xxvi. 1.

κεχρυσωμένη χρυσίῳ καὶ λίθῳ τιμίῳ. *λίθῳ τιμίῳ* is generally said to depend on *κεχρυσωμένη* by a *zeugma*, "from which the reader must mentally supply some such participle as *κεκοσμημένη*" (Swete). But *χρυσοῦν* appears to be used in a loose way in the LXX as = "to cover or adorn"; for *χρυσοῦν χρυσίῳ* (2 Chron. iii. 10), *καταχρυσοῦν χρυσίῳ* (Ex. xxv. 11, 13; 2 Chron. iii. 4, ix. 17), *περιχρυσοῦν χρυσίῳ* (1 Kings x. 18) are renderings of צִפָּה (= to overlay) when followed by זָהָב. Similarly *χρυσοῦν χρυσίῳ* of חִפָּה followed by זָהָב in 2 Chron. iii. 7, 8. When followed by נחשת it is actually rendered *καταχαλκωμένα χαλκῷ* in 2 Chron. iv. 9, and when followed immediately by אבן יקרה in 2 Chron. iii. 6, by *κοσμεῖν*. Hence we should render *κεχρυσωμένη* here by "covered."

χρυσίῳ . . . καὶ μαργαρίταις. Cf. T. Jud. xiii. 5, *καὶ ἐκόσ-*

μησεν αὐτὴν ἐν χρυσίῳ καὶ μαργαρίταις. These words are said of the father of Bathshua who so adorned her in order to seduce Judah.

ἔχουσα ποτήριον χρυσοῦν ἐν τῇ χειρὶ αὐτῆς. These words are modelled on Jer. xxviii. (li.) 7, *ποτήριον χρυσοῦν Βαβυλὼν ἐν χειρὶ κυρίου, μεθύσκον πᾶσαν τὴν γῆν· ἀπὸ τοῦ οἴνου αὐτῆς ἐπίοσαν ἔθνη.*

γέμον βδελυγμάτων καὶ τὰ ἀκάθαρτα. Here *καὶ τὰ ἀκάθαρτα* is either to be taken with R.V. as "even the unclean things of her fornication," or as governed by *ἔχουσα*, just as the words that follow—*καὶ ἐπὶ τὸ μέτωπον*—are dependent on this participle. Cf. Cebes, *Tab.* v., *ὁρᾷς οὖν παρὰ τὴν πύλην θρόνον τινὰ κείμενον κατὰ τὸν τόπον . . . ἐφ' οὗ κάθηται γυνή, πεπλασμένη τῷ ἤθει καὶ πιθανὴ φαινομένη, ἣ ἐν τῇ χειρὶ ἔχει ποτήριόν τι; ὁρῶ, ἀλλὰ τίς ἐστιν αὕτη; ἔφην· Ἀπάτη καλεῖται, φησίν, ἡ πάντας τοὺς ἀνθρώπους πλανῶσα. εἶτα τί πράττει αὕτη; τοὺς εἰσπορευομένους εἰς τὸν βίον ποτίζει τὴν ἑαυτῆς δύναμιν. τοῦτο δὲ τί ἐστι τὸ ποτόν; πλάνος, ἔφη, καὶ ἄγνοια* (from Jerram's text).

5. καὶ ἐπὶ τὸ μέτωπον αὐτῆς ὄνομα γεγραμμένον. Roman harlots wore a label with their names on their brows: cf. Seneca, *Controv.* i. 2 (quoted by Wetstein), "Stetisti puella in lupanari . . . stetisti cum meretricibus . . . nomen tuum pependit a fronte"; Juv. vi. 122 sq., "Tunc nuda papillis Constitit auratis titulum mentita Lyciscae."

μυστήριον. This word indicates that the following name is not to be taken literally, but to be interpreted *πνευματικῶς* (xi. 8). This can be done only by the initiated. Babylon is the mystical name for Rome. Many scholars take it as part of the inscription.

ἡ μήτηρ τῶν † πορνῶν †. As we see from the critical note, the Vg. and Prim. read *πορνιῶν, i.e. πορνειῶν.* This is not improbably the original reading. At all events it forms an excellent parallel to *βδελυγμάτων.* If the text is derived from a Hebrew source, then *πορνῶν* = זֹנוֹת, which is a wrong punctuation for זְנוּת = *πορνείας.*[1] Thus Rome is the mother of harlotry and the world's idolatries. With this statement we might compare Tacitus, *Ann.* xv. 44, where he speaks of Rome as the city "quo cuncta undique atrocia aut pudenda confluunt celebranturque."

6. καὶ εἶδον τὴν γυναῖκα μεθύουσαν ἐκ τοῦ αἵματος τῶν ἁγίων καὶ ἐκ τοῦ αἵματος τῶν μαρτύρων Ἰησοῦ.

The text refers to the Neronic persecution described so vividly by Tac. *Ann.* xv. 44, "Igitur primum correpti qui fatebantur, deinde indicio eorum multitudo ingens haud perinde in crimine incendii quam odio humani generis convicti sunt. Et pereuntibus addita ludibria, ut ferarum tergis contecti laniatu canum

[1] It is noteworthy that Wellhausen mistranslates *πορνῶν* as "harlotries." It was a right instinct, however, that led him to this mistranslation.

interirent aut crucibus affixi, aut flammandi, atque ubi defecisset dies, in usum nocturni luminis urerentur." This verse, either in part or as a whole, is from the hand of our author, who thus gives a Christian character to an originally Jewish source and transforms an oracle of Vespasian's date into a prophecy of the destruction of Rome in the last days (see Introd. § 5).

μεθύουσαν ἐκ τοῦ αἵματος. This conception of a nation drunk, not with wine but with blood, was familiar to the literature of the ancient world. Thus Josephus (*Bell.* v. 8. 2) writes of his infatuated countrymen besieged by the Romans: *ἔτι γὰρ παρῆν ἐσθίειν ἐκ τῶν δημοσίων κακῶν καὶ τὸ τῆς πόλεως αἷμα πίνειν.* The metaphor is also found in a fragment of Euripides preserved in Philo, *Leg. Alleg.* iii. 71, *ἐμπλήσθητί μου | πίνουσα κελαινὸν αἷμα*: in Cic. *Phil.* ii. 29, "gustaras civilem sanguinem vel potius exsorbueras"; Suet. *Tib.* 59, "Fastidit vinum quia jam sitit iste cruorem: Tam bibit nunc avide quam bibit ante merum," and in a form more closely related to our text in Plin. *H.N.* xiv. 22, 28, "(Antonius) ebrius jam sanguine civium." But in the LXX we find the best analogies: cf. Isa. xxxiv. 5, *ἐμεθύσθη . . . ἡ μάχαιρά μου*, xxxiv. 7, *μεθυσθήσεται ἡ γῆ ἀπὸ τοῦ αἵματος*: also li. 21; Jer. xxvi. (xlvi.) 10.

καὶ ἐκ τοῦ αἵματος τῶν μαρτύρων Ἰησοῦ. This clause is regarded by the majority of critics as an addition to the original Jewish source. If it is from the hand of our author, his intention seems to have been to give his source a Christian character, though this was hardly necessary when once the source was incorporated in his work. If the *ἅγιοι* are Christian saints, the two clauses are tautologous. The *ἅγιος* who is martyred is of necessity a *μάρτυς*. On this word see note on ii. 13. It is possible, but improbable, that the *ἅγιοι* represent the Jewish martyrs who fell in the war of 66–70. This was the meaning of the clause in the original source.

7. καὶ ἐθαύμασα ἰδὼν αὐτὴν θαῦμα μέγα. καὶ εἶπέν μοι ὁ ἄγγελος Διὰ τί ἐθαύμασας; ἐγὼ ἐρῶ σοι τὸ μυστήριον τῆς γυναικὸς καὶ τοῦ θηρίου τοῦ βαστάζοντος αὐτήν, τοῦ ἔχοντος τὰς ἑπτὰ κεφαλὰς καὶ τὰ δέκα κέρατα. The Seer is naturally astonished at the fearful vision he has just seen, just as the inhabitants of the earth will be astonished when they see the reality, xvii. 8. In xvii. 1–2 he was promised a vision of the *judgment* of the Great Harlot. This vision is given in xviii., but since the Great Harlot had not heretofore been mentioned, the mystery of the Great Harlot is beheld by the Seer in a vision, xvii. 3–6, and interpreted in xvii. 18, which originally followed on xvii. 7. See Introd. to this Chap. § 6.

For a linguistic parallel to *τὸ μυστήριον τῆς γυναικός* cf. i. 20; and for a like dialogue between the angel and the Seer, cf vii.

13–14. We should observe here that the angel promises an interpretation of the woman and the Beast with seven heads and ten horns, and in this order. But the mystery of the woman is not explained till xvii. 18, and the angel at once proceeds to set forth the meaning of the Beast. Our author is here using sources, and has freely recast them to suit his own purpose. In our text the Beast is Nero *redivivus*, but in the sources used by our author we have seen that this was not so (see Introd. § 4). In the source behind xvii. 3–10 the Beast was originally the Roman Empire, as it still is in xvii. 3 (see note *in loc.*). In the second source, xvii. 11–17, the Beast was obviously Nero returning from the East at the head of the Parthian kings in order to destroy Rome. But our text as it stands represents the expectation of Nero returning as a demonic king from the abyss. This interpretation is indubitably set forth in xvii. 8, which is a recast of the older tradition identifying the Beast with the Empire, and in xvii. 14 which comes directly from our author.

8–18. An interpretation of the vision, in the course of which the older materials of the source are recast with additions in order to depict the expectation of the Neronic Antichrist who was to come up from the abyss.

8. τὸ θηρίον ὃ εἶδες ἦν καὶ οὐκ ἔστιν καὶ μέλλει ἀναβαίνειν ἐκ τῆς ἀβύσσου, καὶ εἰς ἀπώλειαν ὑπάγει· καὶ θαυμασθήσονται οἱ κατοικοῦντες ἐπὶ τῆς γῆς, ὧν οὐ γέγραπται τὸ ὄνομα ἐπὶ τὸ βιβλίον τῆς ζωῆς ἀπὸ καταβολῆς κόσμου, βλεπόντων τὸ θηρίον ὅτι ἦν καὶ οὐκ ἔστιν καὶ πάρεσται.

Thus the verse ran originally: *τὸ θηρίον ὃ εἶδες . . .* (original lost) *καὶ θαυμασθήσονται οἱ κατοικοῦντες ἐπὶ τῆς γῆς, ὧν οὐ γέγραπται τὸ ὄνομα ἐπὶ τὸ βιβλίον τῆς ζωῆς ἀπὸ καταβολῆς κόσμου, βλεπόντων τὸ θηρίον.* In the original form of this verse the Beast symbolized the Empire, as it still does in xvii. 3, and in xiii. 3–10 originally. But here our author has omitted the description of the Beast which came after *εἶδες*, and substituted *ἦν καὶ οὐκ ἔστιν . . . ὑπάγει*, and again after *βλεπόντων τὸ θηρίον* added *ὅτι ἦν . . πάρεσται* in the place of quite a different clause that stood in the source, as we shall see presently.

But not only has some description of the Beast at the beginning of this verse been displaced by the additions of our author, but something has also been lost or displaced at the close of the verse by another of his additions. For, as it stands, 8 simply states that the faithless inhabitants of the earth shall marvel when they behold the Beast. But there is nothing surprising in this fact; for the Seer marvels in the preceding verse. Hence, since the context implies that they will do something which would be the natural outcome of their ungodliness, we conclude that a clause to the effect that they would worship him has been dislodged by the addition "which was and is not and shall come." Now, if we turn to xiii. 3[c], 8 we find the very clause we are in search of, *καὶ προσκυνήσουσιν αὐτὸν πάντες*. When this clause is restored, the mystery of the beast in the source is sufficiently disclosed. The Beast is clearly the Roman Empire. It is on the Beast, *i.e.* the Empire, that the woman, *i.e.* Rome, is seated. But the changes introduced by our author have transformed the significance of the Beast. The Beast now means the demonic Nero returning from the abyss, and it is clearly the intention of our author that 11 should be taken in this sense.

The Beast is now the Neronic Antichrist coming up from the abyss, as in xiii. 3, 12, 14. In these passages he is represented as the hellish antitype of Christ. In *ὅτι ἦν καὶ οὐκ ἔστιν καὶ πάρεσται* there is a parody of the divine name *ὁ ὢν καὶ ὁ ἦν καὶ ὁ ἐρχόμενος* in i. 4, 8, iv. 8, while the *οὐκ ἔστιν* and the parallel descriptions, *ὡς ἐσφαγμένην εἰς θάνατον*, xiii. 3, and *ὃς ἔχει τὴν πληγὴν τῆς μαχαίρας*, xiii. 14, are intended to allude to the death of Christ.

In the Introd. to xiii., vol. i. p. 337, I have, I think, proved that this verse is a doublet of xiii. 3[c], 8—and that both are Greek versions of the same Hebrew original. Since xvii. 8 in some form belonged to xvii. 3–10, it is from this Hebrew source that xiii. 3[c], 8 is derived. When our author incorporated his Greek version of this source in xiii. 3[c], 8 he added *τοῦ ἀρνίου τοῦ ἐσφαγμένου*. Bousset is of opinion that a redactor in close dependence on xiii. 8, or the same writer who wrote xiii. (in the opinion of Bousset our author), composed xvii. 8; but all the evidence when closely examined points in a different direction.

βλεπόντων where we expect *βλέποντες* may be due to *ὤν*, or to a not unnatural rendering of בִּרְאֹתָם.

9–10. ὧδε ὁ νοῦς ὁ ἔχων σοφίαν· αἱ ἑπτὰ κεφαλαὶ ἑπτὰ [ὄρη εἰσίν, ὅπου ἡ γυνὴ κάθηται ἐπ᾽ αὐτῶν. **10.** καὶ] βασιλεῖς [ἑπτά] εἰσιν· οἱ πέντε ἔπεσαν, ὁ εἷς ἔστιν, ὁ ἄλλος οὔπω ἦλθεν, καὶ ὅταν ἔλθῃ ὀλίγον αὐτὸν δεῖ μεῖναι.

9. ὧδε ὁ νοῦς κτλ. = "here is needed the intelligence which is wisdom." It relates to what follows, as in xiii. 18, and comes from the hand of our author.

ὄρη . . . αὐτῶν καί. This is an obvious addition to the text, but it appears to be a very ancient one and may have gone back to the Johannine school, as its Hebraic character shows: *i.e.* *ὅπου . . . αὐτῶν*. Bousset (p. 416) suggests that our author himself made this addition, when he found that he could discover no historical interpretation of xvii. 10–11. This addition, how ever, is wholly unsuitable; for the seven heads do not belong to the woman (*i.e.* Rome) but to the Beast. But the gloss *interprets the heads as if they were an adjunct of the woman, whereas they belong to the Beast.* This absolute misconception of the text is fatal to the genuineness of these words. Again our author in the genuine sections uses *καθῆσθαι* only in the participle (see note on iii. 21) and *καθίζειν* in the finite tenses and infinitive. But there is another objection; for it is clear that, of the two conflicting explanations given in immediate connection, only one can stand—in this case the latter. The idea conveyed of the gloss was a familiar one. "The city of seven hills" was a familiar expression in classical writers: cf. Horace, *Carm. Sec.* 7, "Di, quibus septem placuere colles"; Virg. *Aen.* vi. 782, "Septemque una sibi muro circumdabit arces," *Georg.* ii. 534; Martial, iv. 64, "septem dominos montes"; Cicero, *Ad Att.* vi. 5, *ἐξ ἄστεος ἑπταλόφου*: Propertius, iii. 10. See Wetstein *in loc.*

10. βασιλεῖς [ἑπτά [1]] κτλ. For *βασιλεῖς* as applied to Roman emperors see 1 Pet. ii. 13, 17; 1 Tim. ii. 2. We have here a very clear intimation of the date of this source. Five emperors have already fallen, one is, and another is yet to come. This source was probably written, therefore, under the sixth emperor. Before we can ascertain who this emperor was, we must decide whether we shall include or exclude in our reckoning Galba, Otho, and Vitellius, and with what emperor we shall begin. First of all we may safely exclude the above three emperors from our consideration. Suetonius (*Vesp.* i.) describes their reigns as "rebellio trium principum." Next, though Suetonius, Josephus, and 4 Ezra xi. 12, 13, xii. 14, 15 (see Box, p. 262 sq.), begin with Cæsar, it seems clear here that our text begins with Augustus, as does Tacitus. The first five emperors are Augustus, Tiberius, Caligula, Claudius, Nero. The emperor who "is" is Vespasian, 69–79 A.D., and the one who "is not yet come," Titus, 79–81. Titus thus fulfilled the prediction, *ὅταν ἔλθῃ ὀλίγον κτλ.*

ὅταν ἔλθῃ ὀλίγον κτλ. The ground for this expectation is most probably that assigned by Wellhausen (*Analyse*, 28). "Titus is assumed to be the coming seventh and last: he as the destroyer of Jerusalem will be overtaken by vengeance after a short reign." [2]

But what are we to make of this reckoning in its present

[1] On the order of the numerals see note on viii. 2. When the gloss *ὄρη . . . ἐπ' αὐτῶν καί* was incorporated in the text, *ἑπτά* was of necessity added after *βασιλεῖς*

[2] Another explanation of this prophecy is that the writer of this source knew of the hopeless condition of Titus' health: cf. Suetonius, *Titus*, 7; Dio Cassius, lxvi. 26. 2; Plutarch, *De tuenda sanitate praecepta*, c. 3, p. 123 D (quoted from Bousset). Another is that there was a traditional view that the empire must have seven emperors before its destruction. As the sixth was now living, the Seer necessarily predicts a seventh.

context? Our author has taken over this source and that which follows, but he is writing in the reign of Domitian. If he took xvii. 10 seriously, Domitian must have been for him the sixth emperor, and he could only have justified this view, as Bousset points out (p. 416), by a very artificial method of reckoning, *i.e.* by beginning with Galba, the successor of Nero: Galba, Otho, Vitellius, Vespasian, Titus, Domitian. But we may safely reject this reckoning as impossible, and assume that here, as frequently elsewhere, our author has taken over material that in some one or more respects served his purpose, though in others it was unsuitable. Owing to its unintelligibleness from the historic point of view, some scribe added a geographical explanation in xvii. 9.

11–17. On the source behind these verses see Introd. § 5.

11. καὶ τὸ θηρίον, ὁ ἦν καὶ οὐκ ἔστιν, καὶ αὐτὸς ὄγδοός ἐστιν καὶ ἐκ τῶν ἑπτά ἐστιν, καὶ εἰς ἀπώλειαν ὑπάγει.

This verse presents some difficulty. We have already sought to show (Introd. § 4–5) that xvii. 11–17 is a new source used by our author, referring to the return of Nero from the East at the head of the Parthian kings. Only the latter part of this source is preserved in our text, and this is edited and brought up to date by the addition of ὃ ἦν καὶ οὐκ ἔστιν and καὶ εἰς ἀπώλειαν ὑπάγει in xvii. 11 (see similar addition in xvii. 8), and other changes subsequently. In the original source the Beast was the living Nero returning from the East: in our text the Beast has become Nero *redivivus*, as in xvii. 8. This is the view accepted by such scholars as Ewald, De Wette, Hilgenfeld, Vischer, Völter, Spitta, Holtzmann, Weizsäcker, Bousset. On the other hand, it has been maintained recently by J. Weiss and Swete and Moffatt that the Beast is to be identified with Domitian. Moffatt regards this verse as "a parenthesis added by John to bring the source up to date . . . since the death of Titus had not been followed by the appearance of the Nero-antichrist" . . . "Domitian, the eighth emperor, under whom he writes, is identified with the true Neronic genius of the empire." (Cf. Eus. *H.E.* iii. 20; Tert. *Apol.* 5: "portio Neronis de crudelitate." *De Pallio*, 4, Subneronem. To these we might add Juv. iv. 37 sq., "Calvo serviret Roma Neroni"; Mart. xi. 33, etc. Moffatt seeks to explain the words ἐκ τῶν ἑπτά by showing that Domitian was closely associated with the imperial power already (Tac. *Hist.* iii. 84, iv. 2, 3; cf. Jos. *Bell.* iv. 11. 4, etc.), and points out that whereas it was said of the Neronic Antichrist in xvii. 8, ἀναβαίνειν ἐκ τῆς ἀβύσσου, no such expression is used here. Thus Moffatt recognizes the true Nero *redivivus* in xvii. 8, 14, and a second Nero in the person of Domitian in xvii. 11, and maintains that they are not to be identified. That the juxtaposition of Domitian as a second Nero and Nero *redivivus* is awkward, Moffatt admits, but says it is "inevitable under the circumstances." But his arguments are unconvincing. The *ὃ ἦν καὶ οὐκ ἔστιν* taken together with *ἐκ τῶν ἑπτά* admits of only one interpretation. The person so described "was and is not" (*ἦν καὶ οὐκ ἔστιν*). But Domitian *ἔστιν*. Of him our author cannot say *οὐκ ἔστιν*. Moreover, the pre-existence ascribed to Domitian in *ὃ ἦν* is also inexplicable. Nor can he in any intelligible sense be described as *ἐκ τῶν ἑπτά*. Finally, if we interpret xvii. 12–17 of the Parthian invasion, there is no ground in comparative religion or history for representing Domitian as in any sense its leader. The addition of *καὶ μέλλει ἀναβαίνειν ἐκ τῆς ἀβύσσου* is here wholly unnecessary. *ὃ ἦν καὶ οὐκ ἔστιν* has the same force as the like expressions in xiii. 3, 12, 14.

εἰς ἀπώλειαν ὑπάγει. The issue of the impending conflict is certain. The Antichrist, though he thinks he is accomplishing his own purposes, is accomplishing the purposes of God, and is all the time marching to his own destruction, which is also the purpose of God.

12–13, 17–16, 14. The destruction of Rome by Nero *redivivus* and his Parthian allies (12–13, 17, 16), and the destruction of the latter by the Lamb (14).

12. καὶ τὰ δέκα κέρατα ἃ εἶδες δέκα βασιλεῖς εἰσίν, οἵτινες βασιλείαν οὔπω ἔλαβον, ἀλλὰ ἐξουσίαν ὡς βασιλεῖς μίαν ὥραν λαμβάνουσιν μετὰ τοῦ θηρίου.

The kings are symbolized by the horns, and are thus differentiated from the emperors who are symbolized by the heads of the Beast. Who are these kings? Various answers have been given. 1. They are said to be unknown powers belonging to the future which as confederates of the returning emperor will arise and overthrow Rome (Weizsäcker and Holtzmann). Swete's interpretation belongs partly to this class. "The ten kings . . . represent forces which arising out of the empire itself . . . would turn their arms against Rome and bring about her downfall." 2. The governors of the senatorial provinces who held office for a year (*μίαν ὥραν*). So Ewald, Volkmar, Hilgenfeld, Hausrath, Mommsen, B. Weiss, Briggs, Selwyn. Bousset states that the expressions *τὴν δύναμιν καὶ τὴν ἐξουσίαν αὐτῶν τῷ θηρίῳ διδόασιν*, xvii. 13, and the parallels in xvii. 17 are against this view; but this is not necessarily so. These governors possessed a certain delegated authority (*ὡς βασιλεῖς*), and only for a year (*μίαν ὥραν*). But again this interpretation has not the support of xvi. 12 or of the universal expectation that was then current in the East and in the Roman Empire. The phrase *δοῦναι τὴν βασιλείαν αὐτῶν τῷ θηρίῳ* shows that these have actual kingdoms, and so the text could not apply to Roman officials. 3. The

Parthian satraps (Eichhorn, De Wette, Bleek, Bousset, J. Weiss, Wellhausen, Scott, Moffatt). According to xvi. 12, the Parthians had several kings or satraps. It is stated that there were as many as fourteen, but the number ten here is not to be pressed. According to the current belief of the generation that followed the death of Nero, it was held that Nero had escaped to the East, and that he would return against Rome at the head of the Parthian hosts. That this belief was taken seriously is proved by the fact that three pretenders appeared between 69–88 A.D. under Nero's name as claimants of the imperial throne. For the evidence see App. to this chapter (p. 80). Since this belief had firmly established itself both in the Gentile and Hellenistic Jewish worlds within the first decade after Nero's death, since, further, it is attested actually in our text in xvi. 12, there can be little doubt that the source in xvii. 12–17 is to be explained thereby. But in the present context, in which Nero is a demon from the abyss, it is possible that these kings are, as Bousset suggests, regarded by our Seer as demonic powers.

δέκα βασιλεῖς. Cf. Dan. vii. 24, *καὶ τὰ δέκα κέρατα αὐτοῦ δέκα βασιλεῖς ἀναστήσονται* (Theod.).

βασιλείαν οὔπω ἔλαβον. These words referring to the Parthian satraps are intelligible from the standpoint of the world empire of Rome. They hold a quasi-kingly power (*ὡς βασιλεῖς*) for a brief span (*μίαν ὥραν*), since the Antichrist's power will speedily be brought to an end.

13. οὗτοι μίαν γνώμην ἔχουσιν, καὶ τὴν δύναμιν καὶ ἐξουσίαν αὐτῶν τῷ θηρίῳ διδόασιν. The Greek structure of this verse is still more manifest than that which precedes.

μίαν γνώμην ἔχουσιν—a good Greek idiom. Cf. Thuc. ii. 86, *γνώμην ἔχοντες . . . μὴ ἐκλιπεῖν*, Herod. i. 207; ii. 56, etc.

The unanimity of the Parthian kings is explained in xvii. 17.

15. [καὶ εἶπεν μοι Τὰ ὕδατα ἃ εἶδες, οὗ ἡ πόρνη κάθηται, λαοὶ καὶ ὄχλοι εἰσὶν καὶ ἔθνη καὶ γλῶσσαι.]

This is a gloss explanatory of xvii. 1, where the Harlot City is said to sit *ἐπὶ ὑδάτων πολλῶν*. But since it was not Rome but the literal Babylon that was so situated, the glosser, after the analogy of Isa. viii. 7, Jer. xlvii. 2, interprets the many waters here as referring to the peoples over which Rome ruled. In xvii. 1 the phrase *ἐπὶ ὑδάτων πολλῶν* is simply taken over from Jer. See note *in loc.* The style is not that of our author. He never uses οὗ but *ὅπου*: cf. ii. 13 (*bis*), xi. 8, xii. 6, 14, xx. 10. Nor is the enumeration *λαοὶ κτλ.* that of our author. See note on v. 9. He uses *φυλαί* instead of *ὄχλοι*. Again we should expect *καθίζει* in our author and not *κάθηται*. See note on 9 and on iii. 21.

17. ὁ γὰρ θεὸς ἔδωκεν εἰς τὰς καρδίας αὐτῶν ποιῆσαι τὴν γνώμην αὐτοῦ, [καὶ ποιῆσαι μίαν γνώμην] καὶ δοῦναι τὴν βασιλείαν αὐτῶν τῷ θηρίῳ, ἄχρι τελεσθήσονται οἱ λόγοι τοῦ θεοῦ.

This verse explains the remarkable unanimity of these kings. It was due to God, not to any mere earthly policy, and it would last till the oracles of the prophets regarding Rome were accomplished, and the Antichrist and the kings met in the last great battle with the Lamb, xvii. 14. Even the wrath of men is made to praise Him. There is no real dualism in the universe. The very powers of evil ultimately subserve the purposes of God and are then destroyed. (Cf. xvii. 14.) Since the Beast, which in the source meant the living Nero returning from the East at the head of the Parthians, has become in our author the demonic Nero, it is probable that his attendant hosts are also to be regarded as of demonic origin.

ἔδωκεν εἰς τὰς καρδίας αὐτῶν. For this Hebraism (= נתן אל-לבב) cf. Neh. vii. 5. There is a closely related idiom in Jer. xxxi. (xxxviii.) 33; 1 Thess. iv. 8; Heb. viii. 10.

[καὶ ποιῆσαι μίαν γνώμην.] I have, with Alford, bracketed this clause as an early gloss from xvii. 13. It is superfluous after *ποιῆσαι τὴν γνώμην αὐτοῦ*, which is really explained by *καὶ δοῦναι κτλ.*

τελεσθήσονται οἱ λόγοι τοῦ θεοῦ. In their present context these prophecies must relate not only to the destruction of Rome by Nero and the Parthians as in the source, but to the overthrow of the power of the Beast and his Parthian allies.

16. καὶ τὰ δέκα κέρατα ἃ εἶδες καὶ τὸ θηρίον, οὗτοι μισήσουσιν τὴν πόρνην, καὶ ἠρημωμένην ποιήσουσιν αὐτὴν καὶ γυμνήν, καὶ τὰς σάρκας αὐτῆς φάγονται, καὶ αὐτὴν κατακαύσουσιν ἐν πυρί.

I have restored this verse to the place which it had originally in the source and in our author, *i.e.* after xvii. 17, which in its turn followed immediately on xvii. 13. The Harlot City was to be destroyed by the forces of evil themselves. As the Beast is demonic and the horns are conceived as part of him, these kings appear also to have a demonic character in their present context.

The author of this source must have had Ezek. xxiii. 25–29 before him, but not the LXX. He reproduces the thought but not the form of the Hebrew. Thus *μισήσουσιν τὴν πόρνην* is a free rendering of xxiii. 29, ועשו אותך בשנאה, which the LXX translates literally. Next with *ἠρημωμένην ποιήσουσιν αὐτὴν καὶ γυμνήν* cf. xxiii. 26, והפשיטוך את-בגדיך (*ἐκδύσουσίν σε τὸν ἱματισμόν σου*, and xxiii. 29, ולקחו כל-יגיעך ועזבוך ערם). With *αὐτὴν κατακαύσουσιν ἐν πυρί* cf. xxiii. 25, תאכל באש. All these statements are made by Ezekiel with regard to Jerusalem, which at one moment is spoken of as a woman stripped of her garments and left naked, and at another as a city burnt with fire. The writer here uses the same figures of Rome.

ἠρημωμένην ποιήσουσιν. For construction, see Introd. § 3, p. 67.

τὰς σάρκας αὐτῆς φάγονται: cf. xix. 18, Ps. xxvii. 2, τοῦ φαγεῖν τὰς σάρκας μου. Mic. iii. 3, κατέφαγον τὰς σάρκας τοῦ λαοῦ μου: 2 Kings ix. 36, καταφάγονται οἱ κύνες τὰς σάρκας Ἰεζάβελ· σάρκες denotes the fleshy parts of the body.

κατακαύσουσιν ἐν πυρί: cf. xviii. 8; Jer. vii. 31; Nah. iii. 15. These words can only refer to the city whom the woman represents. Death by fire was not the punishment of the harlot, unless she were a priest's daughter: cf. Lev. xxi. 9.

14. οὗτοι μετὰ τοῦ ἀρνίου πολεμήσουσιν,
καὶ τὸ ἀρνίον νικήσει αὐτούς,
ὅτι κύριος κυρίων ἐστὶν καὶ βασιλεὺς βασιλέων,
καὶ οἱ μετ' αὐτοῦ κλητοὶ καὶ ἐκλεκτοὶ καὶ πιστοί.

This verse is manifestly added by our author to the source he is using. But this verse could not have been inserted in its present position by our author; for it treats of the destruction of the forces appointed by God for Rome's destruction, which they effect in 16. In xvii. 17, 16, according to the MSS text, the ten horns and the Beast are represented as executing a divine judgment on the Harlot City and as destroying Rome after they had already themselves been destroyed (xvii. 14). Hence this verse belongs rightly after 16. I have restored it accordingly. With *μετὰ τοῦ ἀρνίου πολεμήσουσιν . . . νικήσει αὐτούς* compare xiii. 7, which is from his hand. For *κύριος . . . βασιλέων* cf. xix. 16. The subject of this vision, *i.e.* the Parthian kings and their destruction (12–13, 17, 16, 14), has been in part referred to in xvi. 12, and is regarded as already accomplished in xix. 13, where the words *περιβεβλημένος ἱμάτιον βεβαμμένον αἵματι* speak of the vesture of the Divine Warrior as already dipped in blood (*i.e.* in that of the Parthian kings) before the Messianic campaign against the kings of the earth in xix. 11–21.

The concluding line describes the armies who followed the Lamb, *i.e.* "the called, elect, and faithful." That these should crush hostile nations we learn from ii. 26, 27, and their descent from heaven to do so is seen in a vision in xix. 14. Hence they are a martyr host of warriors. It was a well-known Jewish expectation that the righteous would take part in the destruction of the wicked: cf. 1 Enoch xxxviii. 5, xc. 19, xci. 12 for the period of the sword, when the wicked are given into the hands of the righteous, *op. cit.* xcv. 7, xcvi. 1, xcviii. 12, xcix. 4, 6; Wisd. iii. 8. The martyrs are not here engaged on a mission of revenge, but in the fulfilment of a righteous retribution.

In xv. 4 the vision—which is in reality a prophecy—shows that the thought of revenge has wholly passed from the minds of the glorified martyrs. But the nations there referred to are those that are contemporary with the Millennial Reign. See the third note further on.

κύριος κυρίων . . . βασιλέων. This title recurs in xix. 16. In both instances it is used of the Son. The combination of these titles as applied to God is found first in 1 Enoch ix. 4, ὁ θεὸς τῶν θεῶν καὶ (ὁ) κύριος τῶν κυρίων καὶ ὁ βασιλεὺς τῶν βασιλευόντων. (So the two Greek versions in Syncellus, whereas the Ethiopic implies βασιλέων for βασιλευόντων.) It is worth observing that 1 Tim. vi. 15 has βασιλεὺς τῶν βασιλευόντων. These titles occur often separately as applied to God, κύριος τῶν κυρίων, Deut. x. 17; ὁ βασιλεὺς τῶν βασιλέων: 1 Enoch lxiii. 4, lxxxiv. 2; 2 Macc. xiii. 4. See Bousset's *Rel. d. Judenthums*, 306.

The use of such titles in reference to Marduk in Babylonian literature is noted by Zimmern, *K.A.T.*³ 373 sq., 390. Marduk is actually named "Lord of Lords, King of Kings." "King of Kings" was a designation of the Babylonian and Persian kings: cf. Ezek. xxvi. 7; Ezra vii. 12; Dan. ii. 37: of the Egyptian kings, Diod. Sic. i. 55. 7, βασιλεὺς βασιλέων καὶ δεσπότης δεσποτῶν Σεσόωσις. But this title is far outbid by those given to Domitian: "Dominus et deus noster." Suet. *Domit.* 13: cf. Mart. v. 8.

οἱ μετ' αὐτοῦ κλητοὶ κτλ. κλητοὶ and ἐκλεκτοί occur only here in the Apocalypse. We are to understand πολεμήσουσιν and νικήσουσιν from what precedes. The followers of the Lamb who have been called and chosen will manifest their loyalty and share in the Lamb's victory (cf. xii. 11). According to this context those who answer the call are elected and prove their loyalty: cf. 2 Pet. i. 10, σπουδάσατε βεβαίαν ὑμῶν τὴν κλῆσιν καὶ ἐκλογὴν ποιεῖσθαι. But these loyal followers of the Lamb belong already to the heavenly hosts; for they accompany Him from heaven: cf. xix. 14. They are called πιστοί as their Leader is called πιστός (i. 5).

18. καὶ ἡ γυνὴ ἣν εἶδες ἔστιν ἡ πόλις ἡ μεγάλη ἡ ἔχουσα βασιλείαν ἐπὶ τῶν βασιλέων τῆς γῆς.

Our author knows at last the interpretation of the chief figure in the vision. The woman is the city Rome, the empress of the entire world.

This verse belonged to the source A: see Introd. to Chap., § 5, and had its place immediately after xvii. 7, but was transferred to its present position in order to introduce the great chapter of the downfall of Rome.

On the phrase ἡ πόλις ἡ μεγάλη, see note on xi. 8.

Additional Note on xvii.

The Antichrist, Beliar,[1] *and Neronic Myths, and their ultimate Fusion in early Christian Literature.*

This question bristles with problems. Many of these, it is true, have been solved and others are on the way to solution. Nevertheless, many lie still in the background and have not as yet yielded up their secret to research. The chief workers in this field have been Gunkel and Bousset. While the services of the former have been at times brilliant, they have at the same time showed a lack of sound judgment. In the latter respect Bousset in his *Antichrist Legend* (translated from the German, 1896) and in the *Offenbarung Johannis*[5], 1906, has made an admirable contribution, and proved that outside Daniel and Revelation there was an independent tradition of the Antichrist myth coming down from ancient times and diffused through many lands. A study of such articles as Creation, Dragon, Leviathan, Serpent in the *Encyc. Biblica* will show that the Creation Story passed through a long development within the domain of Hebrew and Jewish thought, and further study proves that such an expression as "the great dragon, the ancient serpent, who is called the Devil and Satan" (Rev. xii. 9), finds one of its sources ultimately in the myth that underlies the Creation story. But the present study cannot take account of the manifold traces of this development discoverable in the O.T. (see Gunkel, *Schöpfung und Chaos*—a book full of suggestion, but in many of its conclusions, especially as regards Revelation, demonstrably wrong). It must be strictly limited to the ideas of the Antichrist and kindred conceptions that prevailed within Judaism and Christianity from 200 B.C. to 100 A.D. or thereabouts.

In a study of the present subject in 1900 (see *Ascension of Isaiah*, pp. li–lxxiii) I pointed out that, whilst Bousset's and Gunkel's works (above cited) were most helpful and stimulating in many directions, they did not deal satisfactorily with the relations of Beliar and the Antichrist, and that their account of the fusion of the latter with the Neronic legend was wanting in lucidity and consistency. This defect Bousset has from his own standpoint partially remedied in *Rel. d. Judentums im Neutest. Zeitalter*[2], 1906, and his article on "Antichrist" in Hastings' *Encyc. of Religion and Ethics*, i. 578 sqq. Here he has vastly improved on his earlier studies, and removed many of the defects to which I took objection in 1900. But, notwithstanding these advances on Bousset's part, I feel constrained to republish here the main part

[1] This is the form that Belial takes in Jubilees, Testaments XII Patriarchs, the Sibylline Oracles, Martyrdom of Isaiah.

of my study of 1900 with such additions and improvements as the work of the intervening years has naturally brought with them.

If we can succeed in establishing with approximate accuracy the dates when the Antichrist, Beliar, and Neronic myths originated and became fused together, we acquire means for determining the dates of the fragments of such myths as have secured an entrance into the work of our author.

The aim, therefore, of the present note is to touch briefly on the history of the Antichrist, Beliar, and Neronic myths, before the fusion of any one of them with another, or of each with all: and next to give the passages from Jewish and Christian literature where such fusion is attested and their approximate dates. Thus I shall deal with—

I. *The independent development of the Antichrist, Beliar, and Neronic myths.*

II. *The fusion of the Antichrist myth with that of Beliar, and subsequently and independently with the Neronic myth.*

III. *The fusion of all these myths together.*

I. *The independent development of the Antichrist, Beliar, and Neronic myths.*

i. *The Antichrist myth.*—The term "Antichrist" is comparatively late though the idea signified by it is early. Thus it is not attested till far on in the first century of our era; for it is found in the N.T. only in the Johannine Epistles—1 John ii. 18, 22, iv. 3; 2 John 7. The idea, however, can be traced back to the second century B.C., and appears first in the Book of Daniel. This conception takes two forms: (*a*) the individual Antichrist, and (*b*) the collective Antichrist.

(*a*) *A God-opposing individual.*—In Daniel we find the individual Antichrist (the king of the North, xi. 40) appearing at the head of mighty armies, with which he crushes certain nations and preserves others, persecutes the saints (vii. 25), putting numbers of them to death (viii. 10), sets up in the Temple "the abomination that maketh desolate" (*i.e.* the heathen altar over the altar of burnt-offering, viii. 13, ix. 27, xi. 31, xii. 11), "magnifies himself above every god" (xi. 36: cf. 2 Thess. ii. 4), and after a reign of three and a half years (vii. 25 sq.) meets his end (xi. 45). The historical figure here referred to was Antiochus IV. Epiphanes (*i.e.* (God) made manifest). The idea, which may in part have existed already and which became impersonated in Antiochus disassociated itself from the historical figure of Antiochus, and through its enlargement and enrichment in the Book of Daniel established itself as a permanent expectation in Judaism. In the earliest literature, therefore, where the idea appears, it implies *a being of human origin* (though claiming divine prerogatives), whereas Beliar, who came subsequently to be identified with the Antichrist, was originally *a superhuman or Satanic being.*

The next historical character to whom epithets belonging to the Antichrist are applied, is Pompey the Great, who committed the unpardonable act of profaning the Temple by entering the Holy of Holies after his conquest of Jerusalem. Thus in the Pss. of Solomon (70–40 B.C.), Pompey is called "the Dragon" (ὁ δράκων, ii. 29). There may be here an unconscious allusion to the Dragon myth (see Cheyne's art. "Dragon" in the *Encyc. Bib.* i.). He is described as "the sinner," ii. 1 (ὁ ἁμαρτωλός), the personification of sin (cf. 2 Thess. ii. 3, ὁ ἄνθρωπος τῆς ἁμαρτίας—so the inferior Uncials): "the lawless one," xvii. 13 (ὁ ἄνομος), an attribute of Beliar (cf. 2 Thess. ii. 3, ὁ ἄνθρωπος τῆς ἀνομίας, ℵB). But since his soldiers are designated "the lawless ones" (xvii. 20, οἱ ἄνομοι), the epithet may mean no more than heathen, as in 1 Cor. ix. 21; 2 Cor. vi. 14; Acts ii. 23. The epithet "lawless," if technically used, is proper to the Beliar myth.

This expectation may have been influenced by the action of the emperor Caligula (37–41 A.D.), when he ordered the governor Petronius to erect his statue in the Temple. If he had persisted in this act of profanation, the Jews would undoubtedly have regarded it as a fulfilment of the prediction of the setting up of "the abomination of desolation" in the Temple. This phrase was, as we are aware, first applied to the heathen altar set up by Antiochus in the Temple (1 Macc. i. 54), and probably also to the image of Olympian Zeus beside it (cf. Taanith iv. 6). Bousset suggests that "the ever recurring expectation of later times, that Antichrist would take his place in the Temple of Jerusalem, dates . . . from this period."

The next reference to the Antichrist is to be found in 2 Bar. xxxvi. 5, xxxix. 3, xl. 1, 2, according to which the head of the Roman Empire was to be brought before the Messiah and destroyed, and still another in 4 Ezra v. 6, where the reign of the Antichrist is foretold: "Et regnabit quem non sperant, qui inhabitant super terram."

(*b*) *A God-opposing power, or the collective Antichrist.*—So far we have cited our authorities as testifying to a single individual Antichrist. But with the expectation of an individual Antichrist that of a collective Antichrist, (α) secular, or (β) religious, is often involved.

(α) Thus in Dan. vii. 7 sqq., 19 sqq. the Fourth Empire (*i.e.* the Greek or Macedonian) is the collective Antichrist. The identity of the Seleucidae or Greek rulers of Syria with the Fourth Kingdom appears in the Sibylline Oracles,

iii. 388–400 (before 140 B.C.). But at the close of the first cent. B.C. or the beginning of the first cent. A.D. the prophecy of Daniel was reinterpreted, and, since Syria had now ceased to be a world power, the Fourth Empire was identified with the new world power Rome. This is first seen in the Assumption of Moses (7–30 A.D.), where the overthrow of Rome by Israel is predicted :

x. 8. "Then thou, O Israel, shalt be happy,
And thou shalt go up against the eagle,
And its neck and wings shall be destroyed."[1]

Lest his contemporaries should misunderstand Dan. vii. 17–19, 23 sqq. as referring to the Greek Empire, the Seer in 4 Ezra xii. 11–12 expressly states that this passage refers to the Roman Empire. This is the universal view of the first century A.D. Cf. 2 Bar. xxxvi.–xl. ; 4 Ezra v. 3–4, xi. 40 sqq. It is attested in the N.T.: see the Little Jewish Apocalypse incorporated in Mark xiii. (especially 14 = Matt. xxiv. 15 = Luke xxi. 20), and in the sources behind xiii. 1–10 (see § 8 in the Introd. to xiii.), xvii. 3–10, where it is symbolized by the Beast in our Apocalypse. But in our text the meaning of the symbol has been changed : it stands only in part for the Roman Empire, but mainly for Nero *redivivus*, the demonic Antichrist coming up from the abyss, in xiii. 3 and similarly in xvii. 1–10; but the original meaning of the symbol still survives in xiii. 1–2, xvii. 3. In the Ep. Barn. iv. 4–5 (100–120 A.D.) the Fourth Kingdom is Rome : so also in Hippolytus (220 A.D.), and in the Talmud—*Aboda Zara*, 1[b].

(*β*) The collective Antichrist of a religious origin. In the Johannine Epistles of the N.T. (1 John ii. 18, 22, iv. 3; 2 John 7) the Antichrist is the collective name for the false teachers who have gone forth from the bosom of the Church as deceivers (πλάνοι). This conception is not to be confounded with that of pseudo-Christ (ψευδόχριστος) of Matt. xxiv. 24; Mark xiii. 22. The individual Antichrist of the religious type is probably referred to in John v. 43, "If another shall come in his own name, him ye will receive."

Again the original source lying behind xiii. 11–14, 16–17

[1] Here the words "its neck and wings" have been transposed from line 2. The transmitted text runs :

"And thou shalt go up against (*i.e.* ועלית על) the necks and wings of the eagle,
And they shall be destroyed"

(where "implebuntur" of the MS = συντελεσθήσονται, which should have been rendered "delebuntur" here). We have here an early form of the Eagle Vision such as we find in 4 Ezra xi.

was a Jewish Apocalypse directed against the individual Antichrist in the form of the False Prophet (see Introd. to Chap. xiii. § 8, vol. i. pp. 342–344). In our text it has been transformed into a collective Antichrist, *i.e.* the heathen imperial priesthood, and designated the second Beast in subordination to the first in xiii. 1–10. Originally this Antichrist was conceived as independent and without any Antichrist beside him.

ii. In the O.T. Beliar does not appear as a proper name (see "Beliar" in the Bible Dictionaries). Beliar first attains to personality in the second century B.C. Thus, according to the Test. XII Patriarchs, Beliar rules over souls that are constantly disturbed (T. Dan iv. 7), or which yield to the evil inclinations (T. Ash. i. 8), but flees from those that keep the law (T. Dan v. 1). The Messiah will make war on Beliar and take from him the souls he had led captive (T. Dan v. 10), and Beliar will be bound (T. Levi xviii. 12), and cast into the fire (T. Jud. xxv. 3), and the spirits subject to him will be punished (T. Levi iii. 3). This conception is very like that of Satan—a fact which becomes clearer still in Jubilees i. 20, where Beliar (like Satan: cf. 1 Chron. xxi. 1; 1 Enoch xl. 7; Rev. xii. 10) is said to be the accuser of the faithful before God. This identification of Beliar and Satan appears in the Christian pseudepigraph, *The Questions of Bartholomew* (ed. Bonwetsch, 1897), iv. 25. In 2 Cor. vi. 15, Beliar seems a synonym for Satan. Hence we may conclude that towards the close of the second century B.C. Beliar was regarded as a Satanic spirit, and as naught else, until the Beliar myth coalesced with that of the Antichrist.

iii. *The Neronic myth in its earliest form.*—Here our task is simply to show that soon after the death of Nero the myth became current that (*a*) Nero had not really died, but was still living; and (*b*) that he would soon return from this far East to take vengeance on Rome.

(*a*) When Nero with the help of a freedman committed suicide and was cremated (Suet. *Nero*, 49), so great was the public joy that the people thronged the streets in holiday attire (*op. cit.* 57). All, however, did not share in the belief of Nero's death. Thus Tacitus (*Hist.* ii. 8) writes that there were many who pretended and believed that he was still alive; and Suetonius (*Nero*, 57) declares that edicts were issued in his name as though he were still alive and would return speedily to destroy his enemies. As early as 69 A.D. an impostor appeared under his name and headed a rebellion against Rome (Tac. *Hist.* ii. 8, 9).

(*b*) That Nero had taken refuge in the East probably formed a constituent of the myth from the outset—a point on which evidence will be furnished later. Predictions had been made during Nero's lifetime that the East would be the scene of his future greatness: some of these represented J rusalem as the seat of his empire; others promised him the sovereignty of the world (Suet. *Nero*, 40). Probably such vaticinations as these, combined with the fact that Nero had already established friendly relations with the Parthian king Vologeses I. (Suet. *Nero*, 57), led Nero, as the end drew nigh, to think of fleeing to the Parthians (*op. cit.* 47).

In conformity with this expectation we find that a second pseudo-Nero appeared under Titus on the Euphrates, about 80 A.D., and was recognized by the Parthian king Artabanus (Zonaras, xi. 18). Finally, about 88 A.D. a third pretender came forward among the Parthians and all but succeeded in hurling Parthia against Rome (Tac. *Hist.* i. 2; Suet. *Nero*, 57). This Nero myth, thus firmly rooted in the Gentile world, passed over to the Jewish. The Jewish source, lying behind Rev. xvii. 12–17 (*i.e.* xvii. 11[a], 12–13, 17, 16) and written probably in the reign of Titus, embodies this expectation and predicts the destruction of Rome by the Parthians under the leadership of Nero, who is there called "the beast." This expectation of a Parthian invasion of the West is explicitly stated in xvi. 12. With these passages Rev. ix. 13–21 should be compared, though here we have a demonic form of the myth. The Sibylline Oracles, v. 143–148 (71–74 A.D.—so Zahn and Bousset), prove that this myth had established itself in the eschatology of Hellenistic Judaism. According to the passage just referred to, the flight of Nero from Rome to the Parthians is mentioned, and in v. 361–364 his return to destroy Rome. Early in the next decade we find other testimonies to the prevalence of this myth: see Sibyll. Or. iv. 119–122, where Nero is described as a fugitive to Parthia, and iv. 137–139, where he is described as returning to assail the West at the head of a vast host.

It is possible that the statement in the Talmud (*Yoma*, 10[a]), to the effect that Rome would be destroyed by the Persians, is an echo of this early expectation.

II. *The fusion of the Antichrist myth* (i.) *with that of Beliar before 50 A.D.; and* (ii.) *independently with that of Nero redivivus, 88–100 A.D.*

i. As a result of this fusion the Antichrist is regarded as (*a*) *a God-opposing man armed with miraculous powers*—this appears to have been effected on Christian soil before 50 A.D.; (*b*) a purely Satanic power before 70 A.D.

(*a*) 2 Thess. ii. 1–12, according to the usual interpretation, presents an indubitable instance of this fusion. Thus, on the one hand, we have Beliar. "The man of lawlessness" (ὁ ἄνθρωπος τῆς ἀνομίας) is all but certainly a translation of Beliar; for ἀνόμημα is the LXX rendering of it in Deut. xv. 9, and ἀνομία in 2 Kings xxii. 5, and παράνομος is frequently found as its equivalent, when it is used as an epithet: Deut. xiii. 13; Judg. xix. 22, xx. 13; 2 Kings xvi. 7, etc.

In the next place it is Beliar appearing as the Antichrist; for the words "he that opposeth himself . . . against all that is called God" (ὁ ἀντικείμενος . . . ἐπὶ πάντα λεγόμενον θεόν) form an excellent definition of the Antichrist. Since 2 Thess. is now generally (and certainly by the present writer) regarded as an authentic writing of St. Paul, we have here the earliest evidence for the fusion of these ideas (*circ.* 50 A.D.), and also for *the humanization of the Beliar myth through its fusion with that of the Antichrist*; for hitherto Beliar had been conceived as a Satanic or superhuman being. The Antichrist thus comes to be conceived as *a God-opposing man armed with Satanic powers.*

We should next observe that in 2 Thess. ii. 1–12 the myth appears to have a purely *religious* significance and not a *political* one, as in Rev. xiii. 1–10, xvii. Thus in 2 Thess. ii. 6, 7 the Roman Empire is referred to as the power which checks the manifestation of the Antichrist, whereas in Rev. xiii. 1–10 it is the Roman Empire that stood originally in the source of this passage and that still stands in the background as the Antichrist, while the demonic Nero stands in the foreground as this being. In no case could 2 Thess. ii. 1–12 have been written after 70 A.D. This section is a Christian transformation of a current Judaistic myth.

Another phase of this expectation appears in Rev. xiii. 11–17. In the source of this passage the Antichrist was conceived similarly to that in 2 Thess. ii. But by our author this conception was recast and interpreted of the priesthood, which was attached to the cultus of the Caesars, and had the chief seat of its activities in the province of Asia. This Antichrist—in our author symbolized by the second Beast—is a false teacher and prophet. Hence this conception is akin to that which prevails in the Johannine Epistles: 1 John ii. 18, 22, iv. 3; 2 John 7. Though both in the Epistles and Rev. xiii. 11–17 the Antichrist is human, in the latter passage he is armed with Satanic powers and "deceiveth them that dwell on the earth by reason of the signs which it was given him to do in the sight of the beast" (xiii. 14). His task is to make the inhabitants of the earth worship the first Beast (*i.e.* the Beliar Nero), whose death-stroke had been healed (xiii. 12). This subordinate Antichrist is designated as "the false prophet" in xvi. 13, xix. 20, xx. 10. Thus a conception which had originally grown up in Jewish and Christian circles, and, referring to a Jewish Antichrist, had a purely religious significance, was recast by our author and reinterpreted of a heathen corporation, the Imperial priesthood, which was in part religious and in part political in its aims.

Sibylline Or. ii. 167 sq. (*circ.* 200 A.D.) should probably be cited under this head, where it is said that Beliar will come and work many portents before men.

(*b*) *The Beliar Antichrist = a purely Satanic power before 70 A.D.* (*or 30 A.D.*).

This stage of the myth is attested in Rev. xi. 7, where as the Beast from the abyss he makes war with and kills the witnesses. The Antichrist in this passage makes his advent *in Jerusalem* (xi. 8), and therefore before 70 A.D. This phase of the myth was *originally* independent of that which appears in Rev. xiii. and xvii., where it has been fused together with the Neronic myth. But in its present context in xi. it is treated as identical with the conception in xiii. and xvii. and is used proleptically in reference to it.

We should probably not be wrong in recognizing in the Assumption of Moses x. 1, 2 an instance of this compound conception.

1. "And then His kingdom shall appear throughout all His creation,
And then Satan shall be no more,
And sorrow shall depart with him.
2. Then the hands of the angel shall be filled
Who has been appointed chief,
And he shall forthwith avenge them of their adversaries."

If this passage comes rightly under this head, then the fusion of the ideas of Beliar and Antichrist must be anterior to 30 A.D.

ii. *Fusion of the Antichrist myth with that of the Nero redivivus.*—This fusion could not have taken place before the first half of Domitian's reign, when the last Neronic pretender appeared. As soon, however, as the hope of the return of the living Nero could no longer be entertained, the way was prepared for this transformation of the myth. The living Nero was no longer expected, but Nero restored to life from the abyss. This expectation appears in Rev. xiii., xvii. But it is questionable if this classification is right, and the very much conflated conceptions of the Antichrist in these chapters had best been reckoned under III. The simple Neronic myth needs some infusion of the Beliar myth in order to develop the expectation of Nero *redivivus*, or Nero as a demonic power.

III. *Fusion of the Antichrist, Beliar, and Neronic myths in various degrees and forms.*

From this fusion the myth emerges in three forms, which

owe their diversity in the main to the three variations of the Neronic myth which enter into and affect the combination. These are: (i.) *Incarnation of Beliar as the Antichrist in Nero still conceived as alive.* The Antichrist has here a political significance, and is human. (ii.) *Incarnation of Beliar in the form of the dead Nero.* The Antichrist is here a Satanic being. (iii.) *Incarnation of Beliar as the Antichrist in Nero redivivus.*

(i.) *Incarnation of Beliar as the Antichrist in Nero still conceived as living*—before 90 A.D.—We have seen above from documentary evidence that before 80 A.D. the myth had gained wide circulation both among Gentiles and Jews, that Nero was still living in the East, and would speedily return to avenge himself on Rome. We have further seen that long before 80 A.D. the minds of both Jews and Christians were familiar with the expectation of the Antichrist pure and simple, and of the Antichrist possessing the attributes of Beliar or Satan, and so denoting a God-opposing man armed with miraculous powers, or a truly Satanic being. So strong was the tendency of such mythical currents to merge in a common stream that it is not surprising to find this coalescence achieved in Sibyll. Or. iii. 63–74. This passage is unhappily of uncertain date, though no doubt before 90 A.D., since Nero is still regarded as alive. Its significance, however, cannot be mistaken. Beliar comes as Antichrist and is descended from Augustus (ἐκ Σεβαστηνῶν). That this descendant of Augustus is Nero there seems no room for doubt. The lines are:

> ἐκ δὲ Σεβαστηνῶν ἥξει Βελίαρ μετόπισθεν
> καὶ † στήσει † ὀρέων ὕψος, στήσει δὲ θάλασσαν . . .
> καὶ νέκυας στήσει καὶ σήματα πολλὰ ποιήσει . . .
> ἀλλ' ὁπόταν μεγάλοιο θεοῦ πελάσωσιν ἀπειλαί,
> καὶ δύναμις φλογέουσα δι' οἴδματος εἰς γαῖαν ἥξει,
> καὶ Βελίαρ φλέξει καὶ ὑπερφιάλους ἀνθρώπους
> πάντας, ὅσοι τούτῳ πίστιν ἐνεποιήσαντο.

It is possible, however, that the Σεβαστηνοί are the inhabitants of Σεβαστή, *i.e.* Samaria. In that case the text would come under II. i. (*b*).

ii. *Incarnation of Beliar as Antichrist in the form of the dead Nero.*—In due time the belief that Nero was still alive in the East began to die. The time of its extinction must naturally have varied according to temperament and locality. It is accordingly difficult to assign definite dates. Since, however, the latest pretender to the Neronic rôle came forward in 88 A.D., we may not unreasonably infer that from that year the belief began to lose its grip on the common folk, and to decline steadily till it finally disappeared. No doubt during the next twenty years or more it crops up sporadically, but even during that period its place has been taken by two rival and stronger forms of the same myth.

These new forms may have already been evolved in the later years of Vespasian. At all events they are not later than 90–100 A.D. Now that the belief that Nero was still alive had already been abandoned, there were two courses of development open for this myth, in case the Neronic element was still to be retained. Either Beliar must come in the form of the dead Nero, or Nero must be recalled to life by a Satanic miracle as in (iii.). The first course is adopted by the writer of the Ascension of Isaiah, the second by our author in xiii., xvii. The passage in the Ascension, iv. 2–4, is as follows:

"And after (the age) is fulfilled, Beliar, the great ruler, the king of this world, will descend, who hath ruled it since it came into being; yea he will descend from his firmament in the likeness of a man, a lawless king, the slayer of his mother, who himself (even) this king 3. Will persecute the plant which the Twelve Apostles of the Beloved have planted. Of the Twelve one will be delivered into his hand. 4. This ruler in the form of that king will come, and there will come with him all the powers of this world," etc.

(iii.) *Incarnation of Beliar as the Antichrist in Nero redivivus.*—The chief authority attesting this expectation is Rev. xiii., xvii. in their present form as they left our author's hand. But we shall first deal shortly with others in the Sibylline Oracles. In Sibyll. Or. v. 28–34 (written in the reign of Hadrian) the description of the Antichrist involves all the above elements. Thus it is Nero *redivivus* that is described; for the author of the lines is writing two generations after Nero's death. In the next place he is called in semi-mythological language "the serpent" (herein we have the Beliar element), and finally he makes himself equal to God. The lines bearing on our subject are v. 28–29, 33–34.

πεντήκοντα δ' ὅτις κεραίην λάχε, κοίρανος ἔσται,
δεινὸς ὄφις . . .
ἀλλ' ἔσται καὶ ἄϊστος ὀλοίιος· εἶτα ἀνακάμψει
ἰσάζων θεῷ αὐτόν.

v. 214–227 belongs more clearly to this division. According to this passage, Nero is to return aloft, upborne by the Fates. His achievements are portrayed in 219–225. In Book viii., of which lines 4–429 belong to the close of the second century, the various myths have so thoroughly coalesced that Nero is no longer regarded as a man but as a Satanic monster. He has become the Dragon (viii. 88, *πορφυρεός τε δράκων*), and assumed the monster's form (157, *θῆρα μέγαν*).

It is needless here to pursue the ramifications of this myth further in this and later literature than to state, that so thoroughly did the Neronic element in the composite Antichrist conception gain the upper hand in the East, that in Armenian the word Nero became and remains the equivalent for Antichrist.

We shall now return to the most important testimonies of this subject, *i.e.* in Rev. xiii., xvii. We need not here deal with them in detail, since they are fully discussed already. Here we have the most vigorous and illuminating conception of the Antichrist in all literature, although, as we have seen in our study of these chapters, our author was to a considerable extent indebted to existing sources in their composition. But though the elements of the Antichrist were drawn for the most part from disparate sources, the result is no mere mosaic, no laboured syncretism of conflicting traits, but a marvellous portrait of the great God-opposing power that should hereafter arise, who was to exalt might above right, and attempt, successfully or unsuccessfully for the time, to seize the sovereignty of the world, backed by hosts of intellectual workers,[1] who would uphold his pretensions, justify all his actions, and enforce his political aims by an economic warfare,[2] which menaced with destruction all that did not bow down to his arrogant and godless claims. And though the justness of this forecast is clear to the student who approaches the subject with some insight, and to all students who approach it with the experience of the present world war, we find that as late as 1908, Bousset in his article on the "Antichrist" in Hastings' *Encyclopædia of Religion and Ethics*, writes as follows: "The interest in the (Antichrist) legend . . . is now to be found only among the lower classes of the Christian community, among sects, eccentric individuals, and fanatics."

No great prophecy receives its full and final fulfilment in any single event or series of events. In fact, it may not be fulfilled at all in regard to the object against which it was primarily delivered by the prophet or Seer. But, if it is the expression of a great moral and spiritual truth, it will of a surety be fulfilled at sundry times and in divers manners and in varying degrees of completeness. The present attitude of the Central Powers of Europe on this question of might against right, of Cæsarism against religion, of the state against God, is the greatest fulfilment that the Johannine prophecy in xiii. has as yet received. Even the very indefiniteness regarding the chief Antichrist in xiii. is reproduced in the present upheaval of

[1] This is the second Beast in xiii.—the false prophet.
[2] The measures described in xiii. 16–17.

evil powers. In xiii. the Antichrist is conceived as a single individual, *i.e.* the demonic Nero; but, even so, behind him stands the Roman Empire, which is one with him in character and purpose, and is itself the Fourth Kingdom or the Kingdom of the Antichrist—in fact, the Antichrist itself. So in regard to the present war, it is difficult to determine whether the Kaiser or his people can advance the best claims to the title of a modern Antichrist. If he is a present-day representative of the Antichrist, so just as surely is the empire behind him, for it is one in spirit and purpose with its leader—whether regarded from its military side, its intellectual, or its industrial. They are in a degree far transcending that of ancient Rome "those who are destroying the earth" (Rev. xi. 18).

CHAPTER XVIII.

§ 1. *The Contents and Character of this Chapter.*

This chapter, which deals with the doom of Rome, opens with a prophetic prelude, in which the Seer looks far forward and sees the destruction of Rome as already accomplished, and the earth's proud capital as the haunt of every unclean thing—both demonic and belonging to this world.[1] This prelude, described as an angelic utterance from heaven (1–3), is proleptic, since in the rest of the chapter various stages in the actual destruction are described.

In 4–8 there follows another voice addressed to the faithful[2] (4–5), and to the ministers of God's wrath,[3] who were assembled for the destruction of Rome.

We now come to the three threnodies pronounced respectively over burning Rome by the kings (9–10), by the merchant princes of the earth (11–13, 15–16), and by the shipowners and sailors of all the world (17–19). Each in turn bewail the doom of the great city in whose wantonness and luxury and wealth they had all shared.

The chapter closes with a song of doom preluded by a symbolic action on the part of a strong angel. This dirge is uttered by the Seer who wrote the Oracle, which John has utilized here for his own purposes. At its close he has added 20, 23^{f}–24, in which he appeals to heaven and to the martyrs,

[1] As John had not the opportunity of revising his great Apocalyse, several traces of the expectations belonging to the Vespanianic period survive in this Jewish source. According to John's own view, the smoke of Rome was to go up till the world's end (xix. 3), but not so in this source (xviii. 2).

[2] Another element testifying to the origin of the source in Vespanian's time. The faithful had all been removed from the earth at the close of xiii.

[3] In the original source—Nero and the Parthians.

apostles and prophets already there, to rejoice over the destruction of Rome. This appeal is answered in xix. This last part of the chapter was evidently found by our author in a very confused condition. It should be read as follows (as we have shown in § 6): 21, 14, 22^{abcd}, 23^{cd}, 22^{efgh}, 23^{ab}, 20, 23^{f}, 24.

As we have already stated, John has here used a source belonging to the Vespasianic period, and written soon after the destruction of Jerusalem. It was apparently written originally in Hebrew, and found by John in a Greek translation. The grounds for these statements are given in the sections that follow. To the same Vespasianic source xvii. 1^{b}–7, 18, 8–10 (in part) originally belonged.

§ 2. *The Diction, Idiom, and Style of xviii. 2–23 is not that of our author.*

The style of this chapter has none of our author's characteristic abnormal constructions (see 2). It has, on the other hand, constructions which are wholly against his usage (see 3). This chapter contains a great many *ἅπαξ λεγόμενα* so far as the rest of the N.T. is concerned (see footnote on 1), and also peculiar usages of certain words (see 5) not only unknown in the rest of the N.T. and the LXX, but almost unknown elsewhere. The style is most carefully elaborated, and in this respect different from that of our author. Our author is, of course, a stylist, but with him style is a wholly secondary consideration. His theme had wholly gained possession of him, and being the greatest of all themes it naturally expresses itself in great and noble words. But the writer of xviii. 2–23 is no less conscious of the claims of form than he is of the subject-matter of his vision. He is a conscious stylist. Moreover, the order of his words is less Semitic than that of any other chapter in the Apocalypse from our author's hand. Thus the verb frequently follows after the subject or the object, or both combined: cf. 3, 7, 8, 11, 14, 15, 17. In xvii. 1^{c}–2, 3^{b}–7, 8–10, the earlier part of this source, the order is Semitic, but this seems owing to the revision it has undergone at the hands of our author before he incorporated it in his text.

Finally, this source has influenced our author (see 7).

1. *Diction.*—The source begins with 2. It is introduced by 1, every phrase of which is from our author. Thus *μετὰ ταῦτα εἶδον* is a characteristic phrase: *εἶδον ἄλλον ἄγγελον καταβαίνοντα ἐκ τοῦ οὐρανοῦ* is found in x. 1 and again in xx. 1. On *ἔχοντα ἐξουσίαν* cf. ix. 3, xvi. 9, xx. 6; and on *ἐφωτίσθη ἐκ τῆς δόξης αὐτοῦ*, cf. xxi. 23, *ἡ γὰρ δόξα τοῦ θεοῦ ἐφώτισεν αὐτήν.* The style of 2–23 is not that of our author, nor the diction nor the idiom.

The *diction* is in the main different. I have added a list of phrases and clauses common to xviii. and the rest of the book. Now from this list must be withdrawn those given under 20, 23, 24, since either originally or in their present form they are from our author's hand. Next, those given under 3^{b}, 10, 16 are repeated from the earlier part of the same source, xvii. 1–10, but not found elsewhere in the Book. Again, this old Vespasianic source has not unnaturally influenced our author's diction: hence the clauses given in 2^{a}, 3^{a} are the source of xiv. 8, and the rare use of *βύσσινον* in 12 appears to be the source of our author's use of it in xix. 8, 14. Thus the clauses with a diction akin to that in our author are those given under 4 (8), 9, 21 (below). But the clauses which in these verses are common to this source and our author are not distinctive. On the other hand, xviii. has a large number of *ἅπαξ λεγόμενα*, so far as the rest of our author and the N.T. are concerned.[1]

2. ἔπεσεν, ἔπεσεν Βαβυλὼν ἡ μεγάλη: cf. xiv. 8, which, however, appears to be borrowed from this source.

3. ἐκ τοῦ οἴνου [τοῦ θυμοῦ] τῆς πορνείας αὐτῆς πεπότικεν πάντα τὰ ἔθνη—the source of xiv. 8^{c}. οἱ βασιλεῖς τῆς γῆς μετ᾿ αὐτῆς ἐπόρνευσαν: cf. 9, xvii. 2, where the clause has already occurred.

4. ἤκουσα ἄλλην φωνὴν ἐκ τοῦ οὐρανοῦ λέγουσαν: cf. x. 4, 8, xi. 12, xiv. 2, etc.

8. διὰ τοῦτο: cf. vii. 15, xii. 12. ἐν πυρὶ κατακαυθήσεται: cf. xvii. 16.

9. κόψονται ἐπ᾿ αὐτῇ: cf. i. 7.

10. ἡ πόλις ἡ μεγάλη: cf. 16, 19, xvii. 18—all belonging to the same source.

12. βυσσίνου: cf. 16, xix. 8, 14, where this use of *βύσσινον* as a noun appears derived from the use in this source.

16. ἡ περιβεβλημένη . . . μαργαρίτῃ: repeated with slight variations from xvii. 4—both belonging to the same source.

17. ἔστησαν. Our author would have used ἐστάθησαν or εἱστήκεισαν. See vol. i. p. 272.

20. εὐφραίνου: cf. xii. 12. οὐρανέ. Our author uses this word in the sing. οἱ ἅγιοι κ. οἱ ἀπόστολοι καὶ οἱ προφῆται. The order is unusual: contrast xi. 18, xviii. 24. ἔκρινεν: cf. xvi. 6.

21. εἷς (cf. viii. 13, xix. 17) ἄγγελος ἰσχυρός: cf. v. 2, x. 1. ἔβαλεν εἰς: very frequent. οὐ μὴ εὑρέθῃ ἔτι: cf. 22, 24, xii. 8, xiv. 5.

23. ἐπλανήθησαν πάντα τὰ ἔθνη: cf. xx. 3, 8, xii. 9, xiii. 14.

[1] Thus we have *φυλακή* in xviii. 2: *στρήνους* in xviii. 3 (cf. *στρηνιάω* in 7, 9, also ἅπ. λεγ.), *διπλώσατε*, and *διπλᾶ* and *διπλοῦν* as nouns in 6, *σιρικοῦ*, *θύινον*, *ἐλεφάντινον*, *μαρμάρου* in 12, and in the same verse *κοκκίνου* as a noun (cf. 16, xvii. 4), *κιννάμωμον*, *ἄμωμον*, *σεμίδαλιν* [*ῥεδῶν*, *σωμάτων* in this sense] in 13, *ὀπώρα*, *λιπαρά* in 14, *πορφυροῦν* as a noun in 16 (xvii. 4), *ἐργάζονται* (in this sense) in 17, *τιμιότητος* in 19, *μύλινον*, *ὁρμήματι* in 21, *μουσικῶν*, *σαλπιστῶν* in 22.

24. προφητῶν καὶ ἁγίων: cf. xi. 18. ἐσφαγμένων: cf. v. 6, 9, 12, vi. 9, xiii. 8.

2. The style of xviii. 2–23 exhibits *none* of the abnormal constructions[1] so frequent in our author, is far more normal than that of our author, and is comparatively good Greek. In fact the writer of this source was a conscious stylist.

3. Whilst this source has none of our author's characteristic abnormal constructions, it contains *constructions which are wholly against his usage.* Thus οὐαί *cum nom.* in 10, 16, 19, whereas it appears in our author only *cum acc.* ἐν ἰσχυρᾷ φωνῇ in 2 is both as regards the epithet and the order in this phrase unexampled in our author (see note *in loc.*). αὐτῆς αἱ ἁμαρτίαι in 5 is an example of the unemphatic position of αὐτός not elsewhere in our author save in one Uncial (A) in xxi. 3 (see vol. ii. p. 208, footnote). κράζειν ἐν . . . φωνῇ in 2 is against our author's usage, who never inserts the ἐν here: cf. vi. 10, vii. 2, 10, x. 3, xix. 17. In xviii. 4 the order ἐκ τῶν πληγῶν αὐτῆς ἵνα μὴ λάβητε (ℵACQ) is unparalleled in our author. Hence some later authorities transpose ἐκ τ. πληγῶν αὐτῆς after λάβητε. Again, ἡ μεγάλη πόλις in 21 is unparalleled in our author in this phrase (see note *in loc.*). The attraction of the relative in xviii. 6, ποτηρίῳ ᾧ ἐκέρασεν, is against his usage: cf. i. 20. Even the title of Babylon in xviii. 10, ἡ πόλις ἡ ἰσχυρά, is against our author's use, who calls it ἡ μεγάλη in xiv. 8, xvi. 19, a title which appears also in this source in xvii. 5, xviii. 2, 10, 21. Finally, in xviii. 7 we find κάθημαι where our author would have used καθίζω: see note on iii. 21; and οὐ μή, xviii. 14, with εὑρήσουσιν, where he would use εὕρωσιν.

4. The accumulation of participles is a frequent characteristic of this source—without any real parallel in the rest of the Book. Thus in xviii. 9–10 we have οἱ . . . πορνεύσαντες καὶ στρηνιάσαντες ὅταν βλέπωσιν . . . ἀπὸ μακρόθεν ἑστηκότες . . . λέγοντες, all dependent on the subject of the principal verb. In 15, οἱ πλουτήσαντες . . . κλαίοντες καὶ πενθοῦντες, λέγοντες, similarly dependent on the subject of the principal verb: in 18, βλέποντες . . . λέγοντες: in 19, κλαίοντες καὶ πενθοῦντες, λέγοντες. The same accumulation of participles is to be found in the earlier fragment of this source, *i.e.* xvii. 1^c–2, 3^b–7, 18, 8–10. Thus in xvii. 3 we have γυναῖκα καθημένην ἐπὶ θηρίον . . . γέμοντα . . . ἔχων: in 4, περιβεβλημένη . . . καὶ κεχρυσωμένη . . . ἔχουσα: in 7, τοῦ βαστάζοντος, τοῦ ἔχοντος: in 8, οἱ κατοικοῦντες . . . βλεπόντων.

5. The use of neuter adjectives in the sing. as nouns is

[1] Thus the syntax is carefully observed as regards gender and number. Even λέγων (λέγοντες, etc.) always agrees with the noun on which it depends; contrast our author's use: i. 11, iv. 1, v. 12, 13, ix. 14, x. 8 (*bis*), xi. 1, 15, xiv. 7, xix. 1, 6.

characteristic of this source: *i.e.* βύσσινον = "fine linen" in xviii. 12, 16. This usage occurs only once in the LXX in Dan. x. 5^c. Occasionally τὰ βύσσινα is used in this sense in the LXX. Similarly πορφυροῦν in xvii. 4, xviii. 16, κόκκινον in xvii. 4, xviii. 12, 16, σιρικόν, xviii. 12, and διπλοῦν in xviii. 6, are used as nouns, although, save in the case of σιρικόν and διπλοῦν, such a use of these words in the sing. seems unattested elsewhere. σιρικόν is found in Arrian and Strabo as a noun, and διπλοῦν appears to be used similarly in the LXX in Ex. xxii. 7, 9. For certain adjectives employed in this way in the rest of the N.T. see Robertson, *Gram.* 653 sq., who, however, as the rest of the N.T. grammarians, fails to notice most of the above words.

6. The order of this source is less Semitic than that of our author: see above.

7. *This source appears to have influenced our author.*—As regards xviii. 2–23, it has become clear that it is not our author's production, as we have found also with regard to xvii. 1^c–2, 3^b–7, 18, 8–10. Now this source, dating from the time of Vespasian, had been in our author's hands and was apparently laid under contribution by him. Thus xiv. 8 is composed simply of xviii. 2^b, 3^a put together. Again our author's peculiar use of βύσσινον in xix. 8, 14 as a noun appears due to this same use in xviii. 12, 16 (see 5. above). The fact that this use of βύσσινον is characteristic of this source and borrowed by our author gains support by its use of πορφυροῦν (xvii. 4, xviii. 16), κόκκινον (xvii. 4, xviii. 12, 16), σιρικόν (xviii. 12), and διπλοῦν (xviii. 6) as nouns, although, save in the case of the σιρικόν and διπλοῦν, such a use seems unattested elsewhere. διπλᾶ and τὰ κόκκινα are found elsewhere. Since, therefore, our author appears to have been influenced by this source in the above respects, it is possible that he may have been also influenced by it in his use of ἰσχυρός, which occurs 4 times in xviii. and 5 times in the rest of our author. Three of these five times it occurs in the phrase ἄγγελος ἰσχυρός found also in xviii. 21. But οὐκ . . . ἔτι, which is 6 times in xviii., occurs 9 times in the rest of our author and belongs to his vocabulary. His use of διὰ τοῦτο, vii. 15, xii. 12, is not to be traced to xviii. 8, seeing that it is a very common phrase, being found 15 times in the Johannine Gospel and 3 times in the Epistles.

§ 3. *The Greek appears to be a translation from a Hebrew source.*

The evidence for the hypothesis is not conclusive. It will be found in the notes on 8, 19, 22 in connection with the words and phrases πένθος, ἐκ τῆς τιμιότητος, and μουσικῶν. The use of δυνάμεως in 3 may suggest חיל = "wealth."

§ 4. *The text has suffered great dislocations—in some degree comparable to those in xxii. Translation of xviii. 21–24 in its reconstructed order.*

One of these dislocations—that of 14—was observed by early scholars like Beza and Vitringa, which they restore after 23^{d}. But the present writer thinks that 14 should be read immediately after 21: 20 he finds is also out of place. It should be replaced after 23^{ab}. The various elements of 22–23 have been disarranged, as is shown in the notes.

21–24 should be read in the following order: 21, 14, 22$^{a\text{-}d}$, 23^{cd}, 22$^{e\text{-}h}$, 23^{ab}, 20, 23^{f}, 24.

21. And a strong angel took up a stone as it were a great millstone, and cast it into the sea, saying:

"Thus with violence shall be cast down,
Babylon the great city,
And shall no more be found.

(The Seer's dirge over Babylon.)

14. And the fruits which thy soul lusted after
Are gone from thee:
And all the dainties and the splendours
Are perished from thee.
[And men shall find them no more at all].

22$^{a\text{-}d}$. And the voice of the harpers and singers
<Shall be heard no more in thee>,
And <the voice> of the fluteplayers and trumpeters
Shall be heard no more in thee.

23^{cd}. And the voice of the bridegroom and the bride
Shall be heard no more in thee:
22^{ef}. And no craftsman of whatsoever craft
Shall be found any more in thee:

22^{gh}. And the voice of the millstone
Shall be heard no more in thee:
23^{ab}. And the light of the lamp
Shall shine no more in thee.

(The Seer's appeal to heaven and its inhabitants to rejoice over the doom of Rome.)

20. Rejoice over her, thou heaven,
And ye saints and ye apostles and ye prophets;
For God hath judged your judgment upon her;

23f. For with *her* sorcery had all the nations been deceived:
24. And in her was found the blood of the prophets and saints
And of all that had been slain upon the earth."

§ 5. *xviii. was written in the time of Vespasian* [1]

This statement can be proved by means of 2, 4, 6–8.

(*a*) For first of all 2 presupposes the fires of Rome to have been long extinct, and its ruins to have become the abode of every unclean spirit, bird, and beast. Now such a supposition even in a vision was not possible for the Seer writing in 95 A.D. He was then looking forward to the destruction of Rome as one of the *last* great acts in the judgment of the world. Moreover, the fires which should consume Rome, xviii. 9, 15, 18, were *never, so long as the earth lasted, to be extinguished*, xix. 3. Hence, however we explain xviii. 2, it was written at an earlier date than the Apocalypse as a whole. But, whereas the prophecy in 2 is merely proleptic and therefore not at variance with xviii. 8, 15, 18, it is really irreconcilable with xix. 3, which declares that the smoke of Rome's ruins will go up till the world's end. The former gives the expectation of a Jewish Seer in Vespasian's time, the latter that of our author John in 95 A.D.

(*b*) In the note on 4 I have shown that the presupposition underlying it runs counter to the expectation of our Seer, that after chap. xiii. all the faithful had been put to death. But in this verse a considerable body of the faithful is presumed to be actually present in Rome. Such a presumption would be justifiable in Vespasian's time after the fall of Jerusalem, to which period xviii. can most reasonably be assigned.

(*c*) In 6–8 the same Vespasianic standpoint is transparent. We have such an expectation here as would be naturally entertained by a zealous Jew after the destruction of Jerusalem.

§ 6. *xviii. preserved in a corrupt condition and adapted by our author to his own purpose.*

The dislocation of 14 and 20 and of several clauses in 21–24 from their original contexts shows how profoundly the original source has suffered (see § 4). There is no reason to suppose that these dislocations were due to our author. Either they were already present in his source, or they are due to accidental disarrangement subsequently. It should be borne in mind that, if the present writer's hypothesis is sound as to the death of John when he had completed xx. 3, we are to regard i.–xx. 3 as never having undergone a final revision at his hands. In fact we have in i.–xx. 3, the first sketch of a great work, portions of which

[1] On a variety of grounds Sabatier, Rauch, Spitta, Weyland, Bousset, J. Weiss, Wellhausen, and Moffatt accept the Vespasianic date of xviii.

have been most carefully worked out from the visions of many years, while others show not a few inequalities and inconsistencies that a final revision would have removed.

As regards the corruptions in the text we have already (§ 3) sought to explain those in 8, 19, 22 by means of a Hebrew background. The ungrammatical clause (καὶ ἵππων κτλ.) in 13 is merely a gloss. 23^{e}, if it belonged to the original source, is at all events in its wrong context where it stands. 24 is from the hand of John as well as the phrase καὶ οἱ ἀποστολοί in 20.

§ 7. *xviii. and xvii. 1^{c}–2, 3^{b}–7, 18, 8–10 are a Greek translation of one and the same Hebrew source.*

We have already come to the conclusion that xvii. 1^{c}–2, 3^{b}–7, 18, 8–10, and xviii. 2–24 are of a Vespasianic date, and that the Greek of these sections is apparently a translation (not made but revised by John) from a Hebrew original. Since xvii. 1^{c}–2, 3^{b}–7, 18, 8–10, and xviii. 2–23, which are closely connected by their peculiar and in some respects unique diction, deal with the same subject and belong to the same date, we conclude that they are from the same hand. The former served as an introduction to the latter. xvii. 1 gives the title of xviii. τὸ κρίμα τῆς πόρνης τῆς μεγάλης τῆς καθημένης ἐπὶ ὑδάτων πολλῶν. Next, xvii. 2 (μεθ' ἧς ἐπόρνευσαν οἱ βασιλεῖς τῆς γῆς, καὶ ἐμεθύσθησαν οἱ κατοικοῦντες τὴν γῆν ἐκ τοῦ οἴνου τῆς πορνείας αὐτῆς) is repeated in substance and in part verbally in xviii. 3, ἐκ τοῦ οἴνου τοῦ θυμοῦ τῆς πορνείας αὐτῆς πεπότικεν πάντα τὰ ἔθνη, and 23, ἐν τῇ φαρμακίᾳ σου ἐπλανήθησαν πάντα τὰ ἔθνη. Next, clauses from xvii. 4 (περιβεβλημένη πορφυροῦν[1] καὶ κόκκινον, καὶ κεχρυσωμένη χρυσίῳ καὶ λίθῳ τιμίῳ καὶ μαργαρίταις) are repeated almost word for word in xviii. 16, ἡ περιβεβλημένη . . . πορφυροῦν καὶ κόκκινον καὶ κεχρυσωμένη . . . λίθῳ τιμίῳ καὶ μαργαρίτῃ. Again, ποτήριον . . . ἐν τῇ χειρὶ αὐτῆς γέμον βδελυγμάτων in xvii. 4 is recalled by ἐν τῷ ποτηρίῳ ᾧ ἐκέρασεν in xviii. 6; Βαβυλὼν ἡ μεγάλη in xvii. 5 by a kindred clause in xviii. 10; and ἡ πόλις ἡ μεγάλη in xvii. 18 by the same phrase in xviii. 10, 16, 19.

Hence xvii. 1^{c}–2, 3^{b}–7, 18, 8–10, and xviii. appear to be derived from one and the same Hebrew source.[2] With this he has combined another source, xvii. 11–13, 17, 16, which foretold the destruction of Rome by Nero and the Parthians. xvii. 2 gives the title of the Vision in xviii., *i.e.* the Doom of Rome; this judgment is preceded by a vision of Rome before its overthrow in

[1] It is important to observe that πορφυροῦν used as a noun seems to occur only in xvii. 4 and xviii. 16, that κόκκινον is used as a noun in the sing. in xvii. 4^{b}, xviii. 12, 16—a most rare use, though it is found in the LXX and elsewhere as a noun in the plural. See § 2. 5 above.

[2] The order of the words in xviii. while in the main Semitic, is not as decidedly so as in xvii. 1^{c}–2, 3^{b}–7, 18, 8–10. The latter has been thoroughly revised by our author.

xvii. 3–7, 18, 8–10, and by a *prophecy* of the coming destruction of Rome by fire at the hands of Nero and the Parthians, *i.e.* xvii. 12–13, 17, 16. It is not till we come to xviii. that the promise of the Angel of the Bowls in xvii. 1, *δείξω σοι τὸ κρίμα τῆς πόρνης*, is fulfilled. xviii. is a vision of Rome's doom, which is *foretold* in xvii. 16.

1–3. The proclamation of the doom of Babylon by the first angel. This proclamation is proleptic. The angel's words regard Rome's doom as already accomplished far in the past.

From 2[cde] it appears that the fires that consumed it have long since been quenched, and that it has become the abode of unclean birds and demons. See the note on these clauses below.

1. ἄλλον ἄγγελον. This angel is distinguished from the angel mentioned in xvii. 1, 7, who is the *angelus interpres*.

ἡ γῆ ἐφωτίσθη ἐκ τῆς δόξης αὐτοῦ. This is a direct rendering of Ezek. xliii. 2, הארץ הֵאִירָה מכבדו, where the LXX has *ἡ γῆ ἐξέλαμπεν ὡς φέγγος ἀπὸ τῆς δόξης*. Here the Targum has ארעא נהרת מזיו יקריה. Thus the brightness of God's glory is here attributed to an angel. See further on this "brightness" in note on xxi. 23. On this use of *ἐκ* = "by reason of," cf. viii. 13, xvi. 11.

2. ἔκραξεν ἐν ἰσχυρᾷ φωνῇ. The diction in this phrase is unexampled in our author: the order is most exceptional. See note on x. 3.

ἔπεσεν ἔπεσεν Βαβυλὼν ἡ μεγάλη. This clause has already occurred in xiv. 8 (see note). The Greek here, with the exception of the epithet, is an independent rendering of Isa. xxi. 9.

2[cde]. These three clauses are to be taken proleptically in reference to 9, 15, 18: otherwise they occasion difficulty; for in 9, 15, 18, Rome is seen in the Seer's vision to be consumed by fire: whereas these clauses presuppose the fires of Rome to have been long extinct, and the ruins to have become the hold of unclean birds and demons. xiv. 11 refers not to the city Rome, but to the eternal torment of the worshippers of the Beast in the next world. On the other hand it is impossible to reconcile 2[cde] with xix. 3, which represents the smoke of her burning as going up for ever and ever, *i.e.* to the end of the world. This last is our author's own expectation. Here that of his source conflicts with it: see Introd. to this Chap., § 5.

ἐγένετο κατοικητήριον δαιμονίων . . . μεμισημένου: cf. Isa. xiii. 21–22 (*δαιμόνια ἐκεῖ ὀρχηθήσονται*); Jer. li. 31, "Babylon shall become . . . a dwelling for jackals"; 1 Bar. iv. 35, *κατοικηθήσεται ὑπὸ δαιμονίων*. In Isa. xxxiv. 11, 13[b], 14–15, Jer. l. 39, there is a list of unclean birds and beasts that are to inhabit Edom or Babylon given: cf. Zeph ii. 14. The *δαιμόνια* are the ציים, or more probably the שׂעירים (Isa. xiii. 21, xxxiv. 14).

ὀρνέου ἀκαθάρτου: cf. Deut. xiv. 12–19.

3. The nations as a whole, the rulers of the earth and its merchants, were involved in the sin of Rome.

ἐκ τοῦ οἴνου [τοῦ θυμοῦ] τῆς πορνείας αὐτῆς. I have here with much hesitation bracketed τοῦ θυμοῦ, although it has the support of the best MSS. But the extraordinary diversity among the authorities points to some corruption in the above text. See notes on xiv. 8, xvii. 2. In the latter passage we have an exact parallel to xviii. 3^{ab}; for 3^{a} (cf. 23^{d} ὅτι ἐν τῇ φαρμακίᾳ σου ἐπλανήθησαν πάντα τὰ ἔθνη) corresponds to ἐμεθύσθησαν οἱ κατοικοῦντες τ. γῆν ἐκ τοῦ οἴνου τῆς πορνείας αὐτῆς. 3^{b} corresponds almost *verbatim* with xvii. 2^{a}, μεθ' ἧς ἐπόρνευσαν οἱ βασιλεῖς τῆς γῆς.

οἱ βασιλεῖς τῆς γῆς. Their lamentation over Rome is given in 9–20, as that of the merchants in 11–13, 15–16.

πεπότικεν. This reading, supported by a few cursives, appears to be the true one, though in the cursives only a happy conjecture. It explains the impossible readings of אACQ. It is also required by the context: otherwise Rome is represented only as passively evil. πέπτωκαν though originating in a scribal error seemed to derive support from ἔπεσεν. As Babylon fell, so did the nations.

οἱ ἔμποροι τῆς γῆς. This phrase, which is peculiar to this chapter in the N.T. (cf. 11, 15, 23), is significant. All the merchants of the world are involved in the overthrow of Rome. The long list of merchants who traded with Tyre, according to Ezek. xxvii. 9–25, was in the mind of our author.

ἐκ . . . αὐτῆς ἐπλούτησαν: cf. 15.

τῆς δυνάμεως = "wealth"—a meaning which is found also in the LXX of Deut. viii. 17, Ruth iv. 11, where δύναμις is a rendering of חיל. In Isa. lxi. 6 it is rendered by ἰσχύς = "wealth." This meaning is to be found in Xen. *Cyr.* vii. 4. 34, etc., 2 Cor. viii. 3, and the Papyri.

τοῦ στρήνους αὐτῆς = "of her wantonness." Here and in 2 Kings xix. 28. Cf. στρηνιᾶν in 9, and καταστρηνιᾶν τοῦ Χριστοῦ, "to wax wanton against the restrictions prescribed by Christ," in 1 Tim. v. 11.

4–8. The second voice, which comes from heaven itself. 4–5 are addressed to the faithful, and 6–8 to the ministers of God's wrath who were seen by the Seer to be assembling for the work of destruction.

4. No justifiable meaning can be attached to this verse as it stands. As we have repeatedly seen heretofore (cf. also ver. 20), the presupposition of the Seer is that after xiii. all the faithful had been put to death. In xv. 2–4 the army of martyrs is seen in its completeness in a vision before the throne of God, while the Seven Bowls are poured down on a wholly heathen world. In the present verse, therefore, indeed in the present chapter, we have a document that belongs, as a large body of modern scholars have recognized, to the time of Vespasian. This oracle dealt with the destruction of Rome. Völter (*Offenbarung Johannis*, 1904), J. Weiss and Erbes ascribe this oracle to a Christian source written respectively about 60, 70 and 80 A.D. On the other hand, Vischer, Schoen, Weyland, Spitta trace it, and rightly in the opinion of the present writer, to a Jewish source. Whether Jewish or Christian originally, it is partially adapted to its present context by the mention of the "apostles" in 20, and by the addition of 24.

ἄλλην φωνήν. The words that follow—ὁ λαός μου—seem to suggest that it is God that speaks. But 5 is against this conclusion. Cf. xvi. 1 for a like difficulty. It may, however, be Christ that speaks.

ἐξέλθατε ἐξ αὐτῆς ὁ λαός μου. These words appear to be a reproduction of Jer. li. (xxviii.) 45, צאו מִתּוֹכָהּ עַמִּי. Since they are not found in ℵABQ* of the LXX and in Q^mg are rendered by *ἐξέλθετε ἐκ μέσου αὐτῆς λαός μου*, this clause seems to have been translated directly from the Hebrew, and independently of the LXX.

There are, it is true, many parallels in the O.T. to the above clause in our text. Cf. Jer. xxvii. (l.) 8, *ἀπαλλοτριώθητε ἐκ μέσου Βαβυλῶνος . . . καὶ ἐξέλθατε*: xxviii. (li.) 6, *φεύγετε ἐκ μέσου Βαβυλῶνος, καὶ ἀνασώζετε ἕκαστος τὴν ψυχὴν αὐτοῦ καὶ μὴ ἀποριφῆτε ἐν τῇ ἀδικίᾳ αὐτῆς*: Isa. xlviii. 20, *ἔξελθε ἐκ Βαβυλῶνος*: lii. 11, *ἀπόστητε, ἀπόστητε, ἐξέλθατε ἐκεῖθεν . . . ἐξέλθατε ἐκ μέσου αὐτῆς*: cf. also 2 Bar. ii. 1, "Retire from this city"; Matt. xxiv. 16, *τότε οἱ ἐν τῇ Ἰουδαίᾳ φευγέτωσαν ἐπὶ τὰ ὄρη*. The last quotation belongs to the Little Apocalypse, and refers, of course, to Jerusalem.

συνκοινωνήσητε ταῖς ἡμαρτίας: cf. Eph. v. 11, *μὴ συνκοινωνεῖτε τ. ἔργοις . . . τ. σκότους*: 1 Tim. v. 22, *μηδὲ κοινώνει ἁμαρτίαις ἀλλοτρίαις*. These words deal with the guilt of sharing in the sin of Rome, as the words that follow deal with the punishment that such guilt must entail.

ἐκ τῶν πληγῶν αὐτῆς, "some of her plagues."

5. ἐκολλήθησαν . . . ἄχρι τ. οὐρανοῦ. These words are, apparently, a reminiscence of Jer. li. 9, נגע אל השמים משפטה. If so, then *ἐκολλήθησαν* is simply to be rendered (as in the A.V. and R.V. and the Vulg., pervenerunt) "have reached." This rendering of נגע is very rare,—see Lam. ii. 2 and Zech. xiv. 5, *ἐνκολληθήσεται* (יַגִּיעַ) *φάραγξ ὀρέων ἕως Ἰασός*,—but the meaning belonging to this Hebrew verb is clearly the one required by our context. We might also compare with our text 1 Esdr. viii. 72, *αἱ δὲ ἄγνοιαι ἡμῶν ὑπερήνεγκαν ἕως τοῦ οὐρανοῦ*: cf. Ezra ix. 6; also 4 Ezra xi. 43, "Et ascendit contumelia tua ad altissimum et superbia tua ad fortem." If this rendering is right, then we are not to attempt to render ἐκολλήθησαν κτλ. as "have grown together into such a mass as to reach the heaven." It would be extraordinary if God was not mindful of the sins of Rome (5^b) till they pressed in a mass against the roof of heaven. To such an extravagant conception the parallelism καὶ ἐμνημόνευσεν ὁ θεὸς τὰ ἀδικήματα αὐτῆς would form a singular anticlimax—a piece of sheer bathos. Hence we infer that ἐκολλήθησαν is here = הגיעו, and that the rendering is independent of the LXX in Jer. li. (xxviii.) 9, ἤγγικεν εἰς οὐρανὸν τὸ κρίμα αὐτῆς. The rendering of the two Syriac Versions here is very infelicitous, *i.e.* "have cleaved to." This rendering of κολλᾶσθαι is found once more in the Syriac Versions, namely, in Luke x. 11, but there it is very felicitous.

On the other hand, it must be conceded that κολλᾶσθαι is the general rendering of דבק in the LXX. If it presupposes this Hebrew word here, then our text is not a reminiscence of Jer. li. 9. But even so, the context is against the meaning belonging to דבק. Such a passage as 1 Bar. i. 20, ἐκολλήθη εἰς ἡμᾶς τὰ κακὰ καὶ ἡ ἀρά, does not support our text in the sense of "cleave unto." Even in this passage of Baruch ἐκολλήθη probably presupposes a corrupt Hebrew text. See Whitehouse in Charles, *The Apoc. and Pseud.* i. 578, and Kneucker *in loc.* The Syriac Version of Baruch = ותבא (= et pervenerunt), while the Greek = ותדבק. Dan. ix. 11, with which 1 Bar. i. 15–ii. 17 is closely related, supports the former.

αὐτῆς αἱ ἁμαρτίαι. On this vernacular use of the genitive of **αὐτός** see notes on ii. 2, 19, and in vol. ii. 208, footnote.

ἐμνημόνευσεν ὁ θεός κτλ. Cf. xvi. 19, Βαβυλὼν ἡ μεγάλη ἐμνήσθη ἐνώπιον τοῦ θεοῦ.

6. In its present context this verse is to be taken as addressed to Nero *redivivus* and the hosts that followed him: cf. xvii. 11–17. But it is not to be forgotten that already Rome has for the most part been destroyed in xvi. 19 by a great earthquake, and its entire destruction by fire foretold in xvii. 16. The present chapter, taken by itself, shows no consciousness of the first of these judgments. But the destruction of Rome by fire is proclaimed in xviii. 8, 9, 15. Hence the description of the final overthrow of Rome in xviii. 21 must be taken as purely figurative.

ἀπόδοτε αὐτῇ ὡς καὶ αὐτὴ ἀπέδωκεν κτλ., *i.e.* deal out to her the same measure that she dealt to others. Cf. Jer. xxvii. (l.) 29, ἀνταπόδοτε αὐτῇ κατὰ τὰ ἔργα αὐτῆς· κατὰ πάντα ὅσα ἐποίησεν ποιήσατε αὐτῇ: 15. ἐκδικεῖτε ἐπ' αὐτήν· καθὼς ἐποίησεν, ποιήσατε αὐτῇ: Ps. cxxxvi. 8, μακάριος ὃς ἀνταποδώσει σοι τὸ ἀνταπόδομά σου ὃ ἀνταπέδωκας ἡμῖν. On this principle of *lex talionis* see the notes in my edition of *Jubilees* on iv. 31, xlviii. 14.

διπλώσατε διπλᾶ: cf. Isa. xl. 2, ἐδέξατο ἐκ χειρὸς κυρίου διπλᾶ τὰ ἁμαρτήματα αὐτῆς: Jer. xvi. 18, ἀνταποδώσω . . . διπλᾶς τὰς κακίας αὐτῶν. διπλοῦν διπλᾶ is an extraordinary expression. Cf. Aesch. *Agamem.* 537, διπλᾶ δ' ἔτισαν Πριαμίδαι θἀμάρτια.

But in Aeschylus the διπλοῦς is used purely as an adjective, whereas in our text it is a noun. For this use cf. Ex. xxii. 3, 6, 8. In the first passage we have διπλᾶ in the LXX (שנים), in the second τὸ (?) διπλοῦν, and in the third διπλοῦν, *i.e.* ἀποτίσει διπλοῦν τῷ πλησίον. Cf. also Zech. ix. 12, διπλᾶ ἀνταποδώσω.

ἐν τῷ ποτηρίῳ κτλ.: cf. xiv. 8, xvii. 4. This cup is the cup of the wrath of God. Cf. 2 Bar. xiii. 8, in which the Romans also are addressed.

> "Ye who have drunken the strained wine
> Drink ye also of its dregs,
> The judgment of the Lofty One
> Who has no respect of persons."

7. In this verse it is a question whether the speaker is a heavenly being or the Seer who wrote this vision.

ὅσα . . . τοσοῦτον. The torment and grief (or "misfortune") of Rome are to be proportionate to her self-glorification and wantonness. Cf. Isa. iii. 16, 17, ἀνθ' ὧν ὑψώθησαν αἱ θυγατέρες Σειὼν . . . καὶ ταπεινώσει ὁ θεὸς ἀρχούσας θυγατέρας Σειών: Prov. xxix. 23, ὕβρις ἄνδρα ταπεινοῖ: Luke xiv. 11, etc. On the probability that πένθος, which occurs twice in this verse, is to be rendered "misfortune" or "calamity," or that it is a translation of a corrupt form in the Hebrew original, see note on ver. 8.

ὅτι ἐν τῇ καρδίᾳ αὐτῆς λέγει . . . ἴδω. These lines reproduce freely Isa. xlvii. 7, 8, . . . ותֹּאמְרִי לעולם אהיה גברת האֹמְרָה בלבבה . . . לא אשב אלמנה ולא אדע שכול. But the LXX is not followed, which here gives εἶπας Εἰς τὸν αἰῶνα ἔσομαι ἄρχουσα . . . ἡ λέγουσα ἐν τῇ καρδίᾳ αὐτῆς . . . οὐ καθιῶ χήρα οὐδὲ γνώσομαι ὀρφανείαν. We should observe that for κάθημαι we should expect καθίζω (see note on iii. 21) if this chapter were from the hand of our author. As a parallel to our text, the boast of Tyre in Ezek. xxviii. 2 should be compared and also the self-glorification attributed to Rome in 2 Bar. xii. 3.

8. Because of (ὅτι . . . διὰ τοῦτο) Rome's pride and self-confidence she shall be overthrown suddenly.

ἐν μιᾷ ἡμέρᾳ ἥξουσιν. Isa. xlvii. still influences our writer; for these words are derived from the Massoretic ver. 9, where the LXX (B) renders ἥξει . . . ἐπὶ σὲ ἐν τῇ φαρμακίᾳ σου. But אA etc. agree with Mass. It is noteworthy that εἷς is postpositive in ix. 12, 13, but prepositive in viii. 13, xvii. 12, 13, 17, xviii. 8, 10, 16, 19, xix. 17.

† θάνατος καὶ πένθος καὶ λιμός †. We might compare vi. 8. It must be confessed that *πένθος* ("mourning") cannot with any justice be reckoned under the category of plagues. But first of all the presence of *λιμός* suggests that *θάνατος* here as in vi. 8 and frequently in the O.T. = דבר, "pestilence." In that case the natural order would be *λιμὸς κ. θάνατος κ. πένθος*. Now returning to *πένθος*, it is possible that it should be rendered here according to a rare meaning by "calamity," "misfortune" (cf. Pindar, *Isth.* vi. (vii.) 51, *ἔτλαν δὲ πένθος οὐ φατόν*: Herod. iii. 14). If so, we should translate "famine and pestilence and misfortune." But the error may be due to a corruption in the Semitic original. Thus *πένθος* = אבל, corrupt for חֶבֶל. If this is right, we obtain an excellent sense—"famine and pestilence and destruction." The approach of the Parthians from the East under Nero would cut off food supplies from Rome and lead to famine, in the train of which pestilence would soon follow. The third plague would then prepare for the destruction of Rome by fire. Or, since the writer has, as has been shown on 7, borrowed freely from Isa. xlvii. 7, 8, it is possible that אֵבֶל (= *πένθος*) may be a corruption of שכול in Isa. xlvii. 8—"famine and pestilence and loss of children." But the former restoration is to be preferred.

ἐν πυρὶ κατακαυθήσεται. The judgment of Rome by fire, which according to xvii. 16 is to be executed by Nero and the Parthian kings, is here declared to come from God in the first instance. On the judgment by fire cf. Jer. l. 32, li. 25, 30, 32, 58.

ἰσχυρὸς ὁ θεὸς ὁ κρίνας αὐτήν. The translator of this chapter is fond of the word *ἰσχυρός* = cf. 2, 10, 21. Outside this chapter it occurs only five times in the Apocalypse: cf. Jer. xxvii. (l.) 34, *ὁ λυτρούμενος αὐτοὺς ἰσχυρός . . . κρίσιν κρινεῖ πρὸς τοὺς ἀντιδίκους αὐτοῦ*. This *κρίνας* points to the fact that the decree of judgment has already been passed on Rome.

9–19. The dirge chanted over the conflagration of Rome by the kings, 9–10, by the merchant princes of the earth, 11–16, and the shipowners and sailors of the world, 17–19. The author is influenced by the doom song pronounced by Ezekiel over Tyre, Ezek. xxvi.–xxviii.

9–10. Cf. Ezek. xxvi. 16–17, where the princes of the sea mourn over Tyre.

κλαύσονται καὶ κόψονται ἐπὶ αὐτῇ: cf. 2 Sam. i. 12, *ἐκόψαντο . . . καὶ ἔκλαυσαν . . . ἐπί*. Hence our text = "shall weep and mourn over" (= ויבכו ויספדו על). See also 11, 15, 19.

οἱ βασιλεῖς τῆς γῆς: cf. vi. 15 (see note), xvii. 2, 18, xviii. 3. These kings are the heads of the heathen nations. Foremost amongst them are princes subject to or in alliance with

Rome; for, as the next clause shows, they have been deeply affected by her influence. They are distinct from the Parthian kings who destroy Rome, xvii. 16.

οἱ μετ' αὐτῆς πορνεύσαντες: cf. xvii. 2, xviii. 3. στρηνιάσαντες. They too had lived wantonly like Rome: cf. 3.

ὅταν βλέπωσιν . . . αὐτῆς. This clause recurs in 18.

τῆς πυρώσεως. The prophecy of Rome's destruction by fire is dwelt on again and again: cf. xvii. 16, xviii. 8, 18.

10. ἀπὸ μακρόθεν: cf. 15 (see note), 17; Matt. xxvi. 58; Mark v. 6, viii. 3, etc.

διὰ τὸν φόβον . . . αὐτῆς. This phrase recurs in 15.

οὐαὶ οὐαὶ ἡ πόλις κτλ. This construction is not found in the N.T. except in Luke vi. 25^b; but it occurs frequently in the LXX: cf. Isa. v. 8, 11, 20, 21, 22; Hab. ii. 6, 12, 19; Zeph. ii. 5; Amos v. 18, where the R.V. rightly renders: "woe unto." Hence the rendering here, as in these passages, should be, "Woe, woe to the great city." The construction suggests the writer's acquaintance with the LXX. Our author's construction is *οὐαί* with the dat.: cf. viii. 13.

μιᾷ ὥρᾳ: cf. 8, 16, 19.

11–16. The merchants of the earth take up their dirge over Rome

11. οἱ ἔμποροι τῆς γῆς. In Ezek. xxvii. 12–24 the various nations that had commercial relations with Tyre are enumerated.

κλαίουσιν καὶ πενθοῦσιν ἐπ' αὐτῇ: cf. 9, 15, 19; Mark xvi. 10; Luke vi. 25; Jas. iv. 9. This combination is found in Neh. i. 4.

γόμον = ship's freight or cargo: cf. Acts xxi. 3. The vastness of the commerce of Rome may be inferred from the following passages, which are all taken from Wetstein; Galen, *De Antidot*, i. 4, *ἐὰν ἐν Ῥώμῃ κατοικῶμεν, εἰς ἣν ἐξ ἁπάντων τῶν ἐθνῶν καθ' ἕκαστον ἐνιαυτὸν ἐξικνοῦνται πάμπολλα . . . εἰς ἣν τὰ πανταχόθεν ἧκε καλὰ διὰ παντὸς ἔτους*: Pliny, *H.N.* vi. 26, "Minima computatione millies centena millia sestertium annis omnibus India et Seres peninsulaque illa imperio nostro adimunt": Aristides, *In Rom.*, p. 200, *ἄγεται δὲ ἐκ πάσης γῆς καὶ θαλάττης, ὅσα ὧραι φύουσι, καὶ χῶραι ἑκάσται φέρουσι, καὶ ποταμοί, καὶ λίμναι, καὶ τέχναι Ἑλλήνων καὶ βαρβάρων· ὥστε εἴ τις ταῦτα πάντα ἐπιδεῖν βούλοιτο, δεῖ αὐτὸν ἢ πᾶσαν εἰσελθόντα τὴν οἰκουμένην οὕτω θεάσασθαι, ἢ ἐν τῇδε τῇ πόλει γενόμενον . . . τοσαῦται δὲ ἀφικνοῦνται δεῦρο κομίζουσαι παρὰ πάντων ὁλκάδες, ἀνὰ πᾶσαν μὲν ὥραν, πᾶσαν δὲ φθινόπωρον περιτροπήν, ὥστ' ἐοικέναι τὴν πόλιν κοινῷ τινι τῆς γῆς ἐργαστηρίῳ. φόρτους μὲν ἀπ' Ἰνδῶν, εἰ βούλει δὲ καὶ τῶν εὐδαιμόνων Ἀράβων τοσούτους ὁρᾶν ἐστίν, ὥστε εἰκάζειν γυμνὰ τὸ λοιπὸν τοῖς ἐκεῖ λελεῖφθαι τὰ δένδρα. . . . Ἐσθῆτας δ' αὖ Βαβυλωνίας, καὶ τοὺς ἐκ τῆς ἐπέκεινα βαρβάρου κόσμους. . . . Πάντα ἐνταῦθα συμπίπτει,* ἐμπορίαι, ναυταλίαι, γεωργίαι, μετάλλων κάθαρσις, τέχναι ὁπόσαι εἰσί τε καὶ γεγένηνται, πάντα ὅσα γεννᾶται καὶ φύεται. ὅ τι δ' ἂν μὴ ἐνταῦθα ἴδοι τις, οὐκ ἔστι τῶν γενομένων ἢ γιγνομένων. In the Talmud, *Qidd.* 49^b, it is stated that "Ten measures of wealth came down into the world: Rome received nine, and all the world one."

Since 23^e cannot stand in its present context, it may originally have stood after 11^a, and so this verse may have run as follows:

11^a "And the merchants of the earth weep and mourn over her,
23^e For thy merchants were the princes of the earth,
11^b For no man buyeth their merchandise any more."

12-13. These two verses give a list of the articles imported by Rome from all quarters of the world. Holtzmann has recognized that the first four articles mentioned (*i.e.* precious stones) harmonize rhythmically with the next four, consisting of costly garments. But further examination of the passage shows that it consists, according to the present text, of nine lines. That the first four of these consist of two couplets there can be no doubt, but great difficulty attaches to the method of dealing with the remaining five lines. If they are to be retained as they stand, it might be best to regard them as consisting of a tristich and a distich:

"And cinnamon and spice and incense,
And ointment and frankincense and wine,
And oil and fine flour and wheat:
And beasts and sheep [and horses
And chariots and slaves] and souls of men."

But it is probable that the words I have bracketed are an interpolation; for (1) their syntax—genitives where there ought to be accusatives—is wholly anomalous. It is without a real parallel in the abnormal style of our author, and is still more at variance with the much more grammatical style of this chapter, which, as we have elsewhere seen, comes from an independent source. (2) The same ideas are repeated in immediate proximity under different forms; for "slaves" and "souls of men" are here synonymous.

κτήνη, as is shown in the notes on 13 = draught cattle, *i.e.* horses, asses, etc., and thus the mention of horses separately, as in the present text, is wholly gratuitous. Now, if we excise as a gloss, which has crept in from the margin, the words "and horses and chariots and slaves," we get rid of the anomalous syntax, and of the meaningless repetitions in the last line, and recover the original text of 12–13, consisting of four stanzas of two lines each. The last stanza then would be:

> "And oil and fine flour and wheat,
> And beasts and sheep and souls of men."

The dramatic forcibleness of what seems at first a purely prosaic list of imports is in the highest degree impressive, closing as it does in the climax—

> "And beasts and sheep and souls of men."

12. On the various articles mentioned in 12–13 the Bible Dictionaries should be consulted. Most of them are to be found in the imports of Tyre: Ezek. xxvii. 12–24, *i.e.* gold, silver, precious stones, fine linen, purple, brass, iron, all spices, oil, wheat, cattle, sheep, horses, and the souls of men.

βυσσίνου: cf. xix. 8.

σιρικοῦ (so the uncials. The usual form is *σηρικοῦ*). This word (= "silk") is a *ἅπ. λεγ.* in Biblical Greek, but it was used frequently by Greek writers after Alexander's time. How commonly it was used in Rome about 70 A.D. may be inferred from the words of Josephus (*B.J.* vii. 5. 4), who describes the triumphant army of Vespasian and Titus as being clothed *ἐν ἐσθῆσιν σηρικαῖς, ἐστεφανωμένοι δάφναις*.

καὶ πᾶν ξύλον θύινον. The construction here changes and *ξύλον* is governed directly by *ἀγοράζει*. This change may be due not to a slip on the part of the translator, but to a right rendering of his text. The *οὐδεὶς ἀγοράζει* is to be taken closely with *πᾶν ξύλον* (= כל־עץ . . . לא יקנה איש) = "no one buyeth any thyine wood." Hence *καὶ πᾶν ξυλον θύινον* should be rendered "or any thyine wood" and not as in the A.V. and R.V. "and all thyine wood." Of course it is possible that the translator ought to have rendered *παντὸς ξύλου*, but, so far as the Hebrew before him went, the acc. was not only a possible but probably the right rendering.

θύινον. This wood most probably came from *Thuia articulata*, a tree which grew in N. Africa. It was known to the Greeks as *θύα*, *θύον*, or *θυία*, to the Romans as *citrus*. It was much used in the making of costly tables: cf. Martial, xiv. 87, "Mensa citrea." Seneca (quoted by Swete from Mayor on Juv. i. 137) had (according to Dio, lxi. 10. 3) 300 such tables with ivory feet.

ἐλεφάντινον. Ivory was largely used, as Swete states, by wealthy Romans in the decoration of furniture, quoting Juv. xi. 120 sqq.

13. κιννάμωμον. In the O.T. cinnamon appears thrice among aromatic spices. It is the *Cassia lignea* and was imported, as it still is, from China. It was much used in Rome, as we can infer from Plautus, Propertius, Lucan, Martial.

ἄμωμον. This perfumed unguent was derived from a shrub of Eastern origin (Virg. *Ecl.* iv. 25, "Assyrium vulgo nascetur amomum"). It was well known at Rome: Mart. viii. 77: "Si sapis, Assyrio semper tibi crinis amomo splendeat": Statius Silv. i. 113: "Nec pingui crinem deducere amomo cessavit" (quoted by Wetstein). Theophrastus, ix. 7, is uncertain whether it was derived from Media or India. Pliny, *H.N.* xii. 28, mentions this costly unguent for the hair.

θυμιάματα. See v. 8, **λίβανος**: cf. viii. 3.

σεμίδαλιν (= סֹלֶת). This word, meaning fine flour, is not found elsewhere in the N.T. though frequent in the LXX. Pliny, *H.N.* xiii. 21, refers to it: "Similago ex tritico fit laudatissimo."

σῖτον. Egypt was the granary of Rome.

κτήνη. This word generally means flocks and herds, but it can also mean draught cattle or beasts for riding: hence horses or asses: cf. Luke x. 34; Acts xxiii. 24. That *κτῆνος* could mean "a horse" is to be inferred also from Gen. viii. 19, where the Hebrew is רֶמֶשׂ, which clearly the Greek translators read as רֶכֶשׁ (= "horse"), and from Num. xvi. 32, where the translators again read רכשׁ instead of רְכוּשׁ (= "substance"). From these facts we conclude that *κτήνη* means all kinds of cattle for draught or riding. Hence there is no real need for the word *ἵππων* which follows, as it is already included in *κτήνη*. Horses are mentioned among the imports of Tyre in Ezek. xxvii. 13 sq.

[**καὶ ἵππων . . . σωμάτων.**] I have already given in the introductory note on 12–13 the grounds on which these words are to be excised as an interpolation. The absolutely anomalous genitive here is, so far as I am aware, universally explained by inserting *γόμον* before it. Thus Holtzmann and Bousset remark here that as in 12 the gen. passes over into the acc., so here the acc. returns again into the gen. But, as I have shown on 12, the acc. can not only be accounted for, but probably justified: whereas nothing can justify the present genitives between a series of accusatives preceding and an acc. following. They are therefore to be regarded as an interpolation.

ῥεδῶν. The *ῥέδη* came, according to Quintilian (i. 5. 5), from Gaul and was a vehicle with four wheels (Isid. *Etym.* xx. 12). Cicero used it, and apparently it became fashionable at Rome.

σώματα. This word is used to translate נְפָשׁוֹת ("souls") in the LXX of Gen. xxxvi. 6. It is also used elsewhere in the LXX in the sense of "slaves": cf. Gen. xxxiv. 29; Tob. x. 11 (*σώματα καὶ κτήνη*); Bel 32 (Theod.), *δύο σώματα καὶ δύο πρόβατα*: 2 Macc.

viii. 11. This non-Attic usage of the word arose apparently in Egypt, as the Papyri show, and later established itself in Greek generally. Hence a slave dealer is called a *σωματέμπορος* and a slave house *σωματοτροφεῖον*.

ψυχὰς ἀνθρώπων. This phrase is borrowed from Ezek. xxvii. 13, *οὗτοι ἐνεπορεύοντό σοι ἐν ψυχαῖς ἀνθρώπων* (בנפש אדם). The phrase occurs also in 1 Chron. v. 21, but there it does not mean slaves as here.

14. This verse, as Vitringa, and in modern times Ewald (2nd ed.), Volkmar, B. Weiss, and Moffatt have recognized, is here out of place. These scholars have restored it after 23[d], but the present writer is of opinion that it originally stood after 21, where he has restored it in this edition.

15. This verse resumes the dirge of the merchants over Rome, from which the writer had turned aside to describe the nature and extent of their commerce with Rome.

οἱ ἔμποροι τούτων — *i.e.* the merchants who dealt in the merchandise mentioned in 12–13: cf. 23. This phrase in itself, as B. Weiss observes, unconditionally excludes the presence of 14 where it stands in the text.

οἱ πλουτήσαντες ἀπ' αὐτῆς: cf. 3, 19.

ἀπὸ μακρόθεν στήσονται: cf. 10, *ἀπὸ μακρόθεν ἑστηκότες*: 17, *ἀπὸ μακρόθεν ἔστησαν*.

διὰ τὸν φόβον τοῦ βασανισμοῦ αὐτῆς. This phrase has already occurred in 10.

κλαίοντες κ. πενθοῦντες: cf. 9, 11, 19.

16. On this construction of οὐαί see note on 10. ἡ πόλις ἡ μεγάλη: cf. 10, 19, xvii. 18. ἡ περιβεβλημένη πορφυροῦν καὶ κόκκινον. Repeated from xvii. 4. κεχρυσωμένη χρυσίῳ . . . μαργαρίτῃ, Repeated from xvii. 4. μιᾷ ὥρᾳ ἠρημώθη. Repeated in 19. A corresponding clause in the dirge of the kings is found in 10.

17–19. Dirge of the seafolk. Cf. Ezek. xxvii. 28–29 on Tyre.

17. κυβερνήτης. This word means "shipmaster" or captain as distinct from *ναύκληρος* = "shipowner." In Acts xxvii. 11 we have *τῷ κυβερνήτῃ καὶ τῷ ναυκλήρῳ* = "the captain and the shipowner." Cf. Plutarch, *Moralia*, 807 B, *ναύτας μὲν ἐκλέγεται κυβερνήτης καὶ κυβερνήτην ναύκληρος*: Artemidorus, i. 37, *ἄρχει δὲ . . . πρωρέως ὁ κυβερνήτης, κυβερνήτου δὲ ὁ ναύκληρος*. The word *κυβερνήτης* is a rendering of חֹבֵל in Ezek. xxvii. 8, 27, 28, where it means "pilots." In Jon. i. 6 it means "a sailor," for the captain is called רַב הַחֹבֵל, or "chief of the sailors."

ὁ ἐπὶ τόπον πλέων = "Every one that saileth any whither" (R.V.). Cf. Acts xxvii. 2, *πλεῖν εἰς τοὺς κατὰ τὴν 'Ασίαν τόπους*. But the expression is a strange one, and there is much to be said for Nestle's (*Textual Criticism of the N.T.*, p. 168) correction of τοπον into πὀτον, *i.e.* πόντον. At all events Primasius supports this emendation: "omnis super mare navigans."

ὅσοι τὴν θάλασσαν ἐργάζονται, "gain their living by the sea" (R.V.), lit. "work the sea." This is good classical Greek. Thus Hesiod (*Theog.* 440) has οἳ γλαυκὴν δυσπέμφελον ἐργάζονται: Dion. Hal. *A.* iii. 46, τὴν αὐτὴν εἰργάζετο . . . θάλασσαν: Appian, *Pun.*, p. 2, τὴν θάλασσαν . . . ἐργαζόμενοι. For abundant illustrations of this idiom, see Wetstein *in loc.* What the Hebrew equivalent of the clause is is uncertain: possibly הַסֹּחֲרִים אֶת־הַיָּם = "who trade on the sea": cf. Gen. xxxiv. 10, 21, xlii. 34. The corresponding phrase ἐργάζεσθαι τὴν γῆν is also good Greek and likewise good Hebrew: cf. Gen. ii. 5, 15, iii. 23, iv. 2; but the verb used in this connection עָבַד would not serve for the clause in our text.

ἀπὸ μακρόθεν ἔστησαν. Cf. 10, 15.

18. βλέποντες τὸν καπνὸν τῆς πυρώσεως αὐτῆς. This is the exact equivalent of the ὅταν . . . αὐτῆς clause in 9.

18–19. The last clause of 18 and the first clause of 19 are dependent on Ezek. xxvii. 30–32. Thus τίς ὁμοία τῇ πόλει τῇ μεγάλῃ recalls Ezekiel's words with regard to Tyre, xxvii. 32, "who is like unto Tyre?" Here מִי כְצוֹר is rendered in the LXX by τίς ὥσπερ Τύρος; Next, ἔβαλον χοῦν ἐπὶ τὰς κεφαλὰς αὐτῶν is from xxvii. 30, "They shall cast up dust upon their heads" (יַעֲלוּ עָפָר עַל־רָאשֵׁיהֶם). Here the LXX presupposes quite a different and corrupt text (ἐπιθήσουσιν ἐπὶ τὴν κεφαλὴν αὐτῶν γῆν καὶ σποδὸν στρώσονται). The same Hebrew clause is found in Josh. vii. 6 and Lam. ii. 10. In the former passage the LXX renders it almost as in our text. Even ἔκραξαν κλαίοντες καὶ πενθοῦντες seems to be suggested by Ezek. xxvii. 30, 31, "they shall cry" (LXX κεκράξονται) . . . "they shall weep" (LXX —A only—κλαύσονται). But the combination κλαίοντες καὶ πενθοῦντες has already occurred in the text in 11, 15.

οὐαὶ ἡ πόλις. See note on 10.

ἐπλούτησαν. Cf. 3, 15.

† ἐκ τῆς τιμιότητος αὐτῆς ὅτι μιᾷ ὥρᾳ ἠρημώθη †. The text is here corrupt. This becomes apparent, if we compare the corresponding clauses in the woes pronounced by the kings in 10, ὅτι μιᾷ ὥρᾳ ἦλθεν ἡ κρίσις σου, and by the merchants in 16, ὅτι μιᾷ ὥρᾳ ἠρημώθη ὁ τοσοῦτος πλοῦτος. These parallel clauses lead us to expect a definite subject to be added after ἠρημώθη in 19 as there is after the verbs in 10, 16. Now we discover in the corrupt phrase ἐκ τῆς τιμιότητος αὐτῆς, the subject needed for ἠρημώθη, *i.e.* ἡ τιμιότης αὐτῆς. Thus the final clause of the text should run: ὅτι μιᾷ ὥρᾳ ἠρημώθη ἡ τιμιότης αὐτῆς. Thus this clause is brought into line with the corresponding clauses in 10,

16, and the woe pronounced by the seafolk falls naturally into three lines as the woe of the kings in 10.

"Woe, woe unto the great city,
Wherein were made rich all that had their ships at sea;
For in one hour are her precious things laid waste."

The corruption can be explained best through the Hebrew. The original = כי בשעה אחת נשם הוֹנָהּ. The corruption could have arisen through an accidental doubling of the ם (hence מֵהוֹנָהּ) and the subsequent transposition of מהונה before כי in order to give some intelligible sense to the passage. Hence מהונה כי בשעה אחת נשם the source of our corrupt text.

21–24. This section, embracing as it does 14 and 20, consists of a song of doom preluded by a symbolic action, the original idea of which is derived from Jer. li. 63, 64. This dirge is not put in the mouth of some particular class. The speaker is the Seer who wrote the original oracle, which has been utilized here by our author. Some attempts here have been made to adapt it to its new context. Thus the insertion of the phrase *καὶ οἱ ἀπόστολοι* in 20 is due to our author, and most probably the last clause of 23 and the whole of 24. The penultimate clause of 23 is either a gloss or should probably be restored after the first clause in 11. A line has probably been lost in 22.

21. καὶ ἦρεν εἷς ἄγγελος ἰσχυρός κτλ. Here as in v. 2, x. 1 we have the phrase *ἄγγ. ἰσχυρός*. The writer had Jer. li. 63, 64 in his mind: "And it shall be, when thou hast made an end of reading this book, that thou shalt bind a stone to it, and cast it into the midst of the Euphrates: and thou shalt say, Thus shall Babylon sink and shall not rise again." There may also be a reminiscence of Ezekiel's words with regard to Tyre, xxvi. 21. Cf. also *Or. Sib.* v. 158 sqq., on the destruction of Babylon by a great star.

λίθον ὡς μύλινον μέγαν. The particle ὡς shows that it is not a millstone that is referred to here, but that what the Seer saw in the vision recalled the idea of such a stone. The stone was probably the *μύλος ὀνικός*, seeing it is defined as *μέγας*. To turn such a stone an ass was needed.

οὕτως ὁρμήματι βληθήσεται. It is not quite clear what *ὁρμήματι* means here. It is rendered by Weizsäcker and Swete "with a rush": cf. Deut. (LXX) xxviii. 49; 1 Macc. vi. 33. This rendering is in keeping with the symbol of the boulder hurled down into the sea, but it is not in keeping with the thing symbolized—the destruction of Rome by fire by Nero and the Parthians. The rendering of the A.V. and Holtzmann, "with violence," suits the figure, but how it can be justified is not clear.

Perhaps *ὅρμημα* has here the meaning which belongs to it in the LXX in Hos. v. 10 (also in Symm.), Amos i. 11, Hab. iii. 8, *i.e.* "indignation" = עברה. This would suit the attitude alike of heaven and the Parthian hosts towards Rome. But the matter is uncertain.

ἡ μεγάλη πόλις. The order of the words as regards this particular adjective is not that of our author (see note on xvi. 1) nor of the rest of the source here used by him.

οὐ μὴ εὑρεθῇ ἔτι. Cf. Ezek. xxvi. 21 in reference to Tyre.

14. This verse forms the opening stanza of the Seer's dirge over Rome. It consists of four stanzas of four lines each. These four stanzas are followed by two stanzas of three lines each. The text has suffered owing to one or perhaps two disturbing glosses and the loss of a line in the second stanza.

ὀπώρα—ripe fruit. This word, like the Hebrew קיץ, means first late summer or autumn, and next the fruits that then ripen. Cf. Jer. xl. 10, 12. The phrase σου τῆς ἐπιθυμίας τῆς ψυχῆς is a literal rendering of אַוַּת נַפְשְׁךָ (cf. Deut. xii. 15, 20, 21, xiv. 26, Hebrew and LXX). The unemphatic or vernacular use of *σου* here should be observed. That *σου* is unemphatic is shown independently by its absence from the parallel verse. *σου* follows *ψυχῆς* in the LXX.

τὰ λιπαρά. This phrase denotes the things that belong to a rich and sumptuous mode of life. Possibly food is specially referred to here. At all events *λιπαρός* is, in the few cases where it occurs in the LXX, a rendering of שָׁמֵן, which primarily and generally means oil or fat. It is used in Ezek. xvi. 13, Prov. xxi. 17, as a sign of luxury, and refers undoubtedly to rich food. Cf. also Isa. xxx. 23.

τὰ λαμπρά. It is difficult to assign a definite meaning to this phrase. Probably it indicates the well-ordered magnificence in which the "pride of life" exhibits itself. Perhaps we might render "the splendours."

καὶ οὐκέτι . . . εὑρήσουσιν. There can hardly be a doubt as to this clause being a gloss. Without it the stanza consists of four lines, as do the three succeeding stanzas. See Introd. to this Chap., § 4. We should observe that our author uses *οὐ μή* with the aorist subjunctive.

22–23. These verses have suffered severely in the course of transmission. We have already seen that 20 (see p. 92) should be restored after 23^{b}. After a dirge of four stanzas of four lines each (= 14, 22, 23^{a-d}) the Seer in the original source calls upon heaven and the saints on earth to rejoice over the doom of Rome. But this is not all. In 22 there has been a loss of some words, while in 23 there is an addition to the text which is not only meaningless but is also against the structure of the stanza.

22. This verse consists of two stanzas of four lines each. But the second line of the first stanza and one of the words of the third line have been lost. These losses can, however, easily be restored. It is obvious, from a comparison of the remaining stanzas, that *φωνὴ κιθαρῳδῶν καὶ μουσικῶν καὶ αὐλητῶν καὶ σαλπιστῶν* is too long: in fact these words are but the relics of three lines, and the whole stanza is to be read as follows:

καὶ φωνὴ κιθαρῳδῶν καὶ μουσικῶν
<οὐ μὴ ἀκουσθῇ ἐν σοὶ ἔτι·>
καὶ <φωνὴ> αὐλητῶν καὶ σαλπιστῶν
οὐ μὴ ἀκουσθῇ ἐν σοὶ ἔτι.

The omission may have been due to a lazy scribe, who failed to see that he was transcribing verse, and thought that the sense was not affected by his compression of the text. The student of MSS is not unacquainted with such arbitrary proceedings.

φωνὴ κιθαρῳδῶν καὶ † μουσικῶν † = "the voice of the harpers and singers." The writer had Ezekiel's words against Tyre (xxvi. 13) in his mind:

"I will cause the noise of the songs to cease
And the sound of thy harps shall be no more heard."

He adopted the words "shall be no more heard," and instead of speaking of "harps" changes this word into "harpers" and "songs" into "singers," though as we shall see presently the text used by the Greek translator may have been corrupt here. Thus the first two lines would be somewhat as follows:

וְקוֹל מְנַגְּנִים וְשָׁרִים
לא יישמע בך עוד

while the next two lines would speak similarly of the fluteplayers and trumpeters.

But to return to *μουσικῶν*, it will be seen that I have rendered it "singers" on the strength of the context (*i.e.* that we must here have a specific and not a generic term) and of Ezek. xxvi. 13 (quoted above). Now in classical Greek *μουσικός* never appears to mean "a singer," nor in later Greek, unless it is a translation from the Hebrew It has been thought by some scholars that in 1 Macc. ix. 39, 41, *ὁ νύμφιος ἐξῆλθεν καὶ οἱ φίλοι αὐτοῦ . . . μετὰ τυμπάνων καὶ μουσικῶν καὶ ὅπλων πολλῶν . . . καὶ μετεστράφη . . . φωνὴ μουσικῶν αὐτῶν εἰς θρῆνον*, the word *μουσικῶν* may mean "singers"; but the fact that it stands between *τυμπάνων* and *ὅπλων* does not favour this view. Cf. Gen. xxxi. 27, *μετὰ μουσικῶν* (= שִׁירִים) *καὶ τυμπάνων*. In 1 Esdr. iv. 63 the meaning is uncertain: *ἐκωθωνίζοντο μετὰ μουσικῶν* (= "songs" or "musical instruments") *καὶ χαρᾶς*: But cf. v. 2, 59, Dan. iii. 5, 7, 10, 15, where it = "musical instruments," or "music." However, if it be conceded that the word in some of these passages means "singers," then this otherwise unattested meaning, appearing as it does in translations from the Hebrew, is in some way due to the Hebrew text. Only in one case does *μουσικός* appear as = "a singer," in a passage which none of the commentators has noticed, *i.e.* T. Jud. xxiii. 2, *τὰς θυγατέρας ὑμῶν μουσικὰς καὶ δημοσίας ποιήσετε*. Here the Greek is a translation from the Hebrew, and even here the rendering "minstrels" would accord better alike with the context and the etymology than "singers."[1] In other passages in the LXX *μουσικά* = "songs." Cf. Gen. xxxi. 27; Ezek. xxvi. 13; Sir. xxii. 6, xxxv. 3, 5, 6, xliv. 5, xlix. 1. From this examination of the word it follows that *μουσικῶν* means either "song" or "music," but never save in T. Jud. xxiii. 2 does it mean "singer" or rather "minstrel." And yet our text makes the meaning of "singers" indispensable. Hence we conclude either that *μουσικῶν* here = "singers,"—a meaning difficult to justify,—or that it is an error due to a corruption in the source. That is, *μουσικῶν* = שִׁירִים, corrupt for שָׁרִים = "singers." The rendering "minstrels" (R.V.) is here inadmissible; for we cannot have a *generic* term such as "minstrel" occurring in the midst of a list of *specific* terms.

αὐλητῶν. The fluteplayer (tibicen) was in much request on the Roman stage, and at Roman festivities as well as at funerals.

σαλπιστῶν. The trumpeter (tubicen) had his part in the Roman games, in the theatre and at funerals.

22^e-h^–23. The order of these verses seems to be wrong. We should expect that the dirge, having begun with the luxuries of life and dwelt on their being brought to an end, would proceed in due gradation to the destruction of the barest necessities of life. And this expectation is confirmed by Jer. xxv. 10, which the Seer had in his mind: "I will take from them the voice of mirth and the voice of gladness, the voice of the bridegroom and the voice of the bride, the sound of the millstones and the light of the candle." If this view is right, as the present writer believes, we should rearrange as follows:

23^cd^. And the voice of the bridegroom and the bride
Shall be heard no more in thee:

[1] Observe that in Eccles. ii. 8 שָׁרִים וְשָׁרוֹת is rendered by the LXX *ᾄδοντας καὶ ᾀδούσας*, and not by *μουσικοὺς καὶ μουσικάς*, which would mean "male and female minstrels."

22[e-h]. And no craftsman of whatsoever craft
Shall be found any more in thee.

And the voice of the millstone
Shall be heard no more in thee:
23[ab]. And the light of the lamp
Shall shine no more in thee.

Thus the rejoicings attendant on marriage would no more be known; the arts of civilized life would come to an end; the familiar sounds of the household mill to be heard in every hamlet would be no more heard, and the light of every lamp would be extinguished. It will be observed that by this rearrangement our text reproduces the order in Jer. xxv. 10.

23[cd]. φωνὴ νυμφίου καὶ νύμφης. See the quotation from Jer. xxv. 10 given above. Cf. also vii. 34, xvi. 9, xxxiii. 11.

22[e-h]. τεχνίτης κτλ. This line would embrace skilled workers in every kind of material.

φωνὴ μύλου (=קוֹל רֵחַיִם, Jer. xxv. 10). It will be observed that for *φωνὴ μύλου* the LXX reads *ὀσμὴν μύρου*, presupposing קול ריח.

23[ab]. φῶς λύχνου (=אוֹר נֵר, Jer. xxv. 10). At this stage the Seer is not thinking of the brilliant lights and torches borne by slaves as they escorted the wealthy Romans to their homes, but simply anticipating the hour when all lights—even the meanest—will be extinguished for ever.

20. Restored to its rightful place at the close of the writer's dirge over Rome, this appeal to heaven and the saints to rejoice over its destruction is most appropriate, and forms a fitting introduction to xix., which contains the heavenly response, whereas this apostrophe, standing as it does in the MSS, comes in most awkwardly between two descriptive passages as Moffatt has already recognized. The whole verse is to be ascribed to John: Moffatt assigns it to the hand of a Christian editor.

There are, it is true, some difficulties in the style. Thus from xi. 18, xviii. 24, we should expect *οἱ προφῆται . . . καὶ οἱ ἅγιοι*. But the fuller phrase here, *οἱ ἅγιοι κ. οἱ ἀπόστολοι κ. οἱ προφῆται*, may account for the difference of order. Again, *κρίμα seems* here to have the sense of lawsuit or case—a meaning not found elsewhere in our author: cf. xvii. 1, xix. 2, where it = sentence, judgment. But even here it can bear the latter meaning: "God hath judged your judgment (*i.e.* the judgment due to you) upon her." On the other hand, *εὐφραίνεσθαι* belongs to the diction of our author: cf. xii. 12, and the use of the singular *οὐρανός* is characteristically that of John. Hence 20 is from the hand of John: likewise 23[f]-24.

This call of the Seer to heaven and its inhabitants to rejoice over the accomplished doom of Rome is formed of two tristichs: 20, 23^f–24.

εὐφραίνου. Modelled apparently on Jer. li. 48 (וְרִנְּנוּ עַל בָּבֶל שָׁמַיִם), which is not found in the LXX.

οἱ ἅγιοι καὶ οἱ ἀπόστολοι καὶ οἱ προφῆται: cf. xvi. 6. These must be the blessed in heaven—martyrs, apostles, and prophets: cf. xii. 12, where those addressed are the angelic hosts.

ἔκρινεν—τὸ κρίμα ὑμῶν ἐξ αὐτῆς = "hath judged your case against her" (lit. "at her cost"). This phrase is found in Lam. iii. 59, שָׁפְטָה מִשְׁפָּטִי, "judge Thou my cause." With the idiom *ἐξ αὐτῆς* cf. Ps. cxix. 84 (LXX), but here the present Hebrew text has בְּ and not מִן. Or, as is suggested above, *κρίμα ἐξ αὐτῆς* may here be taken in the sense of judgment. *ἐξ αὐτῆς* is probably to be taken as the equivalent of מִיָּדָהּ: cf. xix. 2; 2 Kings ix. 7.

23^e. [**ὅτι οἱ ἔμποροί σου ἦσαν οἱ μεγιστᾶνες τῆς γῆς.**] This line, which is based on Isa. xxiii. 8, סֹחֲרֶיהָ שָׂרִים . . . נִכְבַּדֵּי־אָרֶץ where the LXX has *οἱ ἔμποροι αὐτῆς . . . ἄρχοντες τῆς γῆς*. But in its present context there is no place for this line, being against the parallelism. It is also meaningless. There is no ground for saying that God destroyed Rome because its merchants were the great ones of the earth. The real reason is given by the next *ὅτι* clause. It is possible that this line may be a fragmentary survival of the original ending of the source used by our author. Perhaps it should be read immediately after the first clause in 11, "and the merchants of the earth—for thy merchants were the princes of the earth—weep," etc. This would be analogous to the descriptive clause added in 9 after the phrase "the kings of the earth."

23^f–24. This stanza, consisting of three lines, gives the grounds for the destruction of Rome: her leading astray of the nations by her sorcery, and her bloodguiltiness in respect of the prophets and saints and of all the righteous, who had been slain by her throughout the world.

23^f. ὅτι ἐν τῇ φαρμακίᾳ † σου † ἐπλανήθησαν πάντα τὰ ἔθνη: cf. 3^a. The *σου* is here corrupt for *αὐτῆς*. The corruption can be explained by the dislocation of the text and the influence of the preceding occurrences of the second personal pronoun. **ἐν τῇ φαρμακίᾳ κτλ.** Cf. Nah. iii. 4, where Nineveh is called "the mistress of witchcrafts (*ἡγουμένη φαρμάκων*), that selleth nations through her whoredoms and families through her witchcrafts." Cf. also Isa. xlvii. 12, where analogous charges are brought against Babylon.

24. While there is some doubt as to the provenance of 23^f

(*i.e.* the first line of the closing stanza), there can be none as to that of the last two lines. The *προφῆται καὶ ἅγιοι* are the Christian prophets and saints, and the subject of the last line is the universal martyrdom of the Christians apprehended by our author and regarded as accomplished at the close of xiii.

προφητῶν καὶ ἁγίων. See note on xvi. 6, xviii. 20.

αἷμα προφητῶν κτλ.: cf. Ezek. xxiv. 6, *ὦ πόλις αἱμάτων*: Jer. li. (LXX, xxviii.) 35, *τὸ αἷμά μου ἐπὶ τοὺς κατοικοῦντας Χαλδαίους, ἐρεῖ Ἰερουσαλήμ.* In Matt. xxii. 35 a like charge is brought against Jerusalem: *ὅπως ἔλθῃ ἐφ' ὑμᾶς πᾶν αἷμα δίκαιον ἐκχυννόμενον ἐπὶ τῆς γῆς.* The Seer here is not thinking only of the martyrs under the Neronian persecution, nor yet of such as had already fallen under Domitian (see list of passages referring to this persecution in Lightfoot, *Ep. Clem.* i. 104–115) at the time of writing; he is rather from the standpoint of the Seer looking back on the universal martyrdom of the Christian Church as a fact already accomplished. The diction used—*πάντων τῶν ἐσφαγμένων ἐπὶ τῆς γῆς*—shows that it is of the martyrs that our author is thinking; for *σφάζω* has this connotation in our author's language: cf. v. 6, 9, 12, vi. 9, xiii. 8. xiii. 3 is no exception, for the Beast is therein caricaturing the Lamb. On the other hand, in vi. 4 *σφάζω* is used in a more special sense.

CHAPTER XIX.

§ 1. *Its Import.*

No real difficulty emerges in this chapter either as regards its authorship or its relation to the chapters that precede and follow it. There can be no question as to the Johannine authorship of xix. 1–8[a], 9[a], 11–21 from the standpoint of its style and diction (§ 2), and there can be no doubt as to the relevancy and indispensableness of its subject-matter (§ 4). Alike from its form and substance it receives unequivocal attestation.

The chapter opens with the response (1–3) that the heavenly hosts make *to the appeal of the Seer* in xviii. 20, who thunder forth as with the mighty voice of a great multitude their exultation over the destruction of the Harlot City and God's avenging of the saints which she had slain. The theme is taken up afresh by the Elders and the Living Creatures and by the angel of the altar of incense, 4, xvi. 5[b]–7. The echoes of the closing words of this anthem have hardly ceased to reverberate, when at the summons of *a voice from the throne* (5) the glorified host of martyrs burst forth with, as it were, the voice of many waters and the voice of mighty thunderings into glad thanksgivings (6–7), for that now at length the Lord God Omnipotent reigneth upon the earth and the advent of the kingdom of Christ is at hand. Thus, whereas the angels rejoice over the vindication of divine justice, the martyred host rejoice in that the kingdom of Christ is at hand with fresh stores of mercy and salvation for the sons of men (cf. xv. 4).

At this stage we should have expected a vision bearing on the destruction of the Parthian kings, mention of which was made proleptically in xvii. 14 (see § 4 *ad fin.*); but this vision may have been displaced by the interpolation 9ᵇ–10 (see § 2).[1]

Now that the Harlot City (and the Parthian kings) have been destroyed, there remains only the execution of judgment on the kings of the earth who had shared in the spiritual fornication and abominations of Rome (11–21). These are slain with the sword that proceeded out of the mouth of the Word of God, and the Beast and the False Prophet that deceived them were cast into the lake of fire.

§ 2. *The Diction and Idiom.*

There can be no doubt whatever that xix. 1–8ᵃ, 11–21 comes from the hand of our author. Alike (*a*) the diction and (*b*) the idioms are his, as is shown fully in the notes on the various verses, but it will not be unhelpful to show in the case of a few verses how intimately every verse is bound up with what precedes.

(*a*) *Diction.*—**1.** μετὰ ταῦτα ἤκουσα. Frequent in our author. ὡς φωνὴν μεγάλην: cf. i. 15, vi. 1, 6, ix. 9, etc. *μέγας* is the adjective generally connected with *φωνή*: see xvi. 1, note.

ὄχλου πολλοῦ . . . λεγόντων: cf. vii. 9. *ὄχλος πολὺς* . . . ἑστῶτες. Observe the same construction *κατὰ σύνεσιν*. *ἡ σωτηρία* καὶ ἡ δόξα καὶ ἡ δύναμις τοῦ θεοῦ ἡμῶν: cf. iv. 11, v. 12, vii. 10, xii. 10.

2. ἀληθιναὶ καὶ δίκαιαι αἱ κρίσεις αὐτοῦ: cf. xv. 3.

ὅτι ἔκρινεν τὴν πόρνην τὴν μεγάλην: cf. xvii. 1; also 5, 16. ἥτις ἔφθειρεν τὴν γῆν: cf. xi. 18. ἐν τῇ πορνείᾳ αὐτῆς: cf. xiv. 8, xvii. 2, xviii. 3. ἐξεδίκησεν τὸ αἷμα . . . ἐκ: cf. vi. 10.

3. καὶ ὁ καπνὸς αὐτῆς ἀναβαίνει κτλ.: cf. xiv. 11 (xviii. 9, 18).

4. ἔπεσαν οἱ πρέσβυτεροι οἱ εἰκ. τέσσαρες: cf. iv. 10, v. 8, xi. 16. ἔπεσαν οἱ πρεσβύτεροι . . . καὶ προσεκύνησαν: cf. xi. 16. τ. καθημένῳ ἐπὶ τ. θρόνῳ: see note on iv. 2.

XVI. 5ᵇ–7. See notes on p. 120 sqq

XIX. 5. φωνὴ ἀπὸ τοῦ θρόνου ἐξῆλθεν: cf. xvi. 17 for the more usual order. οἱ δοῦλοι αὐτοῦ . . . μεγάλοι: almost a verbal reproduction of xi. 18, though with a limitation of meaning.

[1] 8ᵇ is a gloss and 9ᵇ–10 an interpolation (see notes *in loc*), which may have displaced a vision of the destruction of the Parthian kings and their hosts by the Lamb and the glorified martyrs. See § 4, *ad finem*.

6. ὡς φωνὴν ὄχλου πολλοῦ: see note on i. ὡς φωνὴν ὑδάτων πολλῶν: cf. i. 15, xiv. 2. ὡς φωνὴν βροντῶν: cf. vi. 1. ἐβασίλευσεν κύριος ὁ θεός, ὁ παντοκράτωρ: cf. xi. 17, εὐχαριστοῦμέν σοι, κύριε, ὁ θεός, ὁ παντοκράτωρ . . . ὅτι . . . ἐβασίλευσας.

7. δώσομεν τὴν δόξαν: see note on xi. 13. ἦλθεν ὁ γάμος: cf. xi. 18 for same use of verb. ἡτοίμασεν ἑαυτήν: cf. xxi. 2, ἡτοιμασμένην ὡς νύμφην, also ix. 7, 15, xvi. 12.

8. περιβάληται βύσσινον: cf. for construction vii. 9, 13, x. 1.

9ᵇ–10. See notes *in loc.*

11. πιστὸς κ. ἀληθινός: cf. xxii. 6. πολεμεῖ: only used outside our author once in the N.T., whereas he uses it six times.

12. οἱ δὲ ὀφθαλμοὶ αὐτοῦ ὡς φλὸξ πυρός: repeated from i. 14: ἔχων . . . αὐτός—a gloss, though the diction is Johannine.

14. τὰ στρατεύματα: cf. ix. 16. ἐνδεδυμένοι βύσσινον:[1] cf. i. 13, xv. 6.

15. ἐκ τοῦ στόματος ἐκπορεύεται ῥομφαία ὀξεία: cf. 21, i. 16, ii. 12. ποιμανεῖ αὐτοὺς ἐν ῥάβδῳ σιδηρᾷ: cf. ii. 27, xii. 5. πατεῖ τ. ληνὸν τοῦ οἴνου τ. θυμοῦ κτλ.: cf. xiv. 19–20, τ. ληνὸν τ. θυμοῦ τ. θεοῦ . . . καὶ ἐπατήθη ἡ ληνός.

16. βασιλεὺς βασιλέων κτλ.: cf. xvii. 14.

17. ἔκραξεν φωνῇ μεγάλῃ: see note on xiv. 15. πετομένοις ἐν μεσουρανήματι: cf. viii. 13, xiv. 6.

18. χιλιάρχων: cf. vi. 15. ἐλευθέρων . . . μεγάλων: cf. xiii. 16.

19. τ. βασιλεῖς τ. γῆς: cf. vi. 15 (xvi. 14), xxi. 24. συνηγμένα ποιῆσαι τ. πόλεμον μετά: cf. xvi. 14, 16, xx. 8.

20. ὁ ψευδοπροφήτης: cf. xvi. 13, xx. 10. ὁ ποιήσας τὰ σημεῖα: cf. xiii. 13, 14. ἐπλάνησεν κτλ.: cf. xiii. 14, xx. 3, etc. λαβόντας τ. χάραγμα τ. θηρίου: cf. xiv. 11, xx. 4 (xvi. 2, note). προσκυνοῦντας τ. εἰκόνα: cf. xiii. 14, xiv. 9; see note on vii. 11. ἐβλήθησαν . . . εἰς τ. λίμνην τ. πυρὸς . . . θείῳ: cf. xx. 10, xxi. 8.

21. τῇ ῥομφαίᾳ . . . ἐξελθούσῃ ἐκ τ. στόματος αὐτοῦ: see on 15.

(*b*) *Idiom.*—There are no idoms against our author's usage, while those that follow are characteristic of him.

1. ὡς φωνήν: cf. *passim.* ὄχλου . . . λεγόντων: cf. vii. 9.

2. ἥτις = ἡ in 2: cf. i. 12, xii. 13, xvii. 12. ἐξεδίκησεν τὸ αἷμα . . . ἐκ: cf. vi. 10.

[1] βύσσινον is used as a noun only once in the LXX in the sing., Dan. x. 5ᶜ; in the plural in the LXX in Dan. x. 5ᵇ, xii. 6, 7; Isa. iii. 23: but in our author only in sing.; cf. xix. 8ᵃᵇ, 14, xviii. 12, 16. This use of adjectives as nouns *in the sing.* is characteristic of the writer of xviii. Thus he uses βύσσινον as a noun in 12, 16, πορφυροῦν as a noun in 16, and in xvii. 4—which is from the same source, whereas the Fourth Gospel uses it as an adj. (cf. xix. 2, 5), κόκκινον as a noun (rare except in plural) in 12, 16 and in xvii. 4, but as an adj. in xvii. 3. I do not know of any other instances of πορφυροῦν as a noun. σιρικόν in 12; here only in Biblical Greek, though used by Plutarch, Strabo, etc.

4. προσεκύνησαν τῷ θεῷ: see note on vii. 11.

τῷ καθημένῳ ἐπὶ τῷ θρόνῳ: see note on iv. 2. οἱ μικροὶ καὶ οἱ μεγάλοι: cf. xi. 18.

5. αἰνεῖτε τῷ θεῷ: a Hebraism; see note *in loc.*

6. ὡς φωνὴν ὄχλου . . . λεγόντων: see note on 1.

8. ἐδόθη αὐτῇ ἵνα: cf. ix. 5.

11. ὁ καθήμενος ἐπ' αὐτόν: see note on iv. 2.

12. ἐπὶ τ. κεφαλὴν αὐτοῦ: cf. x. 1, xiv. 14 (see Introd. to xiv. § 3).

13. περιβεβλημένος—a participle used as a finite verb: see note on iv. 7, vol. i. p. 104.

14. αὐτῷ ἐφ' ἵπποις. The dat. after ἐπί here seems due to *αὐτῷ*: cf. our author's usage where *καθημένου* is followed by gen. in 18, 19, 21, and where *καθημένῳ* is followed by dat.: iv. 9, v. 13, vii. 10, etc.

15. ποιμανεῖ: here used as equivalent to "will break": see note on ii. 27.

16. ἐπὶ τὸν μηρὸν . . . γεγραμμένον: cf. iii. 12, *γράψω ἐπ' αὐτὸν τὸ ὄνομα.*

18. καθημένων ἐπ' αὐτῶν: cf. 19, 21: see note on iv. 2.

20. προσκυνοῦντας τ. εἰκόνα: see note on vii. 11.

§ 3. *xix. 9^b–10 an Interpolation.*

See note *in loc.*

§ 4. *The Structure of the Book requires xix. 1–4, xvi. 5^b–7, xix. 5–8, 9^a, 11–21.*

xix. 1–4, xvi. 5^b–7, xix. 5–8 is the heavenly response to the Seer's appeal in xviii. 20. 9^a contains the fourth of the seven beatitudes. The contents of xix. 11–21, which have already been proleptically described in xiv. 14, 18–20, xvi. 14, 16, are here seen in their due chronological connection, as the necessary prelude to xx.–xxii. The kings of the earth, who had shared in the idolatries and abominations of Rome, here meet with just doom, while the Beast and the False Prophet are cast down into the lake of fire. Only one more event must intervene before the advent of the heavenly Jerusalem, and this—the chaining of Satan—is witnessed in xx. 1–3.

There appears, however, to be a lacuna in this chapter. Where the interpolation (9^b–10) stands we should expect a vision relating to the destruction of the Parthian kings. In xviii. we have the vision of the destruction of the Harlot City which had in an earlier chapter been spoken of proleptically as though already accomplished: cf. xiv. 8. In xix. 11–21 we have a vision of the destruction of the kings of the earth and the final doom of the Beast and the False Prophet in their due chronological sequence, save in one respect, and this is, that after the destruction of Rome and before the destruction of the kings of the earth there ought to be a vision of the destruction of the Parthian kings—a destruction that has already been referred to proleptically in xvii. 14 (see 12–13, 17, 16, 14). A short vision to this effect may have been displaced by the interpolation xix. 9^b–10.

§ 5. *The Method of our author elsewhere in this Book is observed here.*

In xix. 1–8 our author pursues the method already familiar to us in preceding chapters, in accordance with which over against a vision of the tribulation of the faithful is set one of their deliverance and triumph, or over against a vision of coming judgment on the enemies of Christ is set one of the ultimate blessedness of the redeemed.

Thus xix. 1–4, xvi. 5^b–7, xix. 5–8, which sets forth the joy of the angels on the dooms just executed on Rome and the joy of the glorified martyrs on the impending advent of the kingdom, is not only a heavenly response to the appeal of the Seer in xviii. 20, but the counterpart we expect of the dread judgments culminating in xvii.–xviii. With this notable contrast we might compare earlier analogous contrasts on this Book. Thus xv. 2–3, which comes in reality immediately after xiii. (since xiv. is entirely proleptic), brings out the glaring contrast between the universal martyrdom of the faithful in xiii. and the blessed inheritance on which they entered forthwith in heaven itself. Also in xiv. 1–5 we have a parallel to xv. 2–3 in contrast to xiii., where the visions were of such a nature as to daunt the faithfullest heart, as they foretold the destruction of all God's servants. In like manner xi. 14–18 comes in as a contrast to the tribulations depicted in xi. 1–13 and the still darker visions that follow in xii.–xiii., claiming as it does that already, however great may appear the triumph of the Antichrist, it is but a passing one, and that the issues of the strife are already made known to the hosts of heaven. Once more, after the account of the Seals is placed the vision of the great multitude in heaven, vii. 9–17.

On every ground, therefore, whether we regard the diction, the idioms, the due development of events in the Book, or the method pursued in this chapter, we conclude that it is the undoubted product of his pen.

1–8. Thanksgivings in heaven. The closing appeal in xviii. 20 to heaven to rejoice in that God had judged the great Harlot

City is answered by an exultant anthem voiced by a great multitude of angels (1–3) which is closed by the four and twenty Elders and the Cherubim with the response, "Amen, alleluia" (4–5). They had already voiced their thanksgivings in two anthems on the same subjects in xi. 15–18. Hence here they simply give utterance to their approval of the theme of the angels' song. And whereas a voice from earth summoned the heavenly hosts to the duty of thanksgiving in that the doom of the Harlot City is already accomplished in 1–5, now in 6–8 a voice from the throne summons the glorified martyrs in heaven to the glad service of thanksgiving, whereupon there arose as it were the voice of a great multitude and of many waters and of mighty thunderings proclaiming that the Lord God Omnipotent had become King, and that the advent of the heavenly Jerusalem was at hand. It is fitting that the last song in the Apocalypse should come from the lips of the martyrs.

1. The thanksgiving in this verse has been explained by some interpreters as coming from the glorified martyrs, as in xii. 10–12; but the context and our author's usage is against this interpretation. The context is against it; for the faithful, who appear to embrace only the glorified martyrs, do not offer their thanksgiving till 6–8. Further, our author's usage is against it. In such a series of thanksgivings those of the angels could not be omitted, and, if the alleluia in 1 is ascribed to the glorified martyrs, then we have such an omission, while in 6–8 there would then be a duplication of the praises of the martyrs. Furthermore (see notes on iv. 4, v. 11), if any reference to the angels' thanksgiving is made in our text, it must come in 1; for the mention of the Elders and the Living Creatures (*and in this order*) in 4 shows that the Seer is beginning his description with the outer ranks of the heavenly beings and proceeding inwards towards the throne. Thus, as in vii. 11, we have first angels, then the Elders, then the Living Creatures.

If the same order were observed as in vii. 9–11, we should have 6–8 before 1–5: in other words, the thanksgivings of men, then of angels, then of the Elders, and finally of the Living Creatures. But the order is otherwise here, and the change is instructive. Whereas in an earlier chapter, vi. 10, the cry of the faithful was for vengeance on their persecutors, here (cf. xv. 4) their sole theme of thanksgiving is that now at last "the Lord God Omnipotent reigneth," and that "the marriage of the Lamb is come." This prepares the reader for what is to follow in the speedy removal (in xix. 11–21) of all that prevents the advent of the heavenly Jerusalem. Hence 6–8 comes rightly at the close of 1–5. On the other hand, it is noteworthy that in 1–5 the theme of the angels' song is one of profound thanksgiving for

God's righteous judgment of Rome and His avenging of the blood of the martyrs. This thanksgiving follows naturally and immediately in response to the appeal in xviii. 20.

ὡς φωνὴν μεγάλην. With *ὡς φωνήν* cf. i. 15 (v. 11), vi. 1, 6, ix. 9, xiv. 2, xix. 6. *μεγάλη* is the usual adjective our author connects with *φωνή* (see xvi. 1, note). With *ὄχλου πολλοῦ*, cf. vii. 9. **λεγόντων.** A construction *κατὰ σύνεσιν* with *ὄχλου* exactly as we find it in vii. 9—*ὄχλος . . . ἑστῶτες.* **Ἁλληλουιά.** As this word is a transliteration of הַלְלוּיָהּ, the *η*, where we should have *ε*, is strange. The same irregularity is to be found in *Γεθσημανεί*, which according to Dalman (*Gram.* p. 152, note 3), Delitzsch, and others is derived from גַּת שְׁמָנֵי. This transliteration came into use before the Christian era amongst Hellenistic Jews, as Swete remarks, since it is found in 3 Macc. vii. 13; Tob. xiii. 18. In the LXX it is found frequently at the beginning and end of certain Pss.: see Swete, *Intr. to O.T. in Greek*, p. 250.

ἡ σωτηρία καὶ ἡ δόξα καὶ ἡ δύναμις τοῦ θεοῦ ἡμῶν. In xii. 10 we find *ἡ σωτηρία* and *ἡ δύναμις* conjoined, and in iv. 11, vii. 12, *ἡ δόξα* and *ἡ δύναμις* (also in v. 12, but in the reverse order): in vii. 10, *ἡ σωτηρία* alone. This construction *ἡ σωτηρία . . . τοῦ θεοῦ ἡμῶν* has already occurred in xii. 10, the more usual being that which is found in i. 6 (*αὐτῷ ἡ δόξα*), vii. 10.

2. ἀληθιναὶ καὶ δίκαιαι αἱ κρίσεις αὐτοῦ. This clause has, if we have concluded rightly, been reproduced in xvi. 7, which belongs to a dislocated passage, *i.e.* xvi. 5–7. A distant parallel occurs in xv. 3, *δίκαιαι καὶ ἀληθιναὶ αἱ ὁδοί σου.* These words define the reason for this hymn of praise—the righteousness of God's judgments as exemplified in the destruction of the Harlot City.

ὅτι ἔκρινεν τὴν πόρνην τὴν μεγάλην. This clause is a justification of the preceding *ὅτι* clause. It recalls xvii. 1, *τὸ κρίμα τῆς πόρνης τῆς μεγάλης.* On *ἔκρινεν* cf. xviii. 8, 20, and on *τῆς πόρνης τ. μεγάλης* cf. xvii. 1, 5, 15, 16.

ἥτις ἔφθειρεν τὴν γῆν: cf. xi. 18, *διαφθεῖραι τοὺς διαφθείροντας τὴν γῆν*, and the note thereon. The pronoun *ἥτις* appears here to be simply the equivalent of *ἥ*. It definitely determines who the Harlot is. For this usage of *ὅστις* see note on xi. 8. **ἐν τῇ πορνείᾳ αὐτῆς.** This is the first charge brought against Rome. It has corrupted the whole earth, cf. xiv. 8, xvii. 2, xviii. 3. The second charge is that stated in the words **ἐξεδίκησεν τὸ αἷμα τῶν δούλων κτλ.** These words recall the complaint of the martyrs in vi. 10, *οὐ . . . ἐκδικεῖς τὸ αἷμα ἡμῶν ἐκ τῶν κατοικούντων ἐπὶ τῆς γῆς*, and now recognize the consummation of divine justice: cf. xi. 18. The idiom itself is found in 2 Kings ix. 7, *ἐκδικήσεις* (ונקמתי) *τὰ αἵματα τῶν δούλων μου . . . ἐκ χειρὸς* (מיד) *Ἰεζάβελ.*

Cf. also Deut. xxxii. 43. τῶν δούλων αὐτοῦ recalls xviii. 24—the prophets and saints.

3. καὶ δεύτερον εἴρηκαν. "And a second time they say." The second utterance or antistrophe from the lips of the same multitude consists not only of the word ἀλληλουιά, but also of the words that follow καὶ ὁ καπνὸς . . . αἰώνων. These words correspond to the tetrastich that follows the first ἀλληλουιά in 1-2.

καὶ ὁ καπνὸς αὐτῆς κτλ. This clause recalls xviii. 8 (ἐν πυρὶ κατακαυθήσεται) and xviii. 9, 18 (τὸν καπνὸν τῆς πυρώσεως αὐτῆς). Cf. also xiv. 11, καὶ ὁ καπνὸς τοῦ βασανισμοῦ αὐτῶν εἰς αἰῶνας αἰώνων ἀναβαίνει. The καί is not to be taken here as a mere conjunction. We can only secure the right meaning of the clause that follows if καί is taken as a Hebraism: *i.e.* "Hallelujah; for the smoke thereof goeth up for ever and ever." This clause therefore is a circumstantial clause introduced by καί (=וְ) and gives a statement of the concomitant conditions, which justify the action denoted by the principal verb (הללו־יה). See *Oxford Hebrew Dict.* p. 253.

εἰς τοὺς αἰῶνας τῶν αἰώνων. This expression is equivalent here to 1000 years. For, since the advent of the Millennial Kingdom is already at hand, and since the earth is to be destroyed at its close, it follows that even the smoking ruins of Rome will cease to exist at that date. Contrast this meaning with that which it bears in xxii. 5, where it denotes eternity.

4. Now that the angelic hosts have sung their two paeans of triumph, the Elders and the Living Creatures too take their share in the praises of heaven with the words, Ἀμήν, Ἁλληλουιά, followed by xvi. 5^b–7, which belongs here.

In iv. 8, 11, xi. 15–18 the Cherubim and the Elders offer their praises independently; in v. 9 together, as in the verse before us; in v. 14 the Cherubim pronounce the "amen" at the close of the doxology of all creation. In the present text both orders unite together (as in v. 9) in singing the antistrophe (consisting like the strophe 1^b–2 of two stanzas of three lines each), 3^c, xvi. 5^b–7.

προσεκύνησαν τῷ θεῷ. Our author uses the dative when speaking of the highest form of worship: see note on vii. 11. τῷ καθ. ἐπὶ τῷ θρόνῳ—also a characteristic usage of our author: see note on iv. 2.

Ἀμήν, ἀλληλουιά. These words form the close of Ps. cvi. 48, אָמֵן הַלְלוּ־יָהּ, where they are rendered in the LXX by γένοιτο, γένοιτο. Cf. also Neh. v. 13.

XVI. 5^b–7. These verses, which in the MSS follow after xvi. 5^a, do not belong to xvi., but have in this edition been restored to their original context after xix. 4. Either what originally followed was lost (cf. loss in xvi. 10), or else it was deliberately removed by the Johannine editor and these verses substituted in their stead.

(1) The first ground for regarding these verses as an interpolation in their present context is that they limit the incidence of the Third Plague and probably that of the Second to the adherents of the Roman Empire. But, if the Second and Third Plagues are studied apart from these verses, the fact that their incidence is universal for sea and land cannot be questioned any more than that of the Fourth Plague, the Sixth, and the Seventh. We have already seen that the First also affects all the earth. Hence all the Bowls are universal in their incidence save the Fifth, just as all the Seals are likewise universal save the Fifth.

(2) The main point of these verses was not understood by the Johannine editor. Rightly understood they mean: God is righteous, inasmuch as He has made those who shed the blood of the prophets and saints to shed each other's blood (*αἷμα αὐτοῖς δέδωκας πεῖν*, xvi. 6^b) and stirred up the kings of the East against the great Harlot City Rome to destroy it, and eat her flesh (*τὰς σάρκας αὐτῆς φάγονται*, xvii. 16). Now this judgment of Rome is not referred to till we come to the vision in xvii. 12–13, 17, 16: hence xvi. 5^b–7 cannot rightly occur till after xvii., nor in fact till after xviii., which describes the destruction of Rome.

(3) Since xvi. 5^b–7 does not belong to xvi. and cannot justly be used till after xviii., we have two further points to determine: *i.e.* (*a*) Are these verses from our author; and, if so, (*b*) what was their original context?

(*a*) The passage is genuine. In xvi. 5 on *ὁ ὢν καὶ ὁ ἦν* cf. xi. 17 (*n.*): on *ὅσιος* as applied to God cf. xv. 4, *ὅτι μόνος ὅσιος*: on *ταῦτα ἔκρινας* cf. vi. 10, xix. 2. **6.** On *αἷμα ἁγίων κ. προφητῶν* cf. xi. 18, xviii. 24, xix. 2: on *ἄξιοί εἰσιν* cf. iii. 4 and xiv. 5 for exactly the same asyndetic construction. **7.** On *κύριε ὁ θεός, ὁ παντοκράτωρ* cf. i. 8, iv. 8, xi. 17, xv. 3, xix. 6, xxi. 22. Here we should observe that the divine title in 5 and this title in 7 are already conjoined in xi. 17: on *ἀληθιναὶ κ. δίκαιαι αἱ κρίσεις σου* cf. xix. 2 where the words recur exactly as here; also in xv. 3 (in reverse order).

Thus the passage is undoubtedly Johannine.

(*b*) All the evidence is in favour of restoring it immediately after *ἀλληλουιά* in xix. 4. Thus we have: first two stanzas of three lines each, xix. 1^b–2, followed by one of two in xix. 3, and parallel with these two other stanzas of three lines each in xix. 4^c, xvi. 5^b–6 followed by another of two in xvi. 7^{bc}. The structure is thus perfectly symmetrical.

The Song of the Angels.

XIX. 1^b. Ἀλληλουιά·
Ἡ σωτηρία καὶ ἡ δόξα καὶ ἡ δύναμις τοῦ θεοῦ
ἡμῶν,
2. Ὅτι ἀληθιναὶ καὶ δίκαιαι αἱ κρίσεις αὐτοῦ·

Ὅτι ἔκρινεν τὴν πόρνην τὴν μεγάλην,
Ἥτις ἔφθειρεν τὴν γῆν ἐν τῇ πορνείᾳ αὐτῆς,
Καὶ ἐξεδίκησεν τὸ αἷμα τῶν δούλων αὐτοῦ ἐκ χειρὸς
αὐτῆς.

3. Καὶ δεύτερον εἴρηκαν·
Ἀλληλουιά·
Καὶ ὁ καπνὸς αὐτῆς ἀναβαίνει εἰς τοὺς αἰῶνας τῶν
αἰώνων.

The Song of the Elders and the Cherubim.

4^c. Ἀμήν, ἀλληλουιά·
XVI. 5^b. Δίκαιος εἶ, ὁ ὢν καὶ ὁ ἦν,
Ὅσιος ὅτι ταῦτα ἔκρινας.

6. Ὅτι αἷμα ἁγίων καὶ προφητῶν ἐξέχεαν,
Καὶ αἷμα αὐτοῖς δέδωκας πεῖν·
Ἄξιοί εἰσιν.

7. Καὶ ἤκουσα τοῦ θυσιαστηρίου λέγοντος
Ναί, κύριε, ὁ θεὸς ὁ παντοκράτωρ,
Ἀληθιναὶ καὶ δίκαιαι αἱ κρίσεις σου.

At first sight it might appear an objection that this doxology is addressed directly to God, whereas the doxology in xix. 1^b–2 is not so directed, but God is spoken of in the third person. But this objection is groundless; for in iv. 8 the doxology speaks of God in the third person, whereas that which follows in iv. 11 is addressed directly to God. The same change of persons is found in the two thanksgivings in connection with the Lamb in v. 9–10 and v. 12. Here also the Elders and the Cherubim join together, as in v. 9, in this great anthem of praise. Again it is noteworthy that the doxologies of the twenty-four Elders are always elsewhere in our author (cf. iv. 11, v. 9, xi. 17) addressed directly to God, just as they are above in xix. 4^c, xvi. 5^b–6. Thus what at first sight appears to be an objection turns out to be evidence in favour of the above restoration.

(4) The reader will recognize at a glance the similarity of construction between the doxology in xix. 1–2 and that of the Elders and Living Creatures in xix. 4^c, xvi. 5^b–6, both of which consist of two stanzas of three lines each, and that in each case

these stanzas are followed by one of two lines. They both also deal with the same subject—thanksgiving over the fall of Rome.

XVI. 5[b]. ὁ ὢν καὶ ὁ ἦν. See note on i. 4.

ὅσιος. Cf. xv. 5. So the best authorities: "holy"—in apposition to δίκαιος. If with ℵP we read ὁ ὅσιος the phrase is to be taken as a vocative, "Thou Holy One." It represents God as faithful in His relation to men. See Trench (*Synon.*[8] p. 316) on the relation of δίκαιος and ὅσιος in Classical Greek. On this attribute of God cf. 1 Enoch i. 2, 3, x. 1, xiv. 1, xxv. 3, xxxvii. 2, cxxxiv. 1, xcii 2, xciii. 11, xcviii. 6, civ. 9.

6. αἷμα . . . ἐξέχεαν. Cf. Ps. lxxix. 3.

ἁγίων καὶ προφητῶν. We should expect the reverse order: cf. xviii. 24, xxii. 9.

αἷμα αὐτοῖς δέδωκας πεῖν. This expression has a technical sense in the O.T. and later books. Thus in Isa. xlix. 26 we have = "I will feed them that oppress thee with their own flesh, and they shall be drunken with their own blood." In that time "no man spareth his own brother" (Isa. ix. 19). This is the so-called Period of the Sword: cf. Ezek. xxxviii. 21, "I will call for a sword against him . . . every man's sword shall be against his brother"; Hag. ii. 22, "I will destroy the strength of the kingdoms . . . every-one by the sword of his brother"; Zech. xiv. 13; 1 Enoch xxxviii. 5, xcviii. 12, xcix. 4, 6: Jub. xxiii. 19; 2 Bar. xlviii. 32, lxx. 6–7; Mark xiii. 8. Thus the meaning of the clause in our text is that God would cause internecine war to arise amongst the Antichristian nations, *i.e.* between Rome and the nations of the East; for the latter, as the Seer has already testified in xvii. 12–13, 17, 16, would invade the West and destroy Rome. But the Johannine editor was wholly ignorant of the force of these words and took them in a literal and material sense: As Rome had shed the blood of the saints, so it should drink actual blood! whereas they mean that the doom pronounced by God on those who had martyred the prophets and the saints would be that they should fall by each other's hands, and thus they should eat each other's flesh (xvii. 16) and drink each other's blood (xvi. 6). We should observe that the two ideas in Isa. xlix. 26 are thus adopted by our author. πεῖν = πιεῖν: cf. Blass, *Gram.* 23.

ἄξιοί εἰσιν. Contrast the use of this phrase in iii. 4, and for the absence of the copula xiv. 5.

7. ἤκουσα τοῦ θυσιαστηρίου λέγοντος. This clause must be taken in connection with the statements made in reference to this altar, *i.e.* the altar of incense in the preceding chapters. In vi. 10 the souls of the martyrs are represented as beneath this altar, and from thence their prayers go forth to God. In viii. 3–4 the prayers of all the saints that are still upon earth are offered up upon it. In ix. 13 this altar first appears in connection with judgment, where it is conceived as initiating the second Woe by ordering the four angels of punishment to be let loose. In xiv. 18, which represents a period chronologically later, *i.e.* when the roll of the martyrs is complete, an angel goes forth from this altar and delivers to the Son of Man the divine command to undertake the judgment of the earth. In the present passage the altar confirms the doxologies just uttered (*ναί*), and declares that in the destruction of Rome the truth and righteousness of God are vindicated. Thus at last the prayers of the martyrs and of the saints are fulfilled.

XIX. 5. φωνὴ ἀπὸ τοῦ θρόνου. This voice directed to God's servants in heaven (*i.e.* the martyrs) seems to be that of one of the Cherubim or of the Elders, and not of an angel, since the two first orders were the nearest to the throne. In no case should the voice be ascribed to Christ, as in that case we should have not *τῷ θεῷ ἡμων* in the words that follow, but *τῷ θεῷ μου*, as in iii. 12.

αἰνεῖτε τῷ θεῷ ἡμῶν (=הַלְלוּ לֵאלֹהֵינוּ). *αἰνεῖν* takes the acc. elsewhere in the N.T. and all but universally in the LXX. In the half-dozen or more of cases where *αἰνεῖν* takes the dative in the LXX, we can explain it in 1 Chron. xvi. 36, xxiii. 5, 2 Chron. xx. 19 as a reproduction of the Hebrew idiom הלל ליהוה or הודה ליהוה. Still more remarkable is the careful following of the text in Ezra iii. 10, where *αἰνεῖν* takes the acc. as הלל does in the Hebrew, and in iii 11, where *αἰνεῖν τῷ κυρίῳ* is a rendering of הלל ליהוה. In 2 Chron. v. 13, *αἰνεῖν τῷ κ.* is a translation of הודה לי״; also in vii. 3. Hence it is not improbable that this Hebrew idiom was in the mind of our author when he wrote, *αἰνεῖτε τῷ θεῷ ἡμῶν.* The dative is also found in Pss Sol. v. 1, *αἰνέσω τῷ ὀνόματί σου.*

αἰνεῖτε . . . πάντες οἱ δοῦλοι αὐτοῦ, καὶ οἱ φοβούμενοι αὐτόν, οἱ μικροὶ καὶ οἱ μεγάλοι. Cf xi. 18, *τοῖς δούλοις σου καὶ τοὺς φοβουμένους τὸ ὄνομά σου, τοὺς μικροὺς καὶ τοὺς μεγάλους.* First of all, our text is influenced by Ps. cxxxv. 1, הללו־יה . . . עבדי יהוה (LXX, *αἰνεῖτε . . . δοῦλοι Κύριον*), and 20, יראי יהוה (LXX, *οἱ φοβούμενοι τὸν κύριον*). In the usage of our author the phrase *δοῦλοι* (*τοῦ θεοῦ*) represents the most notable servants of God—the Christian prophets (cf. i. 1, x. 7, xi. 18, xxii. 6) and martyrs (cf. vii. 3, xix. 2), and the servants of God generally in ii. 20, xxii. 3. The context therefore must decide its special significance in each case.

We have next to discover who these servants of God are. They can hardly be said to compose the Church universal; for (1) the presupposition of xviii. 20, *εὐφραίνου . . . οὐρανέ*, is that only those who are in heaven should take part in the thanksgivings over the fall of Rome. (2) The words, further, *φωνὴ ἀπο τοῦ θρόνου*, have the same implication. They are addressed to those in heaven. If the voice were addressed to those on earth we shall expect *φωνὴ ἐκ τοῦ οὐρανοῦ*: cf. x. 4, 8, xi 12, xiv. 2, 13, xviii. 4 In xxi. 3 God tabernacles with men = hence this phrase has not the same significance there that it has in the earlier chapters. (3) We have found that all the faithful had been removed from the earth after chap. xiii.

Thus since the divine command is issued only to the servants (*δοῦλοι*) of God in heaven, these can only be the glorified martyrs, who have already been described as "a mighty multitude which no man could number" in vii. 9. The martyrs have already been so designated in vii. 3, xix. 2. It is used elsewhere also of the Christian prophets, and also of God's servants generally (see above).

So much then appears clear. The anthems of thanksgiving in xix. 1–8 are sung only by those actually in heaven—angels and glorified martyrs. We have now to deal with the further description of the latter, which is given in the next line.

καὶ οἱ φοβούμενοι αὐτὸν, οἱ μικροὶ καὶ οἱ μεγάλοι. If we accept the *καί* (with AQ min^{omn} vg. syr.$^{1, 2}$ Prim.) we must render it as "even"; for there is no question here of two distinct classes of the faithful in heaven: there are only the martyrs. The martyrs are described here as *οἱ δοῦλοι αὐτοῦ*, as in the angels' song in 2. This being so, the phrase *καὶ οἱ φοβούμενοι αὐτόν* is not a strong one as descriptive of the martyrs. *καὶ οἱ φοβ. αὐτόν . . . μεγάλοι* appears to be derived from Ps. cxiv. 13 (cxiii. 21) originally. The phrase *οἱ φοβούμενοι τὸ ὄνομά σου* bears another meaning in xi. 18. There the whole body of the faithful are referred to; xi. 18^{d-g} refers to the events subsequent to the final judgment, and to all the orders of the faithful who then enter into the everlasting Kingdom of God. Hence *καὶ οἱ φοβούμενοι τὸ ὄνομά σου* denotes a class of the faithful quite distinct from the other classes there enumerated. But in the present context only one class is mentioned, *i.e.* that of the martyrs.

6. Response of the martyr host to the divine command.

ὡς φωνὴν ὄχλου πολλοῦ. See note on ver. 1. **ὡς φωνὴν ὑδάτων πολλῶν**: cf. i. 15, xiv. 2. **ὡς φωνὴν βροντῶν ἰσχυρῶν**: cf. vi. 1 (x. 3). **λεγόντων.** This is the best attested reading (AP and many cursives). Presumably our author took it in immediate connection with *βροντῶν*. Cf. like irregularities in iv. 1, *φωνὴ . . . λέγων*: in ix. 13, *φωνὴν . . . λέγοντα*. *λέγοντες* (Q and many cursives) is, though parallels in our author's use (cf. v. 11, xiv. 6–7) could be adduced, probably a correction.

ὅτι ἐβασίλευσεν . . . χαίρωμεν καὶ ἀγαλλιῶμεν. For the same connection of ideas cf. Ps. xcvii. 1 יהוה מלך תגל הארץ (xcvi. 1, *ὁ κύριος ἐβασίλευσεν, ἀγαλλιάσεται ἡ γῆ*). With *ἐβασίλευσεν*: cf.

xi. 15, 17. With the destruction of Rome the reign of God is established on earth. Cf. Pss. Sol. ii. 34, 36, v. 21, 22, xvii. 1, 4, 38, 51, where the like thought of the kingship of God prevails. This is the second great stage in the destruction of evil in the universe. The first was achieved when Satan was cast down from heaven (chap. xii.).

κύριος ὁ θεὸς ὁ παντοκράτωρ. A favourite designation of God in our author. Cf. i. 8, iv. 8, xi. 17, xv. 3, xvi. 7, xxi. 22. Against (A 1, 49, 95 al. me. arm.) other authorities add *ἡμῶν* after *θεός* owing to the influence of 1, 5. But this is against the usage of our author in this phrase, and the context itself is against its insertion. When ὁ *παντοκράτωρ* does not immediately follow, as in iv. 11, we have ὁ *κύριος καὶ* ὁ *θεὸς ἡμῶν*, where Dr. D'Arcy suggests there may be a reference to the blasphemous title assumed by Domitian, "Dominus et Deus noster."

7. χαίρωμεν καὶ ἀγαλλιῶμεν. For the same combination cf. Matt. v. 12, *χαίρετε καὶ ἀγαλλιᾶσθε*. *ἀγαλλιᾶν* is found in the N.T. only here and in Luke i. 47. Elsewhere in the N.T. and in the LXX the middle form is used. The classical form is *ἀγάλλομαι*.

δώσομεν τὴν δόξαν. See note on xi. 13.

ἦλθεν ὁ γάμος τοῦ ἀρνίου. *ἦλθεν* is used proleptically in xi. 18, but not to the same extent here; for Rome is already overthrown: the impenitent nations, the Beast and the False Prophet are on the eve of being cast into the lake of fire, the Millennial Kingdom on the eve of being set up, and the heavenly Jerusalem—the bride—of coming down from heaven. In fact, *ἦλθεν* refers here to the time just preceding the advent of the Millennial Kingdom, whereas in xi. 18 to the period that follows on its close. Cf. xiv. 7, 15, where it also occurs.

ὁ γάμος τοῦ ἀρνίου. As God in the O.T. is the Bridegroom of Israel (cf. Hos. ii. 16; Isa. liv. 6; Ezek. xvi. 7 sq.), in the N.T. this symbolism is transferred to Christ and the Church, which in our author is symbolized by the heavenly and the New Jerusalem: cf. xxi. 9–10, xxii. 17, xxi. 2. This figure of marriage denotes *the intimate and indissoluble communion of Christ with the community, which He has purchased with His own blood* (v. 6, 9, vii. 17, xiv. 1). *This communion is reached first in its fulness by the martyrs*, who reign with Christ for 1000 years in the Holy City, which comes down from heaven, and are yet in a mysterious way identified with the Holy City xxi. 9, xxii. 17, *i.e.* the Church, the Bride of Christ. The Gentiles converted during these 1000 years belong also to the Church. *When the New* (*καινή*) *Jerusalem descends* in xxi. 2 after the final judgment and the creation of a new heaven and a new earth, *it has become a symbol for the Church Universal.*

It is worth observing that the heavenly (or New?) Jerusalem is symbolized by a woman in 4 Ezra ix. 38 sqq., x. 25–50.

But to return to the term *γάμος*, we meet with the above symbolism in other parts of the N.T. Thus the marriage feast (*γάμοι*) is made by the king for His Son in Matt. xxii. 2 sqq.; the bride chamber is mentioned Matt. xxii. 10 (*νυμφών*), and the wedding garment (*ἔνδυμα γάμου*), xxii. 11; the sons of the bride-chamber, Mark ii. 19; the bridegroom (*νυμφίος*), Mark ii. 19, Matt. xxv. 1; and his friends (John iii. 29) and the bride (*νύμφη*) in Matt. xxv. 1 (D). In 2 Cor. xi. 2 the same symbolism occurs, *ἡρμοσάμην γὰρ ὑμᾶς ἑνὶ ἀνδρὶ παρθένον ἁγνὴν παραστῆσαι τῷ Χριστῷ*: Eph. v. 25, 32, *οἱ ἄνδρες, ἀγαπᾶτε τὰς γυναῖκας, καθὼς καὶ ὁ Χριστὸς ἠγάπησεν τὴν ἐκκλησίαν . . . τὸ μυστήριον τοῦτο μέγα ἐστίν, ἐγὼ δὲ λέγω εἰς Χριστὸν καὶ εἰς τὴν ἐκκλησίαν.*

ἡ γυνὴ αὐτοῦ. Here *ἡ γυνή* is used as equivalent to *ἡ μεμνηστευμένη* (= מְאֹרָשָׂה), as in Deut. xxii. 23; Matt. i. 20. In xxi. 9 of our text the *τὴν γυναῖκα* appears to be a gloss.

ἡτοίμασεν ἑαυτήν. A favourite word in our author (ix. 7, 15, xii. 6, xvi. 12, xxi. 2 (viii. 6)). Only the destruction of the Antichristian kings and nations, the casting of the Beast and the False Prophet into the lake of fire (xix. 11–21), and the chaining of Satan in the abyss (xx. 1–3), must intervene before the actual bridal, before the full spiritual communion of Christ and His Church is accomplished in the descent of the Holy City in xxi. 9 sqq.

8. καὶ ἐδόθη αὐτῇ ἵνα περιβάληται βύσσινον = "And it had been given unto her that she should array herself in fine linen." This privilege was already accorded to the martyr Church in vi. 11. *περιβάλλεσθαι βύσσινον, ἱμάτια, στολάς* are favourite expressions in our author: cf. iii. 18, vii. 9, 13, x. 1, xviii. 16, etc. Our author uses also the phrase *ἐνδύεσθαι βύσσινον*: cf. 14, xv. 6 (?). In the words *ἐδόθη αὐτῇ ἵνα περιβάληται κτλ.*, and in the preceding clause *ἡτοίμασεν ἑαυτήν*, we have presented God's part and man's part in the work of redemption: cf. Phil. ii. 12–13, *τὴν ἑαυτῶν σωτηρίαν κατεργάζεσθε, θεὸς γάρ ἐστιν ὁ ἐνεργῶν ἐν ὑμῖν καὶ τὸ θέλειν καὶ τὸ ἐνεργεῖν.* The words *καὶ ἐδόθη . . . καθαρόν* could be taken as part of the martyrs' song. But both the context and the parallelism are in favour of regarding them as a remark of the Seer.

βύσσινον: cf. 14, xviii. 12. Here used as a noun, as in Dan. (LXX) x. 5. On the meaning of this "fine linen" see note on iii. 5, vi. 11, vol. i. p. 184 sq.

λαμπρὸν καθαρόν: cf. xv. 6. The vesture of the saints stands out in strong contrast with that of the Harlot in xvii. 4, xviii. 16.

[**τὸ γὰρ βύσσινον τὰ δικαιώματα τῶν ἁγίων ἐστίν.**] This is regarded by some scholars as the close of the anthem: if so, it is a prosaic one. Of course it might be urged that it does not come from the heavenly choir, but is an explanation of the Seer himself, as the preceding clause itself appears to be. But this can hardly be maintained. As we have seen in the note on xiv. 13, the righteous acts (so δικαιώματα: cf. xv. 4; Rom. v. 18; 1 Bar. ii. 19) of the saints are regarded by our author as the manifestation of the inner life and as practically identical with character—the character a man takes with him when he leaves this life. Neither his righteous acts nor his character are to be regarded as the garment of the soul of the martyrs; for, though they had already this character they are described as without such garments for a time, even in heaven: see vi. 11. As a fitting clothing of the souls of the martyrs, God assigns them spiritual bodies, vi. 11 (see note), which in iii. 5 (see note) and here are described as white garments or shining pure garments. The individuals also who compose the Church or Bride at this period are the martyrs. If this view is right, then 8^b is a gloss. In a limited sense it is a correct gloss, since the spiritual bodies will be in keeping with the character or righteous acts of the saints.

Alford regards the entire verse as an explanation of the Seer. But the objections to 8^b hold nevertheless.

9^b–10. This passage, which is in part a doublet of xxii. 8–9 but rewritten and given quite a different meaning, is bracketed as an interpolation.

1. The clause οὗτοι οἱ λόγοι οἱ ἀληθινοὶ τοῦ θεοῦ εἰσίν (9) is rather inept here, seeing that the words referred to are *the triumphant songs of the angels and martyrs in heaven.* In xxii. 6, on the other hand, they are full of significance, coming in as they do at the close of the Book and giving it a solemn attestation. In xxi. 5 the authenticity of the phrase can hardly be maintained.

2. xix. 10 is in part a doublet of xxii. 8–9. This fact in itself is only of importance when combined with others.

3. xix. 10 is rewritten from xxii. 8–9 by the editor and given a less general meaning. In xxii. 8–9 the angel is a fellow-servant of the prophets and *of all Christians.* In xix. 10 he is a fellow-servant only of the prophets and those endowed with the prophetic spirit.

4. If xix. 10 were original, the action of the Seer in xxii. 8–9, in again prostrating himself before the angel, would be incomprehensible. But if xix. 10 is an interpolation, then xxii. 8–9 is intelligible and in its right context at the close of the Book.

5. προσκυνῆσαι αὐτῷ (10) is not used elsewhere in our author of simple homage or even of a θρησκεία τῶν ἀγγέλων (Col. ii. 18).

but only of divine worship (see note on vii. 11). We should, if this phrase were from our author's hand, have προσκυνῆσαι αὐτόν. In xxii. 8 no such breach of our author's usage is committed.

The above difficulties are against the direct authorship of the Seer. The most natural hypothesis as to their insertion here is that they were inserted by the disciple who edited the whole work, who, though he repeats some clauses from John's own hand, supplements them with others from his own. This hypothesis would explain the misuse of the phrase προσκυνῆσαι αὐτῷ in this context, and the addition of the final clause ἡ γὰρ μαρτυρία Ἰησοῦ ἐστὶν τὸ πνεῦμα τῆς προφητείας. For this clause gives the preceding one, τῶν ἐχόντων τὴν μαρτυρίαν Ἰησοῦ, a new meaning. In itself the latter means the whole body of believers generally, but when the last clause of 10 is added it means the limited body of Christian prophets. By this gloss the exact parallelism of xix. 9–10 with xxii. 8–9 is destroyed, for there the angel represents himself as the servant of the prophets and the whole Christian community.

9a. καὶ λέγει μοι Γράψον Μακάριοι οἱ εἰς τὸ δεῖπνον τοῦ γάμου τοῦ ἀρνίου κεκλημένοι.

This beatitude is the fourth of our author's *seven* beatitudes. But there is a difficulty in κεκλημένοι; for throughout the Millennial Reign all men alike are "called" to share in the kingdom: cf. xiv. 7, xv. 4, xxii. 17. There is no blessedness in being called (cf. Luke xiv. 24, οὐδεὶς . . . τ. κεκλημένων γεύσεταί μου τοῦ δείπνου), unless a man accepts the call and is found faithful—is "chosen" ἐκλεκτός and found faithful πιστός (cf. xvii. 14). The words of our Lord can hardly have been unknown to our Seer; πολλοὶ γάρ εἰσιν κλητοί, ὀλίγοι δὲ ἐκλεκτοί (Matt. xx. 16, xxii. 14). But κεκλημένοι has not this technical meaning here, but simply that of "invited." Here, as in Matt. xxii. 2 sq., the guests and the Bride are one and the same. But, though the guests or the faithful might (as Israel in the O.T. in relation to Yahweh) be rightly designated the Bride, as, for example, in xxi. 9 (cf. Eph. v. 27), at the beginning of the Millennial Kingdom, since the words Bridegroom and Bride symbolize the close relation between Christ and the Church at all times, yet the realization of the things so symbolized is always partial and imperfect till the number of the saints is complete. Hence not till then has the time come for the Wedding Feast and for the Bride to become the Wife of the Lamb. It is to this feast, therefore, that the faithful are "invited"; and all such as are then invited naturally accept, for they are all saints. So the writer of 4 Ezra ii. 38–41 rightly connects the Marriage Supper and the completion of the roll of the saints: "Videte numerum signatorum in convivio Domini.

Qui se de umbra saeculi transtulerunt, splendidas tunicas a Domino acceperunt. Recipe, Sion, numerum tuum . . . Filiorum tuorum . . . plenus est numerus . . . populus tuus, qui vocatus est ab initio." As Dalman (*Words of Jesus*, 118 sq.) points out, *κεκλημένοι* = מְזֻמָּנִים: cf. Babba Bathra, 75^b: "those who are *invited* go up to the Jerusalem of the age to come"; Midr. Tehill. 14[7], where Jacob is "invited to the heavenly banquet" (מְזֻמָּן לִסְעוּדָה). With the beatitude in our text cf. *μακάριος ὅστις φάγεται ἄρτον ἐν τῇ βασιλείᾳ τοῦ θεοῦ* (Luke xiv. 15).

κεκλημένοι. *καλεῖν* always means "to name" in our author except here and in xvii. 14, where the meaning our author attaches to *κλητοί* is seen from its context: *κλητοὶ καὶ ἐκλεκτοὶ καὶ πιστοί*. Here these three epithets refer to the same persons.

οὗτοι οἱ λόγοι οἱ ἀληθινοὶ τοῦ θεοῦ εἰσίν. See 1 in the note on 9^b–10.

10. ἔπεσα ἔμπροσθεν τῶν ποδῶν αὐτοῦ: cf. xxii. 8. *πίπτειν* followed immediately by such phrases as *πρὸς τ. πόδας*, i. 17, *ἐνώπιον*, iv. 10, v. 8, vii. 11, *ἐπὶ τὰ πρόσωπα*, xi. 16, is used of the divine worship of God or the Lamb. Hence in *ἔπεσα ἔμπροσθεν τ. ποδῶν αὐτοῦ* the same worship seems implied. It is strange that the phrase *προσκυνεῖν ἔμπροσθεν* is used simply of homage. See note on xxii. 8.

προσκυνῆσαι αὐτῷ. On this usage (contrary to that of our author) see 5 in the note on 9^b–10 and vii. 11 note.

ὅρα μή . . . ἀδελφῶν σου. See xxii. 9, where these words occur in their right context.

τῶν ἐχόντων τὴν μαρτυρίαν Ἰησοῦ. This phrase is found already in xii. 17. It is certainly in the phraseology of our author. Cf. vi. 9, *τὴν μαρτυρίαν ἣν εἶχον*, and i. 2, 9, xx. 4, where we have the phrase *ἡ μαρτυρία Ἰησοῦ*. In *τὴν μαρτυρίαν Ἰησοῦ* the question arises whether we have in *Ἰησοῦ* the subjective or objective genitive, *i.e.* the testimony borne by Jesus, or the testimony which men bear to Jesus. The former, according to i. 2, xii. 17, means the sum of the revelation made by him, and should naturally be the meaning of the phrase here. But the words that follow, *ἡ γὰρ μαρτυρία Ἰησοῦ κτλ.*, require us to make them mean "the witness to Jesus." Hence it follows that the *γάρ* is here to be taken in an explanatory sense: "now the witness to Jesus is the spirit of prophecy." Thus the angel declares that he is the fellow-servant of John, and of those who share with him the prophetic spirit. This is not the meaning of the parallel passage in xxii. 10.

There is, however, the possibility that *ἡ γὰρ μαρτυρία . . . προφητείας* may have been a marginal gloss on *τὴν μαρτυρίαν Ἰησοῦ*, which was subsequently incorporated in the text. It certainly comes in very awkwardly after *τῷ θεῷ προσκύνησον*.

It should have preceded it. If this clause was a gloss, then the words σύνδουλός σού εἰμι καὶ τῶν ἀδελφῶν . . . Ἰησοῦ and xxii. 9[ab] would be practically equivalent in meaning. Even so, many of the objections to the originality of xix. 9[b]–10 still remain.

11–21. Cf. xiv. 14, 18–20, and xvi. 13–16 for proleptic accounts of this destruction of the kings and the nations by Christ and His angels. See note on 14. 11–21 deals with the victory of Christ and His angels over the Beast, the False Prophet, and the kings of the earth. With this victory of the Messiah cf. 1 Enoch lxii. 2; 2 Bar. xxxix.–xl., lxxii.; 4 Ezra xii. 32, xiii. 38. This destruction of the remaining active foes of the Messianic Kingdom comes in here of necessity after that judgment has been executed on Rome and before the inauguration of the Millennial reign. This corresponds to the judgment of the Sword at the beginning of the Messianic Kingdom in 1 Enoch l. 2, xc. 19, xci. 12, xcv. 7, xcvi. 1, xcviii. 12. Though the destruction of the Parthian kings is foretold proleptically in xvii. 14, it is nowhere subsequently described.

11. εἶδον τὸν οὐρανὸν ἠνεῳγμένον: cf. Ezek. i. 1, *καὶ ἀνεῴχθησαν οἱ οὐρανοί*: 2 Bar. xxii. 1; 3 Macc. vi. 18; Matt. iii. 16; John i. 51, *ὄψεσθε τὸν οὐρανὸν ἀνεῳγότα*.

As we learn from what follows, it is only the nations that are *hostile* to Christ that are to be destroyed. For the attitude of Judaism to the Gentiles in the O.T. and Apocryphal and Apocalyptic literature, see my *Eschatology*², 165, 246, 296, 297, 332, 361, also Sibyll. Or. iii. 740; Tob. xiii. 11, xiv. 6 sq.; Test. XII. Patr. (see Index, p. 242, in my edition), and Volz, *Judische Eschatologie*, 322–325.

ἵππος λευκὸς καὶ ὁ καθήμενος ἐπ' αὐτόν: repeated from vi. 2, but the two riders are quite distinct. Here there is no question as to the personality of the present Rider. He is the Messiah—"the Word of God." The very epithets that are applied to Him have occurred before in the same connection: cf. iii. 14, *ὁ μαρτὺς ὁ πιστὸς καὶ ἀληθινός*. See also i. 5, iii. 7. This same combination of epithets is used by Christ (the Logos) in xxii. 6, *οὗτοι οἱ λόγοι πιστοὶ καὶ ἀληθινοί*. For this combination of epithets cf. also 3 Macc. ii. 11. The Messiah as a man of war appears in Pss. Sol. xvii. 23–27; Philo, *De Praem. et Poena*, 16, *στρατραρχῶν καὶ πολεμῶν ἔθνη . . . χειρώσεται*.

ἐν δικαιοσύνῃ κρίνει καὶ πολεμεῖ. This description of the righteousness of the Messiah is brought forward very distinctively in Isa. xi. 3 sq.: "He shall not judge after the sight of his eyes . . . 4. but with righteousness shall he judge (ושפט בצדק) the poor, and reprove with equity the meek of the earth. 5. And righteousness shall be the girdle of his loins and faithfulness the girdle of his reins." In 1 Enoch he is designated as "the Righteous One" (xxxviii. 2), "the Righteous and Elect One" (liii. 6), "the Elect One of righteousness and faith" (xxxix. 6). Cf. also Pss. Sol. xvii. 31, *κρινεῖ . . . ἔθνη ἐν σοφίᾳ δικαιοσύνης αὐτοῦ*: also in 35 he is described as a *βασιλεὺς δίκαιος καὶ διδακτὸς ὑπὸ θεοῦ*: cf. also 36, 41: Ps. xcvi. 13; Acts xvii. 31.

12. οἱ δὲ ὀφθαλμοὶ αὐτοῦ ὡς φλὸξ πυρός. Repeated from i. 14: cf. ii. 18.

ἐπὶ τ. κεφαλὴν αὐτοῦ διαδήματα πολλά. Here as always, except in xii. 1, our author uses *ἐπὶ τ. κεφαλήν* and not *ἐπὶ τ. κεφαλῆς*. See note on Introd. to xii., vol. i. p. 300 sq. As King of kings (16) the Messiah wears many diadems. The Dragon (xii. 3) and the Beast (xiii. 1) wear respectively seven and ten. According to 1 Macc. xi. 13, Ptolemy wore two diadems on entering Antioch—one for Egypt and one for Asia.

12ᶜ. [ἔχων ὄνομα γεγραμμένον ὃ οὐδεὶς οἶδεν εἰ μὴ αὐτός.] Though the diction is Johannine (on *ἔχων . . . γέγραμμένον* cf. 16, and with *ὃ οὐδεὶς οἶδεν* cf. ii. 17) this clause appears to be interpolated. The objections are three. First, there is a break in the thought. We should not expect a reference to the name here in the midst of a description of the person and dress. Moreover, the statement that no one knows His name save Himself is flatly contradicted in the next verse (13^b), where the words *καὶ κέκληται τὸ ὄνομα αὐτοῦ Ὁ Λόγος τοῦ θεοῦ* cannot be explained away (see note *in loc.*). Finally, by the omission of this clause the parallelism is restored.

12. οἱ δὲ ὀφθαλμοὶ αὐτοῦ ὡς φλὸξ πυρός,
καὶ ἐπὶ τὴν κεφαλὴν αὐτοῦ διαδήματα πολλά,
13. καὶ περιβεβλημένος ἱμάτιον βεβαμμένον αἵματι,
καὶ κέκληται τὸ ὄνομα αὐτοῦ Ὁ Λόγος τοῦ θεοῦ.

The interpolated line may have originated in a marginal gloss. We have now to inquire what meaning can be attached to this gloss. Some interpreters have thought the unknown designation to be *ὁ κύριος*, Phil. ii. 11; others (as Ewald and Volkmar) have taken it to be the tetragrammaton; others a really mysterious name known only to Christ Himself, comparing ii. 17, *ὄνομα καινὸν γεγραμμένον ὃ οὐδεὶς οἶδεν εἰ μὴ ὁ λαμβάνων*, and iii. 12. As regards this last interpretation scholars are again divided. Swete is of opinion that all created beings are excluded from the knowledge of this name. Alford thinks that the knowledge of this name is withheld till the final and complete union of Christ and His Church. In favour of this view we might compare Asc. Isa. ix. 5: "This is . . . the Lord Christ, who will be called Jesus in the world, but His name thou canst not hear till thou hast ascended out of thy body." Others, as Bousset, that this knowledge is withheld because of the power that attaches to such knowledge. The Messiah alone has a name which carries with it power over heaven and earth, and as no one knows this name but Him, so He is the sole possessor of the power bound up with the name. This last interpretation belongs undoubtedly to the reign of magic, and is found among the Gnostics. This idea underlies Gen. xxxii. 29 and Judg. xiii. 17 sq. It was a very widespread idea among many ancient nations that the man who knew the name of a god or a demon possessed certain powers over him. Hence the name was concealed: cf. Heitmüller, *Im Namen Jesu*, 162 sqq.; Giesebrecht, *Gottesname*, 23, 45, 100 (the last reference is from Gunkel's *Genesis*[3], p. 362: Jevons, *Introd. Hist. Religion*, p. 361).

ὃ οὐδεὶς κτλ.: cf. ii. 17, iii. 12.

13. καὶ περιβεβλημένος ἱμάτιον βεβαμμένον αἵματι. This clause has created no little difficulty. But, if we hold fast to the following facts, the difficulty can be surmounted. The first is that in the leader of the heavenly hosts we have to do—not with the Slain One, but the Slayer. The Word of God has come to execute divine judgment. Hence the idea that the blood on His Vesture is His own (cf. i. 5, v. 9, vii. 14, xii. 11) cannot be entertained. When our author wishes to express a thought of this nature, he speaks of the *ἀρνίον . . . ὡς ἐσφαγμένον* (v. 6). Now this being so, how are we to explain the *ἱμάτιον βεβαμμένον αἵματι*? In whose blood is the vesture of the Divine Warrior dipped? If it is not His Own, no more is it that of the kings of the earth and their armies (15, 18); for the judgment of the sword as regards these has not yet begun, and the garments of the heavenly armies are still white and pure (14). A comparison with Isa. lxiii. 1–3—which passage is in the mind of our author—confirms this conclusion: "Who is this that cometh from Edom, with red garments from Bozrah? . . . 2. Wherefore art thou red in thine apparel, and thy garments like him that treadeth in the winefat? 3. I have trodden the winepress alone . . . yea, I trod them in my anger . . . and their lifeblood is sprinkled upon my garments." Here the redness of the garments is due to the blood of those who have already been slain, exactly as in our text. Since, therefore, the redness of the vesture in 13 is not due to the warfare in 11–21, there remains only one other possible explanation, and this is that *the blood on His vesture is that of the Parthian kings and their armies*, whom He had already destroyed, and whose destruction had already been proleptically prophesied in xvii. 14. In this strife He was supported by the glorified martyrs (*οἱ μετ' αὐτοῦ κλητοὶ καὶ ἐκλεκτοί κτλ.*).

ἱμάτιον βεβαμμένον αἵματι. These words are freely based on Isa. lxiii. 3, ויז נצחם על־בגדי (= "and their blood is sprinkled on my garments"). Here *βεβαμμένον* (AQ, etc.) is to be accepted and not *ῥεραντισμένον*, *ἐρραμμένον*, or the other variants from *ῥαίνω* and *ῥαντίζω*; for, whereas both these latter verbs are used in the LXX to render נזה (the Hebrew verb in Isa. lxiii. 3), and whereas Aquila and Symmachus do render it by *ῥαντίζω* in Isa. lxiii. 3, but no translator ever renders it by *βάπτω*, it follows that, though there were possible grounds for changing *βεβαμμένον* into *ἐρραμμένον*, there were none for changing *ἐρραμμένον* into *βεβαμμένον* from the standpoint of Isa. lxiii. 3, whence the idea was derived. Our author thus deals freely with Isa. lxiii. 3. That such a free reproduction was not unknown in Judaism we might infer from the late Palestinian Targum on Gen. xlix. 11, which recounts the victory of the Messiah over His enemies: "How beauteous is the king Messiah, who is about to arise from the house of Judah. He hath bound his loins and gone forth to war against those that hate him: kings and princes shall be slain: he will make red the rivers with the blood of their slain . . . his garments will be dipped in blood (לבושׁי מעגנין באדמה)."

καὶ κέκληται τὸ ὄνομα αὐτοῦ Ὁ Λόγος τοῦ θεοῦ. This line has been taken by Völter, Spitta, Hilgenfeld, Bousset, and others to be the addition of a scribe or reviser. Now it is manifest that either 12[c] (*ἔχων ὄνομα . . . ὃ οὐδεὶς οἶδεν κτλ.*) or the present clause must be of this nature. But, whereas we found that 12[c] was open to serious objections on various contextual grounds, no objection of such a nature can be brought against the present clause, which accordingly comes from the hand of our author. We have here another of the numerous instances of community of diction between the Apocalypse and the Fourth Gospel, in many of which there is no community of meaning. For the Logos here is a Warrior, and our text reminds us of Wisd. xviii. 4–25, especially of xviii. 15, *ὁ παντοδύναμός σου λόγος ἀπ' οὐρανῶν ἐκ θρόνων βασιλείων ἀπότομος πολεμιστὴς εἰς μέσον τῆς ὀλεθρίας ἥλατο γῆς ξίφος ὀξὺ τὴν ἀνυπόκριτον ἐπιταγήν σου φέρων.* We might compare also the later Jewish conception, מֵאמַר and *ὁ λόγος τοῦ θεοῦ* in Heb. iv. 12. Although the ideas underlying the words are different, in the latter passage this word is said to be "sharper than any two-edged sword."

14. καὶ τὰ στρατεύματα κτλ. To 14[a] conjoined with 16[b] we have remarkable parallels in xvii. 14, but there the enemies of the Lamb are the Parthian kings, who are also referred to in xvi. 12. Here we have a conflict on a larger scale, as in xiv. 14, 18–20, xvi. 13–16. See notes on xiv. 14, 18–20, xvi. 12–16, xvii. 14.

A study of the chief passages (ii. 26–27, xiv. 14, 18–20, xvi. 12–16, xvii. 14, xviii., xix. 11–21) dealing with the destruction of the world powers helps us to understand the expectations of the Seer as to (*a*) the order in which the world powers were to be destroyed before the Millennium, and (*b*) the nature of the heavenly armies which destroyed these powers.

(*a*) *The destruction of Rome was to come first, next that of the Parthians, and finally that of the remaining hostile powers.*—In xiv. 8–11 the destruction of Rome is foretold, followed immediately (for xiv. 12–13 belongs after xiii. 15 or 18) by that of the hostile nations, xiv. 14, 18–20. The same sequence of events is found in xviii. (the destruction of Rome) and xix. 11–21 (that of the hostile nations). But the sequence of events can be determined more definitely. Thus in xvi. 12 the forces led by the Parthian kings are clearly distinguished from those of the remaining hostile nations in xvi. 13–16; and that these two divisions of the hostile heathen world, which survived the destruction of Rome, were to be separately destroyed, we infer from xvii. 14, according to which, immediately after the destruction of Rome, Christ and His armies would destroy its destroyers, *i.e.* the Parthians.

(*b*) *The heavenly armies were to be composed of angels and* (*in certain cases if not in all*) *of the glorified martyrs.*—The armies of the Word of God are described in xix. 14 (τὰ στρατεύματα τὰ ἐν τῷ οὐρανῷ . . . ἐφ' ἵπποις λευκοῖς). In xiv. 14, 18–20 the presence of these heavenly horsemen is presupposed in xiv. 20 (ἄχρι τῶν χαλινῶν τ. ἵππων). So far as these passages go, we should conclude that the heavenly armies were composed of angels only. But this is not so. Quite clearly in xvii. 14 it is stated that the armies of the Lamb will be "the called and elect and faithful," a description which cannot be applied to angels. Now since this war of the Lamb on the Parthians is subsequent to the destruction of Rome, and therefore to the universal martyrdom of the faithful, it follows that this army is composed of the glorified martyrs, who had come down from heaven with Christ for that purpose. That they should share in this task we have already learnt from ii. 27, where of the individual martyr (ὁ νικῶν) it is stated ποιμανεῖ αὐτοὺς ἐν ῥάβδῳ σιδηρᾷ, the very words, which in xix. 15 are used of Christ Himself. That the martyrs take part in the judgment of all the hostile nations cannot be affirmed in so many words, though the comparison of ποιμανεῖ κτλ. in both ii. 27 and xix. 15 points probably to this conclusion. Moreover, the comparison of xvii. 14 (where Christ is called κύριος κυρίων καὶ βασιλεὺς βασιλέων, and His army is composed of glorified martyrs) and of xix. 14[a], where His followers are the armies of heaven and His name is βασιλεὺς βασιλέων κ. κύριος κυρίων (16[b]), may point in the same direction.

Some of the chief expectations of our Seer relative to the judgment of the hostile nations may be briefly summarized as follows.

The Parthian kings are referred to in xvi. 12, xvii. 12–13, 17, 16, and their destruction by the Lamb and the glorified martyrs in xvii. 14^{a-c}. The other hostile kings of the world are mentioned: their gathering to Armageddon in xvi. 13–16, and their destruction by One like a son of man, xiv. 14, 18–20, by the Word of God with the armies of heaven in xix. 11–21. In these last two passages the Divine Leader is said to tread the winepress of the wrath of God (xiv. 19, xix. 15). Finally, at the close of the Millennial Kingdom there is the destruction of the unrepentant nations by fire sent down from heaven, xx. 7–10.

For the idea of armies in heaven cf. Test. Levi iii. 3; 2 Enoch xvii.; 2 Esdr. xix. 6, *σοὶ προσκυνοῦσιν αἱ στρατεῖαι τῶν οὐρανῶν* (where the armies are the stars); Matt. xxvi. 53.

The heavenly armies, which are not definitely mentioned in the parallel account (xiv. 14, 18–20) but are implied in the words *ἄχρι τῶν χαλινῶν τῶν ἵππων*, have descended with Christ from heaven. In ii. 27 (see note), xvii. 14 (see notes) they appear to be the faithful: in ii. 27 the foes they destroy are the hostile nations generally: in xvii. 14 the Parthian kings.

ἐνδεδυμένοι βύσσινον λευκόν. For the phrase cf. i. 13, xv. 6.

15. In 15^{abc} are combined thoughts and words which are drawn from Isa. xi. 4 and Ps. ii. 9. But this combination is already found in Pss. Sol.

xvii. 26. *ἐκτρίψαι ὑπερηφανίαν ἁμαρτωλῶν ὡς σκεύη κεραμέως, ἐν ῥάβδῳ σιδηρᾷ συντρίψαι πᾶσαν ὑπόστασιν αὐτῶν·*

27. *ὀλοθρεῦσαι ἔθνη παράνομα ἐν λόγῳ στόματος αὐτοῦ.*

39. *πατάξει γὰρ γῆν τῷ λόγῳ τοῦ στόματος αὐτοῦ.*

καὶ ἐκ τοῦ στόματος αὐτοῦ ἐκπορεύεται ῥομφαία ὀξεία: cf. i. 16, ii. 12.

ἵνα ἐν αὐτῇ πατάξῃ τὰ ἔθνη. From Isa. xi. 4, *καὶ πατάξει γῆν τῷ λόγῳ τοῦ στόματος αὐτοῦ, καὶ ἐν πνεύματι διὰ χειλέων ἀνελεῖ ἀσεβῆ*, cf. Pss. Sol. xvii. 26–27, 39 (quoted above). Wisd. xviii. 22, *ἐνίκησε τὸν ὄχλον οὐκ ἰσχύι τοῦ σώματος οὐχ ὅπλων ἐνεργείᾳ ἀλλὰ λόγῳ τὸν κολάζοντα ὑπέταξεν*: 1 Enoch lxii. 2, "The word of his mouth slays all the sinners." All these passages imply that the sword that proceeds out of the mouth of the Messiah is simply a figure for forensic or judicial condemnation.

καὶ αὐτὸς ποιμανεῖ αὐτοὺς ἐν ῥάβδῳ σιδηρᾷ: cf. ii. 27 (see note), xii. 5. From Ps. ii. 9. The *αὐτός* in this and the next clause is emphatic. Neither here nor in ii. 27, xii. 5 has *ποιμαίνειν* a favourable meaning.

In these three passages it connotes punishment and destruction. Contrast, on the other hand, its meaning in vii. 17. See note on ii. 27. Hence render "break them with an iron rod."

καὶ αὐτὸς πατεῖ τὴν ληνὸν κτλ. Here, though accompanied by hosts of angelic warriors, the action of the Messiah alone is dwelt upon, just as in xiv. 19 sq. and in similar words. Only here and in xiv. 19–20 is the *ληνός* of divine judgment spoken of in our author. The two ideas of the winepress (xiv. 19) and the cup of wrath (xiv. 10) are here combined, and mean that from the winepress trodden by Christ flows the wine of the wrath of God, of which his enemies are to be made to drink. It is a case of mixed metaphors.

16. [ἐπὶ τὸ ἱμάτιον καὶ] ἐπὶ τὸν μηρὸν αὐτοῦ κτλ. Of this text there is no satisfactory explanation. Düsterdieck, B. Weiss, and Holtzmann think that the title is inscribed on the girdle; Swete, that "it is displayed on His habit where it falls over the thigh"; Grotius imagines a sword on the hilt of which the name was inscribed. Wellhausen, recognizing the unintelligibleness of the text, proposes ἵππον instead of ἱμάτιον and makes the αὐτοῦ refer to the ἵππον. Horses were branded on the thigh amongst the Greeks: see Wetstein *in loc.* But the idea of such an inscription on a horse cannot be entertained. If, therefore, we are to gain any satisfactory meaning here, we can only do so by following our chief Uncial A, Cassiodorus, and some Ethiop. MSS, which omit the words I have bracketed above. If A is right, the chief Syriac Version (s^1) would probably be the first stage in the interpolation of the text; for s^1 here places the two phrases ἐπὶ τὸ ἱμάτων αὐτοῦ and ἐπὶ τ. μηρὸν αὐτοῦ side by side without the connecting καί. Thus the first phrase would appear to have originated in a marginal gloss owing to 13^a (περιβεβλημένος ἱμάτιον κτλ.). The final stage in the corruption of the text is that which all the remaining authorities attest. At this stage the first αὐτοῦ is omitted and the καί inserted.

Our text now runs ἐπὶ τ. μηρὸν αὐτοῦ. For the occasional appearance of names and inscriptions on the thighs of statues we have evidence in Greek and Roman authors (see Wetstein from whom these quotations are derived). Thus in Cicero, *Verr.* iv. 43, we find: "Signum Apollinis pulcherrimum, cujus in femore literulis minutis argenteis nomen Myronis erat inscriptum." Also in Pausanias, *Eliac. extr.*, τὸ ἀνάθημα . . . ἀνδρὸς εἰκὼν . . . ἐλεγεῖον δὲ ἐπ' αὐτὸ γεγραμμένον ἐπὶ τοῦ μηροῦ: "Justinus (4 cent. A.D.?), xv. 4, 5: Figura anchorae, quae in femore Seleuci nata cum ipso parvulo fuit. 9. Originis ejus argumentum etiam in posteris mansit, siquidem filii nepotesque ejus anchoram in femore veluti notam generis naturalem habuere."

The Seer sees in the vision the Divine Warrior and His heavenly horsemen—not halting but *sweeping downward from heaven and onward* against the serried armies of the Beast, False Prophet, and the kings of the earth, and, as they thunder along, their garments stream behind them, and so on the thigh of the Leader is disclosed the name: "King of kings and Lord of lords."

βασιλεὺς βασιλέων κτλ. See note on xvii. 14.

17–21. An angelic summons to all the birds of prey to

hasten to the scene of slaughter of all the mighty of the earth. The overthrow and final doom of the Beast and the False Prophet.

17. ἕνα (cf. viii. 13) ἄγγελον ἑστῶτα ἐν τῷ ἡλίῳ. What was the original idea underlying this phrase is unknown. It is generally explained that the angel took this central position in mid heaven in order to deliver from thence his message of victory and his summons to the birds of prey.

καὶ ἔκραξεν φωνῇ μεγάλῃ. See note on xiv. 15.

λέγων πᾶσι τοῖς ὀρνέοις τοῖς πετομένοις ἐν μεσουρανήματι (cf. viii. 13, xiv. 6) Δεῦτε συνάχθητε εἰς τὸ δεῖπνον . . . τοῦ θεοῦ. 18. ἵνα φάγητε σάρκας βασιλέων . . . καὶ σάρκας ἰσχυρῶν. This passage is clearly based on Ezek. xxxix. 17, where the LXX reads *εἰπὸν παντὶ ὀρνέῳ πετεινῷ . . . Συνάχθητε καὶ ἔρχεσθε . . . ἐπὶ τὴν θυσίαν μου . . . καὶ φάγεσθε.* 18. *κρέα γιγάντων . . . καὶ αἷμα ἀρχόντων.* 20. *καὶ . . . ἵππον καὶ ἀναβάτην.* It is obvious, however, that our author is giving an independent rendering of the Hebrew: observe *δεῦτε συνάχθητε* (בֹּאוּ הֵאָסְפוּ) with *συνάχθητε καὶ ἔρχεσθε*, and *ἰσχυρῶν* in our text with *γιγάντων*, and *ἵππων κ. τῶν καθημένων ἐπ' αὐτῶν* with *ἵππον καὶ ἀναβάτην* in Ezek. xxxix. 20.

Our author here borrows his imagery from the slaughter wrought by God in Ezek. xxxix., and yet the final overthrow of Gog and Magog in our author is adjourned to the close of the Millennial reign in our author.

τὸ δεῖπνον τὸ μέγα τοῦ θεοῦ. See Gressmann, *Ursprung der Israelit. Jüd. Eschatologie*, 136–141.

18. τῶν καθημένων ἐπ' αὐτῶν. Here the reading *αὐτῶν* (PQ min[fere omn]) is to be followed. A with two cursives and ℵ read respectively *αὐτούς* and *αὐτοῖς*—which are both corrupt. Cf. 19, 21. ἐλευθέρων τε καὶ δούλων. See note on xiii. 16. μικρῶν καὶ μεγάλων. See note on xiii. 16.

19–21. The Beast, the False Prophet, and the kings of the earth overthrown and cast into the lake of fire.

19. τὸ θηρίον—*i.e.* Nero-antichrist. See xi. 7 (note), xiii. 3 (note on various stages of the Neronic myth).

τοὺς βασιλεῖς τῆς γῆς: cf. xiv. 14, 18–20 (though not here specifically mentioned), xvi. 14 (note), xvii. 2, 18, xviii. 3. These are to be carefully distinguished from the Parthian kings, xvi. 12, xvii. 12–13, 17, 16, who are destroyed by the Lamb (and the glorified martyrs). See also note on 14 above.

τὰ στρατεύματα αὐτῶν. For *αὐτῶν* A and a few cursives read *αὐτοῦ*. This is perhaps right. Though they are the subjects of the kings, they are the armies of the Beast.

συνηγμένα ποιῆσαι τὸν πόλεμον. For the diction cf. xvi. 14, 16, xx. 8.

τοῦ στρατεύματος αὐτοῦ. Though the heavenly army is described in the plural as στρατεύματα, it is here very significantly described as a single host. While the opposing hosts of evil are moved by a variety of conflicting aims, the heavenly host is actuated by one only.

20. With the Beast and the False Prophet we might compare Ahriman and Azi-Dahâka in the Zend religion, which influenced Judaism from the East. Cf. De la Saussaye, *Lehrb. d. Religionsgeschichte*², ii. 206 (ii. 226 in 3rd ed.): "Zuletzt bleibt noch der Kampf zwischen himmlischen und höllischen Geistern übrig. Alle Ameshas Spentas ringen da mit ihren teuflischen Gegengeschöpfen und vernichten sie gänzlich: Ahriman selbst und die Schlange Azhi zu bändigen, wird die Sache Mazda's und Sraosha's sein. Als Priester erheben sich die beiden Götter, mit Gebet und Gebetschnur überwältigen sie die Bösen und stürzen sie und ihr Versteck in den glühenden Strom. Dann ist die Welt vollkommen rein, das Universum nur von Mazda's Wesen erfüllt, und alles, was lebt, geht in die Unsterblichkeit und himmlische Vollkommenheit ein (Bahman Yasht, 43; Bundehesh, 30)." See also Böklen, *Die Verwandschaft d. jüd.-christichen mit der parsischen Eschatologie*, 127 sqq.

ἐπιάσθη. The Attic form of this verb is πιέζω, but in late Attic πιάζω is also found. The classical meaning was to press, weigh down, stifle, etc. But its later meaning, as here, is to seize, lay hold of. πιάζω, which occurs only here in our author, is a favourite word in the Fourth Gospel, being found there eight times and only four times throughout the rest of the N.T. (one of these being in Luke vi. 38, where it retains the ancient classical form and meaning).

ὁ ψευδοπροφήτης. See xiii. 11 sqq. notes, xvi. 13, xx. 10. The False Prophet represented the priesthood of the Imperial cult, which practised all kinds of magic and imposture to beguile men to worship the Beast.

ἐπλάνησεν τοὺς λαβόντας τὸ χάραγμα κτλ. Only those who had received this mark were an easy prey to the False Prophet. On the τὸ χάραγμα see note on xiii. 16: cf. xiv. 9 sqq., xvi. 2 (note), xx. 4.

προσκυνοῦντας τὴν εἰκόνα αὐτοῦ. Though weakly attested ℵ* 28, 39), this seems to be the right reading: see note on vii. 11. Possibly the dative is right. In that case the text would mean that divine worship was actually offered to the image.

τὴν λίμνην τοῦ πυρός: cf. xx. 10, xxi. 8. On this final abode of punishment for Satan, the Beast, the False Prophet, and wicked men, see note on ix. 1.

τῆς καιομένης ἐν θείῳ. The genitive here can only be explained as a slip on the part of the writer. Contrast xxi. 8—τῇ λίμνῃ τῇ καιομένῃ. On ἐν θείῳ in this conjunction cf. xiv. 10, xx. 10, xxi. 8.

21. οἱ λοιποὶ ἀπεκτάνθησαν κτλ., *i.e.* the kings of the earth and their armies. These kings and their armies had been affected by the Caesar-worship: cf. xiv. 9 sq. They were not, like the Beast and the False Prophet, cast forthwith into Gehenna. Their physical life was destroyed by the sword, *i.e.* by the sword of the Word of God (cf. ver. 15), and their spirits no doubt consigned to Hades. In the judgment all the dead are raised (xx. 12), and then death and Hades and all the wicked are cast into the lake of fire (xx. 14–15). In the Test. of Hezekiah—a work incorporated in the Ascension of Isaiah, *i.e.* iii. 13^b–iv. 18, and written before 100 A.D.—a different sequence is anticipated: Asc. Isa. iv. 14, "The Lord will come with His angels and with the armies of the holy ones from the seventh heaven . . . and He will drag Beliar (*i.e.* the Antichrist) into Gehenna *and also his armies*."

πάντα τὰ ὄρνεα ἐχορτάσθησαν κτλ. Cf. 17 sq.; also 1 Enoch xlvi. 4–6.

CHAPTER XX. 1–3.

INTRODUCTION.

§ 1. *Contents.*—Now that Rome has fallen (xviii.), the hostile nations been destroyed, and the two Beasts cast into the lake of fire (xix. 19–20), there remains no obstacle to the manifestation of the kingdom save the presence of Satan still on earth. Hence to his activities an end is put by his being cast down into the abyss and chained there for 1000 years (xx. 1–3). The destinies of Satan are determined by the chief events in the life of Christ. In xii. Satan's expulsion from heaven is connected with the birth and ascension of Christ. On the earth, as he had only a short time, he raged furiously against Christ's followers, but on Christ's Second Advent and His overthrow of Satan's agents, Satan too is cast down from the earth into the abyss and the Millennial Kingdom established. At the close of this kingdom Satan is loosed from the abyss and finally conquered and cast into the lake of fire, and the new heaven and the new earth appear, wherein is the joint throne of God and the Lamb.

That xx. 1–3 comes from our author's hand there can be no doubt, as the diction and idiom prove.

§ 2. *Diction and idiom.*

1. εἶδον ἄγγελον καταβαίνοντα ἐκ τοῦ οὐρανοῦ. The whole clause has already occurred in x. 1, xviii. 1, and the last four words also in iii. 12, xvi. 21, xxi. 2, 10.

τὴν κλεῖν τῆς ἀβύσσου: cf. ix. 1.

2. τὸν δράκοντα ὁ ὄφις ὁ ἀρχαῖος. The same words in the same characteristic and anomalous construction have already occurred in xii. 9. ὅς ἐστιν Διάβολος καὶ ὁ Σατανᾶς. Cf. xii. 9, ὁ καλούμενος Διάβολος καὶ ὁ Σατανᾶς.

ἔδησεν αὐτόν Cf. ix. 14, δεδεμένους.

3. ἔβαλεν αὐτὸν εἰς τὴν ἄβυσσον. For this use of βάλλειν cf. ii. 10, viii. 5, 7, 8, xii. 9, xix. 20, etc.

ἔκλεισεν: cf iii. 7, 8, xi. 6, xxi. 25. ἐσφράγισεν—seven times elsewhere in our author. ἐπάνω: cf. vi. 8. ἵνα μὴ πλανήσῃ ἔτι τὰ ἔθνη: cf. xiii. 14, xii. 9. ἄχρι *cum subj.*—a rare use: cf. 5, vii. 3, xv. 8. τελεσθῇ: cf. 5, 7, x. 7, xv. 1, 8.

§ 3. *Order of words.*—Wholly Semitic.

1–3. The binding of the Dragon in the abyss for 1000 years.

1. καὶ εἶδον.—See note on iv. 1.

τὴν κλεῖν τῆς ἀβύσσου. See notes on i. 18, ix. 1. The abyss is regarded only as a temporary abode of punishment. Satan is finally cast into the lake of fire, xx. 10.

ἅλυσιν μεγάλην. ἅλυσις seems to be used here to denote a chain or bond by which the body is bound. In Mark v. 4 and frequently elsewhere it signifies hand fetters as opposed to πέδαι. See note of Lightfoot on Phil., p. 8.

ἐπὶ τὴν χεῖρα. It is hard to explain the use of ἐπί here. The best parallel is to be found in v. 1, ἐπὶ τὴν δεξιὰν . . . βιβλίον. But in this latter case the idea implied is that the book is lying on the palm of the hand. It is perhaps best to regard the present instance as a loose use of ἐπί, which does not admit of any exact explanation. It is practically here equivalent to ἐν (cf. i. 16 with i. 20), and indeed ἐν is read here by ℵ 38 syr.[1, 2]. Another difficult use of ἐπί, but with the dative, occurs in xxii. 16, where, however, the best authorities have ἐν.

2. τὸν δράκοντα, ὁ ὄφις ὁ ἀρχαῖος. For a like anacolouthon cf. i. 5. See note on xii. 9 on the identification of the old serpent and the devil. Gunkel on Gen.[3] iii. 1 maintains that the text there implies that originally the serpent was an evil demon hostile to God and man and possessing a snakelike form. He further points out in support of this view that in 2 Kings xviii. 4 divine worship is offered to a snakelike form by the faithless Israelites, and that heathen gods and demons were frequently so conceived in the ancient world.

ἔδησεν αὐτὸν χίλια ἔτη. This idea of binding the powers of evil in prison for an undefined period is already found in Isa. xxiv. 22, and of their final judgment in xxiv. 23. These powers consist of the host of heaven and the kings of the earth This idea of the angels and the kings of the earth being judged together reappears in 1 Enoch liii. 4–liv. 5, and the idea of the binding of the fallen angels in a place of temporary punishment till the day of the final judgment is found in 1 Enoch xviii. 12–16, xix. 1–2, xxi. 1–6, from which the final place of their punishment —an abyss of fire—is carefully distinguished, x. 13–15, xviii. 11, xxi. 7–10, liv. 6, xc. 24–25. Their leader Azazel is bound in a place by himself (x. 4–5) as a preliminary punishment, but at the final judgment is to be cast into a place of everlasting punishment (x. 6). In nearly all cases the evil spirits are spoken of in 1 Enoch as being "bound" in a preliminary place of punishment, just as in Isa. xxiv. 22 and in our text.

In the Zend religion the same idea is found. According to the Bundehesh iii. 26 (cf. xiii. 77) the evil serpent Azi-Dahâka was smitten by Thraêtaona and fettered in the mountain Damâvand for 9000 years, *S.B.E.* iv. 9 (note), 226, 245 sq., v. 234, 397, xviii. 110, 201, etc. He was released by Ahriman, *S.B.E.* v. 233–235, and reigned for 1000 years, v. 150, xxiv. 103, but was slain by Sâm or Keresâsp, v. 235. After the renovation of the world there would be no Azi-Dahâka, xviii. 118. But, since these Iranic myths belong to various periods before and after the Christian era, there is no ground for tracing any direct connection.

χίλια ἔτη. Before the year 100 B.C. it was generally believed in Judaism that the Messianic Kingdom would last *for ever* on the present earth. Sometimes the conception was universalistic in character, especially in the greater prophets of the O.T., as Jeremiah, the Second Isaiah, Jonah, Malachi; but in others, as in Ezekiel, Haggai, Zechariah, Joel, it was particularistic. The idea of the everlastingness of this kingdom on earth persisted, as we have above said, till about 100 B.C. For such it appears to be in 1 Enoch lxxxiii.–xc., vi.–xxxvi., but by the date just mentioned the earth had come to be regarded in Judaism as wholly unfit for the manifestation of this kingdom except in a temporary character. The dualism which had begun to affect the religious forecasts of religious thinkers in the 2nd cent. B.C. succeeded in leavening wholly their expectations in the 1st. As a consequence of this breach between the things of earth and the things of heaven, the writers of this century were forced to entertain new conceptions of the kingdom. Hence in 1 Enoch xci.–civ., Pss. Sol. i.–xvi., the Messianic Kingdom is declared to be of temporary duration on the present earth, and the goal of the risen righteous to be not this transitory kingdom, but heaven itself after the final judgment, which from this period forwards was conceived of as taking place not at the beginning, but at the close of the Messianic Kingdom. Thus it is that the Millennium in our text, as in 2 Baruch and 4 Ezra, is really a late and attenuated form of the old Jewish expectation of an eternal Messianic Kingdom on the present earth. For a fuller treatment of this question the reader can consult my *Eschatology*[2], pp. 103, 106–108, 110 sq., 113–116, 219 sq., 223, 248, 250 sq.

We have next to consider the duration of this kingdom. Apparently nowhere in earlier or contemporary literature is the duration of 1000 years assigned to the Messianic Kingdom save here. Its duration is not defined in 1 Enoch xci.–civ.; Pss. Sol. xi. 1 sqq.; Sibyll. Or. iii. 1–62; Jubilees xxiii. 27–29; Assumption of Moses x. 7; 2 Bar. xxix. 4–xxx. 1, xxxix. 7, xl. 3, lxxii. 2–4; 4 Ezra xiii. 32, 36. In 4 Ezra vii. 28 it is definitely said to last 400 years.

3. ἔβαλεν αὐτὸν εἰς τ. ἄβυσσον καὶ ἔκλεισεν. On the ἄβυσσος see ix. 1, note.

ἔκλεισεν καὶ ἐσφράγισεν ἐπάνω αὐτοῦ, *i.e.* closed the abyss and sealed it over him. Our text recalls the Prayer of Manasseh, 2–4, and the two passages are distantly connected, though our Seer has no thought of this passage nor of the myth that it presupposes.

For, whereas it is a literal Satan overcome by an angel that is presupposed in our text, it is a mythological monster that is overcome by God in the Prayer of Manasseh. What was originally a mythological idea concerning the uprising of the Chaos monster (*i.e.* the sea) against God at the world's beginning, had long ere our Seer's time been transformed into an eschatological expectation, *i.e.* the rebellion of Satan against God at the world's close, and his being cast into the abyss. The mythological idea is quite clearly set forth in the above-mentioned Prayer of Manasseh: *ὁ ποιήσας τὸν οὐρανὸν καὶ τὴν γῆν σὺν παντὶ τῷ κόσμῳ αὐτοῦ, ὁ πεδήσας τὴν θάλασσαν τῷ λόγῳ τοῦ προστάγματός σου, ὁ κλείσας τὴν ἄβυσσον καὶ σφραγισάμενος αὐτὴν τῷ φοβερῷ καὶ ἐνδόξῳ ὀνόματί σου.*

πλανήσῃ ἔτι τὰ ἔθνη. As he had done before: cf. xiii. 14, xvi. 13. See also xii. 9. As these words point to the future, they imply that there would still be heathen nations after the Messianic judgment executed in xix. 19–21. Now that Satan's chief agents, the Beast and the False Prophet, were cast into the lake of fire and Satan himself bound in the abyss, the time for the Millennial reign has arrived and for the evangelization of the surviving heathen nations: see xiv. 7, xv. 4, xxii. 17. The astonishing part in our Seer's forecast is that the preaching of the Gospel during the Millennium will only in part be successful, though the active impersonations of evil have been wholly removed from the earth for this period. The implication is that each man carries in his own bosom the possibilities of his own heaven and his own hell.

δεῖ: cf. i. 1, iv. 1.

XX. 4–XXII. THE TEXT INCOHERENT AND SELF-CONTRADICTORY AS IT STANDS.

XX. 4–XXII. These chapters have hitherto been a constant source of insurmountable difficulty to the exegete. They are full of confusion and contradiction if the text is honestly dealt with. And yet the Apocalypse exhibits, except in a few passages, and especially in chap. xviii., a structural unity and a steady development of thought from the first chapter to the close of xx. 3. Now this is just what we should expect in an Apocalypse which is designed to be a philosophy of history and religion from the standpoint of the author. It was a combination of *vision and reflection.* Though the book of a prophet did not necessarily show any structural unity or steady development of thought, it was far otherwise with the apocalyptist, in whose writings such characteristics were indispensable. While the ordinary man saw only the outside of things in all their incoherence and isolation, the apocalyptist sought to get behind the surface and penetrate to the essence of events, the spiritual motives and purposes that underlay and gave them their real significance—in fact, to lay bare their origin, course, and consummation. It was thus, in short, a Semitic philosophy of religion, and as such it was ever asking Whence? Wherefore? Whither? Apocalyptic, and not prophecy, was the first to grasp the great idea that all history, alike human, cosmological, and spiritual, is a unity—a unity following naturally as a corollary of the unity of God preached by the prophets.

I have emphasized these two points—structural unity and orderly development of thought to the final consummation of all things—as pre-eminently the characteristics of apocalyptic and not of prophecy or of any other form of writing in the Bible. This being so, we are all the more astonished that the three closing chapters of the Apocalypse are all but wholly wanting in these characteristics, and—so far from advancing steadily to the consummation that all the preceding chapters postulate—exhibit many incoherencies and self-contradictory elements.

To some of these I drew attention in my first edition of the Book of Enoch in 1893, where on p. 45 I wrote as follows: "We have here (*i.e.* Rev. xxi. 1, 2) a new heaven and a new earth, and a New Jerusalem coming down from heaven: yet in xxii. 15 all classes of sinners are said to be without the gates of the city. But if there were a new earth this would be impossible." This is only one of the many difficulties that confront the serious student of these chapters. Now to make the problem before us clear it will be best to deal shortly with a few of the passages which make it impossible for us to accept the text as it stands.

1. In xx. 7–10, after the close of the Millennial Kingdom, Satan is loosed, and the heathen nations (Gog and Magog), which have refused to accept the Christian faith, march against Jerusalem and the camp of the saints, but are destroyed by fire from heaven. Satan also is cast finally into the lake of fire and brimstone, to be tormented there for ever and ever. *Thus the prime source of evil and his deluded followers (Gog and Magog) are removed finally from the world, and their power to influence the world for evil made impossible for ever.*

2. In xx. 11–15 the old earth and the old heaven are given over to annihilation. Then the final judgment takes place, and all the dead are judged according to their works, and death and Hades are cast into the lake of fire, together with all those whose names are not found written in the book of life. *At this stage we have arrived at the final condemnation and destruction of all evil, together with the destruction of death itself.*

3. Now that all evil and death itself are cast into the lake of fire, the new heaven and the new earth come into being, and the New Jerusalem comes down from heaven, and God Himself dwells with men (xxi. 1–4).

It is clear from this passage that we have arrived at the closing scene of the great world struggle between good and evil, and that henceforth there can be neither sin, nor crying, nor pain, nor death any more. In fact, there can be no place at all for these in the universe of God—the new heaven and the new earth, and the New Jerusalem that cometh down from God to the new earth.

The conclusion just arrived at is inevitable, if there is a steady development in the visions of the Seer. Now since such a development is manifest in chaps. i.–xx. 3, when certain verses and glosses are excised and a few disarrangements of the text set right—expecially in xviii.—we naturally conclude that our author will not lightly fall into contradictions, even of a minor sort, in the last three chapters. But unhappily this is not our experience as we study them ; and at last we stand aghast at the hopeless mental confusion which dominates the present structure of these chapters, and are compelled to ask if they can possibly come from his hand, and, in case they do, to ask further, if they have been preserved as they left his hand. But we must first justify the above statement, though we shall adduce here only the main contradictions in these chapters.

1. Inasmuch as according to our text the New Jerusalem does not come down from heaven till Satan is bound for ever in the lake of fire, and all sin and death itself are at an end, and the place of the old world has been taken by a new and glorious

world, wherein there is neither spot nor blemish nor any such thing, how is it that we are told that, outside the gates of the Holy City which has come down from God to the new earth, there are "the dogs and the sorcerers, and the fornicators, and the murderers, and the idolaters, and every one that loveth and maketh a lie" (xxii. 15)? A greater contradiction in thought and statement is hardly conceivable. But, if this statement were made in connection with the Millennial Kingdom which was to be established before the Final Judgment, everything would be intelligible.

2. Again, since the new earth is inhabited only by the blessed, on whom the second death could have no effect, and since these are all righteous, and God Himself tabernacles among them, how is it that in xxii. 2 the leaves of the tree of life are said to be for the healing of the nations? This statement can have no meaning unless it applies to the period of the Millennial Kingdom. During Christ's reign of 1000 years the surviving nations have still a further period of grace accorded to them. This evangelizing of the nations during this period has already been proclaimed in xiv. 6–7, xv. 4. It is thrice elsewhere referred to in the last two chapters, *i.e.* xxi. 24, xxii. 14, 17.

3. Only on the supposition that the Millennial Kingdom is still in existence can we explain xxi. 24–27:

"And the nations shall walk by the light thereof:
And the kings of the earth do bring their glory into it.
And the gates thereof shall not be shut day *or night.*[1]
And they shall bring the glory and the honour of the nations into it:
And there shall not enter into it anything unclean, or he that maketh an abomination or a lie;
But only they which are written in the book of life of the Lamb."

Now from the above contradictions—the solution of which is in part already suggested—it follows either that (*a*) a considerable part of xx.–xxii. is not from the hand of our author, or that, (*b*) if it is from his hand, it is disarranged.

Now the first solution (*a*) is that adopted by most of the leading German scholars of the past thirty years. Thus while Völter (*Die Offenbarung Johannis*, 1904), Weyland (*Omverkingsen Compilatie-Hypothesen toegepast op de Apocalypse van Johannes*, 1908), and J. Weiss (*Die Offenb. des Johannes*, 1908) assume that xx.–xxii. is derived from three different sources, and Spitta (*Die Offenb. des Johannes*, 1889) finds traces of four authors,

[1] A necessary emendation. The corruption in the text arose from the present disorder, and the influence of xxii. 5, "and there shall be no more night," where this clause is wholly justifiable.

Erbes (*Die Offenb. Johannis*, 1891) and, on the whole, Bousset (1906), are content with two. Bousset, in fact, regards xx.–xxii. as the work of our author, with the exception of the fragment xxi. 9–xxii. 5.

But, even though for the time being we accepted as a working hypothesis any one of the theories of these scholars based on a plurality of authorship, we have still two insuperable difficulties to face. (α) The first of these is that *the more closely we study i.–xx. 3, the more convinced we become of the structural unity of these chapters*—a fact which does not exclude the occasional use and adaptation of sources—*and the clear and masterly development in thought, working up steadily to a climax. This being so, how is it that xx.–xxii. shows no such orderly development, but rather a chaos of conflicting conceptions?* (β) But the second difficulty is still greater. The hypotheses of the above scholars, with the partial exception of Bousset, break down hopelessly in the face of the general linguistic unity of xx.–xxii. In fact, these scholars had failed to make a thorough study of the style, vocabulary, and grammar of the Apocalypse. Bousset, it is true, has done much to compensate for the deficiencies of his predecessors in this field, but a deeper study of his materials would have precluded his assuming the existence of xxi. 9–xxii. 5 as an independent source, seeing that it is internally self-contradictory and that yet *linguistically it is from the hand of our author.* To the conclusion, in fact, that, with the exception of a few verses, chaps. xx.–xxii. are from the same hand to which we owe the bulk of the preceding chapters, a close and prolonged study has slowly but irresistibly brought me. If, then, this is so, we must conclude that the text in xx.–xxii. *is disarranged in an astonishing degree and does not at present stand in the orderly sequence originally designed by our author.*

To what cause, we must now ask, is this almost incredible disorder due? It cannot be accounted for by accidental transpositions of the text in the MSS—a phenomenon with which the students of MSS in every ancient language are familiar. For no accident could explain the intolerable confusion of the text in xx. 4–xxii., and apparently the only hypothesis that can account for it is that which a comprehensive study of the facts forced upon me in the beginning of 1914, and this is that *John died either as a martyr or by a natural death, when he had completed i.–xx. 3 of his work, and that the materials for its completion, which were for the most part ready in a series of independent documents, were put together by a faithful but unintelligent disciple in the order which he thought right.*

This hypothesis we shall now proceed to establish by adequate proofs.

1. First of all it is a matter beyond dispute that xxii. 15, xxi. 27, which state that outside the gates of the Heavenly Jerusalem evil in every form exists, but that it can in no wise pass within the gates of the Holy City, prove that *the Heavenly Jerusalem here referred to was to descend before the disappearance of the first earth and the first heaven and the final judgment* described in xx. 11–15. A kindred expectation is found in 4 Ezra vii. 26–28, where the Heavenly Jerusalem,[1] the Messiah, and those who had been translated to heaven without seeing death, are to be manifested together on the earth for 400 years. The same view appears in the same work in xiii. 32–36. In this latter passage evil in every form exists outside the Heavenly City.

From later Jewish sources we are familiar with the connection of the rebuilt Jerusalem and the temporary reign of the Messiah. The advent of the Messiah determines the hour when the Temple and therefore Jerusalem should be rebuilt (Shemoth rab. c. 31). According to the Targum on Isa. liii. 5 (cf. Bammidbar rab. c. 13) the Messiah Himself was to build it.

From the above facts we conclude that in our author the account of the Heavenly Jerusalem (xxi. 9–xxii. 2, 14–15, 17) should have followed immediately on xx. 3 as the seat of the Messiah's Kingdom.

2. Verses xxi. 24–26, xxii. 2, 14–15, 17 assume that the nations are still upon earth, that the gospel is preached to them afresh from the Heavenly Jerusalem, that they are healed thereby of their spiritual evils, their sins washed away, that they can enter the Heavenly City and eat of the tree of life which was therein. And to this salvation they are bidden of the Spirit and the Heavenly Jerusalem (*i.e.* the bride, xxii. 17).

Now this expectation is derived from the Old Testament. In Zech. xiv. 16 sqq., when the blessed era sets in, the nations are to go up yearly to keep the Feast of Tabernacles at Jerusalem. In Tob. xiv. 6 the conversion of the Gentiles is to synchronize with the rebuilding of Jerusalem in a fashion far transcending all that Seer or prophet had hitherto dreamt of—when its gates should be "builded with sapphire and emerald," and all its walls "with precious stones," and its streets "paved with carbuncle and stones of Ophir" (xiii. 16–17). Similarly in 1 Enoch (161 B.C.) we find it prophesied that the conversion of the surviving Gentiles would follow on the setting up of the Holy City, which was to be done by none other than God Himself. Next, in the Test. XII Patriarchs the conversion of

[1] Box, it is true, regards vii. 26, which tells of the manifestation of the Heavenly Jerusalem, as an interpolation; but the evidence of our text and later Judaism supports the connection of the Messiah and the Holy City.

the Gentiles is associated with the advent of the Messiah, T. Levi xviii. 9, T. Jud. xxiv. 5, and that of the New Jerusalem in T. Dan v. 12. Like expectations are expressed in the Sibyll. Or. iii. 751–59, 767–95; 1 Enoch xlviii. 4 (where the Messiah is described as the light of the Gentiles); Pss. Sol. xvii. 27, 32.

Thus in many books in Judaism the hope is entertained, as in our text, that the Gentiles would turn to the worship of the true God, when either the earthly Jerusalem was rebuilt or a Heavenly Jerusalem set up on earth, or when the Messiah established His Kingdom upon the earth. It is true that Judaism associated this expectation with the First Advent of the Messiah; for it looked for no second. But in Christianity it was different. What had not been realized on the First Advent of Christ is, according to many a Christian prophet and Seer, as also to our author, to be realized in a far higher degree when Christ came the second time in glory.

That the conversion of the heathen nations in our text, therefore, was to be accomplished in connection with the Heavenly City, which as the seat of the Millennial Kingdom was to descend on the earth before the Final Judgment, needs no further demonstration.

3. The facts just stated in the preceding paragraph, that the Gentiles shall still be upon the earth on the advent of the Heavenly City, and have a right to enter therein, are already postulated in the earlier chapters of the Apocalypse. Thus in xv. 4 we read in the song sung by the triumphant martyrs before the throne of God—

"Who shall not fear, O Lord,
And glorify Thy name?
For Thou alone art holy;
For all the nations shall come
And worship before Thee;
For Thy righteous acts shall have been made manifest."

Again, in xiv. 6–7 the Seer recounts a vision in which he hears an angel proclaiming the coming evangelization of the nations of the world:[1] "And I saw another angel flying in mid heaven, having an eternal gospel to proclaim unto them that dwell on the earth, and unto every nation and tribe and tongue and people, saying with a great voice,

[1] A somewhat analogous expectation is found in 1 Cor. xv. 23–28, where we have an account of the Messianic Kingdom. This kingdom is heralded by the resurrection of Christ: it is apparently established on Christ's (second) Advent with the risen righteous (23). Then follows the reign of Christ, in the course of which every evil power is overthrown (24[b]–28). Then comes the end (the general resurrection, final judgment, the destruction of the old world and the creation of the new).

Fear God and give Him glory;
For the hour of His judgment is come:
And worship Him that made the heaven and the earth
And the sea and fountains of waters."

Now, *according to the present form of the text of the last three chapters of our book, these prophecies*, which definitely foretell the evangelization of the nations of the world and their acceptance of the Gospel preached, *remain wholly unfulfilled.* In fact, according to the present text, the nations are simply annihilated before the advent of the Heavenly City. On the other hand, if the account of the Heavenly Jerusalem as given in xxi. 9 to xxii. 2, 14–15, 17 is restored immediately after xx. 3, then these prophecies are fulfilled; for the nations, according to this account, walk by the light thereof, and the kings of the earth do bring their glory into it, and yet outside its gates there is still evil of every kind.

4. Again, in xi. 15 we read—

"The Kingdom of the world is become the Kingdom of our Lord and of His Christ,
And He shall reign for ever and ever."

These words quite clearly assume that the rule of God and Christ will be extended over the whole world of the nations. But, as the text at present stands, not a single nation is mentioned as being brought beneath its sway, while in the verses (xx. 9–10) that precede the description of the Final Judgment (xx. 11–15) we are led to infer that they are wholly destroyed by fire from heaven. That is one way of establishing authority over the neutral or hostile nations, but it is not God's way. We have only to read chaps. xxi.–xxii., which deal *ostensibly* with events occurring only after the absolute destruction of all the nations and of the first heaven and the first earth, when we discover the nations, that had presumably passed out of existence, going up in pilgrimage to the Heavenly Jerusalem, each under its own king, passing within its blessed portals, bringing their glory and honour into it, receiving spiritual healing in the Holy City, and assimilating the divine truths that make them heirs to immortality, that is, eating of the tree of life. That all the nations do not avail themselves of these privileges is plainly asserted in the text; for outside the gates are sorcerers and whoremongers and idolaters and whosoever loveth and maketh a lie.

On this ground again we must transpose the description of the Holy City before the Final Judgment, and regard it as the seat of the Millennial Kingdom.

5. The city that is spiritually designated Sodom and Egypt (xi. 8) cannot be called "the beloved city" as in xx. 9, nor can

it become the seat of the Millennial Kingdom. Much less can the ruins of such a polluted city become the abode of Christ and of the risen martyrs come down from heaven to reign with Him for a thousand years.

6. Again, as we study xxi.–xxii. we discover that there are in reality two descriptions of the Heavenly City, and not one, as has hitherto been universally assumed. The Seer has two distinct visions, and they deal not with one and the same city, but with two quite distinct cities. The first (xxi. 9 to xxii. 2, 14–15, 17) presupposes the existence of the present earth. Thus the Seer tells how the angel, that had showed him the destruction of the great world-capital Rome in xvii., came again to him and carried him off *to a great high mountain* to show him the Heavenly City that was to take the place of Rome as the metropolis of the world. The very first words of the vision presuppose the co-existence of the Heavenly Jerusalem and the present earth. This city the Seer beheld coming down from heaven to earth (*i.e.* the first heaven and the first earth). It becomes the great spiritual centre of the world. The nations flock up to it from every side to share in its spiritual blessings, its gates are open day and night, and yet none of the evil individuals or nations that are without may enter into it (xxi. 24–27).

It is manifest that since sin, and therefore death, prevail outside the gates of the Heavenly City, the present order of things still prevails, the first heaven and the first earth are still in being.

But there is another Heavenly City (xxi. 1–4[c], xxii. 3–5) described by our author, quite distinct from that just dealt with. The angel in xxi. 9 has apparently had no direct part in mediating this new vision. The vision, just as those in xx. 1–3, 11–15, xxi. 1, seems to be independent of any angelic agency. With regard to this Heavenly City there can be no question as to the hour of its manifestation. The very first words of the text imply that the vision of the Seer has outleapt the bounds of time, when the former heaven and earth have vanished for ever. This second Heavenly City does not appear *till the first heaven and the first earth have vanished and their place been taken by the new heaven and the new earth.* Hence as distinguished from the first Heavenly City, it is designated "new," *i.e.* καινή, that is, of a new sort or quality as distinct from the first, just as the second heaven and the second earth are themselves described as "new" (καινός and καινή). This epithet is never applied to the Heavenly City described at such length in xxi. 9–xxii. 2, 14–15, 17. Sin, of course, no longer exists in this new world. Hence there is no more crying, nor mourning, nor pain, nor curse, nor death (xxi. 4[abc], xxii. 3[a]), though round about the first Heavenly City —close even to its very gates—sin in every form and death did exist, and even within its stately walls sorrow for sin and repentance were never absent, for the nations of the earth flocked to it from every side to be healed of their spiritual ills and infirmities (xxi. 24–26, xxii. 2).

7. It is finally to be observed that, since the earthly Jerusalem was in ruins, and never in the opinion of the Seer to be rebuilt, a new city was of necessity to take its place as the seat of Christ's Kingdom and the abode of the blessed martyrs, who were to come down from heaven to reign for a thousand years with Him. Since this new city was to be the abode of Christ on His Second Advent from heaven, and of the martyrs coming down from heaven with Him in their glorified bodies, it follows that the new city must be from heaven also, if it was to be a fit abode for its inhabitants from heaven. Even as early as 161 B.C. (as we have already mentioned above), we have a like expectation in 1 Enoch xc. 28–38, where it is said in the vision that God Himself set up the New Jerusalem, to be the abode of the Messiah and the transformed and glorified Israel. A like expectation is attested in a work almost contemporary with our author, *i.e.* 4 Ezra, as we have already shown.

8. To the revision of John's literary executor we may probably ascribe the non-Johannine combinations *τ. καθήμενον ἐπ' αὐτοῦ* in xx. 11, where, though only A and some cursives attest this reading, they are to be followed; *ὁ καθήμενος ἐπὶ τ. θρόνου* in xxi. 5, where, since every MS is wrong, the error must go back to the editor; *τῶν πεπελεκισμένων . . . καὶ οἵτινες οὐ προσεκύνησαν* in xx. 4, where the *οἵτινες* is thrust in against John's usage (see i. 5, note). Possibly the normal construction *τ. λίμνῃ τῇ καιομένῃ πυρὶ καὶ θείῳ* in xxi. 8 may be due to him: contrast that in xix. 20. Again in xxi. 6 instead of *τῷ διψῶντι δώσω* the Johannine idiom is *τῷ διψῶντι δώσω αὐτῷ* (see note *in loc.*).

From the above facts the conclusion is inevitable that after xx. 3 *our author had intended to add a description of the Heavenly Jerusalem that was to come down from heaven to earth and be the habitation of Christ and the martyrs that accompanied Him from heaven in their glorified bodies: and also that this very description has been preserved in certain sections of xxi.–xxii.*

We have next to determine the extent of this description. Now even the cursory reader will observe that there are two accounts of the Heavenly Jerusalem in these chapters, which have been rudely thrust together by the Seer's literary executor.[1] A

[1] We might compare 2 Corinthians, which is now recognized by the learned world as consisting of two mutilated Epistles of St. Paul edited together as one, the last four chapters belonging to the earlier Epistle. In Cicero's letters Professor Purser shows that in several cases exactly the same phenomenon may be found.

close study of these chapters will show that the section xxi. 9–xxii. 2 constitutes a unity, though incomplete in itself, as we shall see presently, and gives a description of the Heavenly Jerusalem that was to be the centre of the Millennial Kingdom. Two further fragments of this description are to be found in xxii. 14–15 and 17. This description fits in perfectly with the conditions of the Millennial reign of Christ and the martyrs for a thousand years. It is conceived of as a period of beneficent rule and evangelizing effort in regard to the surviving nations who visit the Heavenly Jerusalem and bring all their glory and honour into it. Wickedness, of course, still exists without it. but nothing that is unclean, nor any liar or abominable person, is permitted to enter into it (xxii. 15, xxi. 27).

So far the first description. But what are we to make of the second, which begins with xxi. 1? Only the *disjecta membra* of this description remain. Two fragments of it are recoverable in xxi. 1–4^{c} and xxii. 3–5. These should be read together, as the first clause of xxii. 3 forms the fourth line of the stanza, the first three lines of which are preserved in xxi. 4^{abc}. In this second description the former heaven and earth have passed away for ever, with all the sin and sorrow and pain that prevailed on the former earth. Death itself shall be no more throughout the new heaven and the new earth and the New Jerusalem (xxi. 4). And whereas in the Heavenly Jerusalem that came down from God for the Millennial Kingdom the saints who had been martyred reigned only a thousand years, in the later New Jerusalem they are to reign for ever and ever (xxii. 5). It is noteworthy that even the very diction of xxi. 1–4^{abc} and of xxii. 3–5 testifies to the fact that they form part of one and the same poem. Thus οὐκ ἔσται ἔτι, which occurs three times in xxi. 1^{c} 4^{bc}, recurs twice in xxii. 3^{a} 5^{a} (contrast xxi. 26) and not elsewhere throughout our author. οὐκ . . . ἔτι occurs nine times in connection with other verbs. Thus while οὐκ ἔσται ἔτι is confined to xxi. 1–4^{abc}, xxii. 3–5, it is to be observed that οὐκ . . . ἔτι is characteristic of our author in the N.T., since outside our author it occurs in the N.T. only six times and twice of these in quotations.

We have now dealt with the chief difficulties in xx.–xxii. There are, of course, many of a subordinate nature affecting the original order of the text in xxii., but they are treated shortly in the introductions to the various sections of the rearranged translation that follows. Chaps. xx.–xxii. should provisionally be read in the following order:

xx. 1–3. Vision of the chaining of Satan for a thousand years.

xxi. 9–xxii. 2, 14–15, 17. Vision of the Heavenly Jerusalem

which comes down to be the abode of Christ and the glorified martyrs, and the centre of a new evangelization of the nations for a thousand years.

xx. 4–6. Vision of the glorified martyrs who reign with Christ for a thousand years.

xx. 7–10. Vision of the loosing of Satan, and the attack of Gog and Magog on the Beloved City; of the destruction of Gog and Magog, and the casting of Satan into the lake of fire.

xx. 11–15. Vision of the great white throne; of the vanishing of the former heaven and earth; of the judgment of the dead, and of the casting of death and Hades into the lake of fire.

xxi. 5^a, 4^d, 5^b, $1–4^{abc}$, xxii. 3–5. The outworn world has vanished: God creates a new world. Vision of the new heaven and the new earth: of the New Jerusalem descending from God to the new earth, in which the saints are to reign for ever.

xxi. 5^c 6^b–8. Admonition of God conveyed through the Seer to his contemporaries.

xxii. 6–7, 18^a, 16, 13, 12, 10. Declaration of Christ as to the truth of the words of the Seer; His assurance of His almighty power and His speedy advent; and His command to the Seer to publish the prophecy: for the time is at hand.

xxii. 8–9, 20. John's testimony and closing words regarding Christ.[1]

xxii. 21. The closing benediction.

VISION OF THE HEAVENLY JERUSALEM.

XXI 9–XXII. 2, 14–15, 17: *Vision of the Heavenly Jerusalem coming down from heaven to be the abode of Christ and of the glorified martyrs, who are to reign with Him for 1000 years, and to be the centre of a new evangelization of the nations.*

This vision forms (I.) an integral part of the Book, and (II.) is from the hand of the Seer. Since the question has already been discussed (see pp. 144–154) we shall sum up shortly the evidence for the above statements.

I. The vision forms an integral part of the Book.

1. There must be a fitting seat on earth for the kingdom of Christ during the Millennial reign with the glorified martyrs in their heavenly bodies. This city while obviously supramundane, as befitting Christ and the glorified saints, must yet be accessible to the actual dwellers on the earth, as in fact it is: cf. xxi. 24–27, xxii. 14–15, 17.

2. Such a kingdom or centre of the evangelization of the heathen nations is clearly foretold in xv. 3–4, and implied in v. 10,

[1] xxii. 11, 18^d–19 are most probably later additions.

xiv. 7. Without such a kingdom there would be a lacuna in the Book.

3. As one of the angels of the Seven Bowls showed the doomed city of the Antichrist to the Seer (xvii.–xviii.), so the same angel, or one of the same Seven, shows him the blessed city of the Christ (xxi. 9).

Thus so far as the subject-matter goes, the presence of this vision is indispensable.

II. It is from the hand of the Seer. Full evidence of this statement is given in the notes, but sufficient evidence will here be adduced to establish this point.

1. First, as to *diction.*

XXI. 9. καὶ ἦλθεν . . . δείξω σοι agrees exactly with xvii. 1. With φιάλας τῶν γεμόντων τῶν ἑπτὰ πληγῶν cf. xv. 7. τ. νυμφὴν τ. γυναῖκα τοῦ ἀρνίου is prepared for in xix. 7–8.

10. ἀπήνεγκεν . . . πνεύματι. So also in xvii. 3. τὴν πόλιν τ. ἁγίαν Ἰερουσαλήμ : cf. xxi. 2. καταβαίνουσαν ἐκ τ. οὐρανοῦ ἀπὸ τ. θεοῦ : cf. iii. 12, x. 1, xxi. 2, etc. ἔχουσαν τ. δόξαν τοῦ θεοῦ (also in 23): cf. xv. 8.

11. ὡς λίθῳ ἰάσπιδι : cf. iv. 3, *ὅμοιος . . . λίθῳ ἰάσπιδι.* Now we know (see vol. i. p. 36) that our author several times uses *ὅμοιος* as the equivalent of ὡς. κρυσταλλίζοντι : cf. iv. 6, *ὁμοία κρυστάλλῳ.*

13. ἀπὸ ἀνατολῆς : cf. vii. 2, xvi. 12.

15. ὁ λαλῶν μετ᾽ ἐμοῦ : cf. xvii. 1.

18. ὑάλῳ (*ὕαλος*, 21) : cf. *ὑάλινος*, iv. 6, xv. 2.

22. Observe the divine title so frequent in our Book.

23. οὐ χρείαν ἔχει : cf. iii. 17, xxii. 5. φαίνωσιν : cf. i. 16, viii. 12.

24. περιπατήσουσιν : cf. ii. 1, iii. 4, xvi. 15.

26. τὴν δόξαν καὶ τ. τιμήν : cf. iv. 9, 11, v. 12, 13.

27. γεγραμμένοι ἐν τ. βιβλίῳ τῆς ζωῆς : cf. xx. 12, 15. ποιῶν βδέλυγμα (cf. xxi. 8) καὶ ψεῦδος : cf. xxii. 15.

XXII. 1. λαμπρόν : cf. xv. 6, xix. 8. ποταμόν . . . ὡς κρύσταλλον : cf. iv. 6, *θάλασσα . . . ὁμοία κρυστάλλῳ*, and see above on xxi. 10. ἐκπορευόμενον ἐκ τ. θρόνου : cf. iv. 5.

14. πλύνοντες τ. στολὰς αὐτῶν. So vii. 14. ἐξουσία—a favourite Johannine word though here used with a slightly different meaning.

15. φαρμακοὶ . . . εἰδωλολάτραι. For the same list of four see xxi. 8, though in a different order.

17. νύμφη : cf. xxi. 2, 9. ἔρχου : cf. vi. 1. διψῶντι : cf. xxi. 6. ὕδωρ ζωῆς δωρεάν : cf. xxi. 6.

2. *Technical use of idioms.*

(*a*) Anomalous constructions : cf. xxi. 9, φιάλας τῶν γεμόντων. 14. τὸ τεῖχος . . . ἔχων. (*b*) Participle = finite verb, ἔχων = ἔχει, xxi. 12, 14 : cf. iv. 1, etc. (*c*) Delicate distinction of our author preserved between ὕδωρ ζωῆς and ξύλον ζωῆς in xxii. 14.

17. This distinction is not made, so far as I am aware, in any other book before 100 A.D.: cf. vii. 17, xxi. 6 on *ὕδωρ ζωῆς*, and ii. 7 (note) on *ξύλον ζωῆς*. (*d*) Observe how the difficult phrase **ὁ φωστὴρ αὐτῆς ὅμοιος . . . λίθῳ ἰάσπιδι** (xxi. 11) is explained by the clause in iv. 3, *ὁ καθήμενος ὅμοιος . . . λίθῳ ἰάσπιδι* (see note on xxi. 11). (*e*) The use of **ὡς** and **ὅμοιος** as equivalents: cf. xxi. 11, 18, where *ὅμοιος* is used in this sense, and xxi. 11, 21, xxii. 1, where *ὡς* is so used. Observe also that whereas we have **ὕδωρ ζωῆς δωρεάν** in xxii. 17, we find **τοῦ ὕδατος τῆς ζωῆς δωρεάν** in xxi. 6—a fact which points to xxi. 6 having been written subsequently to xxii. 17. (*f*) The order observed by our author as to numerals but nowhere else rigidly observed, is attested in every instance in this vision. Thus our author also places *δώδεκα* after its noun when the noun is otherwise unqualified: so also in xxi. 12 (*bis*), *πυλῶνας δώδεκα*, *ἀγγέλους δώδεκα*, and *καρποὺς δώδεκα*, xxii. 2; but before it when the noun has a dependent genitive: so also in xxi. 12, *δώδεκα ὀνόματα τῶν δώδεκα ἀποστολῶν*. Finally, when the subject of a clause consists of *δώδεκα* preceded by the article and followed by a noun, and the same numeral recurs in the predicate with a noun, the *δώδεκα* precedes the noun. So also in xxi. 21, *οἱ δώδεκα πυλῶνες δώδεκα μαργαρῖται*. See note on viii. 2.

XXI. 9–21. An angel of the Seven Bowls shows to the Seer the Heavenly Jerusalem which is to be the seat of the Millennial Kingdom.

9. καὶ ἦλθεν . . . φιάλας. Repeated from xvii. 1. **φιάλας τῶν γεμόντων.** This is certainly an extraordinary construction even in our author. It is best, perhaps, to explain it as an oversight. **καὶ ἐλάλησεν . . . δείξω σοι.** Repeated from xvii. 1.

τὴν νύμφην [τὴν γυναῖκα] τοῦ ἀρνίου. The phrase in brackets is with Bousset to be excised. It can be explained as a marginal gloss on *τ. νύμφην* based on xix. 7. The great variation in the MSS points to this phrase being an intrusion.

10. καὶ ἀπήνεγκέν με ἐν πνεύματι. This clause has already occurred in xvii. 3, and the phrase that follows here, *ἐπὶ ὄρος μέγα*, suggests the present earth just as explicitly as does *εἰς ἔρημον* in xvii. 3. The implication is that the present earth and the Heavenly Jerusalem would coexist. But there is no such implication in regard to the New Jerusalem. The former heaven and earth have already vanished (xxi. 1). Ezek. xl. appears to have been in the mind of our author when he committed this vision to writing. 10^a is practically an echo of Ezek. xl. 2, "In the visions of God brought he me . . . and set me down upon a very high mountain." Here, as the LXX renders *ἤγαγέν με ἐν ὁράσει θεοῦ . . . καὶ ἔθηκέν με ἐπ' ὄρος ὑψηλὸν σφόδρα*, our author has thought of the Hebrew only. On this very high mountain (cf. Ezek. xvii. 22; Isa. ii. 2) stood what appeared to be the structure of a city.

There he met a man with a measuring line (Ezek. xl. 3) wherewith he measured the Temple.

ἐπὶ ὄρος μέγα καὶ ὑψηλόν. Paradise and a lofty mountain are associated together in 1 Enoch xxiv. sq., and again in lxxxvii. 3, and probably in Jub. iv. 26. But this association may go back to primitive times, when the mountain of God (Ezek. xxviii. 14, Ps. xlviii. 2) was associated with the glorified Jerusalem (Isa. ii. 2); see Oesterley, *Evolution of Mess. Idea*, p. 129 sqq.

τὴν πόλιν τὴν ἁγίαν Ἰερουσαλήμ. If we compare this phrase with that in xxi. 2, which refers to the New Jerusalem which descends after the Judgment and the creation of the new heaven and the new earth, we observe that it is word for word the same save that the latter adds the significant word *καινήν*. This seems to imply that the Heavenly City is itself renewed or replaced by another.

But there are other questions which call for discussion in connection with this conception. We have four titles of this future abode of the blessed in our author: 1. *ἡ πόλις τοῦ θεοῦ μου* (iii. 12). 2. *ἡ πόλις ἡ ἁγία Ἰερουσαλὴμ καινή* (xxi. 2.), or *ἡ καινὴ Ἰερουσαλήμ* (iii. 12). 3. *ἡ πόλις ἡ ἁγία Ἰερουσαλήμ* (xxi. 10). 4. *ὁ παράδεισος τοῦ θεοῦ μου* (ii. 7). This list we can at once reduce to three by referring to iii. 12, where 1 and 2 are identified. Next, by comparing xxi. 10 and ii. 7, we are enabled to identify 3 and 4; for both these are the seat of the *ξύλον ζωῆς* (cf. xxii. 2). We have now to consider in what relation does (α) *ἡ πόλις ἡ ἁγία Ἰερ.* (= *ὁ παράδεισος τοῦ θεοῦ μου*) stand to (β) *ἡ πόλις ἡ ἁγία Ἰερ. καινή* (= *ἡ πόλις τοῦ θεοῦ μου*). Are they really different or are they identical? They are closely related in the mind of our author, but *they are not identical.*

(α) The first, *i.e. ἡ πόλις ἡ ἁγία Ἰερουσαλήμ*, is the seat of the Millennial Kingdom. It contains the tree of life (ii. 7, xxii. 2). At the close of the Millennial Kingdom and before the Final Judgment, when both the heaven and the earth vanish, its removal from the earth is presupposed together with Christ and the glorified martyrs. This removal from the earth is not expressly stated, but it is undoubtedly presupposed. There are analogous expectations in contemporary Judaism. Thus in 2 Bar. vi. 6–10 it is said that even the sacred vessels of the Holy of Holies were removed by angels before the destruction of Jerusalem in 70 A.D. For an analogous account see 2 Macc. ii. 4–8. In 4 Ezra vi. 2–3, iii. 6, moreover, where the main source (= S: see Box) identifies the heavenly and earthly Paradises, Paradise, which had been prepared by God before the creation of the world, was placed afterwards on the earth as Adam's abode, iii. 6, but withdrawn after Adam's fall (see Box on *4 Ezra*, p. 197). Hence we might reasonably conclude that it is the same city—the Holy City, Jerusalem—that is spoken of in xxi. 10 sqq. and in xxi. 2, but *that it has been transformed* (καινή) in order to adapt it to the new heaven and the new earth. Further, in this connection we might remark that just as the Heavenly Jerusalem is associated with the manifestation of Christ on earth in our text, so also we find the same association in 4 Ezra vii. 26, xiii. 36. It is true that Box rejects both these passages as interpolations. But if it was believed that the heavenly Paradise had come down to earth to be Adam's abode, there could be no objection to the hope that the Heavenly City should come down to be the abode of the Messiah.

(β) But, though the Holy City, Jerusalem, has been removed from the earth before the Final Judgment, when the former heaven and earth vanish into nothingness, this city is not to be absolutely identified with "the Holy City, New Jerusalem," which comes down from the new heaven to the new earth to be the *everlasting* abode of the blessed. This new city is either wholly new in every respect, or it is the former city *transformed*. It belongs to the new creation, xxi. 5^b. As opposed to the former Holy City, this Holy City is "new" (καινή); that is, it is here contemplated not under aspects of time but of *quality*: it is new as set over against that which is in some respects materialistic, or outworn, or marred, or unfit.

In β, as we have already remarked, there is an identification of ἡ καινὴ Ἰερουσαλήμ (iii. 12) and ἡ πόλις τοῦ θεοῦ. It seems as if β is distinguished also in another respect from α. There is no mention of the presence of the tree of life in β, though this is a characteristic feature of α. But the tree of life is unnecessary in β, since death itself is wholly at an end, xxi. 4^b, and the blessed live in the light of God's presence and reign for ever and ever, xxii. 5.

In the conception of the New Jerusalem our author has fused together 1 and 2 and discarded 4 (see above). But these ideas were originally very different, as the following notes will show.

1. *The city of God.*—The idea of the heavenly city or the *city of the gods*, found in many nations of the ancient world, was taken over by Judaism.

The city of the gods was originally suggested by the heaven with the sun and moon and the twelve signs of the Zodiac and the twelve gates through which they were conceived to pass, on the north three gates, on the east three gates, on the south three gates, and on the west three gates. There was also the great Milky Way, which was conceived as the great street of the heavenly city.

It has been said that our author had before him the description of Ezekiel's city (Ezek. xlviii. 31 sqq.) with its twelve gates, three in each of the four walls, and that this description with the enumeration of the twelve precious stones in the high priest's breastplate (Ex. xxviii. 17 sqq., xxxix. 10 sqq.) was all that our author drew upon in the ideas and facts of the past for his own description of the Heavenly City. But our text itself refutes such a view. For the fact that in this city are twelve gates,[1] which are respectively composed of the twelve precious stones, shows that some of the ideas in our text go back ultimately to the heavenly city itself. There is some hint of this connection in 1 Enoch lxxii. 2 sqq., lxxv. 6, lxxxii. 4 sqq., where there are said to be twelve portals in the heaven through which the sun, moon, and stars go forth at different seasons. The connection is here very slight, but the connection between these gates and the precious stones mentioned in our text recalls the fact that Philo (*De Monarchia*, ii. 5 : cf. *Vita Mos.* iii. 14) and Josephus (*Ant.* iii. 7. 7) interpret the twelve precious stones on the breastplate of the high priest of the signs of the Zodiac ; and Kircher (*Oedipus Aegyptiacus*, 1653, II. ii. 177 sq.) has shown that according to Egyptian and Arabian monuments these stones correspond to these signs.

The peculiar shape of the city, that it is equally long, broad, and high, may possibly be explained from this standpoint ; for to the human vision the heaven appears to be of this character. We might here compare the Holy of Holies in Solomon's Temple, which was a cube, being 20 cubits each way : cf. 1 Kings vi. 20.

But our author disassociates (see p. 167 sq.) the Heavenly Jerusalem from this ethnic conception of the city of the gods, which had impressed itself slowly, and perhaps for the most part imperceptibly, on the Judaism of the past. As the stars were naturally compared with precious stones, and as we have just seen that a clear association between the signs of the Zodiac and certain precious stones was established before the Christian era, it is not improbable that in Isa. liv. 11–12, where the earthly Zion is referred to, we have traces of the heavenly city :

"Behold I will set thy bases in rubies,
And thy foundations in sapphires.
And I will make of jasper thy pinnacles,
And thy gates of carbuncles, and all thy border of jewels"

(Box's translation) ; and also in Tob. xiii. 16–18,

"And the gates of Jerusalem shall be builded with sapphire and emerald,

[1] The Babylonians were already familiar with the idea of heavenly gates ; see Zimmern, *KAT*³, p. 619.

And all thy walls with precious stones.
The towers of Jerusalem shall be builded with gold,
And their battlements with pure gold.
The streets of Jerusalem shall be paved
With carbuncle and stones of Ophir,
And the gates of Jerusalem shall utter hymns of gladness,
And all her houses shall say, Hallelujah."

In a much later work, Sibyll. Or. v. 420 sq., we find

καὶ πόλιν ἣν ἐπόθησε θεός, ταύτην ἐποίησεν
φαιδροτέραν ἄστρων τε καὶ ἡλίου ἠδὲ σελήνης.

Now from the contents of these passages it appears clear that we have to do not with the heavenly city of God, but with the earthly Jerusalem, and yet the descriptions reflect the characteristics of the heavenly city.[1]

2. *Paradise.* — Paradise[2] is very variously conceived at different times and in different writings. First of all the term is used of the Garden of Eden in Gen. ii.–iii. In the 2nd cent. B.C. it has become the abode of the righteous and elect after this life, and is called the Garden of Righteousness, or of the Righteous, or the Garden of Life, 1 Enoch lx. 8, 23, lxi. 12, and is situated at the ends of the earth, lxv. 2, cvi. 8 (lxxxix. 52), or on the N.W., lxx. 3, lxxvii. 3, or to the east of the seven great mountains, xxxii. 1–2, xxiv. 1–4 sqq. In Test. Levi xviii. 10, 2 Bar. li. 10–11, 2 Enoch ix. 1 sqq., xlii. 2–4, Paradise does not become the abode of the righteous till the Advent of the Messiah or the last judgment, 1 Enoch xxii. In nearly all these passages it is the heavenly and not the earthly Paradise that is meant, or rather the earthly Paradise has assumed a heavenly character. In 2 Enoch viii. 1–6 the heavenly and earthly Paradises are mentioned in succession. The earthly Paradise was created on the third day, Jub. ii. 7, 2 Enoch xxx. 1, whereas according to later Judaism the heavenly Paradise is described as existing before the world either actually or in the thought of God, Pesach. 54^a; Ned. 39^b.

In 4 Ezra (source S) the heavenly and the earthly Paradises are identified. This Paradise was prepared by God before the Creation as Adam's first abode, iii. 6 (cf. 2 Bar. iv. 3), but afterwards withdrawn from the earth and reserved for the righteous after the final Judgment. In this author Paradise has become identical with heaven and is set over against Gehenna, 4 Ezra

[1] See Zimmern, *KAT*^{3}, p. 619; Gunkel, *Zum Verständniss des NT.*, p. 48 sqq.; Bousset *in loc.*; Jeremias, *Babylonisches im NT.*, p. 68.

[2] The Talmudists are almost unanimous in maintaining that there was both a heavenly and an earthly Paradise. The Rabbis distinguish between Gan and Eden. Thus Samuel bar Naḥman declares that Adam dwelt only in the Gan, whereas no mortal eye had ever seen Eden (Ber. 34^b).

vii. 36–38, 123. See Box, *4 Ezra*, 195 sqq. But in 2 Bar. iv. 3 the two Paradises are distinguished apparently; for Adam did not live in the heavenly Paradise, but only enjoyed the vision of it before his fall.

3. *The New Jerusalem.*—In the O.T. such passages as Isa. liv. 11 sq., lx. 10–14, Hag. ii. 7–9, Zech. ii. 1–5, refer only to the earthly Jerusalem, though in Isa. liv. this conception has been influenced by the conception of the city of God. In Tob. xiii. 16–18 this influence is still clearer, while in 2 Bar. iv. 2–4 the heavenly Jerusalem is definitely affirmed and distinguished from the earthly and likewise from Paradise. But it is an error to suppose, as some do, that it was only after the destruction of the earthly Jerusalem that the idea of the heavenly was evolved, for we find it clearly stated early in the second century B.C. in 1 Enoch xc. 29, where God Himself builds what is symbolically called "the New House" on the site of the earthly Jerusalem, which He had removed. In 2 Bar. iv. 3 the manifestation of this city is connected with the manifestation of God, just as in 4 Ezra vii. 26, xiii. 36 the heavenly Zion is to appear along with the Messiah, and in our own text the Holy City, Jerusalem, with Christ and the glorified martyrs. If the heavenly Paradise could appear on earth for Adam, it was only natural that the heavenly Jerusalem should appear on earth for Christ—the Second and greater Adam. Finally, we should observe that the transference of the tree of life from Paradise to Jerusalem, 1 Enoch xxv. 4–5, implies the identification even at this early date of Paradise and Jerusalem: also in Test. Dan v. 12,

> "And the saints shall rest in Eden (*i.e.* Paradise),
> And in the New Jerusalem shall the righteous rejoice."

καταβαίνουσαν . . . τοῦ θεοῦ. For parallel phrases in our author see above, p. 155.

τὴν δόξαν τοῦ θεοῦ. See note on 23, xviii. 1.

11. ὁ φωστὴρ αὐτῆς = "the light thereof." This phrase is practically equivalent to that which immediately precedes, *i.e.* *ἔχουσαν τὴν δόξαν τοῦ θεοῦ*. The city is lighted up by the glory of God Himself, and this light was "like a most precious stone as it were a jasper (*ὅμοιος λίθῳ τιμιωτάτῳ, ὡς λίθῳ ἰάσπιδι*). *ὁ φωστὴρ αὐτῆς* does not mean "the luminary thereof" and is not equivalent to *ὁ λύχνος αὐτῆς* in 23, but is to be rendered as given above. This is clear when the words that follow *ὅμοιος λίθῳ . . . ὡς λίθῳ ἰάσπιδι* are compared with iv. 3, where "He that sat on the throne" is described as being "to look upon like a jasper stone" (*ὅμοιος λίθῳ ἰάσπιδι*). Thus the light that pervades the Holy City is in colour like to that which flashes through the nimbus that surrounded the throne of God (iv. 3). Moreover, we are told that it is the glory of God that gives light to the city (xxi. 23, ἡ γὰρ δόξα τοῦ θεοῦ ἐφώτισεν αὐτήν). This use of φωστήρ = light, is very rare. Cf. 1 Esdr. viii. 79. Thayer quotes *Anthol.* 11. 359 as another instance of this use.

12. ἔχουσα = ἔχει. See p. 155 *ad fin.* The second ἔχουσα is an ordinary participle.

τεῖχος. Cf. 2 Enoch lxv. 10, "And there shall be to them a great wall that cannot be broken down."

πυλῶνας δώδεκα. Twelve gates, as in the city of Ezekiel: cf. Ezek. xlviii. 30 sqq., corresponding to the Twelve Tribes. In 1 Enoch xxxiii.–xxxv. there is a similar distribution of the gates of heaven whence the stars issue. In Classical Greek πυλών meant a gatehouse, gatetower, or porch, and was, therefore, distinct from πύλη. It has this meaning in Acts xii. 13, τὴν θύραν τοῦ πυλῶνος: cf. *ibid.* xii. 14; Matt. xxvi. 71. But it came in late Greek (see the LXX) to mean simply a large gate: cf. Luke xvi. 20; Acts x. 17, xiv. 13. It is in this sense that it appears to be used by our author—in all eleven times. This is clear from xxi. 21, οἱ δώδεκα πυλῶνες δώδεκα μαργαρῖται. He does not use πύλη. In the LXX πυλών is often used as a rendering of פֶּתַח and sometimes of שַׁעַר, while πύλη very often renders שַׁעַר and sometimes פֶּתַח. Hence it is no guide here. It is noteworthy that whereas the Fourth Gospel does not use πυλών or πύλη, it employs θύρα many times in the same sense (x. 1, 2, 7, 9, xviii. 16, xx. 19), as does our author (iii. 8, 20, iv. 1).

ἀγγέλους δώδεκα. Cf. Isa. lxii. 6, "I have set watchmen upon thy walls, O Jerusalem."

ὀνόματα ἐπιγεγραμμένα κτλ. The twelve gates are entrusted respectively to the Twelve Tribes, and the names of the latter inscribed respectively on these gates, as in Ezek. xlviii. 31, "The gates of the city (LXX, πύλαι τῆς πόλεως) shall be after the names of the tribes of Israel." If the gates bear the names of the Twelve Tribes, the names of the Twelve Apostles (14) are engraven on the foundations. Thereby the Seer maintains the continuity of the O.T. and the Christian Church.

13. The order of the points of the compass in this verse are E.N.S.W., whereas in Num. ii. 3 sqq. it is E.S.W.N. and in Ezek. xlviii. N.E.S.W. How the gates were respectively inscribed we have no means of determining.

14. τεῖχος . . . ἔχων. See above, p. 155 *ad fin.*

θεμελίους δώδεκα. Since there are twelve gates, the wall surrounding the City is divided into twelve sections, each section of which rests upon a single foundation stone. These twelve foundation stones consist of twelve precious stones, which are enumerated in 19 sq., and form apparently an unbroken and continuous basement.

ἐπ᾽ αὐτῶν δώδεκα ὀνόματα τ. δώδεκα ἀποστόλων. Elsewhere in the N.T. we have a similar combination of the Christian and Jewish Churches. In Matt. xix. 28, καθήσεσθε καὶ ὑμεῖς ἐπὶ δώδεκα θρόνους κρίνοντες τὰς δώδεκα φυλὰς τοῦ Ἰσραήλ, which may contain a reminiscence of T. Jud. xxv. 1. A remote parallel is to be found in Eph. ii. 20, ἐποικοδομηθέντες ἐπὶ τῷ θεμελίῳ τῶν ἀποστόλων καὶ προφητῶν, ὄντος ἀκρογωνιαίου αὐτοῦ Χριστοῦ Ἰησοῦ. In Eph. the whole spiritual Church is the theme of St. Paul: here it is only the foundations of the wall that encircles the Holy City. We have really a nearer parallel in Heb. xi. 10. ἐξεδέχετο γὰρ τὴν τοὺς θεμελίους ἔχουσαν πόλιν, ἧς τεχνίτης . . . ὁ θεός.

τῶν δώδεκα ἀποστόλων. The Twelve are here referred to as a corporate body, and there is no hint as to its exact composition. "The absence of Paul's name," as Moffatt remarks, "is no more significant than the failure to emphasize that of Peter."

15. This and some of the verses that follow have been suggested by Ezek. xl. 3 sqq. The measuring in each case has to do with the respective ideal cities of the O.T. prophet and the N.T. Seer, and not as in xi. 2, where the actual Jerusalem is referred to. The act of measuring here has none of the meanings given in the note on xi. 1. The measures are given to the Seer in order to elucidate the vision.

16. ἡ πόλις τετράγωνος. Babylon, according to Herodotus (i. 178), was a square (τετράγωνος), each side of the square being 120 stades. The Greeks regarded the square as a symbol for perfection: cf. Simonides in Plato's *Prot.* 344 A, ἄνδρ᾽ ἀγαθόν, χερσί τε καὶ ποσὶ καὶ νόῳ τετράγωνον, ἄνευ ψόγου τετυγμένον, χαλεπὸν ἀλαθέως: Aristotle, *Rhet.* iii. 11. 2, τὸν ἀγαθὸν ἄνδρα φάναι τετράγωνον: cf. *Eth. Nic.* i. 10, 11, ἀγαθὸς ἀληθῶς καὶ τετράγωνος ἄνευ ψόγου. κεῖται = "stood." Cf. iv. 2; Jer. xxiv. 1, δύο καλάθους . . . κειμένους (מוּעָדִים): John ii. 6, xix. 29.

ἐπὶ σταδίους δώδεκα χιλιάδων. This reading, which is that of AQ and most of the cursives, is very difficult. ἐπὶ σταδίους is in itself the usual classical construction, but the genitive (so ℵP) also is found: see Thuc. ii. 90; Xen. *Cyr.* ii. 4. 2, ἐγένοντο τὸ μέτωπον ἐπὶ τριακοσίων . . . τὸ δὲ βάθος ἐφ᾽ ἕκατον. But how, if we adopt the σταδίους, are we to explain δώδεκα χιλιάδων? Winer (p. 244 n.) describes it as a genitive of quality and compares πηχῶν (see Blass, p. 99, n. 1) in the next line. But the cases are not analogous. If it is original, it is perhaps to be rendered "to the length of furlongs of the amount of 12,000." Possibly, however, σταδίους is a primitive error and ℵP have rightly emended the text: ἐπὶ σταδίων δ. χ. = "at 12,000 furlongs." Cf. xiv. 20, ἀπὸ σταδίων χιλίων ἑξακοσίων.

δώδεκα χιλάδων. 12,000 stades = nearly 1500 miles. This is either the length of one side of the square or of the four sides combined, but the words that follow are in favour of the former view. These huge figures are not, of course, to be taken literally. Our Seer is using the language of symbolism. When dealing with the subject of Paradise later Jewish writers make statements of a kindred nature. Amongst the more moderate computations is that found in Sibyll. Or. v. 251 (88–130 A.D.):

ἄχρι δὲ καὶ Ἰόπης τεῖχος μέγα κυκλώσαντες
ὑψόσ' ἀείρονται ἄχρι καὶ νεφέων ἐρεβεννῶν.

Here the circumference of the city would be about 280 miles.

A larger estimate (quoted from Wetstein) appears in the Shir R. vii. 5, where it is said that Jerusalem would be enlarged till it reached the gates of Damascus, and exalted till it reached the throne of God (ix. 1). In the Baba Bathra, 75[b], its height is defined as twelve miles. But the imagination is wholly baffled by the amazing figures in Taanith, 10[a], where the whole world is declared to be the sixtieth part of the Garden, and the Garden the sixtieth part of Eden.

17. ἑκατὸν τεσσεράκοντα τεσσάρων πηχῶν. This wall of 144 cubits is wholly out of proportion in view of the gigantic magnitude of the City. It cannot rightly be described as μέγα καὶ ὑψηλόν in connection with the City, and so it may be either a fragmentary and now unintelligible survival of some archaic element, or else merely a poetical detail, and without symbolic significance. But if we might take the wall as an outer line of defence distinct from the City, then it could well serve as a defence against the entrance of the wicked and unclean (xxi. 27, xxii. 15).

μέτρον ἀνθρώπου ὅ ἐστιν ἀγγέλου. The measures used by the angel are those in common use amongst mankind. This is not unreasonable, since both angels and men are fellow-servants of God (xix. 10, xxii. 9).

18–XXII. 2. This section is in verse, and deals with the appearance and character of the City.

18–21. The materials of which the city is constructed.

18. ἡ ἐνδώμησις . . . ἴασπις. ἐνδώμησις found only here and in Joseph. *Ant.* xv. 9. 6 (ἡ δὲ ἐνδόμησις ὅσον ἦν ἐβάλλετο κατὰ τῆς θαλάσσης διακοσίους πόδας), and in a pre-Christian inscription, τὴν ἐνδώμησιν τοῦ τεμένους (Dittenberger's *Sylloge Inscript. Graec.*[2] 583, 31, quoted from Moffatt), appears to mean materials or fabric. Thus not only was the radiance that came forth from Him that sat on the throne (iv. 3) of a jasper hue, and likewise that of the whole atmosphere of the Holy City (xxi. 11), but the wall itself was constructed of jasper. This structure of jasper was based on twelve precious stones, each of which formed one-twelfth of the entire foundation (cf. 12, 19).

ἡ πόλις χρυσίον καθαρόν κτλ. The city itself was composed of transparent gold.

19. The twelve precious stones which compose the twelve foundations of the wall correspond on the whole to those that were set in gold on the high priest's breastplate in Ex. xxviii. 17–20, xxxix. 10–13 (cf. also Ezek. xxviii. 13 on the dress of the King of Tyre, where, however, in the Hebrew only nine stones are mentioned though twelve are given in the LXX).

Whereas, according to Ex. xxviii. 17 sqq., the names of the Twelve Tribes were written on the twelve stones on the high priest's breastplate, in our text the names of the Twelve Tribes are written, as in Ezek. xlviii. 31, on the twelve gates; but it is the names of the Twelve Apostles that are written on the twelve precious stones which form the foundations of the wall of the City. By means of xxi. 13, where the order in which the angel measured the four sides of the city (*i.e.* E.N.S.W.), and xxi. 19–20, where the twelve stones are enumerated, we are able to discover the probable order in which these foundations were laid. This order has nothing whatever to do with the order given in Ex. xxviii. 17 sqq., as Myers, *Encyc. Bib.* iv. 4811, and Bousset, following the same principle in his commentary, assume; nor is it to be explained from any accidental inversion or misreading of the twelve stones arranged in four lines, each line containing three stones. Bousset's explanation is as follows. Our author read the second three stones in Ex. xxviii. 17 sq. before the first three, and the fourth three before the third three, and thus arrived at the following order:

I.	ἄνθραξ	σάπφειρος	ἴασπις
II.	σάρδιον	τοπάζιον	σμάραγδος
III.	χρυσόλιθος	βηρύλλιον	ὀνύχιον
IV.	λιγύριον	ἀχάτης	ἀμέθυστος.

Next, he or his source had read the stones in I. and II. from right to left, and in III. and IV. from left to right. Now, only in the last resort could such a complicated hypothesis—in itself a confession of failure—be accepted.

While rejecting such an hypothesis, it is advisable to state the actual relations between our text and Ex. xxviii. 17–20. 1. Our author has not followed the LXX of Ex. xxviii. 17 sqq., seeing that his list differs in the renderings of four of the Hebrew words. 2. Our author's list presupposes a transposition of the sixth and twelfth stones, *i.e.* the יַהֲלֹם (=τοπάζιον) and יָשְׁפֵה (=ἴασπις). This was probably the original Hebrew order (see *Encyc. Bib.* iv. 4810). 3. It is not credible that, using as he did the Hebrew text first hand, he should accidentally invert the order of the first and second rows and of the third and fourth, and in addition read the first pair of rows from right to left and the second pair from left to right. *In short, the order of the stones in our text cannot be explained from the order in Ex. xxviii. 7–20.* We have now to discover the grounds which gave rise to the difference in order between our text and Ex. xxviii. 17–20. First of all let us arrange the list of stones in 19–20 in conjunction with the sides of the city as they were measured by the angel.

Now whereas in Num. ii. the tribes are arranged in a square, the sides of which look E.S.W.N., and the gates of the Holy City in Ezek. xlviii. which bear the names of the Tribes are enumerated in the order N.E.S.W., we are tempted to ask why does the angel adopt an apparently capricious order and measure the sides of the Holy City E.N.S.W.? I know of no certain explanation, but it is possible that we may discover some ground for it, if we take the reconstructed list of the Tribes in vii. 5–8 and combine it with xxi. 13. As a result of this combination we have the following result :

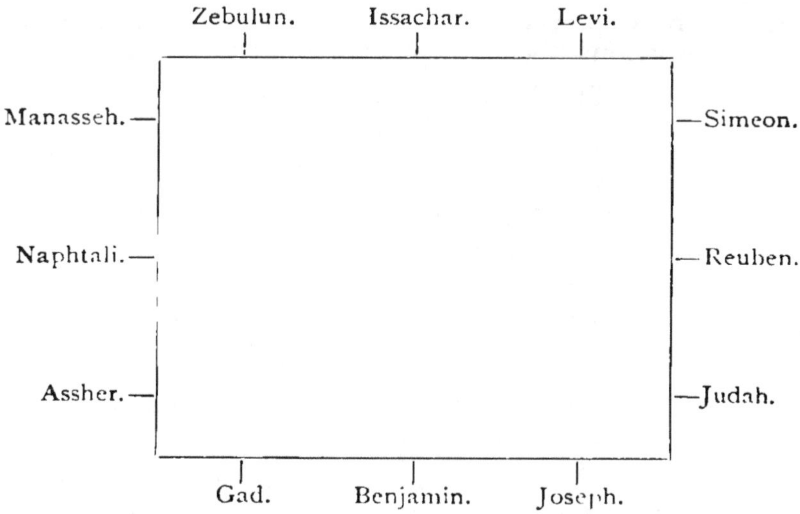

In this diagram we see that the six sons of Leah, *i.e.* Judah, Reuben, Simeon, Levi, Issachar, Zebulun (see vol. i. p. 208), are arranged along the E. and N. Immediately adjoining the children of Leah come the children of Rachel in our author's list, Joseph and Benjamin (see i. 208), and since the S. was preferred to the W. among the Jews, and the angel measures the city in the order E.N.S.W. (xxi. 13), these two must be arranged along the S. Next (see i. 208) come the sons of Leah's handmaid, *i.e.* Gad and Assher. These take the next position of honour, *i.e* S.W.S. and W.S.W.

This solution of the difficulties of vii. 5–8, xxi. 13, 19–20 has this recommendation, that it explains all three passages as part of one coherent conception. If it is rejected, some other explanation must be discovered, else the direction pursued by the angel in measuring the walls—E.N.S.W.—is highly capricious.

The angel measures the walls in the order E.N.S.W. Now, let us take the twelve stones enumerated in 19–20 and beginning with the S.E. corner place the first three on E., which the angel measured first, the second three on N., which the angel measured next, the third three on S., which the angel measured next, and the fourth three on W., as is done below. But it is not till we combine these data with the following fact that we arrive at the solution of the problem. This fact is that, according to Kircher's *Oedipus Aegyptiacus*, II. ii. 177 sq. (1653), each of the twelve precious stones[1] in our text is connected respectively with one of the twelve signs of the Zodiac on Egyptian and Arabian monuments. That this connection was already recognized by the Jews we learn from the express statements of Philo and Josephus (see references in note, p. 159). The following table (from Kircher) gives the connections between the signs and the precious stones

1. The Ram—the amethyst.
2. The Bull—the hyacinth.
3. The Twins—the chrysoprase.
4. The Crab—the topaz.
5. The Lion—the beryl.
6. The Virgin—the chrysolite.
7. The Balance—the sardius.
8. The Scorpion—the sardonyx.
9. The Archer—the smaragdus.
10. The Goat—the chalcedon.
11. The Water-carrier—the sapphire.
12. The Fishes—the jasper.

In the diagram that follows I have placed the precious stones in the order suggested by our text in 13, 19–20 and added the signs of the Zodiac with which they were respectively connected. Now, if we read the signs of the Zodiac as there given in the order prescribed in 19–20 we arrive at the following result. *The signs or constellations are given in a certain order, and that exactly the reverse order of the actual path of the sun through the signs.* Thus we have the Fishes, Water-carrier, Goat, Archer Scorpion, Balance, Virgin, Lion, Crab, Twins, Bull, Ram ; for the order to be followed is that given in xxi. 13, *i.e.* E.N.S.W. But in the apparent movement of the sun, the sun is said when

[1] In Pliny's *H.N.* xxxiii. the definite number twelve is connected with precious stones.

crossing the equator towards the north to be at the first point of the Ram, thirty days later it enters the Bull, and so on through the Twins, Crab, Lion, etc., till it reaches the Fishes. Now *this cannot be an accident.* The conclusion that our author is acquainted with these current beliefs as to the connection of the twelve precious stones with the signs of the Zodiac, and the sun's progress through the signs of the Zodiac cannot in the face of the above facts be questioned, while the further fact that he gives the stones in exactly the reverse order to that required by astronomical science, shows that he regards *the Holy City which he describes as having nothing to do with the ethnic speculations of his own and past ages regarding the city of the gods.* Thus he deliberately disconnects the Holy City with the city of the gods, in which the twelve gates were connected with the twelve precious stones and the signs of the Zodiac, (1) by connecting the gates of the Holy City with the names of the Twelve Tribes, and by representing each gate as composed of a single pearl, and (2) by using the twelve precious stones in an ornamental sense and describing them as engraved with the names of the Twelve Apostles.

Table giving the stones of the foundations in their probable order and their probable equivalents in Ex. xxviii. 17–20.

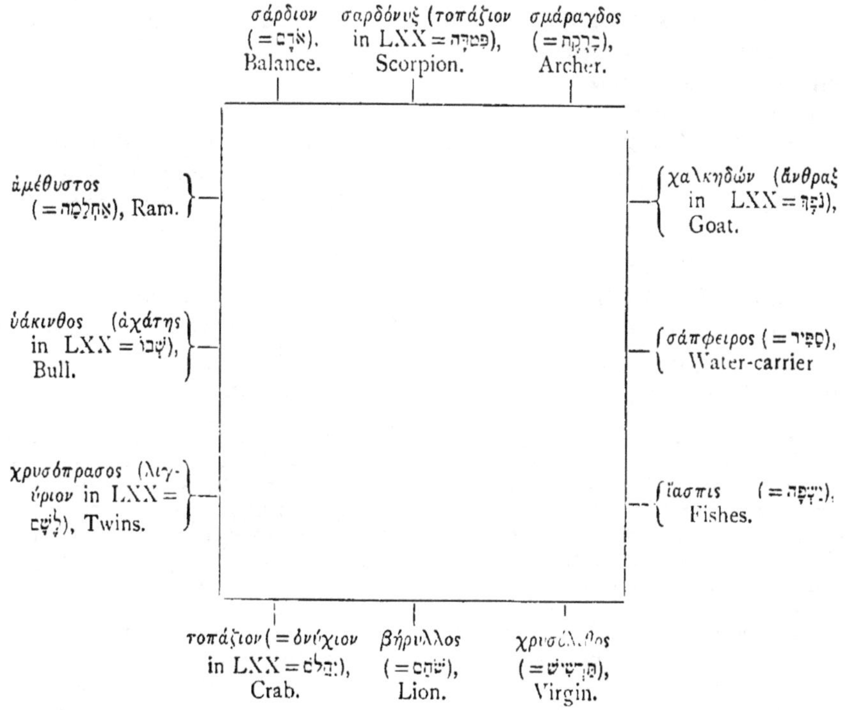

In the above diagram it will be observed that our author has rendered the Hebrew words נפך, פטדה, לשם, and שבו respectively by *χαλκηδών*, *σαρδόνυξ*, *χρυσόπρασος*, and *ὑάκινθος*, whereas the LXX in Ex. xxviii. 17–20 renders them respectively by *ἄνθραξ*, *τοπάζιον*, *λιγύριον*, *ἀχάτης*. Of the twelve stones enumerated in our text[1] three have already been mentioned, the *ἴασπις*, *σμάραγδος*, and *σάρδιον* in iv. 3, while *ὑάκινθος* is implied in ix. 17.

ἴασπις. This was probably of a green or emerald colour. See iv. 3.

σάπφειρος. This stone "is identified (Theophr. 37; cf. 55, *κύανος σκύθης*, and Pliny, *H.N.* xxxvii. 120) with the opaque blue 'lapis lazuli' of Turkestan" (*Encyc. Bib.* iv. 4805).

χαλκηδών. This word occurs only here in Biblical Greek. This gem is taken to be of a green colour (=a copper silicate), and as we have seen already is substituted for *ἄνθραξ* (a red garnet) in the LXX.

σμάραγδος. See note on iv. 3.

20. σαρδόνυξ (=the פטדה). If we may identify this stone with the topaz, it was, according to Strabo (770), translucent and golden coloured (*χρυσοειδὲς ἀποστίλβον φέγγος*) or yellow green; according to Pliny (*H.N.* xxxvii. 8), yellow green (e virenti genere). The LXX renders פטדה by *τοπάζιον* in Ex. xxviii. 17–20. But the *σαρδόνυξ* was properly a variety of the *ὄνυξ* in which the white background was variegated by layers of red or brown (Pliny, *H.N.* xxxvii. 23). But what is the Hebrew?

σάρδιον. See iv. 3 (*n.*).

χρυσόλιθος (=תרשיש). This gold stone is hard to identify: it may be golden yellow and opaque—*i.e.* yellow jasper or yellow serpentine: or it may be golden yellow and translucent (see *Encyc. Bib.* iv. 4807). These stones are described by Pliny, *H.N.* xxxvii. 42, as "aureo fulgore translucentes."

βήρυλλος (=שֹׁהַם). This is thought to be the malachite by Myres in the *Encyc. Bib.* iv. 4808, "with its wavy . . . bands and cloudy patches of light vivid and dark green." In Ex. xxvii. 20, xxxix. 13, שהם is rendered by *ὀνύχιον*.

[1] The identification of the Greek with the Hebrew names for these precious stones is in several cases purely hypothetical. This is in part due to the confusion of the order in the Massoretic. Although the same order in the four rows on the high priest's breastplate is given in Ex. xxviii. 17–20 and xxxix. 10–13 both in the Massoretic and the LXX respectively, yet the LXX implies a transposition of ישפה and יהלם. But the confusion is further aggravated by the two accounts in Josephus, *Ant.* iii. 7. 5 and *Bell.* v. 5, 7, which differ from each other as to the order of the stones in the third and fourth rows, and while the first account gives for the first stone in the first row *σαρδόνυξ*, the second gives *σάρδιον*. Since Josephus states (*Ant.* iii. 7. 5) that the names of the Twelve Tribes were engraven on the stones, each stone having the honour of a name in the order in which they were born, this confusion is all the more disturbing.

τοπάζιον. See under *σαρδόνυξ* above.

χρυσόπρασος. This word, which does not occur in the LXX, which has *λιγύριον*, is the Greek equivalent of לשם. It was probably of a greenish yellow colour. According to Pliny, *H.N.* xxxvii. 20, it was like the beryl but paler: "vicinum genus huic (beryllo) est pallidius, et a quibusdam proprii generis existimatur vocaturque chrysoprasus."

ὑάκινθος (*i.e.* שבו, where LXX has *ἀχάτης*). According to Pliny, *H.N.* xxxvii. 41, it was of a violet colour, resembling the amethyst but less bright: "ille emicans in amethysto fulgor violaceus dilutus est in hyacintho."

ἀμέθυστος (*i.e.* אחלמה)—a transparent purple quartz.

21. οἱ δώδεκα πυλῶνες . . . μαργαρῖται. Cf. Sanh. 100ª: "Rabbi Jochanan sat one day and preached: One day will the Holy One—blessed be He—bring precious stones and pearls thirty cubits long by thirty cubits broad and excavate (openings) in them of ten cubits (in breadth and) twenty cubits in height, and they shall stand in the gates of Jerusalem": cf. also Baba Bathra 75ᵇ. **ἀνὰ εἷς ἕκαστος.** This is a "barbaric" construction: cf. Matt. xxvi. 22, etc. For this distributive use of *ἀνά* cf. iv. 8, John ii. 6; but the *ἀνά* is here an adverb, not a preposition. In *καθ' εἷς* in Mark xiv. 19, Rom. xii. 5 the *κατά* is an adverb also (Robertson, pp. 460, 555). A somewhat parallel construction is found in Eph. v. 33, *καθ' ἕνα ἕκαστος* (Blass, p. 179). **ἡ πλατεῖα.** Probably to be taken generically "the streets," as *ξύλον ζωῆς* in xxii. 2. **χρυσίον καθαρόν.** The whole city is described as "pure gold" in ver. 18. **ὡς ὕαλος διαυγής.** This may be rendered either "transparent as glass" or "as it were transparent glass." The latter is decidedly weak, but either is admissible: cf. i. 14, iv. 6, ix. 9, xv. 2, xxii. 1. *διαυγής* is found only here in the N.T. and not at all in the LXX. It occurs in Philo, Lucian, Plutarch, Apollonius Rhodius.

22. In the Holy City there would be no temple (see note on vii. 15), nor ark of the covenant—the restoration of which was so eagerly looked for by the Jews; for that the Lord God would be the Temple thereof and the Lamb the Ark of the Covenant thereof. The absolute destruction of the earthly temple was foretold by our Lord, Mark xiii. 2; John iv. 21; but even the heavenly temple so often referred to in the earlier chapters would have no place as the Heavenly Jerusalem. This verse like those which precede and follow it was originally a tristich, but some words have been lost after *καὶ τὸ ἀρνίον*. Not improbably the missing words are to be recovered from xi. 19, and thus the last two lines may have run

> *ὁ γὰρ κύριος, ὁ θεὸς ὁ παντοκράτωρ, ναὸς αὐτῆς ἐστίν,*
> *καὶ τὸ ἀρνίον ἡ κιβωτὸς τῆς διαθήκης αὐτῆς.*

The temple that was in the first heaven will disappear (cf. vii. 15, xi. 19). God Himself is henceforth the only Temple, and Christ the Ark of the Covenant. By this restoration the complete parallelism between 22 and 23 is restored. In vii. 9–16 the vision is concerned with the martyr host before the throne of God in heaven, still incomplete and still growing with fresh accessions from the great tribulation on the earth. This host serve God day and night in the temple in heaven, but this temple has no part in the Heavenly Jerusalem: still less in the New; for it belongs to the former things that have passed away (xxi. 4[d]). See note on xxi. 3. In the Ep. Barn. xvi. the idea of anything but a spiritual temple is looked upon with disfavour. Man, when redeemed, forms the habitation of God—"a spiritual temple built up to the Lord" (*πνευματικὸς ναὸς οἰκοδομούμενος τῷ κυρίῳ*).

Our restoration of the missing words *ἡ κιβωτὸς τῆς διαθήκης αὐτῆς* is confirmed by Jer. iii. 16, where it is prophesied that on the advent of the kingdom of God "the ark of the covenant of the Lord" (ארון ברית יהוה) should no longer be thought of nor needed nor restored. That the Jews of the century before the Christian era expected the restoration of the ark on the advent of the kingdom is clear from 2 Macc. ii. 4 sqq., where it is told that the ark had not been destroyed but had been hidden by Jeremiah on Mount Nebo with a view to its safe keeping. That this belief was current in the first century A.D. is to be inferred from 2 Bar. vi. 7–9, where the ark and certain other holy things belonging to the first temple are said to have been hidden by angels in the earth till the Messianic kingdom was established. That this expectation persisted long afterwards in Judaism we learn from Bammidbar rabba 15. For another kindred legend see Yoma, 54[a]. Against such materialistic expectations our author declares boldly that there will be no restoration of the ark of the covenant, for that its place was taken by the Lamb.[1]

23. With the whole verse cf. Isa. lx. 19 sqq., *καὶ οὐκ ἔσται σοι ἔτι ὁ ἥλιος εἰς φῶς ἡμέρας, οὐδὲ ἀνατολὴ σελήνης φωτιεῖ σοι τὴν νύκτα ἀλλ' ἔσται σοι Κύριος φῶς αἰώνιον . . . οὐ γὰρ δύσεται ὁ ἥλιός σοι, καὶ ἡ σελήνη σοι οὐκ ἐκλείψει, ἔσται γὰρ Κύριός σοι φῶς αἰώνιον.* As in Isaiah the sun and moon do not cease to exist: their splendour is simply put to shame by the glory of God Himself: cf. Isa. xxiv. 23. Our author does not seem to have used the LXX here.

οὐ χρείαν ἔχει τοῦ ἡλίου οὐδὲ τῆς σελήνης . . . αὐτῇ: cf. xxii. 5; Isa. lx. 19 sq. Here the glory of God—see 11, *ἔχουσαν τὴν δόξαν*

[1] The ark was at all events a symbol of the divine presence. To the popular mind, however, it was more; it was conceived as the actual abode of Jahveh: cf. Num. x. 35, 36; 2 Sam. xv. 25.

τοῦ θεοῦ (note)—lights up the Heavenly City, and not the sun and moon as we see from the next clause, though these still give light to the world outside the City. Cf. Midrash Tillin, xxxvi. 2, "Neque in mundo futuro necesse habebunt lumen solis interdiu, aut lunae noctu" (Wetstein).

ἡ δόξα τοῦ θεοῦ ἐφώτισεν αὐτήν: cf. 11, xviii. 1. The "glory" of God manifests itself in light. This *δόξα* is probably the זִיו or brightness which went forth from the Shekinah or the glory (יקרא) of God: cf. Targ. Jer. 1 on Ex. xxxiii. 11, זיו אפין, and Jarg. Jon. on Ezek. xliii. 2, where we have "the brightness of His glory" (זיו יקרא). The brightness of Moses' face (זיו איקונין דאנפוי), according to Jarg. Jer. 1 on Ex. xxxiv. 29, was derived from the brightness of the glory of the Shekinah of Yahveh (מן זיו איקר שכינתא דיי). This last expression will explain xviii. 1, where it is said of an angel, *ἡ γῆ ἐφωτίσθη ἐκ τῆς δόξης αὐτοῦ*: cf. xxi. 3, note.

καὶ ὁ λύχνος αὐτῆς τὸ ἀρνίον. Here *ὁ λύχνος αὐτῆς* is the predicate and corresponds to *ἐφώτισεν αὐτήν* in the preceding line, just as *τὸ ἀρνίον* is the parallel to *ἡ δόξα τοῦ θεοῦ*. There is no comparison here with the sun and moon as Bousset suggests.

24–27. The necessity of interpreting these verses with regard to the present earth and the nations surviving the advent of the Millennium has already been pointed out (see p. 146 sqq.). The evangelizing of the nations is already foretold in xiv. 7 by an angel flying in the midst of heaven, and the going up of the nations to worship God is proclaimed as an event of the future by the glorified martyrs in heaven (xv. 4). The Seer at last beholds in vision the fulfilment of these prophecies. Unless we explain xxi. 9–xxii. 2, 14–15, 17 as the Heavenly City which was to come down from heaven to be the seat of the Millennial reign, then the prophecies in xiv. 7, xv. 3 remain unfulfilled.

The conversion of the Gentiles to Judaism was looked for by Zechariah, ii. 11, viii. 23, and the writer of Isa. lxv.–lxvi.; Dan. vii. 14; Tob. xiii. 11, xiv. 6; 1 Enoch x. 21, xc. 32 sqq.; Test. Levi xviii. 9; Test. Jud. xxv. 5; Test. Asher vii. 3; Test. Naph. viii. 4; Pss. Sol. xvii. 32; 4 Ezra xi. 46, amongst other Jewish writers. This expectation became a central truth of Christianity, but the conversion of the heathen nations is to be due, not to Judaism, but to Christianity.

24. This verse consists of a stanza of three lines, the second line of which is corrupt. The whole stanza is based on Isa. lx. 3, 11—not on the LXX of these verses, which runs as follows:

> 3. καὶ πορεύσονται βασιλεῖς τῷ φωτί σου,
> καὶ ἔθνη τῇ λαμπρότητί σου.

11. *καὶ ἀνοιχθήσονται* **αἱ πύλαι** *σου διὰ παντός,*
ἡμέρας καὶ νυκτὸς οὐ κλεισθήσονται
εἰσαγαγεῖν **πρός σε** *δύναμιν* **ἐθνῶν,**
καὶ **βασιλεῖς** *αὐτῶν ἀγομένους.*

The words in heavy type have their equivalents in our text, in 24–25, but our author has here rendered the Hebrew independently of the LXX. We might compare Pss. Sol. xvii. 34–35.

διὰ τοῦ φωτός. Here *διά* may be rendered "amidst" or "by."

25. ἡμέρας † νὺξ γὰρ οὐκ ἔσται ἐκεῖ †. The obelized clause was probably a marginal gloss originally, based on xxii. 5, which subsequently displaced the true text, *καὶ νυκτός.* In xxii. 5 the definite statement is made that there shall be no longer any night at all. That is what we should expect in the New Jerusalem and the new heaven and the new earth. But there are the following objections to this clause in its present context. 1. We should expect *ἡμέρας καὶ νυκτός* as in Isa. lx. 11, on which the text is confessedly based. 2. The parallelism is against it. 24–25 form a tristich occurring in the midst of a succession of tristichs, and the last line of this tristich is formed of 25. Hence instead of

καὶ οἱ πυλῶνες αὐτῆς οὐ μὴ κλεισθῶσιν ἡμέρας, νὺξ γὰρ οὐκ ἔσται ἐκεῖ

we should read

καὶ οἱ πυλῶνες αὐτῆς οὐ μὴ κλεισθῶσιν ἡμέρας καὶ νυκτός.

3. We should then have the familiar phraseology of our author: cf. iv. 8, vii. 15, xx. 10.

It might, of course, be urged that the adverb *ἐκεῖ* justifies the clause in the present context by limiting the statement to the city itself. But this emphatic use of *ἐκεῖ* implies clearly that day and night alternate as usual outside the City. What meaning is then to be attached to *ἡμέρας*? Does this word denote the unbroken day that prevails *within the City*, or the usual period of light without it? The obelized clause introduces hopeless confusion into the context.

26. Based on Isa. lx. 11. See on 24: cf. also lx. 5, "the wealth of the nations shall come unto thee." Here the LXX differs: *ὅτι μεταβαλεῖ εἰς σὲ πλοῦτος θαλάσσης καὶ ἐθνῶν καὶ λαῶν. καὶ ἥξουσίν σοι ἀγέλαι.*

27. The unclean and the abominable and the liars are still on the earth, but, though the gates are open day and night, they cannot enter.

οὐ μὴ εἰσέλθῃ . . . πᾶν κοινόν: cf. LXX of Isa. lii. 1, *οὐκέτι προστεθήσεται διελθεῖν διὰ σοῦ ἀπερίτμητος καὶ ἀκάθαρτος*; xxxv 8, *οὐ μὴ παρέλθῃ ἐκεῖ ἀκάθαρτος*: also Ezek. xliv. 9. That our author is using the Hebrew text and not the LXX is evident here; for though *ἀκάθαρτος* has already occurred four times, he does not use it here but *κοινός*. But there seems to be some primitive error in the text. Alike the passages in the O.T., of which our text is a reminiscence, and the following phrase *ποιῶν βδέλυγμα* lead us to expect *πᾶς κοινός* instead of *πᾶν κοινόν*. Moreover, the final clause *εἰ μὴ οἱ γεγραμμένοι* presupposes only persons to be mentioned here. If this is right, then we should render: "and there shall in no wise enter into it any that is unclean or that maketh an abomination or a lie." כָּל־טָמֵא could represent *πᾶς κοινός* or *πᾶν κοινόν*.

ποιῶν βδέλυγμα. Contrast Babylon (xvii. 4) which was full of *βδελύγματα*: cf. xxi. 8. **ποιῶν . . . ψεῦδος**: and xxii. 15, *πᾶς φιλῶν καὶ ποιῶν ψεῦδος*.

εἰ μὴ οἱ γεγραμμένοι (= כִּי עִם־הכתובים). This construction, as I have pointed out above, implies that only persons should be mentioned in the two preceding lines: *i.e., οὐ μὴ εἰσέλθῃ εἰς αὐτὴν πᾶς κοινὸς καὶ ποιῶν βδέλυγμα*.

τῷ βιβλίῳ τῆς ζωῆς τοῦ ἀρνίου. See notes on iii. 5, xiii. 8.

CHAPTER XXII.

1–2. The description of the Heavenly City that descends from heaven for the Millennial reign is continued in these verses. The *καὶ ἔδειξέν μοι* points back to xxi. 9, 10, where the same phrase occurs. In this vision the spirit of the Seer is actually translated (cf. xvii. 3) to the Heavenly City, which is shown to him by an angel (cf. xvii. 1). There is no such translation of the Seer's spirit in the vision of the New Jerusalem that is to descend from heaven after the Judgment and the creation of the new heaven and the new earth (xxi. 5^a, 4^d, 5^b, 6^a, $1–4^{abc}$, xxii. 3–5). This latter vision is part and parcel of the vision of the Judgment: cf. *καὶ εἶδον* in xxi 1, 2 with the same phrase in xx. 11, 12. In this vision there is no angelic intermediary. The Seer sees the great white throne and Him that sat thereon (xx. 11, 12): he hears God proclaiming the end of the old world and the creation of the new (xxi. 5^a, 4^d, 5^b): he sees the new heaven and the new earth and the descent of the New Jerusalem, and hears a great voice from the throne declaring that God Himself will henceforth abide with men (xxi. 1–3).

1. καὶ ἔδειξέν μοι: cf. i. 1, iv. 1, and the preceding note.

ποταμὸν ὕδατος ζωῆς. Has "the river of the water of life" the same spiritual significance as "the fountains (or 'fountain') of the waters (or 'water') of life" in vii. 17, xxi. 6 and "the water of life" in xxii. 17? It is probable, since the river goes forth from the throne of God, and "the fountains of the waters of life" may be conceived as forming the source of this river in the throne of God. But it is noteworthy that no spiritual significance is attached to this river here, whereas the tree of life (xxii. 2) is full of significance in this respect.

Whatever the relation of "the river of life" and "the fountains of the waters of life" may be in our author, their origin and meaning were originally different. The idea of the river in the Heavenly City springs ultimately from the river in the Garden of Eden (Gen. ii. 10). The object of the river in Eden was simply to supply the garden richly with water. When, however, we come down to Ezekiel, we find that the river which flowed forth from beneath the Temple in the coming Kingdom of God was possessed of healing powers as regards the natural products of the earth (Ezek. xlvii. 8-11). Zechariah (xiv. 8) speaks of these waters as issuing forth from Jerusalem eastward and westward, but attributes no transforming influence to them. Perhaps Ps. xlvi. 5 might be cited here, but both the text and its meaning are uncertain. Lastly, in 2 Enoch viii. 5 it is stated that the river in Paradise in the third heaven flows from beneath the tree of life and divides into four streams of honey and milk and oil and wine. Thus so far as the O.T. and Judaistic literature down to 100 A.D. are concerned, this river in Paradise was not associated with any powers of spiritual transformation such as we find frequently with the phrase "fountain of life" or "water of life."

So far for "the river of the water of life." Turning now to the phrase "fountain of life," we find that this and analogous phrases had in Jewish literature a spiritual significance—cf. Jer. ii. 13; Prov. x. 11, xiii. 14, xiv. 27, xvi. 22; Ps. xxxvi. 10; 1 Enoch xcvi. 6—just as they have in our author.

λαμπρὸν ὡς κρύσταλλον. For *λαμπρός* cf. xv. 6, xix. 8, xxii. 16, and with *ὡς κρύσταλλον* cf. iv. 6, *ὁμοία . . . κρυστάλλῳ*—the two phrases being exact equivalents (see vol. i. p. 36).

2. ἐκπορευόμενον: cf. Ezek. xlvii. 1, *καὶ ἰδοὺ ὕδωρ ἐξεπορεύετο ὑποκάτωθεν τοῦ αἰθρίου κατ' ἀνατολάς*: also 8; Zech. xiv. 8.

τοῦ θρόνου τοῦ θεοῦ καὶ τοῦ ἀρνίου. There is no difficulty in this conception nor is there any ground for regarding *καὶ τοῦ ἀρνίου* with the most recent German critics as an addition. This idea with regard to the Messiah is pre-Christian: cf. 1 Enoch li. 3, "And the Elect One shall in those days sit on My throne." Likewise the Elect One is described as sitting on "the throne of glory, xlv. 3, lv. 4, and as sitting on the throne of His (*i.e.* God's) glory," lxii. 3, 5 (cf. li. 3). Similarly the Lord of Spirits places the Elect One "on the throne of glory" (lxi. 8), "on the throne of His glory," lxii. 2. This throne is called the Son of Man's throne, lxix. 27, 29. Finally, it is to be observed that though the Lord of Spirits places the Elect One on the throne of glory in lxi. 8, and he judges all men, yet in lxi. 9, the praises of all are directed to the Lord of Spirits. On the other hand, in xxii. 3 of our text the phrase *καὶ τοῦ ἀρνίου* may be an addition, though there is no conclusive evidence for so regarding it.

ἐν μέσῳ τῆς πλατείας αὐτῆς. This phrase can be taken either with what precedes or with what follows. 1. In the former case we are to translate as in the R.V. "he shewed me a river . . . in the midst of the street thereof." The next sentence then proceeds: "And on this side of the river and on that." Here *ἐντεῦθεν καὶ ἐκεῖθεν* have a prepositional force as in Dan. xii. 5 (Theod.), *εἷς ἐντεῦθεν τοῦ χείλους τοῦ ποταμοῦ* (הֵנָּה לִשְׂפַת הַיְאֹר): cf. *ἔνθεν καὶ ἔνθεν τῆς κιβωτοῦ*, מִזֶּה וּמִזֶּה לָאָרוֹן, in Jos. viii. 33. According to this view the river runs down the midst of the great heavenly way, and is flanked on either side by the trees of life. 2. But it is possible to take the passage differently and connect the words *ἐν μέσῳ τῆς πλατείας αὐτῆς* with what follows, and treat *ἐντεῦθεν καὶ ἐκεῖθεν* as genuine adverbs (cf. Ezek. xlvii. 7, *δένδρα πολλὰ σφόδρα ἔνθεν καὶ ἔνθεν* (מזה ומזה), and John xix. 18, *ἐντεῦθεν καὶ ἐντεῦθεν*). The resulting construction is quite grammatical but the sense is unsatisfactory: "Between the street of the City and the river on either side of it was there the tree of life." These words presuppose that there was a space between the street and the river, and suggest that they ran side by side. There are two possible ways of conceiving the arrangement of the trees of life. Either these trees are arranged in two rows, one on either bank of the river (one row thus coming between the street and the river), or they are placed on either side of the space that lies between the street and the river. The unsymmetrical character of 2. is certainly against it.

ξύλον ζωῆς. See note on xxii. 14. This expression is used here collectively. In Gen. i. 11 sq. עֵץ is used collectively. Hence our author departs here from the conception of a single tree of life as in Gen. ii. 9, iii. 22; 1 Enoch xxiv. 4, xxv. 4–6—perhaps under the influence of Ezek. xlvii. 7, *καὶ ἰδοὺ ἐπὶ τοῦ χείλους τοῦ ποταμοῦ δένδρα πολλὰ* (עץ רב) *σφόδρα ἔνθεν καὶ ἔνθεν*, and 12, *ἐπὶ τοῦ χείλους αὐτοῦ ἔνθεν καὶ ἔνθεν· πᾶν ξύλον βρώσιμον . . . καὶ ἔσται ὁ καρπὸς αὐτῶν εἰς βρῶσιν καὶ ἡ ἀνάβασις αὐτῶν εἰς ὑγίειαν.*

ποιοῦν καρποὺς δώδεκα. This is suggested by Ezek. xlvii. 12, which speaks of fresh fruit being produced every month.

κατὰ μῆνα ἕκαστον ἀποδιδοῦν τὸν καρπὸν αὐτοῦ. This is a free rendering of Ezek. xlvii. 12, לָחֳדָשָׁיו יְבַכֵּר, where the LXX (AQ, other uncials omitting) has *τῆς καινότητος αὐτοῦ πρωτοβολήσει*—a fact which proves our author's independent use of the Hebrew text. The greater part of this verse is based on Ezek. xlvii. 12.

τὰ φύλλα τοῦ ξύλου εἰς θεραπείαν τῶν ἐθνῶν. Here again our author draws directly from Ezek. xlvii. 12, עָלֵהוּ לִתְרוּפָה, which the LXX has rendered *ἀνάβασις αὐτῶν* (= עֲלֹתָם (?): cf. Ezek. xl. 6) *εἰς ὑγίειαν*. The nations here are those that have survived the visitations in chap. xix. and are evangelized by the inhabitants of the Heavenly City.

14–15. This is the next fragment of the description of the Heavenly City which is to be the seat of the Millennial Kingdom. The persons referred to here are the nations who are contemporaries of this kingdom.

14. οἱ πλύνοντες τὰς στολὰς αὐτῶν. See additional note on vi. 11, vol. i. p. 187 sq.

The phrase is the equivalent spiritually of *οἱ νικῶντες*. Each class alike has endured and overcome, and as access to the tree of life is here promised to those who have cleansed their robes, so in ii. 7 the right to eat of the tree of life is given to those who have overcome.

ἵνα ἔσται . . . καὶ . . . εἰσέλθωσιν. On this combination of the future and subjunctive cf. iii. 9. *ἵνα* is frequently followed by the future in our author: cf. vi. 4, 11, viii. 3, ix. 5, xii. 6, xiii. 12, xiv. 13.

The *καί* here = "and so"; for the faithful must first enter the City before they can eat of the tree of life: "that they may have the right to the tree of life and so may enter, etc." To *ἵνα ἔσται ἡ ἐξουσία αὐτῶν ἐπὶ τὸ ξύλον τῆς ζωῆς* we have a remarkable parallel in 1 Enoch xxv. 4, *οὐδεμία σὰρξ ἐξουσίαν ἔχει ἅψασθαι αὐτοῦ μέχρι τῆς μεγάλης κρίσεως*.

τὸ ξύλον τῆς ζωῆς. See note on ii. 7.

15. ἔξω. There can be no question as to the meaning of this term here. Our author clearly states that *outside* the City or the gates of the City are all classes of sinners. We might compare Ps. ci. 7, "He that worketh deceit shall not dwell within my house." In the Pss. of Solomon xvii. 29 the writer declares of the Messiah:

> "And he shall not suffer unrighteousness to lodge in their midst,
> Nor shall there dwell with them any that knoweth wickedness."

Nay, more, like Joel iii. 17 (*ἀλλογενεῖς οὐ διελεύσονται δι' αὐτῆς οὐκέτι*) the writer of this Psalm maintains the exclusion of the Gentiles in 31, "And the sojourner and the alien shall dwell with them no more." But in our author race distinctions are taken no account of. Character alone is decisive of a man's fitness or unfitness.

οἱ κύνες. If we compare this verse with xxi. 8 we observe that they are practically doublets. Thus the οἱ φαρμακοὶ καὶ οἱ πόρνοι καὶ οἱ φονεῖς καὶ οἱ εἰδωλολάτραι as well as πᾶς ποιῶν ψεῦδος are repeated almost verbally in xxi. 8. To τοῖς δειλοῖς καὶ ἀπίστοις in xxi. 8 there is no equivalent, but we may reasonably infer with Swete that the κύνες of the verse before us denote the same persons as the ἐβδελυγμένοις in xxi. 8. In other words, the persons referred to were either heathens or Jews stained with the abominable vice which excluded them from the Heavenly Jerusalem, the Spiritual Israel. Anciently the word was used to denounce the moral impurities of heathen worship: cf. Deut. xxiii. 18, "Thou shalt not bring the hire of a whore or the wages of a dog unto the house of the Lord thy God." Here "dog" is the technical term for a קָדֵשׁ, or male prostitute, according to the inscription in the temple of Astarte at Larnaka. It was likewise employed by the Jews of the 1st century A.D. to designate the heathen: cf. Matt. xv. 22 sq. In Phil. iii. 2 St. Paul applies the term to the Judaizing faction in the Christian Church (βλέπετε τοὺς κύνας). See Lightfoot, who well paraphrases iii. 2–3: "*We* are the children, for we banquet on the spiritual feast which God has spread before us: *they* are the dogs, for they greedily devour the garbage of carnal ordinances, the very refuse of God's table."

On οἱ φαρμακοὶ . . . καὶ οἱ εἰδωλολάτραι see xxi. 8 (notes).

πᾶς φιλῶν καὶ ποιῶν ψεῦδος. Cf. xxi. 8, πᾶσι τοῖς ψευδέσιν. Unless we attach to ποιῶν here the sense of doing with regard to a certain object or end, we should have an anticlimax in the phrase before us. The meaning then would be: "every one that loveth and maketh falsehood his systematic object." In this case ὁ ποιῶν ψ. would differ from ὁ πράσσων ψ. The latter would mean simply "one who tells lies," "one who practises lying," whereas the former would mean rather "one who lies deliberately with an object" (see Plato, *Charmides*, 162*d*, on this meaning of ποιεῖν as distinguished from πράσσειν). The φιλῶν ψεῦδος denotes one who loves lying for its own sake. Here we might compare Rom. i. 32, οὐ μόνον αὐτὰ ποιοῦσιν ἀλλὰ καὶ συνευδοκοῦσιν τοῖς πράσσουσιν.

17. This is the last verse belonging to the description of the Heavenly Jerusalem, xxi. 9–xxii. 2, 14–15, 17. It cannot belong to any other section of the work. It deals with the evangelization of the heathen nations as foretold in xiv. 7, xv. 4, and implied in xi. 15.

This expectation is in harmony with most O.T. prophecies—as in the Second Isaiah, Haggai, Zechariah, Daniel, and also in the Apocryphal literature—in Sirach, 1 Enoch, Testaments XII Patriarchs. See my *Eschatology*, and Wicks, *The Doctrine of God* (in the indexes of both).

τὸ πνεῦμα. πνεῦμα has many different meanings in our author. 1. Either alone, as in xiii. 15, or with ζωῆς appended, xii. 11, it simply means "life." 2. It means personalized living beings either (*a*) as angels, τὰ πνεύματα τοῦ θεοῦ, iii. 1, iv. 5, v. 6: (*b*) as men, though in the passages that follow it is the spiritual element that is alone emphasized, ἐν πνεύματι, i. 10, iv. 2, xvii. 3, xxi. 10, ὁ θεὸς τῶν πνευμάτων τῶν προφητῶν, xxii. 6: (*c*) as unclean spirits or demons, πνεύματα ἀκάθαρτα, xvi. 13, xviii. 2, πν. δαιμονίων, xvi. 14. 3. It means the Spirit of Christ. Thus in τὸ πνεῦμα λέγει, ii. 7, 11, 17, 29, iii. 6, 13, 22, xiv. 13[c] (where ναί, λέγει τὸ πνεῦμα—the utterance of the Seer—answers like an echo the voice from heaven in xiv. 13[ab]) it is the Spirit of Christ speaking through the Seer. For in all the Seven Letters the Speaker is Christ: cf. ii. 1, 8, 12, etc. Similarly in the present passage, xxii. 17, it is the Spirit of Christ that is speaking through John. Thus the entire phrase τὸ πνεῦμα καὶ ἡ νύμφη means concretely "Christ and the Church in the Heavenly Jerusalem"—that is the Church after the Second Advent, not before it: see next note. In such expressions of the prophet the human intermediary is wholly overlooked, and his utterance assigned directly to the Spirit, just as in the O.T. the prophet introduced his message with the words: "Thus saith the Lord." We might compare 1 Tim. iv. 1, where τὸ πνεῦμα ῥητῶς λέγει means in concrete language: "a certain prophet says expressly": cf. Acts xxi. 11.

ἡ νύμφη. In xxi. 9 at the beginning of the description of the Heavenly Jerusalem this City is called ἡ νύμφη: cf. xxi. 2. Thus the term has a double meaning: it can denote either the Heavenly Jerusalem or its inhabitants, *i.e.* the Spiritual Israel, which is to be the Bride of Christ, just as Israel in the O.T. was conceived of as the Bride of Yahweh. It is as the Spiritual Israel, as the Church triumphant in the Heavenly Jerusalem, that the Bride evangelizes the earth afresh—an evangelization which was promised in xiv. 7, xv. 4, and which, when it is accomplished, will make true in fact what was already declared as accomplished in the counsels of heaven in xi. 15, ἐγένετο ἡ βασιλεία τοῦ κόσμου τοῦ κυρίου ἡμῶν καὶ τοῦ Χριστοῦ αὐτοῦ. England can mean either a certain geographical expanse of country or the people who live in it. See xix. 9[a], p. 129.

ἔρχου. Cf. vi. 1. This word seems to be taken universally as the reply of the Church to the voice of Jesus in ver. 12. But, as we have seen above, the Bride is the Heavenly Jerusalem or its blessed inhabitants in the Millennial Kingdom and not the

Church before the Advent. Thus Christ has already come in this vision. Further, in line 17^c, there can be no question that ἐρχέσθω refers to the coming of him that is athirst to Christ. It is, therefore, only natural, apart wholly from the force of the term ἡ νύμφη, to take ἔρχου in 17^ab in the same sense: *i.e.* as the invitation of the Spirit of Christ, of the Heavenly Jerusalem, and of those who accepted the message, to the world of men that were still thirsting for life and truth or were willing to accept them. Cf. John vi. 35, ὁ ἐρχόμενος πρὸς ἐμὲ οὐ μὴ πεινάσῃ, καὶ ὁ πιστεύων εἰς ἐμὲ οὐ μὴ διψήσει πώποτε: vii. 37, ἐάν τις διψᾷ, ἐρχέσθω πρός με καὶ πινέτω. Cf. the Didache, x. 6, in the post-Communion prayer of the Church.

> "Let grace come (ἐλθέτω)
> And let this world go.
> Hosanna to the Son of David,
> If any one is holy, let him come (ἐρχέσθω):
> If any one is not, let him repent.
> Come, Lord (*i.e.* μαραναθά)."

We have here a spiritual adaptation of certain parts of our text. Here, since the Second Advent of Christ is still in the distance, the prayer "Come, Lord" can be taken eschatologically as well as spiritually.

καὶ ὁ ἀκούων κτλ. The call was to be taken up by such as heard it and repented. The hearer is to be regarded as one who heard and accepted. **ὁ διψῶν ἐρχέσθω.** Cf. Isa. lv. 1 (כל־צמא לכו למים); John vii. 37, ἐάν τις διψᾷ, ἐρχέσθω πρός με καὶ πινέτω. Cf. also xxi. 6 of our text.

ὕδωρ ζωῆς δωρεάν. The phrase recurs in xxi. 6 where it rightly has the article τοῦ ὕδατος τῆς ζωῆς δωρεάν—a fact which points to xxi. 6 as really coming later in the text.

CHAPTER XX. 4–15.

§ 1. *Contents.*

This section follows naturally on the elaborate description of the Heavenly Jerusalem, which had come down from heaven to be the abode of Christ and the glorified martyrs. After this vision we have another vision of the glorified martyrs who alone had part in the first resurrection (xx. 4–6). Then, at the close of the Millennial Kingdom, Satan is loosed and leads Gog and Magog to the assault of the Beloved City, whereupon follows their destruction by fire from heaven, and Satan is cast into the lake of fire (7–10). This section closes with a vision of the great white throne, before whose presence the former heaven and earth had vanished, of the raising of the righteous and wicked from the "treasuries" and from Sheol to be judged, and the casting of death and Hades into the lake of fire (11–15).

This section has suffered from a transposition of the text in 4. Most probaby 13 stood originally before 12. Glosses have been added at the close of 12 and 14, and the text tampered with in 13 on dogmatical grounds. 13[a] is meaningless as it stands. 4–15 with the above exceptions comes from the hand of John as we shall now show alike by its diction and idiom. That it forms an organic and indispensable element of the Book is obvious.

§ 2. *Diction.*

4. διὰ τ. μαρτυρίαν Ἰησοῦ καὶ διὰ τ. λόγον τ. θεοῦ: cf. i. 2, 9, vi. 9, xii. 11. οὐ . . . τὸ θηρίον οὐδὲ τ. εἰκόνα αὐτοῦ: cf. xiv. 9. τὸ χάραγμα ἐπὶ τ. μέτωπον καὶ ἐπὶ τ. χεῖρα: cf. xiii. 16. ἐβασίλευσαν κτλ.: cf. v. 10.

5. ἔζησαν = "came to life": cf. ii. 8 (xiii. 14). ἄχρι τελεσθῇ: cf. xv. 8, xvii. 17, xx. 3.

6. ὁ δεύτερος θάνατος: cf. ii. 11, xxi. 8. ἱερεῖς . . . βασιλεύσουσιν: cf. i. 6, v. 10.

7. ἐκ τῆς φυλακῆς: cf. ii. 10 for phrase.

8. πλανῆσαι τὰ ἔθνη: cf. xii. 9, xiii. 14 (xviii. 23), xix. 20, xx. 3, 10. ἐν ταῖς τέσσαρσι γωνίαις τῆς γῆς: cf. vii. 1 for the phrase. συναγαγεῖν αὐτοὺς εἰς τ. πόλεμον: cf. xvi. 14 for the phrase.

10. ὁ διάβολος ὁ πλανῶν: cf. xii. 9, ὁ Σατανᾶς ὁ πλανῶν. ἐβλήθη εἰς τ. λίμνην τοῦ πυρός: cf. xix. 20, xx. 14, 15. ὅπου καί: cf. xi. 8. βασανισθήσονται: cf. ix. 5, xiv. 10. ἡμέρας καὶ νυκτός: cf. iv. 8, vii. 15, etc. εἰς τ. αἰῶνας τ. αἰώνων: cf. i. 6, 18, iv. 9, etc.

11. ἔφυγεν . . . καὶ . . . οὐχ εὑρέθη: cf. xvi. 20, ἔφυγεν καὶ . . . οὐχ εὑρέθησαν. τόπος οὐχ εὑρέθη αὐτοῖς: cf. xii. 8.

12. ἑστῶτας ἐνώπιον τ. θρόνου: cf. vii. 9, ἑστῶτες ἐνώπιον τ. θρόνου, viii. 2, etc. γεγραμμένων ἐν τοῖς βιβλίοις: cf. i. 3. ἐν αὐτῇ γεγραμμένα: xiii. 8, xx. 15, xxi. 27.

13. ἐκρίθησαν ἕκαστος κατὰ τὰ ἔργα αὐτῶν. For ἕκαστος with plural verb cf. v. 8 (cf. John xvi. 32), and for κατὰ τὰ ἔργα, ii. 23.

14. ἐβλήθησαν εἰς τ. λίμνην τοῦ πυρός: cf. 10, 15, xix. 20.

15. εὑρέθη . . . γεγραμμένος: cf. iii. 2 for construction. ἐν τ. βίβλῳ τῆς ζωῆς: cf. iii. 5, xxi. 27.

§ 3. *Idioms.*

4. προσεκύνησαν τὸ θηρίον: see note on vii. 11.

ἐπὶ τὸ μέτωπον καὶ ἐπὶ τ. χεῖρα: see note on xiii. 16, vii. 3.

5. ἄχρι with subj.: cf. ii. 25, note, vii. 4, xv. 8, etc.

6. ἐπὶ τούτων . . . οὐκ ἔχει ἐξουσίαν: cf. ii. 26.

8. ὧν . . . αὐτῶν: cf. iii. 8, vii. 2, 9, ix. 11, etc.

13. ἔδωκεν = "gave up"—a Hebraism in this sense = נתן.

In two cases the text abandons our author's idiom owing to the ignorance of the editor.

4. Abandonment of the author's idiom by insertion of οἵτινες by editor in τῶν πεπελεκισμένων . . . καὶ οἵτινες οὐ προσεκύνησαν. See note on i. 5.

11. τὸν καθήμενον ἐπὶ αὐτοῦ: see note on iv. 2. Our author wrote ἐπὶ αὐτόν, but of our author's unique treatment of this phrase the editor of xxi. 4–xxii. was ignorant.

4–6. *Vision of the glorified martyrs who reign with Christ for a thousand years.*

4. The construction of this verse is difficult. Thus we have two clauses, καὶ ἐκάθισαν ἐπ' αὐτούς, καὶ κρίμα ἐδόθη αὐτοῖς, intervening between εἶδον and its accusative τὰς ψυχάς. But not only is the construction irregular, but the sense is hopelessly uncertain from the standpoint of our author. For if we ask who are those who seat themselves on the thrones, no satisfactory answer can be given. It is not the glorified martyrs; for they are first referred to in the words τὰς ψυχὰς τῶν πεπελεκισμένων. And yet from iii. 21, where it is said that the martyrs are to share the throne of Christ, we should expect them to be referred to here and to sit on the thrones as Christ's assessors. Somewhat in favour of this view is Christ's promise to His Apostles in Matt. xix. 28, καθήσεσθε καὶ ὑμεῖς ἐπὶ δώδεκα θρόνους. Likewise in Dan. vii. 9 (LXX Theod.), ἐθεώρουν ἕως ὅτε (ὅτου, Theod.) θρόνοι ἐτέθησαν, and vii. 26 (Theod.), τὸ κριτήριον ἐκάθισεν (LXX, ἡ κρίσις καθίσεται), and vii. 22 (Theod.), καὶ τὸ κρίμα (LXX, τὴν κρίσιν) ἔδωκεν (+ τοῖς, LXX) ἁγίοις (+ τοῦ, LXX), ὑψίστου, we have passages which not only speak of the function of judgment as assigned by the Most High to the saints, but appear to have suggested the clauses in our text. Cf. 1 Cor. vi. 2 sq., οὐκ οἴδατε ὅτι οἱ ἅγιοι τὸν κόσμον κρινοῦσιν . . . ὅτι ἀγγέλους κρινοῦμεν.

Thus owing both to the ungrammatical structure of the text and its unintelligibleness it is not improbable that θρόνους, καὶ ἐκάθισαν ἐπ' αὐτούς καὶ κρίμα ἐδόθη αὐτοῖς καὶ was originally a marginal gloss based on Daniel, or rather that this passage has got displaced and should be restored after καὶ ἐπὶ τὴν χεῖρα αὐτῶν. By adopting the latter alternative, as the present editor has done, we restore sanity to the text by making it at once grammatical and intelligible, and recovering the lost parallelism of the passage: *i.e.*

καὶ εἶδον τ. ψυχὰς τ. πεπελεκισμένων διὰ τ. μαρτυρίαν Ἰησοῦ
  καὶ διὰ τ. λόγον τοῦ θεοῦ,
καὶ [οἵτινες] οὐ προσεκύνησαν τὸ θηρίον
  οὐδὲ τ. εἰκόνα αὐτοῦ,
καὶ οὐκ ἔλαβον τὸ χάραγμα ἐπὶ τὸ μέτωπον
  καὶ ἐπὶ τ. χεῖρα αὐτῶν
<καὶ εἶδον> θρόνους καὶ ἐκάθισαν ἐπ' αὐτους
  καὶ κρίμα ἐδόθη αὐτοῖς.

This signifies that authority is now vested in the hands of the righteous, and not in those of the oppressors of the Church as aforetime.

τῶν πεπελεκισμένων, *i.e.* beheaded by the *πελεκύς*—the instrument of capital punishment in republican Rome. Cf. Diod. Sic. xix. 101, *ῥαβδοίσας ἐπελέκισε κατὰ τὸ πάτριον ἔθος*. Joseph. *Ant.* xiv. 7. 4, *Σκιπίων δέ, ἐπιστείλαντος αὐτῷ Πομπηίου ἀποκτεῖναι Ἀλέξανδρον τὸν Ἀριστοβούλου, αἰτιασάμενος τὸν νεανίσκον ἐπὶ τοῖς τὸ πρῶτον εἰς Ῥωμαίους ἐξημαρτημένοις τῷ πελέκει διεχρήσατο*. In vi. 9, xviii. 24 we find *ἐσφαγμένων*, the word used in connection with the Lamb that was sacrificed, v. 6, 9, 12, xiii. 8.

διὰ τ. μαρτυρίαν Ἰησοῦ καὶ διὰ τ. λόγον τ. θεοῦ. These phrases are found in the opposite order in i. 2, 9, vi. 9. Cf. xii. 11.

[οἵτινες] οὐ προσεκύνησαν κτλ. These had all suffered martyrdom according to xiii. 15. The clause gives a further definition of those who had been faithful unto death. To regard these as forming a second class of the faithful, *i.e.* the surviving faithful, is against the actual statement in xiii. 15, and the presuppositions that underlie xiv.–xix. (see pp. 4, 26, 40, 96 *ad fin.*) and also against the immediate context; for in that case we should have to attach two conflicting meanings to *ἔζησαν* which immediately follows: *i.e.* "lived again" and "continued to live" according as we connect it with the first class, the actual martyrs, or the second class, the confessors. Moreover, the opening words of 5, *οἱ λοιποὶ τῶν νεκρῶν*, clearly imply that the persons referred to in 4 were among the *νεκροί* according to the usual phraseology.

[οἵτινες]. This is probably an addition made by the disciple who edited these last chapters. See note on i. 5^b–6. By its omission we should recover our author's *normal* resolution of the participle into a finite verb, *i.e.* *τ. πεπελεκισμένων . . . καὶ οὐ προσεκύνησαν* = "who had been beheaded and had not worshipped."

προσεκύνησαν τὸ θηρίον κτλ. See vii. 11 *n.*

τὸ χάραγμα ἐπὶ τ. μέτωπον καὶ ἐπὶ τ. χεῖρα. See xiii. 16 (*n.*), vii. 3 (*n.*).

ἔζησαν, *i.e.* "came to life" (cf. ii. 8, xiii. 14; Rom. xiv. 9) in human parlance, though in their life in heaven they had been more truly alive than when they had been on earth. With this first resurrection or manifestation of the glorified martyrs in the Millennial Kingdom we should compare that of all the departed saints with Christ in 1 Thess. iv. 14–17, and that of certain saints who had been taken up alive into heaven in 4 Ezra vii. 28 (cf. vi. 26). This line resumes briefly the preceding eight lines.

ἐβασίλευσαν μετὰ τοῦ Χριστοῦ χίλια ἔτη. Cf. v. 10. The earliest authorities for the belief in a temporary kingdom of the Messiah are 1 Enoch xci.–civ. (xciii. 1–14, xci. 12–19), Pss. Sol. xi., xvii.; Sibyll. Or. iii. 1–62; Jub. xxiii. 27–29, 31, 11; 2 Bar. xxx., xl. 3, lxxiv. 2, xii. 34; 1 Cor. xv. 23–28. The limits assigned to its duration are various. In 4 Ezra vii. 28 sq. this kingdom is to endure for four hundred years, and to come to a close with the death of the Messiah and all His companions, and the world is to return to primeval silence—a statement apparently without parallel for its explicitness in Jewish literature. In 2 Bar. xxx., on the other hand, Christ returns in glory to heaven at the close of the Messianic reign. In 2 Enoch xxxii. 2–xxxiii. 2 there is a reference to a period of Sabbatic rest of a thousand years after the close of six thousand years of the world's history. Barnabas, *Ep.* xv. 2–8, accepts this view, and adds that the Son of God will appear at the close of the six thousand years to put an end to the reign of the Lawless one, to judge the wicked and to change the sun, moon, and stars. At the close of the Millennial period there will be the beginning of another world (*ἄλλου κόσμου ἀρχήν*). See my *Eschatology*², pp. 248, 250 sq., 270 sq., 301 sq., 330, etc. Weber², 373. The reckoning of a thousand years was based on a combination of Gen. i. 2 and Ps. xc. 4 = 2 Pet. iii. 8. From this it was concluded that as each day of creation stood for a world-day of a thousand years, so the history of the world would embrace a world-week of seven thousand years, six thousand years till the final judgment and a thousand years of blessedness and rest.

5. οἱ λοιποὶ τῶν νεκρῶν οὐκ ἔζησαν. Therefore not even the righteous, who had died a peaceful death, have part in this first resurrection. We should observe that John, who must have been well acquainted with the traditional and current belief, that the righteous survivors would be blessed on the advent of the kingdom, deliberately ignores it. This can only mean, as has been frequently shown in the preceding pages (see p. 183), that John held that there would be no righteous survivors on the advent of the kingdom. The traditional belief is attested in Dan. xii. 12; Pss. Sol. xvii. 50; Sibyll. Or. iii. 371; 1 Thess. iv. 17; 1 Cor. xv. 51–52; Asc. Isa. iv. 15.

αὕτη ἡ ἀνάστασις ἡ πρώτη. This must not be construed in a purely spiritual sense and taken to mean a death to sin and a new birth unto righteousness. 1. The earliest expounders of the Apocalypse, such as Justin Martyr, Tertullian, Irenæus, Hippolytus, and Victorinus, quite rightly take the words in a literal sense of an actual reign of Christ with the glorified martyrs on earth. The spiritualizing method which emanated from Alexandria put an end to all trustworthy exegesis of the Apocalypse, when adopted in its entirety with reference to the Apocalypse. The meaning assigned by the votaries of this method became wholly arbitrary, and every student found in the Apocalypse what he wished to find (see my *Studies in the Apocalypse*, 8, 9, 10, 12, 13, 14, 28, 30, 36, 38, 48, etc.). The earliest expounders were right, as they were in close touch with the apostolic time.

2. Moreover, the Talmud, and other Jewish writings, and specially the Jewish Apocalypses, attest a literal reign—and no other—of the Messiah, so far as they deal with the question.

3. The context itself is wholly against taking the words in a spiritual sense; for (*a*) this resurrection is obviously the guerdon of martyrdom, and begins *not with the beginning of the Christian life but after its earthly close.* (*b*) As Alford rightly urges: "no legitimate treatment of it (*i.e.* the text itself) will extort what is known as the spiritual interpretation now in fashion. If, in a passage where *two resurrections* are mentioned, where certain ψυχαὶ ἔζησαν at the first, and the rest of the νεκροὶ ἔζησαν only at the end of a specified period after the first,—if in such a passage the first resurrection may be understood to mean *spiritual* rising with Christ, while the second means *literal* rising from the grave;—then there is an end of all significance in language, and Scripture is wiped out as a definite testimony to anything." Hence attempts to revive the spiritualizing interpretation of the Millennial Kingdom are to be deplored from every standpoint.

But since the first resurrection embraces only the glorified martyrs, who return to earth to share the Millennial Kingdom with Christ in the Jerusalem which comes down from heaven, it is different in character from the second. For only the faithful who had undergone martyrdom have part in it, whereas at the second resurrection the rest of the faithful and all the unfaithful rise to judgment. As we shall see on xx. 12, these two classes appear before the great white throne, the former, as we must conclude, in their glorified spiritual bodies, and the latter simply as disembodied souls—*i.e.* naked.

6. By meeting martyrdom on behalf of their faith the martyrs are admitted to share in the Millennial Kingdom, are not subject to the second death, and accordingly are exempt from the Judgment that is to follow on the close of the kingdom. Moreover, their priestly character in bringing the knowledge of

God and Christ to the nations during the Millennial Kingdom appears to be referred to in the expression *ἱερεῖς τοῦ θεοῦ καὶ τοῦ Χριστοῦ* (see below).

μακάριος καὶ ἅγιος. *Μακάριος* is used seven times—in each case in connection with a beatitude—cf. i. 3, xiv. 13, xvi. 15, xix. 9, xx. 6, xxii. 7, 14. *ἅγιος* though of frequent occurrence is not used in this connection elsewhere in our author. Hence it is possible, as Wetstein suggests, that *ἅγιος* refers to the blessed in their priestly capacity (*ἱερεῖς τοῦ θεοῦ*) and *μακάριος* in their kingly (*βασιλεύσουσιν*). The combination "blessed and holy" is found in Jub. ii. 23.

ὁ ἔχων μέρος ἐν. Cf. John xiii. 8, *οὐκ ἔχεις μέρος μετ' ἐμοῦ*: also in xxi. 8 in a different form, *τὸ μέρος αὐτῶν*, and xxii. 19.

ἐπὶ τούτων. For *ἐπί* in this sense with the genitive cf. ii. 26 [xi. 6], [xiv. 18].

ὁ δεύτερος θάνατος. This death is defined in xxi. 8 (cf. Matt. x. 28). It is mentioned already in ii. 11 as a punishment, from which those, who are faithful to the end, are exempt. In xx. 14 it is clearly an interpolation.

οὐκ ἔχει ἐξουσίαν. Cf. ii. 26, vi. 8, ix. 3, etc.

ἱερεῖς τοῦ θεοῦ καὶ τοῦ Χριστοῦ. Cf. i. 6, *ἱερεῖς τῷ θεῷ*. Now it is to be observed that in i. 6 (see note *in loc.*), v. 10, and here the priesthood and the kingship of those whom John addressed are conjoined (in 1 Pet. ii. 9 they are combined in one expression, *βασίλειον ἱεράτευμα*). But it is further noteworthy that v. 10 (*ἐποίησας αὐτοὺς . . . βασιλείαν καὶ ἱερεῖς καὶ βασιλεύουσιν ἐπὶ τῆς γῆς*) and the present passage *connect the priesthood with a special period of kingship, i.e.* that which they are to exercise in the Millennial Kingdom, and share with Christ (xx. 6) on the earth (v. 10). These facts suggest that *the priestly offices of the blessed in the Millennial Kingdom have to do with the nations*, who are to be evangelized during this period (xiv. 6–7, xv. 4), and this suggestion receives some support from xxii. 5 where, when the eternal reign of all the saints after the Judgment is mentioned (*βασιλεύσουσιν εἰς τ. αἰῶνας τ. αἰώνων*), there is not the remotest reference to any special or other priesthood of the faithful.

βασιλεύσουσιν μετ' αὐτοῦ. The scene of this reign is given in the proleptic vision, v. 10, as *ἐπὶ τῆς γῆς*.

7–10. *Close of the Millennial Kingdom and of its evangelizing activities. Thereupon follow the loosing of Satan, the march of Gog and Magog—all the faithless upon the earth—against the Beloved City, their destruction by supernatural means, and the casting of Satan into the lake of fire.* The Seer does not say what became of the Heavenly Jerusalem, but its withdrawal from the earth with Christ and the glorified martyrs before the

Judgment is presupposed, while its return to the new earth in a renewed form is definitely stated in xxi. 2. Since "the Beloved City" in xx. 9 is the Heavenly Jerusalem, the saints referred to in the same verse include the risen martyrs and the converts from among the nations.

The same order of events appears in Sibyll. Or. iii. 662–701, *i.e.* the advent of the Messiah, the establishment of His kingdom, the attack of the nations on Jerusalem, and the destruction of the invading hosts by God. In certain sections (A^1, A^2, A^3) of 2 Baruch (1st century A.D.; see my edition, pp. liii. sqq.) the writers look forward to a temporary Messianic kingdom preceded by the Messianic woes, a beneficent domination of the world by the Messiah preceded by the destruction of the antichristian powers, and of such heathen powers as had been in any way associated with them. In the Son of Man Vision in 4 Ezra xiii. the Messianic woes come first (xiii. 30–31), then the manifestation of the Messiah (xiii. 32), the assault of the heathen nations on the Messiah, and their destruction by Him, xiii. 33–34, and the manifestation of the Heavenly Jerusalem, xiii. 36. For yet another scheme of the last things see 4 Ezra iv. 56–v. 13^a, vi. 11–28, vii. 26–44 (Box's edition, p. 111). According to a contemporary of our author, R. Eliezer ben Hyrkanos or R. Eliezer the Great, the woes of the Messiah were to come first, then the day of Gog and Magog, and then the Judgment. If we pass on to the Coptic Apocalypse of Elias (a Jewish work edited by a Christian, 2nd century A.D.) we find the order of events as follows: the destruction of Antichrist and his adherents, the advent of Christ with His saints, the creation of the new heaven and the new earth and the Millennial Kingdom! In the Hebrew Apocalypse of Elijah (3rd century A.D.) Gog and Magog appear after a Messianic reign of forty years. On their annihilation follow the Judgment and the descent of Jerusalem from heaven.

It will be observed that, though each of the works above cited differs in some respect from our text, in some respects they all agree with it.

It is obvious at a glance that our author here forsakes the apocalyptic style and adopts the prophetic. But he has already done so in 6^{cd}, and in 9–10 he reverts to his apocalyptic style. Further, there are no grounds in this section itself for assuming a source, since there is not a single construction at variance with our author's style, though there are new phrases as might be expected in describing new events.

7. λυθήσεται. Cf. *λυθῆναι* in 3 and the same verb in ix. 14 used in the same sense. ἐκ τ. φυλακῆς αὐτοῦ. Cf. ii. 10 [xviii. 2] for the word *φυλακή*.

8. **ἐξελεύσεται** (cf. iii. 12, vi. 2, 4, ix. 3, etc.) **πλανῆσαι τὰ ἔθνη.** In 3 Satan was cast into the abyss, *ἵνα μὴ πλανήσῃ ἔτι τὰ ἔθνη.*

ἐν ταῖς τέσσαρσι γωνίαις τῆς γῆς. Cf. vii. 1 where this phrase has already occurred.

τὸν Γὼγ καὶ Μαγώγ. Three matters call for consideration here: 1. The names. 2. The duplication of the invasion by and the judgment of the heathen nations, *i.e.* before and after the setting up of the Messianic Kingdom. 3. The comprehension of these terms in our text. 1. Magog first appears in Gen. x. 2 as a son of Japheth, but in the Mass. of Ezek. xxxviii. 2 Magog is represented as the land from which Gog came: *i.e.* "Gog of the land of Magog." The LXX (*ἐπὶ Γὼγ καὶ τὴν γῆν τοῦ Μαγώγ*) and Peshitto, however, have "toward Gog and (+'toward,' Pesh.) the land of Magog," a reading which prepares the way for the later view current in Judaism, which conceived Gog and Magog to be two different leaders. In Ezek. xxxix. 6 Magog seems to be the name of a people. Gog is the foe whose invasion from the north had been prophesied by Jeremiah (iii.–vi.) and by Zephaniah (i. 7), but whose coming had hitherto been looked for in vain. The name Gog is undoubtedly ancient; for it is found in the Tel Amarna letters (1400 B.C.) in the form Gâgaja as a designation of the northern nations. In Jubilees viii. 25 the land of Gog is mentioned. Gog is identified with the Scythians by Josephus (*Ant.* i. 6. 1) and by the Chronicles of Jerachmeel (xxxi. 4). In Jub. vii. 19, ix. 8, Magog appears as a son of Japheth, as in Gen. x. 2. The same idea that underlies the LXX of Ezek. xxxviii. 2 is definitely set forth in Sibyll. Or. iii. 512, 519:

> *αἰαῖ σοι, Γὼγ καὶ πᾶσιν ἐφεξῆς ἅμα Μαγώγ . . .*
> *Ὕψιστος δεινὴν ἐπιπέμψει ἔθνεσι πληγήν.*

and 319 sq.:

> *αἰαῖ σοι, χώρα Γὼγ ἠδὲ Μαγὼγ μέσον οὖσα*
> *Αἰθιόπων ποταμῶν, πόσον αἵματος ἔκχυμα δέξῃ.*

By the second century B.C. this invasion of Palestine by the two peoples Gog and Magog was clearly expected.

2. The duplication of the attack on Jerusalem (see p. 46), *i.e.* before and after the establishment of the Messianic Kingdom and of the judgment on the heathen nations. The first attestation of this conception is, of course, in Ezek. xxxvii. 21–xxxix. In xxxvii. 21–28 the kingdom with the Messiah, the son of David, is established after the Captivity. Thereupon follows the final attack of the heathen nations upon it in xxxviii.–ix. In the fragment, 1 Enoch lvi. 5–8, we have a description of such an attack. In 4 Ezra xiii. 5, 8–9, 28–35 there is another account

of this final assault of the heathen nations on the Messiah and on Mount Zion, or the Heavenly City, xiii. 35–36 (cf. 6), just as in our text.

In many of the authorities it is only the hostile heathen hosts that are destroyed: cf. Pss. Sol. xvii. 32; 2 Bar. lxxii. 4; Tobit xiii. 11, xiv. 6 sq.; Sanh. 105a; but in most Jewish writings after 100 A.D. a harsher view prevails as to the future destiny of all the Gentiles.

Gog and Magog are frequently mentioned in Rabbinic works. These nations march against God and the Messiah, Aboda-zara, 3^b. This war and the last judgment were to last twelve months according to the Rabbi Aqiba, Edujoth, ii. 10. Other references to Gog and Magog will be found in Ber. 7^b and also in the Targ. Jer. on Num. xi. 26, where it is recorded that Medad prophesied: "In fine extremitatis dierum Gog et Magog et exercitus ejus ascendent contra Jerusalem, et per manus regis Messiae cadent, et septem annis integris ignem accendent filii Israel ex eorum instrumentis bellicis" (cf. also Targ. Jon. *in loc.*). In the Targ. Jon. on Ex. xl. 11, Num. xxiv. 17, Gog's armies are mentioned, and in the Targ. Jer. on Deut. xxxii. 39 and on Isa. xxxiii. 22. See Weber, Bousset, and Volz *in loc.*

3. The terms "Gog and Magog" comprehend all the faithless upon the earth. These are all destroyed by fire from heaven in 9. *Hence the earth is left without inhabitant at the close of the Millennial Kingdom.* Since the faithful at the close of the thousand years withdraw from the earth along with the Heavenly Jerusalem, *there is no longer upon the earth any in whom is the breath of human life.* At this point our Apocalypse agrees with 4 Ezra vii. 29–30, which declares that the world will revert "into the primeval silence . . . like as in the first beginnings, so that no man is left": cf. 2 Bar. iii. 7, "Shall the world return to its nature (of aforetime) and the age revert to primeval silence?"

συναγαγεῖν αὐτοὺς εἰς τὸν πόλεμον. This phrase has already occurred in xvi. 14.

ὧν ὁ ἀριθμος αὐτῶν ὡς κτλ. On the Hebraism iii. 8, xiii. 8, 12, etc. On the metaphor ὡς ἡ ἄμμος τῆς θαλάσσης, cf. Gen. xxii. 17; Jos. xi. 4; Judg. vii. 12, etc. The phrase ἡ ἄμμος τῆς θαλάσσης has already occurred in a literal sense in xii. 18.

9. ἀνέβησαν. Cf. 1 Enoch lvi. 6 sq. where the Parthians and Medes are mentioned:

> "And they shall go up and tread under foot the land of His
> elect ones . . .
> But the city of My righteous shall be a hindrance to their
> horses."

Also Zech. xii. 3. ἀναβαίνω is the word always used in connection with the pilgrims *going up* to Jerusalem. We might compare the "Songs of the Ascents"—the title of certain of the later Psalms sung by the pilgrims as they approached the Holy City. Cf. Ezek. xxxviii. 9, 11, 16 of the going up of Gog to Jerusalem. Bousset and Gunkel explain the *ἀνέβησαν* of the march of Gog and Magog from the outlying periphery of the earth to the mountain of God lying in the centre of the earth.

ἐπὶ τὸ πλάτος τῆς γῆς. There are two ways of rendering these words. 1. "Through the breadth of the earth." This phrase is found in the LXX of Hab. i. 6 (in connection with the march of the Chaldean army against Jerusalem) where it is a translation of לְמֶרְחֲבֵי אֶרֶץ. 2. It is suggested that this phrase describes the goal, towards which Gog and Magog were marching, *i.e.* Jerusalem, which in Ezek. xxxviii. 12 is called the centre or navel of the earth. Wellhausen suggests that the Greek phrase before us = אֶרֶץ פְּרָזוֹת (Ezek. xxxviii. 11) and is actually identical with טבור הארץ = *ὄμφαλος τῆς γῆς* (xxxviii. 12).

ἐκύκλευσαν. Here and in John x. 24 only in the N.T.

τὴν παρεμβολὴν τῶν ἁγίων. *i.e.* the same as the Heavenly City. If the heathen nations had the daring to attack the supernatural Messiah and His elect (xvii. 14) it is not surprising that they should assault His city.

τὴν πόλιν τὴν ἠγαπημένην. The "Holy City" is rightly here designated "the beloved." For a thousand years it has been the seat of Christ's Kingdom and the centre of the evangelizing efforts of the Church. Thus its record stands out in strong contrast with that of the earthly Jerusalem, which according to our author "is called spiritually Sodom and Egypt" (xi. 8). As such it rightly perished at the hands of the antichristian power of Rome. But far other is the destiny of "the beloved city." When Gog and Magog have been destroyed by fire and Satan cast down into the lake of fire, the Holy City, which had come down from heaven, is presupposed to be withdrawn from the sphere of the former heaven and the former earth, and after that it has itself been renewed (observe xxi. 2, *τὴν πόλιν τὴν ἁγίαν Ἰερουσαλὴμ καινήν*) to return from heaven from God to the new earth.

That an assault on Christ and the Holy City should be deemed an inconceivable event by a few scholars can only be due to their want of acquaintance not only with Jewish and Christian Apocalyptic but even with the text of our author. For in our author we find the Parthian kings making war upon the Lamb and the elect (xvii. 14), while in xix. 19 the kings of the earth and their armies levy war on Christ and His hosts from heaven (xix. 14). These passages refer to events at the initiation of the Millennial Kingdom. In 4 Ezra xiii., as in our text, the heathen nations (xiii. 5, 33, 34) assail the Messiah, who came flying with the clouds of heaven (xiii. 3) and brought with Him the Heavenly Jerusalem (xiii. 6, 35, 36), but with a flaming breath from His lips He burnt them all up so that there was nothing more to be seen of them "save only dust of ashes and smell of smoke" (xiii. 10–11, 38). We have here almost a perfect parallel to the account in our text from what was practically a contemporary Jewish source. For we have a supernatural Messiah, a Heavenly Jerusalem established on Mount Zion, an assault of the heathen nations, and their destruction by fire. There is, of course, one outstanding difference between the two accounts, *i.e.* that whereas these events are connected with the first advent of the Messiah in the Jewish document, they are incidents belonging to the second advent of Christ in the Christian Apocalypse.

Likewise in 4 Ezra xii. 32–34 we have a description of the Messiah destroying the heathen nations — especially Rome. Similarly in 2 Bar. xl. 1 sq., lxxii. 2 sqq. That He is a supernatural Messiah whom the nations have attacked is to be inferred from the description in 4 Ezra xiii. 3[b], 26, xiv. 9, and 2 Bar. xxx. 1. We have already become familiar with this conception of the Messiah in 1 Enoch xxxvii.–lxxi.

κατέβη πῦρ ἐκ τοῦ οὐρανοῦ. Cf. Ezek. xxxviii. 22, *πῦρ καὶ θεῖον βρέξω ἐπ' αὐτὸν (τὸν Γώγ) καὶ ἐπὶ πάντας τοὺς μετ' αὐτοῦ*: xxxix. 6, *ἀποστελῶ πῦρ ἐπὶ Γώγ*, and the references given in the preceding note from 4 Ezra in exactly analogous circumstances: 2 Thess. i. 8, ii. 8; Asc. Is. iv. 18. So far as words go, a perfect parallel to *κατέβη . . . αὐτούς* is found in 2 Kings i. 10.

κατέφαγεν αὐτούς. All the hosts of Gog and Magog are burnt up—that is all the faithless upon the earth (see note 3 on 8 above). At the close of 10 we are left to infer that the Holy City has withdrawn with all the faithful from the earth. Thereupon follows the Judgment of *the risen dead* by God Himself, from whose presence the former outworn heaven and earth vanish into nothingness.

10. ὁ διάβολος ὁ πλανῶν. Cf. xii. 9, *ὁ Σατανᾶς ὁ πλανῶν*: [xiii. 14] xix. 20. **ἐβλήθη εἰς τὴν λίμνην κτλ.** Cf. xix. 20. **ὅπου καί.** Cf. xi. 8: also (for *ὅπου* without *καί*) ii. 13, *ὅπου . . . ἐκεῖ*. xii. 6, 14. Cf. xvii. 9. **βασανισθήσονται** (cf. ix. 5, xiv. 10). **ἡμέρας καὶ νυκτός** (cf. iv. 8, vii. 15, xii. 10, xiv. 11). **εἰς τοὺς αἰῶνας τῶν αἰώνων** (i. 6, 18, iv. 9, 10, v. 13, vii. 12, x. 6, xi. 15, etc.).

11–15. *Vision of the great white throne and of Him who sat thereon. Disappearance of the former heaven and earth. Judgment of the dead. Death and hell cast into the lake of fire.* This vision consists of four stanzas of three lines each. This vision has suffered at the hands of interpolators.

11. εἶδον θρόνον μέγαν. As distinct from those mentioned in

iv. 4, xx. 4, this throne is designated μέγαν. Moreover, whereas God has assessors seated on adjoining thrones in Dan. vii. 9, here He judges alone. With this line and the text which refers to God we might compare Isa. vi. 1, "I saw the Lord sitting upon a throne . . . and His train filled the temple." In our text there is not the same explicitness. God is referred to indeed under the unmistakable designation ὁ καθήμενος ἐπὶ τὸν θρόνον, but *the place of the judgment is not specified.* The latter is only natural; for before the judgment has taken place (12–15) *the former heaven and earth have vanished into nothingness* (11[bc]). Hence the great white throne is conceived as the only thing (save the Heavenly Jerusalem which was to be renewed) that survives the annihilation of all that belongs to the first heaven and the first earth, and as situated somewhere in illimitable space. It is before this great white throne that the risen *souls* clothed in spiritual bodies and unclothed, *i.e.* those of the righteous and of the wicked, appear. Since this throne was created before the world (Berisheth rab. i.), as the eternal place of God, it could well be conceived as surviving the world's annihilation. According to 4 Ezra vii. 33 also, "the Most High shall be revealed upon the throne of judgment" after the first world has disappeared (vii. 31; see p. 198). It was different, however, in earlier Apocalypses, where the Messianic Kingdom was everlasting on the present earth and was of necessity preceded by the Final Judgment. In such cases the Final Judgment took place upon the earth, and the throne of judgment was set up in Palestine, 1 Enoch xc. 20. In Joel iii. 2, 12, 14–16 and 1 Enoch liii. 1 the valley of Jehoshaphat is the scene of this judgment and the agents are the angels (Joel iii. 13).

The Final Judgment is reserved in our text for God Himself; but this Judgment has to do only *with the dead, or rather those risen from the dead, both good and bad*, whereas *the judgment of the living* in xiv. 14, 18–20, xvii. 14, xix. 11–21, xx. 7–10 is committed wholly to Christ. In assigning the Final Judgment exclusively to the Father even in this limited form (see, however, xxii. 13, 12) our author stands apart from the doctrine presented in John v. 22, οὐδὲ γὰρ ὁ πατὴρ κρίνει οὐδένα, ἀλλὰ τὴν κρίσιν πᾶσαν δέδωκεν τῷ υἱῷ, and Matt. vii. 22, 23, xvi. 27, xxv. 31–46; Acts xvii. 31; 2 Cor. v. 10. Cf. 1 Enoch xlv. 3, lxix. 27; 2 Bar. lxxii. 2–6. On the other hand, God alone is mentioned in this relation in Matt. vi. 4, 6, 14, 15, 18, xviii. 35, while St. Paul sometimes ascribes the Final Judgment to God, Rom. xiv. 10, and sometimes to Christ, 2 Cor. v. 10.

λευκόν. This epithet may point to the absolute equity of the Judgment. Or since according to our text and 4 Ezra vii. 31 the first world and all that belongs to it have vanished, and according to 4 Ezra vii. 41–42, "there is neither sun nor moon nor stars . . . neither shining nor brightness nor light, but only the *splendour of the glory of the Most High*" (=זיו כבוד עליון), the throne of God is lighted up with the splendour of the Shekinah, and hence it is the centre of light in the illimitable vastness of space. Whether this is so or not, it is the glory of God alone that lights up the universe. See note on *τ. δόξαν τοῦ θεοῦ*, xxi. 10; also xxi. 23, note.

οὗ ἀπὸ τοῦ προσώπου ἔφυγεν ἡ γῆ καὶ ὁ οὐρανός. Cf. xvi. 20. When we take this line in connection with that which follows, it is clear that there is here taught the literal vanishing of the former heaven and earth into nothingness. As I have shown in my *Eschatology*², 127–128, the older doctrine in the O.T. was the eternity of the present order of things. This was the received view down to the 2nd century B.C. From the 1st century B.C. onward in Judaism and Christianity, the transitoriness of the present heaven and earth was universally accepted. Cf. Mark xiii. 31, *ὁ οὐρανὸς καὶ ἡ γῆ παρελεύσονται.*

From the words before us we must conclude that before the Judgment began both *heaven and earth had vanished into nothingness.* This conclusion is of great importance when we come to deal with 13. That this was a contemporary Jewish doctrine we find from 2 Enoch lxv. 6, "when all creation visible and invisible . . . shall end, then every man goes to the great judgment." See also 4 Ezra vii. 31–36 (in the note on 13 below) where the same view is taught.

καὶ τόπος οὐχ εὑρέθη αὐτοῖς. See xii. 8 *n.*

12. Since the verses that precede and follow 12 consist each of three lines, we naturally expect that 12 originally consisted of three lines also. When we examine the text we discover one or two disturbing glosses. When these are excised this verse is parallel in structure to that which precedes and that which follows it. But this verse should be transposed after 13, since it presupposes it.

τοὺς νεκρούς, *i.e.* the rest of the dead who had no share in the first resurrection. Only the dead appear before the great white throne. As Christ had judged the quick in a series of judgments (see note on 11), so God Himself judges all the dead save those who had part in the first resurrection. From 11 taken in conjunction with 13 it is to be concluded that our author has no thought here of a bodily resurrection—save in the case of the righteous dead, who would naturally as in 1 Cor. xv. appear in their spiritual bodies. As regards the wicked, however, the case is different. These would appear simply as disembodied souls—"naked"—in a spiritual environment without a body—without the capacity for communication with or means of expression in that environment. Every wicked soul, therefore, would be thus shut up within itself and form its own hell even before it was cast into the lake of fire.

[τοὺς μεγάλους καὶ τοὺς μικρούς.] Elsewhere our author writes *τοὺς μικροὺς καὶ τοὺς μεγάλους*: cf. xi. 18, xiii. 16, xix. 5, 18 (the usual order in the O.T.). But he may have here deliberately changed the order to emphasize the judgment which awaits the great ones of the earth, and which they so often escaped on earth. In the O.T. the order *τ. μεγ. καὶ τ. μικρούς* is found in Jonah iii. 5, but in 1 Sam. v. 9; Jer. vi. 13, xxxi. 34; Ps. cxv. 13 we have the usual order *τοὺς μικροὺς καὶ τοὺς μεγάλους*.

καὶ βιβλία ἠνοίχθησαν. These books contain a record of all that men have done: cf. Dan. vii. 10, *βίβλοι ἠνοίχθησαν*: 1 Enoch[2] xc. 20, "The other took the sealed books and opened those books before the Lord of the Sheep"; 4 Ezra vi. 20, "The books shall be opened before the face of the firmament"; 2 Bar. xxiv. 1, "Behold the days come and the books shall be opened in which are written the sins of all who have sinned"; Asc. Isa. ix. 22. On these books see my note on 1 Enoch[2] xlvii. 3, which deals with three distinct classes of heavenly books, two of which are mentioned in our text.

καὶ ἄλλο βιβλίον ἠνοίχθη ὅ ἐστιν τῆς ζωῆς. This book is the register of the righteous. Cf. 1 Enoch xlvii. 3, "The books of the living were opened before Him" (see note *in loc.*; also on iii. 5 of the present text). The explanatory clause looks like a gloss. Seeing that this book has already been mentioned with the article in iii. 5, xiii. 8, xvii. 8, such a clause is needless at all events. The relation of the book of life and the books is well stated by Alford. These "books and the book of life bore independent witness to the fact of men being or not being among the saved: the one by inference from the works recorded: the other by inscription or non-inscription of the name in the list. So the books could be as the 'vouchers' for the book of life."

[κατὰ τὰ ἔργα αὐτῶν]. This phrase is a mere tautology here. It is interpolated from 13, where it rightly occurs. If the dead are judged, *ἐκ τῶν γεγραμμένων ἐν τοῖς βιβλίοις*, that is the same thing as saying *ἐκρίθησαν ἕκαστος κατὰ τὰ ἔργα αὐτῶν* (13).

13. This verse should be transferred before 12.

καὶ ἔδωκεν † ἡ θάλασσα † τοὺς νεκροὺς τοὺς ἐν † αὐτῇ †,
καὶ ὁ θάνατος καὶ ὁ ᾅδης ἔδωκαν τοὺς νεκροὺς τοὺς ἐν αὐτοῖς,
καὶ ἐκρίθησαν ἕκαστος κατὰ τὰ ἔργα αὐτοῦ.

This stanza betrays in its present form a hopeless confusion of thought, which can only be due to deliberate change of the text. The context cannot admit of a resurrection of the physical body from the sea—seeing that the sea and everything pertaining to it had vanished. And yet this is the only natural meaning of 13^a. Hence, if 13^a is original and we hold fast to the natural sense, 11^b cannot be original. But the originality of 11^b cannot be questioned, for xxi. 4^d, 5 presuppose it. Accordingly we must either interpret 13^a in a wholly non-natural sense as defining not the place of departed souls but the means by which certain men perished, *i.e.* the sea, and 13^b as giving the intermediate abode of *all souls*, which had died on sea or land, save only those of the martyrs. The general sense then would be : all souls together with their bodies—even those lost at sea (13^a)—are given up by Hades for judgment before the great white throne.

But it is only by a quite illegitimate *tour de force* that such a meaning can be wrested from the words. 13^a clearly presupposes the sea at once as existing and delivering up the *bodies* that had been engulfed in it, at the same time that Hades is represented as delivering up the *souls* that were in it. Body and soul would thus be reunited. The only natural meaning, then, of 13^{ab} is in conflict with the unmistakable statement in 11^b that sea is now non-existent, and with the presupposition that underlies the entire book, *i.e.* that the wicked rise as disembodied souls (see additional note on vi. 11).[1] Only the righteous are to possess

[1] The doctrine of a bodily resurrection is consistently taught in 1 Enoch xxxvii.–lxxi. There the general resurrection takes place before the Judgment, while the former heaven and the former earth still subsist. In lxi. 5 we find an account of the resurrection of

"Those who had been destroyed by the desert,
And those who had been devoured by the beasts,
And those who had been devoured by the fish of the sea."

Here quite distinctly a physical resurrection is described. Further in the same work in li. 1 the body and soul are raised separately and reunited at the Final Judgment. In the case of the righteous a transformation of the physical body into a spiritual is presupposed in the rest of this section (lxii. 15, 16).

"And in those days shall the earth also give back that which was entrusted to it,
And Sheol also shall give back that which it has received,
And hell (= Abaddon) shall give back that which it owes."

Cf. also Ps.-Philo, *de Biblic. Antiquitatibus*, iii. 10 :

"Reddet infernus (= Hades) debitum suum,
Et perditio (=Abaddon) restituet paratecen suam,
Ut reddam unicuique secundum opera sua."

There is a remarkable parallelism here with our text (13). The doctrine of a physical resurrection is enforced dogmatically in 2 Bar. xlix.–li. and Sanh. 91^a. This was the orthodox Rabbinic belief, and it is expressed in the ancient Benediction (Ber. 60^b) still recited by the pious Jew every morning: "O my God, the soul which Thou gavest me is pure : Thou didst create it . . . and Thou wilt take it from me, but wilt restore it unto me hereafter . . . Blessed art Thou, O Lord, *who restores' souls to dead bodies*" (see Singer, *Authorised Daily Prayer Book—Hebrew and English*, p. 5).

But this crass materialistic doctrine does not belong to the N.T. Such a

bodies, *i.e.* spiritual bodies. Finally, Sheol in our author is the abode, not of righteous but of wicked or indifferent souls. As we shall see presently, righteous souls (save those of the martyrs) were preserved in "the treasuries."

Hence we conclude that in *ἡ θάλασσα τοὺς νεκροὺς τοὺς ἐν αὐτῇ* there is a deliberate change of *τὰ ταμεῖα* into *ἡ θάλασσα* in order to introduce the idea of a physical resurrection. These *ταμεῖα* (or "treasuries") contained the souls of the righteous (with the exception of the martyrs who were already in heaven), whereas *ᾅδης* was the abode of the wicked souls. Thus we should have:

> "And the treasuries gave up the dead that were in them,
> And death and Hades gave up the dead that were in them,
> And they were judged every man according to their works."

Our text thus, like the Pauline Epistles, teaches a resurrection of persons ("the dead" so called), not a resurrection of dead bodies even though in company with souls. The personality of the righteous is complete—the soul clothed with a spiritual body: the personality of the unrighteous is incomplete—the soul is without a body—without the power of expressing itself or receiving impressions from without. Sin is ultimately self-destructive.

That such deliberate perversions of the text took place early—probably in the 2nd century A.D.—I shall show presently. In the meantime it is our task to prove that in apocalyptic circles, to which our author belonged, it was *the accepted belief* that the souls of the righteous were preserved in certain "treasuries." The word "treasuries" (in the Latin of 4 Ezra promptuaria, and in the Syriac of 4 Ezra and 2 Baruch ܐܘܨܪ̈ܐ) clearly goes back to the Hebrew אוצרים, which is used also in the Talmud occasionally in this sense, and which in the Midr. rabba on Ecclesiastes iii. 21 (Weber², 338) is said to be placed in the heavenly height. These treasuries are first referred to in 1 Enoch c. 5, though not by name:

> "And over all the righteous and holy He will appoint guardians from among the holy angels,
> To guard them as the apple of an eye,

doctrine has no part in the Pauline Epistles, Hebrews, or in the Fourth Evangelist, nor does it find any countenance in our author, though it was enforced by many of the Fathers in the Christian Church from the 3rd century onward in opposition to Gnosticism, and other more legitimate doctrines within the Church on this question.

Until He makes an end of all wickedness and all sin,
And though the righteous sleep a long sleep, they have nought to fear."

To these treasuries only the souls of the righteous were admitted. From this passage in 1 Enoch (early in the 1st century B.C.) we come down to two Jewish works practically contemporary with our author, *i.e.* 2 Bar. and 4 Ezra. In 2 Bar. xxi. 23, we have a remarkable confirmation of the above emendation of 13[a]; for in xxi. 23 the angel of death is mentioned, then Sheol as the intermediate abode of wicked souls, and then the treasuries of the souls of the righteous. These treasuries are to be opened after the close of the Messianic Kingdom, 2 Bar. xxx. 2, and the souls of the righteous to come forth at the Final Judgment. In 4 Ezra iv. 41–42 we find a second confirmation of the above restoration of 13[a].

"And he said unto me: Sheol and the treasuries of souls are like the womb: 42. For just as she who is in travail makes haste to escape the anguish of the travail; even so do these places hasten to deliver what has been entrusted to them from the beginning." Here as Sheol (cf. viii. 53) is the abode of unrighteous souls, so the treasuries are the abode of righteous souls (cf. iv. 35, vii. 80). These treasuries were to restore the souls of the righteous at the Final Judgment, vii. 32, 95. These treasuries are likewise designated "habitations" (habitacula: cf. "mansions" or "abiding places," μοναί, John xiv. 2) in vii. 85, 101, 121.

We have thus proved that towards the close of the 1st century A.D. as well as earlier and later the souls of the righteous were conceived of as being guarded and at rest (cf. 1 Enoch c. 5; 4 Ezra vii. 95) in certain places called "treasuries," and that from these the souls of the righteous came forth at the Final Judgment.

Such a conception as the above would suit our text perfectly; for the Final Judgment has come, and *since it is a judgment both of the righteous and the wicked, we expect some reference to the former in our text. By the proposed restoration we recover this reference.*

But the evidence in favour of this restoration is not yet complete. For an examination of our author's use of the word ᾅδης shows that he uses it in a bad sense *as the temporary abode of wicked souls.* This is evident from the next verse (xx. 14), where it is said that death and Hades are cast down into the lake of fire. Hence ᾅδης bears no neutral complexion in our author. Had it done so, it would simply have vanished into nothingness like the earth (11[b]), but it is hurled into the abyss where Satan and his servants are tormented for ever and ever.

Thus, unless the text is restored as above suggested, there

would only be a judgment of wicked souls, but by the above restoration we have a General Judgment of the righteous and the wicked.

It is significant that in 4 Ezra vii. 31–36 we find an analogous depravation of the text with a like object, that is, to introduce the idea of a physical resurrection. As might be expected, the thought of the text is thereby hopelessly confused. In vii. 31–36 we have a description in couplets of the new heaven and the new earth taking the place of the old which as corruptible *had passed away*.

31. "And it shall be that after seven days the Age,
which is not yet awake, shall be aroused,
And that which is corruptible shall perish."[1]
32[a]. . . . .
[b]. . . . .
32[c]. And the treasuries shall restore those that were committed unto them.
33. And the Most High shall be revealed upon the throne of judgment.[2]
And compassion shall pass away
And longsuffering shall disappear.[3]
34. But judgment alone shall remain,
Truth shall stand and faithfulness flourish.
35. And recompense shall follow,
And the reward be made manifest."

Box, following Kabisch, has through a strange misconception obelized 32[c] as an interpolation. But manifestly 32[ab] is the intruder.

ἔδωκεν . . ἔδωκαν. Here διδόναι is used absolutely like נתן =

[1] Here a couplet has been displaced and another interpolated to introduce the idea of a physical resurrection.

32[a]. "And the earth shall restore those that sleep in her,
[b]. And the dust those that are at rest therein."

Seeing that the new world has already displaced the old in 31 this couplet is wholly at variance with the context. Its aim is to assert the resurrection of the body, to rejoin the souls which come forth from the treasuries, 32[c]. But since the treasuries are prepared for righteous souls only (cf. iv. 35, vii. 80, 95; 2 Bar. xxi. 23, xxx. 2; 1 Enoch c. 5) the text would then teach only a resurrection of the righteous. But every couplet that follows proves that we have here a *general resurrection*. The lost couplet clearly spoke of Sheol giving up the souls of the wicked for judgment, as the treasuries in 32[c] yield up the souls of the righteous.

[2] The Syriac here interpolates "And then cometh the end" against all the other versions.

[3] The Syriac adds "And pity shall be afar off" against the Latin and the first Arabic versions. The Syr. is supported by the Eth. and Arab[2]. The line appears to be a doublet.

"to give up." It is not a classical use, nor so far as I am aware a Hellenistic one.

ὁ θάνατος καὶ ὁ ᾅδης. As pointed out in the preceding note, ᾅδης can be here only the abode of unrighteous souls (as in 1 Enoch lxiii. 10 xcix. 11, ciii. 7; Pss. Sol. xiv. 6, xv. 11), seeing that in the next verse it is cast into the lake of fire. Death and Hades have already been found together in i. 18 (*n.*), vi. 8: also in Ps.-Philo, *De Bibl. Antiquitatibus.* In the latter work the destruction of death and Hades are followed as in our text by the creation of a new heaven and a new earth.

"Et extinguetur mors,
Et infernus (= Hades) claudet os suum . . .
Et erit terra alia et caelum aliud."

The alia and aliud here obviously go back to ἕτερος which as distinguished from ἄλλος involves a distinction in kind. While ἄλλος simply asserts the negation of identity, ἕτερος asserts the negation of likeness in kind. In 2 Bar. xxi. 23, when Sheol and the treasuries have yielded up the souls in them, the new world promised by God was to be manifested, xxi. 25. This accords with the order of events in our text, xx. 13, xxi. 1 In 2 Enoch lxv. 10 it is said that "all corruptible things shall pass away, and there shall be eternal life."

ἐκρίθησαν ἕκαστος κατὰ τὰ ἔργα αὐτῶν. Cf. ii. 23; Ps. xxviii. 4 lxii. 13; Jer. xvii. 10; Matt. x. 32, 33.

14–15. These two verses originally formed the concluding stanza of this section. The text as it stands is impossible. The statement *οὗτος ὁ θάνατος δεύτερός ἐστιν, ἡ λίμνη τοῦ πυρός* can only be made in reference to human beings, who have undergone the first death, *i.e.* the physical one. Hence, if it belongs to the text, it does not do so in its present position. Here, though a number of cursives, the Sahidic Version and Primasius omit this line, the grounds for its rejection in its present position are not to be sought in textual evidence, since its intrusion is anterior to all such evidence. The real grounds for its rejection are that the statement is absolutely devoid of meaning. Even if death and Hades be regarded as persons, we cannot conceive (cf. Haussleiter, *Die Lateinische Apocalypse*, 213) how the words *ὁ θάνατος ὁ δεύτερος* can be applied to them. Moffatt suggests that this line was displaced from its original position after 15. There are, in fact, only these two alternatives. Either (1) the line is to be rejected as a gloss, and we must read as follows:

καὶ ὁ θάνατος καὶ ὁ ᾅδης
ἐβλήθησαν εἰς τὴν λίμνην τοῦ πυρός,
καὶ εἴ τις οὐχ εὑρέθη ἐν τῇ βίβλῳ τῆς ζωῆς γεγραμμένος
ἐβλήθη εἰς τὴν λίμνην τοῦ πυρός.

Or (2) what appears here as the first and second lines must be read as the first, and what appears here as the third and fourth lines must be read as the second, and *οὗτος ὁ θάνατος ὁ δεύτερός ἐστιν, ἡ λίμνη τοῦ πυρός* be read as the third. This latter arrangement is not free from serious objections. These are two. First, there does not appear any reasonable ground for the misplacement of the clause. In the next place, the clause in itself is an unmeaning mis-statement. The lake of fire is not the second death, but the second death is the lot of those who are cast into the lake of fire. The right definition of the second death is given in xxi. 8. The present writer, therefore, regards the clause as originally a marginal gloss drawn from xxi. 8 and subsequently incorporated into the text.

14. ἐβλήθησαν εἰς τὴν λίμνην τοῦ πυρός. Cf. 10, xix. 20; Petr. Apoc. 8, *λίμνη τις ἦν μεγάλη πεπληρωμένη βορβόρου φλεγομένου ἐν ᾧ ἦσαν ἄνθρωποί τινες ἀποστρέφοντες τὴν δικαιοσύνην.*

[**οὗτος ὁ θάνατος κτλ.**] See note above and cf. xxi. 8.

15. ἐν τῇ βίβλῳ τῆς ζωῆς κτλ. Cf. xxi. 27, iii. 5, note. **τὴν λίμνην τοῦ πυρός.** See note on ix. 1 on the significance of this phrase.

CHAPTER XXI. 5^a, 4^d, 5^b, 6^a, 1–4^{abc}, XXII. 3–5.

Introduction.

The New Heaven, the New Earth, and the New Jerusalem, with its blest inhabitants.

§ 1. Now that all evil has been destroyed for ever, and all evil agents have been cast into the lake of fire, that the former heaven and earth have vanished, the final judgment brought to a close, and death and Hades destroyed, God creates a new heaven and a new earth, and summons into being the New Jerusalem. In this city, which would never know tears, nor grief, nor crying, nor any pain nor curse, God will dwell with men, and His throne, which is also that of the Lamb, will be in it, and His servants, whose character, as God's own possession, shall henceforth be blazoned on their brows, shall serve Him and they shall see His Face. And God will cause the light of His Face to shine upon them in perpetual benediction, and they shall reign for ever and ever.

That this section was written by our author is undeniable. It forms the natural climax and the fitting close to all that has gone before, and the nature of the blessedness of the new heaven and the new earth and the new city is in keeping with all that is foreshadowed in the earlier visions of the Seer. The diction and the idiom are our author's.

§ 2. *Diction.*

XXI. 4^d. τὰ πρῶτα ἀπῆλθαν: for this use of ἀπελθεῖν cf. ix. 12, xi. 14, xxi. 1. παρελθεῖν is used in this connection in Synoptics and St. Paul: cf. Mark xiii. 31 = Matt. xxiv. 35 = Luke xxi. 33; 2 Cor. v. 17, τὰ ἀρχαῖα παρῆλθον.

5^b. καινὰ ποιῶ πάντα. These words summarize the action of God on the world. The faithful receive a new name, ii. 17, iii. 12; they sing a new song, v. 9, xiv. 3; and a new heaven, earth, and a new city are created to be their habitation, xxi. 1, 2.

6^a. γέγοναν. Cf. xvi. 17, φωνὴ . . . λέγουσα Γέγονεν.

1. ὁ πρῶτος οὐρανός. For this position of πρῶτος cf. ii. 5. ἀπῆλθαν. See note on xxi. 4^d above.

2. τὴν πόλιν τ. ἁγίαν: cf. xxi. 10. Ἰερουσαλὴμ καινήν: cf. iii. 12. καταβαίνουσαν ἐκ τ. οὐρανοῦ ἀπὸ τοῦ θεοῦ: cf. iii. 12, xxi. 10. ἡτοιμασμένην ὡς νύμφην: cf. xix. 7.

3. φωνῆς μεγάλης ἐκ τοῦ θρόνου: cf. xvi. 17, xix. 5. σκηνώσει: cf. vii. 15, xii. 12, xiii. 6. αὐτοὶ λαοὶ αὐτοῦ ἔσονται καὶ αὐτὸς ἔσται θεὸς αὐτῶν: cf. xxi. 7^bc.

4^ab. ἐξαλείψει κτλ.: cf. vii. 17. οὐκ ἔσται ἔτι: cf. xxii. 3, 5. πόνος: cf. xvi. 10, 11.

XXII. 3. οὐκ ἔσται ἔτι: cf. xxi. 4^a. ὁ θρόνος τοῦ θεοῦ καὶ τοῦ ἀρνίου: cf. xxii. 1. οἱ δοῦλοι αὐτοῦ λατρεύσουσιν: cf. vii. 15.

5. οὐκ ἔχουσιν χρείαν φωτὸς λύχνου κτλ.: cf. xxi. 23. βασιλεύσουσιν εἰς τ. αἰῶνας τ. αἰώνων: cf. xx. 4.

Idiom.

Johannine: **XXII.** 4. τὸ ὄνομα αὐτοῦ ἐπὶ τῶν μετώπων: see notes on vii. 3, xiii. 16.

5. οὐχ ἔχουσιν χρείαν . . . φῶς ἡλίου: cf. iii. 17 for this extraordinary construction. Φωτίσει ἐπ' αὐτούς: a pure Hebraism: see note *in loc.* Contrast construction in xviii. 1, xxi. 23.

Non-Johannine: **XXI.** 5. ὁ καθήμενος ἐπὶ τῷ θρόνῳ: see note on iv. 2.

God will Create the World afresh—Heaven, Earth, and the Holy City. This New Jerusalem—which is not created till after the Millennial Kingdom—is always spoken of as belonging to the future (*i.e.* every verb is in the future): whereas the Jerusalem described in xxi. 9–xxii. 2, 14–15, 17 is described as already existing, though as yet in heaven.

XXI. 5^a, 4^d, 5^b. *God's Declaration at the close of the Final Judgment.*

"*The former things have passed away:*
Behold I make all things new."

We have already (see pp. 151–153) shown that xxi. 1–4^c and

xxii. 3–5 belong together and form a description by the Seer of the New Jerusalem which is to be the eternal abode of the blessed. This poem consists of six stanzas, the first two of three lines each and the remaining four of four lines each. Next, since it is obvious that xxi. 4^d, 5^{ab} do not really belong to what follows nor yet to what precedes in the present text, these dislocated lines, as representing the words of Him, from whose presence the former heaven and earth had vanished into nothingness, who has just judged the world (xx. 11–15), and who has cast all wickedness into the lake of fire, at once claim their rightful position as forming the close of the first creation and the beginning of the new.

> **5^a.** καὶ εἶπεν ὁ καθήμενος ἐπὶ † τῷ θρόνῳ †,
> **4^d.** τὰ πρῶτα ἀπῆλθαν,
> **5^b.** Ἰδοὺ καινὰ ποιῶ πάντα.

This restoration of the order of the text is supported by the remarkable parallel in 2 Cor. v. 17, *εἴ τις ἐν Χριστῷ, καινὴ κτίσις· τὰ ἀρχαῖα παρῆλθεν, ἰδοὺ γέγονεν καινά.* St. Paul here, it is true, refers to the new or spiritual creation of the individual. But in this respect man is a microcosm—an epitome of the universe or the macrocosm.

5^a. καὶ εἶπεν. The Speaker here as in i. 8, xvi. 1, 17, is God Himself, and He speaks, not to the Seer—hence no *μοι* is added as generally elsewhere in our author: cf. vii. 14, xvii. 7, xxi. 6, xxii. 6—but to the entire world of the blessed. The words are most probably conceived as pronounced from the great white throne at the close of the Final Judgment.

† ἐπὶ τῷ θρόνῳ †. We have an error here traceable probably to the disciple of the Seer who edited xx. 4–xxii. When he makes an addition, he generally makes a mistake. Cf. xix. 10, *προσκυνῆσαι αὐτῷ*, which should be **αὐτόν**. We should, of course, have *ἐπὶ τὸν θρόνον*: see iv. 2, note.

The words *ὁ καθήμενος ἐπὶ τ. θρόνον* go back to xx. 11, where God is so described at the beginning of the Final Judgment. Now that character has attained finality and all men have entered on the issues of their conduct, and death and Hades have come to an end, He that sitteth on the throne makes the solemn pronouncement with regard to all that the past: *τὰ πρῶτα ἀπῆλθαν.* The first world and all that essentially belongs to it as distinct from the second and spiritual world have vanished for ever.

4^d. τὰ πρῶτα ἀπῆλθαν. With **τὰ πρῶτα** cf. xxi. 1, *ὁ γὰρ πρῶτος οὐρανὸς καὶ ἡ πρώτη γῆ ἀπῆλθαν.* With *ἀπῆλθαν* cf. ix. 12, xi. 14, xxi. 1. That *τὰ πρῶτα ἀπῆλθαν* is to be taken immediately in connection with Ἰδοὺ *καινὰ ποιῶ πάντα* is obvious in itself. But there is some external evidence that confirms the combination of 4^d and 5^b; for, while it is recognized on all hands that Isa. xliii. 18, 19 was in the mind of our author here, we find on turning to this passage that the two main ideas in 4^d and 5^b are already brought together (though in a more primitive and limited form), and set forth as a divine utterance as here:

18. μὴ μνημονεύετε τὰ πρῶτα
καὶ τὰ ἀρχαῖα μὴ συλλογίζεσθε·
19. Ἰδοὺ ἐγὼ ποιῶ καινά.

The two ideas are also brought together in 2 Cor. v. 17, τὰ ἀρχαῖα παρῆλθεν, ἰδοὺ γέγονεν καινά.

5^b. Ἰδοὺ καινὰ ποιῶ πάντα. On the idea of a new heaven and a new earth cf. Isa. lxv. 17, lxvi. 22; Ps. cii. 25–26: see note on xxii. 1 of our text. But in the current Apocalypses this idea was a familiar one. Thus in 1 Enoch xci. 16 (before 170 B.C.?) we find:

"The first heaven shall depart and pass away,
And a new heaven shall appear";

in lxxii. 1 (before 110 B.C.): "Till the new creation is accomplished which dureth till eternity"; in xlv. 4 (94–64 B.C.):

"And I will transform the heaven and make it an eternal blessing and light,
And I will transform the earth and make it a blessing";

Jub. i. 29 (before 107 A.D.): "From the day of the creation till the heavens and the earth are renewed"; also in 2 Bar. lvii. 2 (before 70 A.D.):

"And belief in the coming judgment was then generated,
And hope of the world that was to be renewed was then built up,
And the promise of the life that should come hereafter was implanted";

xliv. 12 (after 70 A.D.). "And the new world which does not turn to corruption those who depart to its blessedness"; xxxii. 6: "When the Mighty One will renew His creation"; 4 Ezra vii. 75: "Until those times come in which Thou shalt renew Thy creation." In the N.T. cf. Matt. xix. 28; Acts iii. 21; 2 Pet. iii. 13. The passage in Barnabas vi. 13 (λέγει δὲ κύριος Ἰδοὺ ποιῶ τὰ ἔσχατα ὡς τὰ πρῶτα) has nothing in common with our text.

5^c. [καὶ λέγει· Γράψον ὅτι οὗτοι οἱ λόγοι πιστοὶ καὶ ἀληθινοί εἰσιν]. As these words cannot be assigned to God, they are assigned to an angel. But if we accept this explanation we should here have an instance of bathos—an error in style of which our author is never guilty. When God Himself declares in the hearing of the Seer that He recreates the world, His words do not require to be confirmed either directly or indirectly by any angel or archangel. The clause *οὗτοι οἱ λόγοι . . . ἀληθινοί* is repeated from xxii. 6, where it is full of significance in the mouth of Christ. *ὅτι* may (1) introduce a statement or (2) give a reason. But it is not used in the first sense elsewhere in our author after *γράψον*, cf. ii. 1, 8, 12, 18, iii. 1, 7, 14, xiv. 13. Even if we take it in the second sense ("because") the bathos of the statement still remains unrelieved. Hence 5^{c} appears to be an interpolation. That Christ should solemnly authenticate the truth of these visions in xxii. 6 is wholly fitting.

[6^{a}. **καὶ εἶπέν μοι Γέγοναν.**] Cf. xvi. 17. See note on xxi. 5^{b} (English translation: see vol. ii. 443, note 3). An interpolation? If original, the words come from God or from the *angelus interpres.* The Seer hears God's first declaration: "Behold I make all things new," and following immediately thereupon the words: "They have become (new)." After this the Seer sees the new heaven and the new earth and the New Jerusalem (xxi. $1–4^{abc}$, xxii. 3–5). On the form *γέγοναν* see Blass, *Gram.* p. 46.

XXI. $1–4^{abc}$, XXII. 3–5. *The vision of the new heaven and the new earth and the descent of the New Jerusalem adorned as a bride for her husband. God is to tabernacle with men, and never more is there to be grief or pain or tears or death, and all the faithful are to reign for ever and ever.*

1. εἶδον οὐρανὸν καινὸν καὶ γῆν καινήν. On the meaning of *καινός* as distinguished from *νέος* see iii. 12, note. On the new heaven and the new earth see the note on xxi. 4^{d} above, p. 203. In Isa. lxv. 17 the actual phrase used by our author is found: "For behold I create a new heaven and a new earth" (כי־הנני בורא שׁמים חדשים וארץ חדשה) where the LXX has *ἔσται γὰρ ὁ οὐρανὸς καινὸς καὶ ἡ γῆ καινή.* Wetstein quotes the Debarim rab. S. xi.: "Cum Moses ante obitum oraret, coelum et terra et omnis ordo creaturarum commotus est. Tunc dixerunt: Fortasse adest tempus a Deo praestitutum, quo renovandus est orbis universus (לחדשׁ את עלמו). Exivit autem vox dicens illud tempus nondum advenisse." See Volz, 296 sqq.; Bousset, *Rel. d. Jüdenth.* 268 sq.

ὁ γὰρ πρῶτος οὐρανὸς καὶ κτλ. This disappearance of the first heaven and the first earth has already been referred to: cf. xx. 11^{b}.

καὶ ἡ θάλασσα οὐκ ἔστιν ἔτι. The earliest parallel to this statement is found in Test. Levi (109–106 B.C.), iv. 1: "Now know that the Lord shall execute judgment upon the sons of men. Because when the rocks are being rent . . . and the waters dried up." Next in the Assumption of Moses, x. 6:

"And the sea shall retire into its abyss,
And the fountains of waters shall fail,
And the rivers shall dry up."

Also in Sibyll. Or. v. 159, 160, 447, ἔσται δ' ὑστατίῳ καιρῷ ξηρός ποτε πόντος: viii. 236, πᾶσα θάλασσα οὐκέτι πλοῦν ἕξει. All these passages point not wholly to any Semitic horror of the sea in itself, but in some degree perhaps unconsciously to its mythological connection with the Babylonian myth of the Creation, in which the sea is the water monster Tiâmat, the special opponent of the gods. The omission of the sea by John may thus be owing to its evil associations, many traces of which survive in the O.T. See articles Dragon, Leviathan, Rahab, Serpent, in the *Encyc. Biblica.* A remarkable parallel in Plutarch's *De Iside et Osiride* 7 should be observed. There the sea is regarded as an alien element in nature, fraught with destruction and disease: ὅλως δὲ καὶ τὴν θάλατταν ἐκ πυρὸς ἡγοῦνται καὶ παρωρισμένην, οὐδὲ μέρος οὐδὲ στοιχεῖον ἀλλ' ἀλλοῖον περίττωμα διεφθορὸς καὶ νοσῶδες.

2. τὴν πόλιν τὴν ἁγίαν Ἰερουσαλὴμ καινήν. This city is either wholly distinct from that described in xxi. 9–xxii. 2—the seat of the Millennial Kingdom—or it is that city wholly transformed and hence described καινήν: see xxi. 10, note. Since God re-creates all things, xxi. 5^b, the Holy City is either transformed or created afresh as are the heaven and the earth. This city is clearly distinguished from that in xxi. 9–xxii. 2. In the latter the saints reign for a thousand years, and the tree of life stands in the street thereof in order that all who were worthy might eat thereof, that is, attain to immortality. But in this city there is no mention of the tree of life: it is not needed; for all its inhabitants are immortal (xxi. 4^b) and reign with God for ever and ever (xxii. 5). With this New Jerusalem we might compare Heb. xii. 22, Ἰερουσαλὴμ ἐπουρανίῳ: Gal. iv. 26, ἡ δὲ ἄνω Ἰερουσαλήμ: and Phil. iii. 20, ἡμῶν γὰρ τὸ πολίτευμα ἐν οὐρανοῖς ὑπάρχει.

καταβαίνουσαν ἐκ τοῦ οὐρανοῦ ἀπὸ τοῦ θεοῦ. Cf. iii. 12, xxi. 10.

ἡτοιμασμένην ὡς νύμφην. Cf. xxi. 9; Isa. xlix. 18, lxi. 10.

τῷ ἀνδρὶ αὐτῆς. Cf. 2 Cor. xi. 2; Eph. v. 23.

3. φωνῆς μεγάλης ἐκ τοῦ θρόνου. The throne is that in xix. 11. The speaker is probably one of the Cherubim.

Ἰδοὺ ἡ σκηνὴ τοῦ θεοῦ μετὰ τῶν ἀνθρώπων,
καὶ σκηνώσει μετ' αὐτῶν.

The word σκηνή here has nothing to do with the Tabernacle (משכן). For in Jewish writings there is no expectation of the restoration of the *Tabernacle* in the Heavenly Jerusalem. Its place is always taken by the Temple (cf. Weber[2], 375–77). But, since our author expressly states (xxi. 22) that there will be no Temple in the Holy City, that is to be the seat of the Millennial Kingdom, it follows that he could not have looked for a restored Tabernacle in the New Jerusalem which was to be the everlasting abode of the blessed. The word *σκηνή* has already occurred twice. In xiii. 6 it means God's dwelling, *i.e.* heaven, or rather (?) "His Shekinah" (see note *in loc.*). In xv. 5, where it is found a second time, we have seen that the text is either corrupt or interpolated; for *ὁ ναὸς τῆς σκηνῆς τοῦ μαρτυρίου ἐν τῷ οὐρανῷ* is an intolerable, because an unintelligible, expression.

What, then, is the meaning of *σκηνή* here? The context appears certainly to favour the interpretation suggested by Dr. Taylor (*Pirke Aboth*[2], p. 44). "The two ('Shekinah' and 'Memra') are brought together by St. John . . . *ὁ Λόγος σὰρξ ἐγένετο, καὶ ἐσκήνωσεν ἐν ἡμῖν* (John i. 14). The word *σκηνή* and its derivatives are chosen on account of their assonance with the Hebrew to express the Shekinah and its dwelling with men—compare especially Rev. xxi. 3: *Ἰδοὺ ἡ σκηνὴ τοῦ θεοῦ μετὰ τῶν ἀνθρώπων καὶ σκηνώσει μετ' αὐτῶν.*" Even in xiii. 6, where our author is adapting to a new situation an earlier source, the probability is that he gives a new meaning to the phrase *τὴν σκηνὴν αὐτοῦ*, *i.e.* "His Shekinah."

Moreover, in Lev. xxvi. 11 we have a confirmation of the above view. Here the Targum regards the Tabernacle simply as the manifestation of the divine presence. The Hebrew (ונתתי משכני בתככם) "I will set my tabernacle among them"—LXX *καὶ θήσω τὴν διαθήκην* (F, *σκηνήν*) *μου ἐν ὑμῖν*—is paraphrased by the Targ. Jon. ואיתן שכינת יקרי בניכון, "I will set the Shekinah of My glory among you." In the next verse we have "the glory of My Shekinah." The word Shekinah which is used as a periphrasis for the divine name is closely associated with the conception of the divine glory (יקרא, איקר, Heb. יקר) as we see from the last two passages and throughout the Targums. Cf. also Targ. Jon. on Gen. xlix. 1, "the glory of the Shekinah of Yahweh": or simply "the glory of God" as in Onk. on Gen. xviii. 33. It is employed also as a rendering of "face" when used of God: cf. Deut. xxxi. 18, where אסתיר פני ("I will hide my face") is rendered אסלק שכנתי, "I will remove my Shekinah": and of "name" in the same connection: cf. Targums of Onk. and Jon. on Ex. xx. 24.

In the Mishnah and Talmud the Shekinah is the mediator of God's presence and activity in the world. Wherever ten persons pray together, the Shekinah is in the midst of them (Pirke Aboth iii. 9 (150–200 A.D.); Berach. 6[a]): also where three are gathered together to administer justice or where two meet to study the Law (Pirke Aboth iii. 9). Where a man and his wife lead a pious life the Shekinah is present. Before Israel sinned the Shekinah dwelt in each individual (Sota, 3[b]): and this relation was possible afterwards: cf. Pirke Aboth iii. 9.

From the Shekinah proceeded a brilliancy or splendour (*i.e.* זיו). In this the blessed were to share in the next word: cf. Berach. 17[a], "They delighted themselves in the brightness of the Shekinah (נהנים מזיו השכינה). On this "brightness," which is apparently rendered by our author by δόξα, see note on xxi. 23.

As our author thought in Hebrew, this line and the next would probably have run in his mind as

הנה שכינת אלהים עם בני האדם
וישכן עמהם

σκηνώσει μετ' αὐτῶν κτλ. On σκηνοῦν used of the inhabitants of heaven, cf. xii. 12, xiii. 6: see also vii. 15. With the thought compare Lev. xxvi. 11, καὶ θήσω τὴν διαθήκην (F, σκηνήν: so Mass. משכני) μου ἐν ὑμῖν . . . 12 . . . καὶ ἔσομαι ὑμῖν θεὸς καὶ ὑμεῖς ἔσεσθέ μου λαός. Ezek. xxxvii. 27, καὶ ἔσται ἡ κατασκήνωσίς μου ἐν αὐτοῖς καὶ ἔσομαι αὐτοῖς θεὸς καὶ αὐτοί μου ἔσονται λαός: xliii. 7; Zech. ii. 14 (10), viii. 3, κατασκηνώσω ἐν μέσῳ Ἰερουσαλήμ.

λαοὶ αὐτοῦ. If this reading is original the idea appears to be the same as that underlying John x. 16, where though there is but one flock (ποίμνη) and one Shepherd, there are many folds (αὐλαί). Each λαός forms a fold in the flock, of which God is the Shepherd. Possibly, however, λαοί may simply mean as in the vernacular "people." But John does not so use λαοί, and λαός seems to be the original reading. See crit. note on Greek text *in loc.*

καὶ αὐτὸς † ὁ θεὸς μετ' αὐτῶν ἔσται αὐτῶν θεός †.

The above text appears in three forms in the MSS, and none of them is satisfactory. **1.** That which is preserved in אQ and many cursives and omits αὐτῶν θεός can hardly be original, independently of its weak attestation; for not only is the parallelism against it (cf. also xxi. 7), but without **αὐτῶν θεός** the line becomes an otiose repetition of the idea in the first two lines. The preceding line, καὶ αὐτοὶ λαοὶ αὐτοῦ ἔσονται, requires some such parallelism as θεὸς αὐτῶν.

2. Since, then, the shortened form of the text in אQ cannot be accepted, we have next to consider that attested by A, vg, $s^{1.\,2}$—καὶ αὐτὸς ὁ θεὸς μετ' αὐτῶν ἔσται αὐτῶν θεός. Although the line is rather full, the sense is not unsatisfactory = "And He—God with them—shall be their God," or "God Himself shall be with them—their God." But this *unemphatic* position of **αὐτῶν** before θεός (*i.e.* the vernacular use of the possessive pronoun—see

Abbott, *Gram.* p. 419 sqq.) is against our author's usage and is not what we expect here.[1] Since in the preceding line the αὐτοῦ in λαοὶ αὐτοῦ has its normal possessive force in this position, we should expect θεὸς αὐτῶν in the present line. As "they shall be His peoples," so He shall be "their God."

3. Instead of αὐτῶν θεός, which is against our author's usage and also against the context, which here requires a real possessive, P and some cursives read θεὸς αὐτῶν. This is the reading the context leads us to expect, but its attestation is of the poorest character. It can only, therefore, be regarded in the light of a scribal emendation.

From the above examination of the MSS it follows that the original text has not been preserved in any MS. The corrupt readings appear to be due to the incorporation of what was really a marginal gloss on xxi. 3[bc], *i.e.* ὁ θεὸς μετ' αὐτῶν. The original may have been (*a*) καὶ αὐτὸς αὐτῶν θεὸς ἔσται, where the αὐτῶν would be emphatic owing to its proximity to αὐτός (see Abbott, *Gram.* p. 421, note 1), or (*b*) καὶ αὐτὸς ἔσται θεὸς αὐτῶν. In any case the sense would be: "And He will be their God." The usage of our author would certainly be in favour of (*b*): cf. xxi. 7.

4. καὶ ἐξαλείψει κτλ. See note on vii. 17. **καὶ ὁ θάνατος οὐκ ἔσται ἔτι.** The idea of this line—but not the diction—is suggested by Isa. xxv. 8[a], "He hath annihilated death for ever" (בלע המות לנצח), which section of Isaiah possibly belongs to the 2nd century B.C. Cf. 1 Cor. xv. 54, κατεπόθη ὁ θάνατος εἰς νῖκος. It will be observed that, whereas Aquila and Theodotion incorrectly render לָנֶצַח as an Aramaic phrase by εἰς νῖκος and the LXX by ἰσχύσας, our author gives the right sense in a paraphrastic form. For first century A.D. testimonies to the belief in the coming destruction of death, cf. 2 Enoch lxv. 10, "All corruptible things shall vanish and there shall be eternal life," and 4 Ezra viii. 53; 2 Bar. xxi. 23. See also Moed Qaton, iii. 9, where it cites Isa. xxv. 8.

Since death is destroyed (cf. xx. 14), there is no longer any need of the tree of life. All the faithful have won everlasting life. There can be no more death, there can be only "more life and fuller."

οὔτε πένθος οὔτε κραυγὴ οὔτε πόνος οὐκ ἔσται ἔτι. Cf. Isa. xxxv. 10, li. 11. "and sorrow and sighing (יגון ואנחה) shall flee

[1] αὐτῶν though occurring very frequently in our author is never elsewhere found in this unemphatic position in our text; nor is αὐτοῦ. αὐτῆς is found once in xviii. 5, but there in a source used by our author. σου is found several times in this position: see ii. 2, 19, notes. This unemphatic use of the genitive of αὐτός, though very frequent in the Fourth Gospel, does not belong to our author.

away." In our text the subject consists of three elements, and so also does the LXX of Isa. xxxv. 10 and li. 11, but the words of the LXX differ from those in our text, *ἀπέδρα ὀδύνη καὶ λύπη καὶ στεναγμός*. See also Isa. lxv. 19[b]; 1 Enoch x. 22, xxv. 6; 2 Enoch lxv. 8–9 (A), "They will live eternally, and then, too, there will be amongst them neither labour nor sickness nor humiliation nor anxiety nor need."

XXII. 3[a]. **καὶ πᾶν κατάθεμα οὐκ ἔσται ἔτι.** This verse forms the fourth line of the stanza, the first three lines of which—xxi. 4[abc]—we have just dealt with. That this verse belongs to that stanza, not only the subject matter, but the very diction is evidence. Thus *οὐκ ἔσται ἔτι*, which is not found in our author outside the description of the New Jerusalem (xxi. 1–4[abc], xxii. 3–5), has already occurred twice in this stanza, *i.e.* xxi. 4[bc]. The words themselves are based on Zech. xiv. 11 (וחרם לא־יהיה עוד) but not on the LXX. The word *κατάθεμα* (syncopated from *καταvάθεμα*) means here, as the context shows, a curse, *i.e.* an accursed thing, and not an accursed person. In itself *κατάθεμα* could mean the latter, as *ἀνάθεμα* (= חֵרֶם) can: cf. Gal. i. 8; 1 Cor. xvi. 22; Rom. ix. 3.

καὶ ὁ θρόνος τοῦ θεοῦ καὶ τοῦ ἀρνίου κτλ. On this conception of "the throne of God and of the Lamb," see note on xxii. 1. Owing to the fact that in the next line only God the Father is spoken of, critics have inferred that *καὶ τοῦ ἀρνίου* is here an intrusion. But, as I have shown in the note on xxii. 1, we find in 1 Enoch lxi. 8, 9 an excellent parallel; for, though the Elect One (*i.e.* the Messiah) is seated on God's throne as Judge in lxi. 8, in lxi. 9 the praises of all present are addressed to God and not to the Elect One. Moreover, in our text, xx. 6[e], the *αὐτοῦ* refers to only one of the two Divine Beings in 6[d]. Cf. iii. 21, which speaks of Christ as seated on God's throne, while in iii. 19 the O.T. words of Yahweh are used by Christ as His own. **οἱ δοῦλοι αὐτοῦ λατρεύσουσιν κτλ.** Cf. vii. 15, note.

4. ὄψονται τὸ πρόσωπον αὐτοῦ. Cf. Matt. v. 8; Heb. xii. 14. This vision of God, which was withheld from Moses (Ex. xxxiii. 20, 23), is promised to the faithful in Messianic times in Jerusalem in T. Zeb. ix. 8, *ὄψεσθε αὐτὸν ἐν Ἰερουσαλήμ*—a promise which appears also in Ps. lxxxiv. 7 (LXX and Vulg.) *ὀφθήσεται ὁ θεὸς τῶν θεῶν ἐν Σιών*. But this is not the vision face to face that is designed in our text and also in 4 Ezra vii. 98. In the latter passage the vision of God constitutes the seventh and supreme bliss of the righteous.

"They shall rejoice with boldness,
Be confident without confusion,
Be glad without fear;

For they are hastening to behold the face of Him whom in life they served,
And from whom they are destined to receive their reward in glory."

The capacity for such vision involves likeness of character: cf. 1 John iii. 2. Moffatt aptly compares Plutarch (*De Iside*, 79), who writes that the souls of men after death "migrate to the unseen" and "hang as it were upon Him (God), and gaze without ever wearying, and yearn for that unspeakable, indescribable beauty."

καὶ τὸ ὄνομα αὐτοῦ ἐπὶ τῶν μετώπων αὐτοῦ. See notes on vii. 3, xiii. 16, xiv. 1. Cf. also iii. 12.

5. καὶ νὺξ οὐκ ἔσται ἔτι. Darkness is at an end for ever. This clause appears to be the source of the corruption in xxi. 25. The expectation here expressed is not found in the O.T. but as regards heaven at all events is definitely taught in Philo, *De Josepho*, 24: εἰ γοῦν βουληθείη διακύπτειν εἴσω τις τῶν πραγμάτων, εὑρήσει τὸν οὐρανὸν ἡμέραν αἰώνιον, νυκτὸς καὶ πάσης σκιᾶς ἀμέτοχον, ἅτε περιλαμπόμενον ἀσβέστοις καὶ ἀκηράτοις ἀδιαστάτως φέγγεσιν. Cf. also 2 Bar. xlviii. 50. But the conception in our text is infinitely finer. The light of the New Jerusalem is not due as in Philo to a multitude of unextinguishable and unadulterated lights, but to the light of God's own presence—always and everywhere present. The conception could be deduced from Isa. lx. 19, "The sun shall be no more thy light by day; neither for brightness shall the moon give light unto thee; but the Lord shall be unto thee an everlasting light."

καὶ οὐχ ἕξουσιν χρείαν φωτὸς λύχνου καὶ φῶς ἡλίου. Cf. xxi. 23^{a}. The future ἕξουσιν (A vg. $s^{1.2}$, Tic.) is to be preferred to ἔχουσιν. All the verbs in this description of the New Jerusalem (xxi. $1–4^{abc}$, xxii. $^{3-5}$) are futures. As contra-distinguished from the heavenly Jerusalem, that was already in being and was to come down from heaven for the Millennial Kingdom, the New Jerusalem, which is not created till after its close, is not yet in being. As regards the former, observe the occasional present and past verbs in xxi. 9–xxii. 2. The phrase φῶς ἡλίου (AP: φωτός ℵ me $s^{1.2}$) had best be regarded as dependent on χρείαν. Such an irregularity is not unfamiliar in our author. In fact we have χρείαν ἔχειν with an acc. in iii. 17 and with a genitive in xxi. 23.

Κύριος ὁ θεὸς φωτίσει ἐπ' αὐτούς. The construction here (φωτίσει ἐπ', ℵA, etc.) differs from that in xxi. 23, ἡ δόξα τοῦ θεοῦ ἐφώτισεν αὐτήν, and in xviii. 1, and the sense differs likewise. In xxi. 23 the meaning is clear: not the physical luminaries, the sun and moon, but "the glory of God did lighten" the Heavenly Jerusalem (cf. also xviii. 1). But here the Greek φωτίσει ἐπ' *αὐτούς* differs from that in xviii. 1, xxi. 23 alike in construction and meaning. First, as regards the construction, it must at once be conceded that it is peculiar. If our author had wished to express the thought "shall shine upon them," "give them light," he would have said *φανεῖ αὐτοῖς*: cf. xxi. 23. Hence later MSS omitted the *ἐπί*, and herein they are followed by WH, Bousset and others. Other editors, such as Alford, Swete, and Moffatt, rightly follow ℵA here, but do not explain the anomaly. We can get a good sense, if we explain it as a Hebraism. When regarded from this standpoint we next recognize that *Κύριος ὁ θεὸς φωτίσει ἐπ᾽ αὐτούς* is a rendering of Ps. cxviii. 27, אֵל יי׳ וַיָּאֶר לָנוּ, where for ויאר our author found יאיר or הֵאִיר, which latter he changed into יאיר. Here the Aramaic Targum and the Syriac, Ethiopic, and Arabic Versions similarly transform the two clauses into one and presuppose the text to have been הֵאִיר and not וַיָּאֶר. Here, therefore, the *ἐπί* reproduces לְ.[1] Having discovered the source of our author's words the discovery of their meaning ceases to be difficult. In Ps. cxviii. 27 the words are a shortened form of the priest's blessing in Num. vi. 25 by the omission of פניו (see *Oxford Hebrew Lexicon*, p. 21^{b}), which in its fuller form recurs several times as the footnote shows. Hence we should here render "The Lord God shall cause His face to shine upon them." Here there is a *personal relation* indicated between God and the blessed individually. In xxi. 23, on the other hand, no such personal relation is indicated. The Holy City is lighted up as a whole by the glory of God instead of by the sun and moon. Thus the Face which the saints will see in xxii. 4 will shine upon them in eternal benediction (xxii. 5).

βασιλεύσουσιν εἰς τοὺς αἰῶνας τῶν αἰώνων. This everlasting reign of the saints in the New Jerusalem stands out in strong contrast with the Millennial reign in the City which came down from heaven before the Final Judgment, xx. 4.

The Epilogue.

xxi. 6^{b}–8, xxii. 6–7, 18^{a}, 16, 13, 12, 10, 8–9, 20–21.

INTRODUCTION.

§ 1. On this epilogue, which contains the declarations of God, of Jesus, and of John, see p. 154. That they come from our author cannot be contested, though they have been transmitted

[1] In Num. vi. 25 we have אֶל (LXX *ἐπί*), in Ps. xxxi. 17; Dan. ix. 17 עַל, and בְּ in Ps. cxix. 135, and אֶת־ in Ps. lxvii. 2. In all cases the LXX renders by *ἐπί*. But the LXX does not use *φωτίζειν* in these passages but *ἐπιφαίνειν*.

in the utmost disorder, and no doubt defectively. The reconstruction here given is, of course, tentative. First of all, xxi. 6^b–8, as containing a declaration of God, singles itself out for consideration. It cannot possibly belong to the period after the Final Judgment; for hope is still held out to the repentant, and the doom of the second death has not yet been pronounced against the finally impenitent. It must, therefore, belong either to the period of the Millennial Kingdom or to that of our author. The thought and language are in favour of the latter hypothesis. Thus ὁ νικῶν in xxii. 7 brings vividly before us the experiences—actual and apprehended—of the faithful in the years 90–96 A.D.: he is the warrior faithful unto death, to whom promise after promise is held out, as in ii. 7, 11, 17, 26, iii. 5, 12, 21, xii. 11, xv. 2. Again, xxi. 6^d, ἐγὼ τῷ διψῶντι δώσω ἐκ τῆς πηγῆς τοῦ ὕδατος τῆς ζωῆς δωρεάν, clearly presupposes xxii. 17 as having *preceded* it; for there we have the divine gift described without the article: ὁ θέλων λαβέτω ὕδωρ ζωῆς δωρεάν. But for the recurrence of the δωρεάν here we might have explained the articles in xxi. 6^d from vii. 17. As regards the sorcerers, fornicators, murderers, and idolaters we are told (xxii. 15) that in the Millennial Kingdom they will be excluded from the Heavenly Jerusalem: here they are adjudged to be cast into the lake of fire (xxi. 8).

Hence xxi. 6^b–8 is to be taken as the divine authentication of the Apocalypse as a whole, which God had given to Jesus Christ to make known to His servants (as stated in i. 1). This declaration of God is then followed by the declaration of Jesus that He had sent His angels to testify these things to the Churches in xxii. 6–7, 18^a, 16, 13, 12, 10, and the Book closes with the testimony of John, xxii. 8–9, 20–21 (see note on i. 1–3). In xxii. 6–21 more than anywhere else in chapters xx.–xxii. we have the *disjecta membra* of the Poet-Seer. We have already assigned xxii. 14–15, 17 to the section dealing with the Heavenly Jerusalem which comes down to earth during the Millennial Kingdom. The re-arrangement of xxii. 6–22 just given is suggested by the text itself and confirmed by i. 1–2 (see note in vol. i. p. 5 sq.), and is therefore not improbably the order intended by the Seer. It is, of course, fragmentary. With a view to its arrangement, we observe first of all that Jesus is the speaker in 12–13, 16, and likewise in 6–7; for in these last two verses the speaker is distinguished from the angel who showed the Seer the things which must shortly come to pass, and the words "behold I come quickly" in 7 are naturally spoken by Christ. Moreover, as Könnecke and Moffatt have recognized, 12–13, 16 can be restored to their original order by reading them as follows: 16, 13, 12. Thus this section is to be read as follows:

6–7, 16, 13, 12. Verse 10—still the words of Christ—comes next, "And He saith unto me, Seal not up the words of the prophecy of this book; for the time is at hand."

I have bracketed 11 as conflicting with xxi. 6b–8, which apparently refer to evangelistic appeals during the Seer's lifetime. xxii. 18a, as coming from Christ, gives His imprimatur to the book. xxii. 8–9 as describing the action of the Seer in relation to the angel at its close, and xxii. 20–21 as giving the Seer's final testimony form the natural close of the Apocalypse.

Traces of the hand of the editor are to be found in two passages: see § 3 *ad fin.* Cf. § 3 in Introduction to xx. 4–15 (p. 182).

§ 2. *Diction.*

XXI. 6. τὸ Ἄλφα καὶ τὸ Ὦ. Cf. i. 8, xxii. 13. ἡ ἀρχὴ καὶ τὸ τέλος: cf. xxii. 13. τῷ διψῶντι (cf. vii. 16) δώσω ἐκ τῆς πηγῆς τοῦ ὕδατος τῆς ζωῆς δωρεάν: cf. xxii. 17, vii 17.

7. ὁ νικῶν: see under § 1. ἔσομαι αὐτῷ θεός: cf. xxi. 3.

8. τοῖς . . . φονεῦσι καὶ πόρνοις καὶ φαρμακοῖς καὶ εἰδωλολάτραις: cf. xxii. 15. τῇ λίμνῃ τῇ καιομένῃ: cf. xix. 20, xx. 10, etc.

ὁ θάνατος ὁ δεύτερος: cf. ii. 11.

XXII. 6. ἀπέστειλεν τ. ἄγγελον αὐτοῦ: cf. i. 1, ἀποστείλας διὰ τ. ἀγγ. αὐτοῦ.

δεῖξαι τ. δούλοις αὐτοῦ . . . ἐν τάχει: a verbal repetition from i. 1.

7. ἰδοὺ ἔρχομαι ταχύ: cf. ii. 16, iii. 11, xvi. 15, xxii. 12. μακάριος ὁ τηρῶν τ. λόγους τ. προφητείας τ. βιβλίου τούτου: a summary of i. 3 (and the last of the seven beatitudes in this Book), xxii. 10, 18.

18a. μαρτυρῶ: cf. i. 2. τ. λόγους τ. προφητείας κτλ.: see on 7 above.

16. ἐγὼ . . . ἔπεμψα κτλ.: cf. i. 1. ἐγώ εἰμι ἡ ῥίζα . . . Δαυείδ: repeated from v. 5. ὁ ἀστήρ . . . ὁ πρωινός: already in ii. 28

13. ἐγὼ τὸ Ἄλφα καὶ τὸ Ὦ: cf. i. 8, xxi. 6. ὁ πρῶτος καὶ ὁ ἔσχατος: cf. i. 17, ii. 8. ἡ ἀρχὴ καὶ τὸ τέλος: cf. xxi. 6.

12. ἰδοὺ ἔρχομαι ταχύ. See on 7 above. ἀποδοῦναι ἑκάστῳ ὡς τὸ ἔργον ἐστὶν αὐτοῦ: cf. ii. 23, δώσω . . . ἑκάστῳ κατὰ τὰ ἔργα ὑμῶν, xx. 13.

10. λέγει μοι: cf. v. 5, vii. 13, x. 9. μὴ σφραγίσῃς: cf. x. 4. τ. λόγους τ. προφητείας τ. βιβλ. τούτου: see on 7 above.

ὁ καιρὸς γὰρ ἐγγύς: cf. i. 3.

8. κἀγὼ Ἰωάννης: cf. i. 1, 4, 9. ἔπεσα προσκυνῆσαι ἔμπροσθεν τῶν ποδῶν: cf. xix. 10, which, however, is a doublet of this passage. Elsewhere John uses *προσκυνεῖν ἐνώπιον*: cf. iii. 9, xv. 4 where this phrase expresses simply homage. τοῦ δεικνύοντος: cf. i. 1, iv. 1, xvii. 1, xxi. 9, 10, xxii. 1, 6.

9. τῶν τηρούντων τ. λόγους τ. βιβλ. τούτου: cf. i. 3, iii. 8, 10, xii. 17, xiv. 12. τῷ θεῷ προσκύνησον: see note on vii. 11.

20. μαρτυρῶν: see 18a above. ναί: see i. 7 (note). ἔρχομαι ταχύ: see on 7 above.

Ἀμήν: see i. 7 (note).

§ 3. *Idioms.*—The constructions are almost wholly normal. Here as elsewhere in xx. 4–xxii. the text has apparently been normalized by the editor of this section.

Johannine xxi. 6. δώσω ἐκ: for this partitive use of ἐκ after διδόναι cf. iii. 9. Not elsewhere in N.T. save in 1 John iv. 13.

8. τοῖς δὲ δειλοῖς . . . τὸ μέρος αὐτῶν: a pure Hebraism: see note *in loc.*.

XXII. 8. ὁ ἀκούων: used here as an aorist or perfect as elsewhere the participle is used in our author: cf. δεικνύοντός, similarly used at the close of this verse.

Non-Johannine xxi. 6. τῷ διψῶντι δώσω. According to our author's universal usage elsewhere we should expect αὐτῷ after δώσω in this connection: cf. ii. 7, 17, 26, iii. 21. Here apparently the editor has omitted it and so normalized the text.

XXI. 8. τῇ λίμνῃ τῇ καιομένῃ may be another such instance: cf. xix. 20.

The Epilogue of the Apocalypse consisting of (1) the declaration of God, xxi. 6b–8: (2) the testimony of Jesus, xxii. 6–7, 18a, 16, 13, 12, 10 [11], [18b–19]: (3) and that of John, xxii. 8–9, 20–21.

Here more than anywhere else in chapters xx.–xxii. have we the *disjecta membra* of the Poet-Seer. These fragments clearly form the Epilogue of the Book, and a study of these fragments leads us to recognize them as coming from three distinct speakers—God, Jesus, and John. In xxi. 6b–8 God is clearly the speaker. In xxii. 12–13, 16, and likewise 6–7, 10, 18a, Jesus is the speaker, for in 6–7 the speaker is distinguished from the angel who showed the Seer the things that must shortly come to pass, and the words "behold I come quickly" in 7 are most naturally spoken by Christ, and likewise 10, 18a. Moreover, as Könnecke (followed by Moffatt) has recognized, 12–13, 16 should be read as follows: 16, 13, 12. Thus the original order of the testimony and declaration of Christ was most probably: 6–7, 16, 13, 12, 10 [11], 18a [18b–19]. The book then closes with the testimony of John xxii. 8–9, 20–21. xxii. 11, 18b–19 appear to be interpolations.

This order, which is suggested by a study of xxii. 6–22, in itself harmonizes with that given in the first two verses of the Apocalypse, where we are told that (1) God has given to Christ this revelation to show unto His servants: (2) that Christ has sent and signified it by His angel to His servant John: (3) that

John has borne witness of the word of God and of the testimony of Christ.

XXI. 6^b–8. *The declaration of God as to His own Being, His willingness to be gracious to the repentant, His promise of being a Father to him that overcometh, and His denunciation of the cravenhearted, the unbelieving and impure as destined to be cast into the lake that burneth with fire and brimstone—the second death.*

6^b. ἐγώ εἰμι τὸ Ἄλφα καὶ τὸ Ὦ. Here as in i. 8 (where see note) these epithets belong to the Eternal Father, whereas in xxii. 13 they are used by Christ of Himself.

ἡ ἀρχὴ καὶ τὸ τέλος. Cf. xxii. 13, see note on i. 8.

ἐγὼ τῷ διψῶντι δώσω ἐκ τῆς πηγῆς κτλ. Based on Isa. lv. 1. See note on vii. 17.

τοῦ ὕδατος τῆς ζωῆς δωρεάν. Observe the articles. We have *ὕδωρ ζωῆς δωρεάν* in xxii. 17—which is explicable if xxii. 17 precedes, but not so if the MSS order of the text were correct. On the distinction between *ὕδωρ ζωῆς* and *ξύλον ζωῆς* see ii. 7, note.

7. ὁ νικῶν κληρονομήσει ταῦτα. The victor is here contrasted with the cravenhearted in 8. The *ταῦτα* here refers to the Millennial blessedness, the new heaven, the new earth, and the New Jerusalem (xxi. 1–4^{abc}, xx. 3–5). Of these "he who conquers" is "the heir" (*κληρονόμος*). The collocation of *κληρονομήσει* in this line and *αὐτὸς ἔσται μοι υἱός* in the next but one shows, as Swete remarks, the close affinity in this respect between our author and St. Paul: cf. Rom. viii. 17, *εἰ δὲ τέκνα, καὶ κληρονόμοι*; Gal. iv. 7, *εἰ δὲ υἱὸς, καὶ κληρονόμος διὰ θεοῦ.*

καὶ ἔσομαι αὐτῷ θεός. This promise was made frequently in the O.T.: first to the founder of the nation, Gen. xvii. 7, 8, while that in the next line, *καὶ αὐτὸς ἔσται μοι υἱός*, is first made in reference to Solomon as a representative of the nation, 2 Sam. vii. 14, and in Ps. lxxxix. 26, 27 in reference to David. Nowhere in the O.T. can the individual *as such* claim God as Father. This claim is first found in Sir. xxiii. 1: later in Wisdom ii. 16 (see note on Jub. i. 24 of my edition). But in the N.T. the normal attitude of the faithful individual to God is that of a son to his heavenly Father. Here only in our author is this conception brought forward. This sonship is realized in some true *degree* in the present life just as surely as the thirst for righteousness (*τῷ διψῶντι*) is in some true measure satisfied here.

8. We have here the list of those who have disfranchised themselves from the Kingdom of God and gone over into the Kingdom of outer darkness. Of these there are mentioned eight classes, which fall into three divisions, the first division comprising three classes, the second three, and the third two.

First division—τοῖς δὲ δειλοῖς[1] καὶ ἀπιστοῖς καὶ ἐβδελυγμένοις. The δειλοί are not "the fearful" as in the A.V. and R.V. but "the cowardly" or "the cravenhearted," who in the struggle with the Beast have played the coward, denied the faith, and rendered worship to Cæsar. δειλία has always a bad meaning, and St. Paul declares, 2 Tim. i. 7: οὐ γὰρ ἔδωκεν ἡμῖν ὁ θεὸς πνεῦμα δειλίας. A man may fear and yet not be δειλός. In fact the most courageous man is he who, notwithstanding his fear of the real dangers that beset his advance, goes sturdily onwards. But this fear in the N.T. is either φόβος—a middle term capable of a good or of a bad interpretation according to the context—or εὐλάβεια. Cf. Phil. ii. 12, μετὰ φόβου καὶ τρόμου τὴν ἑαυτῶν σωτηρίαν κατεργάζεσθε.

τοῖς . . . ἀπίστοις. In our author ἄπιστος means primarily "faithless," "untrustworthy." This is to be inferred from the use of πιστός: cf. i. 5, ἀπὸ Ἰησοῦ Χριστοῦ ὁ μάρτυς ὁ πιστός; ii. 10, γίνου πιστὸς ἄχρι θανάτου; ii. 13, iii. 14, xvii. 14.[2] Thus the ἄπιστος is closely allied to the δειλός that precedes. As such the ἄπιστοι are not coextensive with the δειλοί, for there are other grounds than cowardice for such disloyalty. But the ἄπιστοι owing to the ἐβδελυγμένοι that follows immediately may suggest the idea of immorality: cf. Tit. i. 15, τοῖς δὲ μεμιαμμένοις καὶ ἀπίστοις . . . 16. . . . βδελυκτοὶ ὄντες καὶ ἀπειθεῖς. Furthermore, the ἄπιστοι appear to embrace not only the Christian who denies his faith, but also the pagan who rejects it.

τοῖς . . . ἐβδελυγμένοις. These are those who are defiled with the abominations referred to in xvii. 4, 5, connected with the worship of the Beast and generally with the impurities of the pagan cults, including unnatural vice. Cf. Hos. ix. 10; 2 Enoch x. 4, 5, "This place is prepared for . . . those who on earth practise sin against nature, which is child corruption after the Sodomitic fashion, magic-making, enchantments, and devilish witchcraft . . . lies . . . fornication, murder": Apoc. Pet. 17, οὗτοι δὲ ἦσαν οἱ μιάναντες τὰ σώματα ἑαυτῶν ὡς γυναῖκες ἀναστρεφόμενοι· αἱ δὲ μετ' αὐτῶν γυναῖκες . . . αἱ συγκοιμηθεῖσαι ἀλλήλαις ὡς

[1] In τοῖς δὲ δειλοῖς . . . τὸ μέρος αὐτῶν we have a Hebraism where ל is used in introducing a new subject: see *Oxford Hebrew Lexicon*, p. 514^{b}= לְרַבֵּי לֵב . . . חֶלְקָם. Cf. 1 Chron. xxiv. 1, ולבני אהרן מחלקותם = "And as for the sons of Aaron their courses were": also vii. 1, xxvi. 1, 31 (where the LXX reproduces by the dat.); 2 Chron. vii. 21; Eccles. ix. 4. In Ezra x. 14 the LXX has this construction, though it is not found in the Hebrew, where possibly the ל has been lost: πᾶσιν τοῖς ἐν πόλεσιν ἡμῶν . . . ἐλθέτωσαν, <ל>כל אשר בעָרינו . . . יבא. The more usual construction in Hebrew would be a *nominativus pendens* resumed by חלקם.

[2] This meaning of πιστός, *i.e.* "faithful," "loyal," is also found in 2 Bar. liv. 21 (where see my note), though elsewhere (except possibly in liv. 16) in that book it means "believing": cf. xlii. 2, liv. 5, lvii. 2, lix. 2, lxxxiii. 8 On 4 Ezra in this respect see Box, pp. 67, 143.

ἂν ἀνὴρ πρὸς γυναῖκα This class must obviously comprise all the pagan world that is so defiled. We thus observe that, whereas the first three classes are closely associated in point of character, their comprehensiveness steadily widens from faithless Christians to the whole body of the impure whether Christian or pagan.

καὶ φονεῦσι καὶ πόρνοις καὶ φαρμακοῖς. In xxii. 15 these words are found in the reverse order. These sins have already been referred to in ix. 21, ἐκ τῶν φόνων αὐτῶν οὔτε ἐκ τῶν φαρμάκων αὐτῶν οὔτε ἐκ τῆς πορνείας αὐτῶν (see note). See also Gal. v. 19–21, where πορνεία, φαρμακία and φόνοι (in some MSS) appear amongst many other vices. In 1 Tim. i. 9 we have ἀνδροφόνοις, πόρνοις, and in Jas. ii. 11 φόνος and μοιχεία are combined. The φαρμακοῖς are "sorcerers," as their association with the εἰδωλαλάτραις in the next line shows: cf. ix. 20, 21, where they are similarly associated.

εἰδωλολάτραις καὶ πᾶσι τοῖς ψευδέσιν. Cf. ix. 20, xxii. 15. Idolatry is the cardinal sin against which our author warns his readers. Hence the primary reference is here to Christians. As the idols are lies so all the idolaters are liars. The insincerities of heathenism, the frauds of its priests as well as all the falsities of Christians are here referred to (cf. xiv. 5). Lying and duplicity are denounced in the O.T. but in far stronger terms in the N.T.

τὸ μέρος αὐτῶν. The αὐτῶν resumes the eight classes mentioned in the preceding datives. On these datives see footnote, p. 216. **τῇ λίμνῃ τῇ καιομένῃ κτλ.**: cf. xix. 20, xx. 10, 14, 15 and note on ix. 1: 2 Enoch x. 2, "And there were all manner of tortures in this place . . . 4. This place, O Enoch, is prepared for those who dishonour God, etc." **ὁ θάνατος ὁ δεύτερος.** See note on ii. 11.

The Testimony of Jesus, xxii. 6–7, 16, 13, 12, 10 [11], 18[a] [18[b]–19].

XXII. 6–7. That these are the words of Christ is to be concluded from the declaration in 7, καὶ ἰδοὺ ἔρχομαι ταχύ. Moreover, there is a special fitness that He, who is designated πιστὸς καὶ ἀληθινός in iii. 14, xix. 11, should authenticate the words of the prophecy of this book as πιστοὶ καὶ ἀληθινοί (6).

6. Οὗτοι οἱ λόγοι πιστοὶ καὶ ἀληθινοί. Christ here authenticates the words of the prophecy of this book and as ὁ πιστὸς καὶ ἀληθινός there is a special appropriateness in His so doing. Besides He is therein fulfilling the very task given to Him by God in i. 1, where we are told that God gave Him this revelation in order that He might make it known—ἣν (*i.e.* τὴν ἀποκάλυψιν) ἔδωκεν αὐτῷ (*i.e.* Ἰησοῦ Χριστῷ) ὁ θεὸς δεῖξαι τοῖς δούλοις αὐτοῦ. Cf. 4 Ezra **xv.** 1, 2, "Ecce loquere in aures plebis meae sermones prophetiae, quos immisero in os tuum, dicit Dominus. 2. Et fac ut in charta scribantur, quoniam fideles et veri sunt."

ὁ κύριος ὁ θεὸς τῶν πνευμάτων τῶν προφητῶν. This is certainly a strange expression. Some scholars (Bousset, Moffatt) regard the plural as an archaistic detail (cf. i. 4), according to which there are a variety of angelic spirits that inspire the prophets. If we take this in the sense that various angels were sent at various times to instruct the prophets, it is quite unobjectionable. *πνεύματα* is used of the archangels in our author: cf. iii. 1, iv. 5, etc. But though the sense is unobjectionable, the words themselves can hardly bear this meaning. The *πνεύματα* are best taken with Swete to be the prophets' own spirits filled by the One Spirit mentioned in ii. 7, xiv. 13, xxii. 17. When the prophet spake as a prophet, it was his spirit that was active (i. 10, xvii. 3, xxi. 10). Hence it seems that the text should here be interpreted as a similar expression in 1 Cor. xiv. 32, *πνεύματα προφητῶν προφήταις ὑποτάσσεται*, where it is the prophets' own spirits that are referred to. The divine title in our text has no connection of any kind with the very frequent designation of God in 1 Enoch xxxvii.–lxxi.; 2 Macc. iii. 24, *i.e.* "Lord of Spirits." In Num. xvi. 22, xxvii. 16 the divine title "the God of the spirits of all flesh" (אלהי הרוחת לכל־בשר) has only a general reference to mankind as a whole and not as in our text to the special class of men. τῶν προφητῶν. As in x. 7, xi. 18, xxii. 9, John associates himself here with the Christian prophets.

τὸν ἄγγελον αὐτοῦ. Here Christ speaks of the angel of xvii. 1, xxi. 9 as God's angel, and yet in i. 1, xxii. 16 he is described as Christ's angel. The statements are not incompatible. δεῖξαι τοῖς δούλοις . . . ἐν τάχει. This clause is repeated from i. 1. In fact the words *ἀπέστειλεν τ. ἄγγελον αὐτοῦ δεῖξαι τ. δούλοις αὐτοῦ ἃ δεῖ γενέσθαι ἐν τάχει* combine *δεῖξαι τ. δούλοις αὐτοῦ, ἃ δεῖ γενέσθαι ἐν τάχει* and *ἀποστείλας διὰ τοῦ ἀγγέλου αὐτοῦ* in i. 1.

7. καὶ ἰδοὺ ἔρχομαι ταχύ. Cf. xxii. 12, where as here it is from the lips of Christ; also ii. 5, 16, iii. 11, and xvi. 15, which as we have already seen should be restored after iii. 3ᵃ.

μακάριος ὁ τηρῶν τοὺς λόγους κτλ. This is the last of the seven beatitudes of the book (see note on i. 3). It is a short summary of i. 3, and thus the Book ends as it began in declaring the blessedness of those who have kept the words of the prophecy; but, whereas it is John that pronounces the first beatitude (i. 3), it is Christ that pronounces the last.

18ᵃ. μαρτυρῶ ἐγὼ πάντι τῷ ἀκούοντι τοὺς λόγους κτλ. Here the speaker is, as Swete urges, still Christ, who gives His solemn imprimatur to the Book. Moreover, as in 16—*μαρτυρῆσαι ὑμῖν ταῦτα*—the *τοὺς λόγους* is to be taken as the accusative after *μαρτυρῆσαι* and not after *ἀκούοντι*, as is usually done: "to every-one that heareth I bear witness to the words of the prophecy of this book." As in 7, 10, Christ uses the same phraseology, τ. λόγους τ. προφητείας τ. βιβλίου τούτου.

16. Ἐγὼ Ἰησοῦς ἔπεμψα τὸν ἄγγελόν μου. These words recall i. 1, καὶ ἐσήμανεν ἀποστείλας διὰ τοῦ ἀγγέλου αὐτοῦ, and xxii. 6, ὁ θεὸς . . . ἀπέστειλε τὸν ἄγγελον αὐτοῦ. According to Westcott (Add. Note on John xx. 21) ἀποστέλλω "conveys the accessory notions of a special commission and so far of a delegated authority in the person sent." It is strange that Abbott (*Johannine Vocabulary*, p. 227) ascribes to these verbs almost the contrary meaning: "We are perhaps justified in thinking that ἀποστέλλω means 'sending away into the world at large,' but πέμπω 'sending on a special errand.'" Our author, at any rate, appears to use them as synonyms.

ὑμῖν: cf. also xxii. 6. The angel of Christ attests the contents of this book (ταῦτα) to the members of the Asian Churches. Others think the ὑμῖν refers to the body of prophets in the Johannine school.

ἐγώ εἰμι ἡ ῥίζα καὶ τὸ γένος Δαυείδ: cf. v. 5, ὁ λέων ὁ ἐκ τῆς φυλῆς Ἰούδα, ἡ ῥίζα Δαυείδ: Isa. xi. 1, And there shall come forth a shoot out of the stock of Jesse and a branch out of his roots shall bear fruit; xi. 10; Test. Jud. xxiv. 5.

> "Then shall the sceptre of my kingdom shine forth,
> And from your root shall arise a stem."

In His own person Christ is at once the root, and the stem and branches that spring from the root, and thus combines all the Messianic claims of the Davidic family. Thus He forms the climax of Jewish Messianic expectation. Our author lays more stress on the Davidic descent than Christ did Himself: cf. Matt. xxii. 42–45.

ὁ ἀστὴρ ὁ λαμπρός, ὁ πρωινός. Here Christ is Himself the morning star, which in ii. 28 is promised to the faithful. The idea is ultimately derived from Num. xxiv. 17, "There shall come forth a star out of Jacob," but in the Test. Lev. xviii. 3, and probably in Test. Jud. xxiv. 1, this passage has been definitely associated with the hope of a Messiah from Levi—an expectation that was abandoned early in the first century B.C. As Christ is the realization of all that Israel hoped for in the past (ἡ ῥίζα κτλ.), He contains in Himself the promise (cf. Luke i. 78) of all that is to come (ὁ ἀστὴρ . . . ὁ πρωινός) as "the Light of the world," John viii. 12.

13. In this verse the Son claims all the attributes of the Father. In the next verse (*i.e.* 12) it follows naturally that He designates Himself as the Judge of all the world.

ἐγὼ τὸ Ἄλφα κτλ.: cf. i. 8 (note), xxi. 6, where it is the title used by God of Himself.

ὁ πρῶτος καὶ ὁ ἔσχατος. See note on i. 17, ii. 8—in both cases of Christ.

ἡ ἀρχὴ καὶ τὸ τέλος. This title is used by God of Himself in xxi. 6.

The phrase *ἡ ἀρχὴ καὶ τὸ τέλος* is an abbreviated form of an ancient Orphic saying, which is first recorded in Plato, *Leg.* iv. 7, *ὁ μὲν δὴ θεὸς (ὥσπερ καὶ ὁ παλαιὸς λόγος) ἀρχήν τε καὶ τελευτὴν καὶ μέσα τῶν ὄντων ἁπάντων ἔχων.* Thus Plato in the 4th century B.C. speaks of this saying as even then an ancient one. A scholion on this passage gives the original form of it and an explanation: *θεὸν μὲν τὸν δημιουργὸν σαφῶς, παλαιὸν δὲ λόγον λέγει τὸν Ὀρφικόν, ὅς ἐστιν οὗτος· Ζεὺς ἀρχή, Ζεὺς μέσσα, Διὸς δ' ἐκ πάντα τέτυκται, Ζεὺς πυθμὴν γαίης τε καὶ οὐρανοῦ ἀστερόεντος· καὶ ἀρχὴ μὲν οὗτος ὡς ποιητικὸν αἴτιον, τελευτὴ δὲ ὡς τελικόν, μέσσα δὲ ὡς ἐξίσου πᾶσι παρών.* We might compare the Pauline statement, Rom. xi. 36, *ἐξ αὐτοῦ καὶ δι' αὐτοῦ καὶ εἰς αὐτὸν τὰ πάντα, i.e.* God is the initial cause, the sustaining cause, and the final cause of all things.

This Orphic logion was well known in the ancient world. In the first century A.D. it was familiar to the Palestinian Jews, as we know from Josephus who quotes it in *c. Ap.* ii. 22, *ὁ θεὸς . . . αὐτὸς ἑαυτῷ καὶ πᾶσιν αὐτάρκης, ἀρχὴ καὶ μέσα καὶ τέλος οὗτος τῶν πάντων.* In his *Ant.* viii. 11. 2 it appears in almost the same abbreviated form as in our text: *καὶ τὸν ἴδιον θεὸν . . . ὃς . . . ἀρχὴ καὶ τέλος τῶν ἁπάντων.* In later times it was adopted by the Talmudists and given a Jewish turn in the third century A.D. by Simon ben Lakish, who strove to derive this ancient Greek Orphic saying from the Hebrew word אמת (Jer. Jeb. xii. 13[a]; Gen. R. lxxxi.); "for . . . א is the first, מ the middle, and ת the last letter of the alphabet—this being the name of God according to Isa. xliv. 6, explained Jer. Sanh. i. 18[a], 'I am the first <having had none from whom to receive the kingdom>; I am the middle, there being none who shares the kingdom with me; <and I am the last>there being none to whom I shall hand the kingdom of the world'" (quoted from *Jewish Encyc.* i. 439). It is hardly needful to draw attention to the forced nature of this explanation or to point out that מ is not the middle letter of the Hebrew alphabet—being the 13th from the beginning and the 10th from the end.

Turning now from Jewish to Christian writings, we find that the early Christian writers were well acquainted with this ancient Greek saying. This phrase lies behind the text of the *Κήρυγμα Πέτρου*: *εἷς θεός ἐστιν, ὃς ἀρχὴν πάντων ἐποίησεν καὶ τέλους ἐξουσίαν ἔχει.* Justin Martyr (*Cohort. ad Gent.* xxv.) quotes the saying from Plato but ascribes it to the Law of Moses. Irenaeus (*Haer* iii. 25. 5, "Et Deus quidem, quemadmodum et vetus sermo est, initium et finem et medietates omnium quae sunt habens"; Hippolytus, *Refut. omn. Haer.* i. 19; Clem. Alex. *Protrepb.* vi. 69, *Strom.* ii. 22. § 132; Origen, *c. Cels.* vi. 13; Eusebius, *Praepar. Evang.* xi. 13, *ἀρχὴν αὐτὸς ἔχων καὶ μεσσατον ἠδὲ τελευτήν.*[1]

12. ἰδοὺ ἔρχομαι ταχύ. Cf. iii. 11, xxii. 7, 20. καὶ ὁ μισθός μου μετ' ἐμοῦ. Cf. xi. 18[d]. *ὁ μισθός μου* is here "the reward which I give." Cf. Isa. xl. 10, *ἰδοὺ ὁ μισθὸς αὐτοῦ μετ' αὐτοῦ*: lxii. 11; Wisd. v. 15, *καὶ ἐν κυρίῳ ὁ μισθὸς αὐτῶν.*

ἀποδοῦναι ἑκάστῳ ὡς τὸ ἔργον ἐστὶν αὐτοῦ. Cf. ii. 23, xx. 13; Rom. ii. 6; Prov. xxiv. 12[b] (LXX, *ὃς ἀποδίδωσιν ἑκάστῳ κατὰ τὰ ἔργα αὐτοῦ*); Jer. xvii. 10; Ps. lxi. 13, *ὅτι σὺ ἀποδώσεις ἑκάστῳ κατὰ τὰ ἔργα αὐτοῦ.* Our text seems to have been before 1 Clem. xxxiv. 3.

10. Here also Christ appears to speak, as Bousset recognizes. There is force in His command to issue the Book immediately; "for the time is at hand." As contrasted with Jewish Apocalypses, such as Daniel (cf. viii. 26, xii. 4, 9); 1 Enoch i. 2, xciii. 10, civ. 12; 2 Enoch xxxiii. 9–11, xxxv. 3, etc., which were not to be divulged till distant generations, our Apocalypse is to be made known by the Seer to his contemporaries. The older Apocalypses were referred to as sealed (cf. Dan. viii. 26, in order to explain the withholding of their publication till the actual time of their author.

τοὺς λόγους τ. προφητείας κτλ. Cf. xxii. 7, 18. In all three cases these are the words of Christ: cf. also i. 3. ὁ καιρὸς γὰρ ἐγγύς. This clause and the preceding are combined by our author in i. 3. The same idea underlies the clause *ἔρχομαι ταχύ*, ii. 16, iii. 11, xxii. 7, 12, 20, which is only used by Christ.

[**11.** These words can refer only to the contemporaries of the Seer. But, since xxi. 6–8 refer also to his contemporaries and still proclaim the possibility of free and full forgiveness, this verse appears to be a later addition. In xxi. 6[d] those who thirst after a new life are promised satisfaction, whereas here the door of hope is closed absolutely and finally against every class of sinners. Ver. 11 assumes that finality in character is already arrived at, and an unswerving persistence in good or evil, though there is still some interval between the vision and the Second Advent; for the circulation of the Book among the Churches (ii.–iii.) and the faithful observance of its teaching (xxi. 7, xxii. 7) postulates some such interval. And yet the interval is not expected to be long; "for the time is at hand" (i. 3, xxii. 10). In Dan. xii. 10, 11 no such consideration for the sinner is shown. Besides in our author the whole body of the neutral nations have to be

[1] Cf. the Egyptian prayer quoted by Reitzenstein (*Poimandres*, p. 277): *χαῖρε, ἀρχὴ καὶ τέλος τῆς ἀκινήτου φύσεως.*

evangelized on the Second Advent when the Millennial Kingdom is established: cf. xiv. 6–7, xv. 4, xxii. 2, 17, xxi. 24–26. In the face of such an expectation 11 is an impossibility.

> ὁ ἀδικῶν ἀδικησάτω ἔτι,
> καὶ ὁ ῥυπαρὸς ῥυπανθήτω ἔτι.
> καὶ ὁ δίκαιος δικαιοσύνην ποιησάτω ἔτι,
> καὶ ὁ ἅγιος ἁγιασθήτω ἔτι.

We have already on the ground of their contents rejected these lines. As regards their form and diction there are further objections, though these are not unanswerable in themselves. First, as regards their form, it will be observed that, whereas universally in our author the second line is parallel with, *i.e.* reproduces the first not in identical but in similar terms, or more rarely the second and third lines (as in xxii. 13, 12) reproduce the first, *in 11, however, it is the third line that is parallel antithetically to the first and the fourth that is similarly parallel to the second.* This form of parallelism is not found in our author, though there are approaches to it. It is, however, possible to regard the first and second lines, and the third and fourth as respectively instances of synonymous parallelism. But the antitheses between the ὁ ἀδικῶν and the ὁ δίκαιος and between the ὁ ῥυπαρός and the ὁ ἅγιος and between ἀδικησάτω and δικαιοσύνην ποιησάτω are in favour of our taking the stanza as we have done above. Next the diction is remarkable. Thus ἀδικεῖν, which occurs twice in this stanza, means here "to act unjustly," "to sin," whereas in the nine cases where it occurs previously in our author it means "to hurt," "to damage." Next ῥυπαρός (cf. ἀποθέμενοι πᾶσαν ῥυπαρίαν in Jas. i. 21 in like sense) occurs only here in the N.T. in the sense of internal defilement (cf. Job xiv. 4, τίς γὰρ καθαρὸς ἔσται ἀπὸ ῥύπου; once of external defilement in Jas. ii. 2), ῥυπανθῆναι here only in N.T., and ἁγιασθῆναι, "to purify oneself internally" here only in our author.]

[**18^b–19.** As Porter (*Messages of the Books*, p. 293) remarks, these words form "an unfortunate ending of a book whose value consists in the spirit that breathes in it, the bold faith and confident hope which it inspires, rather than in the literalness and finality of its disclosures." But these clauses, to which there are abundant parallels in other books, as we shall see presently, are not in the opinion of the present editor from the hand of John. For (1) these words presuppose that John looked forward to a long period elapsing before the Second Advent, during which the Book would be exposed not to the errors incidental to transmission but to the deliberate perversion of his message both in the way of additions and omissions.

But we know that John looked for the speedy Advent of

Christ and the Millennial Kingdom—an expectation which is expressed repeatedly in the words ἔρχομαι ταχύ, iii. 11, xxii. 7 12, 20. 2. The style is unlike that of John. Thus we have τῶν λόγων τοῦ βιβλίου τῆς προφητείας ταύτης in 19, whereas, as in xxii. 7, 10, 18, we should expect τ. λόγων τ. προφητείας τ. βιβλίου τούτου. Next after τοὺς λόγους in 18^a we shall expect, not ἐπ' αὐτά, but ἐπ' αὐτούς. Again, instead of ἀφελεῖ . . . τὸ μέρος αὐτοῦ ἀπὸ τοῦ ξύλου τῆς ζωῆς we should expect ἀφελεῖ . . . τὸ μέρος αὐτοῦ ἐν τῷ ξύλῳ τῆς ζωῆς: cf. xx. 6, xxi. 8, or τὴν ἐξουσίαν αὐτοῦ ἐπὶ τὸ ξύλον τῆς ζωῆς: cf. xxii. 14. 3. The nature of the penalty is not what we should expect. The extreme penalty that can befall the evildoer in this Book is not the plagues singly or collectively, but the being cast into the lake of fire. The plagues are concerned with temporal punishments, not with eternal. Exclusion from the tree of life is mentioned, it is true, in 19. 4. 18^b–19 introduce a wrong note in these last verses.

On the above grounds I have bracketed these clauses as an interpolation.

Next, the custom of appending such warnings claims our attention. We first find them in Deut. iv. 2, οὐ προσθήσεσθε πρὸς τὸ ῥῆμα ὃ ἐγὼ ἐντέλλομαι ὑμῖν, καὶ οὐκ ἀφελεῖτε ἀπ' αὐτοῦ: xii. 32: 1 Enoch civ. 10, "And now I know this mystery, that sinners will alter and pervert the words of righteousness in many ways, and will speak wicked words." As opposed to this, Enoch requires that they should "not change or minish aught from my words" (civ. 11). In the Letter of Aristeas (33–41 A.D.?) 310–311, it is said that, when the Greek translation of the O.T. was completed, "they bade them pronounce a curse in accordance with their custom upon any who should make any alteration either by adding anything or changing in any way whatever any of the words which had been written or making an omission. This was a very wise precaution to ensure that the book might be preserved for all the future time unchanged." A terrible judgment is foretold (2 Enoch xlviii. 7–8) for those who tamper with the words of this book. In Josephus (*c. Ap.* i. 8) the writer claims a most faithful transmission of the ancient books of the O.T. δῆλον δ' ἐστὶν ἔργῳ, πῶς ἡμεῖς πρόσιμεν τοῖς ἰδίοις γράμμασι· τοσούτου γὰρ αἰῶνος ἤδη παρῳχηκότος οὔτε προσθεῖναί τις οὐδὲν οὔδε ἀφελεῖν αὐτῶν οὔτε μεταθεῖναι τετόλμηκεν. It was not unusual for writers, Christian and Jewish, to attempt to secure a faithful transmission of their works by appending solemn adjurations that the scribes should in no wise change or tamper with the text. Cf. Irenaeus in Eusebius, *H.E.* v. 20. 2: ὁρκίζω σε τὸν μεταγραψόμενον τὸ βιβλίον τοῦτο . . . ἵνα ἀντιβάλῃς ὃ μετεγράψω καὶ κατορθώσῃς αὐτὸ πρὸς τὸ ἀντίγραφον τοῦτο . . . καὶ τὸν ὅρκον ὁμοίως μεταγράψεις: and Rabbi

Meir in Sota 20[a], "My son, be careful; for it is a divine work: if thou writest, were it but a letter more or less, it is as if thou wert destroying a world."

τὸ μέρος αὐτοῦ ἀπὸ τοῦ ξύλου κτλ. The Holy City mentioned here is that which is associated with the Millennial Kingdom. The tree of life was in this city (xxii. 2).]

8–9, 20–21. *John's testimony and closing words.*

8–9. Of these verses we have already found a doublet in xix. 9–10 (see notes), which was probably from the hand of the disciple that edited the Book after John's death.

8. κἀγὼ Ἰωάννης ὁ ἀκούων καὶ βλέπων. Cf. 2 Cor. xii. 4, *ἤκουσεν ἄρρητα*, Dan. xii. 5, "And I Daniel saw." At the close of his words the author gives his name as at the beginning (i. 1). Observe the participles are in our author's usage equal to aorists or perfects.

ἔπεσα προσκυνῆσαι ἔμπροσθεν τῶν ποδῶν τοῦ ἀγγέλου. See note on xix. 10. Worship in the sense of prostration is here involved, though not divine worship: cf. *προσκυνεῖν ἐνώπιον* in iii. 9, xv. 4 of simple homage. Yet even such homage is refused by the angel. The phrase may be equivalent to *προσκυνῆσαι αὐτόν* (see notes on xix. 9–10 (5°), vii. 11).

τοῦ δεικνύοντός μοι ταῦτα. Cf. i. 1, iv. 1, xvii. 1, xxi. 9, 10, xxii. 1, 6. Here the participle = *δείξαντος*.

9. ὅρα μή· σύνδουλός σού εἰμι κτλ. Our text appears to be the source of Asc. Isa. vii. 21, "And I fell on my face to worship him, but the angel who conducted me (or rather 'showed to me' *i.e. ὃς ἔδειξέ μοι*: for the Ethiopic is capable of this meaning and the Latin and Slavonic Versions = 'instructed me') did not permit me but said unto me: 'Worship neither throne nor angel': and viii. 4–5, 'What is this which I see, my lord?' 5. And he said: 'I am not thy lord but thy fellowservant.'" The Apocryphal Gospel of Matthew iii. 3 (Tischendorf, p. 59) seems also to show signs of the influence of our text: "Benedic me servum tuum. Et dixit ei angelus: Noli te dicere servum, sed conservum meum; unius enim domini servi sumus." Our text is a strong prohibition of angel worship (*θρησκεία τῶν ἀγγέλων*, Col. ii. 18). That this was practised by the Jews before the Christian era is to be inferred from Tob. xii. 15, "I am Raphael, one of the seven angels: 12. When thou didst pray . . . I brought the memorial of your prayer before the glory of the Lord:" Jub. xxx. 20: Test. Dan vi. 2, "Draw near to God and to the angel that intercedeth for you; for he is a mediator between God and man:"[1] Test. Lev. v. 5, where Levi prays to the angel who conducts him to make known to him his name that he might

[1] This idea of an angelic mediator is found already in Job v. 1, xxxiii. 23 sq.; Zech. i. 12.

call upon him in the day of tribulation, and the angel replies: "I (*i.e.* Michael) am the angel who intercedeth for the nation of Israel":[1] 1 Enoch lxxxix. 76.[2] The fact that frequent admonitions against the worship of angels are to be found in Jewish writings confirms the view that this cult did prevail in Judaism. Cf. Mechilta Sect. יתרו, Parash. 10, where R. Ismael ben Elisha (flor. 100 A.D.) forbids the worship of any kind of angels (quoted from Lueken, p. 6): Jer. Berach. ix. 13^a, where men in necessity are bidden to pray to God and not to Michael or Gabriel: Aboda Zara, 42^b, where offerings to Michael are denounced as offerings to the dead. In Shabbath 12^b men are commanded by R. Jehuda (4th century A.D.) not to pray in Aramaic since the angels did not understand Aramaic. On the other hand, in the Jer. Qiddushim at its close (Lueken) permission is given to ask the angels for their intercession. For other proofs that, notwithstanding strong prohibitions against the cult of angels, this cult did survive in Judaism, see Lueken, *Michael*, 6–12.

From Christian sources we know of the prevalence of angelolatry among the Jews: cf. Preaching of Peter (Clem. Alex. *Strom.* vi. 5), *μηδὲ κατὰ Ἰουδαίους σέβεσθε, καὶ γὰρ ἐκεῖνοι . . . οὐκ ἐπίστανται λατρεύοντες ἀγγέλοις*: Celsus in Origen, *c. Cels.* v. 6, *πρῶτον οὖν τῶν Ἰουδαίων θαυμάζειν ἄξιον, εἰ . . . τοὺς . . . ἀγγέλους σέβουσι.*

That this superstition passed from the Jews to the Christians our text is sufficient evidence: cf. also Col. ii. 18; Asc. Isa. vii. 21, viii. 4, 5; Justin Martyr, *Apol.* i. 6, *ἀλλ' ἐκεῖνόν τε, καὶ τὸν παρ' αὐτοῦ υἱὸν ἐλθόντα . . . καὶ τὸν τῶν ἄλλων ἑπομένων καὶ ἐξομοιουμένων ἀγαθῶν ἀγγέλων στρατόν, πνεῦμά τε τὸ προφητικὸν σεβόμεθα καὶ προσκυνοῦμεν*: Athenagoras, *Suppl.* x., xxiv.: Clem. *Hom.* iii. 36.

τῶν προφητῶν καὶ τῶν τηρούντων τοὺς λόγους κτλ. Here, as we have shown in the notes on xix. 9–10, the prophets and the ordinary Christians are practically placed on the same level, whereas in xix. 9–10 the prophets are exalted far above the ordinary Christians, no mention of whom is made.

τῶν τηρούντων τοὺς λόγους. Cf. i. 3, iii. 8, 10, xii. 17, xiv. 12, xxii. 7.

τοῦ βιβλίου τούτου. Cf. xxii. 7, 10 [18, 19]. **τῷ θεῷ προσκύνησον.** See note on vii. 11.

20. λέγει ὁ μαρτυρῶν ταῦτα. Christ is again the Speaker. The *ὁ μαρτυρῶν* goes back to xxii. 18, where Christ solemnly attests the truth of the words of the prophecy of this book.

[1] Cf. Asc. Isa. ix. 23, "Iste est magnus angelus Michael deprecans semper pro humanitate."

[2] The four chief angels are spoken of as intercessors in 1 Enoch ix. 1, 3, the Watchers in xv. 2.

Ναί· ἔρχομαι ταχύ. Here for the third time in this chapter (see 7, 12) our Lord declares that He is coming speedily. On *ναί*, see note on i. 7.

Ἀμήν· ἔρχου, κύριε Ἰησοῦ. On this, the initial and primitive use of *ἀμήν*, which solemnly assents to the utterance of a preceding speaker, cf. v. 14, note, vii. 12, xix. 4. *ἔρχου κύριε* is the Greek equivalent of the Aramaic מָרַנָא תָא (= "our Lord, come").[1] See *Encyc. Bib.* and Hastings' *B.D.* on "Maranatha." The Aramaic is actually found transliterated in 1 Cor. xvi. 22, and in the Didache, x. 6:

> *εἴ τις ἅγιός ἐστιν, ἐρχέσθω·*
> *εἴ τις οὐκ ἔστι, μετανοείτω·*
> *μαραναθά. Ἀμήν.*

κύριε Ἰησοῦ. This designation is found only here and in the next verse in our author.

21. ἡ χάρις τοῦ κυρίου Ἰησοῦ μετὰ πάντων τῶν ἁγίων. This benediction, which is unusual in Apocalypses, is an indication that the Book was intended to be read in the Church services. In the Pauline Epistles *οἱ ἅγιοι* includes the whole body of the baptized. But in our author it appears to embrace only the faithful members of the Church. Cf. v. 8, viii. 3, 4, xi. 18, xiii. 7, 10, xiv. 12, xvi. 6, xvii. 6, xviii. 20, xix. 8, xx. 6, 9. It is not used at all in the Johannine Epistles.

[1] This explanation of Dalman, Wellhausen, etc., is preferable to that which is generally accepted in the Church Fathers, *i.e.* *μαραναθά* = מרן אתא, "our Lord has come."

I. THE TEXT.

The Greek Manuscripts of the Apocalypse.

Uncial MSS containing the Greek Text of the Apocalypse or part of it. The enumeration is that of Gregory, except in the case of ℵAC.

ℵ (iv). Petrograd. Sd. δ 2. ℵ* signifies the original text, where the original scribe or a later one has introduced an emendation. $ℵ^{a}$ $ℵ^{b}$ $ℵ^{ca}$ $ℵ^{cb}$ etc. are various correctors of the MS.[1]

A (v). London. Sd. δ 4. A* signifies as ℵ* above. A** corrector.[2]

C (v). Paris. Sd. δ 3. Contains 1^{1}–3^{19}, 5^{14}–7^{14}, 7^{17}–8^{5}, 9^{16}–10^{10}, 11^{3}–16^{13}, 18^{2}–19^{5}.

025 (ix). Petrograd. Formerly P. Sd. α 3. Contains 1^{1}–16^{12}, 17^{1}–19^{21}, 20^{9}–22^{6}.

046 (x). Rome. Formerly Q or B_2. Sd. α 1070.

051 (ix–x). Athos, Pantokrator 44. Contains 11^{15}–13^{1}, 13^{3}–22^{7}, $22^{15\text{-}21}$ with a commentary of Andreas in cursive. Photographed for Prof. Swete.

052 (x). Athos, Panteleemon. Formerly r 183. Contains 7^{16}–8^{12}.

Greek Cursives of the Apocalypse.[3]

1 (xii–xiii cent.). Maihingen. Formerly r 1. Sd. $A\nu^{20}$.
18 (1364 A.D.). Paris. Formerly r 51. Sd. δ 411.
35 (xi). Paris. Formerly r 17. Sd. δ 309.
42 (xi). Frankfurt a. O. Formerly r 13. Sd. α 107.
60 (x). Cambridge. Formerly r 10. Sd. ϵ 1321.
61 (xvi). Dublin. Formerly r 92. Sd. δ 603.
69 (xv). Leicester. Formerly r 14. Sd. δ 505.
82 (x). Paris. Formerly r 2. Sd. O^{1}.

[1] The photographic facsimile edited by Professor Lake for the Clarendon Press has been used for this edition.

[2] The photographic facsimile edited by Sir Frederic G. Kenyon (1909) has been used for this edition.

[3] Gregory's enumeration of the MSS is adopted in this edition, but for the convenience of those who use Von Soden's text I have added the latter's enumeration.

88 (xii ?). Naples. Formerly r 99. Sd. α 200.
91 (xi). Paris. Formerly r 4. Sd. O^{14}.
93 (x). Paris. Formerly r 19. Sd. α 51.
94 (xiii). Paris. Formerly r 18. Sd. O^{31}.
104 (xi). London. Formerly r 7. Sd. α 103.
110 (xii). London. Formerly r 8. Sd. α 204.
141 (xiii–xiv). Rome. Formerly r 40. Sd. δ 408.
149 (xv). Rome. Formerly r 25. Sd. δ 503.
172 (xiv–xv). Berlin. Formerly r 87. Sd. α 404.
175 (x–xi). Rome. Formerly r 20. Sd. δ 95.
177 (xi). Munich. Formerly r 82. Sd. α 106.
180 (xiv). Rome. Formerly r 44. Sd. ε 1498.
181 (xi). Rome. Formerly r 12. Sd. α 101.
201 (1357 A.D.). London. Formerly r 94. Sd. δ 403.
203 (1111 A.D.). London. Formerly r 181. Sd. α 203.
205 (xv). Venice. Formerly r 88. Sd. δ 500.
209 (xiv ?). Venice. Formerly r 46. Sd. α 1581.
218 (xiii). Vienna. Formerly r 33. Sd. δ 300.
241 (xi). Dresden. Formerly r 47. Sd. δ 507.
242 (xii) Moscow. Formerly r 48. Sd. δ 206.
250 (xi). Paris. Formerly r 121. Sd. O^{10}.
254 (xiv). Athens. Formerly r 122. Sd. $O\Theta^{12}$.
256 (xi). Paris. Formerly r 102. Sd. α 216.
296 (xvi). Paris. Formerly r 57. Sd. δ 600.
314 (xi). Oxford. Formerly r 6. Sd. O^{11}.
325 (xi). Oxford. Formerly r 9. Sd. α 111.
336 (xv). Hamburg. Formerly r 16. Sd. α 500.
337 (xii). Paris. Formerly r 52. Sd. α 205
339 (xiii). Turin. Formerly r 83. Sd. δ 303.
367 (1331 A.D.). Florence. Formerly r 23 Sd. δ 400.
368 (xv). Florence. Formerly r 84. Sd. α 1501.
385 (xv). London. Formerly r 29. Sd. α 506
386 (xiv). Rome. Formerly r 70. Sd. δ 401.
424 (xi). Vienna. Formerly r 34. Sd. O^{12}.
432 (xv). Rome. Formerly r 37. Sd. α 501.
452 (xii). Rome. Formerly r 42. Sd. α 206.
456 (x). Florence. Formerly r 75. Sd. α 52.
459 (1092 A.D.). Florence. Formerly r 45. Sd. α 104.
467 (xv). Paris. Formerly r 53. Sd. α 502.
468 (xiii). Paris. Formerly r 55 Sd. O^{30}.
469 (xii–xiv). Paris. Formerly r 56. Sd. α 306.
498 (xiv). London. Formerly r 97. Sd. δ 402.
506 (xi–xii). Oxford. Formerly r 26. Sd. δ 101.
517 (xi–xii). Oxford. Formerly r 27. Sd. α 214.
522 (1515 A.D.). Oxford. Formerly r 98. Sd. δ 602.
582 (1334 A.D.). Ferron. Formerly r 103. Sd. δ 410.

616 (1434 A.D.). Milan. Formerly r 156. Sd. α 503.
617 (xi). Venice. Formerly r 74. Sd. O^{13}.
620 (xii). Florence. Formerly r 180. Sd. α 207.
627 (x–xi). Rome. Formerly r 24. Sd. α 53.
628 (xiv). Rome. Formerly r 69. Sd. α 400.
632 (xiv). Rome. Formerly r 22. Sd. α 201.
664 (xv). Zittau. Formerly r 106. Sd. δ 502.
680 (xi). Cheltenham. Formerly r 107. Sd. δ 103.
699 (xi). London. Formerly r 108. Sd. δ 104.
743 (xiv). Paris. Formerly r 123. Sd. $A^{\nu 43}$.
757 (xiii–xiv). Athens. Formerly r 110. Sd. δ 304.
792 (xiii). Athens. Formerly r 111. Sd. ε 585.
808 (xii). Athens. Formerly r 112. Sd. δ 203.
824 (xiv). Grottaferrata. Formerly r 113. Sd. δ 404.
866 (xiv). Rome. Formerly r 114. Sd. α 1375.
886 (1454 A.D.). Rome. Formerly r 115. Sd. $A^{\pi\rho 50}$.
919 (xi). Escurial. Formerly r 125. Sd. α 113.
920 (x). Escurial. Formerly r 126. Sd. α 55.
922 (1116 A.D.). Athos. Formerly r 116. Sd. δ 200.
935 Athos. Sd. δ 361.
986 (xiv). Athos. Formerly r 117. Sd δ 508.
1006 Athos. Sd. α 1174.
1064 Athos.
1072 (xiv). Athos. Formerly r 118. Sd. δ 406.
1075 (xiv). Athos. Formerly r 119. Sd. δ 407.
1094 (xiv). Athos. Formerly r 120. Sd. δ 307.
1277 (xi–xii). Cambridge. Formerly r 185. Sd. α 194.
1328 Jerusalem. Sd. α 1470.
1352 Jerusalem. Sd. δ 396.
1384 Andros. Sd. δ 100.
1424 Kosinitza. Sd. δ 30.
1503 Athos.
1551 Athos.
1597 Athos.
1611 (xii). Athens. Formerly r 105. Sd. α 208.
1617 Athos.
1626 Athos.
1652 Athos.
1668 Athos.
1678 Athos.
1685 Serres.
1704 Athos.
1719 Athos.
1728 Athos.
1732 Athos.
1733 Athos.

1734 Athos.
1740 Athos.
1745 Athos.
1746 Athos.
1757 Lesbos.
1760 Serres.
1771 Athos.
1773 Athos.
1774 Athos.
1775 Athos.
1776 Athos.
1778 Saloniki.
1785 Kosinitza. Sd. δ 405.
1795 Kosinitza. Sd. α 215.
1806 Trapezunt. Sd. α 1472.
1824 Rome. Sd. $O^{\alpha 61}$.
1828 (xii). Athens. Formerly r 124. Sd. α 202.
1841 (ix–x). Lesbos. Formerly r 127. Sd. α 47.
1849 (1069 A.D.). Venice. Formerly r 128. Sd. α 110.
1852 (x–xi). Upsala. Formerly r 129. Sd. α 114.
1854 (xi). Athos. Formerly r 130. Sd. α 115.
1857 (xiii). Athos. Formerly r 131. Sd. α 1587.
1859 Athos. Formerly r 371. Sd. α 402.
1862 (ix). Athos. Formerly r 132. Sd. O^{21}.
1864 Athos. Formerly r 327.
1865 Athos. Formerly r 380.
1870 (x). Chalkis. Formerly r 133. Sd. α 54
1872 (xii). Chalkis. Formerly r 134. Sd. α 209.
1876 (xv). Sinai. Formerly r 135. Sd. α 504.
1888 Jerusalem. Formerly r 495. Sd. α 118.
1893 Jerusalem. Formerly r 500. Sd. α 117.
1894 Jerusalem. Formerly r 501. Sd. α 1670.
1903 Athos. Formerly r 513.
1918 (xiv). Rome. Formerly r 39. Sd. α 403.
1934 (xi). Paris. Formerly r. 64. Sd. O^{15}
1948 (xv). Rome. Formerly r 78. Sd. α 505.
1955 (xi). London. Formerly r 93. Sd. α 119.
1957 (xv). Rome. Formerly r 91. Sd. α 1574.
2004 (x). Escurial. Formerly r 142. Sd. α 56.
2014 (xv). Rome. Formerly r 21. Sd. $A\nu^{51}$.
2015 (xv). Oxford. Formerly r 28. Sd. α 1580.
2016 (xv). London. Formerly r 31. Sd. α 1579.
2017 (xv). Dresden. Formerly r 32. Sd. α 1582.
2018 (xiv). Vienna. Formerly r. 35. Sd. $A\nu^{46}$.
2019 (xiii). Vienna. Formerly r 36. Sd. $A\nu^{36}$.
2020 (xv). Rome. Formerly r 38. Sd. α 1573.

2021 (xv). Rome. Formerly r 41. Sd. α 1572.
2022 (xiv). Rome. Formerly r 43. Sd. $A\nu^{401}$.
2023 (xv). Moscow. Formerly r 49. Sd. $A\nu^{56}$.
2024 (xv). Moscow. Formerly r 50. Sd. α 1584.
2025 (xv–xvi). Paris. Formerly r 58. Sd. α 1592.
2026 (xv–xvi). Paris. Formerly r 59. Sd. $A\nu^{501}$.
2027 (xiii–xiv). Paris. Formerly r 61. Sd. α 1374.
2028 (1422 A.D.). Paris. Formerly r 62. Sd. $A\nu^{54}$.
2029 (xvi). Paris. Formerly r 63. Sd. $A\nu^{66}$.
2030 (xii). Moscow. Formerly r 65. Sd. α 1272.
2031 (1301 A.D.). Rome. Formerly r 67. Sd. $A\nu^{41}$.
2032 (xi–xii). Rome. Formerly r 68. Sd. $A\nu^{11}$.
2033 (xvi). Rome. Formerly r 72. Sd. $A\nu^{60}$.
2034 (xv). Rome. Formerly r 73. Sd. $A\nu^{50}$.
2035 (xvi). Florence. Formerly r 77. Sd. $A\nu^{605}$.
2036 (xiv). Rome. Formerly r 79. Sd. $A\nu^{40}$.
2037 (xiv). Munich. Formerly r 80. Sd. $A\nu^{15}$.
2038 (xvi). Munich. Formerly r 81. Sd. $A\nu^{600}$.
2039 (xii). Dresden. Formerly r 90. Sd. α 1271.
2040 (xi–xii). Parham (Curzon). Formerly r 95. Sd. $A\rho^{11}$.
2041 (xiv). Parham (Curzon). Formerly r 96. Sd. α 1475.
2042 (xiv–xv). Naples. Formerly r 100. Sd. $A\nu^{400}$.
2043 (xv). Petrograd. Formerly r 101. Sd. $A\nu^{57}$.
2044 (1507 A.D.). Vienna. Formerly r 136. Sd. $A\nu^{601}$.
2045 (xv). Vienna. Formerly r 137. Sd. $A\nu^{55}$.
2046 (xv). Vienna. Formerly r 138. Sd. $A\nu^{58}$.
2047 (1543 A.D.). Paris. Formerly r 139. Sd. $A\nu^{67}$.
2048 (xi–xii). Paris. Formerly r 140. Sd. α 1172.
2049 (xvi). Athens. Formerly r 141. Sd. α 1684.
2050 (1107 A.D.). Escurial. Formerly r 143. Sd. α 1273.
2051 (xvi). Madrid. Formerly r 144. Sd. $A\nu^{68}$.
2052 (xvi). Florence. Formerly r 145. Sd. $A\nu^{64}$.
2053 (xiii). Messina. Formerly r 146. Sd. $O^{\alpha 31}$.
2054 (xv–xvi). Modena. Formerly r 147. Sd. $A\nu^{500}$.
2055 (xv). Modena. Formerly r 148. Sd. $A\nu^{53}$.
2056 (xiv–xv). Rome. Formerly r 149. Sd. $A\nu^{49}$.
2057 (xv). Rome. Formerly r 150. Sd. α 1576.
2058 (xiv). Rome. Formerly r 151. Sd. $O^{\alpha 40}$.
2059 (xi). Rome. Formerly r 152. Sd. $A\nu^{10}$.
2060 (1331 A.D.). Rome. Formerly r 153. Sd. $A\nu^{42}$.
2061 (xv–xvi). Rome. Formerly r 154. Sd. α 1538.
2062 (xiii). Rome. Formerly r 155. Sd. $O^{\alpha 30}$.
2063 (xvi). Rome. Formerly r 157. Sd. $A\nu^{61}$.
2064 (xvi). Rome. Formerly r 158. Sd. $A\nu^{62}$.
2065 (xv). Rome. Formerly r 159. Sd. $A\nu^{503}$.
2066 (1574 A.D.). Rome. Formerly r 160. Sd. $A\nu^{63}$.

2067 (xv). Rome. Formerly r 161. Sd $A\nu^{52}$.
2068 (xvi). Venice. Formerly r 162. Sd. $A\nu^{65}$.
2069 (xv–xvi). Venice. Formerly r 163. Sd. $A\nu^{59}$.
2070 (1356 A.D.). Athos. Formerly r 164. Sd. $A\nu^{403}$.
2071 (1622 A.D.). Athos. Formerly r 167. Sd. $A\nu^{70}$.
2072 (1798 A.D.). Athos. Formerly r 168. Sd. $A\nu^{80}$.
2073 (xiv). Athos. Formerly r 169. Sd. $A\nu^{47}$.
2074 (x). Athos. Formerly r 170. Sd. $A\nu^{1}$.
2075 (xiv). Athos. Formerly r 171. Sd. $A\nu^{48}$.
2076 (xvii). Athos. Formerly r 172. Sd. α 1570.
2077 (1685 A.D.). Athos. Formerly r 174. Sd. $A\nu^{71}$.
2078 (xvi). Athos. Formerly r 176. Sd. α 1686.
2079 (xiii). Athos. Formerly r 177. Sd. α 1373.
2080 (xiv). Patmos. Formerly r 178.
2081 (xii). Patmos. Formerly r 179. Sd $A\nu^{21}$.
2082 (xvi). Dresden. Formerly r 182. Sd. α 1682.
2083 (1560 A.D.). Leyden. Formerly r 184. Sd. $A\nu^{602}$.
2084 Constantinople. Formerly r 506. Sd. α 1586.
2087 Basel.
2091 Athens. Formerly r 511. Sd. $A\nu^{502}$.
2116 Athens. Sd. $A\rho^{70}$.
2136 Moscow. Sd. ε 700.
2138 Moscow. Sd. α 116.
2186 Athos. Sd. $A\nu^{23}$.
2195 Athos. Sd. α 508.
2196 Athos. Sd. α 1687.
2254 Athos. Sd. $A\nu^{604}$.
2256 Athos. Sd. α 1577.
2258 Athos. Sd. α 1770.
2259 Athos. Sd. $A\nu^{12}$.
2286 Athos. Sd. $A\nu^{22}$.

There are thus 223 Cursives according to the above enumeration, which is based on Gregory's list, *Griechischen Handschriften des NT.* (pp. 48–122).[1]

[1] In his list of MSS of the Apocalypse on pp. 360–361 there are six omissions and two or more wrong insertions. Von Soden (*Schriften des NT.* I. i 289) reckons the number of Cursives as 222. Thus with the seven Uncials there are altogether 230 (or 229) Greek MSS of the Apocalypse.

II. THE TEXT.

THE MSS AND VERSIONS COLLATED FOR THIS EDITION: ABBREVIATIONS: SYMBOLS: ITACISMS.

UNCIALS.—Of the Uncials A and ℵ have been collated afresh from photographs of these MSS published by Kenyon and Lake respectively. For the readings of C, 025, 046 the editor is dependent on Tischendorf, and for 051 on the readings given in Swete's edition under the number 186.

CURSIVES.—The following 22 Cursives have been specially photographed for this edition: 18, 35, 149, 175, 205, 325, 337, 386, 456, 468, 617, 620, 632, 866, 919, 920, 1849, 1934, 2004, 2020, 2040, 2050. Of these the following are defective: 205, 337, 468, 866, 919, 920, 2040, 2050.

205. Defective: xviii. 14 ἀπῆλθεν ἀπὸ σοῦ . . . xx. 9 τὴν παρεμβολὴν τ. ἁγίων, *i.e.* one page lost through carelessness of the photographer.

337. Defective: x. 4–xi. 1 and xxii. 17 λέγουσα to end wanting.

468. Defective: xix. 18 καὶ σάρκας ἰσχυρῶν . . . xxii. 17 εἰπάτω ἔρχου wanting.

866. Defective: contains only vi. 17 ἡμέρα τ. ὀργῆς . . . xiii. 12 τοῦ θηρίου πᾶσαν.

919. Ends with xix. 6 ὑδάτων πολλῶν καὶ ὡς.

920. Ends with xxii. 1 καὶ ἔδειξε.

2040. Ends with the words καὶ τόπος, xx. 11. Photographs incomplete.

2050. Defective. Omits vi. 1 καὶ εἶδον . . . xix. 21 ἐκ τῶν σάρκων αὐτῶν.

These 22 Cursives are generally quoted as **22**, or **21**, **20**, **19**, accordingly as one or more are defective. See under "Abbreviations" below.

For the readings of most of the remaining Cursives cited in this edition the author is indebted to Tischendorf's *NT. Graece* (ed. oct. 1872) and to Hoskier's *Concerning the Date of the Bohairic Version* (1911) for select readings from the following 26 Cursives: 180, 181, 256, 337, 367, 368, 467, 582, 664, 680, 743, 1075, 1948, 2014, 2025, 2026, 2028, 2029, 2030, 2031, 2032, 2033, 2034, 2037, 2038, 2043. Where readings from the Cursives cited by Tischendorf are not to be found in Tischendorf, they are derived from Hoskier.

CORRECTIONS ON THE MSS—

A* = original text. A** = correction and similarly in the Cursives.

ℵ* = original text. The lead of Tischendorf has been followed in distinguishing the different hands engaged in correcting ℵ. On these different correctors (as many as fifteen ranging from the iv to the xii Century) and their dates see Lake, *Codex Sinaiticus*, pp. xvii–xxiv. Lake differs from Tischendorf in differentiating certain of the correctors. Into this vexed question it is not necessary to enter here.

VERSIONS.—For a short description of these Versions see the Introduction to vol. i.

Latin.

Tyc = "Tyconius' Text of the Apocalypse, a partial restoration," published by Prof. Souter in the *J.T.S.*, April 1913.

Pr = Text of Primasius in *Die lateinische Apocalypse*, edited by Haussleiter, 1891.

fl = Palimpsestus floriacensis in Haussleiter's volume just mentioned.

gig = Codex Gigas. A fresh collation made by Dr. Karlsson in 1891 for Bp. John Wordsworth of Salisbury, and put at my service by his collaborator—Professor White.

vg = Vulgate (editio minor), edited by H. J. White, 1911.

Syriac.

s^1 = Philoxenian Version, edited by John Gwynn, 1897.

s^2 = Harkleian or Syriac Vulgate.

s sometimes is used to indicate the consensus of s^1 and s^2.

Armenian.

$arm^{1.2.3.4}$ = Old Armenian MSS edited by F. C. Conybeare, 1907.

arm^a = Armenian Vulgate.

Egyptian.

bo = Bohairic Version of the New Testament, vol. iv., edited by G. Horner, 1905.

sa = Sahidic Version. Partial collation furnished to the editor by G. Horner.

Ethiopic.

eth = Ethiopic Version, edited by J. P. Platt (new edition), 1899.

ABBREVIATIONS AND SYMBOLS—

Or^s=the Greek text, which accompanies the recently discovered Scholia of Origen on the Apocalypse, *i.e.* in Harnack's edition, *Der Scholien-Kommentar des Origenes zur Apokalypse Johannis*, 1911. This text is not Origen's, though the Scholia probably are. It should be numbered as Cursive 2293 (x cent.).

Or$^{Mt. iv. 314}$=Origen's text of the Apoc. in his Commentary on Matthew, vol. iv. p. 314, in Lommatzsch's edition. Similarly Or$^{Cel. xx. 117}$ means Origen's text of the Apoc. in *Contra Celsum*, vol. xx. p. 117, of Lommatzsch's edition. Origen's works are occasionally quoted to show that Or^s cannot be his text.

⌜ ⌝ Words so enclosed are taken by the Editor to have greater claims to be the original than the alternative printed in the margin.

† † Words so enclosed are corrupt. The Editor's restoration is occasionally given in the margin.

< > Words so enclosed are restored by the Editor.

[ ] Words so enclosed are interpolated.

+ =add

> =omit.

∼ =transpose.

pr =prefix.

22 (—18. 35)=the 22 Cursive MSS collated for this edition less by the two MSS 18. 35. Where certain of these MSS are defective the symbol may be **21** or **20** or **19** or **18** or even **17**.

Words in heavy type in the text are restorations of the original text as in $3^{1. 7. 14}$.

ITACISMS.—Itacisms are not recorded in the case of the Cursives nor yet of the Uncials excepting A and ℵ, and not even the itacisms of these in such common instances as ι for ει (ἴδον for εἶδον). Such itacisms as ε for αι or *vice versa* in these two MSS are recorded, since this itacism has in one case led to a corruption of the text. Thus Gwynn and Swete have rightly recognized that πέσῃ ἐπί in 7^{16} is corrupt for παίσῃ ἔτι, the corruption being due originally to the miswriting of παισῃ as πεσῃ. In 9^5 Aℵ write πεσῃ for παισῃ—a fact unrecorded by Tischendorf. In fact A writes πεσ- twice for παισ- out of the five times where it occurs in the N.T. and ℵ three times. Other common unrecorded itacisms are ι for η and ο for ω, or *vice versa*.

III. THE TEXT AND APPARATUS CRITICUS.

Chapter I.

ΑΠΟΚΑΛΥΨΙΣ ΙΩΑΝΝΟΥ.

1. Ἀποκάλυψις Ἰησοῦ Χριστοῦ ἣν ἔδωκεν αὐτῷ ὁ θεὸς δεῖξαι τοῖς
δούλοις αὐτοῦ, ἃ δεῖ γενέσθαι ἐν τάχει, καὶ ἐσήμανεν ἀποστείλας διὰ
τοῦ ἀγγέλου αὐτοῦ τῷ δούλῳ αὐτοῦ Ἰωάννῃ, 2. ὃς ἐμαρτύρησεν τὸν
λόγον τοῦ θεοῦ καὶ τὴν μαρτυρίαν Ἰησοῦ Χριστοῦ, ὅσα εἶδεν.

Title.

αποκαλυψις Ιωαννου (Ιωανου ℵ) ℵC>A 205. 2004 | Ιωαννου αποκαλυψις 175. 337. 920. 2040 | η αποκ. του αγιου Ιωαννου bo | αποκ. Ιωαν. του θεολογου (+ην εν Πατμω τη νισω εθεασατο 620) 325. 620 : αποκ. του αγ. Ιωαν. του θεολογου 18. 35. 386. 456. 468. 2020 Or^{8} | Ιωαν. του θεολ. και ηγαπημενου αποκ. 1934 | αποκ. (+του αγιου 919) Ιωαν. του θεολ. και ευαγγελιστου 046. 919 | αποκ. η εγενετο εις τον (+αγιον s^{1}) Ιωαν. τον ευαγγ. (+υπο του θεου s^{2}) εν Πατμω τη νησω εις ην εβληθη υπο Νηρωνος Καισαρος s$^{1.2}$ | η αποκ. του αποστολου Ιωαν (+και ευαγγελιστου 025) 025 vg | αποκ. του αγ. αποστ. Ιωαν. του θεολ. 632 | αποκ. του αγ. Ιωαν. του αποστ. κ. ευαγγ. του θεολ. ην ιδεν εν πατμω τη νησω κυριε ευλογ. 2050.

1. αποκ. . . . την μαρτ. Ι. Χ.] αποκαλυψις Ιωαννου του ευαγγελιστου arm^{4} : αποκ. Ιωαννου καθως ειδεν Ι. Χ. eth | ην εδωκεν . . . οσ εμαρτυρησεν] της γεναμενης εις εμε Ιωαννην τον αποστολον του κηρυξαι 2050 | ην] δι ης arm$^{2.3^{**}a}$ | αυτω] αυτη 046 | δουλοις] αγιοις ℵ* | κ. εσημ.] significans Tyc : κ. επεμψεν eth | αποστειλας] nuntianda Pr fl : >eth : +αυτα bo | του >88. 2015 | τω δουλω αυτ. > 1854 Or^{8} : του δουλου αυτ. A | Ιωανει ℵ* |.

2. ver. 2 >arm^{1} | οσ εμαρτ. τ. λ.] μαρτυριαν του λογου arm^{3} | του θεου >Pr | Χριστου >181 | οσα >2040 : +τε 1 : ην arm^{4} | ειδεν]+και ατινα εισι και ατινα (or α : >620) χρη γενεσθαι μετα ταυτα 1. 88. 104. 181. 205. 209. 432. 468. 620. 632**. 1957. 2015. 2020. 2023. 2024. 2037. 2041. 2067 al : +και ατινα εισιν 42 : |.

3. Μακάριος ὁ ἀναγινώσκων
καὶ οἱ ἀκούοντες τοὺς λόγους τῆς προφητείας
καὶ τηροῦντες τὰ ἐν αὐτῇ γεγραμμένα,
ὁ γὰρ καιρὸς ἐγγύς.

4. Ἰωάννης ταῖς ἑπτὰ ἐκκλησίαις ταῖς ἐν τῇ Ἀσίᾳ·

Χάρις ὑμῖν καὶ εἰρήνη ἀπὸ ὁ ὢν καὶ ὁ ἦν καὶ ὁ ἐρχόμενος, (*a*)
5. καὶ ἀπὸ Ἰησοῦ Χριστοῦ ὁ μάρτυς ὁ πιστός,
ὁ πρωτότοκος τῶν νεκρῶν καὶ ὁ ἄρχων τῶν βασιλέων τῆς γῆς.

Τῷ ἀγαπῶντι ἡμᾶς καὶ λύσαντι ἡμᾶς ἐκ τῶν ἁμαρτιῶν ἡμῶν ἐν τῷ αἵματι αὐτοῦ,

(*a*) The MSS add here an early interpolation: *καὶ ἀπὸ τῶν ἑπτὰ πνευμάτων τῶν ἐνώπιον τοῦ θρόνου αὐτοῦ.* See vol. i. 11–13.

3. μακαριος] pr *και* eth : + *ει* 2050 : *μακαριοι* arm^{4} bo | *ο αναγιν. και* >arm^{4} : *οι αναγινωσκοντες* bo | *ο ακουων* gig arm$^{1.2.3a}$ | *τ. λογ. τ. προφ. κ. ο ακουων* arm^{2a} | *τ. λογ. τ. προφ.* >arm^{4} | *τουσ λογ.*] + *τουτους* C : *τον λογον* ℵ 046. 2042 | *προφητιας* ℵC 93. 104. 314 : + *ταυτης* 104. 336. 468**. 620 gig vg s$^{1.2}$ arm^{2a} bo : + *τουτου τ. βιβλιου* eth | *και*^{2}] + *οι* 2040 | *τηρουντεσ*] *ποιουντεσ* arm^{4} : *τηρων* gig arm$^{1.2.3a}$ | *εν αυτη* >fl : *επ αυτησ* 2050 bo | *ο γαρ κ. εγγ.* >arm$^{1.3}$ | *καιρ. εγγ.* >2050 |.

4. Ιωαννης] *Ιωανησ* ℵ : pr *α εγραψε* eth : + scribens haec Tyc | *ταισ*^{2}] + *ουσαισ* 2050 | *ειρηνη*] + multiplicetur Tyc | *απο . . . ερχομ.*] a deo patre Tyc | *απο ο ων* AℵC 025. 1. 60. 82. 88. 104. 181. 314. 336. 424. 432. 620. 628. 632**. 1957. 2015. 2020. 2023. 2036. 2037. 2041. 2050. 2067 : *απο του ο ων* 61.^{mg} 429. 617. 1934 : ab eo qui est fl gig vg s$^{1.2}$ bo : *απο θεου ο ων* 046. **21** (−432. 620. 628. 632**. 2020. 2050) al^{mu} Or^{s} : *απο κυριου ο ων* 2016 | *ο*^{3} >2050 | *ερχομ.*] + omnipotens Pr | *και*^{4} >s^{2} | *των*^{2} Aℵ 88. 241. 2036 : *α* C 046. **21** (−205. 620. 2020) al^{pm} Or^{s} s$^{1.2}$ arm^{3} : *α εστιν* 025. 1. 205. 620. 2020. 2023 al arm^{2a} : *α εισιν* 2019 arm^{4} | *αυτου* >2018 bo : *του θεου* 88. 2015. 2036 Pr fl : *Ιησου Χριστου* eth |

5. και απο Ι. Χ.] et a filio hominis Tyc : >eth | *οσ μαρτυς πιστοσ εστιν* 172. 2018 Pr gig vg arm^{4} eth | *ο πρωτοτ.*] "who is eldest" arm$^{2.3a}$: + *εκ* 1. 1957. 2041 al | *των νεκρων*] "among the dead" arm$^{1.2.3a}$ | *αρχων*] *μαρτυσ* 2050 : + *παντων* bo | *βασιλειων* ℵ* (corr. by scribe himself to *βασιλεων*) arm$^{1.2.3a}$ Or^{s} | *τω* (>ℵ*) *αγαπωντι* AℵC 046. **21** (−205) al^{pl} Or^{s} arm^{4} : *τω αγαπησαντι* 025. 1. 61.^{mg} 88. 205. 1957. 2015. 2019. 2036. 2037. 2038. 2041. 2067 : *οσ ηγαπησεν* 172. 2018 fl gig vg arm$^{1.2.3a}$ bo | *ημασ*^{1}] >2050 : *υμας* eth | *λυσαντι* AℵC 1. 88. (104). 181*. 314. (620). 628. 2015. 2019. 2020. 2036. 2050 Or^{s} Pr fl s$^{1.2}$ arm : *λουσαντι* 025. 046. **21** (−620. 2020. 2050) al^{pl} gig vg eth : *ελουσεν* 172.

6. καὶ ἐποίησεν ἡμᾶς βασιλείαν, ἱερεῖς τῷ θεῷ καὶ πατρὶ αὐτοῦ,
αὐτῷ ἡ δόξα καὶ τὸ κράτος εἰς τοὺς αἰῶνας τῶν αἰώνων· ἀμήν.

7. Ἰδοὺ ἔρχεται μετὰ τῶν νεφελῶν,
καὶ ὄψεται αὐτὸν πᾶς ὀφθαλμὸς καὶ οἵτινες αὐτὸν ἐξεκέντησαν,
καὶ κόψονται ἐπ' αὐτὸν πᾶσαι αἱ φυλαὶ τῆς γῆς. ναί, ἀμήν.(*a*)

(*a*) The MSS add here an early interpolation. 8. Ἐγώ εἰμι τὸ Ἄλφα καὶ τὸ Ὦ, λέγει Κύριος ὁ θεός, ὁ ὢν καὶ ὁ ἦν καὶ ὁ ἐρχόμενος, ὁ παντοκράτωρ. See vol. ii. Eng. trans., footnote, *in loc.*

2018 bo : λυσαντι κ. των τησ αμαρτιασ κιλιδων λουσαντι τη εκχυσει του ζωοποιου αιματοσ κ. υδατοσ κ. ποιησαντι ημασ βασιλειον ιερατευμα κ. λουσαντι ημασ απο των αμαρτιων εν τ. αιματι αυτου. και εποιησεν ημασ βασιλειαν ιερεισ κτλ. 104. 620. (336. 459 628) | ημασ^{2} >ℵ* : υμας eth | εκ AℵC 1. 61.^{mg} 88. 181. 2015*. 2019. 2020. 2036. 2037. 2038. 2050. 2067 : απο 025. 046. **21** (−620. 2020. 2050) 250 al^{pl} Or^{s} Pr fl gig vg bo? | τ. αμαρτ.] peccato Pr | ημων] υμων eth : >A 1. 181. 336. (620). 2067 Pr | εν τ. αιμ. αυτ. >arm$^{1.\,3*}$ |.

6. εποιησεν AℵC 025. **21** (−386. 456. 468. 866) 250. 2037. 2038. 2067 Or^{s} s$^{1.\,2}$ bo eth : ποιησαντι 046. 42. 69. 104. 325.^{cor} 336. 367. 385. 456. 459. 468. (620). 2019 | ημασ ℵ 025. 046 al^{pl} Pr gig vg^{d} (s$^{1.\,2}$) arm : ημιν A 42. 325**. 367. 456. 468. 517. 2016. 2020 : ημων C : υμας eth : regnum nostrum fl : nostrum regnum vg$^{(-d)}$: >325* | βασιλειαν ιερεισ Aℵ*C **21** (−325. 456. 468. 2050) 250 al^{pm} fl vg$^{(-d)}$: βασιλειαν και ιερεισ ℵ^{c} 88 Pr gig vg^{d} : "worthy of his kingdom and priests" arm$^{1.\,3.\,4}$: βασιλειαν ιερατικην s$^{1.\,2}$: βασιλειαν αγιαν eth : βασιλειον ιερεισ 046. 2050 : βασιλεισ και ιερεισ 025. 1. 2015. 2019. 2036. 2038. 2067 al arm$^{2.\,3**a}$: βασιλειον ιερατευμα 42. 61*. 69. (325). 367. 456. 468. 517. (620). 1854 Or^{s} bo^{vi} | και^{2} >arm$^{1.\,4}$ bo | αυτου >fl arm^{1} | αυτω . . . αμην >Pr arm^{1} | κ. το κρατος . . . αμην >arm^{1} | τ. αιωνας] τον αιωνα ℵ* | των αιωνων ℵC 046 al^{pl} Or^{s} fl gig vg s$^{1.\,2}$ arm$^{2.\,3a}$: >A 025. 88. 325. 456. 468*. 498. 2015. 2036. 2037. 2050 bo | αμην >218 |.

7. μετα] επι C sa eth | των>250. 2018. 2038 | νεφελων] + αμην 35 : + coeli gig arm$^{1.\,2.\,3a}$ | οψεται] AC 025. 046 al^{pl} Or$^{Mt.\,iv.\,314}$ Pr fl gig vg eth : οψονται ℵ 1. 181. 2038. 2067 Or^{s} s$^{1.\,2}$ arm bo | αυτον^{1} > 1. 205. 209 arm$^{1.\,3}$ | πασ] παντεσ s$^{1.\,2}$ arm : + ο 172 : παντεσ, πασ bo | οφθαλμοσ και >arm^{1} | οφθαλμοι s$^{1.\,2}$ arm$^{2.\,3.\,4a}$ | αυτον^{2} >ℵ* | κοψονται] οψονται (-εται Pr) Pr fl bo arm$^{1.\,(3*)}$: οψονται και κοψονται eth | επ αυτον > 1. 241* arm^{1} : επ >ℵ* 2050 Or^{s} Pr fl bo | πασαι . . . γησ] omnis terra Pr | ναι] + και s^{1} | ναι αμην >fl arm^{1} : ναι> bo | αμην] + και λεγει arm^{1} |.

8. το αλφα AℵC 025. 046. **21** (−620. 632. 2020) al

9. Ἐγὼ Ἰωάννης, ὁ ἀδελφὸς ὑμῶν καὶ συνκοινωνὸς ἐν τῇ θλίψει
καὶ βασιλείᾳ καὶ ὑπομονῇ ἐν Ἰησοῦ, ἐγενόμην ἐν τῇ νήσῳ τῇ
καλουμένῃ Πάτμῳ διὰ τὸν λόγον τοῦ θεοῦ καὶ τὴν μαρτυρίαν Ἰησοῦ.
10. ἐγενόμην ἐν πνεύματι ἐν τῇ κυριακῇ ἡμέρᾳ, καὶ ἤκουσα ⸀φωνὴν ὀπίσω μου
μεγάλην ὄπισθέν μου⸃ ὡς σάλπιγγος λεγούσης φωνὴν
μεγάλην

11. Ὃ βλέπεις γράψον εἰς βιβλίον,
καὶ πέμψον ταῖς ἑπτὰ ἐκκλησίαις,

gig arm$^{2.4a}$ bo : το α 1. 88. 241. 385. 620. 632. 2020. 2023. 2037. 2038. 2039. 2042. 2067 al Or^{8} Pr fl vg : + και εγω ℵ* | το^{2}] I am arm$^{1.3}$ | ω] + (η) αρχη και (το) τελοσ ℵ* 1. 61.^{mg} (88). 172. 205. 250. 1854. (2015). 2018. (2019. 2023. 2036. 2037). 2038. 2050 Or$^{Mt.\,v.\,2}$ Or^{8} gig vg bo | λεγει Κυριος ο θεος > 2050 | λεγει > 88 | ο θεοσ > arm^{1} : + και 620 arm$^{2.3a}$ | και ο ην > arm^{4} : "and who is" arm$^{2.3a}$: "unto aeons" arm^{1} | ο^{4} > 1934 | ερχομ.] + και 386 : + κυριοσ arm$^{1.2a}$ | ο^{5} > 046. 2015. 2036 |.

9. εγω] + ειμι bo : και εγω eth | Ιωανησ ℵ* | συνκοινωνοσ ℵC 025. 2036 al : συγκοιν. A 046. 205. 250. 468. 2020. 2037. 2038. 2050. 2067 al s^{1} : κοινωνοσ **21** (– 205. 468. 2020. 2050) al^{mu} s^{2} : + υμων s$^{1.2}$ eth | και βασιλεια AℵC 046 al^{pl} Or^{8} Pr fl gig vg arm$^{1.2.3a}$: κ. εν τη βασιλ. (+ υμων eth) 025. 1. 104. 205. 620. 2023. 2038. 2067 al eth : τησ βασιλειασ arm^{4} : οτι η βασιλεια bo : > s$^{1.2}$ | και υπομ. εν. Ιησ. > arm$^{1.4}$ | και^{3}] + εν τη s^{1} | υπομ.] + τη s$^{1.2}$: + σου ησαν bo : + δια την υπομονην υμων eth | εν Ιησου ℵ* C 025. 2020. 2050 Or$^{Mt.\,iv.\,18}$ gig vg s^{1} bo : εν Χριστω A : εν Ιησ. Χριστ. ℵ$^{c.c}$ Pr vg^{d} s^{2} eth : Ιησου Χριστου 1. 205. 1854. 2015. 2036 : εν Χριστω Ιησου 046. **21** (– 205. 2020. 2050) al^{pl} Or^{8} fl arm$^{2.(3)a}$ | καλουμενη > 1 : επικαλουμενη 2050 : λεγομενη 141 : | δια$^{(1)}$] και C | θεου] κυριου 620 | και την μαρτ. AC 1. 91. 172. 242. 325*. 424. 432. 1934. 2015. 2016. 2018. 2020. 2036 Pr gig vg arm$^{2.4a}$ bo : και δια τ. μαρτ. ℵ 025. 046. **21** (– 325*. 1934. 2020) al^{pl} Or^{8} fl s$^{1.2}$ arm$^{1.3}$ eth | Ιησου Aℵ*C 025. 181. 2015. 2019. 2020. 2036. 2050 fl gig vg arm^{4} : Χριστου arm^{1} : Ιησου Χριστου ℵ$^{c.c}$ 046. **21** (– 2020. 2050) al^{pl} Or^{8} Pr s$^{1.2}$ arm$^{2.3a}$ bo |.

10. **εγεν. εν πνευμ.**] "and (> a) there was in me the spirit (holy 1)" arm$^{1.2.3.a}$: pr εγω A : pr εγω Ιωαννησ gig : pr και s^{1} | εν πνευματι εν τη > 2050 | φων. μεγ. οπισθεν (336. 2020 οπισω) μου A 336. 2020. 2067 arm^{1} eth : οπισω μου φων. (+ σαλπιγγος 2015) μεγ. ℵC 025. 205. (2015). 2037 al Pr fl gig vg s$^{1.2}$ arm^{2a} bo : φων. οπ. μου μεγαλ. 046. 2040 al^{pl} Or^{8} : φωνησ οπ. λεγουσησ μοι ωσ σαλπιγγοσ μεγαλησ 2050 : φωνησ μεγ. 336. (2050). 2067 | οπισθεν μου > arm^{4} | σαλπιγγοσ] pr φωνη arm$^{1.3.4}$ eth |.

11. **λεγουσης**] λεγουσαν ℵ$^{c.c}$ Pr fl s$^{1.2}$ arm^{4} : λαλουσησ 920.

εἰς Ἔφεσον καὶ εἰς Σμύρναν καὶ εἰς Πέργαμον καὶ εἰς Θυάτειραν
καὶ εἰς Σάρδεις καὶ εἰς Φιλαδελφίαν καὶ εἰς Λαοδικίαν.

12. Καὶ ἐπέστρεψα βλέπειν τὴν φωνὴν ἥτις ἐλάλει μετ᾽ ἐμοῦ.
καὶ ἐπιστρέψας εἶδον ἑπτὰ λυχνίας χρυσᾶς,
13. καὶ ἐν μέσῳ τῶν λυχνιῶν ὅμοιον υἱὸν ἀνθρώπου,
ἐνδεδυμένον ποδήρη καὶ περιεζωσμένον πρὸς τοῖς μαστοῖς ζώνην χρυσᾶν·

2039. 2040 : φωνουσησ 2020 : > 104 : + μοι 1854. (2050) arm$^{1.3}$ bo eth : + εγω αλφα κ. το ω πρωτοσ κ. ο εσχατοσ (και) (025. 104) 620 : + εγω ειμι το α κ. το ω (ο) πρωτοσ κ. (ο) εσχατοσ (και) 1. 61* 336. 628. 2019. 2020. 2023 | ο βλεπ. > ℵ* | ο] α 172. 424. 2018. 2020 Pr s^1 bo | βλεπεισ] βλεπησ 2040 : ακουσει bo | εισ] + το ℵ | και πεμψον > arm^4 : et mittem fl | και^1 > ℵ* bo | εκκλησιαισ] + ταισ εν τη ασια bo : + ταισ (ουσαισ) arm | εν Εφεσω . . . εν Σμυρνα κτλ. arm | εισ^2 · · · ^{7} > bo : εισ$^{2.3}$ > arm^2 | και^2 · · · ^{5} > Pr : και^2 > 149. 201. 2015. 2042. 2067 | και εισ Σμυρν. post Θυατειρ. pon ℵ | Σμυρναν C 025. 046. **21** (– 205. 620. 2040) al s^2 : Smyrnam fl : Smirnam Pr gig : μυρναν A 1. 177. 205. 620. 628. 920. 2017. 2018. 2024. 2040** : μυραν 104*. 2040* : Ζμυρναν ℵ vg s^1 : Ζμυρνα arm | Περκαμον 2050 : | εισ Θυατειραν (-τιραν AC : -τηραν 046. 2050) (AC 046) 69. 110. 172. 314. 424. 1854. 1957. 2018. 2020. (2050) : Tyatyram fl : Tyathiram gig : Thyatiram vg : εισ Θυατειρασ 1. 2038 : εισ Θυατειρα (-τηρα 620. 632) ℵ **21** (– 205 2020. 2050) 250. 2037. 2067 al : εν Θυατειροισ 025. 205. 209. 2019 : Tiatirae Pr : Thyatera bo | και^5] + και 2040 | κ. εισ Σαρδ. > ℵ* : post Λαοδ. pon ℵ^c | Σαρδ.] αρδεισ 620 : | Φιλαδελφιαν AℵC 025. 046. 104. 205. 456. 522. 620. 919. 920. 1849. 1955. 2004. 2015. 2017. 2039. 2042. 2050 bo : Φιλαδελφειαν **21** (– 205. 456. 620. 919. 920. 1849. 2004. 2050) al^{pl} : "Phrygia" arm^1 | Λαοδικιαν AℵC 110*. 205. 2015. 2042. 2050 al bo : Λαοδικειαν 025. 046. **21** (–205. 2050) al^{pl} : Laudatiae Pr |.

12. και] AℵC 025. 205. 632**. 2020. 2050 Pr fl gig Cyp vg s$^{1.2}$ bo : εκει 2016 : και εκει 046. **21** (– 205. 632**. 2020. 2050) al^{pl} | επιστρ. βλεπ. . . . και επιστ. ειδον] conversus respexi ut viderem . . . et vidi Pr fl : επεστρεψα εβλεψα bo | βλεπ.] ιδειν 2050 (s^1) | τ. φων . . . εμου] τον λαλουντα μοι 2050 | ελαλει ℵC 046 al^{pl} Pr fl gig vg (s^2) arm$^{2.3.4}$: λαλει A arm^1 : ελαλησε 025. 1. 104*. 620. al s^1 | μετ εμου] μοι arm^3 | επιστρεψασ > 2050. (Pr fl) arm^1 | λυχν. επτ. χρυσ. 2050 : > arm^1 |.

13. και^1 > arm^1 | εμμεσω AC 2004 : μεσον ℵ | των AC 025. 1.

14. ἡ δὲ κεφαλὴ αὐτοῦ καὶ αἱ τρίχες λευκαὶ ὡς ἔριον λευκόν,(*a*)
καὶ οἱ ὀφθαλμοὶ αὐτοῦ ὡς φλὸξ πυρός,
15. καὶ οἱ πόδες αὐτοῦ ὅμοιοι χαλκολιβάνῳ ὡς ἐν καμίνῳ † πεπ-
υρωμένης †,
καὶ ἡ φωνὴ αὐτοῦ ὡς φωνὴ ὑδάτων πολλῶν.

(*a*) MSS add a gloss *ὡς χιών*. See vol. i. 28.

181. 205. 459. 2015. 2020. 2037. 2038. 2042. 2050. 2067 Tyc Pr fl s arm$^{1.\,2.\,4\,a}$ bo : *των επτα* ℵ 046. **21** (– 205. 2020. 2050) al^{pl} Or^{s} gig vg arm^{3} | *λυχν.*] + *των χρυσων* 172. 250. 424. 2018. 2023 gig vg$^{g.\,v}$ arm^{4} | *ομοιον*] *ομοιωμα* A s^{1} (= *ωσ ομοιωμα*) bo sa : *ομοιοσ* 1854 | *του υιου του ανθρ.* s^{2} | *υιον* ℵ 046. 1. 35. 61*. 69. 104. 110. 172. 175 177. 201. 250. 325. 337. 386. 456. 617. 620. 1934. 2015. 2016. 2018. 2021. 2042. 2050 al : *υιω* AC 025 18. 205. 468. 632. 919. 920. 1849. 1854. 2004. 2020. 2037. 2038. 2040. 2067 al^{pl} Or^{s} Pr Cyp fl gig vg arm | *ανθρωπου*] + *και* s^{1} | *ενδεδυμενοσ . . . περιεζωσμενοσ* 1854 | *ποδηρη* ℵC 025. 046 min fere omn : *ποδηρην* A (2050) | *προσ*] *εν* 172. 2018. 2020 : *επι* Pr fl bo : inter Tyc | *μαστοισ* C 025. 046. 250. 2037.^{mg} al^{pl} : *μαζοισ* A 35. 60. 432. 1957. 2015. 2023. 2036. 2037*. 2038. 2041. 2067 : *μασθοισ* ℵ 104. 205. 209. 385. 498. 620. 632. 2042. 2050 : + *αυτου* s$^{1.\,2}$ bo eth | *χρυσαν* Aℵ*C : *χρυσιν* 620 : *χρυσην* ℵ^{c} 025. 046 min omn^{vid} |.

14. η δε κεφ. . . . τριχ.] "but the hair of his head" arm^{4} | *τριχεσ*] *τριχαισ* 2050 : + *αυτου* s^{1} arm^{2} | *λευκαι* > Pr fl arm$^{1.\,2.\,3\,a}$ sa | *ωσ*^{1} Aℵ 35. 175. 386. 617. 620. 632. 920. 1934. 2020. 2040 al^{mu} Or^{s} : *ωσει* C 025. 1. 1957. 2015. 2023. 2036. 2037. 2038. 2041. 2042. 2050. 2067 al : *ωσπερ* 205. 209. 242 : *και ωσ* 046. 18. 250. 325. 337. 456. 468. 919. 1849. 2004 al | *ωσ εριον . . . οφθ. αυτ.* > arm^{2} | *εριον*] + *και* 110 s^{1} | *λευκον*] *καθαρον* arm^{4} : > 110 Pr fl Cyp s^{1} : + *και* 2019. 2050 gig vg s^{1} arm$^{3**\,a}$ eth | *ωσ χιων* > arm$^{1.\,2.\,3.*\,4}$ | *ωσ*^{2}] *ωσει* (2019). 2020. 2042 : *και* bo : aut (corrupt for ut) Tyc. | *και*^{2} > Pr *ωσ*^{3} > 517 |.

15. *και* > 104. 620 Pr | *ομοιοι*] *ομοιωσ* 920 | *χαλκολιβ.*] *χαλκωλιβανω* 025. 104. 175. 620. 2017. 2042. 2050 : aurichalco (auricalco Pr) Libani Tyc Pr : aurocalco fl : auricalco gig : orichalco vg : "burnished brass" bo : + *και* gig | *ωσ . . . πεπυρ.* > 498. arm$^{1.\,3*.\,4}$ | *ωσ* > s^{1} arm$^{2.\,3**\,a}$ | *εν*] *εκ* Pr fl | *πεπυρωμενησ* AC Cyp Pr fl : *πεπυρωμενω* ℵ 205. 209. 336. 620. 628. 2050 gig vg s$^{1.\,2}$: *πεπυρωμενοι* 025. 046. **21** (– 205. 620. 2050). 250. 2037. 2038. 2067 al^{pl} Or^{s} : ignitos velut in fornace ignis Tyc : "refined amidst a furnace fiery" arm$^{2.\,3**\,a}$ | *κ. η φων. . . . υδ. πολλ.* > arm^{4} | *υδατων πολλων*] *πληθουσ λαου* 2050 (cf. Dan. 10^{6}) |.

16. *καὶ ἔχων ἐν τῇ δεξιᾷ χειρὶ αὐτοῦ ἀστέρας ἑπτά,*
καὶ ἐκ τοῦ στόματος αὐτοῦ ῥομφαία δίστομος ὀξεῖα ἐκπο ρευομένη,
καὶ ἡ ὄψις αὐτοῦ ὡς ὁ ἥλιος φαίνει ἐν τῇ δυνάμει αὐτοῦ.

17. Καὶ ὅτε εἶδον αὐτόν, ἔπεσα πρὸς τοὺς πόδας αὐτοῦ ὡς νεκρός·
καὶ ἔθηκεν τὴν δεξιὰν αὐτοῦ ἐπ' ἐμὲ λέγων

Μὴ φοβοῦ· ἐγώ εἰμι ὁ πρῶτος καὶ ὁ ἔσχατος,
18. *καὶ ὁ ζῶν καὶ ἐγενόμην νεκρὸς,*

καὶ ἰδοὺ ζῶν εἰμὶ εἰς τοὺς αἰῶνας τῶν αἰώνων,
καὶ ἔχω τὰς κλεῖς τοῦ θανάτου καὶ τοῦ ᾅδου.

16. και^{1} > 1854 bo sa | *εχων* ℵ^{c}C 025. 046. **21** (– 2050) 2037. 2038. 2067 al^{pl} Or^{s} s$^{1.2}$: *ειχεν* ℵ* 172 250. 424. 2018. 2019 : habebat Pr fl gig vg arm : > A 2021. 2050 | *εν τ. δ. χ. αυτ.* ~ arm^{4} | *εν* > 2050 | *δεξ. χειρι. αυτ.* AℵC 025. 35. 61. 69. 172. 175. 181. 205. 209. 242. 250. 432. 617. 1934. 1957. 2016. 2017. 2018. 2019. 2023. 2036. 2037. 2038. 2041 al^{p} : *δεξια αυτ. χειρι* **21** (– 35. 175. 205. 617. 920. 1934. 2040. 2050) al^{pl} Or^{s} : *χειρι* > 60. 920. 2015. 2040. 2050 Tyc Pr fl gig vg arm^{2} : *χειρι αυτ. τη δεξια* 046 | *αστερεσ* A 1934. 2021 | *ρομφ. διστ.*] *πνευμα* s^{1} | *οξεια* > 205. 209. 242. 2050 arm$^{1.3.4}$ (bo) | *εκπορευομ.*] pendentem Tyc | *φαινει ωσ ο ηλιοσ* ℵ Pr Cyp fl arm^{4} bo : "like the sun flashing appeared" arm$^{1.2.3a}$ | *ο* > 205. 209. 241. 432. 498. 628. 632. 2020. 2042 | *φαινει*] *φαινων* 2067 : "was flashing" arm^{4} | *εν τη δυν. αυτ.* > arm |.

17. *επεσα* AℵC 025. 046. 35. 205. 325. 337. 456. 620. 632. 2020. 2050 : *επεσον* 18. 175. 386. 617. 919. 920. 1849. 1934. 2004. 2037. 2040 al | *προσ*] *εισ* ℵ 42 : *επι* 2033 s^{1} | *ωσ*] *ωσι* ℵ* : *ωσει* ℵ^{c} arm : *και ωσ* Or^{s} bo | *εθηκεν* AC 025. 046. **21** (– 35. 205. 2050) al^{pl} Or^{s} : posuit Pr gig vg : *επεθηκεν* ℵ 1. 35. 61.^{mg} 205. 2015. 2023. 2036. 2037. 2038. 2050. 2067 : inposuit fl Cyp | *δεξ αυτ.* Aℵ*C 025. 046. **21** (– 35. 205) al^{pl} Pr fl gig vg arm eth + *χειρα* ℵ$^{c.c}$ 1. 35. 61 205. 1957. 2015. 2037. 2038. 2041. 2067 s$^{1.2}$ | *λεγων*] + *μοι* 1 al^{p} arm$^{1.2.3}$ | *μη φοβ* > ℵ* : + *Ιωαννε* Pr | *ο πρωτ.*] *ο πρωτοτοκοσ* A : "beginning" arm$^{1.2}$ | *ο εσχ.*] *ο* > 2050 |.

18. *κ. ο ζων* > Pr gig : "I am life" arm$^{1.2.3a}$ | *και*^{1} > ℵ* bo arm | *εγεν. νεκρ.*] : "I am (+ same^{3}) who died" arm$^{1.2.3a}$: + *και ειπεν μοι* eth | *ιδου* > arm^{3} | *των αιωνων* > 2020 | *αιωνων* Aℵ* C 025. 2019. 2050 2067 Pr Cyp fl gig vg bo arm$^{1.2a}$: + *αμην* ℵ^{c} 046. **21** (– 2020. 2050) 250. 2037. 2038 al Or^{s} s$^{1.2}$ arm^{3} : > 2020 | *την κλειδα* s^{1} | *κλεισ* AℵC 025. 35. 205. 250. 325. 456. 468. 620. 632. 2020. 2037. 2038 al. : *κλειδασ* 046. **21** (– 35. 205. 325. 456.

19. γράψον οὖν ἃ εἶδες
καὶ ἃ εἰσὶν
καὶ ἃ μέλλει γίνεσθαι μετὰ ταῦτα.
20. τὸ μυστήριον τῶν ἑπτὰ ἀστέρων οὓς εἶδες ἐπὶ τῆς δεξιᾶς μου
καὶ τὰς ἑπτὰ λυχνίας τὰς χρυσᾶς· οἱ ἑπτὰ ἀστέρες ἄγγελοι τῶν ἑπτὰ
ἐκκλησιῶν εἰσίν, καὶ αἱ λυχνίαι αἱ ἑπτὰ [ἑπτὰ] ἐκκλησίαι εἰσίν.

468. 620. 632. 2020) al^{mu} Or^{8} | του θαν. κ. τ. αδ. AℵC 025. 046. **21** al^{pl} Tyc Pr fl gig vg s$^{1.2}$ (bo) arm eth : του αδ. κ. τ θαν. 1. 2015. 2019. 2036. 2037. 2038 al |.

19. ουν > 1. 498. 620. 2020. 2050 arm$^{1.2.3a}$ | α] ο s$^{1.2}$ | ειδεσ] οψει bo : ορασ arm$^{1.2.3a}$ | και α εισιν > arm$^{1.3}$ bo | και^{1} > arm$^{2.4a}$ | α^{2} > 2050 | και^{2} > bo | α^{3} > s^{1} | μελλει] δει 2050 : δει μελλειν ℵ* : δει μελλει C : δει 2050 | γινεσθαι Aℵ^{c} **21** (– 35. 386. 468. 617. 632. 2050). 250 al^{pl} Or^{8} : γενεσθαι ℵ*C 025. 046. 35. 61. 69. 314. 386. 468. 617. 632. 1957. 2015. 2019. 2023. 2036. 2037. 2038. 2041. 2042. 2050. 2067 |.

20. ουσ AℵC 025. 1. 110. 181. 205. 209. 2037**. 2038. 2050 : ων 046. **21** (– 205. 2050). 250. 2037*. 2067 al^{pl} Or^{8} | ειδεσ] ορασ arm^{2} | επι τησ δεξ. ℵC 025. 046. 250. 2037. 2067 min omn^{vi} Or^{8} s^{1} arm^{4} bo : εν τη δεξια A 2038 Pr fl gig vg s$^{1.2}$ arm$^{2.3a}$ eth : εν τη χειρι arm^{1} | κ. των επτα λυχνιων 498 Pr fl arm^{2} | τασ^{1} > 18 385. 429*. 522. 919. 920. 1849. 1955. 2004. 2039. 2040. 2042 | τασ χρυσασ > 498 s^{1} : των χρυσων Pr arm^{2a} : + ταυτα εστιν 201 : + ταυτα εισιν 93. 386 | αστερεσ] + επτα bo | αγγ. . . . εισιν] αγγ. εισιν των επτ. εκκλ. 498 Pr fl gig vg : των επτ. εκκλησιων εισιν οι αγγελοι arm^{2a} | εισιν^{1} > ℵ* | και αι λυχν. αι επτα. . . . εισιν > 632* | αι λυχν. αι επτα AC 025. 046 al^{pl} gig vg s$^{1.2}$ eth : αι λυχν. επτα 218. 429 2018. 2019 : επτα λυχν. ℵ* 1. 61.^{mg} 367. 2038 : αι επτα λυχν. ℵ^{c} 35. 205. 250. 632**. 1854. 1957. 2020. 2037. 2050. 2067 al Or^{8} | αι επτα] + ασ ειδεσ 025. 1. (35). (61.^{mg}). 69.^{mg} (205). 1955. (1957). 2036. 2037. 2038. 2067 bo : + αι χρυσαι 2050 : + αι χρυσαι ασ ειδεσ s^{1} : + αι 172. 241. 250. 424. 2020 arm | επτα^{6} > 104. 498 Pr fl (arm^{4}?). Only these authorities attest the original text (see vol. i. 34–35; vol. ii., Eng. trans., footnote, *in loc.*). The **αἱ ἑπτά** belongs to **ἐκκλησίαι**.

Chapter II.

1\. Τῷ ἀγγέλῳ τῷ ἐν Ἐφέσῳ ἐκκλησίας γράψον
Τάδε λέγει ὁ κρατῶν τοὺς ἑπτὰ ἀστέρας ἐν τῇ δεξιᾷ αὐτοῦ,
ὁ περιπατῶν ἐν μέσῳ τῶν ἑπτὰ λυχνιῶν τῶν χρυσῶν,

1\. **τω αγγελω τω εν Εφεσω εκκλησιασ**] Since John's usage elsewhere attests the originality of this unique grammatical construction (see *Gram.* in vol. i.), I add here a summary of the documentary evidence for it in 2^{1} and in the six other passages where it originally occurred, $2^{8.\,12.\,18}$ $3^{1.\,7.\,14}$. This evidence is sufficient to establish the originality of *τω αγγελω τω* in all seven passages: when reinforced by the evidence of John's usage elsewhere, it is irresistible. I have accordingly restored the original reading in $3^{1.\,7.\,14}$ where the Greek MSS fail us.

2^{1} *τ. αγγ. τω*] AC (2019) s^{1} arm^{4} Pr (though he reads: angelo ecclesiae Ephesi). In the note Pr. refers to the peculiar construction in the text: Dativo hic casu ecclesiae posuit, non genetivo; ac si diceret Scribe angelo, huic ecclesiae, ut non tam angelum et ecclesiam separatim videatur dixisse, quam qui sit angelus exponere voluisse, unam videlicet faciens angeli ecclesiaeque personam. 2^{8} *τ. αγγ. τω*] A (2040 *τ. αγγ. τησ ο*) $arm^{4\,a}$. 2^{12} *τ. αγγ. τω*] 2050 s^{1} $arm^{4\,a}$ sa. 2^{18} *τ. αγγ. τω*] A $Epiph^{bis}$ Pr $s^{1.\,2}$ $arm^{4\,(\beta.\,\gamma)}$. C > $τω^{2}$ but does not replace it by *τησ*. 3^{1} *τ. αγγ. τω*] Pr $s^{1.\,2}$ arm^{4}. 3^{7} *τ. αγγ. τω*] Pr arm^{4}. 3^{14} *τ. αγγ. τω*] arm^{4}.

The difficulty of the reading led to the occasional omission of *εκκλησιασ* in 2^{18} (A), 3^{14} (919. 920. 2040), 3^{1} (s^{2}), 3^{7} (arm^{4}). It is interesting to observe how the evidence for the original reading grows weaker as the text advances. The assurance of the scribes grows as they write. On the individual passages the chief variants are given below.

τω αγγ.] *τοισ αγγελοισ* $arm^{1.\,2}$: pr *και* Pr fl gig : bo sa eth begin $2^{1.\,8.\,12.\,18}$ $3^{1.\,7.\,14}$ with *και* (> bo sa) *γραψον* | *τω εν Εφεσω εκκλησιασ* AC : *τω τησ εν Εφ. εκκλ.* 2019 : *τω εν Εφεσω εν τη εκκλησια* arm^{4} : *τω εν εκκλησια Εφεσου* s^{1} : *τησ εν Εφεσω εκκλ.* ℵ 025. 046 min fere omn Or^{8}: Ephesi ecclesiae gig vg : ecclesiae Ephesi Pr bo : *τησ Εφεσιων εκκλησιασ* 1. 2020 fl $arm^{1.\,2.\,3\,a}$ *λεγει*] + *κυριοσ* 172. 250. 424. 522. 2018. 2039 | *κρατων*] + *παντα και* s^{2} | *δεξια*] *χειρι* Tyc s^{1} : *δεξια χειρι* 172. 250. 2018 $arm^{1.\,3.\,4}$ bo sa | *αυτου*] + *χειρι* ℵ* | $ο^{2}$] *και* $arm^{1.\,2.\,3\,a}$ | *εν μεσ.*] *εμμεσω* AC : *επι* 1 | *επτα* > 498. 620. 628. 2020 Tyc s^{1} $arm^{1.\,2}$: ∼ *τ. λ. τ. επτα χρυσ.* 2042 | *χρυσων* ℵ 025. 046 min fere omn : *χρυσεων* AC : *χρυσιων* 2050 |.

2. Οἶδα τὰ ἔργα σου, καὶ τὸν κόπον καὶ τὴν ὑπομονήν σου,
καὶ ὅτι οὐ δύνῃ βαστάσαι κακούς,
καὶ ἐπείρασας τοὺς λέγοντας ἑαυτοὺς ἀποστόλους καὶ οὐκ εἰσίν,
καὶ εὗρες αὐτοὺς ψευδεῖς·

3. καὶ ὑπομονὴν ἔχεις
καὶ ἐβάστασας διὰ τὸ ὄνομά μου
καὶ οὐ κεκοπίακες.

4. ἀλλ' ἔχω κατὰ σοῦ ὅτι τὴν ἀγάπην σου τὴν πρώτην ἀφῆκας.

5. μνημόνευε οὖν πόθεν πέπτωκας,
καὶ μετανόησον καὶ τὰ πρῶτα ἔργα ποίησον·
εἰ δὲ μή, ἔρχομαί σοι
καὶ κινήσω τὴν λυχνίαν σου ἐκ τοῦ τόπου αὐτῆς.(*a*)

(*a*) MSS add gloss ἐὰν μὴ μετανοήσῃς.

2. οιδα] ειδον 337 eth | κ. τ. κοπ. >385. 429. 522 | κ. τ. υπομ. σου κ. τ. κοπ. σου 632 | τον κοπον AC 025. 35. 60. 181. 205. 209. 432. 1957. 2015. 2019. 2023. 2036. 2037. 2038. 2041. 2042 Pr gig vg s^{2} : τουσ κοπουσ arm$^{1\,a}$: τον κοπον σου ℵ 046. **21** (−35. 205). 250. 2067 Or^{s} s^{1} : τουσ κοπουσ σου arm$^{2.\,3.\,4}$ bo | σου^{2} >Pr arm$^{1.\,2\,a}$ | και^{3} >A bo : +οιδα arm^{1} | ου δυνη βαστ.] ου βασταζεισ arm$^{1.\,3}$ | δυνησῃ 2042 : δυνει 620. 2050 | βασταξαι 025. 1. 2020. 2038 | κακον bo | και^{4}] ουσ arm^{1} | εαυτουσ >181. 2067 : +ειναι vg$^{c.\,f}$ arm^{a} | αποστολ. Aℵ*C 025. 94. 337. 2038 vg arm$^{1.\,2.\,3.\,4}$: +ειναι ℵ$^{c.\,c}$ 046. **21** (−337) al^{mu} Or^{s} Pr gig vg^{v} s$^{1.\,2}$ | και ευρ. αυτ. ψ.] κ. ευρεθησαν ψευδαποστολοι bo |.

3. και υπομ. εχ. >218. 424. 2018 | υπομ. εχ. (+κ. θλιψισ πασασ ℵ*) κ. εβαστ. AℵC 046. **21** (−35. 205. 620. 2020). 250 al^{mu} Or^{s} vg s$^{1.\,2}$ arm^{4} : et habuisti patientiam et tolerasti Pr : εβαστ. (εβαπτισασ 1. 61.^{mg} 2037) κ. υπομ. εχ. (1) 35. (61.^{mg}). 1957. 2015. 2020. 2023. 2036. (2037). 2038. 2067 al : εβαστ. με κ. υπομ. εχ. 025. 104. 205. 209. 336. 459. 620 : υπομ. εχ. κ. εβαστ. αυτουσ gig bo | εχεισ] habuisti Pr | κ. εβαστ. >432 | δια >314. 2016 | και ου κεκοπιακεσ AC (s$^{1.\,2}$) : κ. ουκ. εκοπιασασ ℵ 025. 046. **21** (−620. 2020). 250. 2037 al^{pl} Or^{s} : et non (nec Pr) defecisti Pr gig vg : και κεκοπιακασ 336. 432. 628. 2020 arm$^{2\,a}$: καικοπιακασ 1 : και κεκοπιασασ 620 |.

4. αλλ AC 025. 1. 385. 620. 2015. 2020 2037. 2038. 2042. 2050. 2067 Or^{s} : αλλα ℵ 046. **21** (−205. 620. 2020. 2050). 250 al : και 205 | εχω κατα σου]+ολιγα gig | την πρωτην σου αγαπην A | αφηκασ Aℵ$^{c.\,c}$ 025. 046 al omn^{vid} : αφηκεσ ℵ*C |.

5. μνημονευσον 1854. 2020 | ουν >Pr s^{1} arm$^{1.\,2.\,4\,a}$ eth | ποθεν] οθεν 386 : πωσ bo | πεπτωκασ (−εσ ℵ) AℵC 046. **21** (−35. 205. 620). 250 al^{mu} Or^{s} Pr Cyp s^{2} : εκπεπτωκασ 025. 1. 35. 104. 205. 620. 1957. 2015. 2023. 2036. 2037. 2038. 2041. 2067 gig vg s^{1} | κ. μεταν. > s^{1} arm^{3} | κ. τ. πρ. εργ. ποιησον >bo

6. ἀλλὰ τοῦτο ἔχεις ὅτι μισεῖς τὰ ἔργα τῶν Νικολαϊτῶν, ἃ κἀγὼ
μισῶ. 7. Ὁ ἔχων οὖς ἀκουσάτω τί τὸ πνεῦμα λέγει ταῖς ἐκκλησίαις
Τῷ νικῶντι δώσω αὐτῷ φαγεῖν ἐκ τοῦ ξύλου τῆς ζωῆς ὅ ἐστιν ἐν τῷ
παραδείσῳ τοῦ θεοῦ.

8. Καὶ τῷ ἀγγέλῳ τῷ ἐν Σμύρνῃ ἐκκλησίας γράψον
Τάδε λέγει ὁ πρῶτος καὶ ὁ ἔσχατος,
ὃς ἐγένετο νεκρὸς καὶ ἔζησεν·

9. Οἶδά σου τὴν θλίψιν καὶ τὴν πτωχείαν,
ἀλλὰ πλούσιος εἶ,
καὶ τὴν βλασφημίαν ἐκ τῶν λεγόντων Ἰουδαίους εἶναι ἑαυτοὺς
καὶ οὐκ εἰσίν, ἀλλὰ συναγωγὴ τοῦ Σατανᾶ.

eth | εργα]+σου gig arm | σοι AℵC 025. 2050 gig vg s^{1} bo sa : > 181. 2041 arm$^{1.2a}$: + ταχυ 046. **21** (–2050). 250. 2037. 2038. 2067 al^{pl} Or^{s} Pr s^{2} arm^{a} : +ταχει 1 | κινησω]+ κατα σου 325. 456 | εκ τ. τοπ. αυτ. >s^{1} | εαν] ει 35 | μετανοησεισ (-σισ 1) 35. 104. 498. 620. 2050 : μετανοησ 205 : μετανοησῃ Tyc |.

6. εχεισ] +αγαθον Pr | οτι μισ.] οτι μισησ 2040 | α > A arm^{2} : sicut Pr | καγω] εγω s^{1} arm$^{1.2.3a}$ eth |.

7. ουσ] ωτα s$^{1.2}$: +ακουειν bo eth : aures audiendi Pr arm$^{1.2.4}$ | ακουετω 617 | πνευμα]+αγιον arm$^{1.2.4}$ eth | ταισ]+επτα A | εκκλ.]+ταισ επτα C : +και s^{1} | αυτω AC 025. 046. **21** (–35. 205) Or^{s} Pr Cyp vg s^{2} arm eth : >ℵ 35. 60. 205. 209. 1957. 2023. 2041 Tyc gig vg^{d,v} s^{1} | εν τω παραδ. Aℵ*C 046. **21** (–35. 205) al^{mu} Tyc Pr Cyp vg s$^{1.2}$ arm$^{1.2.3.4}$: εν μεσω τω παραδεισω ℵ$^{c.c}$ 025 : εν μεσω του παραδεισου 1. 35. 61.^{mg} 205. (εμεσω 205). 250. 1957. 2015. 2018. 2019. 2023. 2036. 2037. 2038. 2041. 2067 gig arm^{a} bo | του θεου AℵC 025. 1. 61.^{mg} 205. 2015. 2019. 2036. 2037. 2038. 2067 s^{1} arm^{a} : +μου 046. **21** (–205) al^{mu} Or$^{Ex.\ ix.\ 130}$ Or^{s} Tyc Pr gig Cyp vg s^{2} arm$^{1.2.3.4}$ bo eth |.

8. τω εν] See note on 2^{1}. τω A arm^{4} : τησ ℵC 025. 046. **21** min^{rell} Or^{s} eth : τησ+ο 2040 | εν Σμυρνησ εκκλησιασ A : Smirnae ecclesiae gig (vg) bo : ecclesiae Smirnae Pr s^{1} : εν Ζμυρνη εκκλησιασ ℵ : εν Σμυρνη εκκλ. C 025. 046. **21.** 250. 2038. 2067 al^{mu} s^{2} arm^{4} (Ζμ.) : τησ εκκλ. του Σμυρναιου arm$^{1.3a}$: εκκλησιασ μυρναιων 1 : Σμυρναιων εκκλησιασ 2015. 2036. 2037 : Σμυρ. AC 025. 046 min$^{omn\ vid}$ gig s^{2} arm$^{1.2.3a}$ bo : Ζμυρ. ℵ vg s^{1} arm^{4} | πρωτοσ] πρωτοτοκοσ A | ο^{2} > 2016. 2020. 2041 | ο εσχ.] "without end" arm^{1} : +ο πρωτοσ των νεκρων 69 | οσ AℵC 025. 046. 35. 205. 468**. 620. 632. 2020. 2050 Pr gig vg s$^{1.2}$ arm$^{1.2.4a}$ bo : >18. 175. 325. 337. 386. 456. 468*. 617. 919. 920. 1849. 1934. 2004. 2040 al^{mu} | εζησεν] vivit gig vg : revixit Pr |.

9. σου AC 025. 93. 241. 250^{com} Pr gig vg s^{1} bo sa eth : +τα εργα και ℵ 046. **21.** 250. 2037. 2038. 2067 Or^{s} Tyc s^{2}

10. μὴ φοβοῦ ἃ μέλλεις πάσχειν.
ἰδοὺ μέλλει βάλλειν ὁ διάβολος ἐξ ὑμῶν εἰς φυλακήν,
ἵνα πειρασθῆτε καὶ ἕχητε θλίψιν ἡμερῶν δέκα.

γίνου πιστὸς ἄχρι θανάτου,
καὶ δώσω σοι τὸν στέφανον τῆς ζωῆς.

11. Ὁ ἔχων οὖς ἀκουσάτω τί τὸ πνεῦμα λέγει ταῖς ἐκκλησίαις. Ὁ
νικῶν οὐ μὴ ἀδικηθῇ ἐκ τοῦ θανάτου τοῦ δευτέρου.
12. Καὶ τῷ ἀγγέλῳ τῷ ἐν Περγάμῳ ἐκκλησίας γράψον
Τάδε λέγει ὁ ἔχων τὴν ῥομφαίαν τὴν δίστομον τὴν ὀξεῖαν

arm : + τα εργα κ. την υπομονην arm^{4} | πτωχειαν 025. 046. **21** (– 620) Or^{s} : πτωχιαν A ℵ C 1. 498. 620 : + σου gig vg s^{1} bo eth | την βλασφ.] + την ℵ s$^{1.2}$: τασ βλασφημιασ arm$^{1.2.3a}$: blasphemaris Pr gig vg : "I found not one" bo | εκ A ℵ C 046. **21** (– 35. 205) al^{mu} Pr gig vg s$^{1.2}$ bo : > 025. 1. 35. 205. 1957. 2015. 2019. 2023. 2036. 2037. 2038. 2041. 2067 Or^{s} | εαυτ. ιουδ. 2015. 2036 (s^{1}) | Ιουδαιων ℵ*C 2050 arm^{1} | εαυτουσ ειναι 2019 | ειναι > 468** s^{1} | εαυτ. > 336. 620. 628 : αυτουσ 314. 2016. 2019 | κ. ουκ εισιν > arm^{1} | σατανα] + εισιν ℵ$^{c.c}$ Pr gig vg arm$^{1.2.3}$ |.

10. μη AC 046. 2020. 2023. 2050. 2067 bo : μηδεν ℵ 025. **21** (– 2020. 2050) Or^{s} Pr gig vg s$^{1.2}$ eth | α] ων 35 | μελλεισ] θελεισ arm^{a} | πασχειν A ℵ C 025. 1. 35. 104. 172. 205. 468* (πασχει 620). 1957. 2015. 2018. 2019. 2023. 2036. 2041 : παθειν 046. **21** (– 35. 205. 468*. 620). 2067 al^{mu} Or^{s} | ιδου A ℵ C 025. 1. 18. 61. 69. 104. 250. 620. 2018. 2019. 2020. 2036. 2037. 2038 al^{mu} Pr gig vg s^{1} arm bo : + δη 046. **21** (– 18. 205. 620. 2020. 2050). 2067 Or^{s} s^{2} : + γαρ 2050 eth : + και 205 | ο διαβ. βαλ. 920. 2020. 2040 s$^{1.2}$ eth | βαλλειν A ℵ^{c}C 025. 18. 35. 205. 250. 919. 920. 1849. 2004. 2020 al : βαλειν 046. 175. 325. 337. 386. 456. 468. 617. 620. 632. 1934. 2037. 2040. 2050. 2067 al Or^{s} : βαλλειν βαλιν ℵ* | εξ υμ. ο διαβ. ℵ 1. 2037. 2067 al gig | εξ] αφ 1854 | ινα πειρασθ.] ινα πειραθητε 1 : ινα πειρασθη 920 | κ. εχ. θλιψ. > gig | εχητε A 1854. 2019. 2038 Pr (bo) : εχετε C 025. 1. 181. 2050 : εξητε 110 : εξετε ℵ 046. **21** (– 2050) Or^{s} Tyc vg s$^{1.2}$ | θλιψ.] + μεγαλην 2050 | δεκ. ημ. Tyc gig | ημερων A ℵ C 025. 1. 35. 104. 172. 205. 250. 620. 1957. 2015. 2037. 2038. 2050. 2067 al : dierum Pr : ημερασ 046. **21** (– 35. 205. 620. 2050) al^{mu} Or^{s} Tyc s$^{1.2}$: diebus gig vg | γινου > ℵ* | γινεσθε . . . πιστοι . . . υμιν s^{1} | αχρει 2050 | μεχρι 632. 2020 |.

11. ουσ] ωτα s$^{1.2}$ arm$^{1.4}$: + ακουειν bo eth : + audiendi Pr arm$^{1.4a}$ | το] + αγιον arm$^{1.2}$ eth | τ. εκκλ. > arm^{1} | ο νικων] ο γαρ νικων bo |.

12. **τω αγγ.**] τοισ αγγελοισ arm$^{1.2.3}$ | τω εν Π. εκκλ. 2050 (save that it reads Περκαμω) : see note on 2^{1} : τω εν εκκλησια

13. Οἶδα ποῦ κατοικεῖς,
ὅπου ὁ θρόνος τοῦ Σατανᾶ,
καὶ κρατεῖς τὸ ὄνομά μου,
καὶ οὐκ ἠρνήσω τὴν πίστιν μου

καὶ ἐν ταῖς ἡμέραις † Ἀντίπας,† ὁ μάρτυς μου,
ὁ πιστός μου, ὃς ἀπεκτάνθη παρ' ὑμῖν
ὅπου ὁ Σατανᾶς κατοικεῖ.

14. ἀλλ' ἔχω κατὰ σοῦ ὀλίγα,
ὅτι ἔχεις ἐκεῖ κρατοῦντας τὴν διδαχὴν Βαλαάμ,
ὃς ἐδίδασκεν τῷ Βαλὰκ βαλεῖν σκάνδαλον ἐνώπιον τῶν υἱῶν
Ἰσραήλ,
φαγεῖν εἰδωλόθυτα καὶ πορνεῦσαι.

Περγαμου s^{1} : τω εν τη Περγαμου εκκλησια ? arm^{4a} : τω εν τ. εκκλ. II. sa : τησ εν Περγαμω εκκλησιασ all Greek MSS (– 2050) Or^{8} : τησ Περγαμαιων (Περγαιων^{1}) εκκλησιασ arm$^{1.2}$: Pergami ecclesiae gig vg s^{2} bo : eccles. Perg. Pr eth | λεγει] + κυριοσ 205 | τ. οξ. τ. διστ. s$^{1.2}$ eth |.

13. οιδα AℵC 025. 2020. 2050 Tyc Pr gig vg s^{1} arm$^{1.2.4}$ bo sa eth : + τα εργα σου και 046. **21** (– 2020. 2050 [σου τα εργα και 325. 456]) al^{pl} Or^{8} s^{2} arm^{3a} | που] και οτι arm^{a} | κρατεισ] εκρατησασ bo : κρατουσιν arm$^{1.3*}$ | μου^{1}] σου ℵ* | ηρνησω] + nomen meum et gig | την πιστ.] τον πιστον arm^{3} | και^{3} AC 1957. 2050 gig vg s^{1} bo eth : > ℵ 025. 046. **21** (– 2050) al^{pl} Pr arm$^{2.3.4a}$ | εν ταισ] αυταισ 325* : in illis Pr | ημεραισ AC vg s^{1} : + ταυταισ arm$^{1.2}$: + εν ταισ ℵ* : + αισ 046. **21** (– 35. 205. 620. 2040. 2050) al Or^{8} (arm^{3**a}) : + εν αισ ℵ^{c} 025. 1. 35. 104. 205. 250. 620. 1957. 2018. 2023. 2036. 2037. 2038. 2041. 2067 (s^{2}) (arm^{4}) : + in quibus fuit gig : + εμαισ 1. 61.^{mg} : + μου (εν) αισ 2040. (2050) | Αντιπασ ℵ*C 025. 046. **21** (– 325. 337. 456. 2050) al^{mu} vg : Antiphas Pr : Anthipas arm^{3**a} : Antipax gig : Αντειπασ Aℵ$^{c.c}$ 42. 82. 93. 325. 337. 367. 452. 456. 498. 2021. 2024**. 2050 Or^{8} : ἀντεῖπασ s$^{1.2}$ arm^{4} bo : > eth | ο μαρτ.] και ο μαρτυσ 172. 2032 s^{1} : πασ μαρτυσ arm$^{2(1)}$ | μου^{3} > 181. 2019 arm^{1} bo : + και Pr | ο πιστοσ] + οτι πασ μαρτυσ (+ μου s^{1}) πιστοσ 2059 s^{1} : οτι μαρτυσ μου πιστοσ (> γ) πασ ο πιστευων arm$^{β.γ.δ}$ | μου^{4} AC 61. 69. 2050 Or^{8} s^{2} : > ℵ 025. 046. **21** (– 2050) Pr gig vg (arm) bo | οσ αν εκτανθη 2050 : ο απεκτανθη 205 : ον απεκτειναν bo eth | οσ > 172. 314. 2016 | παρ υμιν] παρ υμων 920. 2040 s^{1} arm^{3**4a} : εξ υμων arm^{2} : + εκει 632 | οπου ο Σατ. κατοικ. > 2020 s^{1} |.

14. αλλ. AℵC 025. 35. 205. 620. 2020 2050 al Or^{8} : αλλα 046. **21** (– 35. 205. 620. 2020. 2050) 250. 2038. 2067 al | κατα σου > ℵ* : + λεγειν Pr arm^{3**4} | ολιγα > arm$^{1.2.3*}$ eth | οτι . . . κρατ.] ονοματα κρατουντα bo | οτι > C Pr vg s^{2} | εχεισ] εχει

15. οὕτως ἔχεις καὶ σὺ κρατοῦντας τὴν διδαχὴν Νικολαϊτῶν
ὁμοίως.

16. μετανόησον οὖν·
εἰ δὲ μή, ἔρχομαί σοι ταχύ,
καὶ πολεμήσω μετ᾽ αὐτῶν ἐν τῇ ῥομφαίᾳ τοῦ στόματός μου.

17. Ὁ ἔχων οὖς ἀκουσάτω
τί τὸ πνεῦμα λέγει ταῖς ἐκκλησίαις.

Τῷ νικῶντι δώσω αὐτῷ τοῦ μάννα τοῦ κεκρυμμένου,
καὶ δώσω αὐτῷ ψῆφον λευκήν,
καὶ ἐπὶ τὴν ψῆφον ὄνομα καινὸν γεγραμμένον
ὃ οὐδεὶς οἶδεν εἰ μὴ ὁ λαμβάνων.

A | διδαχην] + του 42. 468. 2019. 2020 | εδιδασκεν Aℵ C 025. 1. 2015. 2036. 2037. 2050. 2067 al Pr gig vg : εδιδαξεν 046. **21** (−2050) al[mu] Or[s] s[1.2] arm[1.2.3a] bo : διδασκει arm[4] | τω Βαλ. AC 104 : εν τω Βαλ. 1. 94 : τον Βαλ. ℵ[c] **21** (−35*). 250. 2037. 2038 Or[s] : εν τω Βαλααμ τον Βαλ. 025. 35*. 2067 et comm. in 250. 2037. 2067 : Βαλ. 046 : > ℵ* | Βαλακ Aℵ[c] 025. **21** (−386. 620. 1849. 2040**. 2050) Or[s] : Balac gig vg arm : Βαλαακ C 046. 620. 1849. 1854. 2040**. 2050 : Balaac Pr : Βαλααμ 386 | βαλειν] βαλλειν ℵ[c] : εμβαλειν 2050 : βασιλει A | των] τε 2050 | φαγειν AℵC 025. 1. 35. 205. 522. 632*. 1957. 2015. 2019. 2020. 2023. 2036. 2050 Or[Num. x. 242] Pr gig vg s[1] arm : του φαγ. 42. 325. 336. 367. 456. 468. 620. 628 : και φαγ. 046. 18. 175. 250. 337. 386. 617. 632**. 919. 920. 1849. 1934. 2004. 2040. 2067 al Or[s] (s[2]) | ειδωλοθ. > vg arm[2] : ειδωλοθυτον 1854 : de sacrificiis Pr |.

15. σ**υ κρατ.**] ο κρατων 2050 | κρατουντασ] κρατουντα bo : > arm[1.2.3a] | Νικολ. AC 046. 18. 175. 325. 386. 456. 468. 617. 919. 1849. 2004 al : των Νικολ. ℵ 025. 1. 35. 104. 205. 337. 620. 632. 920. 1934. 1957. 2015. 2020. 2040. 2050 al (arm[4a] bo) : "of Nicolaus" arm[1.2.3] | ομοιωσ AℵC 046. **21** (−35. 468. 2020) Or[s] Pr gig vg s[1.2] (arm[4]) : ο μισω 1. 61.[mg] : ην μισω 2037 arm[a] : ομοιωσ ο (ω 468 : ην 2067) μισω 025. 35*. 42. 181. 468. 2038. 2067 : > 2020 arm[1.2.3] bo sa eth |.

16. ουν AC 046. **21** (−35) al[mu] arm[1a] bo eth : μονον arm[3] : > ℵ 025. 1. 35. 61. 69. 1957. 2015. 2019. 2023. 2036. 2037. 2038. 2041 Or[s] Pr gig vg s[1.2] arm[2] | ει δε μη] και bo | σοι > 61. 69. 181. 2020. arm[1.2.3a] eth : συ ℵ* | πολεμ.] εκπολεμησω 205 | αυτων] σου 2050 Pr : αυτου arm[2.3] | εν > Tyc | του στομ. μου > arm[1] : + και εν τη απειλη η φιλανθρωπια 104. 336. 459. 620. 628 (from the Comm. of Andreas) |.

17. ουσ] ωτα s[1.2] : + ακουειν bo eth : aures audiendi Pr arm[1.3.4] | πνευμα] + αγιον arm[1.3] eth | εκκλησ.] + οτι bo | τω

18. Καὶ τῷ ἀγγέλῳ τῷ ἐν Θυατείροις ἐκκλησίας γράψον
Τάδε λέγει ὁ υἱὸς τοῦ θεοῦ,
ὁ ἔχων τοὺς ὀφθαλμοὺς ὡς φλόγα πυρός,
καὶ οἱ πόδες αὐτοῦ ὅμοιοι χαλκολιβάνῳ,
19. Οἶδά σου τὰ ἔργα,
καὶ τὴν ἀγάπην καὶ τὴν πίστιν καὶ τὴν διακονίαν καὶ τὴν ὑπομονήν σου,
καὶ τὰ ἔργα σου τὰ ἔσχατα πλείονα τῶν πρώτων.

νικωντι ℵ 025. 046. **21** (– 620. 2050) al^{pl} : *τω νικουντι* AC : | *αυτω* AC 025. 046 $min^{fere\ omn}$ Or^s : > ℵ 61^{txt} Tyc gig $vg^{d.\ v}$ s^1 : + *φαγειν* 025. 1. 35. $61.^{mg}$ 104. 205. 468. 620. 632. 1957. 2015. 2023. 2036. 2037. 2038. 2041. 2067 Or^s Tyc gig $arm^{4\ a}$: + *του φαγειν* 42. 69 : + "food" $arm^{1.\ 2.\ 3}$ | *του μαννα* AC **21** (– 35. 205. 468. 620. 632. 2050) al Or^s : *μαννα* 69 : *το μαννα* 046 gig vg $arm^{2.\ 3}$: *εκ του μαννα* ℵ 468*. 1957. 2019. (2050) Tyc Pr $s^{1.\ 2}$ $arm^{4\ a}$ bo : *απο του μαννα* 1. 35. $61.^{mg}$ 104. 205. 468**. 620. 632. 2015. 2023. 2036. 2037. 2038. 2041. 2067 : *απο του ξυλου* 025 : *απο του ξυλου τησ ζωησ* arm^1 : + *φαγειν* 172. 250. 2018. 2050 | *του κεκρ.*] *το κεκρυμμ νον* 2050 gig vg | *δωσω αυτω*^{2} > ℵ 2020 arm^a | *λευκ. κ. επι τ. ψηφ.* > s^1 | *ψηφ.*^{2}] *ψημον* C | *καινον*] *κενον* C 175. 2040 | *γεγραμμ.*] *εγγεγραμμενον* 919 : > Pr : + *επ αυτην* bo | *ο ουδεισ . . . λαμβ.* > 1 | *ο* > ℵ* | *οιδεν*] *ειδεν* 205. 209 bo : + *αυτω* 2050 |.

18. *τω εν Θυατειροισ εκκλησιασ*] See note on 2^1. *τω εν Θυατ.* A : *εν Θυατ. εκκλησιασ* C : *τω αγγ. τησ εκκλ. τω εν Θυατ.* $Epiph^{455}$: ecclesiae qui est Tyatirae Pr : *τω εν εκκλησια τη εν Θυατ.* s^1 : *τω τησ εκκλησιασ τησ εν Θυατ.* s^2 : qui in Theatrea ecclesia $arm^{4\ (\beta.\ \gamma)}$: *τησ εν Θυατ. εκκλησ.* ℵ 025. 046 min omn^{vid} Or^s : Tyatirae ecclesie gig : Thyatirae ecclesiae vg : ecclesiae Thyaterae bo : *των Θυατιραιων* $arm^{1.\ 2}$: *τησ Θυατειρων εκκλησ.* 2020 (arm^3) | *Θυατειροισ* ℵ 1. 18. 35. 175. 205. 250. 386. 468. 617. 919. 920. 1934. 2004. 2037. 2040. 2067 : *Θυατιροισ* AC : *Θυατηροισ* 025. 149. 201. 632. 1849. 1955. 2036. 2050 : *Θυατειρων* 2020 : *Θυατηρη* 046. 620 : *Θυατειρη* 69. 93. 104. 110. 177. 325. 337. 456. 498. 2021 : Thyatirae vg : Tyatire gig | *εκκλησιασ* > A arm^1 | *τουσ οφθαλμ.* A 2019. 2020 Pr gig vg ($arm^{2.\ 3.\ 4}$) : *τον οφθαλμον* s^1 : + *αυτου* ℵC 025. 046. **21** (– 2020). 250. 2037. 2038 al^{pl} Or^s s^2 ($arm^{1\ a}$) | *φλογα*] *φλοξ* ℵ Pr : *λαμπαδασ* 1854 | *χαλκω λιβανω* 025. 104. 175. 620. 2050 : auricalco Pr : eramento thurino gig : orichalco vg : "unto brass of Libanan" s^2 $arm^{1.\ 2.\ 3^*\ 4}$: "unto brass smelted" $arm^{3^{**}\ a}$: "burnished brass" (*χαλκολιβανοσ*) bo eth |.

19. *τα εργ. και* > 181 | *την* (> 2020) *πιστ. κ. τ. αγαπ. κ. τ διακ.* 18. 242. 2040 : *την αγαπ. κ. τ. διακ. κ. τ. πιστ.* 1 | *κ. τ. αγαπ.*] + *σου* s^1 bo eth | *την*^{2} > C 2020 | *πιστ.*] + *σου* s^1 bo eth | *την διακονιαν και* > ℵ* | *την*^{3} > 2020 | *διακονιαν*] + *σου* s^1 bo

20. ἀλλὰ ἔχω κατὰ σοῦ
ὅτι ἀφεῖς τὴν γυναῖκα Ἰεζάβελ, ἡ λέγουσα ἑαυτὴν προφῆτιν,
καὶ διδάσκει καὶ πλανᾷ τοὺς ἐμοὺς δούλους
πορνεῦσαι καὶ φαγεῖν εἰδωλόθυτα.
21. καὶ ἔδωκα αὐτῇ χρόνον ἵνα μετανοήσῃ,
καὶ οὐκ ἠθέλησεν μετανοῆσαι ἐκ τῆς πορνείας αὐτῆς.
22. ἰδοὺ βάλλω αὐτὴν εἰς κλίνην,
καὶ τοὺς μοιχεύοντας μετ' αὐτῆς εἰς θλίψιν μεγάλην,(a)

(a) Interpolation follows here: ἐὰν μὴ μετανοήσουσιν ἐκ τῶν ἔργων αὐτῆς. See Eng. trans. vol. ii. footnote, *in loc.* ἐὰν μή is not followed by the indicative in our author.

eth | την⁴ >A 2019 | σου² >ℵ 2023 Pr | σου³] + και 1 | πλειονα] χειρονα 175. 617*. 1934 |.

20. αλλα A 046 min mult : αλλ ℵC 025 35. 69. 104. 175. 205. 314. 385. 617. 620. 1934. 1957. 2015. 2016. 2020. 2037. 2038. 2050. 2067 al Or^{s} | εχω] λεγω arm$^{1.2.3a}$ | κατα σου AC 025. 046. **21** (−35*. 632*. 2050). 250 al^{mu} Tyc vg s^{2} bo eth : σοι arm$^{1.2.3a}$: + πολυ ℵ 35*. 181. 632*. 2019. 2022. 2038. 2050 gig s^{1} arm^{4a} : + πολλα 2015. 2036 Pr Cyp : + ολιγα 1 | αφεισ Aℵ*C 025. 046. **21** (−2020. 2040. 2050). 2037. 2038. al^{mu} Pr Cyp gig vg : αφηκασ ℵ^{c} 506. 2019. 2050. 2067 Tyc s$^{1.2}$ arm bo eth : αφιησ 241. 250. 424. 2018. 2040 : ποθεισ 2020 | γυναικα ℵC 025. 1. 104. 205. 468*. 620. 2019. 2020. 2038. 2050 Tyc gig vg arm$^{2.3a}$ bo eth : + σου A 046. **21** (−205. 468*. 620. 2020. 2050) al^{mu} Or^{s} Pr Cyp s$^{1.2}$ arm$^{1.4}$: την Ιεζαβελ A : Ιαζαβελ ℵ* : Zezabel Pr Cyp arm$^{1.2.4a}$ | η λεγουσα Aℵ*C : η λεγει 046. **21** (−35*. 205. 2020. 2050). al^{mu} Or^{s} gig vg bo eth : την λεγουσαν ℵ^{c} 025. 1. 35*. 205. 1854. 2019. 2020. 2038. 2050 : "who declared" arm$^{1.3.4a}$ | εαυτην AC 025. **21** (−620) : αυτην ℵ 046. 104. 141. 336. 620. 628 | προφητιν Aℵ^{c}C **21** (−620. 919. 2004. 2040. 2050) al^{mu} Or^{s} : prophetissam gig : προφητειαν ℵ* : προφητην 025. 046. 104. 172. 620. 919. 2004. 2019. 2038. 2040. 2041*. 2050 : propheten Tyc Pr Cyp vg : + ειναι ℵ 2050 s^{1} arm^{4} | κ. διδασκει] διδασκειν Pr Cyp vg : και διδασκαλον? bo | πλανα] πλαναν Pr Cyp vg | ειδωλοθ. φαγ. 1. 2019 | ειδωλοθ.] το ειδωλοθυτον? arm$^{1.3.4a}$: de idolothytis vg (bo) : de sacrificiis (−ficio gig) Pr Cyp gig : >arm^{2} |.

21. v. 21 >205 | και¹ >Pr arm$^{1.4}$ | αυτη] αυτην 2040 | μεταν.] μετανοησει 620. 2050 | κ. ου θελ. μεταν. >ℵ* (arm^{a}) : κ ει μεν θελει μεταν. 2020 : κ. ου μετενοησεν (post αυτησ) 1 arm$^{1.2.3}$ | ηθελησεν A Pr Cyp eth : θελει ℵ*C 025. 046 min^{omn} Or^{s} gig vg s$^{1.2}$ | πορνειασ C 025. 046. **21** : πορνιασ Aℵ | αυτησ] ταυτησ ℵ : αυτων κ. ου μετενοησαν arm^{a} |.

22. ιδου] ειδ' ου 2020 : + εγω 1 | βαλλω AC **21** (−325.

23. καὶ τὰ τέκνα αὐτῆς ἀποκτενῶ ἐν θανάτῳ.
καὶ γνώσονται πᾶσαι αἱ ἐκκλησίαι
ὅτι ἐγώ εἰμι ὁ ἐραυνῶν νεφροὺς καὶ καρδίας
καὶ δώσω ὑμῖν ἑκάστῳ κατὰ τὰ ἔργα ὑμῶν.
24. ὑμῖν δὲ λέγω τοῖς λοιποῖς τοῖς ἐν Θυατείροις,
ὅσοι οὐκ ἔχουσιν τὴν διδαχὴν ταύτην,
οἵτινες οὐκ ἔγνωσαν τὰ βαθέα τοῦ Σατανᾶ, ὡς λέγουσιν,
οὐ βάλλω ἐφ' ὑμᾶς ἄλλο βάρος·
25. πλὴν ὃ ἔχετε κρατήσατε ἄχρι οὗ ἂν ἥξω.

456. 468*. 632. 2020. 2050). 1. 250. 2037. 2038. 2067 Pr Cyp vg arm : βαλω ℵ^{c} 025. 046. 325. 456. 468*. 632. 2020. 2050 Or^{s} gig bo eth : καλω ℵ* | κλινην] φυλακην A : καμινον arm$^{1.2.3a}$: luctum *cod. ap.* Pr : "pains of a couch" arm^{4} | μοιχευσαντασ 61. 69 Pr Cyp | μετ αυτησ] αυτην 2050 | μεγαλ. > arm^{3} : maximam Pr Cyp vg arm^{a} | μετανοησουσιν Aℵ : μετανοησωσιν C 025. 046. **21** (– 2050) al^{pl} Or^{s} : μετανοησει 2050 : μετανοηση 469 Pr Cyp bo sa eth | εκ. τ. εργ. αυτ. > bo sa | αυτησ ℵC 025. 046. **21** (– 35*. 205. 468. 632) al^{mu} Or^{s} Pr Cyp gig vg s^{2} arm^{4} eth : αυτων A 1. (35*). 61.^{mg} 181. 205 468. 632. 2019. 2023*. 2036. 2037. 2038. 2067 vg$^{d.v}$ s^{1} arm$^{1.2.3a}$ |.

23. και^{1} > A 620 arm^{1} bo sa | αυτησ] αυτων 205. 209 arm$^{2**.3a}$ | εν] εωσ 468* | θαν.] θυμω 2019 | ερauνων AC : ερευνων ℵ 025. 046 min omn^{vid} : scrutator Cyp Pr | νεφ. κ. καρδ.] καρδ. κ. νεφ. arm$^{1.(2).3.4}$ bo eth : renis et cordis Pr | καρδιαν s^{1} (arm^{2}) | αποδωσω 2050 | υμιν > arm$^{1.2.3}$ bo | κατα > arm$^{1.2.3}$ | τα εργα] εργα C : την καρδιαν 2050 | υμων Aℵ^{c}C 025. **21** (– 2020. 2050) Pr gig vg s$^{1.2}$ arm^{4} eth : αυτου 046. 2020. 2050 vg$^{c.d}$ arm$^{1.2.3}$ bo sa : αυτων arm^{a} : > ℵ* |.

24. δε > 468 s^{1} | τοισ λοιπ.] τοισ εν λοιποισ ℵ* | τοισ^{1} > 82 94. 2041 | τοισ εν τοισ Θυατ. λοιποισ 2050 | τοισ εν Θυατ.] των Θυατιραιων arm$^{1.2.3}$ | τοισ^{2} > 205 arm^{4} | Θυατειροισ ℵ* $^{et\ c.c}$ **21** (– 149. 620. 632. 2050) : Θυατιροισ AC : Θυατηροισ 025. 620. 632. 2050 : Θυατηριοισ 149 : Θυατηραισ 046 : Θυατειραισ 61. 69 : Θυατειρη ℵ^{c} : Thyatirae vg : Tyatirae Pr : Tyatire gig | οσοι] οτι 205 : οστισ gig | ουκ^{1} > ℵ* | εχουσιν] εχει gig : εμαθετε arm$^{1.2.3}$ | οιτινεσ ουκ] ουδε Tyc | ουκ^{2} > arm^{1} | εγνωσαν] εγνωτε Tyc arm^{3a} | βαθεα AC 046. **21** (– 205. 2050). 250. 2067 al^{mu} : βαθη ℵ 025. 1. 205. 2015. 2019. 2036. 2037. 2038. 2050 : (το) βαθοσ bo : altitudinem Tyc Pr : altitudines gig vg | ωσ λεγ. > arm^{4} | ωσ] α arm$^{1.2.3a}$ | βαλλω AC 025. **21** (– 337. 632. 2050) al^{mu} Tyc gig arm^{4} : βαλω ℵ 046. 1. 61. 69. 177. 337. 632. 1957. 2023. 2050 Or^{s} Pr vg arm$^{1.2.3a}$ bo eth |.

25. πλην ο] ο ουν s^{1} : "more than what" arm$^{1.2.3}$ | κρατησατε] "and is with you" arm$^{1.2.3}$ | αχρι ℵC 69. 177. 2087 : αχρισ

26. Καὶ ὁ νικῶν καὶ ὁ τηρῶν ἄχρι τέλους τὰ ἔργα μου,
δώσω αὐτῷ ἐξουσίαν ἐπὶ τῶν ἐθνῶν,
27. καὶ ποιμανεῖ αὐτοὺς ἐν ῥάβδῳ σιδηρᾷ
ὡς τὰ σκεύη τὰ κεραμικὰ συντρίβεται,
ὡς κἀγὼ εἴληφα παρὰ τοῦ πατρός μου,
28. καὶ δώσω αὐτῷ τὸν ἀστέρα τὸν πρωινόν.

29. Ὁ ἔχων οὖς ἀκουσάτω
τί τὸ πνεῦμα λέγει ταῖς ἐκκλησίαις.

025. 046. **21** al^{pl} : ου > 2050 : εωσ A 241 | αν ηξω ANC 025. 35. 205. 468. 620. 632. 2020 2050 Tyc Pr gig vg s$^{1.2}$ bo : ανοιξω 046. 18. 175. 325. 337. 386. 456. 617. 919. 920. 1849. 1934. 2004. 2040 al^{pl}.

26. και^1 > 104. 336. 522. 620. 628. 2020 arm$^{1.2.3}$ | ο^2 > 2020 | τηρων] κρατων 468* | αχρι τελ. > s^1 | τα εργα μου αχρει τελουσ 2050 eth | εξ. επι τ. εθν.] επι > ℵ* : τα εθνη Tyc |.

27. κ. ποιμ.] ποιμαινειν (1854) s^1 : et reget gig vg : κ. ποιμανουσιν arm$^{1.2.3}$ | αυτουσ] αυτον arm^2 | σιδηρα] + και συντριψει αυτουσ 2050 : + και Tyc arm$^{1.2}$ | ωσ σκευοσ κεραμικον arm^{2a} bo | συντριβεται AℵC 1. 104. 2020. 2037. 2038. 2050 al^p. Possibly a slip of the author for συντριβονται or rather συντριβησονται : συντριβησεται 025. 046. **21** (– 2020. 2050) al^{mu} Or^s : confringentur Pr vg (s^2) : comminuentur Tyc : συντριψετε s^1 (an itacism for συντριψεται) : confringet eas (placed before ωσ^1) gig : συντριψει (-ουσιν arm$^{1.2.3}$) αυτουσ (αυτον arm^2) arm bo eth | ωσ^2] ουτωσ γαρ s^1 | καγω] εγω arm$^{1.2.3a}$ |.

28. αυτω] αυτοισ arm$^{2.4}$ | πρωινον ℵC 025 al omn fere : προινον A 046. 2038 |.

29. v. 29 > Pr | ουσ] ωτα s$^{1.2}$: + ακουειν bo eth : aures audiendi arm$^{1.3.4}$ | πνευμα] + αγιον arm$^{1.3}$ eth |.

Chapter III.

1. Καὶ τῷ ἀγγέλῳ τῷ ἐν Σάρδεσιν ἐκκλησίας γράψον
Τάδε λέγει ὁ ἔχων τὰ ἑπτὰ πνεύματα τοῦ θεοῦ
καὶ τοὺς ἑπτὰ ἀστέρας,
Οἶδά σου τὰ ἔργα,
ὅτι ὄνομα ἔχεις ὅτι ζῇς καὶ νεκρὸς εἶ.

1. και^1 > Pr | τω αγγ.] τοισ αγγελοισ arm$^{1.2.3.}$ | τω εν Σ. εκκ.]. See note on 2^1. ecclesiae qui est Sardis Pr : τω εν τη εκκλησια Σαρδεων s^1 : τω εν Σαρδ. s^2 : τω εν (ταισ) Σαρδησια εκκλησιαισ arm^4 : τησ εν Σ. εκκ. Aℵ 025. 046 min^{omn} Or^s : ecclesiae Sardis (Sard. eccl. gig) gig vg bo eth : τησ Σαρδικων (Σαρδαιων 2. a) εκκλ. arm$^{1.2.3a}$: τησ εν Σαρδ. εκκλησιαισ C | επτα > 181.

2. γίνου γρηγορῶν, καὶ στήρισον τὰ λοιπὰ ἃ ἔμελλον ἀποθανεῖν,
τὰ ἔργα οὐ γὰρ εὕρηκά σου ⸢ἔργα⸣ πεπληρωμένα ἐνώπιον τοῦ θεοῦ μου.

3a. b. μνημόνευε οὖν πῶς εἴληφας καὶ ἤκουσας,
καὶ τήρει καὶ μετανόησον.

xvi. 15. Ἰδοὺ ἔρχομαι ὡς κλέπτης.
μακάριος ὁ γρηγορῶν καὶ τηρῶν τὰ ἱμάτια αὐτοῦ,
ἵνα μὴ γυμνὸς περιπατῇ,
καὶ βλέπωσιν τὴν ἀσχημοσύνην αὐτοῦ.

2015 | του θεου >386 | εργα] + και Pr s¹ | ονομα] + "of the health" bo | οτι ζησ A𝔖C 025. 35. 205. 250. 620. 2020. 2037. 2038. 2050. 2067 al^mu Or^s Tyc Pr gig vg s² arm^1. 2. 3. 4 bo : και ζησ 046. **21** (–35. 205. 620. 632. 2020. 2050) al^p : και οτι ζησ 632 s¹ : ζωντοσ arm^a | και³] + οτι s¹ |.

2. γινου] και γινου s¹ : γενου 1854 | γρηγορ.] εγρηγορων ℵ* : vigilans et stabilis Pr | στηρισον AC 025. 35. 175. 337. 468**. 617. 919. 920. 1849. 1934. 2004 2020. 2040 al Or^s : στηριξον ℵ 046. 1. 18. 205. 250. 632. 2037. 2038. 2050. 2067 al Tyc Pr gig vg s¹ bo eth : στηριζων 620 : τηρησον 42. 141. 201. 325. 385. 386. 429. 456. 468*. 522. 2015. 2019. 2036 s² : πληρωσον arm^1. 2. 3 | τα λοιπα >Tyc eth : τουσ λοιπουσ (οι) s² | α] οι s²: οτι arm^a : ει δε μη? bo | εμελλον AℵC 025. 172. 181. 250. 424. 468. 2015. 2018. 2019. 2020 2036. 2037. 2038. 2050. 2067 Or^s Tyc Pr gig vg s² arm⁴ : ε(or η)μελλεν 1.^mg 104. 336. 620 : η(or ε)μελλεσ 046. **21** (–468. 620. 2020. 2050). 93. 201. 498 al s¹ : μελλεισ arm^a bo | αποθανειν AℵC 025. 1.^mg 620. 919*. 2020. 2050 al^mu Or^s (αποθνησκειν 468. 2015. 2019. 2036. 2037) Tyc Pr gig vg s^1. 2 arm^4 a bo : αποβαλλειν 046. **21** (–35. 468. 620. 919*. 2020. 2050) : αποβαλειν 35. 1957. 2023 | ευρηκα] ευρηκαν 046 : invenio vg : + σε οτι s¹ | πεπληρ. τ. εργ. σου 141 s¹ | εργα AC 1.^mg : τα εργα ℵ 025. 046. **21** al^pl Or^s | πεπληρωμενα >201. 386 | ενωπιον] + κυριου 35. 205 | μου >1. 205. 2038. 2067 al^p Pr s¹ arm^1. 3 a |.

3^a. b. μνημονευε] pr και eth | ουν >ℵ 69 Pr gig s¹ arm^1. 2. 3. 4 eth | ηκ. κ. ειληφασ 2050 s¹ | κ. ηκουσ. κ. τηρει AℵC 025. 1. 35. 104. 172. 250. 468. 620. 1957. 2020. 2037. 2038. 2041. 2050. 2067 gig vg s² arm^2. 4 bo : κ. ηκουσασ τηρει s¹ : ηκουσασ τηρει arm^a : et audita custodi Pr : >046. **21** (–35. 468. 620. 2020. 2050) al^mu | και τηρει >arm³ eth |.

xvi. 15. ιδου] ωσ Pr arm³ | ερχομαι] ερχεται ℵ* (sed corr. prim. man.) 241. 2020 Pr s¹ arm³ : + εξαιφνης eth | κλεπτησ] + ταχυ 2019 : + και 205 | ο] οτε ℵ* | τηρων] τιμων 1849 | περιπατει 104. 522. 2015 : περιπατηση 2020 : περιπατησει 2019 | βλεπουσι 1. 2015. 2019. 2036. 2038 : videat Pr | βλεπ. τ. αισχ. αυτ.] "their shame appear" arm^1. 2. 3 a |.

3^{c}. ἐὰν οὖν μὴ γρηγορήσῃς
ἥξω ὡς κλέπτης,
καὶ οὐ μὴ ⸂γνῷς⸃ γνωσῃ
ποίαν ὥραν ἥξω ἐπὶ σέ·

4. ἀλλὰ ἔχεις ὀλίγα ὀνόματα ἐν Σάρδεσιν
ἃ οὐκ ἐμόλυναν τὰ ἱμάτια αὐτῶν,
καὶ περιπατήσουσιν μετ' ἐμοῦ ἐν λευκοῖς,
ὅτι ἄξιοί εἰσιν.

5. Ὁ νικῶν οὕτως περιβαλεῖται ἐν ἱματίοις λευκοῖς,
καὶ οὐ μὴ ἐξαλείψω τὸ ὄνομα αὐτοῦ ἐκ τῆς βίβλου τῆς ζωῆς,
καὶ ὁμολογήσω τὸ ὄνομα αὐτοῦ ἐνώπιον τοῦ πατρός μου
καὶ ἐνώπιον τῶν ἀγγέλων αὐτοῦ.

3^{c}. **ουν** > 620 | *γρηγορ.* Aℵ^{c} etc. : *γρηγορησεισ* 104. 620 : *μετανοησησ* ℵ* Pr : *μετανοησησ μηδε* (*και* bo) *γρηγορισεισ* 2050 bo | *ηξω*^{1}] pr. veniam et subitabo adventum meum ad te Pr | *ηξω* AC 025. 1. 35*. 181. 468**. 2015. 2037. 2038. 2067 vg$^{c. d. f. g}$ arm^{a} bo : + *επι σε* ℵ 046. **21** (−35*. 468**) al gig vg$^{a. v}$ s$^{1. 2}$ arm^{4} eth | *γνωσ* AC 025. 1. 35. 175. 205. 468**. 617. 1934. 2037. 2038. 2067 al : *γνωση* ℵ 046. **21** (−35. 175. 205. 468**. 617. 620. 1934. 2050) Or^{s} : *γνωσει* 104. 620. 459. 2050 : nescies gig vg : non scies Pr | *ποιαν ωρ. ηξ.*] "my coming" arm^{a} | *ποιαν ωραν*] *οιαν ωραν* (ℵ*) : *ποια ωρα* 181. 367. 632. 2050 |.

4. **αλλα** AℵC 69. 468. 2020 Or^{s} : *αλλ* 025. 046 min pl : > 35*. 205 arm^{a} | *εχεισ*] *εχω* s^{1} arm^{4} bo | *εχ. ολ. ονομ.* AℵC 025. 1. 35. 205. 2015. 2020. 2037. 2038. 2050 al Or^{s} (Pr) vg s$^{1. 2}$ eth : *εχ. ον. ολ.* gig : *ολιγ. εχ. ονομ.* 046. **21** (−35. 175. 205. 2020. 2050) al : *ολιγ. ονομ. εχ.* 61. 69. 175. 314. 522. 2016 : + *και* 1 | *α* AℵC 025. 046. **21** (−35. 205. 468. 2020) al Or^{s} gig : *οι* 1. 35. 205. 209. 432. 468. 2015. 2020. 2036. 2037. 2038. 2067 Pr vg : *αι* 522 | *το ιματιον* Pr | *αυτ.*] *εαυτων* C : + *μετα γυναικοσ* bo eth | *περιπατησ.*] *περιπατησου* A : *περιπατουσιν* 620. 2050 vg$^{a. f. v}$ s^{1} arm^{a} : ambulaverunt Pr vg^{d} arm^{2} | *μετ εμου* > arm$^{4 a}$: *ενωπιον μου* s^{1} | *οτι*] *και* s^{1} | *οτι . . . εισιν*] eth om. here and trans. after *λευκοισ* in ver. 5 | *εισιν*] + *και αναπαυσιν ουκ εχουσιν . . . κ. ο ερχομενοσ* (from 4^{8}) 35* |.

5. **ουτωσ** Aℵ*C 18. 35. 456. 920. 1849. 2004 al Or^{s} Pr gig vg s$^{1. 2}$ arm$^{4 a}$ bo : *ουτω* 325 : *ουτοσ* ℵ^{c} 025. 046. **21** (−18. 35. 325. 456. 920. 1849. 2004. 2050). 250. 2037. 2038. 2067 : *αυτοσ* 2050 : *ουτοσ ουτωσ* 467 | *περιβαλ.*] *περιβαλλεται* C s$^{1. 2}$: *περιβεβληται* 2050 : *περιβαλουσιν αυτον* ? bo : > eth | *εξαλειψω*] *απαλειψω* 2020 : *εξαλειψουσιν* bo sa | *το ονομ. αυτ. . . . ομολογησω* > 1. 2015 | *αυτου*$^{1. 2.}$] *αυτων* s^{2} arm bo | *εκ τ. βιβλ.*] *εν βιβλω* 2040 | *τ. ζωησ*] *των ζωντων* 920. 2040 | *το ον. αυτ.*^{2}] *αυτον* gig | *ενωπ.*^{1}] *εμπροσθεν* ℵ | *κ. ενωπ. τ. αγγ. αυτ.* > 325. 456 |.

6. Ὁ ἔχων οὖς ἀκουσάτω
τί τὸ πνεῦμα λέγει ταῖς ἐκκλησίαις.

7. Καὶ τῷ ἀγγέλῳ τῷ ἐν Φιλαδελφίᾳ ἐκκλησίας γράψον
Τάδε λέγει ὁ ἅγιος, ὁ ἀληθινός,
ὁ ἔχων τὴν κλεῖν Δαυείδ,
ὁ ἀνοίγων καὶ οὐδεὶς κλείσει
καὶ κλείων καὶ οὐδεὶς ἀνοίγει,

6. v. 6 > Pr | *ουσ*] *ωτα* s$^{1.2}$: + *ακουειν* bo eth : aures audiendi arm$^{1.3.4}$ | *πνευμα*] + *αγιον* arm$^{1.2}$ eth |.

7. *και*^{1} > Pr | *τω αγγ.*] *τοισ αγγελοισ* arm^{1} | *τω εν Φιλ. εκκλ.*] See note on **2**^{1} : ecclesiae qui est Filadelphiae Pr : *τω εν Φιλαδελφια* arm^{4} : *τησ εν Φιλ. εκκλ.* all Greek MSS Or^{8} : Philadelphiae ecclesiae (gig) vg s^{1} bo : *τησ Φιλαδελφων* (*-φιων* 3) *εκκλησιασ* arm$^{1.2.3a}$ | *Φιλαδελφια* ℵC 025. 046. 205. 325. 386. 456. 919. 920. 1849. 1934. 2004 al^{mu} : *Φιλαδελφιασ* A 620. 2050 : *Φιλαδελφεια* 18. 35. 175. 337. 468. 617. 632. 2020. 2040 al^{mu} | *εκκλησιαισ* ℵ | *λεγει*] + *κυριοσ* 172. 2018 | *ο αγιοσ ο αληθ.* C 025. 046. **21** (− 2050). 2037. 2038. 2067 al^{pl} Or$^{Phil. 36}$ s$^{1.2}$ arm^{4a} bo eth : *ο αγιοσ και αληθ.* 172. 2018 : sanctus et verus Tyc Pr gig vg arm$^{1.2.3}$: *ο αληθ. ο αγιοσ* Aℵ : *ο αληθ.* > 2050 : *ο αγγελοσ αληθινοσ* Or^{8} | *ο*^{3} > 337 | *την* > ℵ* | *κλειν* AℵC 025. 046. **21** (− 35. 205. 468**. 617. 620. 2050). 250 al^{mu} Or$^{Phil. 46}$ Or^{8} : *κλειδα* 1. 35. 69. 172. 205. 468**. 617. 620. 2015. 2019. 2036. 2037. 2038. 2050. 2067 Or$^{Phil. 36}$: (+ omnes eth) claves Pr s^{1} arm eth | *Δᾱδ* A 2020 : *του Δᾱδ* (*Δαῑδ* 632) ℵ **21** (− 620. 2020. 2050). 250. 2037. 2038. 2067 al^{pl} : *του οικου* (from Is. 22^{22}) *του Δαυειδ* bo eth : *του αδου* 104*. 218. 336. 459. 620. 2050 arm$^{1.2.3}$ | *ο ανοιγων*] *και ανυγων* ℵ | *και*^{2} > bo | *κλεισει* AℵC 025. 046. **21** (− 205. 620. 632*) al^{pl} Or$^{Phil. 46}$ Or^{8} arm^{4} bo : *κλειση* 104. 385 : *κλειει* 1. 61.^{mg} 205. 314. 632*. 2016. 2019. 2023. 2037. 2038. 2067 Tyc Pr gig vg s$^{1.2}$: *κλειων* 2015. 2036 (arm^{a}) | *κλει.* (sine add) AℵC 025. (35*). 205. 468**. 632*. 2020. 2050 al Or$^{Phil. 36, Ps xi. 372}$ Tyc Pr gig vg s$^{1.2}$ arm^{4a} bo : + *αυτην* 046. **21** (− 35*. 205. 468**. 632*. 2020. 2050) al^{mu} Or^{8} arm$^{1.2.3}$ | *και* (> A : + *ο* 2015. 2036) *κλειων* Aℵ 025. 1. (35*). 172. 205. 250. 314. 468. (2015). 2018. 2019. 2020. 2023. (2036). 2037. 2038. 2050. 2067 Or$^{Phil. 46}$ Or^{8} (s$^{1.2}$) (bo) : *και κλειει* C 61.^{mg} 2016 al gig arm^{4a} : et qui claudit Pr arm$^{2.3.}$: *κλειει* Tyc vg : *ει μη ο ανοιγων* (+ *και ουδεισ ανοιξει* Or^{8}) 046. **21** (− 35*. 205. 468. 620. 2020. 2050) al Or^{8} : *ει μη ο ανοιγων και κλειων* 42. 104. 432. 459. 620 | *και*^{4}] quod Pr | *ανοιγει* AC 025. 61.^{mg} 205. 2019. 2037. 2038. 2067 Or^{8} Tyc Pr gig vg s$^{1.2}$ arm^{4} : *ανοιγων* 468 (arm^{a}) : *ανοιξει* (− *υξει* ℵ) ℵ 046. **21** (− 205. 468. 620). 250 al^{mu} Or$^{Phil. 46}$: *ανοιξη* 104. 385. 620 |.

8. Οἶδά σου τὰ ἔργα
—ἰδοὺ δέδωκα ἐνώπιόν σου θύραν ἀνεῳγμένην,
ἣν οὐδεὶς δύναται κλεῖσαι αὐτήν—

ὅτι μικρὰν ἔχεις δύναμιν,
καὶ ἐτήρησάς μου τὸν λόγον,
καὶ οὐκ ἠρνήσω τὸ ὄνομά μου.

9. ἰδοὺ διδῶ ἐκ τῆς συναγωγῆς τοῦ Σατανᾶ,
τῶν λεγόντων ἑαυτοὺς Ἰουδαίους εἶναι καὶ οὐκ εἰσὶν
ἀλλὰ ψεύδονται—

ἰδοὺ ποιήσω αὐτοὺς ἵνα ἥξουσιν
καὶ προσκυνήσουσιν ἐνώπιον τῶν ποδῶν σου,
καὶ γνῶσιν ὅτι ἐγὼ ἠγάπησά σε.

10. ὅτι ἐτήρησας τὸν λόγον τῆς ὑπομονῆς μου,
κἀγώ σε τηρήσω ἐκ τῆς ὥρας τοῦ πειρασμοῦ
τῆς μελλούσης ἔρχεσθαι ἐπὶ τῆς οἰκουμένης ὅλης,
πειράσαι τοὺς κατοικοῦντας ἐπὶ τῆς γῆς.

8. οιδ. σ. τ. εργ. >Pr | τ. εργ. σου ℵ s^{2} | εργα] + και την πιστιν σου bo : + και s$^{1.2}$ eth | θυρ. ενωπ. σου ανεωγμ. 920. 2040 | ανεωγμ. AC 046. **21** (– 205. 2020. 2050) al Or^{s} : ηνεωγμ. ℵ 025. 172. 205. 2016. 2018. 2020. 2050 | ην] και 1. 61.^{mg} 2037. 2067 eth : >bo : οτι arm^{2} | αυτην >ℵ (35*) 2023. 2038 Pr gig vg arm^{4a} | οτι] + ου 2020. 2036. 2037 | μικρ. . . . δυν.] pusillas . . . vires Pr | εχεισ] εχει 1. 1957. 2037 | τ. λογ.] τα εργα 920. 2040 : τουσ λογουσ arm$^{2.3a}$ |.

9. ιδου] και ιδου s^{1} | διδω AC : δεδωκα ℵ : διδωμι 025. 046. **21** (– 205. 620. 2050) al^{pl} Or^{s} gig : διδω μοι 205 : διδομι 620. 2050 : δωσω Pr vg bo eth | Σατανα] + εκ Pr s$^{1.2}$ | των λεγ.] τουσ λεγοντασ bo | αλλα >eth | ιδου^{2}] και 1. 181. 2023. 2037. 2038. 2067 | ηξουσιν AℵC 025. 69. 82. 201. 218. 314. 386. 632. 2015. 2016. 2018. 2019. 2036. 2050 arm : ηξωσιν 046. **21** (– 386. 632. 2050). 250. 2037. 2038. 2067 al^{mu} Or^{s} : ηξω 1 | ιδου . . . ηξουσιν >eth | και^{2}] + ποιησω αυτουσ ινα bo | προσκυνησουσιν AℵC 025. 1. 42. 82. 149. 201. 2016. 2036. 2050 arm : προσκυνησωσιν 046. **21** (– 149. 2050). 250. 2037. 2038. 2067 al Or^{s} : + σε (σοι) και πεσουνται bo | ηξ. ενωπ. τ. ποδ. σου κ. προσκυν. Pr | και^{3}] + παντεσ bo | γνωσιν AC 025. 046. **21** (– 2050). 250. 2037. 2038. 2067 gig s^{2} arm$^{3''a}$: γνωσονται 2019. 2050. 2087 vg s$^{1\,vid}$: γνωσωνται 2023 : γνωση ℵ 69 Pr arm^{4} : γνωσει Or^{s} | εγω AℵC 025. 205. 250. 468. 620. 2020. 2037. 2038. 2050. 2067 Or^{s} gig vg s$^{1.2}$ bo eth : >046. **21** (– 205 468. 620. 2020. 2050) al^{mu} Pr | ηγαπισα 149. 2040 | σε] + και 2020 |.

10. οτι] και A arm^{4a} | τον λογον μου και την υπομ. bo eth

11. ἔρχομαι ταχύ· κράτει ὃ ἔχεις·
ἵνα μηδεὶς λάβῃ τὸν στέφανόν σου.
12. Ὁ νικῶν ποιήσω αὐτὸν στύλον ἐν τῷ ναῷ τοῦ θεοῦ μου,
καὶ ἔξω οὐ μὴ ἐξέλθῃ ἔτι,
καὶ γράψω ἐπ' αὐτὸν τὸ ὄνομα τοῦ θεοῦ μου,
καὶ τὸ ὄνομα τῆς πόλεως τοῦ θεοῦ μου,
τῆς καινῆς Ἰερουσαλήμ, ἡ καταβαίνουσα ἐκ τοῦ οὐρανοῦ ἀπὸ τοῦ θεοῦ μου,
καὶ τὸ ὄνομά μου τὸ καινόν.
13. Ὁ ἔχων οὖς ἀκουσάτω
τί τὸ πνεῦμα λέγει ταῖς ἐκκλησίαις.
14. Καὶ τῷ ἀγγέλῳ τῷ ἐν Λαοδικίᾳ ἐκκλησίας γράψον
Τάδε λέγει ὁ Ἀμήν,
ὁ μάρτυς ὁ πιστὸς καὶ ἀληθινός,
ἡ ἀρχὴ τῆς κτίσεως τοῦ θεοῦ,

καγω] *και δια τουτο καγω* eth | *τηρησω* > ℵ : *ετηρησα* arm^{2} eth | *τησ ωρασ τ. πειρασμ. τησ* > 2050 : *τησ ωρασ* > s^{1} bo | *πειρασαι*] + *παντασ* arm$^{1.2.3a}$ bo | *κατοικουντασ* > bo |.

11. *ερχ.*] *ιδου ερχομαι* 468**. 2015. 2019. 2036 al vg$^{d.f.v}$ arm^{1} : *και ιδου ερχ.* eth | *μηδεισ λαβη*] *μη λαβη τισ ταχυ* 104. 336. 459. 620 | *μηδεισ*] (ne) quis alius Pr : (ne) alius Cyp | *λαβη*] *λαβοι* 2050 (arm$^{1.2.3.4}$) | *σου*] + *και* s^{1} arm^{1} eth |.

12. *ο νικων*] *τον νικωντα* arm^{a} | *αυτον*] *αυτω* ℵ* 920 Or^{s} | *εν* > ℵ* arm | *τ. ναω*] *τω ονοματι* 920. 2040 | *μου*^{1} > 385. 2019 Or^{s} s^{1} | *και εξω . . . τησ πολεωσ του θεου μου* > 2050 | *ετι* > ℵ arm^{2} | *επ αυτον* > C 2015 : *επ αυτω* 61*. 2019. 2036. 2037 : super illud Tyc : + *το ονομα μου και* 2020 | *τ. θ. μ. κ. το ονομ.* > 046 | *κ. τ. ον. τησ πολ. τ. θεου μου* > 1. 181 s^{2} : *και δωσω αυτοισ τον οικον μου* arm^{1} | *του θεου μου*^{3} > s^{1} eth : *του πατροσ μου* bo | *τησ καινησ πολεωσ του πατροσ μου* bo | *η καταβαινουσα* Aℵ*C 025. 1. 141. 181. 205. 432. 459. 1854. 2015. 2050. 2087 : *η καταβεννουσα* 025 : *τησ καταβαινουσησ* ℵ^{c} : *η καταβαινει* 046. **21** (– 205. 2050). 250. 2037. 2038. 2067 Or^{s} | *εκ. τ. ουρ.* > s^{1} arm^{1} sa | *εκ* AℵC 025. 046. 1. 35. 205. 325. 337. 456. 468. 2020. 2037. 2038. 2050. 2067 al Tyc Pr gig vg bo : *απο* 18. 175. 386. 617. 620. 632. 919. 920. 1849. 1934. 2004. 2040 al | *του*^{4} > 632 | *απο* > 386. 620 arm$^{2.3.4a}$ | *μου*^{5} AℵC 025. 35. 205. 468. 632. 2050 al Or^{s} Tyc Pr gig vg s$^{1.2}$ arm$^{3.4}$ bo : > 046 **21** (– 35. 205. 468. 620. 632. 2050) al^{mu} arm^{2} : *αυτου* arm^{3**a} | *καινον*] + *και* s^{1} |.

13. v. 13 > Pr | *ουσ*] *ωτα* s$^{1.2}$: + *ακουειν* bo eth : aures audiendi arm$^{1.2.3.4}$ | *τι το πν. . . . εκκλησιαισ* > arm^{4} | *πνευμα*] + *αγιον* arm$^{1.2}$ eth |.

14. **τω αγγ.**] *τοισ αγγελοισ* arm$^{1.2}$ | *τω εν Λαοδ. εκκ.*] See note on 2^{1}. *τω εν Λαοδ. εν εκκ.* arm^{4} : *τησ εν Λαοδ. εκκ.* AℵC

15. Οἶδά σου τὰ ἔργα,
ὅτι οὔτε ψυχρὸς εἶ οὔτε ζεστός.
ὄφελον ψυχρὸς ἦς ἢ ζεστός.
16. οὕτως, ὅτι χλιαρὸς εἶ
καὶ οὔτε ⸀ψυχρὸς οὔτε ζεστός⸣, ζεστὸς οὔτε ψυχρός
μέλλω σε ἐμέσαι ἐκ τοῦ στόματός μου.
17. ὅτι λέγεις ὅτι Πλούσιός εἰμι
καὶ πεπλούτηκα καὶ οὐδὲν χρείαν ἔχω,
καὶ οὐκ οἶδας ὅτι σὺ εἶ ὁ ταλαίπωρος καὶ ὁ ἐλεινὸς
καὶ πτωχὸς καὶ τυφλὸς καὶ γυμνός,

025. 046 min$^{fere\ omn}$: τησ εν Λαοδ. (Λαοδικειασ 919) 919. 920. 2040 : τη εν Λαοδ. εκκλησιασ 18 : Laodiciae ecclesiae gig vg : ecclesiae Laudatiae Pr : τησ εκκλησιασ Λαοδικειασ (-κιασ bo) s^{1} arm^{a} bo : τησ εκκλησιασ Λαοδικεων 1 arm$^{2.3}$ | Λαοδικια A‎ℵC 104. 149. 201. 620 : Λαωδικια 2050 : Λαοδικεια 025. 046. **21** (–149. 620. 2050) : Laudatiae Pr : Lavodike arm^{4} | ο αμην] + και ℵ* | και^{2} A 025. 046. **21** (–620. 2050). 250. 2038. 2067 s^{2} arm : ο 69. 104. 459. 620. 2015. 2036. 2037. 2050 : και ο ℵC 82 bo | αληθινοσ] + και ℵ s^{1} arm$^{1.2.3.a}$ eth | η αρχη] απαρχη 2015. 2036. 2037 : απ αρχησ arm^{4} : + τησ αρχησ arm^{a} : ο απ αρχησ eth | τησ κτισ.] τησ εκκλησιασ ℵ : τησ κτησεωσ 1849 : τησ πιστεωσ 201. 386 | του θεου] + μου gig |.

15. οτι > s^{1} | ζεστοσ . . . ψυχροσ 205. 209 arm$^{1.2.3}$ | ει > ℵ* | οφελον ψυχρ. ησ η ζεστοσ > A 1. 241 arm$^{1.2.3}$ | οφελον] ωφελον 025. 046. 205. 522 : + η s^{1} | ησ] εισ 046. 336. 620. 2017 |.

16. ουτωσ . . . ψυχροσ > arm^{2} | ουτωσ οτι] οτι ουτωσ ℵ bo : οτι 1854. 2019 : sed quia (quoniam Pr) Pr gig vg : και s^{1} | ψυχρ. ουτε ζεστ. A 025. 205. (2050) al vg s^{1} : ζεστοσ ουτε ψυχροσ (ℵ)C 046. **21** (–205. 2050). 1 al^{mu} s^{2} arm^{3} bo : κ. ουτε ζεστοσ ουτε ψυχρ. > 60 Pr gig arm$^{1.2.4.a}$ | και ουτε . . . στοματοσ μου > eth | ουτε^{1} A‎ℵC 025. 046. 205. 617. 632. 2020. 2050 vg arm^{3} : ου **21** (–205. 617. 632. 2020. 2050) al Or^{s} (s$^{1.2}$) | ζεστοσ] + ει ℵ^{c} | ψυχροσ] + ει ℵ* 2050 | μελλω σε εμεσαι εκ τ. στομ. μου] παυσε του στοματοσ σου ℵ* | εμεσαι] εμμεσαι 046. 617. 919. 1934 : εμιν ℵ^{c} : αιμεσαι 2050 : "judge" arm$^{1.2.3}$: + και ελεγχω σε 250. 2020 | του στομ.] τησ καρδιασ bo | μου] σου ℵ* arm$^{1.2.3}$ |.

17. οτι] τι 18 : και eth | οτι^{2} AC 1. 35*. 172. 175. 205. 242. 250. 314. 617. 1934. 2015. 2016. 2018. 2020. 2036. 2037. 2040. 2050 al gig vg s$^{1.2}$ bo : > ℵ 025. 046. **21** (–35*. 175. 205. 617. 1934. 2020. 2040. 2050). 2038. 2067 al Or^{s} Cyp | ειμι] ει s^{1} | κ. πεπλουτ > bo sa | ουδεν AC 181. 2038 : ουδενοσ ℵ 025. 046. **21**. 250. 2037. 2067 Or^{s} | εχω] εχεισ 620 | συ > ℵ* |

18. συμβουλεύω σοι ἀγοράσαι παρ' ἐμοῦ χρυσίον πεπυρωμένον
ἐκ πυρὸς ἵνα πλουτήσῃς,
καὶ ἱμάτια λευκὰ ἵνα περιβάλῃ
καὶ μὴ φανερωθῇ ἡ αἰσχύνη τῆς γυμνότητός σου,
καὶ κολλούριον ἐγχρῖσαι τοὺς ὀφθαλμούς σου ἵνα βλέπῃς.
19. ἐγὼ ὅσους ἐὰν φιλῶ ἐλέγχω καὶ παιδεύω·
ζήλευε οὖν καὶ μετανόησον.

ο[1] > ℵ* 2019. 2050 | ταλ. ει ℵ* 2050 | ο ταλ. . . . ελεινοσ] "weak and miserable" bo : ελεινοσ > eth | ο[2] A 046. **21** (− 18. 205. 632. 920. 2004. 2040. 2050). 250 al Or[s] : > ℵC 025. 1. 18. 61. 69. 205. 241. 632. 920. 2004. 2015. 2019. 2036. 2037. 2038. 2039. 2040. 2050 | ελεινοσ AC 104. 620 : ελεεινοσ ℵ 025. 046. **21** (− 620) al[pl] : αληθινοσ 1854 | κ. γυμνοσ κ. τυφλοσ 104. 110. 336. 620. 632. 2050 gig arm[4. a] eth | κ. τυφλ. > s[1] |.

18. συμβ.] συμβουλευσω 2015 arm[2 (1. 3). a] : consule Tyc | σοι] +ουν 2020 arm[a] bo eth : +λαβε arm[1. 2. 3. a] | αγορασαι] αγορασον 2020 (Tyc) arm[1. 2. 3. a] : λαβειν eth | παρ εμου > 172. 250. 424. 498. 2016. 2018. 2038 | παρ εμ. χρυσ. AℵC 025. 1. 35. 205. 2015. 2019. 2023. 2036. 2037. 2050. 2067 al Or[s] Tyc Cyp gig vg s[1. 2] arm : χρυσ. παρ εμ. 046. **21** (− 35. 205. 2050) al bo sa : +εμον eth | εκ πυροσ] εν πυρι bo eth : εκ πυρασ 046 | πλουτησεισ 620. 2050 | ιματιον λευκον Pr Cyp | λευκα] λαμπρα bo : τιμια arm[1] | ινα περιβαλ.] περιβαλεσθαι s[1. 2] | ινα[2] >Pr gig vg bo eth | περιβαλλη 046. 61. 69. 172. 205. 617. 1934. 2015. 2036*. 2037 : περιβαλει 104. 2050 | φανερωθη] φανη 69 Or[s] : +εν σοι Pr | αισχυνη] ασχημοσυνη 025. 35*. 104. 205. 620. 2019 | κολλουριον A 025. 35. 61.[mg] 205. 522. 632. 920. 1849. 1957. 2004. 2019. 2023. 2038. 2040. 2050 al Or[s] : κουλλουριον 1. 18. 919. 2037 : κουλουριον 385. 2015. 2036 : κολλυριον ℵC 175. 250. 325. 337. 386. 456. 468. 617. 620. 1934. 2020. 2067 al : κολυριον 046 : collirio Pr gig : collyrio Tyc Cyp vg | εγχρισαι (ενχ. ℵ 2050 : εχ. 620) AℵC 94. (104). 336. 459. 468**. 620. (2015). 2019. 2037. 2050 : ἔγχρισαι 104. 2015. s[1. 2] : εγχρισον 025. 1. 35. 61.[mg] 1854. 1957. 2023. 2036. 2038. 2041. 2067 eth : inunge Tyc gig vg : ungue Pr Cyp : "give to" bo : "lay" arm[2. 3. a] : εγχριση 2020 : ινα εγχρισει 046 : ινα εγχριση **21** (− 35. 205. 468**. 620. 2020. 2050) Or[s] : ινα εγχρισησ 205 : +επι 60. 432. 1957. 2041 arm | τ. οφθ. σου >s[1] | βλεπεισ 104. 2050 : βλεψεισ 620 arm[4] |.

19. εγω] οτι εγω arm[1. 3] bo sa | εαν] αν ℵ 2019. 2050 | ζηλευε AC 046. **21** (− 35. 205. 468**. 617. 620. 2020). 250 al[mu] : ζηλου 314. 617. 2016 : ζηλωσον ℵ 025. 1. 35. 205. 468**. 620. 2020. 2037. 2038 2067 al : ζητησον 1957 : rede Pr | ουν > 104. 181. 336. 620. 2015 arm[1. 2. 3] | και[2] >arm[2] | κ. μετανοησον] εισ μετανοιαν eth |.

20. Ἰδοὺ ἕστηκα ἐπὶ τὴν θύραν καὶ κρούω·
ἐάν τις ἀκούσῃ τῆς φωνῆς μου καὶ ἀνοίξῃ τὴν θύραν,
καὶ εἰσελεύσομαι πρὸς αὐτὸν καὶ δειπνήσω μετ᾽ αὐτοῦ
καὶ αὐτὸς μετ᾽ ἐμοῦ.
21. ὁ νικῶν δώσω αὐτῷ καθίσαι μετ᾽ ἐμοῦ ἐν τῷ θρόνῳ μου,
ὡς κἀγὼ ἐνίκησα καὶ ἐκάθισα μετὰ τοῦ πατρός μου ἐν τῷ θρόνῳ αὐτοῦ.
22. Ὁ ἔχων οὖς ἀκουσάτω
τί τὸ πνεῦμα λέγει ταῖς ἐκκλησίαις.

20. ιδου] + εγω $Or^{Jo. ii. 381}$: οτι ιδου bo : και ιδου eth | επι] ante Pr | ακουση] ανοιξει 2050 | ακουση . . . μου και >$Or^{Jo. ii. 381}$ and elsewhere | ανοιξω ℵ : ανοιξει 18. 2050 s^{1} : + μοι $Or^{Jo. ii. 381}$ Pr bo eth | $και^{3}$ ℵ 046. **21** (– 205. 468. 620. 632*. 2020. 2050) al^{mu} Or^{s} Pr s^{1} arm^{4} : > A 025. 1. 104. 205. 468 620. 632*. 2015. 2019. 2020. 2036. 2037. 2038. 2050. 2067 $Or^{Jo. ii. 381}$ gig vg s^{2} $arm^{1. 2. 3. a}$ bo eth | προσ αυτον >s^{1} | δειπνησω] "will dwell" arm^{1} : "will rest" eth | εμου] + in trono meo Pr : + "in my kingdom" $arm^{1. 2. 3}$ |.

21. ο νικων] pr και $s^{1. 2}$ eth | καγω] εγω s^{1} bo eth |.

22. v. 22 >gig | ουσ] ωτα Pr $s^{1. 2}$: + ακουειν bo eth : aures audiendi $arm^{1. 3. 4}$ | πνευμα] + αγιον arm^{1} eth |.

Chapter IV.

1. Μετὰ ταῦτα εἶδον, καὶ ἰδοὺ θύρα ἠνεῳγμένη ἐν τῷ οὐρανῷ, καὶ ἡ φωνὴ ἡ πρώτη ἣν ἤκουσα ὡς σάλπιγγος λαλούσης μετ᾽ ἐμοῦ, λέγων Ἀνάβα ὧδε καὶ δείξω σοι ἃ δεῖ γενέσθαι μετὰ ταῦτα.

1. μετα] pr και $arm^{1. 2. 3. a}$ (bo) eth | $και^{1}$ >Pr bo sa eth | ιδου >eth | θυραν 620. 2050 eth | ηνεωγμενη Aℵ 025. 1. 2016. 2020. 2038. 2067 : ηνεωγμενην 2050 : ανεωγμενη 046. **21** (– 2020. 2050). 250. 2037 al Or^{s} : ηνοιχθη arm^{1} Tyc : >arm^{4} | $και^{2}$] + ιδου ℵ Pr | $η^{1}$ >498. 1957. 2020 | φωνη] + η λαλουσα μετ εμου bo | η πρωτη >s^{1} | ην] ησ 205 : >eth | ωσ] + φωνη bo eth | σαλπιγγα Pr gig $s^{1. 2}$ | λαλουσησ] λαλουσαν ℵ Pr gig : λαλουσα 522 : λεγουσησ 141. 218. 1849. 1955 : ελαλησεν s^{1} $arm^{3 a}$ | λεγων Aℵ* 046. **21** (– 35. 205. 468. 620. 632. 2020). 250 al^{mu} Or^{s} : λεγουσα $ℵ^{c}$ 025. 1. 35. $61.^{mg}$ 205. 468. 632. 1854. 1957. 2020. 2023. 2036. 2037. 2038. 2067 : και λεγουσα μοι 2019 : και λεγουσησ 104. 336. 620 : και λεγουσαν gig : και ελεγεν s^{2} eth | αναβα] αναβηθι A | σοι] σε 205. 386 | α] οσα A | δει] δη 2050 .

2. *εὐθέως ἐγενόμην ἐν πνεύματι·*
καὶ ἰδοὺ θρόνος ἔκειτο ἐν τῷ οὐρανῷ,
καὶ ἐπὶ τὸν θρόνον καθήμενος,
3. *καὶ ὁ καθήμενος ὅμοιος ὁράσει λίθῳ ἰάσπιδι καὶ σαρδίῳ,*
καὶ ἶρις κυκλόθεν τοῦ θρόνου ὅμοιος ὁράσει σμαραγδίνῳ.

4. *καὶ κυκλόθεν τοῦ θρόνου θρόνους εἴκοσι τέσσαρες,*
καὶ ἐπὶ τοὺς ⸀θρόνους εἴκοσι τέσσαρας⸁ πρεσβυτέρους καθημένους

2. ευθεωσ Aℵ* 046. **21** (– 35. 205. 620. 632. 2020) al Or^{s} Pr gig vg s^{2} : *ευθεωσ δε* ℵ^{c} : *και ευθεωσ* 025. 1. 35. 104. 205. 620. 632. 1854. 2020 al s^{1} arm$^{(1.2.4.a)}$ eth : *και* arm^{3} bo | *ιδου*] *ειδον* arm$^{1.2.3}$: *ειδον ιδου* bo : *ιδου ειδον* Pr | *εκειτο* > 2050 bo : positum Pr (arm$^{1.2.3}$) | *εν τ. ουρ. εκειτο* 468 eth | *εν τ. ουρ.* > 632 | *τον θρονον* Aℵ 046. **21** (– 35. 205. 632) al^{mu} Or^{s} : *του θρονου* 025. 1. 35. 205. 632. 1957. 2015. 2019. 2036. 2037. 2038. 2041. 2067 |.

3. κ. ο καθημενοσ Aℵ 025. 046. 42. 61. 93. 104. 337. 452. 468. 506. 2019. 2021. 2050 Or^{s} Tyc gig vg s$^{1.2}$: et his qui sedebat Pr : > **21** (– 337. 468. 2050) al^{mu} arm$^{1.2.3.4}$ bo eth | *ορασι* 205 : *ορασισ* 2050 | *λιθω*] *λιθων* 2020 arm$^{3.a}$: *λιθου* Tyc vg s$^{1.2}$: >arm^{1} bo | *ιασπ. κ. σαρδ. λιθω* Pr | *ιασπιδι*] *ασπιδι* 920 : *ηασπιδι* 2050 : + *σμαραγδω* 337 : + *και σμαραγδω* 046. 42. 180. 452. 468. 506. 1854. 2021 | *και*^{2} > 1854 arm^{1} | *σαρδιω* Aℵ 046. **21** (– 325. 337. 456. 468). 250. 2037. 2067 al^{mu} Or^{s} : sardi Tyc : sardo Pr : *σαρδινω* 025. 1. 632*. 2019. 2038 al gig bo sa eth : sardinis vg^{d} : sardini vg : sardion s^{2} arm$^{2.3.4.a}$: sardon s^{1} : > 1854 | *ιρισ* 025. **21** al^{pl} Or^{s} Pr gig vg bo eth : *ιρεισ* ℵ^{c} 046 : *ιερεισ* Aℵ* 2015. 2036 arm$^{1.2.3.a}$ | *κυκλοθεν*] *κυκλοθε* 920 : *κυκλωθεν* 18. 104. 201*. 205. 336. 620. 632. 2017. 2024. 2036. 2037. 2038. 2039. 2050 : *κυκλω* 241. 2019. 2020 | *θρονου*] + *αυτου* 2020 : + et ipsa sedes gig | *ομοιοσ*^{2} A 025. 1. 35*. 104. 181. 314. 429. 632*. 2019. 2036. 2037*. 2038 Pr vg s$^{1.2}$: *ομοιοι* 2015 arm$^{1.2.3.a}$: *ομοιον* 205 : *ομοια* 35**. 241**. 468***. 620. 632**. 1957. 2016. 2023. 2037**. 2041. 2050. 2067 : *ομοιωσ* ℵ^{c} 046. **21** (– 35. 205. 468**. 620. 632. 2050) al Or^{s} | *ομ. ορ. σμ. κ. κυκ. τ. θρ.* > ℵ* | *ορασει σμαραγδινω* Aℵ^{c} 025. 35. 205. 250. 468**. 620. 2037. 2067 al Pr gig vg : *ορασει μιαγδινω* 2050 : *ορασει σμαραγδων* (*σμαραγδου* arm) s$^{1.2}$ arm$^{1.2.3.a}$: *ορασεισ σμαραγδων* 69 : *ορασισ σμαραγδινων* 046. **21** (– 35. 205. 468**. 620. 632. 2020. 2050) al Or^{s} : *ωσ* (> 632*) *ορασισ σμαραγδου* 241. 632**. 2020 : *ορασεωσ σμαρακδου* (arm^{4}) bo |.

4. και^{1} Aℵ^{c} 025. 1. 35. 205. 468. 620. 632. 2020. 2050 al Or^{s} Pr gig vg s^{1} arm$^{1.2.4.a}$ bo eth : > 046. **21** (– 35. 205.

περιβεβλημένους ἱματίοις λευκοῖς,
καὶ ἐπὶ τὰς κεφαλὰς αὐτῶν στεφάνους χρυσοῦς.
5. καὶ ἐκ τοῦ θρόνου ἐκπορεύονται ἀστραπαὶ καὶ φωναὶ καὶ βρονταί·
καὶ ἑπτὰ λαμπάδες πυρὸς καιόμεναι ἐνώπιον τοῦ θρόνου.(*a*)
6. καὶ ἐνώπιον τοῦ θρόνου ὡς θάλασσα ὑαλίνη ὁμοία κρυστάλλῳ,
καὶ (*b*) κύκλῳ τοῦ θρόνου τέσσαρα ζῷα γέμοντα ὀφθαλμῶν
ἔμπροσθεν καὶ ὄπισθεν·

(*a*) A gloss is added here: ἅ ἐστιν τὰ ἑπτὰ πνεύματα τοῦ θεοῦ. See vol. i. 117.
(*b*) A gloss added here: ἐν μέσῳ τοῦ θρόνου καί. See vol. i. 118.

468. 620. 632. 2020. 2050) s^{2} arm^{3} | κυκλοθε 920 : κυκλω 2015. 2019. 2036. 2037. 2067 : κυκλωθεν 18. 104. 205. 336. 620. 2017. 2039. 2050 | θρονου] + ειδον Tyc arm^{4} | θρονουσ^{1} Aℵ 250. 424. 2018 Tyc : θρονοι 025. 046. **21** al^{pl} Or^{s} s$^{1.2}$ bo | εικοσι^{1}] + και 104 al | τεσσαρεσ A 025 min pl : τεσσαρισ 2020. 2050 | και^{2} >2017 arm^{1} | επι τ. εικ. τ. θρον >ℵ 2017 Tyc arm^{1} | επι τ. θρον. εικ. τεσσ. 025. 35. 632* s$^{1.2}$ arm$^{2.3.4.a}$ bo eth : επι τ. θρον. τουσ εικ. τεσσ. 046 min pl Or^{s} : super thronos viginti quattuor vg (gig) : in quibus seniores sedentes erant xxiiii. Pr : επι τ. εικ. τεσσ. θρον. (>920. 2040) A 93. 94. 920. 2040. 2050 : | εικ. τεσσ^{2} >2020 arm^{1} | τεσσαρασ] τεσσαρισ 2050 | θρονουσ^{2} >920. 2040 : + ειδον 1957. 2023. 2041 al^{vid} | καθ. πρεσβ. 2020 : καθημενοι πρεσβυτεροι Pr (arm$^{2.3.4.a}$) | περιβεβλημενοισ 1934 : περιβεβλημενοι Pr | περιβεβλ. A 025. 35. 2015. 2036. 2037 Pr vg gig : + εν ℵ 046. **21** (−35). 250. 2038. 2067 (s$^{1.2}$) Or^{s} | ιματιω λευκω Pr gig : ιματιοισ >ℵ 2050 arm^{4} | αυτων] εχοντεσ gig : + ειχον arm$^{1.2}$ | χρυσεουσ ℵ.

5. **του θρον.**] των θρονων s^{1} | εκπορευονται] εξεπορευοντο 104. 620 vg^{d} arm bo eth (?) | αστρ. κ. φων. κ. βροντ. Aℵ 025. 046. **21** (−2020). 250. 2037. 2038. 2067 al^{pl} Or^{s} Pr gig vg s^{2} arm$^{2.3.4.a}$ bo : αστρ. κ. βροντ. κ. φων. 1. 385. 2020 : βροντ. κ. αστρ. κ. φων. s^{1} | καιομ. πυροσ 920. 2040 | πυροσ > vg s^{1} arm^{4} | καιομεναι > bo | θρονου^{2} Aℵ 025. 1. 632*. 2019. 2020. 2038. 2050. 2067 Pr gig vg arm bo eth : + αυτου 046. **21** (−456. 632*. 2020. 2050) al^{mu} Or^{s} s^{2} | α εισιν . . . του θρονου >ℵ* 456 | α εστιν] και 61*. 69 Or^{s} | α Aℵ^{c} 025. 1. 201. 386. 2019. 2038. 2050 vg^{g*} s^{2} : αι 046. **21** (−386. 456. 2050). 250. 2037. 2067 al Pr gig vg s^{1} | εστιν A : εισιν ℵ^{c} 025. 046 al$^{fere\ omn}$ | τα Aℵ^{c} 025. 1. 61. 69. 468. 632. 1957. 2015. 2019. 2020. 2036. 2037. 2038. 2050. 2067 arm$^{3.a}$ bo : >046. **21** (−456. 468. 632. 2020. 2050). 250 al^{mu} (s$^{1.2}$) arm$^{1.2.4}$ | τα επτα πνευματα] το αγιον πνευμα eth | πνευματα] "powers (parts 4) of the spirit holy (>3*)" arm$^{1.2.3.4}$ |.

6. **θρονου**] + αυτου 104. 141. 205. 209. 620 | ωσ Aℵ 025. 046. **21** (−386. 632*). 250. 2038 al^{pl} Or^{s} s^{2} bo : >1. 201. 386.

7. καὶ τὸ ζῷον τὸ πρῶτον ὅμοιον λέοντι,
καὶ τὸ δεύτερον ζῷον ὅμοιον μόσχῳ,
καὶ τὸ τρίτον ζῷον ἔχων τὸ πρόσωπον ὡς ἀνθρώπου,
καὶ τὸ τέταρτον ζῷον ὅμοιον ἀετῷ πετομένῳ.
8. καὶ τὰ τέσσερα ζῷα, ἓν καθ' ἓν αὐτῶν ἔχων ἀνὰ πτέρυγας ἕξ,(a)
καὶ ἀνάπαυσιν οὐκ ἔχουσιν ἡμέρας καὶ νυκτὸς λέγοντες
Ἅγιος ἅγιος ἅγιος Κύριος, ὁ θεός ὁ παντοκράτωρ,
ὁ ἦν καὶ ὁ ὢν καὶ ὁ ἐρχόμενος.

(a) The following clause is interpolated here: κυκλόθεν καὶ ἔσωθεν γέμουσιν ὀφθαλμῶν.

632* Tyc Pr arm s¹ | θαλασσαν 620. 2050 : + ωσ eth | υαλινη Aℵ 025. 046. **21** (– 205. 325. 456. 468. 632. 2020. 2040. 2050) υαλινην 2050 : υαληνη 2040 : υελινη 60. 205. 241. 325. 456. 468. 498. 632. 2018. 2020. 2022. 2023 | ομια 205 : ομοιαν 2050 | κρυσταλλω] κρυσταλω 632. 2020 : βηρυλλω arm⁴ : "the whiteness of crystal" arm^{1. 2. 3. a} | εμμεσω A 1854 : "at the side of" (?) eth θρονου²] + μου 2020 | κ. κυκλ. τ. θρον. > 385. 429. 522. 2015. 2050 Tyc arm^{1. 2. 3} bo sa eth | κυκλω] κυκλωθεν 110 | τεσσαρα ℵ 025. 046. **21** : τεσσερα A | οφθαλμουσ 336. 620. 2015. 2019 | εμπροσθεν A min^{fere omn} : εμπροσθε 920 : ενπροσθεν ℵ 025. 046 : ante se Pr | οπισθε 920 |.

7. και¹ > 2050 Pr s¹ | το πρωτον το ζωον 386 | ζωον² > arm¹ | και³ > Pr | εχων . . . ανθρ.] ομοιον ανθρωπω gig arm⁴ : ομοιον προσωπω (ως προσωπον eth) υιου ανθρωπου bo eth | εχων τ. προσ . . . τετ. ζωον > 325. 456 | εχων A 046. 104. 620. 919. 920*. 1849. 2015. 2019 Or⁸ : εχον ℵ 025. **21** (– 325. 456. 620. 919. 920*. 1849. 2050) al : ειχεν arm^{2. a} : ην arm³ : > 2050 arm¹ | το⁵ Aℵ 025. 1. 35. 61*. 205. 2015. 2019. 2020. 2023. 2036. 2037. 2038. 2050 al Or⁸ : > 046. **21** (– 35. 205. 2020 2050) al^{mu} | ως ανθρωπου A 42. 2019 vg s¹ : quasi humanam Pr : ωσ ανθρωποσ 025. 1. 35. 61*. 104. 205. 620. 1957. 2015 2020. 2023. 2036. 2037 2038 2041. 2050 s² : ανθρωπου 046. **21** (– 35. 205. 325. 456. 620. 2020. 2050). 250. 2067 Or⁸ arm^{1. 2. 3. a} : ομοιον ανθρωπου 2018 : ωσ ομοιον ανθρωπω ℵ | και⁴ > Pr | το⁶ > 205 | ζωον⁴ Aℵ 025. 35. 468**. 620. 632. 1849. 2020. 2037. 2038. 2050. 2067 al Or⁸ Pr gig vg s^{1. 2} : > 046. **21** (– 35 468**. 620. 632. 1849. 2020. 2050). 250 al eth (which om. ζωον thrice before) |.

8. τα τεσσ. ζωα > bo | τα Aℵ 025. 18. 35. 205. 620. 632. 919. 920. 1849. 2004. 2040. 2050 al^{mu} Or⁸ : > 046. 175. 325. 337. 386. 456. 468. 617. 1934. 2020. 2037. 2038. 2067 al | εν καθ εν αυτων A 025. 35. 104 172. 181. 205. 250. 620. 2015. 2018. 2036. 2038. 2067 al : singula eorum Tyc gig vg : εν εκαστον αυτων ℵ 2020 s¹ bo eth : εν καθ εαυτο 1. 61.^{mg} : καθ εαυτων 2050 : εν καθ εν 046. **21** (– 35. 205. 620. 2020. 2050) al Or⁸ : singula

9. Καὶ ὅταν δώσουσιν τὰ ζῷα δόξαν καὶ τιμὴν καὶ εὐχαριστίαν
τῷ καθημένῳ ἐπὶ τῷ θρονῷ,
τῷ ζῶντι εἰς τοὺς αἰῶνας τῶν αἰώνων,
10. πεσοῦνται οἱ εἴκοσι τέσσαρες πρεσβύτεροι ἐνώπιον τοῦ καθημένου ἐπὶ τοῦ θρόνου,
καὶ προσκυνήσουσιν τῷ ζῶντι εἰς τοὺς αἰῶνας τῶν αἰώνων,
καὶ βαλοῦσιν τοὺς στεφάνους αὐτῶν ἐνώπιον τοῦ θρόνου, λέγοντες

Pr : + εστωσ 250. 424. 2018 s^{1} | εχων A 1. 42. 61*. 82. 104. 172. 336 429. 522. 620. 919. 1849. 1918. 1955. 2017. 2019 : εχον 046. **21** (– 205. 620. 919. 1849. 2020. 2050). 250. 2037. 2038. 2067 al Or^{s} : εχοντα 025. 2020. 2024. 2050 : εχει 2015 : ειχεν 205 : ειχον ℵ 61.^{mg} Tyc Pr gig vg arm^{4} | ανα πτερ. εξ . . . οφθαλμων] κυκλοθεν απο των ονυχων εσωθεν, γεμοντα οφθαλμων bo : + απο των ονυχων και επανω, πτερ. εξ κυκλοθεν· και εσωθεν γεμουσιν οφθαλμων s^{1} | πτερυγων 046 | κυκλοθεν] + και εξωθεν 046 al^{p} : + εξωθεν 61*. 69 | κ. εσωθεν] εσωθεν και εξωθεν Or^{s} : > 218. 522. 2015. 2018. 2020 arm^{a} | εσωθεν] εξωθεν 1957. 2050 : ante se et retro Pr | γεμοντα 1. 2020 : εχοντα 2037 | οφθαλμουσ 620. 2036. 2037 | και^{3}] quae Pr | ουκ εχουσιν] ουχ εξοσαν ℵ* : non habebant Tyc Pr gig vg$^{a. d}$ arm^{4} | ημ. κ. νυκτ.] αλλα παντοτε 2050 | ημερασ] + τε 632 | λεγοντεσ Aℵ 025. 046. **21** al^{pl} Or^{s} : dicentes Pr gig : λεγοντα 110. 385. 1955. 2023**. 2041 : dicentia vg : + το 2050 | αγιοσ ter Aℵ^{c} 025. 205. 386. 617. 620. 632. 920 2004. 2037. 2038. 2040. 2050. 2067 al Pr gig vg s$^{1. 2}$ arm$^{1. 2. 4}$ bo eth : semel Or^{s} : bis 18. 181 : sexies 141. 2020 : octies ℵ* : novies 046. 35. 175. 250. 325. 337. 456. 468. 919. 1849. 1934 al^{mu} arm$^{3. a}$ | κυριοσ] + σαβαωθ 205 | ο^{1} > ℵ* | ο θεοσ > 2050 Or^{s} arm$^{1. 2}$ | ο θεοσ ο παντ.] σαβαωθ ο παντο. 35*. 104. 620. 1918. 2015. 2019. 2036. 2037 | ο παντ.] των θεων eth | ο^{2} > ℵ 2019 | ο ων κ. ο ην 35. 201. 205. 250. 386. 2016. 2019. 2020. 2023**. 2067 (arm) bo sa | κ. ο ων > 620 | και ο ερχ. > eth .

9. δωσουσιν A 025. 1. 632. 2015. 2019. 2020. 2036. 2037. 2050. 2067 al : δωσωσι(ν) ℵ 046. 61. 69. 104. 181. 205. 620. 1854. 1918. 2017. 2038 Or^{s} : δωσι(ν) **21** (– 205. 456. 468*. 620. 632. 2020. 2050) 250 al : δωσει 42. 141. 517 : δω 325**. 456 : dederunt gig s^{1} arm : dederant Pr | δωσ. τ. ζωα] ζωα δωσουσιν 2050 | δοξαν > ℵ* arm$^{2. a}$ | και^{2} > 2050 arm$^{2. a}$ | ευχαριστειασ A arm$^{1*. 3. a}$: ευχαριστειαν 2015. 2017. 2040 : > 2050 | τω θρονω Aℵ 2050 : (in) trono Pr : του θρονου 025. 046. **21** (– 2050) al Or^{s} : + και προσκυνησουσιν (-σωσιν 2040). 920. 2040 : + και s^{1} | τω ζωντι . . . επι του θρονου > 919. 1849. 2004 | τω ζωντι . . . αιωνων > vg^{a} | των αιωνων > 1854 arm^{1} : + αμην (+ και ℵ) ℵ 2017. 2040* Or^{s} s^{1} arm$^{2. a}$: + ευθεωσ Pr !.

10. πεσουνται . . . τ. αιωνων > 175 arm$^{3. a}$ | πεσουνται . . . και προσκυνησουσιν] καὶ προσκυνησουσιν ενωπιον τ. καθ. . . . οι

11. Ἄξιος εἶ, ὁ κύριος καὶ ὁ θεὸς ἡμῶν,
λαβεῖν τὴν δόξαν καὶ τὴν τιμὴν καὶ τὴν δύναμιν,
ὅτι σὺ ἔκτισας τὰ πάντα,
καὶ διὰ τὸ θέλημά σου ἦσαν καὶ ἐκτίσθησαν.

εικ. τ. πρεσβ. eth | πεσουνται] πιπτουσιν vg^g (procedunt corrupt for procid.) : επιπτον Pr vg^a. d. v (procedebant corrupt for procid.) : επεσον arm¹ | εικ] + και min^p s¹ (arm¹) | τεσσαρεσ] τεσσαρισ 2020. 2050 : τεσσαρεισ 620 | ενωπιον . . . θρονου > bo | του καθ. επι > Pr gig arm | προσκυνησωσιν 18. 2004 : προσκυνουσι 61.^mg : προσεκυνουν vg^a. c. d. f. v : adorabunt (corrupt for adorabant) Pr | εισ τ. αιων. των. αιων. τω ζωντι s¹ | τω ζωντι > arm⁴ | εισ τουσ αιωνασ > arm¹ | αιωνων] + αμην ℵ 205. 2017 s¹ arm² | και βαλλουσιν Aℵ^c(?) 025. **21** (−620). 250. 2067 al Or^s gig vg^a. c. f. g s^1. 2 arm⁴ : κ. βαλλουσιν ℵ* 046. 1. 61.^mg 172. 181. 429. 620. 1854. 2015. 2017. 2019. 2023*. 2036. 2037. 2038 bo : κ. εβαλλον vg^d. v : mittentes Tyc Pr arm^a | αυτου 205 | ενωπ. τ. θρον. > 920. 2040 |.

11. ει] εστιν arm² : + κυριε ℵ | ο κυριοσ Aℵ 046. **21** (−35*. 205. 620. 2020). 250. 2067 al^mu Or^s s^1. 2 arm^2. 3. 4 bo : κυριε 025. 1. 35*. 69. 104. 205. 241. 336. 620. 1854. 1918. 2015. 2019. 2020. 2036. 2037. 2038 Pr gig vg arm^1. a : + ημων s¹ | κ. ο θεοσ ημ > 1 | και¹ > 025. 35*. 69. 104. 205. 241. 336. 620. 1854. 1918. 2015. 2019. 2020. 2036. 2037. 2038. 2067 Pr gig vg arm^1. 2. a bo sa eth | ο² > ℵ 468. 2050 Or^s | ημων Aℵ 025. 104. 205. 620. 2020. 2037. 2038. 2050 al Pr gig vg s¹ arm bo eth : + ο ουρανιοσ 172 : + ο αγιοσ 046. **21** (−205. 620. 2020. 2050). 250. 2067 al^mu Or^s s² | δυναμιν . . . δοξαν . . . τιμην 620 | την² > ℵ | την³ > A | δυναμιν] + και 69 | τα Aℵ 025. 1. 35. 205. 2015. 2019. 2020. 2023. 2036. 2037. 2038. 2050 al : > 046. **21** (−35. 205. 2020. 2050). 250. 2067 al Or^s | παντα] + και δια σου εισιν s² | δια > bo | δια θεληματι σου A : δια του θεληματοσ σου 617 (s¹) : ex voluntate tua (tua potestate Pr) Tyc Pr | ησαν κ. εκτισθ.] haec sunt constituta Pr | ησαν και > 2019 | ησαν Aℵ **21** (−18. 35. 468. 620. 2020. 2050) Or^s Tyc gig vg s^1. 2. arm⁴ : ουκ ησαν 046. 18. 69. 2020 : εισι 025. 1. 35. 104. 172. 250. 468. 620. 1854. 1957. 2018. 2023. 2036. 2037. 2038. 2050. (2067) : εγενετο bo : + παντα eth | εκτισθ. κ. εισι 2067 | κ. εκτισθησαν > A : "and stand sure" arm^1. 2. 3. a : α εκτισθησαν eth |.

CHAPTER V.

1. Καὶ εἶδον ἐπὶ τὴν δεξιὰν τοῦ καθημένου ἐπὶ τοῦ θρόνου βιβλίον
γεγραμμένον ἔσωθεν καὶ ⸂ὄπισθεν⸃, κατεσφραγισμένον σφραγῖσιν ἔξωθεν
ἑπτά. 2. καὶ εἶδον ἄγγελον ἰσχυρὸν κηρύσσοντα ἐν φωνῇ μεγάλῃ
Τίς ἄξιος ἀνοῖξαι τὸ βιβλίον καὶ λῦσαι τὰς σφραγῖδας αὐτοῦ; 3. καὶ
οὐδεὶς ἐδύνατο ἐν τῷ οὐρανῷ ⸂οὐδὲ ἐπὶ τῆς γῆς οὐδὲ⸃ ὑποκάτω τῆς οὔτε ἐπὶ
γῆς ἀνοῖξαι τὸ βιβλίον οὐδὲ βλέπειν αὐτό. 4. καὶ ἔκλαιον πολὺ ὅτι τῆς γῆς
οὐδεὶς ἄξιος εὑρέθη ἀνοῖξαι τὸ βιβλίον οὔτε βλέπειν αὐτό. οὔτε

1. και] + μετα τουτο eth | τ. δεξ.] + και εν μεσω Or^{s} : + του θεου Pr Cyp | βιβλ. γεγραμμ. > ℵ* |. εσωθεν] A 025. 046 min^{omn} Tyc Pr gig vg Cyp Or$^{Ps.\ xi.\ 372,\ Ezek.\ xiv.\ 182,\ Phil.\ xxv.\ 36}$ Or^{s} bo eth : εμπροσθεν ℵ Or$^{Jo.\ i.\ 169,\ Phil.\ xxv.\ 46}$ sa | οπισθεν Aℵ 1. 69 al Or$^{Jo.\ i.\ 169,\ Ezek.\ xiv.\ 182,\ Phil.\ xxv.\ 36,\ 46}$ Cyp s^{2} : εξωθεν 025. 046. **21**. 250. 2037. (2038). 2067 al^{pl} Or^{s} s^{1} arm bo eth : a foris gig : foris Tyc Pr vg : + και οπισθεν και εμπροσθεν 35 : + και οπισθεν 2038 : + και ℵ^{c} 42. 337. 468 arm$^{1.\ 2.\ 3}$ | κατεσφραγ.] εσφραγισμενον 337 : κατεσφιγμενον 920. 2040 |.

2. ειδον] ηκουσα gig : + αλλον 172. 250. 2018. 2050 s^{1} | κηρυσσ. ισχυρον ℵ | κηρυσσοντα] + και λεγοντα eth | εν Aℵ 046. **21** (−35. 2020). 250. 2067 al^{mu} Or^{s} : > 025. 1. 35. 172. 1854. 1957. 2015. 2019. 2020. 2023. 2036. 2037. 2038. 2041 Or$^{Ps.\ xi.\ 372,\ Phil.\ xxv.\ 36}$ | μεγαλη > 1854 : + και λεγοντα (Pr) arm$^{1.\ 2.\ a}$ | τισ] + εστιν 1 vg | αξιοσ Aℵ 025. 35. 205. 2020. 2038. 2050. al^{p} Or^{s} s^{1} : + εστιν 046. **21** (−35. 205. 2020. 2050). 250. 2037. 2067 al Tyc Pr gig Cyp s^{2} |.

3. εδυνατο ℵ **21** (−205. 2040. 2050). 250. 2037. 2038 al : ηδυνατο A 025. 046. 1. 61. 69. 104 2023**. 2036. 2040. 2050. 2067 al Or^{s} : δυναται 205 : + ουτε 2050 Tyc Pr Cyp (arm) | ουρανω Aℵ 025. 1. 35. 172. 205. 241. 632**. 1957. 2015. 2019. 2023. 2037. 2038. 2067 al Or$^{Phil\ xxv.\ 36}$ Tyc Pr Cyp gig vg s^{1} arm bo eth : + ανω 046. **21** (−35. 205. 632**. 2050). 250 al Or^{s} s^{2} | ουδε^{1} A 025. 1. 35. 104. 205 620. 1957. 2015. 2020. 2023. 2036. 2037. 2038 al : ουτε ℵ 046. **21** (−35. 205. 620. 2020). 250. 2067 al^{mu} Or^{s} | επι τ. γησ] εν τη γη s^{1} : + κατω 386 | ουδε υποκ. τ. γησ > ℵ 181. 201. 386. 1854. 2023* arm^{1} eth : post αυτο pon 1. 2037 | ουδε^{2} A 025. 1. 35. 104. 314. 620. 1957. 2015. 2023. 2036. 2037. 2038 : ουτε 046. **21** (−35. 386. 620). 250. 2067 al^{mu} Or^{s} | βιβλιον] + και λυσαι τασ σφραγιδασ αυτου s^{1} | ουδε^{3} 025. 1. 35. 104. 314. 1957. 2015. 2023. 2036. 2037. 2038 : ουτε Aℵ 046. **21** (−35. 205). 250. 2067 al Or^{s} : και 205 s^{1} arm$^{1.\ 2.\ a}$: ου γαρ arm^{3} : sed neque Pr Cyp | βλεπειν] εβλεπον arm^{3} |.

4. v. 4 > A 522. 2050 | και ℵ 025. 1. 181. 2015**. 2019.

5. καὶ εἷς ἐκ τῶν πρεσβυτέρων λέγει μοι Μὴ κλαῖε· ἰδοὺ
ἐνίκησεν ὁ λέων ὁ ἐκ τῆς φυλῆς Ἰούδα, ἡ ῥίζα Δαυείδ, ἀνοῖξαι τὸ
βιβλίον καὶ τὰς ἑπτὰ σφραγῖδας αὐτοῦ. 6. Καὶ εἶδον ἐν μέσῳ τοῦ
θρόνου καὶ τῶν τεσσάρων ζῴων καὶ ἐν μέσῳ τῶν πρεσβυτέρων ἀρνίον
ἑστηκὼς ⸀ἑστηκὸς⸀ ὡς ἐσφαγμένον, ἔχων κέρατα ἑπτὰ καὶ ὀφθαλμοὺς ἑπτά,
ἀπεσταλ-μένα οἵ εἰσιν τὰ ἑπτὰ πνεύματα τοῦ θεοῦ, ⸀ἀπεσταλμένοι⸀ εἰς πᾶσαν τὴν

2038 gig s$^{1.2}$ arm$^{2.4.a}$: +εγω 046. **21** (−2050). 250. 2037. (2067) Or$^{Ezek. xiv. 176 (>Ps. xi. 372)}$ Or^{8} Tyc Pr Cyp vg arm$^{1.3}$ | εκλαιαν ℵ* : εκλεον ℵ^{c} | πολυ] πολυν 046 : πολλοι 1 arm^{a} eth : πολλα 205 : παντεσ bo : >Or$^{Phil. xxv. 36}$ | ευρεθη] ευρεθην 2020 : ευρεθησεται ℵ* | ανοιξαι] +και αναγνωναι 1. 35. 205. 1957. 2019. 2023. 2037. 2038. 2067 arm^{a} | το βιβλ.] την σφραγιδα arm^{1} : και λυσαι arm$^{2.3}$ | βλεπειν αυτο] λυσαι τασ σφραγιδασ αυτου Pr s^{1} |.

5. και^{1}] +απεκριθη 2050 : +ιδου Tyc : +ηλθεν μοι bo | λεγει] ειπεν Cyp vg^{a} s^{1} bo | μοι >205 gig arm^{a} | ιδου] +γαρ 2050 | ο^{2} >ℵ 69. 2015** s^{1} bo sa : +ων 1. 2067 | η ριζα] εκ ριζησ arm bo eth : +του 35. 205. 2023 | ανοιξαι Aℵ 025. 1. 35. 104. 205. 468**. 620. 1957. 2015. 2019. 2020. 2023. 2036. 2037. 2038. 2050. 2067 Or$^{Ps. xi. 372, Phil. xxv. 36}$ Pr gig Cyp vg arm bo eth : ανοιξει s$^{1.2}$: ο ανοιξασ 18. 2039 : ο ανοιγων 046. **21** (−18. 35. 205. 468**. 620. 2020. 2050). 250 al^{mu} Or^{8} | και^{2}] +λυσαι ℵ 2067 arm$^{(1).2.3}$ | επτα > s^{1} arm$^{1.2.3**}$ bo eth | σφραγιδασ] +δι 2040 |.

6. ειδον] ιδου και A : ειδον και ιδου 172. 2018 Tyc vg | εν μεσω . . . ζωων (+και 620) >620 s^{2} | εν μεσω του θρονου] θρονοι Tyc | εμμεσω^{1} A 2050 | και^{2}] +εν μεσω Pr arm | των τεσσ. ζωων] (τα) τεσσαρα ζωα Tyc | εν μεσω^{2} >Pr s^{1} arm$^{4.a}$: εμμεσω A | πρεσβ.] +ωσ arm$^{1.2}$ | εστηκοσ A 025. 046. **21** (−149*. 620. 2004. 2050) al^{mu} Or^{8} : εστηκωσ ℵ 1. 104. 149*. 172. 2004. 2015. 2017. 2019 : εστικωσ 620. 2050 : >2038 arm$^{1.2}$ | ωσ >18. 632*. 920. 2016. 2024. 2040. 2050 arm bo sa | εσφαγμ.] εσφραγισμενον 104. (920*). 2016. 2017. 2020. 2038. 2067 arm^{a**} | εχων Aℵ 046. 104. 429. 620. 919. 2015. 2017. 2019. 2050 Or^{8} : εχον 025. **21** (−620. 919. 2020) al^{mu} | κ. οφθαλ. επτα >2050 | οι Aℵ 1. 172. 205. 2020. 2038. 2067 : α 046 **21** (−205. 2020). 250. 2037 al^{pl} : ατινα 241. 498 | τα > 250. 2037 2067 | επτα^{3} ℵ 046. **21** (−205. 2050) al^{mu} Tyc Pr gig Cyp vg$^{a**.c.v}$ s$^{1.2}$ arm bo : >A 1. 181. 205. 2038. 2050 vg$^{d.f.g.h}$ eth | πνευματα] πνευμα eth : powers arm^{2} : powers of the spirit arm$^{1.3}$: (parts of the seven) graces of the spirit arm^{4} | του θεου πνευματα 1 : του θεου >arm^{1} | θεου] +τα 1. 42. 104. 110. 205. 336. 620. 2036. 2037. 2038 (s$^{1.2}$) arm$^{1.2.3.a}$ bo | απεσταλμενοι A : απεσταλμενα ℵ 1. 205. 2020. 2023. 2036. 2037. 2038. 2050 (s^{2}) : "sent down" bo : αποστελλομενα 046. **21** (−205. 2020. 2050). 250. 2067 al^{mu} Or^{8} s^{1} arm$^{1.2.3.a}$: >arm^{4} |.

γῆν. 7. καὶ ἦλθεν καὶ εἴληφεν ἐκ τῆς δεξιᾶς τοῦ καθημένου ἐπὶ τοῦ
θρόνου. 8. Καὶ ὅτε ἔλαβεν τὸ βιβλίον, τὰ τέσσερα ζῷα καὶ οἱ εἴκοσι
τέσσαρες πρεσβύτεροι ἔπεσαν ἐνώπιον τοῦ ἀρνίου, ἔχοντες ἕκαστος
κιθάραν καὶ φιάλας χρυσᾶς γεμούσας θυμιαμάτων (*a*)
9. καὶ ᾄδουσιν ᾠδὴν καινὴν λέγοντες

Ἄξιος εἶ λαβεῖν τὸ βιβλίον
καὶ ἀνοῖξαι τὰς σφραγῖδας αὐτοῦ,
ὅτι ἐσφάγης,

καὶ ἠγόρασας τῷ θεῷ ἐν τῷ αἵματί σου
ἐκ πάσης φυλῆς καὶ γλώσσης καὶ λαοῦ καὶ ἔθνους,

(*a*) MSS add gloss : *αἵ εἰσιν αἱ προσευχαὶ τῶν ἁγίων.*

7. **και**^{2} >bo | *ειληφεν*] +*το βιβλιον* 1**. 104. 205. 620. 2019. 2050 Pr gig Cyp vg$^{a*. b. c. d. g**}$ s^{1} bo sa : +*αυτο* eth | *εκ*] +*τησ χειροσ* 620 arm$^{1. 2. 3. a}$ | *δεξιασ*] *χειροσ* s^{1} : +*του θεου* Pr Cyp | *του καθ.*] *τησ καθημενου* (sic) ℵ* | *θρονου*] +*το βιβλιον* 250**. 2020. 2037. 2067 Tyc vg |.

8. **ελαβεν**] aperuisset vg | *βιβλιον*] +*και* arm^{3} | *τεσσερα* Aℵ 2020 : *τεσσαρα* 025. 046 al^{pl} : *οι εικ. τεσσ. πρεσβ. και τ. τεσσ. ζωα* eth | *τεσσαρεισ* 620 : *τεσσαρισ* 2050 | *ενωπ. τ. αρν. επεσον* 205 | *επεσαν* Aℵ 1. 104. 325*. 337. 452. 456. 506. 517. 620. 2023. 2050 Or^{s} : *επεσον* 046. **21** (−325*. 337. 456. 620. 2050). 250. 2037. 2038. 2067 al^{mu} | *εκαστοσ εχοντεσ* ℵ | *εχοντεσ*] *και ειχον* arm$^{1. 2. 3. a}$ | *εκαστοσ*] +*αυτων* s$^{1. 2}$ | *κιθαραν*] *κιθαρασ* 1. 104. 205 385. 468. 617. 620. 1957. 2019. 2023. 2037*. 2038. 2041. 2067 Tyc Pr gig Cyp vg | *φιαλασ*] *φυαλασ* 2050 : *φιαλην* s^{1} arm$^{1. 2. 3. a}$ | *χρυσασ*] *χρυσεασ* ℵ : *χρυσην* s^{1} arm$^{1. 2. 3. a}$ | *γεμουσασ*] *μεστασ* 620 bo sa : *γεμουσαν* s^{1} arm$^{1. 2. 3. a}$ | *θυμιαματων*] + supplicationum Pr Cyp | *αι* A 025. **21** (−2050). 25 . 2037. 2038. 2067 al^{pl} s$^{1. 2}$ Or^{s} : *α* ℵ 046. 2019. 2050 | *εισι*] *ησαν* arm^{1} : *εστιν* arm$^{3. a}$ | *αι προσευχαι* A ℵ^{c} 025. 046. 1. 35. 205. 241. 250**. 468. 620. 632**. 1957. 2015. 2019. 2020. 2023. 2036. 2037. 2038. 2041. 2050. 2007 Or$^{Jer. xiv. 463}$ s$^{1. 2}$ arm bo eth : *προσευχαι* ℵ* 18. 61. 69. 172. 201. 218. 386. 424. 632*. 920. 1849. 2040 al^{mu} Or^{s} : *προσευχων* 82. 93. 104. 110. 175. 177. 242. 325. 337. 385. 452. 456. 517 617. 919. 1934. 1955. 2004. 2021. 2024 | *των αγιων*] *οντων αγιων* Or^{s} |.

9. **και**^{1} >s^{1} | *αδουσιν*] *αδωσιν* A : *αδοντεσ* Pr s^{1} : cantabant Tyc arm (bo) : cantaverunt Cyp : +*ωσ* Tyc | *καινην ωδην* Pr Cyp vg | *καινην*] +*και* s^{1} arm | *ει*] +*κυριε* gig vg^{v} : +*κυριε ο θεοσ ημων* arm^{2} | *ανοιξαι*] *λυσαι* s^{1} : resignare gig | *εσφαγησ*] *εσφαγεισ* 620. 2050 : *ηγορ. τω θεω* A (eth see below) : +*ημασ* ℵ 025. 046. **21** (−205. 620. 2040*. 2050). 2037. 2067 al^{pl} Or^{s} s$^{1. 2}$ (arm) bo sa : *ηγορ. ημασ τω θεω* 172. 250. 336. 424. 620. 1918.

10. καὶ ἐποίησας αὐτοὺς τῷ θεῷ ἡμῶν βασιλείαν καὶ ἱερεῖς,
βασιλεύσουσιν καὶ ⸀βασιλεύουσιν⸀ ἐπὶ τῆς γῆς.
11. καὶ εἶδον καὶ ἤκουσα φωνὴν ἀγγέλων πολλῶν κύκλῳ τοῦ
θρόνου,(*a*) καὶ ἦν ὁ ἀριθμὸς αὐτῶν μυριάδες μυριάδων καὶ χιλιάδες
χιλιάδων, 12. λέγοντες φωνῇ μεγάλῃ
ἄξιος ⸀Ἄξιόν⸀ ἐστιν τὸ ἀρνίον τὸ ἐσφαγμένον λαβεῖν τὴν δύναμιν
καὶ πλοῦτον καὶ σοφίαν καὶ ἰσχὺν
καὶ τιμὴν καὶ δόξαν καὶ εὐλογίαν.
13. καὶ πᾶν κτίσμα ὃ ἐν τῷ οὐρανῷ καὶ ἐπὶ τῆς γῆς καὶ ὑποκάτω

(*a*) MSS add a gloss here: *καὶ τῶν ζῴων καὶ τῶν πρεσβυτέρων,*

2016. 2018. 2038. 2050 Pr gig Cyp vg : ηγορ. τω θεω ημων 180. 205. 2040* sa : ηγορ. ημασ (>eth) εν τ. αιμ. σου τ. θεω s$^{1.2}$ eth : εν τω αιματι σου >632 | αιματι] ονοματι 2040* | παντων φυλων κ. γλωσσων κ. λαων κ. εθνων arm$^{2.3.4}$ | και γλωσσησ >s^{1} arm^{1} |.

10. αυτουσ] ημασ Pr gig vg$^{d.f.v}$ arm$^{1.2.3}$: ex iis eth | τω θεω ημων >A | βασιλειαν Aℵ 2050 Pr gig Cyp vg (s^{1}) arm^{4} bo : in regnum dei eth : βασιλεισ 046. **21** (–2050). 250. 2037. 2038. 2067 al^{pl} Or^{8} s^{2} | ιερεισ] ιερατειαν ℵ : +και βασιλεισ s^{1} eth | και^{3} >eth | βασιλευουσιν A 046. 18. 325. 386. 456. 617. 919. 920. 1849. 2004. 2020. 2037. 2040 al s^{2} : βασιλευσουσιν ℵ 025. 1. 35. 82. 91. 110. 172. 175. 177. 205. 250. 314. 337. 429. 468. 620. 632. 1934. 2038. 2050. 2067 Or^{8} al gig Cyp vg s^{1} arm^{4} bo : >eth : βασιλευσομεν Pr vg arm$^{1.2.3}$ |.

11. και ειδον >sa eth | φωνην A 025. 046*. 1. 69. 205. 2023. 2036. 2038 al^{p} Or^{8} Tyc Pr gig vg arm$^{2.3.a}$ bo eth : ωσ φωνην ℵ 046**. **21** (–205. 337). 250. 2037. 2067 al^{mu} s$^{1.2}$ arm^{4} sa : ωσ φωνη 337 | πολλων αγγελων 920. 2040 Pr | πολλων >620 arm^{2} | κυκλω] κυκλοθεν 1 : κυκλωθεν 468** | και^{3}] +κυκλω Pr arm$^{(1).2.(3).a}$ | και των πρεσβ. >1 arm^{1} | και ην ο αριθμ. αυτ. >arm^{3} | μυριαδεσ μυριαδ. και > Pr gig vg | μυριαδ. μυριαδ.] μυριασ μυριασ arm : μυριασ μυριαδων s$^{1.2}$ | και χιλιαδ. χιλιαδων >1854 | χιλιαδεσ] χιλιασ s$^{1.2}$ | χιλιαδων] arm$^{2.3}$: +και s^{1} |.

12. λεγοντεσ] λεγοντων 498. 920. 2020. 2040. 2050 Pr vg : κραζοντεσ arm^{1} | αξιον ℵ 046. **21** min omn^{vid} Or^{8} : αξιοσ A (s^{1}) | εστιν] ει s^{1} | εσφαγμ.] εσφραγισμενον 2020 | την > 2019 arm^{1} | δυναμιν . . . ευλογιαν] "praise and riches and honour and glory" arm^{1} | δυν. και >arm$^{2.a}$ | και^{1} >920. 2020. 2040 | πλουτον Aℵ 025. 1. 35. 205. 2020. 2037. 2050. 2067 al arm eth : τον πλουτον 046. **21** (–35. 205. 920. 2020. 2040. 2050). 250. 2038 al^{mu} Or^{8} : την βασιλειαν bo : divinitatem vg : μεγαλοπρεπειαν arm^{4} : > 920. 2040 | και^{2}] + την 386 bo | και ισχυν > bo arm$^{1.3}$: + και βασιλειαν eth | και$^{4.5.6}$] + την bo | και ευλογιαν >arm$^{1.3}$ |.

13. ο A 046. **21** (–35. 205. 468**. 620) al Or^{8} gig s^{1} bo eth : το ℵ : >620 : +εστιν 025. 1. 35. 172. 205. 250 241. 468**. 2015.

τῆς γῆς καὶ ἐπὶ τῆς θαλάσσης ἐστίν, καὶ τὰ ἐν αὐτοῖς πάντα, ἤκουσα ⌈λέγοντας⌉ λέγοντα

Τῷ καθημένῳ ἐπὶ τῷ θρόνῳ καὶ τῷ ἀρνίῳ
ἡ εὐλογία καὶ ἡ τιμὴ καὶ ἡ δόξα
καὶ τὸ κράτος εἰς τοὺς αἰῶνας τῶν αἰώνων.

14. καὶ τὰ τέσσερα ζῷα ἔλεγον Ἀμήν, καὶ οἱ πρεσβύτεροι ἔπεσαν καὶ προσεκύνησαν.

2018. 2019. 2023. 2036. 2037. 2038. 2041. 2050. 2067 al Pr vg s² (arm) | επι τησ γησ] εν τη γη 1. 2037 Pr s¹ : επι γησ 336. 2015. 2036 | κ. υποκ. τ. γησ A 025. 046. **21** (−920. 2040. 2050). 250. 2037. 2038. 2067 al Pr gig vg^a. c. g**. v s¹· ² arm⁴ eth : >ℵ 69. 181. 218. 241. 920. 2040. 2050 vg^d. f. g* arm¹· ²· ³· ᵃ bo | και⁴] +τα ℵ (bo) eth : +quae sunt vg | επι τησ θαλασσησ (την θαλασσαν 2020) 241. 2015. (2020). 2036. 2037 (εν τη θαλασση ℵ Pr gig vg (s¹· ²) arm bo eth) : +εστι(ν) A **21** (−35. 205. 2020. 2050) al : +α εστιν 025. 046. 1. 35. 205. 429**. 1957. 2023. 2038. 2041. 2050. 2067 al : +οσα εστιν 172. 250. 424. 2018 Or^s : +ο εστιν s¹ | και τα >2019 : et quaecumque sunt Pr | εν²] επ 2020 | αυτοισ] ea vg^a. f. g*. v : eo vg^c. g** : +sunt gig : +και 42. 61. 69. 241. 632. 2015. 2037 | παντα ηκουσα λεγοντασ 025. 18. 314. 2017. 2039. 2050 al^p Or^s : παντα ηκ. λεγοντα A 1. 69. 181. 2038 : παντα και ηκ. λεγοντασ ℵ 424. 429. 2019 gig s¹ (bo) : παντα κ. ηκ. λεγοντων 250. 2018 : παντα κ. ηκ. λεγοντα s² : παντασ ηκ. λεγοντασ **21** (−18. 35*. 2050). 2037 al^mu Tyc Pr vg : παντασ και ηκ. λεγοντασ (−των 172). (172). 522 : παντα κ. παντασ ηκ. λεγοντασ 046 : παντα κ. ηκ. παλιν λεγοντα 35* : παντα λεγοντα eth | τω καθημ.] τον καθημενον s² : ο καθημενοσ arm | τω θρονω A 046. 18. 175. 250. 325. 337. 456. 617. 620. 919. 1849. 1934. 2004. 2050 al : (in) throno Tyc Pr vg : θρονω 141 : του θρονου ℵ 025. 1. 35. 205. 241. 386. 468. 632. 920. 1957. 2015. 2019. 2020. 2023. 2036. 2037. 2038. 2040. 2067 al^mu Or^s : (supra) sedem gig | και⁶ >Aℵ^c s² arm¹· ² | και τω αρνιω >bo | τω αρνιω] το αρνιον arm¹· ²· ³· ᵃ : +η 919 | η ευλογ. . . . κρατοσ] "blessed exalted (>2) and glorified (+and almighty 3)" arm¹· ²· ³ | η¹ >025 | η³ >919* | και το κρατοσ] παντοκρατοροσ ℵ* (cf arm³) : >arm¹· ²· ⁴· ᵃ | των αιωνων >arm² Tyc | αιωνων Aℵ 025. 104. 172. 201. 205. 250. 2018. 2050 al^p Or^s Pr gig vg s¹· ² arm¹· ⁴· ᵃ : +αμην 046. **21** (−205. 2050). 2037. 2038. 2067 al^mu arm³ eth |.

14. κ. τ. τεσσ. ζωα ελεγ. αμην >920. 2040 | τα >205. 620 | τεσσερα A 2020 : τεσσαρα ℵ 025. 046 min^pl Or^s | ελεγον Aℵ 025. 1. 35*. 104. 205. 620. 632. 919. 2015. 2018. 2019. 2020. 2023**. 2036. 2037. 2038. 2050. 2067 al Or^s Pr gig vg s² arm : ελεγεν 172. 250 : λεγοντα 046. 18. 35**. 175. 325. 337. 386. 456.

Chapter VI.

1. Καὶ εἶδον ὅτε ἤνοιξεν τὸ ἀρνίον μίαν ἐκ τῶν ἑπτὰ σφραγίδων,
καὶ ἤκουσα ἑνὸς ἐκ τῶν τεσσάρων ζῴων λέγοντος ὡς φωνὴ βροντῆς
Ἔρχου.
2. καὶ εἶδον καὶ ἰδοὺ ἵππος λευκός,
καὶ ὁ καθήμενος ἐπ᾽ αὐτὸν ἔχων τόξον,
καὶ ἐδόθη αὐτῷ στέφανος,
καὶ ἐξῆλθεν νικῶν καὶ ἵνα νικήσῃ.

468. 617. 1849. 1934. 2004 s^{1} (bo) | *αμην* Aℵ 025. 1. 35*. 69. 314. 2015. 2019. 2020. 2036. 2037. 2038. 2050. 2067 Or^{s} bo sa : *το αμην* 046. **21** (– 35*. 920. 2020. 2040. 2050). 250 al^{mu} | *και*^{2} > arm | *οι*] + *εικοσι τεσσαρεσ* Pr vg^{v} | *επεσαν* Aℵ 025. 1. 104. 110. 172. 250. 337. 429. 468. 620. 2018. 2019. 2023. 2050. 2067 al Or^{s} : *επεσον* 046. **21** (– 337. 468. 620. 2050). 2037. 2038 al^{mu} : + *ενωπιον αυτου* arm$^{1.2.3.a}$ | *επεσαν και* > eth | *προσεκυνησαν*] + viventem in saecula saeculorum Pr vg^{d} : + *αυτον* arm^{1} |.

1. **και**] *μετα ταυτα* bo | *ειδον* > Pr eth | *οτε* AℵC 025. 1. 104. 205. 314. 620. 1957. 2020. 2023. 2036. 2037 al Pr gig s arm^{4} bo : *οτι* 046. **20** (– 205. 620. 2020). 250. 2067 al^{pm} Or^{s} vg arm : > 2038 | *ηνοιξεν*] *ηνυξεν* ℵ | *μιαν* > 1 | *εκ των επτα* AℵC 046. **20** (– 205. 325. 456). 250. 2037. 2067 al^{pm} Or^{s} Pr gig vg s arm$^{2.3.4}$ eth : *επτα* > 025. 1. 205. 314. 325. 456. 2015. 2016. 2023. 2038 al arm^{1} bo sa | *σφραγιδων* > ℵ* (suppl. ℵ^{c}) | *και* > 620 bo sa | *ενοσ εκ* > 1957 : *ενοσ* > 920. 2040 : *εξ ενοσ* arm^{a} : *εκ* > ℵ* 468 | *λεγοντοσ*] *λεγοντων* ℵ : > arm | *ωσ φωνη βροντησ* > Pr eth | *φωνη* AC 046. **20** (– 468. 919. 920. 1849). 250. 2037 al^{pm} Or^{s} bo : *φωνην* ℵ 506. 919. 1957 gig vg arm : *φωνησ* 025. 1. 314. 2016. 2038. 2067 : *φωνῇ* 104. 172. 468. 920. 1849. 1955 | *βροντησ*] *βροντων* s^{1} : + *λεγοντοσ* A : + *λεγουσαν* arm | *ερχου* AC 025. 1. 35. 60. 82. 94. 241. 432. 1957. 2015. 2019. 2020. 2023. 2037. 2038. 2041 Or^{s} vg$^{a.c.g*}$ bo sa : *ερχου* ante *ωσ φων. βροντ.* 2036 : *ερχομαι* arm$^{1.2.3.a}$: *ερχου και ιδε* ℵ 046. **20** (– 35. 2020). 61. 104. 110. 172. 201. 250. 314. 385. 498. 522. 1955. 2016. 2018. 2067 Pr gig vg$^{d.f.g**.v}$ s eth |.

2. **και ειδον** > 046. **20** (– 35. 205. 468. 620). 250 al^{mu} Or^{s} Tyc Pr vg$^{d.f.g**}$: pr *και ηκουσα* s^{1} | *και*^{1} > bo | *επ αυτον*] *επ αυτω* 1. 61 (?). 2037* | *εχων*] habebat vg arm : tenebat Pr | *τοξον*] sagittam Pr | *εξηλθεν*] *επηλθεν* Or^{s} : > arm^{3} | *νικων και ινα νικηση*] ut vinceret et victor exiit Pr | *νικων*] pr *ο* A arm$^{2.4}$ | *και ινα νικηση*] *και ενικησεν* ℵ bo sa : *κ. ινα νικησει* 1. 2023. 2038 : *κ. ινα νικηση* (-*σει* 2019) *και ενικησεν* 2017. 2019 : *κ. ενικησεν κ. ινα νικηση* s^{1} : *νικων και* > eth | *και*^{6} > 506 vg gig s^{2} arm |.

3. Καὶ ὅτε ἤνοιξεν τὴν σφραγῖδα τὴν δευτέραν, ἤκουσα τοῦ δευτέρου ζῴου λέγοντος Ἔρχου.

4. Καὶ ἐξῆλθεν ἄλλος ἵππος πυρρός,

καὶ τῷ καθημένῳ ἐπ' † αὐτὸν † ⌜ἐδόθη αὐτῷ⌝ λαβεῖν τὴν εἰρήνην ἐδόθη [ἐκ] τῆς γῆς,

καὶ ἵνα ἀλλήλους σφάξουσιν,

καὶ ἐδόθη αὐτῷ μάχαιρα μεγάλη.

5. Καὶ ὅτε ἤνοιξεν τὴν σφραγῖδα τὴν τρίτην, ἤκουσα τοῦ τρίτου ζῴου λέγοντος Ἔρχου.

καὶ εἶδον, καὶ ἰδοὺ ἵππος μέλας,

καὶ ὁ καθήμενος ἐπ' αὐτὸν ἔχων ζυγὸν ἐν τῇ χειρὶ αὐτοῦ.

3. **ηνοιξεν**] ηνυξεν ℵ | την σφραγιδα την δευτεραν AℵC 025. 1. 172. 205. 250. 314. 424. 2018. 2023. 2038 Tyc Pr gig vg arm : την δευτεραν σφραγιδα 046. **20** (– 205). 2037. 2067 al^{pl} Or^{s} | ερχου AC 025. 046. **20** (– 205. 386. 468). 1. 61. 69. 82. 104. 110. 314. 336. 385. 498. 522. 1955. 1957. 2015. 2016. 2019. 2023. 2037. 2038. 2041 al^{mu} Or^{s} vg s bo sa : ερχομαι arm : ερχου και ιδε ℵ 141. 172. 201. 205. 250. 386. 424. 468. 1918. 2018. 2022. 2067 Tyc Pr gig vg$^{d. g**. v}$ eth |.

4. **και εξηλθεν**] και (ε)ιδον και ιδου (κ. ιδου > bo sa) εξηλθ. ℵ 250. 424. 2018. 2067 bo sa | αλλοσ > Tyc s^{1} arm^{2} bo sa | πυρροσ ℵC 35. 175 201**. 241. 242. 325. 429. 456. 468. 498. 617. 1849. 1934. 1955. 1957. 2023**. 2024. 2037. 2041. 2067 al^{mu} Tyc Pr gig vg s arm$^{2. a}$: πυροσ A 025. 046. 1. 18. 61. 69. 104. 110. 172. 201*. 205. 250. 314. 337. 385. 386. 620. 632. 919. 920. 2004. 2020. 2038. 2040 Or^{s} | τω καθημενω] pr εν A | επ αυτον AℵC 025. 046. **20** (– 18). 250. 2037**. 2038 al^{pm} Or^{s} : επ αυτω 1. 18. 172. 2015. 2037*. 2067 al^{p} : super eum Tyc Pr : super illum gig vg | αυτω ℵ*C 025. 046. **21** Or^{s} vg s arm bo sa eth. The αυτω should stand in the text : cf. 2$^{7. 17. 26}$ 3$^{12. 21}$. It should be restored (?) in 21^{6} : > Aℵ^{c} 2016 Tyc Pr gig | λαβειν > arm$^{2. 4}$ | εκ τησ γησ ℵC 025. 046. **20** (– 205. 620). 250. 2037. 2067 al^{pm} Or^{s} Tyc Pr gig vg s eth : > ℵ^{c} : εκ > A 104. 205. 209. 336. 620. 1918. 2038 : απο τησ γησ 1. 2019 al^{p} | και ινα AℵC 025. 1. 35*. 172. 205. 250. 2018. 2019. 2020. 2038 al Or^{s} Tyc Pr gig vg s^{2} : και > 046. **20** (– 35*. 205. 2020). 2037. 2067 al^{pm} s^{1} bo | σφαξουσιν AC 1849. 2019 : σφαξωσι(ν) ℵ 025. 046. **20** (– 1849). 1. 250. 2037. 2038. 2067 al^{pl} Or^{s} | μαχαιρα μεγαλη] ∼ A bo sa eth |.

5. **ηνοιξεν**] ηνυξεν ℵ : ηνοιγη s^{1} | την σφραγιδα την τριτην] την **τριτ.** σφραγ. 1. 2019. 2020 al : η σφραγισ η τριτη s^{1} | ηκουσα] ειδον bo | ερχου AC 025. 1. 35. 60. 91. 104 241. 336. 432. 620. 1918. 1957. 2020. 2023. 2036. 2037. 2038 Or^{s} gig vg$^{a. f. g*}$ s^{1} bo : + και ιδε ℵ 046. **20** (– 35. (620). 2020). 61. 69. 110. 172. 181. 201. 250. 314. 385. 498. 522. 1955. 2016. 2018. 2067 Pr

6. καὶ ἤκουσα ὡς φωνὴν ἐν μέσῳ τῶν τεσσάρων ζῴων λέγουσαν
Χοῖνιξ σίτου δηναρίου,
καὶ τρεῖς χοίνικες κριθῶν δηναρίου,
καὶ τὸ ἔλαιον καὶ τὸν οἶνον μὴ ἀδικήσῃς·
7. Καὶ ὅτε ἤνοιξεν τὴν σφραγῖδα τὴν τετάρτην, ἤκουσα φωνὴν τοῦ
τετάρτου ζῴου λέγοντος Ἔρχου.
8. καὶ εἶδον καὶ ἰδοὺ ἵππος χλωρός,
καὶ ὁ καθήμενος ἐπάνω αὐτοῦ ὄνομα αὐτῷ ὁ θάνατος (*a*)
καὶ ἐδόθη αὐτῷ ἐξουσία ἐπὶ τὸ τέταρτον τῆς γῆς.(*b*)

(*a*) Here follows an interpolation : *καὶ ὁ ᾅδης ἠκολούθει μετ' αὐτοῦ.*
(*b*) Here follows an interpolation : *ἀποκτεῖναι ἐν ῥομφαίᾳ καὶ ἐν λιμῷ καὶ ἐν θανάτῳ καὶ ὑπὸ τῶν θηρίων τῆς γῆς.*

vg$^{c. d. g**. v}$ s^2 : + ιδε eth | και ειδον > 046. **20** (– 35. 205. 468**. 620). 61. 69. 110. 172. 181. 201 314. 498. 506. 517. 522. 1955. 2016 al^p Or^s gig vg$^{c. d. g**. v}$ s^1 eth | και ιδου > Pr arm^1 eth : και > bo | ιπποσ] pr αλλοσ arm^1 : pr και εξηλθεν eth | μελασ] μεγασ 919. 2020* | επ αυτον] επ αυτω 1. 2037. 2067 al^p | εχων] habebat Tyc Pr vg arm |.

6. ωσ φωνην AℵC 025. 35*. 181. 314. 2038 Or^s gig vg : ωσ > 046. **20** (– 35*). 250. 2037. 2067 al^{pl} Pr s arm bo sa eth | εν μεσω] εμμεσω AC : εκ μεσου s^1 : μεσον 35. 205 | τεσσαρων] δ' 35 : > s^1 arm^1 | ζωων] + ωσ φωνην αετου bo eth | λεγουσαν] λεγοντων gig vg$^{d. f. g}$ arm | χοινιξ] σχοινιξ 920 | δηναριου^1] + ενοσ Pr gig vg^d | κριθων AℵC 025. 1. 181. 205. 2036. 2038. 2067 s^2 : κριθησ 046. **21** (– 205). 250. 2037. al^{pl} Or^s s^1 | δηναριου^2] pr του A : + ενοσ Pr vg^d : > 69. 181 | και] το δε bo sa | και το ελαιον και τον οινον] ~ 2019 Tyc Pr vg s^1 eth | αδικησησ] αδικησισ 025 : αδικηθησονται arm^1 |.

7. την σφραγιδα την τεταρτην] την τεταρτην σφραγιδα 2020. 2038 : την σφραγ. τ. δ' 35 | ηκουσα] pr και 325. 456 | φωνην Aℵ 1. 35. 1957. 2015. 2019. 2023. 2036. 2037. 2038 al^p Or^s vg s^1 eth : pr την 205 : φωνησ 2067 : > C 025. 046. **20** (– 35. 205). 250 al^{pm} Pr gig s^2 arm bo sa | του τεταρτου ζωου] το τεταρτον ζωον C : τεταρτου > s^1 | ερχου AC 025. 1. 104. 620. 632**. 1957. 2015. 2019. 2020. 2023. 2036. 2037. 2038 al^p Or^s vg$^{a. f. g}$ s^1 bo sa arm^4 : + και ιδε ℵ 046. **20** (– 620. 632**. 2020) 250. 2067 al^{pm} Pr gig vg$^{c. d. v}$ s^2 : + ιδε eth : ερχομαι arm |.

8. και ειδον > 046. **20** (– 35. 205. 386. 468**. 620. 632**). 69. 250. 314 al^{mu} Or^s gig vg$^{c. v}$ arm^1 eth | και ιδου > Pr s^1 eth : και > bo : ιδου > arm^2 | ιπποσ] pr και εξηλθεν eth | ιπποσ χλωροσ] ιππον χλωρον Pr s^1 | χλωροσ] λευκοσ 920. 2040 : pallidus Tyc gig vg (Pr) : "reddish" arm^1 | ο καθημενοσ] ο > C | επανω αυτου] αυτου > C 025. 1. 181. 205 | αυτω] + ην Tyc Pr : αυτου s^1 | ο θανατοσ 025. 046. **20** (– 35. 920. 2040). 250. 2037. 2038.

9. Καὶ ὅτε ἤνοιξεν τὴν πέμπτην σφραγῖδα, εἶδον ὑποκάτω τοῦ θυσιαστηρίου τὰς ψυχὰς τῶν ἐσφαγμένων διὰ τὸν λόγον τοῦ θεοῦ καὶ διὰ τὴν μαρτυρίαν ἣν εἶχον.
10. καὶ ἔκραξαν φωνῇ μεγάλῃ λέγοντες

Ἕως πότε, ὁ δεσπότης ὁ ἅγιος καὶ ἀληθινός,
οὐ κρίνεις καὶ ἐκδικεῖς τὸ αἷμα ἡμῶν
ἐκ τῶν κατοικούντων ἐπὶ τῆς γῆς;

2067 al[pl] Or[Mt. iii. 187] Or[s] : ο > ℵC 35. 336*. 432. 920. 2023. 2040. 2041 : ο αθανατοσ A | ο αδησ] infernus Tyc Pr vg[d. f. v] : inferus vg[a. c. g] : "all Amenti" bo | ηκολουθει ℵC 025. 046. **20** (– 35). 250. 2067 al[pm] Or[s] Tyc Pr gig vg arm[1. 2. 4. a] : ακολουθει 1. 35. 1957. 2015. 2023. 2036. 2037. 2038. 2041 s | μετ αυτου AC 025. 1. 35. 104. 498*. 620. 1957. 2015. 2023. 2036. 2037. 2038 : μετ αυτον s² : αυτω ℵ 046. **20** (– 35. 620) al[pm] Or[s] Tyc Pr gig vg s¹ : αυτοισ (also τισιν) Or[Mt. iii. 187] | εδοθη αυτω 046. **20** (– 35. 468*). 250 al[pm] Or[s] Pr gig vg s[1. 2] arm bo sa eth : εδοθη αυτοισ AℵC 025. 1. 35. 468*. 2015. 2023. 2036. 2037. 2038. 2067 al[p] | το τεταρτον] + μεροσ 452. 2015. 2019. 2036. 2037 : quattuor partes vg | εν θανατω] εν > 325 : εν τη θλιψει bo | υπο των θηριων] το τεταρτον των θηριων A |.

9. την πεμπτην σφραγιδα] AC 025. 046 al : την σφραγ. την ε. ℵ* Tyc vg[c] : την ε. σφραγ. ℵ[c] 35 : την σφραγ. τ. πεμπτην 61. 69 s[1. 2] arm[1. 4. a] | του θυσιαστηριου] + του θεου Tyc Pr Cyp | των εσφαγμενων AC 046. **20** (– 35. 205. 920). 250. 2037 al[pl] Tyc Pr gig Cyp vg s² eth : pr των ανθρωπων ℵ 025. 1. 35. 60. 181. 205. 209. 432. 1957. 2019. 2023. 2038. 2041. 2067 bo sa : τασ εσφαγμενασ s¹ : των εσφραγισμενων 104. 218. 336*. 920 Or[s] | δια τον λογον] pr δια τον θεον και arm¹ | δια² > A Pr gig Cyp bo sa | μαρτυριαν AℵC 025. 1. 241. 632**. 2015. 2019. 2036. 2037. 2038 Pr gig Cyp vg bo : εκκλησιαν 2020 : + του αρνιου 046. **20** (– 632**. 2020). 2067 al[pm] Or[s] s² : + Ιησου s¹ : + Ιησου Χριστου 172. 250. 424. 2018 : + αυτου Pr Cyp arm[1. 2. 3] eth | ην ειχον ℵ[c]] ην εσχον ℵ* |.

10. εκραξαν AℵC 046. **20** (– 35*. 205. 632**. 2020). 250 al[pm] Pr Cyp bo : εκραζον 025. 1. 35*. 205. 632**. 2016. 2019. 2020. 2036. 2037. 2038. 2067 Or[s] gig vg s : ειπον arm[1. 2. 3. a] | φωνη μεγαλη AℵC 025. 1. 35. 104. 205. 385. 620. 632**. 2020. 2037. 2038. 2067 al[mu] Or[s] Pr gig vg Cyp s (arm) bo : φωνην μεγαλην 046. **20** (– 35. 205. 620. 632**. 2020). 250 al[mu] | αληθινοσ] pr ο 1. 172. 429**. 468. 620. (2018). 2037. 2067 | εκδικεισ] εκδικησεισ ℵ | εκ των AℵC 046. **20** (– 35*. 205. 468. 620. 2020). 250 al[pm] Or[s] : απο των 025. 1. 35*. 104. 205. 468. 620. 2015. 2018. 2023. 2037. 2038. 2067 al[p] : και των 2020 | επι τησ γησ] in terris Pr Cyp |.

11. καὶ ἐδόθη αὐτοῖς ἑκάστῳ στολὴ λευκή,
καὶ ἐρρέθη αὐτοῖς ἵνα ἀναπαύσονται ἔτι χρόνον μικρόν,
ἕως πληρωθῶσιν καὶ οἱ σύνδουλοι αὐτῶν καὶ οἱ ἀδελφοὶ αὐτῶν
οἱ μέλλοντες ἀποκτέννεσθαι ὡς καὶ αὐτοί.

12. Καὶ εἶδον ὅτε ἤνοιξεν τὴν σφραγῖδα τὴν ἕκτην·
καὶ σεισμὸς μέγας ἐγένετο,
καὶ ὁ ἥλιος ἐγένετο μέλας ὡς σάκκος τρίχινος,
καὶ ἡ σελήνη ὅλη ἐγένετο ὡς αἷμα·

11. εδοθη . . . στολη λευκη : εδοθησαν . . . στολαι λευκαι Pr vg (Cyp) arm[1] | αυτοισ εκαστω A ℵC 025. 35. 61. 69. 104. 205. 250. 468. 620. 632**. 1957. 2018. 2019. 2020. 2023. 2036. 2067 al[p] arm[4] bo : eis singulis Pr gig Cyp : illis singulae vg : αυτοισ > 82. 91. 93. 181 : εκαστω > 046. **20** (– 35. 205. 468 620. 632**. 2020) al[mu] Or[s] arm[1. 2. 3. a] : εκαστω αυτων (~2037) 2015. 2037 s eth | ερρεθη] ερεθη ℵ 35. 241. 522. 620. 632 : ερρηθη 172. 242. 250. 1957. 2018. 2024. 2039 : εδοθη 2038 | αυτοισ > s[1] | αναπαυσονται A 025. 046. 1. 104. 110. 522. 620. 2015. 2019. 2036. 2038 al[p] : αναπαυσωνται ℵC **20** (– 620). 250. 2037. 2067 al[pl] : αναπνευσωνται 69** : αναπαυσασθαι Or[s] | ετι (επι ℵ) χρον. μικ. ℵC 025. 1. 18. 205 632**. 2015. 2036. 2037. 2038. 2067 vg s[2] bo sa : χρονον ετι μικρον A : ετι χρονον 046. **20** (– 18. 205. 325. 456. 632**. 2020). 250 al[pm] : ετι τινα χρον. μικ. 2020 : ετι μικ. χρον. 241. 2019 eth : εωσ καιρου χρον. μικ. s[1] : χρονον 325. 456 : μικρον Or[s] : ετι μικρον gig : μικ. ετι χρον. Cyp : χρον. μικ. arm | εωσ] + ου 1. 18. 35. 205. 1957. 2015. 2019. 2023. 2036. 2037. 2038. 2041. 2067 al[p] | πληρωθωσιν AC 385 gig vg s arm bo eth : πληρωσωσι(ν) ℵ 025. 046. **20** (– 620. 632. 2040). 1. 250. 2037. 2038. 2067 al[pl] Or[s] : πληρωσουσι 620. 632. 2015. 2016. 2019. 2036. 2040 : impleatur numerus Cyp | και οι συνδουλοι > 2019 : και > 046 Cyp vg bo | και οι αδελφοι] και > 386 | οι μελλοντεσ A ℵC 025. 35. 205. 620 Or[s] vg s[1. 2] bo : pr και 046. **20** (– 35. 205. 620). 2037 al[mu] (Cyp) | οι μελλ. αποκτενν.] qui occidentur gig | αποκτεννεσθαι A ℵC 35. 82. 93. 94. 175. 205. 241. 250. 325. 337. 456. 617. 919. 920. 1955. 2004. 2018. 2024 : + υπ αυτων ℵ* (del. ℵ[c]) : αποκτενεσθαι 18. 42. 91. 104. 110. 172. 242. 385. 386. 468. 506. 620. 632. 1849. 1934. 2015. 2016. 2017. 2019. 2023. 2024. 2036. 2039. 2040. 2041 : αποκτεινεσθαι 025. 046. 1. 61. 69. 336. 429. 498 Or[s] (vel— τενεσθαι) : αποθανειν arm | ωσ και αυτοι] και > 385. 2020 : exemplo ipsorum Cyp |.

12. ειδον > 18. 94. 141. 385. 429. 522. 1849. 1955. 2039. 2040 Tyc eth | οτε ηνοιξεν] οτε ενυξεν ℵ* (ηνυξεν ℵ[c]) : pr και 025. 1. 35**. 42. 61. 69. 181. 205. 209. 432. 468. 1957. 2019. 2023 2041 Pr | την σφραγιδα την εκτην] την εκτ. σφραγ. Pr Tyc σεισμοσ] pr ιδου A vg[v] : φωσ s[1] | μεγασ εγενετο ℵC 025. 046.

13. *καὶ οἱ ἀστέρες τοῦ οὐρανοῦ ἔπεσαν εἰς τὴν γῆν,*
ὡς συκῆ βάλλει τοὺς ὀλύνθους αὐτῆς
ὑπὸ ἀνέμου μεγάλου σειομένη·

14. *καὶ ὁ οὐρανὸς ἀπεχωρίσθη*
ὡς βιβλίον ⸢† ἑλισσόμενον †⸣, ἑλισσο
καὶ πᾶν ὄρος καὶ νῆσος ἐκ τῶν τόπων αὐτῶν ἐκινήθησαν. μενος

15. *καὶ οἱ βασιλεῖς τῆς γῆς καὶ οἱ μεγιστᾶνες καὶ οἱ χιλίαρχοι καὶ*
οἱ πλούσιοι καὶ οἱ ἰσχυροὶ καὶ πᾶς δοῦλος καὶ ἐλεύθερος ἔκρυψαν
ἑαυτοὺς εἰς τὰ σπήλαια καὶ εἰς τὰς πέτρας τῶν ὀρέων.

20. 250. 2037. 2038. 2067 al^{pl} Or^{s} Pr arm^{8} : ∼ A 2016 Tyc gig vg arm^{4} | *εγενετο μελασ* AC 025. 1. 35. 205. 2015. 2019. 2020. 2036. 2037. 2038. 2067 Tyc Pr gig vg arm^{a} : ∼ ℵ 046. **20** (−35. 205. 2020). 61. 69. 104. 110. 172. 201. 250. 314. 498. 522. 1955. 1957. 2016. 2018. 2023. 2041 al^{p} Or^{s} | *ωσ . . . τριχινοσ* >eth | *σακκοσ*] *ασκοσ* s^{1} | *η σεληνη ολη* AℵC 046. **20** (−35. 205). 2067 al^{pm} Or^{s} Tyc (gig) vg s$^{1.2}$ bo eth : "the moon wholly" arm$^{1.2.3.a}$: *ολη* >025. 1. 35. 172. 205. 250. 1957. 2018. 2023. 2037. 2038. 2041. 2067 Pr sa | *ωσ αιμα*] *εισ αιμα* 1934 : *ωσ* >Pr gig arm |.

13. *του ουρανου*] *του θεου* A : >Tyc Pr vg$^{d.f}$: de coelo (post *επεσαν* pon gig bo eth) gig arm bo eth | *επεσαν* AℵC 025. 1. 104. 337. 429. 2015 al^{p} Or^{s} : *επεσον* 046. **20** (−337). 250. 2037. 2038. 2067 al^{mu} arm^{4} : "were shaken down" arm$^{1.2.3.a}$ | *εισ την γην*] *επι την γην* ℵ 241. 468**. 2038 s^{1} : super terram vg arm^{4} (bo) : >gig | *συκη*] + *σειομενη* (Tyc) | *βαλλει* AC 025. 046. 35. 61. 69. 2019. 2023. 2037. 2038. 2067 Tyc Pr gig vg arm^{4} : *αποβαλλει* 2015. 2036 : *βαλει* 1 : *βαλλουσα* ℵ 18. 172. 205. 250. 336. 429. 468. 498. 620. 1918. 2039 Or^{s} s : *βαλουσα* **20** (−18. 35. 205. 468. 620. 2020). 42. 93. 94. 141. 201. 209. 218. 241. 242. 385. 424. 452. 506. 517. 522. 1955. 2016. 2017. 2021 al^{p} : *αποβαλουσα* 2020 | *υπο*] *απο* ℵ 69. 2016** | *ανεμου μεγαλου* AℵC 046. **20** (−35. 205). 250 al^{mu} Or^{s} Pr gig vg : ∼ 025. 1. 35. 2015. 2037. 2038. 2067 : *μεγαλου* >Tyc : *υπο μεγ. σειομενη ανεμου* 205 | *σειομενη*] *σαλευομενη* A 181 : *σειομενου* 456 |.

14. *ο* >1 | *απεχωρισθη*] >arm$^{1.2.3.a}$ bo : *ετακη* s^{1} arm^{4} : *ειλιχθη* eth | *ωσ βιβλιον*] *και ωσ βιβλια* s^{1} | *ελισσομενον* AC 046. 35. 69. 82. 104. 250 337. 468. 2023*. 2040 al^{mu} Or^{s} Tyc Pr gig vg s^{2} bo eth : *ειλισσομενον* 025. 1. 2019. 2023**. 2036. 2037. 2038 : *ελισσομενοσ* ℵ **20** (−35. 337. 468. 632. 2040). 110. 314. 1957. 2016. 2067 al^{p} : *ειλισσομενοσ* 632 : *ελισσοιται* s^{1} : *ειλιχθη* arm bo | *νησοσ*] *νησσοσ* C 046 : *βουνοσ* ℵ : insulae Tyc Pr vg : pr *πασα* s^{1} bo sa | *αυτων* >ℵ | *εκινηθησαν* ℵ*C 025. 046 min^{pl} : *εκινησαν* ℵ* : *απεκεινησαν* A : *εσαλευθησαν* 920. 2040 |.

15. *και*^{3} >A | *χιλιαρχοι . . . πλουσιοι*] ∼ 1. 2019. 2020. 2038

16. καὶ λέγουσιν τοῖς ὄρεσιν καὶ ταῖς πέτραις
Πέσατε ἐφ' ἡμᾶς καὶ κρύψατε ἡμᾶς ἀπὸ προσώπου τοῦ καθη-
μένου ἐπὶ τοῦ θρόνου
καὶ ἀπὸ τῆς ὀργῆς τοῦ ἀρνίου,
17. ὅτι ἦλθεν ἡ ἡμέρα ἡ μεγάλη τῆς ὀργῆς αὐτοῦ,
καὶ τίς δύναται σταθῆναι;

al^{p} | και οι ισχυροι > 1. 181. 2019. 2038 : οι > ℵ 2024. 2040 | και ελευθεροσ AC 046. **20** (– 35. 205. 2020). 250 al^{pm} Or^{8} Pr gig vg s : και πασ ελευθεροσ ℵ^{c} 025. 1. 35. 205. 1957. 2015. 2020. 2023. 2037. 2038. 2041. 2067 : > ℵ* arm^{4} : και παντεσ οι ελευθεροι arm^{a} bo | πετρασ] οπασ arm bo |.

16. και λεγουσιν] dicentes Pr : και ειπον arm$^{1.2.3.a}$ | τοισ ορεσιν και ταισ πετραισ] ~ bo arm^{4} : > Tyc : και ταισ πετραισ > arm$^{1.a}$ | πεσατε A 025. 104. 2015. 2036 Or^{8} : πεσετε C 046. **20** 1. 250. 2037. 2038. 2067 al^{pl} : πεσεται ℵ | κρυψατε] κρυψεται ℵ : κρυψετε 385* | απο προσωπου . . . του αρνιου > arm^{a} | του καθη μενου . . . τησ οργησ > s^{1} | επι του θρονου AC 025. 1. 35. 69*. 104. 205. 241. 468. 632. 1957. 2015. 2019. 2020. 2023. 2036. 2037. 2038. 2067 al^{mu} Or^{8} : επι τω θρονω ℵ 046. **20** (– 35. 205. 468. 632. 2020). 250 al^{mu} : supra sedem gig : super thronum (Pr) vg | απο^{2} ℵ^{c}] επι ℵ* |.

17. οτι > Or^{8}. η ημερα η μεγαλη τησ οργησ αυτου] η μεγαλη τησ οργησ αυτου ημερα 18 | η^{I} > 2004. 2020 | η μεγαλη > 69. 325. 456. 517 | αυτου A 025. 046. **20** (– 2020). 250. 2037. 2038. 2067 al^{pl} Or^{8} Pr arm$^{1.2.3.a}$ bo : αυτων ℵC 2020 gig vg s$^{1.2}$ arm^{4} sa | σταθηναι] σωθηναι 141. 242. 617. 1934 : στηναι 250. 429. 2018. 2019 : + ante illum Pr arm$^{1.2}$ bo |.

Chapter VII.

Καὶ μετὰ

1. ⸀Μετὰ⸁ τοῦτο εἶδον τέσσαρας ἀγγέλους ἑστῶτας ἐπὶ τὰς τέσ-
σαρας γωνίας τῆς γῆς, κρατοῦντας τοὺς τέσσαρας ἀνέμους τῆς γῆς,
ἵνα μὴ πνέῃ ἄνεμος ἐπὶ τῆς γῆς μήτε ἐπὶ τῆς θαλάσσης μήτε ἐπί

1. μετα AC Or^{8} Pr gig vg sa : pr και ℵ 025. 046 **21**. 250. 2037. 2038. 2067 al^{pl} s arm^{3} (bo) eth | τουτο AℵC 046. **21** (– 205. 468. 920. 2040). 250 al^{pm} Or^{8} s arm eth : ταυτα 025. 1. 61. 205. 241. 468. 920. 2015. 2019. 2036. 2037. 2038. 2040. 2067 Pr gig vg bo | τεσσαρασ^{1} C 025. 046. **21** (– 35. 866) Or^{8} : τεσσαρεσ A : δ' ℵ 35. 866 | επι] per Pr | τεσσαρασ^{2} AℵC 046. **21** (– 35) Or^{8} : τεσσαρεσ 025 : δ' 35 | κρατουντασ] pr και 337 s arm$^{1.a}$ | κρατουντασ . . . ανεμουσ τ. γησ > eth | τεσσαρασ^{3} ℵC 025. 046. **21** (– 35) Or^{8} : τεσσαρεσ A : δ' 35 | τησ γησ > 2020. 2037 s^{1} bo sa | πνεη] πνευση ℵ 172. 205. 250 : πνεει 2019.

⸀† τι⸀ δένδρον †. 2. καὶ εἶδον ἄλλον ἄγγελον ἀναβαίνοντα ἀπὸ πᾶν
⸀ἀνατολῆς⸀ ἡλίου, ἔχοντα σφραγῖδα θεοῦ ζῶντος, καὶ ⸀ἔκραξεν⸀ ἀνατολῶν
φωνῇ μεγάλῃ τοῖς τέσσαρσιν ἀγγέλοις οἷς ἐδόθη αὐτοῖς ἀδικῆσαι τὴν ἔκραζεν
γῆν καὶ τὴν θάλασσαν, 3. λέγων Μὴ ἀδικήσητε τὴν γῆν ⸀μήτε⸀ τὴν καὶ
θάλασσαν μήτε τὰ δένδρα, ἄχρι σφραγίσωμεν τοὺς δούλους τοῦ θεοῦ
ἡμῶν ἐπὶ τῶν μετώπων αὐτῶν.

4. Καὶ ἤκουσα τὸν ἀριθμὸν τῶν ἐσφραγισμένων· ἑκατὸν τεσσαράκοντα τέσσαρες χιλιάδες ἐσφραγισμένοι ἐκ πάσης φυλῆς υἱῶν Ἰσραήλ.

(Or^{s}) : πεση 920. 2040 : flarent Pr vg$^{f. v}$ bo | ανεμοσ] pr ο C 61. 69. 506. 522. 632*. 919. 920. 1955. 2040 : >Pr vg$^{f. v}$ arm^{2} : οι ανεμοι bo | επι τησ γησ >A : in terris Pr | επι τησ θαλασσησ] τησ >A : + μητε επι των ποταμων bo | επι τι δενδρον C 046. **21** (−35. 205). 250 al^{pm} Or^{s} (Pr gig vg) : επι παν δενδρον ℵ 025. 1. 35. 205. 1957. 2015. 2019. 2023. 2036. 2037. 2038. 2041 s^{1} : επι δενδρου A : επι (τα) δενδρα s$^{2?}$ arm bo eth |.

2. αλλον αγγελον] ~42. 325. 456. 468. 620. 866. 1934. 1957. 2036 : αλλον >Pr | αλλον . . . αναβαινοντα] και ανεβη αλλοσ αγγελοσ eth | αναβαινοντα] αναβαντα 1 bo | ανατολησ ℵC 025. 046. **21** (−18). 250. 2037. 2038. 2067 al^{pl} Or^{s} s^{2} : ανατολων A 18. 2039 (s^{1}) | σφραγιδα et ℵ^{c}] σφαγιδα ℵ* | θεου] pr του 325. 456. 468. 620. 866 | ζωντοσ] pr του 468 | εκραξεν ℵC 046. **21.** 250. 2037. 2038 al^{pl} Or^{s} Tyc Pr gig vg s arm bo : εκραζεν A 025. 2067 | φωνη μεγαλη] φωνην μεγαλη 866 | τεσσαρσιν et ℵ^{c}] τεσσαρεσ ℵ* : δ´ 35 | αγγελοισ] ζωοισ arm^{4} | οισ εδοθη] eo quod datum esset Pr | αυτοισ >35. 336. 337. 2015. 2023. 2036. 2037 gig vg | αδικησαι] απολεσαι arm$^{1. 2. a}$ |.

3. λεγων] + αυτοισ Pr bo eth | αδικησητε] αδικησεται ℵ : + μητε Or$^{Jo. i. 6}$ | μητε την θαλασσαν C 025. 046. **21** (−866. 2020). 250. 2037. 2067 al^{pl} Or$^{Jo. i. 6}$: μηδε την θ. ℵ 866 2038 : και την θ. A 432. 452. 2020. 2021 Or^{s} bo sa | μητε^{2}] μηδε ℵ 866 | αχρι (-σℵ) AℵC 025. 1. 35. 181. 2038 Or$^{Jo. i. 6}$: αχρισ ου 046. **21** (−35). 250. 2067 al^{pl} Or^{s} : αχρισ αν 94. 2015. 2036. 2037 : ινα arm^{3} | σφραγισωμεν] σφραγισομεν 337. 2016. 2020. : "I shall have sealed" arm^{1} : σφραγισητε bo : σφραγισθωσι eth | ημων >241. 2015. 2039. 2040 Tyc s^{1} bo sa eth |.

4. και ηκουσα . . . εσφραγισμενων >A | τον αριθμον >920. 2040 | εσφραγισμενων] + επι του μετωπου αυτων bo | εκατον . . . εσφραγισμενοι >18. 141. 385. 429. 919. 920. 1849. 2004. 2039. 2040. 2067 | εκατον τεσσ. τεσσαρεσ 025. 205. 386. 620. 866. 1934 : εκατον και τεσσ. τεσσαρεσ C 82. 104. 172. 175. 250. 314. 325. 337. 456. 468. 617. 632. 1957. 2018. 2041 : (εκατον) εκατον και τεσσ. και τεσσαρεσ 498 (2020) : εκατον τεσσ. και τεσσαρεσ 69 : ρ μ δ 046. 1. 35 al^{mu} : εκατον τεσσερακοντα (τεσσαρακοντα A) A*ℵ : εκ. τεσσ. δ´ A** | εσφραγισμενοι AℵC 025. 1. 35.

5^{ab}. ἐκ φυλῆς Ἰούδα δώδεκα χιλιάδες ἐσφραγισμένοι,
ἐκ φυλῆς Ῥουβὴν δώδεκα χιλιάδες, (*a*)
7. ἐκ φυλῆς Συμεὼν δώδεκα χιλιάδες,
ἐκ φυλῆς Λευὶ δώδεκα χιλιάδες,
ἐκ φυλῆς Ἰσσαχὰρ δώδεκα χιλιάδες,
8. ἐκ φυλῆς Ζαβουλὼν δώδεκα χιλιάδες,
ἐκ φυλῆς Ἰωσὴφ δώδεκα χιλιάδες,
ἐκ φυλῆς Βενιαμεὶν δώδεκα χιλιάδες ἐσφραγισμένοι,
5^{c} ἐκ φυλῆς Γὰδ δώδεκα χιλιάδες,
6. ἐκ φυλῆς Ἀσὴρ δώδεκα χιλιάδες,
ἐκ φυλῆς Νεφθαλὶμ δώδεκα χιλιάδες
ἐκ φυλῆς Μανασσῆ δώδεκα χιλιάδες.

(*a*) On the restoration of the original order of the text, see vol. i. 207 sqq.

205. 632*. 2020. 2037. 2038 al^{mu} Or$^{Jo.\ 3\ sq.\ (semel)}$ Tyc Pr gig vg s^2 bo : *εσφραγισμενων* 046. **21** (−35. 205. 632*. 2020). 69. 82. 104. 201. 250. 314. 498. 2016. 2017. 2018. 2036 al^p Or^s : >s^1 sa : + *επι τ. μετωπων αυτων* bo | *υιων Ισραηλ*] *υιων* >arm$^{2.\ 4}$ eth : *Ισραηλιτων* s^2 |.

5$^{a.\ b}$. εσφραγισμενοι AℵC 025. 35. 468. 632. 2020 Or^s Pr gig vg s^2 : *-μεναι* 046. **21** (−35. 468. 632. 2020). 82. 201. 314. 385. 498. 1955. 2016. 2017 al^p : *-μενων* 69. 104. 522 : >s^1 arm$^{3.\ 4}$ bo eth | *Ρουβην* AℵC 025. 046. 175 Or^s : *Ρουβιν* 61. 69. 104. 201. 337. 498. 617. 919. 1955. 2004. 2015 : *Ρουβιμ* 1. 18. 35. 93. 386. 456. 468. 620**. 632. 920. 1849. 2017. 2019. 2020. 2036. 2037. 2038. 2040. 2067 : *Ρουβειμ* 60. 91. 172. 205. 385. 1934. 2018. 2023. 2041 : *Ρουβειν* 250. 2016 : *Ρουβημ* 314. 325. 506. 517. 620*. 866. 2024 : Ruben Pr gig vg : Roubēn bo |.

7. εκ φυλ. Συμ. δωδ. χιλ. >ℵ 172 | *Λευι*] *Λευει* ℵ : *Λευι* et *Ισαχαρ* ~ s^1 | *Ισσαχαρ* Aℵ 025. 61. 104. 385. 522. 919. 1955. 2017 al^p Or^s vg arm$^{1.\ 2.\ 3.\ a}$: *Ισαχαρ* C 046. **21** (−919) s^1 arm^4 bo : Isachar Pr : Ysacar gig |.

8. εκ φυλ. Ζαβ. δωδ. χιλ. > 1849 | *Ζαβουλων . . . Ιωσηφ*] ~ 1934 | *Ιωσηφ . . . Βενιαμειν*] ~ ℵ 2015 | *Βενιαμειν* A 025. 920. 2038 : *Βενιαμιν* ℵC 046. **21** (−456. 620. 866. 920) al^{pl} Or^s Pr gig vg s bo : *Βενιαμην* 242. 456. 620. 866. 2017 | *εσφραγισμενοι* AℵC 025. 35. 205. 468. 632. 2020 Or^s gig vg s^1 bo : *-μεναι* 046. **21** (−35. 205. 468. 632. 920. 2020. 2040) al^{mu} : >920. 2040 Pr s^2 |.

5^{c}. εκ φυλ. Γαδ. δωδ. χιλ. > ℵ | *Γαδ*] *Δαν* 42. 325 (pr man. scripsit in marg.) 336. 456. 620. 866 : *Δαδ* 1 : Gath Pr |.

6. εκ φυλ. Ασηρ δωδ. χιλ. > Or^s | *Νεφθαλιμ* A 046. 61**. 69**. 175. 314 325. 429. 456. 617. 620. 866. 919. 920. 1849. 1955. 2004 al vg : Nephtalim arm$^{1.\ 2.\ 3.\ a}$: Neptalim Pr gig : *Νεφθαλι* ℵ s : *Νεφθαλιν* C : *Νεφθαλημ* 69*. 201. 386. 517. 522 : Ephthalim bo : *Νεφθαλειμ* 025. 1. 18. 35. 61*. 104. 172. 205. 241.

9. Μετὰ ταῦτα εἶδον,
καὶ ἰδοὺ ὄχλος πολύς, ὃν ἀριθμῆσαι αὐτὸν οὐδεὶς ἐδύνατο,
ἐκ παντὸς ἔθνους καὶ φυλῶν καὶ λαῶν καὶ γλωσσῶν,
ἑστῶτες ἐνώπιον τοῦ θρόνου καὶ ἐνώπιον τοῦ ἀρνίου,
† περιβεβλημένους † στολὰς λευκάς, καὶ φοίνικες ἐν ταῖς χερσὶν αὐτῶν·
10. καὶ κράζουσιν φωνῇ μεγάλῃ λέγοντες
Ἡ σωτηρία τῷ θεῷ ἡμῶν
τῷ καθημένῳ ἐπὶ τῷ θρόνῳ
καὶ τῷ ἀρνίῳ.

242. 250. 337. 385. 468. 498. 632. 1934. 1957. 2015. 2016. 2017. 2018. 2019. 2020. 2023. 2024. 2037. 2038 2039. 2040. 2041. 2067 al^{mu} Or^{s} | εκ φυλ. Μαν. δωδ. χιλ. > 620*. 866 | Μανασση ℵ 025. **21** (– 175. 205. 620*. 866). 1. 250. 2067 al^{pl} Or^{s} Pr gig vg arm : Μανασσην C : Μαννασση A : Μονασση 046. 175. 205. 2037. 2038 s : Dan bo |.

9. μετα] pr και s^{1} arm^{1} bo eth | και ιδου ℵ 025. 046. **21**. 250. 2037. 2038. 2067 al^{pl} Or^{s} Tyc gig s^{2} : >A Pr Cyp vg s^{1} bo sa : ιδου >C | οχλοσ πολυσ ℵC 025. 046. **21**. 250. 2037. 2038. 2067 al^{pl} Tyc gig s^{2} : πολυσ >Or^{s} : οχλον πολυν A Pr Cyp vg s^{1} bo | ον et ℵ^{c}] οσ ℵ* : και A | αυτον AℵC 025. 1. 61. 69. 205. 2019 al^{p} Or^{s} s bo : >046. **21** (– 205). 104. 172. 201. 241. 242. 250. 314. 385. 429. 498. 522. 1955. 1957. 2015. 2016. 2017. 2018. 2023. 2024. 2037. 2038. 2039. 2041. 2067 al^{p} Tyc Pr gig Cyp vg | εδυνατο AℵC 046. **21** (– 205. 2040) al^{pl} : ηδυνατο 025. 1. 61. 69. 172. 205. 241. 250. 2015. 2023**. 2037. 2040. 2067 al^{mu} Or^{s} : δυναται 2038 arm^{4} | εκ παντοσ εθνοσ] εκ παντων εθνων Tyc gig vg arm$^{3.\ 4.\ a}$ | φυλων] φυλησ s^{1} Pr Cyp | και λαων και γλωσσων >eth | εστωτεσ Aℵ 025. 1. 35. 205. 1957. 2004. 2019. 2023. 2024. 2037. 2038. 2067 al^{p} s : εστωτασ 046. **21** (– 35. 205. 2004. 2020). 250 al^{mu} Or^{s} : εστωτων C 2020 : εστωτα 93. 1955 : stantes Pr gig Cyp vg | ενωπιον^{1}] επι A | περιβεβλημενουσ Aℵ*C 046. **21** (– 35. 205. 2040). 250 al^{pm} gig : περιβεβλημενασ 242. 2040 : περιβεβλημενοι ℵ^{c} 025. 1. 35. 205. 1957. 2015. 2019. 2023. 2037. 2038. 2067 al^{p} Or^{s} Tyc vg : και περιβεβλημενοι s^{1} : et erant amicti Pr Cyp | φοινικεσ Aℵ^{c}C 025. 1. 35. 104. 172. 205. 250. 2018. 2019. 2020. 2037. 2038. 2067 al^{p} gig vg arm : palmae fuerunt Pr Cyp : φοινικασ ℵ* 046. **21** (– 35. 205. 2020). 61. 69. 201. 241. 242. 314. 385. 429. 498. 522. 1957. 2015. 2016. 2017. 2023. 2024. 2039. 2041 al^{mu} Or^{s} : κιθαραι bo | εν ταισ χερσιν] pr ησαν Pr gig Cyp .

10. **και^{1}** > 1. 2067 bo. **κραζουσιν**] κραζοντεσ 1. 2067 bo s^{1} : εκραζον Pr gig Cyp vg arm | λεγοντεσ] pr και 2067 s^{1} : ελεγον arm^{1} : και ελεξαν arm$^{2.\ 3.\ 4.\ a}$ | τω θεω] του θεου A (in marg.) bo : θεω 1. 2037 (post τω καθ. επι τω θρον.) | τω καθημενω > ℵ*

11. καὶ πάντες οἱ ἄγγελοι ἱστήκεισαν κύκλῳ τοῦ θρόνου καὶ τῶν
πρεσβυτέρων καὶ τῶν τεσσάρων ζῴων, καὶ ἔπεσαν ἐνώπιον τοῦ θρόνου
ἐπὶ τὰ πρόσωπα αὐτῶν καὶ προσεκύνησαν τῷ θεῷ, 12. λέγοντες
Ἀμήν· ἡ εὐλογία καὶ ἡ δόξα καὶ ἡ σοφία
καὶ ἡ εὐχαριστία καὶ ἡ τιμὴ καὶ ἡ δύναμις
καὶ ἡ ἰσχὺς τῷ θεῷ ἡμῶν εἰς τοὺς αἰῶνας τῶν αἰώνων [·ἀμήν]
13. Καὶ ἀπεκρίθη εἷς ἐκ τῶν πρεσβυτέρων λέγων μοι Οὗτοι οἱ
περιβεβλημένοι τὰς στολὰς τὰς λευκὰς τίνες εἰσὶν καὶ πόθεν ἦλθον;
14. καὶ εἴρηκα αὐτῷ Κύριέ μου, σὺ οἶδας. καὶ εἶπέν μοι
Οὗτοί εἰσιν οἱ ἐρχόμενοι ἐκ τῆς θλίψεως τῆς μεγάλης,
καὶ ἔπλυναν τὰς στολὰς αὐτῶν,
καὶ ἐλεύκαναν αὐτὰς ἐν τῷ αἵματι τοῦ ἀρνίου.

(suppl. ℵ^c) : pr και s^1 | επι τω θρονω Aℵ*C 025. **21** (– 205. 468. 632**. 2020). 250. 2067 al^{mu} : επι του θρονου ℵ^c 046. 1. 104. 205. 468. 632**. 2019. 2020. 2036. 2037. 2038 al^{mu} Or^s s^1 : super thronum Pr Cyp vg : supra sedem gig | τω αρνιω] του αρνιου ℵ^c : + εισ τουσ αιωνασ των αιωνων αμην ℵ* (del. ℵ^c).

11. οι > ℵ* (suppl. ℵ^c) | ιστηκεισαν Aℵ (– κισαν ℵ) 025 : εστηκισαν C : ειστηκησαν 046. 104**. 919. 2017. 2018. 2036 : ειστηκεισαν **21** (– 205. 919). 250. 2037. 2067 al^{pl} Or^s : ειστη κεσαν 1. 205 : stabant Tyc Pr gig vg arm bo | κυκλω] ενωπιον bo | επεσαν AℵC 025. 42. 181. 325*. 337. 468. 517. 620. 866 al^p Or^s : επεσον 046. **21** (– 325*. 337. 468. 620. 866). 250. 2037. 2038. 2067 al^{pl} | ενωπιον . . . προσωπον αυτων] επι τ. προσ. αυτων ενωπιον τ. θρον. bo sa eth | του θρονου AℵC 025. 35. 205. 920. 2020. 2037. 2038. 2040. 2067 al Or^s Pr gig vg s^1 arm$^{2.\ 3.\ a}$ bo : + αυτου 046. **21** (– 35. 205. 920. 2020. 2040). 250 al s^2 | επι τα προσωπα] επι προσωπον 1. 2038. 2067 bo : > arm^1 | και προσεκυνησαν τω θεω > s^1 | και επεσαν . . . λεγοντεσ] προσεκυνησαν επι τ. προσωπα αυτων ενωπιον τ. θρονου του θεου λεγοντεσ eth |.

12. αμην] pr αγιοσ αγιοσ αγιοσ 205 | ευλογια . . . δοξα] ~ s^1 eth | και η σοφια > A arm^4 : ante η δοξα pon 506 : post η τιμη κ. η ευχαριστια pon 2067 | η ευχαριστια > η ℵ* (suppl. ℵ^c) | και η τιμη > eth | και η ισχυσ > bo : και η χαρισ arm$^{1.\ 2.\ 4.\ a}$: και η εξουσια arm^3 | τω θεω] του θεου bo : τω κυριω arm^1 : κυριω τω θεω arm^a | αμην > C 2015. 2019 Pr |.

13. απεκριθη] + μοι Tyc gig : λεγει μοι arm$^{1.\ 2.\ 3.\ a}$ eth | εκ > ℵ 1957 | λεγων μοι > gig arm$^{1.\ 2.\ 3.\ a}$ eth : μοι > Tyc arm^4 | τασ στολασ τασ λευκασ] τασ λευκασ στολασ 2015. 2036 | τασ^2 > C | τινεσ εισιν και > eth : εισιν > 1. 181. 2038 | ηλθον] veniunt vg$^{f.\ g}$ arm$^{1.\ 2.\ 3.\ a}$ |.

14. και > bo sa | ειρηκα AℵC 025. 1. 205. 2015. 2019. 2036. 2037. 2038. 2067 al^p Or^s : ειπον 046. **21** (– 205). 250. al^{pm} : dixi Pr gig Cyp vg : λεγω arm^1 | κυριε μου ℵC 025. 046.

15. διὰ τοῦτό εἰσιν ἐνώπιον τοῦ θρόνου τοῦ θεοῦ,
καὶ λατρεύουσιν αὐτῷ ἡμέρας καὶ νυκτὸς ἐν τῷ ναῷ αὐτοῦ,
καὶ ὁ καθήμενος ἐπὶ †τοῦ θρόνου† σκηνώσει ἐπ' αὐτούς.
16. οὐ πεινάσουσιν ἔτι οὐδὲ διψήσουσιν ἔτι,
οὐδὲ μὴ παίσῃ ἔτι αὐτοὺς ὁ ἥλιος οὐδὲ πᾶν καῦμα,
17. ὅτι τὸ ἀρνίον τὸ ἀνὰ μέσον τοῦ θρόνου ποιμανεῖ αὐτούς,
καὶ ὁδηγήσει αὐτοὺς ἐπὶ ζωῆς πηγὰς ὑδάτων·
καὶ ἐξαλείψει ὁ θεὸς πᾶν δάκρυον ἐκ τῶν ὀφθαλμῶν αὐτῶν.

21 (– 205). 250. 2037. 2038. 2067 al^{pm} Or^{s} vg s arm$^{2.3.4}$ bo : *μου* > A 1. 205 Pr gig Cyp arm$^{1.\alpha}$ | *ειπεν*] *λεγει* gig arm^{1} | *οι ερχομενοι*] qui venerunt Tyc Pr Cyp eth : qui veniunt gig vg arm bo | *εκ τησ θλιψεωσ τησ μεγαλησ*] *απο θλιψεωσ μεγαλησ* A | *επλυναν* Aℵ 046. 18. 35. 175. 205. 468**. 617. 620. 632**. 1934. 2020 Or^{s} Tyc gig vg Cyp s arm bo : *επλατυναν* 42*. 82. 201. 325. 337. 385. 386. 429. 452. 456. 468*. 498. 522. 632*. 919. 920. 1849. 1955. 2004. 2021. 2024. 2040 : *επλατειναν* 1 : *ελευκαναν* 2015 : > Pr | *και ελευκαναν αυτασ* > Tyc : "made them glorious" bo | *και*^{4} > 620. 866 | *αυτασ* Aℵ 025. 1. 35. 60. 93. 181. 205. 209. 432. 468. 1957. 2015. 2023. 2036. 2038. 2041. 2067 gig vg Cyp s arm^{4} bo : *αυτουσ* 2037 : > 046. **21** (– 35. 205. 468). 250 al^{mu} Or^{s} Pr arm$^{\alpha}$ |.

15. **δια τουτο**] pr *και* 046*. 2015. 2036. 2037. 2067 | *εισιν*] *ηλθον* eth | *λατρευουσιν*] *δοξαζουσιν* eth | *ο καθημενοσ*] his qui sedet Pr Cyp | *επι του θρονου* Aℵ 1. 61. 172. 205. 250. 385. 2015. 2018. 2019. 2020. 2023**. 2037. 2038. 2067 al^{mu} Or^{s} s^{1} : *επι τω θρονω* 025. 046. **21** (– 205. 2020) al^{mu} : supra sedem gig : in throno Tyc Pr vg Cyp | *σκηνωσει επ αυτουσ*] ℵ$^{c.c}$: *γινωσκει αυτουσ* ℵ* : *γινωσκει επ αυτουσ* ℵ^{c} : habitavit supra illos gig : inhabitavit super eos Cyp : habitat super eos Tyc : inhabitavit in eis Pr : "dwelleth in them" arm$^{1.2.(3).\alpha}$ |.

16. *ετι*^{1} A 025. 046. **21**. 250. 2037. 2038. 2067 al^{pl} Or^{s} gig : > ℵ 2019 Pr vg Cyp s arm$^{3.4.\alpha}$ bo sa | *ουδε*] + *μη* A 61. 69 Or^{s} | *διψησουσιν*] *διψασουσιν* ℵ 385 : *διψησωσιν* 025. 69. 2038 | *ετι*^{2} Aℵ 046. **21** (– 205. 2020). 2067 al^{pl} Or^{s} vg s^{2} arm^{2} bo : umquam Pr Cyp : > 025. 1. 141. 172. 205. 250. 424. 2018. 2019. 2020. 2037. 2038 gig s^{1} arm$^{1.3.4.\alpha}$: + "neither shall they toil" bo | *μη παισῃ ετι*] an emendation of Gwynn and Swete of *μη πεσῃ επι* Aℵ 025. 1. 35. 69. 2015. 2019. 2036 al^{p} : *ου μη πεσῃ επι* 046. **21** (– 35. 2020). 250. 2037. 2038. 2067 al^{pm} Or^{s} : *ου μη πεσηται επι* 2020 | *ο ηλιοσ*] *ο* > 2020. 2037 : "cold" arm$^{1.2.3}$: "shadow" bo | *παν* > Tyc arm : *το* 314. 2016 | *καυμα*] + patientur Pr Cyp |.

17. **ανα μεσον**] *ενωπιον* bo eth | *ποιμανει* Aℵ 025. 046. 1. 35. 61. 69. 104. 205. 314. 429. 468*. 620. 866. 2015. 2019. 2020. 2023**. 2036. 2037. 2038. 2041*. 2067. s arm sa : reget gig vg Cyp : *ποιμαινει* **21** (– 35. 205. 468*. 620. 866. 2020). 42. 82.

CHAPTER VIII.

1. Καὶ ὅταν ἤνοιξεν τὴν σφραγῖδα τὴν ἑβδόμην, ἐγένετο σιγὴ ἐν
τῷ οὐρανῷ ὡς ἡμίωρον.(*a*) 3. καὶ † ἄλλος † (*b*) ἄγγελος ἦλθεν καὶ
τοῦ θυσιασ- ἐστάθη ἐπὶ ⌜τὸ θυσιαστήριον⌝ ἔχων λιβανωτὸν χρυσοῦν, καὶ ἐδόθη
τηρίου αὐτῷ θυμιάματα πολλά, ἵνα δώσει ταῖς προσευχαῖς τῶν ἁγίων πάντων
ἐπὶ τὸ θυσιαστήριον τὸ χρυσοῦν τὸ ἐνώπιον τοῦ θρόνου. 4. καὶ ἀνέβη

(*a*) Verse **2** is restored in what appears to have been its original form after S^{6}. See vol. i. 218–222, 224.
(*b*) Read εἷς.

91. 141. 172. 201. 218. 241. 242. 250. 385. 424. 432. 498. 522. 1955. 1957. 2016. 2017. 2018. 2021. 2023*. 2024. 2039. 2041** Or^{s} : regit Pr : *περιπατει μετ αυτων* bo | *οδηγησει* Aℵ 025. 046. 1. 35. 61. 69. 205. 2015. 2019. 2020. 2036. 2037. 2038. 2067 al^{p} Or^{s} Tyc gig Cyp vg s arm bo : *οδηγει* **21** (− 35. 205. 2020). 42. 82. 91. 104. 250. 385. 429. 2016. 2017 al^{mu} Pr | *ζωησ*] *ζωσασ* 1. 2020. 2036. 2037. 2038. 2067 : *ζωην και επι* s^{1} | *πηγασ*] fontem Pr arm^{a} bo | *και εξαλειψει . . . οφθαλμων αυτων* > 2020 | *εξαλειψει*] *εξελει* 35 | *ο θεοσ* > s^{1} arm$^{2.4}$ | *παν δακρυον*] *παν δρακυον* ℵ* : *παντα τα δακρυα* 69 arm : *δακρυον* eth | *εκ των οφθαλμων* AC 025. 046. **21** (− 325. 456. 468*. 620. 866. 920. 2040). 250. 2038 al^{mu} Pr gig Cyp vg s : *απο των οφθαλμων* ℵ 61. 104. 241 325. 456. 468*. 620. 866. 920. 2015. 2023. 2024. 2036. 2037. 2040. 2067 al^{p} Or^{s} vg$^{d.v}$ |.

1. *και* > Tyc | *οταν* AC : *οτε* ℵ 025. 046. **21**. 250. 2037. 2038. 2067 al^{pl} Or^{s} | *σιγη*] *φωνη* bo | *ημιωρον* AC 337. 498. 1957 : *ημιωριον* (*ειμ-* ℵ) ℵ 025. 046. **21** (− 337. 866). 250. 2037. 2038. 2067 al^{pl} Or^{s} s : semihora Pr gig : media hora Tyc vg : *ωραν* bo |.

3. *αγγελοσ* > s^{1} | *ηλθεν*] *εξηλθεν* 69 : before *αλλοσ* arm$^{1.2}$ | *επι το θυσιαστηριον* A 025. 1. 35. 205. 2019. 2023 al^{mu} : *επι του θυσιαστηριου* ℵ 046. **21** (− 35. 205). 69. 104. 250. 314. 385. 2015. 2016. 2018. 2037. 2067 al^{mu} Or^{s} : *επι του θυσιαστηριον* C : ante altare Tyc gig vg arm^{1} eth : super altarium Dei Pr : "at the altar" arm$^{2.3.4.a}$ | *εχων*] *και ειχεν* arm$^{1.2.a}$ eth : *ειχεν* arm^{3} | *λιβανωτον*] *λιβανον το* C | *θυμιαματα*] supplicamenta Pr | *ινα δωσει* > s^{1} | *δωσει* AℵC 1. 35. 110. 172. 201. 250*. 337. 386. 632. 2015. 2037. 2038. 2040 al^{p} : *δωση* 025. 046. **21** (− 35. 325. 337. 386. 456. 632. 2040). 250**. 2067 al^{mu} Or^{s} : *δω* 69. 314. 325. 456. 2019 | *ταισ προσευχαισ*] *ταισ ευχασ* 205 : orationes gig arm$^{1.2.3.a}$: de orationibus vg$^{d.v}$: "along with the prayers" bo | *θυσιαστηριον*] + *του θεου* Pr | *το ενωπιον*] *το* > ℵ arm$^{1.2.3.a}$ |.

4. *ανεβη ο καπνοσ*] ℵ^{c} : *αναβη καπνοσ* ℵ* : *ο* > 506 : *ανεβη* > arm^{2} | *των θυμιαματων*] supplicationum Pr | *ταισ προσευχαισ*]

ὁ καπνὸς τῶν θυμιαμάτων ταῖς προσευχαῖς τῶν ἁγίων ἐκ χειρὸς τοῦ ἀγγέλου ἐνώπιον τοῦ θεοῦ. 5. καὶ εἴληφεν ὁ ἄγγελος τὸν λιβανωτόν, καὶ ἐγέμισεν αὐτὸν ἐκ τοῦ πυρὸς τοῦ θυσιαστηρίου, καὶ ἔβαλεν εἰς τὴν γῆν, καὶ ἐγένοντο † βρονταὶ καὶ ἀστραπαὶ καὶ φωναὶ † καὶ σεισμός.

2. Καὶ εἶδον † τοὺς ἑπτὰ † (*a*) ἀγγέλους (*b*) καὶ ⸀ἐδόθησαν⸀ αὐτοῖς ἐδόθη † ἑπτὰ † (*a*) σάλπιγγες. 6. καὶ οἱ † ἑπτὰ † (*a*) ἄγγελοι οἱ ἔχοντες τὰς † ἑπτὰ † (*a*) σάλπιγγας ἡτοίμασαν αὐτοὺς ἵνα σαλπίσωσι.

(*a*) Read τρεῖς in the first two cases after the noun but without change of order in the next two. See vol. i. 218–223.

(*b*) The interpolator of viii. 7–12, to whom the changes in the text are due, added here οἱ ἐνώπιον τοῦ θεοῦ ἑστήκασιν. This termination—ασιν—of the perfect does not occur elsewhere in our author, who uses -αν.

orationum Pr s² arm⁴ bo : de orationibus gig vg : συν τ. προσευχαισ eth | χειροσ] χειρων arm^{1. 2. 3. a} | του αγγελου] του > 498. 2020 : των αγγελων 69*. 205 arm^{2. a} : του αρχαγγελου arm¹ | ενωπιον > arm¹ : pr του bo | του θεου > arm^{1. 4} |.

5. ειληφεν] εγεμισεν arm^{1. 2. 3. a} | τον λιβανωτον] το λιβανωτον 104. 141. 205. 218. 424. 2019. 2024 | και εγεμ. αυτον > eth | αυτον] αυτο 104. 205. 218. 424 | του θυσιαστηριου] + του θεου Pr : pr του επι s¹ : "of Gehenna" arm² | εβαλεν ℵ 046. **21** Or^s Pr gig vg s arm bo eth : εβαλλεν 025 : ελαβον A | βρονται κ. αστραπαι κ. φωναι A 336. 2020 s^{2 (d. l. p)} : βρονται κ. φωναι κ. αστραπαι ℵ 046. **21** (– 35. 2020). 69. 110. 172. 250. 314. 385. 2016. 2018 al^p Or^s Pr gig vg s¹ bo eth : φωναι κ. βρονται κ. αστραπαι 025. 1. 35. 2037. 2067 al^{mu} Tyc arm⁴ : φωναι κ. αστραπαι κ. βρονται 104. 2038 : The order of all the MSS is corrupt. We should expect αστραπαι first, since not only in point of fact the lightning is seen before the thunder is heard, but also because this order is preserved always elsewhere in our author: cf. 4⁵ 11¹⁹ 16¹⁸. St. John is an observer of nature, and was not guilty of this blunder. It is due to the interpolator of 8^{7-12}. The original order was αστρ. και φωναι και βρονται as in 4⁵ 11¹⁹ 16¹⁸. The hopeless order of A—βροντ. κ. αστρ. κ. φων.—is most probably due to the interpolator. The readings of ℵ 046 Pr vg s¹, of 025 Tyc, are obvious attempts at correction. | και σεισμοσ > 242. 617. 1934 : σεισμοι 209 Or^s arm^{2. 3} : + μεγασ vg^v arm^{1. a} : + εγενετο μεγασ vg^g |.

2. τουσ επτα > 1. 506 : τουσ > 205 | του θεου > arm¹ : του θρονου 620. 866 arm⁴ | εστηκασιν AℵC 025. 046. **21** (– 35. 325. 456. 468. 2020) Or^s : ειστηκεισαν 35. 468. 2020 s : εστηκεσαν 42. 314. 325. 456. 517 : stabant gig : stant Tyc eth : stantes Pr vg bo | εδοθησαν ℵC 025. 046. **21** (– 18. 919. 920. 1849. 2004. 2040) Or^s Pr gig vg s bo : εδοθη A 18. 172. 919. 920. 1849. 1955. 2004. 2018. 2040. 2041 arm : qui acceperunt Tyc | σαλπιγγεσ] + ινα σαλπισωσι 920. 2040 : tubas Tyc |.

6. οι εχοντεσ A 025. 046. **21** (– 468*. 620. 866). 250. 2037.

13. *καὶ εἶδον καὶ ἤκουσα ἑνὸς ἀετοῦ πετομένου ἐν μεσουρανήματι λέγοντος φωνῇ μεγάλῃ Οὐαί οὐαί οὐαὶ τοῖς κατοικοῦσιν ἐπὶ τῆς γῆς ἐκ τῶν [λοιπῶν] φωνῶν τῆς σάλπιγγος τῶν τριῶν ἀγγέλων τῶν μελλόντων σαλπίζειν.*

[7. Καὶ ὁ *πρῶτος ἐσάλπισεν·*

καὶ ἐγένετο χάλαζα καὶ πῦρ μεμιγμένα ἐν αἵματι,
καὶ ἐβλήθη εἰς τὴν γῆν.
καὶ τὸ τρίτον τῆς γῆς κατεκάη,
καὶ τὸ τρίτον τῶν δένδρων κατεκάη,
καὶ πᾶς χόρτος χλωρὸς κατεκάη.

8. Καὶ ὁ *δεύτερος ἄγγελος ἐσάλπισεν·*

2067 al[pl] s arm[1. 2. 3. a] bo eth : *οι* > ℵ 468*. 620. 866. 2019. 2038 Or[s] arm[4] | *ταο* >arm[a] | *αυτουσ* Aℵ* : *εαυτουσ* ℵ[c] 025. 046. **21**. 250 2037. 2038. 2067 al[pl] Or[s] s[1. 2] bo : *επ αυτουσ* 69 | *σαλπισωσι*] + *τουσ σαλπιγγασ* arm[1. 3] : + *τουσ επτα σαλπιγγασ* arm[2] |.

13. **και** *ειδον* >s[1] eth | *ηκουσα*] + *φωνην* Tyc vg arm[1. 2. a] *ενοσ* >ℵ 025 arm bo sa | *αετου* Aℵ 046. **21** (– 205. 468. 620. 632. 866) 250 al[mu] Or[s] Tyc gig fl s arm[1. 2. 3. 4] bo eth : ut aquilam Pr : *αγγελου* 025. 1. 104. 205. 241. 468. 620. 632. 866. 2015. 2019. 2036. 2037. 2038. 2067 arm[a] | *πετομενου* > bo | *εν μεσουρανηματι*] *εν μεσουρανισματι* 1 : in medio caeli et terrae eth | *λεγοντοσ*] et dicentem Tyc eth | *φωνη μεγαλη*] + *τρισ* 104. 432. 2015. 2023. 2036. 2037. 2041 : *φωνη τρισ* 35. 2019 : *φων. μεγ.* before *λεγοντοσ* gig fl : >Tyc s[1] | *ουαι*] twice only 1. 2038 eth | *τοισ κατοικουσιν* A 025. 1. 35. 104. 205. 2037. 2038. 2067 al[mu] : *τουσ κατοικουντασ* ℵ 046. **21** (– 35. 205). 61. 69. 110. 172. 242. 250. 314. 385. 2016. 2018 al[mu] Or[s] | *εκ των λοιπων φωνων τησ σαλπιγγοσ*] *εκ τησ φωνησ των σαλπιγγων* s[1] : *εκ τ. φωνησ τ. λοιπων σαλπιγγων* s[2] : *φωνων τησ σαλπιγγοσ* > Pr |.

7. **ο** *πρωτοσ* Aℵ 025. 046. **21** (– 2020) al[pm] Or[s] s arm[4] : + *αγγελοσ* 1. 250. 522. 2015. 2019. 2020. 2036. 2037. 2038. 2067 Tyc Pr gig vg arm[1. 2. 3. a] bo eth | *και*[3] >Tyc | *μεμιγμενα* A 046. **21** (– 205. 2020). 250. 2037 al[pl] Or[s] Pr gig vg s : *μεμιγμενον* ℵ 025. 181. 205. 209. 432. 2020. 2038. 2067 Tyc | *εν αιματι*] *εν* >1. 2038 al[p] : *υδατι* 205 s[1. 2] : *εισ αιμα* Pr gig | *εβληθη*] *εβληθησαν* 172. 250. 424. 2018 s[1. 2] | *και το τριτον τησ γησ κατεκαη* >1. 2018 arm[1. 4] | *τριτον*[1]] *δευτερον* arm[2. 3] | *κατεκαη*[1. 2. 3]] *κατεκαυσαν* fl : *κατεκαυσεν* arm[2. 3. a] | *και το τριτον των δενδρων κατεκαη* >046*. 175. 456 al[p] gig arm[3. a] : *και κατεκαη παν δενδρον* eth | *τριτον*[2]] *δευτερον* arm[2] | *κατεκαη*[2] >Tyc arm[2. 3] bo | *και πασ χορτοσ χλωροσ κατεκαη* > arm[a] | *χορτοσ χλωροσ*] *ο χορτ. ο χλωροσ* 104. 201. 386 : *παντα χορτον χλωρον* arm[1. 2. 3] bo | *χλωροσ*] *τησ γησ* s[1] | *κατεκαη*[3] > eth |.

8. **αγγελοσ** >ℵ s[1] | *ωσ*] pr *εγενετο* 920. 2040 s[1] | *πυρι* Aℵ

καὶ ὡς ὄρος μέγα πυρὶ καιόμενον ἐβλήθη εἰς τὴν θάλασσαν,
καὶ ἐγένετο τὸ τρίτον τῆς θαλάσσης αἷμα,
9. καὶ ἀπέθανεν τὸ τρίτον τῶν κτισμάτων τῶν ἐν τῇ θαλάσσῃ τὰ ἔχοντα ψυχάς,
καὶ τὸ τρίτον τῶν πλοίων διεφθάρησαν.
10. Καὶ ὁ τρίτος ἄγγελος ἐσάλπισεν·
καὶ ἔπεσεν ἐκ τοῦ οὐρανοῦ ἀστὴρ μέγας καιόμενος ὡς λαμπάς,
καὶ ἔπεσεν ἐπὶ τὸ τρίτον τῶν ποταμῶν καὶ † ἐπὶ τὰς πηγὰς ⸆ τῶν ὑδάτων,
11. [καὶ τὸ ὄνομα τοῦ ἀστέρος λέγεται ὁ Ἄψινθος]
καὶ ἐγένετο τὸ τρίτον τῶν ὑδάτων ὡς ἄψινθος,
καὶ πολλοὶ τῶν ἀνθρώπων ἀπέθανον ἐκ τῶν ὑδάτων ὅτι ἐπικράνθησαν.

025. 1. 35*. 205. 250. 2020. 2037. 2038. 2067 al^{mu} Or^{s} Tyc Pr gig fl vg s^{2} arm$^{2.4}$: πυροσ bo : >046. **21** (−35*. 205. 2020) al^{pm} s^{1} arm$^{1.3.a}$ | εβληθη] επεσεν s^{1} arm | ωσ οροσ μεγα πυρι] πυρ μεγα ωσ οροσ eth | εγενετο] εγενηθη ℵ | τριτον] δευτερον arm^{2} | αιμα] in sanguinem Pr |.

9. το τριτον^{1}] + μεροσ ℵ 172. 250. 424. 2018. 2019 Pr gig fl vg bo sa eth : το δευτερον arm$^{2.3}$ | των κτισματων] piscium Pr : animalium fl arm^{4} : creaturae vg : pr παντων s$^{1.2}$ bo | των εν τη θαλασση Aℵ 025. 205. 250. 2020. 2037 al^{mu} Or^{s} fl s bo eth : >1. 181 Pr vg : των >046. **21** (−205. 2020). 2038. 2067 al^{mu} : eorum quae in mari creata sunt gig | τα εχοντα ψυχασ] τα εχοντα ψυχην (+ζωησ bo sa eth) ℵ bo sa eth : τα εχοντα τασ ψυχασ 42. 242. 468 : των εχοντων τασ ψυχασ 35* : το εχον ψυχην s^{1} : habentium animas Tyc : >Pr fl | διεφθαρησαν Aℵ 025. (1). 35. 42. 60. 181. 432. 1957. 2015. 2023. 2036. 2037**. 2041 s^{2} arm$^{1.2}$: διεφθαρη 046. **21** (−35. 205). 250. 2038. 2067 al^{pl} Or^{s} s^{1} arm$^{3.a}$: εφθαρη 205 : corruperunt Tyc : periit Pr : interiit gig fl vg |.

10. αγγελοσ >s^{1} | λαμπασ] πυρ eth : +πυροσ bo | και επεσεν^{2} >Pr fl | τριτον] + μεροσ 2019 Pr fl vg bo sa eth | και επι τασ πηγασ των υδατων >A : υδατοσ bo sa |.

11. του αστεροσ] + τουτου Tyc | λεγεται] ελεγετο 104 arm^{4} | ο Αψινθοσ A 025. 046. **21** (−2020). 250 al^{pm} Or^{s} s : ο >ℵ* et c. 1. 69. 104. 2019. 2020. 2037. 2038. 2067 al^{p} | αψινθοσ] ℵ^{c} : αψινθιον ℵ* (+και λεγεται ℵ* del ℵ^{c}) bo : αψινθωσ 2067 : absintium Tyc : absintus Pr : absinthius gig vg$^{a.d.v}$: absentius vg^{f} : absinthus vg^{g} : habsintus vg^{c} : absentium fl : "bitterness" arm$^{1.2.3.a}$: "wormwood" arm^{4} | τριτον] + μεροσ Or^{s} Pr fl gig vg bo eth | εγενετο] γινεται 1. 2019. 2038 al^{p} | ωσ αψινθοσ (-ον Or^{s}) 2038 Or^{s} : sicut absintium (alloe bo) Pr gig vg s^{1} bo sa : quasi absentium fl : εισ αψινθον A 025. 046. **21** (−620. 866. 1934). 250. 2067 al^{pl} s^{2} : εισ αψινθιον ℵ 104. 110. 336. 620. 866. 1934. 2015. 2023. 2036. 2037 gig vg : "bitter" arm^{3} : "into blood

12. Καὶ ὁ τέταρτος ἄγγελος ἐσάλπισεν·
καὶ ἐπλήγη τὸ τρίτον τοῦ ἡλίου
καὶ τὸ τρίτον τῆς σελήνης καὶ τὸ τρίτον τῶν ἀστέρων,
ἵνα σκοτισθῇ τὸ τρίτον αὐτῶν
καὶ † ἡ ἡμέρα μὴ φάνῃ τὸ τρίτον αὐτῆς καὶ ἡ νὺξ † ὁμοίως.]

into wormwood" arm⁴ | εκ των υδατων οτι επικρανθησαν] (ab) amaritudine aquarum (Pr) fl arm[1. 2. a] eth : οτι επικρανθησαν τα υδατα s[1] | εκ των] επι των A |.

12. αγγελοσ > s[1] | επληγη] επληξε arm[1. 2. 3. a] : + και εσκοτισθη eth | το τριτον του ηλιου και > 1934 | τριτον] + μεροσ (thrice in this verse) Pr fl gig vg bo sa eth | και το τριτον τησ σεληνησ > fl | ινα σκοτισθη το τριτον αυτων] + και εσκοτισθησαν s[2] : και εσκοτισθη (– θησαν s[1]) το τριτον αυτων 172. 250. 2018 s[1] arm[1. 3. 4. a] : και εσκοτισθη arm[2] : ινα σκοτισθωσι bo : ut minus lucerent Pr : ινα σκοτ. τ. τριτον αυτων και > eth | η ημερα . . . νυξ] text corrupt : bo alone (και το τρ. αυτων μη φανη ημερασ και ομοιωσ νυκτοσ) either preserves or recovers original sense. Pr fl and eth attempt to recover it. See below. Evidence as follows. η ημερα μη φανη το τριτον (τεταρτον A) αυτησ Aℵ 025. 35. 2037. 2038. 2067 al[mu] Or[s] : και το τριτον αυτησ μη φανη η (> 046. 522) ημερα 046. 175. 325. 337. 456. 468. 617. 620. 866. 1934 al[pm] ; (αυτων for αυτησ 18. 69. 141. 385. 429. 522. 632. 919. 1849. 1955. 2004. 2015. 2024 : αυτοισ for αυτησ 386 : αυτησ > 920. 2040 : το τριτον αυτησ > 2020) : et dies eandem partem amitteret Pr fl : et dies non luceat terciam partem gig : et diei non luceret pars tertia vg : και η ημερα ουκ εφαινε το τριτον αυτησ s[1] : και η ημερα ουκ εφανη και το τριτον arm[1] : "and the third part of them had not light and day" arm[3] : μη φαινωσιν και το τριτον ημερασ και νυκτοσ eth | η νυξ] nocte vg[f. v] : noctis vg[d] bo eth |.

Chapter IX.

< πρῶτος >

1. Καὶ ὁ † πέμπτος † ἄγγελος ἐσάλπισεν·
καὶ εἶδον ἀστέρα ἐκ τοῦ οὐρανοῦ πεπτωκότα εἰς τὴν γῆν,
καὶ ἐδόθη αὐτῷ ἡ κλεὶς τοῦ φρέατος τῆς ἀβύσσου·

1. και . . . εσαλπισεν > 1849 | και ειδον > eth | αστερα . . . πεπτωκοτα] ℵ[c] : αστερασ . . . πεπτωκοτασ ℵ* | αστερα εκ του ουρανου πεπτωκοτα] αστερα πεπτωκ. εκ του ουρ. 920. 2040 arm⁴ : εκ του ουρ. αστ. πεπτ. gig | εισ την γην] επι τησ γησ 498. 2020 s[1] bo sa : προσ την γην 385 | εδοθη] εδωκαν bo | η κλεισ] τασ κλειδασ bo eth | του φρεατοσ] των φρεατων s[1] | τησ αβυσσου > gig |.

2. καὶ ἤνοιξεν τὸ φρέαρ τῆς ἀβύσσου,
καὶ ἀνέβη καπνὸς ἐκ τοῦ φρέατος
ὡς καπνὸς καμίνου μεγάλης,
καὶ ἐσκοτώθη ὁ ἥλιος καὶ ὁ ἀὴρ ἐκ τοῦ καπνοῦ τοῦ φρέατος.

3. καὶ ἐκ τοῦ καπνοῦ ἐξῆλθον ἀκρίδες εἰς τὴν γῆν,
καὶ ἐδόθη αὐταῖς ἐξουσία ὡς ἔχουσιν ἐξουσίαν οἱ σκορπίοι τῆς γῆς.

4. καὶ ἐρρέθη αὐταῖς ἵνα μὴ ἀδικήσουσιν τὸν χόρτον τῆς γῆς
οὐδὲ πᾶν χλωρὸν οὐδὲ πᾶν δένδρον, εἰ μὴ τοὺς ἀνθρώπους
οἵτινες οὐκ ἔχουσιν τὴν σφραγῖδα τοῦ θεοῦ ἐπὶ τῶν μετώπων.

2. **και ηνοιξεν το φρεαρ τησ αβυσσου** A 025. 1. 35. 104. 172. 241. 250. 620. 632. 866. 1957. 2015. 2019. 2020. 2023. 2036. 2037. 2041. 2067 al^{p} Or^{s} Tyc Pr gig fl vg s^{2} arm$^{1.4}$: > ℵ 046. **21** (– 35. 620. 632. 866. 2020). 2038 al^{mu} vg$^{a.d}$ s^{1} arm$^{2.3.a}$ bo eth | και ανεβη] de quo ascendit Pr | καπνοσ εκ του φρεατοσ ωσ > 1. 172. 325. 456. 2018. 2021 | εκ] ℵ^{c} : επι ℵ* | του φρεατοσ] των φρεατων s^{1} | ωσ καπνοσ] ωσ > A : ωσ εκ Pr fl | καπνοσ] ℵ^{c} : καμινοσ ℵ* | μεγαλησ Aℵ 025. 1. 35. 205. 2015. 2036. 2037. 2038. 2067 al^{mu} Tyc Pr vg fl arm$^{1.2.3.a}$ bo eth : καιομενησ 046. **21** (– 35. 205. 2020). 250 al^{mu} Or^{s} s^{2} : μεγαλησ καιομενησ 141. 432. 452. 2019. 2020 (μεγαλου). 2021 gig s^{1} arm^{4} | και^{3}] οσ Pr fl | εσκοτωθη A 61. 69. 181. 2038 : εσκοτισθη ℵ 025. 046. **21.** 250. 2037. 2067 al^{pl} Or^{s} : tenebris obscuravit Pr fl | αηρ] αστηρ 205 | εκ του καπνου του φρεατοσ και > ℵ* (but not ℵ^{c}) Pr fl arm$^{1.2.a}$ | του φρεατοσ] των φρεατων s^{1} : τησ καμινου arm^{3} |.

3. **καπνου**] + του φρεατοσ Tyc vg$^{f.v}$: φρεατοσ arm$^{1.a}$ | εισ] επι arm bo | αυταισ A 025. **21.** 250. 2037. 2038. 2067 al^{pl} Or^{s} : αυτοισ ℵ 046. 104 | εξουσια] + και τα κεντρα αυτων arm^{1} | ωσ εχουσιν εξουσιαν] similis eam quae habent fl : ην εχουσιν s^{1} : ωσ κεντρα σκορπιου arm$^{1.2.a}$: ινα γενωνται ωσ eth | τησ γησ] pr επι s^{2} arm^{3} bo eth : > arm$^{1.2.a}$ |.

4. **ερρεθη** Aℵ 025. **21** (– 35*). 2037. 2038. 2067 al^{pl} Or^{s} : ερρηθη 046. 172. 250. 2018. 2024 : ερεθη 35* | αυταισ A 025. **21** (– 18. 919. 2004). 250. 2037. 2038. 2067 al^{pl} Or^{s} : αυτοισ ℵ 046. 18. 61. 69. 172. 919. 2004. 2039 | αδικησουσιν A 2019 : αδικησωσιν ℵ 025. 046. **21.** 250. 2037. 2038. 2067 al^{pl} Or^{s} Tyc Pr gig fl vg | ουδε παν χλωρον] > ℵ* (ℵ^{c} wrote χλω above δενδρον) Tyc arm : μηδε παν χλωρον 2020 : και παν χλωρον s^{1} | χλωρον . . . δενδρον] ~ bo | παν δενδρον] δενδρα s^{1} : παν > arm^{1} : παντα δενδρα arm$^{2.3.4.a}$ | ει μη τουσ ανθρωπουσ] + μονουσ 1957. 2023. 2041 al^{p} : nisi tantum homines vg arm | σφραγιδα] σφραγιδαν ℵ 82. 866 | του θεου] > 1. 35. 181. 241. 2015. 2036. 2037. 2067 : του Χριστου arm^{1} | μετωπων Aℵ 025. 1. 181. 2015. 2036. 2037. 2038 gig vg$^{a.c.d}$: + αυτων 046. **21.** 250. 2067 al^{pl} Pr vg. fl s arm$^{1.2.4}$ eth |.

5. καὶ ἐδόθη αὐταῖς ἵνα μὴ ἀποκτείνωσιν αὐτούς,
ἀλλ' ἵνα βασανισθήσονται μῆνας πέντε.(a)
6. καὶ ἐν ταῖς ἡμέραις ἐκείναις ζητήσουσιν οἱ ἄνθρωποι τὸν θάνατον
εὑρήσουσιν καὶ οὐ μὴ ⌜εὕρωσιν⌝ αὐτόν,
καὶ ἐπιθυμήσουσιν ἀποθανεῖν
καὶ φεύγει ὁ θάνατος ἀπ' αὐτῶν.
ὅμοιοι 7. καὶ τὰ ὁμοιώματα τῶν ἀκρίδων ⌜ὅμοια⌝ ἵπποις ἡτοιμασμένοις εἰς πόλεμον,
καὶ ἐπὶ τὰς κεφαλὰς αὐτῶν ὡς στέφανοι ὅμοιοι χρυσῷ,
καὶ τὰ πρόσωπα αὐτῶν ὡς πρόσωπα ἀνθρώπων.

(*a*) Text adds gloss: *καὶ ὁ βασανισμὸς αὐτῶν ὡς βασανισμὸς σκορπίου ὅταν παίσῃ ἄνθρωπον.*

5. και εδοθη] et dictum est Pr eth : dictum est fl | *αυταισ* 025. 046. **21** (– 2004). 250. 2037. 2038. 2067 al^{pl} Or^{s} : *αυτοισ* Aℵ 1. 104. 181. 2004 | *αποκτεινωσιν*] *αδικησωσιν* 920. 2040 | *ινα*^{2} > s^{1} | *βασανισθησονται* Aℵ 025. 1. 35. 181. 2019. 2020. 2038 : *βασανισθωσι* 046. **21** (– 35. 2020). 250. 2037. 2067 al^{pl} Or^{s} : cruciarentur Pr (gig) vg fl : cruciarent Tyc arm bo eth | *αυτων ωσ βασανισμοσ* > 149 | *παιση* **21** (– 149. 468*. 620. 866. 920. 2020) Or^{s} Tyc gig fl vg s^{2} arm : *πεση* Aℵ 025. 046. 104. 149. 172. 620. 866. 920. 2020. 2038 al^{mu} : *πεση επ.* s^{1} : *πληξη* 60. 432. 452. 506. 2021. 2022. 2023. 2041** : *δακη* 367. 468* bo sa eth |.

6. *εν ταισ ημεραισ εκειναισ* > Tyc : *εν τη ημερα εκεινη* arm^{1} | *ζητησουσιν*] *ζητουσιν* 60. 82. 93. 110. 175. 325. 452. 456. 468. 517. 1957. 2024. 2041 | *οι ανθρωποι* > Pr | *ευρωσιν* A 025. 35. 172. 181. 205. 209. 250. 424. 2015. 2018. 2023. 2036. 2037 : *ευρησουσιν* ℵ 046. **21** (– 35. 205. 325. 337. 456. 468. 620. 866. 1849). 104. 110. 201. 241. 242. 314. 385. 429. 498. 522. 1957. 2017. 2019. 2024. 2041. 2067 al^{mu} Or^{s} gig fl vg : *ευρησωσιν* 1. 61. 69. 82. 325. 337. 456. 468. 517. 620. 866. 1849 : *ευρουσιν* 2038 : inveniunt Pr | *αποθανειν*] *τον θανατον* 104 | *φευγει* A 025. 1. 35. 181. 2019. 2020. 2067 : *φυγη* ℵ : *φευξεται* 046. **21** (– 35. 2020). 250. 2037. 2067 al^{pl} Or^{s} Pr gig fl vg s arm bo eth | *ο θανατοσ απ αυτων* Aℵ 025. 1. 35. 205. 2015 (> *απ*). 2019. 2020. 2036. 2037. 2067 al^{mu} Pr gig fl vg s arm^{4} : *απ αυτων ο θανατοσ* 046. **21** (– 35. 205. 2020). 250. 2038 al^{mu} Or^{s} arm$^{1.2.3.a}$: *ο θανατοσ* > 104 |.

7. τα ομοιωματα] *το ομοιωμα* gig s arm$^{1.2.3.a}$ bo | *ομοια* 025. 046. **21**. 250. 2037. 2038. 2067 al^{pl} Pr vg : *ομοιοι* ℵ (s) : *ομοιω ματα* A : *ομοιωμα* Or^{s} arm$^{1.2.a}$: *ομοιον* arm^{3} : similes erant fl arm^{4} | *αυτων*] + *ομοιωμα* Or^{s} | *ομοιοι χρυσω* Aℵ 025. 1. 35. 172. 205. 250. 429.^{mg} 2015. 2018. 2019. 2036. 2037. 2038. 2067 al^{p}

8. καὶ εἶχαν τρίχας ὡς τρίχας γυναικῶν,
καὶ οἱ ὀδόντες αὐτῶν ὡς λεόντων ἦσαν,

9. καὶ ἶχαν θώρακας ὡς θώρακας σιδηροῦς,
καὶ ἡ φωνὴ τῶν πτερύγων αὐτῶν ὡς φωνὴ ἁρμάτων,
ἵππων πολλῶν τρεχόντων εἰς πόλεμον.

10. καὶ ἔχουσιν οὐρὰς ὁμοίας σκορπίοις καὶ κέντρα,
καὶ ἐν ταῖς οὐραῖς αὐτῶν ἡ ἐξουσία αὐτῶν
ἀδικῆσαι τοὺς ἀνθρώπους μῆνας πέντε.

11. ἔχουσιν ἐπ' αὐτῶν βασιλέα τὸν ἄγγελον τῆς ἀβύσσου,
ὄνομα αὐτῷ Ἑβραϊστὶ Ἀβαδδών.(a)

(a) Text adds gloss: *καὶ ἐν τῇ Ἑλληνικῇ ὄνομα ἔχει Ἀπολλύων.*
Observe below how Pr fl vg add et Latine habet nomen Exterminans—a fact which shows how glosses arise.

Or^{s} Tyc Pr gig fl vg s (arm): "of colour of gold" bo: χρυσοι 046. **21** (− 35. 205) al^{pm} | και τα προσωπα . . . ανθρωπων > arm^{2} |.

8. ειχαν Aℵ: ειχον 025. 046. **21.** 250. 2037. 2067 al^{pl} Or^{s}: εχοντεσ 2038 Pr fl: > arm$^{1. 2. 3. a}$ | τριχασ^{1}] και αι τριχεσ αυτων (> arm^{3}) arm$^{1. 2. 3. a}$ | τριχασ^{2} > 2020 fl: τριχεσ arm$^{1. 2. 3. a}$ | γυναικων] γυναικοσ arm$^{1. 2. 3. a}$: ut mulieres fl | ωσ^{2}] + οδοντεσ fl vg^{d} | λεοντων] λεοντοσ arm$^{1. 2. a}$ | ησαν > fl s^{1} arm |.

9. και ειχαν . . . σιδηρουσ > 920. 2040 | θωρακασ^{1} > 2020: pectora Pr | ωσ θωρακασ > 18. 919. 1849. 2004 gig | φωνη^{2} > Pr fl arm^{2} | ιππων] pr και 337. 468: > 325. 456. 620. 866 | πολλων > bo | τρεχοντων] ητοιμασμενων bo |.

10. και εχουσιν] και ειχον 2020. 2067 Tyc Pr vg arm$^{1. 2. 3. 4}$: > fl | ουρασ ομοιασ] ουραι ομοιαι fl: ομοιωμα arm^{4} | ομοιασ 025. 046. **21** (− 35. 617). 250. 2037. 2038. 2067 al^{pl} Or^{s} Tyc Pr gig vg s arm$^{1. 2. 3}$ bo: ομοιαισ 617: ομοιοισ Aℵ 69: ομοιωσ 35 | σκορπιοισ] σκορπιω s^{1} arm$^{1. 2. 3. a}$: σκορπιων vg: σκορπιων ησαν fl | κεντρα και εν Aℵ 025. 046. **21** (− 18. 205. 2020) al^{pm} Or^{s} s^{2} arm$^{3. 4}$ bo: κεντροισ και εν Pr fl: κεντρα ην εν vg$^{f. v}$: κεντρα (δε) εν s^{1}: και > 1. 18. 61. 104. 141. 172. 205. 209. 241. 250. 424. 2015. 2018. 2019. 2020. 2036. 2037. 2038. 2039. 2067 Tyc gig vg eth: και εν > arm^{1}: κεντρον (και arm^{2}) εν arm$^{2. a}$ | η εξουσια αυτων Aℵ 025. 35. 172. 205. 209. 250. 424. 2018 al^{p} gig vg bo: pr και 1. 2019. 2038. 2067 Or^{s} (Pr fl) vg^{d} s^{1}: εξουσιαν εχουσιν 046. **21** (− 18. 35. 205). 69. 110. 201. 242. 314. 385. 429. 498. 522. 1955. 1957. 2015. 2016. 2017. 2023. 2024. 2037 al^{mu} s^{2} (pr και 241. 2036): (και) εξουσιαν ειχον arm$^{1. (a)}$: εξουσιαν εχουσαι 18. 61. 2039: > 104 eth | αδικησαι Aℵ 025. 1. 35. 172. 175. 205. 242. 250. 314. 617. 1934. 2015. 2017. 2018. 2019. 2036. 2037. 2038. 2067 al^{p} Or^{s}: pr του 046. **21** (− 35. 175. 205. 617. 1934) al^{mu} | πεντε] sex Pr |.

11. εχουσιν Aℵ 205. 314: pr και 025. 1. 250. 2037. 2038 al Or^{s} gig s: και ειχον 2067 Pr fl vg arm$^{4. a}$: εχουσαι 046. **21** (− 205)

12. Ἡ οὐαὶ ἡ μία ἀπῆλθεν· ἰδοὺ ἔρχεται ἔτι δύο οὐαὶ μετὰ ταῦτα.

al^mu Tyc | επ αυτων βασιλεα A 025. (025* adds in mg. but writes αυτον). 1. 35. 61. 69. 205. 2015. 2036. 2037. 2038. 2067. Tyc Pr gig vg s¹ : επ αυτων βασιλεισ 2019 : εαυτων τον βασιλεα ℵ arm⁴ : βασιλεα επ αυτων 046. **21** (−35. 205). 250 al^mu Or^s s² arm^a : βασιλεα επ αυτον 18. : 72. 452 (επ αυτουσ 104 : υπ αυτων 336) : | βασιλεα] + τον αρχοντα A : > fl | τον αγγελον τησ αβυσσου] τησ αβυσσου τον αγγελον A | τον αγγελον Aℵ 025. 1. 35. 69. 104. 205. 632**. 2015. 2019. 2020. 2036. 2037. 2038. 2067 al^mu Or^s arm^a bo : τον > 046. **21** (−35. 205. 632**. 2020). 250 al^mu | ονομα αυτω] pr ω ℵ : ω ονομα 94 Tyc Pr fl (+est) vg : ονομα αυτου 2067 | αβαδδων Aℵ 025 al^p Tyc vg s¹ : αββααδδων 046. 325. 429. 456. 468. 517. 620. 632. 919. 1849. 1955. 2004 : αββααδων 172. 250. 920. 2018. 2040 : αβααδδων 42. 82. 93. 110. 337. 452. 506. 2020. 2021. 2024 al^p : αββαδων 1. 18. 35. 60. 91. 175. 181. 201. 314. 386. 617. 1934. 2015. 2016. 2023. 2036. 2037. 2038. 2067 Or^s gig arm³ : αββαδδων 2019. 2041 : αβλαδδων 61. 69 : armageddon Pr : ababdon fl : albagos arm^{1. (2)} : nabathdon arm⁴ : magedon bo | και εν τη Aℵ 025. 1. 35. 205. 314. 2019. 2038 al^p gig s¹ : εν δε τη 046. **21** (−35. 205. 325. 456. 468*. 620. 866. 920). 250. 2037. 2067 al^pm Or^s s² : εν τη ελληνικη δε 325. 456. 468*. 620. 866 : εν τη δε τη 920 : graece autem Tyc vg : graeca autem lingua Pr : graeca lingua fl : "who is called in" arm^{1. 2. 3} | ελληνικη] ελληνιδι ℵ 205 : + ρησει 2020. 2067 : συριακη s¹ : "Armenian" arm^{1. 2} | ονομα εχει] ∼ ℵ 2019 gig : ονομα εχων 522 : "is called" arm^{1. 2. 3} : > Pr vg arm^{4. a} eth | απολλυων] pr ο 2038 bo : απολυων 522. 2023* : apolion Tyc : apollion Pr : perdens gig : apollyon fl arm^{3. a} : "destruction" arm^{1. 2} : "destroyer" arm⁴ : + latine perdens Tyc : + et latina lingua nomen habens exterminans Pr fl (vg) : + "who is called destruction in Armenian" arm^{1. 2. 3} |.

12. η ουαι η μια] ουαι μια ℵ* : ουαι η μια ℵ^c : pr ιδου arm | απηλθεν] παρηλθεν 2015. 2036. 2037 arm^{1. 2. 3. a} | ιδου] pr και Tyc Pr fl vg^{c. g. v} : > arm^{1. 2. 3. a} eth | ερχεται Aℵ* **21** (−632**. 2020). 69. 104. 110. 385. 429. 2016. 2023* al^mu Or^s s² arm¹ bo : ερχονται ℵ^c 025. 046. 1. 172. 250. 632**. 2015. 2017. 2018. 2019. 2020. 2036. 2037. 2038. 2067 vg s¹ : secuntur Pr : venient Tyc | ετι] αι 432. 2019. 2037. 2038 : ετι και αι 241 : alii Pr : alia gig : > 1. 104. 498. 2023. 2067 Tyc fl bo eth | δυο] δευτερα 104 : secundum fl arm^{1. 4} bo | μετα ταυτα. και A 025. 1. 35. 172. 205. 250. 632**. 2015. 2020. 2023. 2037. 2038. 2067 al^mu Or^s gig vg s² : also Pr eth but > μετα ταυτα : και μετα ταυτα 046. 69 Tyc : μετα ταυτα και (> και ℵ 469 s¹ bo sa) are joined to ver. 13 by ℵ **21** (−35. 205. 632**. 2020). 110. 241. 242. 385. 469. 2016. 2024. 2039 al^mu s¹ bo sa |.

13. Καὶ ὁ † ἕκτος † ἄγγελος ἐσάλπισεν· <δεύτε-ρος>
καὶ ἤκουσα φωνὴν μίαν ἐκ τῶν κεράτων τοῦ θυσιαστηρίου τοῦ
χρυσοῦ τοῦ ἐνώπιον τοῦ θεοῦ,
14. λέγοντα τῷ † ἕκτῳ † ἀγγέλῳ, ὁ ἔχων τὴν σάλπιγγα <δευτέ-ρῳ>
Λῦσον τοὺς τέσσαρας ἀγγέλους τοὺς δεδεμένους ἐπὶ τῷ ποταμῷ
τῷ μεγάλῳ Εὐφράτῃ.

15. καὶ ἐλύθησαν οἱ τέσσαρες ἄγγελοι
οἱ ἡτοιμασμένοι εἰς τὴν ὥραν καὶ ἡμέραν καὶ μῆνα καὶ
ἐνιαυτόν,
ἵνα ἀποκτείνωσιν τὸ τρίτον τῶν ἀνθρώπων.
16. καὶ ὁ ἀριθμὸς τῶν στρατευμάτων τοῦ ἱππικοῦ δὶς μυριάδες
μυριάδων.

13. και >א (see above) | φωνην μιαν]~69 Or^{s} : φωνησ μιασ א^{c} 2067 : μιαν >א* 2020 arm$^{1.2.3.a}$ bo : φωνην μεγαλην 172. 250. 424. 2018 : vocem, unum vg : unum Tyc Pr gig Cyp | μιαν εκ των κερατων >א* (μιασ εκ των κερατων א^{c}) | κερατων Aא^{c} 2015. 2036 gig vg s^{2} bo sa eth : pr τεσσαρων 025. 046. **21**. 250. 2037. 2038. 2067 al^{pl} Or^{s} Tyc Pr (Cyp) s^{1} arm : ζωων arm$^{2.a}$ | θυσιαστηριου]+dei Pr : arcae Cyp | ενωπιον]+του θρονου bo eth |.

14. λεγοντα Aא* Tyc Pr gig vg Cyp : λεγοντοσ 046. **21** (–35. 205. 468. 2020) al^{mu} Or^{s} : λεγουσαν 025. 1. 35. 104. 172. 205. 468 1957. 2015. 2018. 2019. 2020. 2023. 2036 al^{p} : λεγουσησ א^{c} 2067 : λεγων 141 | εκτω >A 2038 | ο εχων] τω εχοντι 172. 250. 424. 2018 | τεσσαρασ] τεσσαρεσ א 172 | τουσ δεδεμενουσ . . . αγγελοι (ver. 15) >bo, but not sa eth | επι] εν 93. 104. 432 | τω ποταμω > 1849 | τω μεγαλω]+ποταμω 025 : > arm$^{1.2.4.a}$ | ευφρατη] εφρατη 046 : pr τω 468 : eufraten Tyc Pr gig Cyp : Al Frat sa |.

15. ελυθησαν] ελυπηθησαν A | οι ητοιμασμενοι] οι >א 18. 522. 2021. 2039 : οι προητοιμασμενοι 2015. 2036 | και ημεραν A 025. 35. 205. 2037. 2038. 2067 al^{mu} Tyc Pr gig vg Cyp : και εισ την ημεραν 046. **21** (–35. 205. 2020). 250 al^{mu} Or^{s} s eth : και την ημεραν 1957. 2015. 2020. 2023. 2036. 2041 bo sa : >א 1 | ινα]+μη א | τριτον]+μεροσ 432. 2015. 2036. 2037 Pr Cyp gig vg bo sa eth |.

16. του ιππικου Aא 025. 046. 1. 35. 61. 69. 104. 205. 2015. 2019. 2019. 2020. 2023.^{mg} 2036. 2037. 2038. 2067. al^{p} Or^{s} : του ιππου **21** (–35. 205. 386. 2020). 42. 82. 110. 336. 385. 1957. 2018. 2023* al^{mu} : των ιππων 386 | δισ μυριαδεσ . . . αριθμον > arm^{1} | δισ μυριαδεσ μυριαδων A 025. 1*. 205. 2016. 2019. 2038 Or^{s} (Cyp) : δυο μυριαδων μυριαδασ א : μυριαδεσ μυριαδων 046. **21** (–205). 250. 2037. 2067 al^{pm} : myriadis myriadum Tyc : octoginta milia Pr : vicies milies dena milia gig vg | αυτων]+ut

17. ἤκουσα τὸν ἀριθμὸν αὐτῶν. καὶ οὕτως εἶδον τοὺς ἵππους ἐν
τῇ ὁράσει (*a*)
καὶ τοὺς καθημένους ἐπ' † αὐτῶν † ἔχοντας θώρακας πυρίνους
καὶ ὑακινθίνους καὶ θειώδεις,
καὶ αἱ κεφαλαὶ τῶν ἵππων ὡς κεφαλαὶ λεόντων,
καὶ ἐκ τῶν στομάτων αὐτῶν ἐκπορεύεται πῦρ καὶ καπνὸς καὶ
θεῖον.

18. ἀπὸ τῶν τριῶν πληγῶν τούτων ἀπεκτάνθησαν τὸ τρίτον τῶν
ἀνθρώπων,
ἐκ τοῦ πυρὸς καὶ τοῦ καπνοῦ καὶ τοῦ θείου τοῦ ἐκπορευομένου
ἐκ τῶν στομάτων αὐτῶν.
19. ἡ γὰρ ἐξουσία τῶν ἵππων ἐν τῷ στόματι αὐτῶν ἐστιν (*b*) καὶ
<αὐτοῖς> ἐν † αὐταῖς † ἀδικοῦσιν.

(*a*) The text is corrupt and defective: ἤκουσα τ. ἀριθμὸν αὐτῶν may be an intrusion. After ὁράσει we should restore καὶ τοὺς καθημένους ἐπ' αὐτούς, which has been lost through hmt. Next, for καὶ τ. καθημένους ἐπ' † αὐτῶν † ἔχοντας above read καὶ οἱ καθήμενοι ἐπ' αὐτοὺς ἔχοντες.

(*b*) Text adds an interpolation here: καὶ ἐν ταῖς οὐραῖς αὐτῶν, αἱ γὰρ οὐραὶ αὐτῶν ὅμοιαι ὄφεσιν, ἔχουσαι κεφαλάς. See vol. i. p. 253 sq.

occiderent tertiam partem hominum Pr | ηκουσα . . . αυτων > eth. After μυριαδων two lines appear to have been lost.

17. και ουτωσ . . . ορασει > s[1] | ουτωσ > 2020 Tyc Pr arm[1. 2. 3. a] | ιππουσ] ιππικουσ 046. 69 Or[s] | επ] επανω ℵ | εχοντασ] περιβεβλημενουσ bo | υακινθινουσ και θειωδεισ] καρχηδονα θειου s[1] | υακινθινουσ] οιακινθινουσ 325. 456 : ιακινθινουσ 620. 866 : hyacinthinas Tyc : hyacintinas vg : iacintinas Cyp gig : spineas Pr | και θειωδεισ > eth | θειωδεισ] θυωδεισ ℵ* : θιωδεισ ℵ[c] : "god-like" arm[4] | των στοματων] του στοματοσ 35 Tyc Pr gig vg Cyp s[1] arm[1. 2. 3. a] | εκπορευεται] εξεπορευετο 2020. 2067 | πυρ . . . καπνοσ] ~ Tyc | καπνοσ . . . θειον] ~ s[1] |.

18. απο] pr και s[1. 2] arm bo : υπο 1 | των τριων πληγων τουτων] των > C : τριων > ℵ Or[s] arm[1. 2. 3. a] : πληγων > 1. 2038 : των τριων τουτων πληγων 205 | απεκτανθησαν] απεκτανθη 468. 498. 2019. 2020 gig vg Cyp | τριτον] + μεροσ gig vg bo sa eth | εκ του πυροσ AℵC 025. 1. 35. 205. 1957. 2015. 2019. 2020. 2023. 2036. 2037. 2038 Or[s] vg Cyp : απο του πυροσ 046. **21** (− 35. 205. 2020). 69. 104. 250. 2067 al[pm] : pr και s[1] arm[4] | του καπνου Aℵ 046. **21** (− 35*. 866). 69. 104. 110. 250. 385. 2004. 2036. 2067 al[pm] Or[s] vg Cyp bo sa eth : pr εκ C 025. 1. 35*. 314. 2016. 2037. 2038 al[p] gig s : pr απο 866 : > arm[1] | του θειου AℵC 046. **21** (− 35*). 250. 2067 al[pm] Or[s] vg bo sa eth : pr εκ 025. 1. 35*. 314. 2016. 2036. 2037. 2038 al[p] gig s | του εκπορευομενου] εκπορευομενου] > 104 : των εκπορευομενων 2015. 2019. 2020. 2036. 2037. 2067 bo | εκ των στοματων] εκ του στοματοσ 205. 920. 1957. 2040 gig vg Cyp s[1] arm[1. 2. 3. a] |.

19. ιππων] τοπων A | εν τω στοματι αυτων εστιν και εν ταισ

20. καὶ οἱ λοιποὶ τῶν ἀνθρώπων, οἳ οὐκ ἀπεκτάνθησαν ἐν ταῖς
πληγαῖς ταύταις,
⸀οὐδὲ⸁ μετενόησαν ἐκ τῶν ἔργων τῶν χειρῶν αὐτῶν, οὔτε v. οὐ
ἵνα μὴ προσκυνήσουσιν τὰ δαιμόνια καὶ τὰ εἴδωλα
τὰ χρυσᾶ καὶ τὰ ἀργυρᾶ καὶ τὰ χαλκᾶ καὶ τὰ λίθινα καὶ τὰ
ξύλινα,
ἃ οὔτε βλέπειν δύνανται οὔτε ἀκούειν οὔτε περιπατεῖν,
21. καὶ οὐ μετενόησαν ἐκ τῶν φόνων αὐτῶν οὔτε ἐκ τῶν φαρμακιῶν
αὐτῶν
οὔτε ἐκ τῆς πορνείας αὐτῶν οὔτε ἐκ τῶν κλεμμάτων αὐτῶν.

ουραισ αυτων] εν ταισ ουραισ και εν τω στοματι αυτων ην 2020. 2037 : in ore et caudis eorum erat Pr | και εν ταισ ουραισ αυτων > 1. 2019. 2038 | αυτων] των ιππων 385 : + εστιν s^{2} | αι γαρ ουραι . . . αδικουσιν > s^{1} | ομοιαι] > C* : ομοιοι 2023 : erant similes Pr arm$^{1.2.3.4}$ | οφεσιν Aא C 025. 1. 35. 61. 69. 1957. 2015. 2019. 2020. 2023. 2036. 2037. 2038*. 2041. 2067 al^{p} Or^{s} Tyc Pr gig vg Cyp s^{2} arm$^{1.2.4}$ bo : οφει arm^{3} : οφεων 046. **21** (–35. 2020). 250 al^{mu} : ομοιαι των οφεων 2038.^{mg} | εχουσαι] εχουσασ א* : εχουσαισ א^{c} 025. 2019 : εχουσιν C* 2038. 2067 | κεφαλασ] + draconum Pr | αδικουσιν] ηδικουσαν 2020 : ηδικουν Pr arm$^{2.3.4.a}$ bo eth : αδικησουσιν arm^{1} : + ανθρωπουσ πεντε μηνασ bo eth |.

20. οι^{2} > gig arm$^{2.4}$ bo | πληγαισ] + αυτων א | ουδε . . . χειρων αυτων > 919 | ουδε א 046. 61. 69. 2020 : ουτε A 025. 1. 35. 205. 429**. 632**. 2019. 2037. 2038 al^{p} Pr gig vg Cyp bo : ου C **21** (–35. 205. 632**. 919). 104. 110. 172. 241. 242. 250. 314. 385. 429*. 1955. 1957. 2015. 2016. 2017. 2018. 2023. 2024. 2036. 2067 al Or^{s} | των εργων] του εργου s^{1} | προσκυνησουσιν AאC 104*. 452. 2019 : προσκυνησωσιν 025. 046. **21**. 250. 2037. 2038. 2067 al^{pl} Or^{s} : adorarent Pr vg$^{c.d.f.v.}$: adorent gig vg$^{a.g}$ Cyp | τα δαιμονια και] τω δαιμονι η 2020 : > arm^{1} | ειδωλα] + id est simulacra Cyp : + αυτων arm$^{1.2.3.a}$ | χρυσα] χρυσαια א : χρυσια Or^{s} | και τα χαλκα (χαλκεα א) AאC 025. 046. 35. 468**. 2020. Or^{s} Pr gig vg Cyp. s arm bo eth : > **21** (–35. 205. 468**. 2020). 42. 82. 104. 110. 201. 218. 241. 242. 314. 336. 385. 429. 498. 522. 1955. 2016. 2019. 2024. 2039 al^{p} | λιθινα . . . ξυλινα] ~ א 743. 1075 s^{1} bo eth | δυνανται AאC 025. 046*. 18. 35. 104. 149*. 205. 241. 250. 468**. 632. 2004. 2015. 2018. 2019. 2020. 2023. 2024. 2036. 2037. 2067 Or^{s} : δυναται 046**. **21** (–18. 35. 149*. 205. 468**. 632. 2004. 2020). 2038 al^{pl} : > s^{1} | ακουειν . . . περιπατειν] ~ arm^{1} | ουτε ακουειν > Cyp |.

21. μετενοησαν] + εκ τουτων ουτε 2020 | φονων] φωνων gig : φωνησ arm^{3} | ουτε εκ των φαρμακιων αυτων > Cyp arm^{2} | φαρμακιων A 025. 046. 104. 2038 al^{p} Or^{s} : φαρμακων אC **21** (–35. 205. 468**. 632**. 2020). 250 al^{mu} : φαρμακειων 1. 35. 205. 468**. 632**. 2020. 2037. 2038**. 2067 al : "sorcery" arm$^{1.3.a}$:

CHAPTER X.

1. Καὶ εἶδον ἄλλον ἄγγελον ἰσχυρὸν καταβαίνοντα ἐκ τοῦ
οὐρανοῦ, περιβεβλημένον νεφέλην, καὶ ἡ ἶρις ἐπὶ τὴν κεφαλὴν
αὐτοῦ, καὶ τὸ πρόσωπον αὐτοῦ ὡς ὁ ἥλιος καὶ οἱ πόδες αὐτοῦ ὡς
στύλοι πυρός, 2. καὶ ἔχων ἐν τῇ χειρὶ αὐτοῦ βιβλαρίδιον ἠνεῳγμένον.
καὶ ἔθηκεν τὸν πόδα αὐτοῦ τὸν δεξιὸν ἐπὶ τῆς θαλάσσης, τὸν δὲ
εὐώνυμον ἐπὶ τῆς γῆς, 3. καὶ ἔκραξεν φωνῇ μεγάλῃ ὥσπερ λέων
μυκᾶται. καὶ ὅτε ἔκραξεν, ἐλάλησαν αἱ ἑπτὰ βρονταὶ τὰς ἑαυτῶν
φωνάς.

"divination" arm^{4} | πορνειασ] πονηριασ Aℵ* : πορνιασ ℵ^{c} 025. 866 | ουτε εκ των κλεμματων αυτων > Pr s^{1} sa | κλεμματων] factorum Cyp |.

1. **και ειδον . . . καταβαινοντα**] *και μετα ταυτα αλλοσ αγγ. κατεβη* eth | αλλον αγγελον AℵC 172. 205. 250. 2018. 2019. 2020. 2038. 2067 Or^{s} Tyc gig vg s arm$^{1.\,2\,4.\,a}$: ~ 104. 336. (620. 866 αλον) Pr : αλλον > 025. 046. **21** (− 205. 620. 866. 2020). 1. 2037 al^{pm} | ισχυρον > s^{1} arm$^{1.\,2}$ | εκ] απο 337 | και η ιρισ επι την κεφαλην αυτου] > arm^{3} : και η ιρισ > arm^{4} | η (> ℵ^{c}) ιρισ A (-εισ) ℵ^{c} C 046. **21** (− 205. 2020). 250 al^{pm} Or^{s} arm$^{1.\,2.\,a}$ bo : η θριξ ℵ* : η > 025. 1. 104. 205. 522. 2017. 2019. 2020. 2037*. 2067 al^{p} : ιριν 2036. 2037** : ιρην 2038 : εριν 2015 | επι την κεφαλην AC 181 : επι τησ κεφαλησ ℵ 025. 046. **21**. 250. 2037. 2038. 2067 al^{pl} Or^{s} | το προσωπον αυτου] + ην vg | ο ηλιοσ] ο > 2020 | στυλοι] στυλοσ 205. 2020 Tyc vg (− vg^{c}) s^{1} arm |.

2. **και** > 2020 | εχων AℵC 025. 046. **21** (− 35. 205. 468**. 632**. 2020). 250 al^{mu} Or^{s} : κατεχων 2020 : ειχεν 1. 104 205. 241. 468**. 632**. 1957. 2015. 2018. 2019. 2023. 2036. 2037. 2038. 2041. 2067 al^{p} Pr gig vg arm : εχει 35 | βιβλαριδιον Aℵ* C** 025. 1. 2067 al^{p} Or^{s} s : βιβλιδαριον ℵ^{c}C* 35. 60. 61. 69. 104. 205. 241. 432. 468**. 632**. 1957. 2015. 2019. 2020. 2023. 2036. 2037. 2038. 2041 : βιβλιον 046. **21** (− 35. 205. 468**. 632**. 2020). 250 al^{mu} Pr gig : libellum vg | ηνεωγμενον ℵC 025. 104. 172. 205. 218. 250. 424. 2016. 2018. 2038. 2067 : ηνεωγμενων 1 : ανεωγμενον 046. **21** (− 205). 2037 al^{pl} Or^{s} : > A bo | τον δεξιον > C | τησ θαλασσησ] την θαλασσαν 1. 2037. 2038 al^{p} | τον δε ευωνυμον επι τησ γησ > 866 | τησ γησ] την γην 1. 201. 386 |.

3. **ωσπερ**] pr και Tyc arm$^{1.\,3.\,a}$: ωσ οτε vg | μυκαται] rugiens Pr bo | εκραξεν^{2}] + ωσ ℵ* (del ℵ^{c}) : + μεγαλη φωνη arm^{a} | αι επτα βρονται] ℵ^{c} : επτα φωναι ℵ* : αι > 1. 91. 94. 104. 866. 2067 arm | τασ εαυτων φωνασ] ταισ εαυτων φωναισ ℵ 104 gig s^{1} arm$^{3*.\,4.\,a}$: > Pr | τασ εαυτων φωνασ . . . (ver. 4) γραφειν >

4. καὶ ὅτε ἐλάλησαν αἱ ἑπτὰ βρονταί, ἤμελλον γράφειν· καὶ
ἤκουσα φωνὴν ἐκ τοῦ οὐρανοῦ λέγουσαν Σφράγισον ἃ ἐλάλησαν αἱ
ἑπτὰ βρονταί, καὶ μὴ αὐτὰ γράψῃς.
5. καὶ ὁ ἄγγελος ὃν εἶδον ἑστῶτα ἐπὶ τῆς θαλάσσης καὶ ἐπὶ τῆς
γῆς
ἦρεν τὴν χεῖρα αὐτοῦ τὴν δεξιὰν εἰς τὸν οὐρανόν,
6. καὶ ὤμοσεν ἐν τῷ ζῶντι εἰς τοὺς αἰῶνας τῶν αἰώνων,
ὃς ἔκτισεν τὸν οὐρανὸν καὶ τὰ ἐν αὐτῷ, καὶ τὴν γῆν καὶ τὰ ἐν
αὐτῇ,
καὶ τὴν θάλασσαν καὶ τὰ ἐν αὐτῇ, ὅτι χρόνος οὐκέτι ἔσται.
7. ἀλλ' ἐν ταῖς ἡμέραις τῆς φωνῆς τοῦ † ἑβδόμου † ἀγγέλου, ὅταν <τρίτου>
μέλλῃ σαλπίζειν, καὶ ἐτελέσθη τὸ μυστήριον τοῦ θεοῦ, ὡς εὐηγγέλισεν

arm$^{1.2}$ | τασ εαυτων φωνασ . . . (ver. 4) βρονται^{1} >386. 620. 866 |.

4. **οτ**] οσα ℵ 432. 2036. 2037 Pr gig | βρονται^{1}] + voces suas vg^{v} | ημελλον AC 046. 61. 69. 82. 181. 201. 218. 386. 452. 498. 920. 2020. 2024. 2038 Or^{8} : εμελλον ℵ 025. **20** (− 386. 920. 2020). 1. 104. 110. 250. 314. 385. 2015. 2037. 2067 al^{pl} | και οτε . . . γραφειν] "And I heard the things which the seven thunders said: I was about to write them also." bo | εκ του ουρανου] + του εβδομου s^{1} | σφραγισον] nota tibi Pr | α] οσα ℵ 94 : ο s^{1} | επτα >C gig arm^{2} | και^{3} >Tyc vg bo | μη αυτα AℵC 025. 046. **20** (− 35). 250 al^{pm} Or^{8} Tyc Pr gig vg s^{2} arm$^{1.2.3.4}$: αυτα > arm^{a} : μη αυτο s^{1} : μετα ταυτα 1. 35. 60. 181. 432. 1957. 2023. 2036. 2037. 2038. 2041. 2067 | γραψησ] γραφησ 205 Or^{8} : γραφεισ 1. 35. 60. 432. 1957. 2019. 2023. 2036. 2037. 2038. 2041 : γραψεισ 104. 522. 2015 : γραψον 2067 |.

5. **ο αγγελοσ**] τον αγγελον Pr vg$^{a.c.f.g}$ | εστωτα >429. 498. 522. 2016*. 2020 gig | ηρεν] pr οσ s^{1} | την δεξιαν >A 1. 35. 2019. 2038 vg s^{1} | εισ τον ουρανον] in caelo gig |.

6. **και ωμοσεν**] + ο αγγελοσ Tyc | εν τω ζωντι . . . εν αυτη^{2} >Tyc | εν τω ζωντι Aℵ^{c} 025. 1. 35. 104. 175. 205. 314. 617. 1957. 2015. 2016 2017. 2019. 2023. 2036. 2037. 2038. 2067 al^{p} : per viventem Pr gig vg : εν >ℵ* 046. **20** (− 35. 175. 205. 617). 250 al^{pm} Or^{8} | των αιωνων] >1. 181. 241. 632**. 2038. 2067 : + αμην 336. 620. 866. 2019 | και τα εν αυτω >arm^{1} bo | και την γην και τα εν αυτη >A 1. 181 | και τα εν αυτη^{1} >256 arm^{1} bo | εν αυτη^{1}] εν αυτοισ 2015. 2036. 2037 | και την θαλασσαν και τα εν αυτη ℵ^{c}C 025. 046. **20** (− 205. 2020). 250. 2037. 2038. 2067 al^{pm} Or^{8} vg s^{2} arm$^{(1).2.3}$: >Aℵ* 141. 205. 429. 522. 2016. 2017. 2020. 2023 Tyc Pr gig vg s^{1} arm$^{4.a}$ | εν αυτη^{2}] εν αυτοισ arm^{1} | ουκετι εσται] ουκετι εστι ℵ* 141 : ουκ εσται ετι 1. 2036. 2037 : ετι ουκ εσται s^{1} |.

7. **αλλ** >gig bo : ουκ s^{1} | τησ φωνησ >Tyc s^{1} arm^{2} | του

τοὺς ἑαυτοῦ δούλους τοὺς προφήτας. 8. καὶ ἡ φωνὴ ἣν ἤκουσα ἐκ τοῦ οὐρανοῦ πάλιν † λαλοῦσαν μετ' ἐμοῦ καὶ λέγουσαν † Ὕπαγε λάβε τὸ βιβλίον τὸ ἠνεῳγμένον τὸ ἐν χειρὶ τοῦ ἀγγέλου τοῦ ἑστῶτος ἐπὶ τῆς θαλάσσης καὶ ἐπὶ τῆς γῆς. 9. καὶ ἀπῆλθα πρὸς τὸν ἄγγελον λέγων αὐτῷ δοῦναί μοι τὸ βιβλαρίδιον. καὶ λέγει μοι Λάβε καὶ κατάφαγε αὐτό, καὶ πικρανεῖ σου τὴν κοιλίαν, ἀλλ' ἐν τῷ στόματί σου ἔσται γλυκὺ ὡς μέλι.

εβδομου αγγελου] του αγγελου του εβδομου ℵ : του > C | μελλη] μελλει 18. 104. 172. 429. 522. 1849. 1957. 2015. 2016. 2018. 2019. 2036 | και AℵC 025. 046. **20** (– 35**. 386. 468**). 1. 250. 2037. 2038 al^{pl} Or^{s} vg$^{a.g}$ s$^{1.2}$ eth : > 35**. 60. 201. 386. 432. 468**. 1957. 2023. 2041. 2067 Pr gig vg$^{c.f.v}$ bo arm : tunc vg^{d} | ετελεσθη AℵC 025. **20** (– 35**. 205. 468*). 250. 2038 al^{pm} s : + γαρ bo : τελεσθη 1. 35**. 205. 468*. 1957. 2015. 2019. 2023. 2036. 2037. 2041. 2067 Or^{s} : τελεσθει 046. 104 : τελεσθηναι 35* : finietur Pr (gig vg arm) | ωσ] ο 60. 432. 1957. 2015. 2023. 2036. 2037. 2038. 2041. 2067 s^{1} arm$^{1.2.4.a}$: οσ 35 | ευηγγελισεν] ευηγγελισατο 35. 60. 93. 181. 432. 506. 1957. 2015. 2023. 2036. 2037. 2041 Or^{s} | τουσ εαυτου δουλουσ AℵC 025. 35. 205. 2020. 2038 : τουσ δουλουσ εαυτου Or^{s} : τουσ δουλουσ αυτου 046. **20** (– 35. 205. 2020). 250 al^{mu} s^{1} : τουσ αυτου δουλουσ 69. 2019 : τοισ εαυτου δουλοισ 1. 2037. 2067 al^{p} : τοισ αυτου δουλοισ 2015. 2036 : τοισ δουλοισ αυτου 498 gig arm$^{1.2.4}$: per profetas servos suos Pr : per servos suos vg arm$^{3.a}$ bo | τουσ προφητασ] pr και ℵ eth : τοισ προφηταισ 1. 498. 2015. 2036. 2037. 2067 |.

8. και η φωνη ην ηκουσα] και ηκουσα φωνην 104 Pr (gig) vg^{d} s^{1} arm^{4} | λαλουσαν . . . λεγουσαν AℵC 025. 046. 61. 69. 104. 1957. 2019 (+ μοι). 2038 (Pr) gig vg s^{1} arm^{4} : λαλουσα . . . λεγουσα **20**. 1. 250. 2037. 2067 al^{pm} Or^{s} | και λεγουσαν > Pr : + μοι arm^{2} | υπαγε] + και 91. 175. 242. 314. 617. 1934. 2016. 2017 Pr vg^{d} arm$^{2.3}$ | βιβλιον AC 69. 314 Pr gig vg : βιβλαριδιον ℵ 025. 1. 2038. 2067 al^{p} Or^{s} s : βιβλιδαριον 046. **20**. 250. 2037 al^{pm} | ηνεωγμενον AℵC 025. 1. 61. 172. 250. 2018. 2019. 2038. 2067 al : ανεωγμενον 046. **20**. 2037 al^{mu} Or^{s} : > s^{1} | εν χειρι] > C arm^{3} : εν > 314. 2016 : εκ χειροσ 2019 Pr gig vg | θαλασσησ . . . γησ] ∼ s^{1} |.

9. και απηλθα . . . λαβε > s^{1} | απηλθα A 336. 498. 517. 620. 866. 2024 Or^{s} : απηλθον ℵC 025. 046. **20** (– 620. 866). 250. 2037. 2038. 2067 al^{pl} | λεγων αυτω] > Tyc : αυτω > Pr | δουναι AℵC 046. **20** (– 35. 205. 468**. 2020). 250 al^{pm} Or^{s} Tyc Pr gig vg s^{2} arm^{4} : δοσ 025. 1. 35. 205. 468**. 1957. 2015. 2019. 2020. 2023. 2036. 2037. 2038. 2041. 2067 bo | βιβλαριδιον A**C 025. 1. 2038. 2067 al^{p} Or^{s} : βιβλαριον A* : βιβλιον ℵ al^{p} (Pr gig vg) : βιβλιδαριον 046. **20**. 250. 2037 al^{pm} | λαβε και καταφαγε αυτο] λαβε αυτο και καταφαγε ℵ* : λαβε αυτο και καταφαγε αυτο ℵ^{c} eth

10. καὶ ἔλαβον τὸ βιβλαρίδιον ἐκ τῆς χειρὸς τοῦ ἀγγέλου καὶ
κατέφαγον αὐτό, καὶ ἦν ἐν τῷ στόματί μου γλυκὺ ὡς μέλι· καὶ ὅτε
ἔφαγον αὐτό, ἐπικράνθη ἡ κοιλία μου. 11. καὶ λέγουσίν μοι Δεῖ σε
πάλιν προφητεῦσαι ἐπὶ λαοῖς καὶ ἔθνεσιν καὶ γλώσσαις καὶ βασιλεῦσιν
πολλοῖς.

arm^{a} : accipe librum et devora illum vg : λαβε αυτο σοι bo | σου] σοι s^{1} | την κοιλιαν] την καρδιαν A Or^{s} : +σου s^{1} : εν τη κοιλια arm$^{1.2.3.a}$ | εσται γλυκυ] ~Pr : γλυκυ >s^{1} |.

10. και] +οτε Pr | και ελαβον . . . κατεφαγον αυτο >gig | βιβλαριδιον AC 025. 1. 2038. 2067 al^{p} Or^{s} s : βιβλιον ℵ 046. **20** (–35. 205). 250 al^{mu} (vg) : βιβλιδαριον 35. 60. 69. 110. 205. 432. 1957. 2015. 2017. 2019. 2023. 2036. 2037. 2041 : libellum Pr | και ην . . . εφαγον αυτο >Pr arm^{1} | γλυκυ ωσ μελι A 046. 2019 arm^{3} : ωσ μελι γλυκυ ℵC 025. **20.** 250. 2037. 2038. 2067 al^{pl} Or^{s} gig vg s arm^{4} : γλυκυ >arm$^{2.a}$: ωσ μελι >eth | οτε εφαγον αυτο >250. 424. 2018 arm^{2} | επικρανθη] εγεμισθη ℵ Pr gig arm$^{1.2.4}$ | κοιλια] καρδια Or^{s} (but writes κοιλια above) | μου] +πικριασ ℵ^{c} gig arm$^{1.(3).4}$ |.

11. λεγουσιν Aℵ 046. **20** (–35. 205. 468**. 632**. 2020). 250 al^{mu} Or^{s} vg$^{a*.c.g}$ sa : λεγει 025. 1. 35. 104. 205. 241. 468**. 632**. 1957. 2015. 2016. 2020. 2023. 2036. 2037. 2038. 2041. 2067 al^{p} Tyc Pr gig vg$^{a**.d.f.v}$ s arm bo^{vi} eth | παλιν προφητευσαι] ~2020 : παλιν > arm^{2} | λαοισ . . . εθνεσι] ~s | επι λαοισ] επι λαου 617. 920. 2040 s^{2} : επι λαουσ 172 : in populos Pr : populis gig vg | εθνεσιν Aℵ 025. 1. 35. 205. 241. 468*. 2016. 2019. 2020. 2037. 2038. 2067 al^{p} Or^{s} gig vg bo : pr επι 046. **20** (–35. 205. 468*. 2020). 250 al^{mu} s | και γλωσσαισ . . . πολλοισ >arm^{1} | γλωσσαισ] pr επι arm$^{2.3.4.a}$ |.

CHAPTER XI.

1. Καὶ ἐδόθη μοι κάλαμος ὅμοιος ῥάβδῳ λέγων Ἔγειρε καὶ
μέτρησον τὸν ναὸν τοῦ θεοῦ καὶ τὸ θυσιαστήριον καὶ τοὺς προσ-

1. και εδοθη μοι] dedit mihi Pr : εδωκαν μοι bo | καλαμοσ ομοιοσ ραβδω] Aaron virgae similis Tyc : harundinem auream similem virgae Pr bo (m-s^{pl}) eth | ομοιοσ ραβδω] ωσ ραβδοσ 2020 | λεγων Aℵ^{c} 025. **20.** 1. 2038 al^{pm} Tyc Pr gig vg : +μοι 743. 1075. 2067 arm$^{1.2.a}$ bo eth : λεγει ℵ* : και φωνη λεγουσα 2015. 2036. 2037 : pr και ειστηκει (εστηκει ℵ$^{c.c}$: ιστηκει 046) ο αγγελοσ ℵ$^{c.c}$ 046. 60. 61. 69. 104. 172. 250. 424. 432. 1957. 2018. 2023. 2041 Or^{s} s$^{1.2*}$ arm : pr και ο αγγελοσ ειστηκει 2019 | εγειρε Aℵ 025. 046. 175. 325. 456. 620. (866). 920. 1849. 2004. 2037* al

κυνοῦντας ἐν αὐτῷ. 2. καὶ τὴν αὐλὴν τὴν ἔξωθεν τοῦ ναοῦ ἔκβαλε
ἔξωθεν καὶ μὴ αὐτὴν μετρήσῃς, ὅτι ἐδόθη τοῖς ἔθνεσιν, καὶ τὴν πόλιν
τὴν ἁγίαν πατήσουσιν μῆνας τεσσεράκοντα καὶ δύο.
3. καὶ δώσω τοῖς δυσὶν μάρτυσίν μου, καὶ προφητεύσουσιν ἡμέρας
χιλίας διακοσίας ἑξήκοντα † περιβεβλημένους † σάκκους. 4. Οὗτοί
εἰσιν αἱ δύο ἐλαῖαι καὶ αἱ δύο λυχνίαι αἱ ἐνώπιον τοῦ κυρίου τῆς γῆς

Or^{s} : εγειρον 60. 94. 205. 2038 : εγειραι **20** (– 175. 325. 456. 620. 866. 920. 1849. 2004). 1. 250. 2067 al | *και*^{2} > 104 Tyc bo | *μετρησον*] *μετρησαι* 104. 920. 2040 | *του θεου* > arm$^{1.2}$ | *το θυσιαστηριον*] + *του θεου* Tyc Pr : + *αύτου* eth | *εν αυτω*] illud gig arm^{4} |.

2. και την αυλην . . . μετρησησ > gig | *την αυλην την*] ℵ^{c} : *τησ αυλησ τησ* ℵ* : atrium autem (Tyc) vg : ara autem Pr | *εξωθεν*^{1} A 025. 046. **21.** 2067 al^{pl} Or^{s} Tyc Pr vg s^{2} arm$^{1.2.3.a}$ bo : *εσωθεν* ℵ 1. 172. 181. 250. 2018. 2037. 2038 s^{1} | *ναου*] ℵ^{c} : *λαου* ℵ* | *εκβαλε εξωθεν και* > Pr arm^{4} | *εκβαλε*] ℵ^{c} : pr *και* ℵ* : *εκβαλλε* 2037 | *εξωθεν*^{2} Aℵ^{c} 1. 35. 61. 69. 172. 181. 250. 424. 432. 506. 1957. 2015. 2018. 2019. 2023. 2036. 2037. 2038. 2041 Or^{s} s : *εσωθεν* 025 : *εσω* ℵ* arm^{1**} : *εξω* 046. **21** (– 35). 2067 al^{pl} arm$^{1*.3}$ bo : foras Tyc vg : > arm$^{2.a}$ eth | *μετρησησ*] *μετρησισ* 1 : *μετρησεισ* 104. 2036 | *τοισ εθνεσιν*] ℵ^{c} : pr *και* ℵ* | *την πολιν την αγιαν*] *η πολισ η αγια* arm^{1} bo | *την αγιαν* > Pr | *πατησουσιν*] *μετρησουσιν* A : + *εν αυτη* bo : "that they shall trample under foot" arm^{1} | *τεσσερακοντα* Aℵ : *τεσσαρακοντα* 025. **21** (– 35) al^{pl} Or^{s} : *μ´* 046. 1. 35 | *και δυο* A 046 (*β´*). **21** (– 35. 205. 617. 919. 2020). 429. 2067 al^{p} s arm : *και* > ℵ 025. 69. 205. 250. 617. 919. 2018. 2020. 2023. 2037 Or^{s} Tyc Pr gig vg bo : *β´* 1. 35 al^{mu} |.

3. και προφητευσουσιν] ut profetent Pr eth : *προφητευσαι* s^{1} : *και* > bo | *διακοσιασ* > 69 | *εξηκοντα*] + *πεντε* ℵ$^{c.c}$ 69 arm$^{1.2.3}$ | *περιβεβλημενουσ* Aℵ* 025. 046. 35*. 91. 104. 242. 920. 1934. 2015. 2036. 2041 : *-μενοι* ℵ^{c} C **21** (– 35*. 920. 1934). 1. 250. 2037. 2038. 2067 al^{pl} Or^{s} Tyc Pr vg : amictis gig | *σακκουσ*] saccis Tyc Pr gig vg^{v} |.

4. αι δυο ελαιαι και > 1*. 2038 | *αι*^{1}] ℵ^{c} : *οι* ℵ* : > 205 s$^{1.2(?)}$ | *ελαιαι*] *αυλαιαι* A : *αλαιαι* C | *αι δυο*^{2} Aℵ^{c} C 025. 046. **21** (– 205. 620. 866). 250. 2037. 2067 al^{pm} Or^{s} arm : *ε δυο* 620 : *δυο* ℵ* 205. 866 al^{p} s$^{1.2(?)}$ | *αι ενωπιον* AC 025. 046. **21** (– 35. 175. 205. 386. 1934. 2040). 1. 250. 2037. 2067 al^{pl} bo : *οι ενωπιον* 201. 386 : *αι* > ℵ 35. 61. 69. 104. 172. 175. 205. 241. 242. 314. 424. 1934. 2016. 2017. 2018. 2038. 2040 Or^{s} : in conspectu Tyc vg : sub conspectu Pr : coram gig | *του κυριου* ℵC 025. **21** (– 35. 205). 250. 2067 al^{pm} Or^{s} Tyc Pr gig vg s arm$^{3.4}$ bo : *του* > A 046 : *του θεου* 1. 35. 205. 2015. 2019. 2036. 2037. 2038 al^{p} arm^{a} : "the lord God" arm$^{1.2}$ | *τησ γησ*] pr *πασησ* s^{1} arm$^{1.2}$: super terram gig :

† ἑστῶτες †. 5. *καὶ εἴ τις αὐτοὺς θέλει ἀδικῆσαι, πῦρ ἐκπορεύεται
ἐκ τοῦ στόματος αὐτῶν καὶ κατεσθίει τοὺς ἐχθροὺς αὐτῶν.*(a) 6.
*οὗτοι ἔχουσιν τὴν ἐξουσίαν κλεῖσαι τὸν οὐρανόν, ἵνα μὴ ὑετὸς βρέχῃ
τὰς ἡμέρας τῆς προφητείας αὐτῶν, καὶ ἐξουσίαν ἔχουσιν ἐπὶ τῶν
ὑδάτων στρέφειν αὐτὰ εἰς αἷμα καὶ πατάξαι τὴν γῆν ἐν πάσῃ πληγῇ
ὁσάκις ἐὰν θελήσωσιν.*

(a) Text adds a gloss here: *καὶ εἴ τις θελήσῃ αὐτοὺς ἀδικῆσαι, οὕτως δεῖ αὐτὸν ἀποκτανθῆναι.*

> bo | *εστωτεσ* Aℵ*C 046. **21** (–35. 205. 337. 468. 617. 632**. 866. 920. 2020. 2040). 250 al^{mu} Or^{s} s : *εστωταισ* 866 : *εστωσαι* ℵ^{cc} 025. 1. 35. 104. 205. 241. 337. 385. 468. 617. (620). 632**. 920. 1957. 2015. 2019. 2020. 2023. 2036. 2037. 2038. 2040. 2067 al^{p} : stantes Tyc vg : consistentia Pr |.

5. και ει τισ αυτουσ θελει αδικησαι] *και ει τι θελουσι αυτο ποιησουσι* bo? : "and they (he arm$^{2.3.4}$) shall desire (desire arm^{4}) to hurt them" arm | *αυτουσ θελει* AC 025. 046. **21** (–468*). 2037. 2067 al^{mu} Or^{s} Tyc Pr vg s^{2} : ∼ ℵ 172. 250. 468*. 2018 gig : *θελει (αδικησαι) αυτουσ* 69 s^{1} | *θελει*] *θελη* 104. 2038 : *θελησει* Pr arm$^{1.2.3.a}$: voluerit gig vg | *αδικησαι*] + sive occidere Tyc | *πυρ εκπορευεται . . . αδικησαι* > 205 | *εκπορευεται*] *εκπορευσεται* 61. 69 Or^{s} arm$^{1.2.3.a}$: exeat Pr : exiet gig vg | *και* > bo | *κατεσθιει*] devorabit gig vg arm$^{1.2.3.a}$: comburens Pr | *ει τισ*] ℵ^{c} : *η τισ* ℵ* C 1 : *οστισ* 2020 s^{1} arm | *θελησῃ* Aℵ : *θελησει* 2020 Or^{s} arm$^{1.2.3.a}$: *θελει* C 025. 046. **21** (–2020). 250. 2037. 2038. 2067 al^{pl} Pr s arm^{4} : voluerit gig vg | *θελησῃ αυτουσ* AC 025. 046. **21** (–468*). 250. 2037 al^{p} Or^{s} gig vg : ∼ 1. 468*. 2019. 2023. 2038. 2067 al^{mu} Pr s^{2} : *θελησῃ (αδικησαι) αυτουσ* ℵ (s^{1}) | *αδικησαι*] *αποκτειναι* 432. 2015. 2019. 2022. 2036. 2037. 2067 | *ουτωσ*] > A : *ουτω* 18. 205. 617. 632. 919. 920. 1849. 1934. 2004. 2040 | *αυτον*] pr *και* Pr : *αυτουσ* 620. 866 s^{1} arm^{4} | *αποκτανθηναι*] *αδικηθηναι* arm^{4} |.

6. ουτοι] pr *και* s^{1} : *οτι* bo eth | *την εξουσιαν* AC 025 Or^{s} : *την* > ℵ 046. **21**. 250. 2037. 2038. 2067 al^{pl} | *εξουσιαν κλεισαι τον ουρανον* AℵC 025. 1. 35. 205. 2015. 2019. 2023. 2036. 2037. 2038. 2067 al^{mu} Tyc Pr gig (vg) s : + *και* after *εξουσιαν* Or^{s} : *τον ουρανον εξουσιαν κλεισαι* 046. **21** (–35. 205. 2020). 250 al^{mu} : *εξουσιαν τον ουρανον κλεισαι* 69. 498. 2020 | *κλεισαι*] *μετρησαι* arm^{4} | *υετοσ βρεχῃ*] ∼ 1. 2037. 2067 al^{p} : *υετουσ βρεχῃ* 498 : *υετουσ βρεξῃ* 2020 : *υετοσ βρεχει* 429. 522. 2015. 2017. 2019. 2021 : *καταβαινῃ υετοσ* s^{1} arm^{4} : pluat Tyc vg : imbrem pluat Pr : pluat pluvia gig : "they rain" arm^{1} : + *επι την γην* bo eth | *τασ ημερασ*] *εν ταισ ημεραισ* 1. 2037 Tyc Pr (vg) s^{1} arm^{4} : pr *πασασ* bo | *τησ προφητειασ αυτων* 025. **21** (–617. 920. 2040). 250. 2038. 2067 al^{mu} Or^{s} Tyc Pr gig vg s$^{1.2}$ arm : *τησ προφητιασ αυτων* AℵC 046 : *αυτων τησ προφητειασ* 1. 617. 920. 2037. 2040 al^{pl} |

7. Καὶ ὅταν τελέσωσιν τὴν μαρτυρίαν αὐτῶν, τὸ θηρίον τὸ
ἀναβαῖνον ἐκ τῆς ἀβύσσου ποιήσει μετ' αὐτῶν πόλεμον καὶ νικήσει
αὐτοὺς καὶ ἀποκτενεῖ αὐτούς. 8. καὶ τὸ πτῶμα αὐτῶν ἐπὶ τῆς πλατείας
τῆς πόλεως τῆς μεγάλης, ἥτις καλεῖται πνευματικῶς Σόδομα καὶ
Αἴγυπτος, ὅπου καὶ ὁ κύριος αὐτῶν ἐσταυρώθη. 9. καὶ βλέπουσιν
ἐκ τῶν λαῶν καὶ φυλῶν καὶ γλωσσῶν καὶ ἐθνῶν τὸ πτῶμα αὐτῶν

επι των υδατων στρεφειν αυτα] *στρεφειν τα υδατα* s^{1} | *επι των υδατων*] omnium aquarum Pr | *εισ αιμα*] in sanguine gig | *και*] ℵ^{c} : >ℵ* | *εν παση πληγη οσακισ εαν θελησωσιν* AℵC 025. 1. 35. 205. 2015. 2019. 2020. 2023. 2036. 2037. 2038. 2067 al^{p} Or^{s} Pr gig vg s arm$^{1.3.4.a}$ eth : *εν παση πληγη* after *θελησωσιν* 046. **21** (–35. 205. 617. 920. 2020. 2040). 250 al^{mu} | *εν παση πληγη* AℵC 025. **21** (–617. 920. 2040). 1. 2015. 2019. 2023. 2036. 2037. 2038. 2067 al^{pm} Or^{s} Pr s (arm$^{3.a}$) : *εν* >046 al^{p} vg (arm$^{1.4}$) : *εν παση* >gig : >617. 920. 2040 | *εαν*] *αν* C 2020 | *θελησωσιν*] *θελησουσιν* C : *θελωσιν* 69. 498. 2019. 2038 : *θελουσιν* 181 |.

7. *και οταν τελεσωσιν* >617* (but not 617**). 920. 2040 Or^{s} (through homoeotel.) arm$^{2.3}$ | *τελεσωσιν*] *τελεσουσι* 1. 2037. 2067 | *αυτων*] *τησ* (*αυτων και την* eth) *προφητειασ* (-*αν* eth) *αυτων* bo eth | *το θηριον*] + *το τεταρτον* A | *το αναβαινον*] ℵ^{c} : *τοτε αναβαινον* ℵ* : *το αναβαινων* A : quae descendit Tyc | *αβυσσου*] *θαλασσησ* s^{1} | *μετ αυτων πολεμον* AℵC 025. 046. **21** (–205). 250 al^{mu} Or^{s} Tyc Pr (gig vg) s : *πολεμον μετ αυτων* 1. 205. 2019. 2037. 2038. 2067 al^{p} | *νικησει*] *νεικηση* C : *νικηση* 104 : vicit Tyc | *και αποκτενει αυτουσ* > 1. 172. 181. 498. 2019. 2021. 2038 | *και* > bo | *αποκτενει*] occidit Tyc |.

8. *το πτωμα* AC 046. **21** (–35. 205. 2020) al^{mu} Or^{s} Tyc arm$^{3.a}$ bo : *τα πτωματα* ℵ 025. 1. 35. 172. 205. 250 1957. 2018. 2019. 2020. 2023. 2036. 2037. 2038. 2067 al^{p} Pr gig vg s arm$^{1.2.4}$ | *επι τησ πλατειασ*] *επι των πλατειων* s^{1} : in plateis Tyc vg arm^{4} : in platea gig : in medio Pr : "in the midst of their street" arm$^{1.2.(3).a}$: pr *εσται* ℵ$^{c.c}$ bo sa : pr *εασει* 432. 2015. 2022. 2036. 2037 : pr proicitur Tyc : pr ponet Pr : pr jacebunt gig vg$^{d.v}$ arm^{4} : pr posuit eth | *τησ πλατειασ* >eth | *πολεωσ τησ μεγαλησ*] *τησ μεγαλησ πολεωσ* 205 : *εν τη πολει τη μεγαλη* arm$^{1.3}$: + *ριψει* 94 : + *αταφα* 2015. 2036. 2037 : + jacebunt vg$^{a**.c}$ | *Σοδομα*] + *και εγγυσ ο ποταμοσ* ℵ^{c} : Segor arm$^{1.4}$: + *και Βαβυλων* arm^{4} | *και Αιγυπτοσ*] >Pr : *και Γομορρα* 2019 : + *και Βαβυλων* arm$^{1.2}$: "of Khemi" bo | *οπου και*] *και* > ℵ^{c} 1. 61. 69. 104. 172. 181. 250. 424. 919. 2018. 2019. 2038. 2067. s^{1} bo eth | *αυτων*] ℵ^{c} : > ℵ* : *ημων* 1 |.

9. *βλεπουσιν*] *βλεψουσιν* Pr gig vg arm$^{1.2.3.a}$ bo eth | *λαων . . . φυλων*] ~ ℵ s^{1} bo | *φυλων*] pr *των* 046 | *και εθνων*] > 1 Tyc arm^{1} : + "they shall look upon" bo | *το πτωμα . . . ημισυ* > Pr | *το πτωμα* AℵC 046. **21** (–35. 205. 2020. 2040). 250 al^{pm} Or^{s}

ἡμέρας τρεῖς καὶ ἥμισυ, καὶ τὰ πτώματα αὐτῶν οὐκ ἀφίουσιν τεθῆναι
εἰς μνῆμα. 10. καὶ οἱ κατοικοῦντες ἐπὶ τῆς γῆς χαίρουσιν ἐπ' αὐτοῖς
καὶ εὐφραίνονται καὶ δῶρα πέμψουσιν ἀλλήλοις, ὅτι οὗτοι οἱ δύο
προφῆται ἐβασάνισαν τοὺς κατοικοῦντας ἐπὶ τῆς γῆς.
11. Καὶ μετὰ τὰς τρεῖς ἡμέρας καὶ ἥμισυ πνεῦμα ζωῆς ἐκ τοῦ θεοῦ
εἰσῆλθεν ἐν αὐτοῖς, καὶ ἔστησαν ἐπὶ τοὺς πόδας αὐτῶν, καὶ φόβος

Tyc arm$^{1.2.3.a}$: *τα πτωματα* 025. 1. 35. 205. 1957. 2015. 2019. 2020. 2023. 2036. 2037. 2038. 2040. 2041. 2067 gig vg s arm^{4} bo | *και ημισυ* AℵC 025. 35. 429*. 432. 2015. 2023. 2036. 2040 al^{p} Or^{s} Tyc gig vg s arm^{4} : *και* > 046. **21** (– 35. 2040). 250. 2037. 2038. 2067 al^{pm} | *τα πτωματα*] *τα σωματα* 2037 arm^{3} : *το σωμα* 69 : "their bones" arm$^{1.2.a}$ | *αφιουσιν* AℵC 025. 1. 181. 2015. 2019. 2036. 2037. 2038 Tyc vg : *αφησουσιν* 046. **21** (– 2040). 250. 2067 al^{pl} gig s arm bo : *αφιασι* 2040 : *αφιησιν* Or^{s} | *μνημα* (A) ℵ* 025. 046. **21** (– 205). 1. 250. 2037. 2038. 2067 al^{pm} Or^{s} Tyc gig arm$^{1.2.a}$ bo : *μνημειον* C 2019 : *μνηματα* ℵ^{c} 205. 522 al^{p} Pr vg s arm$^{3.4}$ |.

10. οι κατοικουντεσ] pr *παντεσ* bo | *επι τησ γησ*] *επι την γην* 172. 314 : *επι* > 2015. 2036 | *χαιρουσιν*] *χαρησονται* 2020. 2067 Pr gig vg s arm^{4} bo | *επ αυτοισ*] *εν αυτοισ* 2015. 2020. 2036 | *ευφραινονται* AℵC 025. 1. 35*. 181. 205. 2015. 2019. 2036. 2037. 2038. 2040 Or^{s} arm$^{1.2.3.a}$: epulantur Tyc : *ευφρανθησονται* 046. **21** (– 35*. 205. 2040). 69. 104. 110. 250. 314. 2067 Pr gig vg s bo | *και ευφραιν.* > eth | *πεμψουσιν* Aℵ^{c}C 1. 35. 205. 2037**. 2040 al^{mu} Or^{s} Pr gig vg s bo eth : *πεμπουσιν* ℵ 025. 2015. 2019. 2036. 2037*. 2038 Tyc arm$^{2.3.4}$ (sa ?) : *δωσουσιν* 046. **21** (– 35. 205. 2040). 250. 2067 al^{mu} | *αλληλοισ*] *αλληλουσ* C 517 | *ουτοι* > s^{1} | *οι δυο προφηται*] *οι προφηται οι δυο* ℵ : *προφηται* > Pr | *τουσ κατοικουντασ επι τησ γησ*] eos per plagas Tyc |.

11. τασ τρεισ AC 046. **21** (– 35. 468. 1849. 2020). 2037. 2067 al^{pl} Or^{s} s^{2} : *τασ* > ℵ 025. 1. 35. 69. 141. 250. 432. 468. 1849. 1957. 2015. 2018. 2019. 2020. 2023. 2038. 2041 s^{1} arm$^{1.3.4.a}$ bo : > arm^{2} | *ημερασ και ημισυ*] *ημερασ* after *ημισυ* 69. 2015. 2020. 2036. 2037. 2067 : *και* > 69. 2020 : *και ημισυ* > arm$^{1.2}$ | *ημισυ*] *ημισου* Aℵ* : *το ημισυ* C | *ζωησ*] *ζων* s^{1} arm$^{3.a}$: > bo | *εκ του θεου*] > 468*. 617. 632* : *εκ* > arm$^{1.2.4}$ bo | *εκ του θεου εισηλθεν*] *εισηλθεν εκ του θεου* C | *εισηλθεν*] *εισελευσεται* bo eth | *εν αυτοισ* A 94. 2015**. 2019. 2036. 2037. 2040 Or^{s} : *εν* > C 025. 1. 35. 104. 181. 2020. 2038 : *εισ αυτουσ* ℵ 046. **21** (– 35. 2020. 2040). 250. 2067 al^{mu} Tyc Pr gig vg arm bo sa eth : *επ αυτουσ* 1957. 2023. 2041 : s$^{1.2}$ = *εν αυτοισ* or *εισ αυτουσ* | *εστησαν*] *στησονται* 2020 bo eth | *αυτων*] + *και πνευμα ζωησ επεσεν επ αυτουσ* s^{1} | *επεπεσεν* AC 025. 35. 325. 337. 456. 468. 620. 632**. 866. 920. 2037. 2038 al^{p} Or^{s} : *επιπεσειται* 2020 arm$^{1.2.3*}$ bo : *επεσεν* ℵ 046. **21** (– 35. 325. 337. 456. 468. 620. 632**. 866. 920). 250

φώνης μέγας ἐπέπεσεν ἐπὶ τοὺς θεωροῦντας αὐτούς. 12. καὶ ἤκουσαν ⌜φωνὴν
μεγάλης μεγάλην⌝ ἐκ τοῦ οὐρανοῦ ⌜λέγουσαν⌝ αὐτοῖς Ἀνάβατε ὧδε· καὶ ἀνέ-
λεγούσης βησαν εἰς τὸν οὐρανὸν ἐν τῇ νεφέλῃ, καὶ ἐθεώρησαν αὐτοὺς οἱ ἐχθροὶ
αὐτῶν.

13. Καὶ ἐν ἐκείνῃ τῇ ὥρᾳ ἐγένετο σεισμὸς μέγας, καὶ τὸ δέκατον
τῆς πόλεως ἔπεσεν, καὶ ἀπεκτάνθησαν ἐν τῷ σεισμῷ ὀνόματα ἀνθρώ-
πων χιλιάδες ἑπτά, καὶ οἱ λοιποὶ ἔμφοβοι ἐγένοντο καὶ ἔδωκαν δόξαν
τῷ θεῷ τοῦ οὐρανοῦ.

14. Ἡ οὐαὶ ἡ δευτέρα ἀπῆλθεν· ἰδοὺ ἡ οὐαὶ ἡ τρίτη ἔρχεται ταχύ.

2067 al^{p} eth : εγενετο s^{1} | τουσ θεωρουντασ] των θεωρουντων C 025. 35* |.

12. > Pr | ηκουσαν A א C 025. 429** al^{p} vg s : ηκουσα 046. **21** (− 2020). 250. 2037. 2038. 2067 al^{pm} Or^{8} Tyc gig arm bo sa : ακουσονται 2020 | φωνην μεγαλην εκ του ουρανου] de caelo vocem magnam Tyc | φωνην μεγαλην . . . λεγουσαν (λεγουσα 046**) A 046*. **21** (− 35. 205. 2040). 250 al^{pm} Or^{8} : φωνησ μεγαλησ . . . λεγουσησ א C 025. 1. 35. 60. 181. 205. 432. 1957. 2015. 2019. 2023. 2036. 2037. 2038. 2040. 2041. 2067 | αυτοισ] > A 2015 Tyc gig : αυτουσ 2016* | αναβατε A א C 025. 325. 452. 456. 506. 2019 Or^{8} : αναβητε 046. **21** (− 325. 456. 620. 866). 250. 2037. 2038. 2067 al^{pl} : αναβειτε 620. 866 : ascende Tyc : "rise ye up and come up" arm$^{1.2.a}$ | εθεωρησαν] εθεωρουν 498. 2020 s^{1} : "shall see" bo | αυτουσ] "their going up" arm$^{1.2}$ | οι εχθροι] pr παντεσ arm$^{1.2}$ |.

13. και εν A א C 025. 1. 35. 205. 250. 2037. 2038. 2040. 2067 al^{mu} Or^{8} Pr gig vg s arm$^{1.2.a}$ bo eth : και > 046. **21** (− 35. 205. 2040) al^{mu} Tyc arm$^{3.4}$ | ωρα A א C 025. 1. 205. 2019. 2037. 2040 al^{p} Or^{8} Tyc Pr vg s arm$^{1.2.3.a}$ bo eth : ημερα 046. **21** (− 205. 2040). 250 2038. 2067 al^{pm} gig arm^{4} | εγενετο] εσται arm^{2} bo | και το] ωστε το C | δεκατον] γ´ 046 bo : δωδεκατον 175. 2017 : + μεροσ bo eth | επεσεν] επεσαν s^{1} : "was swallowed up" arm$^{1.2.3.a}$ | ονοματα ανθρωπων χιλιαδεσ επτα] numero LXX milia hominum Pr : pr και s^{1} | ονοματα ανθρωπων] > arm^{1} : ονοματα ανθρωποι s^{1} : ανθρωποι arm | οι λοιποι] + ανθρωπων arm^{4} : "after that" arm$^{1.2.3.a}$ | εμφοβοι εγενοντο] ενφοβοι εγεν. C : εν φοβω εγεν. א 69 Or^{8} Pr (sunt missi) s^{1} : in timorem sunt missi vg : "fear (+ great arm$^{1.a}$) was (shall be arm^{2}) in all" arm$^{1.2.3.a}$: "were astounded" arm^{4} | εγενοντο και] γενομενοι 2015. 2036. 2037 | του ουρανου] > Tyc s^{2} : + et terrae Pr : τω εν τω ουρανω s^{1} : "heavenly" arm$^{1.2.3.a}$ |.

14. η ουαι η δευτερα] η^{1} > א^{c} 1. 172 : pr και 386 : pr ιδου arm$^{1.2.4.a}$: ιδου αι ουαι αι δυο s^{1} | απηλθεν] παρηλθεν א 2015. 2036. 2037 : απηλθον s^{1} | ιδου] pr και vg^{a} s^{1} arm^{4} bo : > 104. 205 209. 218. 314. 2018 arm^{3} eth : και arm$^{1.2.a}$ eth | ιδου η ουαι η τριτη ερχεται AC 025. 1. 35. 2019. 2020. 2038 al^{p} Or^{8} Pr (vg) s (bo) : ιδου η τριτη ουαι ερχεται 2015. 2036. 2037 : ιδου ουαι η τριτη ερχεται

15. Καὶ ὁ † ἕβδομος † ἄγγελος ἐσάλπισεν· καὶ ἐγένοντο φωναὶ <τρίτος>
μεγάλαι ἐν τῷ οὐρανῷ λέγοντες

Ἐγένετο ἡ βασιλεία τοῦ κόσμου τοῦ κυρίου ἡμῶν καὶ τοῦ Χριστοῦ αὐτοῦ,
καὶ βασιλεύσει εἰς τοὺς αἰῶνας τῶν αἰώνων.

16. καὶ οἱ εἴκοσι τέσσαρες πρεσβύτεροι οἱ ἐνώπιον τοῦ θεοῦ καθήμενοι ἐπὶ τοὺς θρόνους αὐτῶν ἔπεσαν ἐπὶ τὰ πρόσωπα αὐτῶν καὶ προσεκύνησαν τῷ θεῷ λέγοντες

2040 : η ουαι η τριτη (ταχυ) ερχεται 205 : ιδου ερχεται η ουαι η τριτη ℵ 2019 gig : η ουαι η τριτη ιδου ερχεται 046. **21** (– 35. 205. 2020. 2040). 250. 2067 al^{mu} | ερχεται] veniet vg (arm$^{1.2.3.a}$) : εληλυθε s^{1} : tr. after ταχυ 205 |.

15. και] + οτε arm$^{1.2.3.a}$ | ο εβδομοσ αγγελοσ εσαλπισεν] οι επτα αγγελοι εσαλπισαν arm^{1} | ο > A | και^{2} > arm$^{1.2.4.a}$ | εγενοντο] ℵ^{c} : εγενετο ℵ* arm$^{1.2.3.a}$ | φωναι μεγαλαι] φωνη μεγαλη arm$^{1.3}$ eth : φωνη arm^{a} | εν τω ουρανω] εκ του ουρανου arm$^{1.3}$ bo eth | λεγοντεσ A 046. 18. 61. 69. 82. 93. 110. 314. 325. 336. 429. 432. 452. 456. 506. 517. 522. 617. 620. 866. 919. 920. 1849. 1955. 2004. 2021. 2039 Or^{s} : λεγουσαι ℵC 025. **21** (– 18. 325. 456. 617. 620 866. 919. 920. 1849. 2004). 250. 2037. 2038. 2067 al^{pl} | εγενετο η βασιλεια] εγενοντο αι βασιλειαι 1. 104. 205. 2038 | η βασιλεια] pr πασα arm$^{1.2.a}$ | του κοσμου] huius mundi gig vg : > 2015. 2037 Pr arm$^{1.4}$ | του κυριου ημων] pr και 1934 : του θεου ημων 2015. 2020. Pr : και του θεου ημων s^{1} : του κυριου του θεου ημων bo | και του Χριστου αυτου] Ιησου Χριστου 205. 1934. 2015 (pr του). 2036. 2037 arm$^{1.2}$: και > arm^{4} | βασιλευσει] βασιλευει 69. 172. 325. 336. 456. 517. 620. 866. 2015. 2018. 2036. 2037* : regnavit gig s^{1} | τουσ αιωνασ] + και εισ τουσ αιωνασ arm^{4} : τον αιωνα bo | των αιωνων] + αμην ℵ 94. 141. 181. 2020 vg^{c} arm^{2} bo^{pl} |.

16. οι^{1} > ℵ* A bo | εικοσι τεσσαρεσ AℵC 025. 18. 175. 205. 250. 386. 617. 920. 1849. 1934. 2020. 2037. 2038. 2067 al^{mu} Or^{s} : κδ' 046. **21** (– 18. 175. 205. 386. 617. 920. 1849. 1934. 2020). 1. 104 al^{p} : εικοσι και τεσσαρεσ 429 al^{p} | οι ενωπιον ℵC 025. **21** (– 35*. 205. 2040). 250. 2037. 2067 al^{pl} Or^{s} s arm$^{1.2.4.a}$ bo : qui in conspectu dei sedent Pr (gig) vg : οι > A 046. 1. 35*. 61. 69. 104. 181. 205. 209. 2038. 2040 Cyp arm^{3} | του θεου AℵC 025. 1. 35. 205. 1957. 2015. 2023. 2036 2037. 2038. 2040. 2041. 2067 al^{p} Pr gig fl vg s^{1} arm$^{1.2.4.a}$: pr του θρονου 046. **21** (– 35. 205. 2040). 250 al^{pm} Or^{s} s^{2} arm^{3} | καθημενοι A 025. 1. 35. 104. 632**. 1957. 2019. 2020. 2037. 2038. 2067 al^{p} Pr gig vg Cyp (s) arm bo eth : pr οι 61. 69. 205 Or^{s} : καθηνται ℵ^{c}C 82. 2040 : οι καθηνται ℵ* 046. **21** (– 35. 205. 632**. 2020. 2040). 250 al^{pm} | επι τουσ θρονουσ] επι θρονον arm^{1} | επεσαν . . . τω θεω > arm^{1} | επεσαν . . . αυτων > arm^{4} | αυτων > bo | επεσαν A(ℵ)C 025. 1. 104. 110. 33*. 429. 620. 866. 2016. 2023*. 2067 al^{p} Or^{s} : επεσον

17 Εὐχαριστοῦμέν σοι, Κύριε ὁ θεὸς ὁ παντοκράτωρ,
ὁ ὢν καὶ ὁ ἦν,
ὅτι εἴληφας τὴν δύναμίν σου τὴν μεγάλην
καὶ ἐβασίλευσας.
18*a*. καὶ τὰ ἔθνη ὠργίσθησαν,
b. καὶ ἦλθεν ἡ ὀργή σου,
h. καὶ <ὁ καιρὸς> διαφθεῖραι τοὺς διαφθείροντας τὴν γῆν,
c. καὶ ὁ καιρὸς τῶν νεκρῶν κριθῆναι,
g. τοὺς μικροὺς καὶ τοὺς μεγάλους,
d. καὶ δοῦναι τὸν μισθὸν τοῖς δούλοις σου,
e. τοῖς προφήταις καὶ τοῖς ἁγίοις
f. καὶ τοῖς φοβουμένοις τὸ ὄνομά σου.

046. **21** (– 337. 620. 866). 250. 2037. 2038. (2040) al^{mu} : pr *και* ℵ 2040 | *τα προσωπα*] *το προσωπον* fl bo | *και*^{2} > bo sa | *τω θεω*] > gig : "the Lord God" arm$^{1.2.a}$ | *λεγοντεσ*] *ελεγον* arm^{1} : *και ελεγον* arm$^{2.a}$ |.

17. *σοι*] *σε* 046 | *Κυριε*] *Κυριοσ* ℵ 2038 | *ο θεοσ*] + *ημων* 2015. 2036. 2037 gig vg^{g} arm^{2} | *ο*^{2}] ℵ^{c} : > ℵ* | *ων . . . ην*] ∼ gig eth | *ο ην*] + *και ο ερχομενοσ* 051. 35. 1957. 2015. 2019. 2023. 2036. 2037. 2040. 2041 al^{p} (bo) | *οτι*] pr *και* ℵ*C : *και* arm^{a} : *οσ* arm$^{1.2}$ | *ειληφασ*] *ειληφεσ* C | *σου την μεγαλην* > arm^{1} bo |.

18. *ωργισθησαν*] ℵ^{c} : *ωργισθη* ℵ* : *οργισθησαν* 149. 201. 2015. 2017 al^{p} | *και*^{2}] *οτι* bo | *σου*] + *επ αυτουσ* 2020 | *και διαφθειραι*] *και* > A arm^{2} : quique exterminandi sunt Pr : et conrumpantur fl : *διαφθερεισ* bo | *διαφθειροντασ* Aℵ 046. **21** (– 35 468**). 2037 al^{pl} Or^{s} arm bo eth : *διαφθειραντασ* C 35. 60. 104. 172. 241. 242. 250. 468**. 1957. 2018. 2023. 2041 Pr gig fl vg Cyp s : *φθειροντασ* 025. 1. 2038. 2067 | *καιροσ*] *κληροσ* C : + *τησ κρισεωσ* bo | *των νεκρων*] *των εθνων* 617. 920. 2020 : *τουσ νεκρουσ* bo | *κριθηναι*] > Pr : *κρινεισ* arm^{3} : *κριναι* bo | *τουσ μικρουσ και τουσ μεγαλουσ* Aℵ*C Or^{s} : *τοισ* (pr *και* 2020 gig) *μικροισ και τοισ μεγαλοισ* ℵ$^{c.c}$ 025. 046. **21.** 250. 2037. 2038. 2067 al^{pl} Pr gig fl vg Cyp s^{2} arm : *τοισ μικροισ μετα των μεγαλων* s^{1}. It is possible to explain the variation of tenses as due to the dislocation of lines *h* and *g*. Thus Aℵ*C preserve the acc. (*τουσ μικρουσ* in apposition to the subject of *κριθηναι*) even after the transposition of the line after *και τοισ φοβ. σου*. Next comes the corrector's stage: the acc. is changed into a dat. to agree with *τοισ φοβ.* Possibly the original order was *a*, *b*, *h*, *g*, *c*, *d*, *e*, *f*. The *τουσ μικρουσ κτλ.* would then qualify *τουσ διαφθειροντασ κτλ.* In any case the order in the MSS is wrong. | *δουναι*] + *αυτοισ* bo | *και τοισ αγιοισ* > Pr gig | *τοισ αγιοισ και τοισ* (> ℵ) *φοβουμενοισ*] *τουσ αγιουσ και τουσ φοβουμενουσ* A (a correction?) : *τοισ αγιοισ και* > 051 : *και* > 35*. 205. 2015. 2019. 2036. 2037. 2038 al^{p} arm$^{1.2.a}$ | *αγιοισ*] + *σου* 617. 920. 2020 |.

19. καὶ ἠνοίγη ὁ ναὸς τοῦ θεοῦ ὁ ἐν τῷ οὐρανῷ, καὶ ὤφθη ἡ κιβωτὸς τῆς διαθήκης αὐτοῦ ἐν τῷ ναῷ αὐτοῦ, καὶ ἐγένοντο ἀστραπαὶ καὶ φωναὶ καὶ βρονταὶ καὶ σεισμὸς καὶ χάλαζα μεγάλη.

19. ηνοιγη Aℵ (ηνυγη) C 025. 1. 35. 61. 69. 104. 172. 205. 250. 1957. 2015. 2018. 2019. 2023. 2036. 2037. 2038. 2040. 2067 al[p] Or[s] eth : ηνοιχθη 046. **21** (– 35. 205. 2040) al[mu] | ο εν τω AC 61. 69. 172. 250. 2018. 2020. 2040 Or[s] gig fl arm bo eth : ο > ℵ 025. 046. **21** (– 2020. 2040). 2037. 2038. 2067 al[pl] Tyc vg s | ουρανω] + ανω ℵ* (del. ℵ[c]) | ωφθη] εδοθη C | τησ διαθηκησ αυτου] του θεου arm[a] | αυτου[1] AC 025. 1. 35*. 172. 205. 250. 2015. 2018. 2019. 2036. 2037. 2038. 2040 al[p] gig vg s arm[1. 2. 3. 4] : του κυριου **21** (– 18. 35*. 205 386. 2040). 2067 al[pl] Or[s] : κυριου 046. 18. 104. 1957. 2039 : του θεου ℵ 201. 386 fl eth : > Tyc bo | εν τω ναω] > arm[2] : pr "which is" arm[1. 3] eth | αυτου[2] > s[1] bo | εγενοιτο] ℵ[c] : εγενετο ℵ* | και φωναι και βρονται AℵC 025. 046. **21** (– 2020) Or[s] Pr arm[(1. 2). 3. a] sa eth : φωναι . . . βρονται ~ 69. 172. 250. 498. 2015. 2019. 2020. 2036. 2037 gig fl s (arm[4]) bo : και φωναι > 314. 2016 Tyc : και βρονται > vg | και σεισμοσ AℵC 025. 1. 35*. 205. 2015. 2019. 2020. 2023. 2036. 2040. 2067 al[p] Or[s] Tyc Pr gig fl vg s arm[2. 4. a] eth : και ο σεισμοσ 181 : και σεισμοι 172. 250. 424. 2018. 2037 2038 arm[1] bo sa : > 046. **21** (– 35*. 205. 2020. 2040) al[mu] arm[3] | και χαλαζα μεγαλη > Tyc |.

Chapter XII.

1. Καὶ σημεῖον μέγα ὤφθη ἐν τῷ οὐρανῷ, γυνὴ περιβεβλημένη τὸν ἥλιον, καὶ ἡ σελήνη ὑποκάτω τῶν ποδῶν αὐτῆς, καὶ ἐπὶ τῆς κεφαλῆς αὐτῆς στέφανος ἀστέρων δώδεκα. 2. καὶ ἐν γαστρὶ ⸀ἔχουσα, ἔχουσα

1. και] > Pr : + ιδου bo | περιβεβλημενη] περιβλεπομενη A | η σεληνη] ℵ[c] : την σεληνην ℵ* : η > 1. 175. 498 : + ην 2020 | αστερων] ακανθων s[1] | δωδεκα AℵC 025. 046. **21** (– 35. 337) Or[s] : δεκα δυο 1. 181. 2037. 2067 : ιβʹ 35. 337. 2015. 2017 al[p] : xxii. gig |.

2. εν γαστρι εχουσα] erat praegnans ventre Pr : in utero habebat fl : "she was with child" arm[1. 2. 3. a] | και κραζει ℵ 2040 vg[c. g] : και > A 025. 1. 35. 2015. 2019. 2036. 2037. 2038 : και εκραζεν C Pr fl vg[f. v] : εκραζεν **21** (– 35*. 1849. 2040). 1. 104. 110. 172. 250. 2016. 2067 al[mu] Or[s] vg[d] s[2] : εκραξεν 046. 1849 al[p] arm[4] : εκρακεν 35 ? : και εκραξεν gig arm[1. 2. a] : "who cried out" arm[3*] : et clamans vg[a] s[1] : κραζουσα bo | ωδινουσα] pr και A s eth | και βασανιζομενη] και > bo : et cruciabatur Pr fl : "and in many pains she was nigh" arm[1] | τεκειν] pr του 468**. 2040 |.

καὶ⌉ κράζει ὠδίνουσα καὶ βασανιζομένη τεκεῖν. 3. καὶ ὤφθη ἄλλο
πυρρὸς μέγας *σημεῖον ἐν τῷ οὐρανῷ, καὶ ἰδοὺ δράκων ⌈μέγας πυρρός⌉, ἔχων κεφαλὰς*
ἑπτὰ καὶ κέρατα δέκα, καὶ ἐπὶ τὰς κεφαλὰς αὐτοῦ ἑπτὰ διαδήματα.
4. καὶ ἡ οὐρὰ αὐτοῦ σύρει τὸ τρίτον τῶν ἀστέρων τοῦ οὐρανοῦ, καὶ
ἔβαλεν αὐτοὺς εἰς τὴν γῆν. καὶ ὁ δράκων ἕστηκεν ἐνώπιον τῆς
γυναικὸς τῆς μελλούσης τεκεῖν, ἵνα ὅταν τέκῃ τὸ τέκνον αὐτῆς
καταφάγῃ.

5. καὶ ἔτεκεν υἱόν, ἄρσεν, ὃς μέλλει ποιμαίνειν πάντα τὰ ἔθνη ἐν
ῥάβδῳ σιδηρᾷ· καὶ ἡρπάσθη τὸ τέκνον αὐτῆς πρὸς τὸν θεὸν καὶ πρὸς
τὸν θρόνον αὐτοῦ.

3. μεγασ πυρ(ρ)οσ A 025. 051. 1. 35. 172. 205. 1957. 2015. 2019. 2023. 2036. 2037. 2038. 2040. 2041 al^{p} Tyc vg s^{I} sa eth : ~ℵC 046. **21** (–35. 205. 2040). 250. 2067 al^{mu} Or^{s} Pr gig fl s^{2} arm$^{1.2.3.a}$ (bo) | *μεγασ*] + "exceedingly" arm^{1} : "it is very great" bo | *πυρροσ* Aℵ 025. 051. **21** (–18. 205. 337. 386. 617. 919. 920. 1849. 2004. 2040). 2037. 2038. 2067 al^{mu} Or^{s} : rufus Tyc Pr gig fl vg eth : *πυροσ* C 046. 1. 18. 205. 250. 337. 386. 617. 919. 920. 1849. 2040 s : "fiery" arm$^{1.2.3.a}$: "of colour of fire" bo : > arm^{4} : + *ομοιοσ πυρι* eth | *επι τασ κεφαλασ*] *επι τησ κεφαλησ* 205 (arm$^{1.2}$) : *επι τασ επτα κεφαλασ* arm^{4} | *αυτου*] *αυτων* A 172 | *επτα*^{2} > 1. 181. 2038 |.

4. η ουρα αυτου] > gig : *αυτου* > 1 | *συρει*] trahebat Tyc Pr fl vg | *των αστερων*] ℵ^{c} : + *το τριτον* ℵ* | *του ουρανου*] > 1. 2067 : *των εν τω ουρανω* s^{1} | *αυτουσ*] + *εκ του ουρανου* arm$^{2.4}$ | *εισ την γην* > arm^{4} | *εστηκεν*] *εστηκει* C s : *εστη* 61. 69 | *τησ μελλουσησ τεκειν*] > bo eth : "who wished to bear" arm$^{1.2.3}$ sa | *τεκειν*] *τικτειν* 051. 35. 432. 1957. 2023. 2041 | *τεκη*] + *η γυνη* arm$^{1.2.3.a}$ | *το τεκνον αυτησ* > arm^{4} | *τεκνον*] *παιδιον* 2020 : filium gig vg bo : natum Pr fl | *αυτησ* > bo | *καταφαγη*] + *αυτο(ν)* arm^{3} : + *αυτο(ν) ο δρακων* arm$^{1.2.a}$ | *ινα . . . καταφαγη*] *ινα εαν τεκη το τεκνον ο δρακων καταφαγη αυτο* bo : *ινα οταν τεκη καταφαγη το τεκνον αυτησ* eth |.

5. ετεκεν] + *η γυνη* Tyc arm$^{1.2.3.a}$ | *υιον* > Tyc Pr arm^{a} | *αρσεν* AC : *αρσενα* 025. 2038. 2040 : *αρρενα* ℵ **21** (–2040). 1. 250. 2037. 2067 al^{pl} Or^{s} : *αρενα* 046 | *μελλει ποιμαινειν*] "shall shepherd" arm$^{1.2.3}$: recturus est Pr gig fl vg | *παντα τα εθνη*] *τα εθνη* 205. bo : "his people" arm$^{1.2}$ | *εν ραβδω* AℵC 046. **21** (–35*. 205. 2040). 250. al^{pl} Or^{s} Pr gig fl vg s (bo) : *εν* > 025. 051. 1. 35*. 181. 205. 498. 2015. 2037. 2038. 2040. 2067 | *και*^{2} > Pr | *ηρπασθη* AC 025. **21** (–386. 2040). 1. 69. 104. 250. 2037. 2038. 2067 al^{pl} Or^{s} : *ηρπαχθη* 046 : *ηρπαγη* ℵ 60. 241. 385. 386. 432 1957. 2016. 2023. 2040. 2041 | *τεκνον*] *παιδιον* 2020 | *αυτησ* > bo | *προσ*^{2} > 1. 205. 2019. 2037. 2038 al^{p} |.

6. καὶ ἡ γυνὴ ἔφυγεν εἰς τὴν ἔρημον, ὅπου ἔχει ἐκεῖ τόπον
ἡτοιμασμένον ἀπὸ τοῦ θεοῦ, ἵνα ἐκεῖ ⸀τρέφουσιν⸣ αὐτὴν ἡμέρας χιλίας τρέφωσιν
διακοσίας ἑξήκοντα.
7. Καὶ ἐγένετο πόλεμος ἐν τῷ οὐρανῷ,
ὁ Μιχαὴλ καὶ οἱ ἄγγελοι αὐτοῦ τοῦ πολεμῆσαι μετὰ τοῦ δράκοντος,
καὶ ὁ δράκων ἐπολέμησεν καὶ οἱ ἄγγελοι αὐτοῦ, 8. καὶ οὐκ
⸀ἴσχυσεν,⸣ ἴσχυσαν
οὐδὲ τόπος εὑρέθη † αὐτῶν † ἔτι ἐν τῷ οὐρανῷ.

6. η^{1} >205 | οπου εχει . . . απο του θεου] "where was her place (a place for her arm$^{2.a}$) prepared of God" arm $^{1.2.a}$: "which hath there a place prepared of God" arm^{4} : και (>bo) εισ τον τοπον ον ητοιμασεν αυτη ο θεοσ bo s^{1} eth | εχει] ειχε 2020 fl vg^{d} s | εκει^{1} Aℵ 025. 046. **21** (−2020). 250. 2067. al^{pm} Or^{s} s^{I} arm$^{3.4}$: tr after τοπον 205. 241. 632** gig : >C 051. 1. 69. 2019. 2020. 2037. 2038 al^{p} Pr fl vg s^{2} arm$^{1.2.a}$ | ητοιμασμενον] pr αυτη arm$^{2.a}$: + αυτη arm^{3} | απο του θεου AℵC 025. 1. 35. 1957. 2023. 2037*. 2038. 2040. 2041 : απο >205 : υπο του θεου 046. **21** (−35. 205. 468*. 620. 866. 2040). 250. 2037**. 2067 al^{mu} Or^{s} : υπο θεου 468*. 620. 866 | εκει^{2}] tr after αυτην 468 Pr fl : >051 s^{I} | τρεφωσιν A 025. 1. 18. 205. 250. 617. 2020. 2037. 2040. 2067 al^{mu} Or^{s} : εκτρεφωσιν 046. **21** (−18. 205. 617. 2020 2040) al^{mu} : τρεφουσιν ℵC 051. 2019. 2038 . εκτρεφουσιν 429. 522 : "she may be fed" arm$^{1.a}$ | αυτην] ℵ^{c} : αυτον ℵ* : > 69 arm$^{1.a}$ | χιλιασ διακοσιασ εξηκοντα Aℵ 025. **21** Or^{s} (arm$^{3**.a}$) : + πεντε ℵ^{c} (arm$^{1.2.3*.4}$) : χιλιασ διακοσιασ ξ′ 046 : ασξ′ 2015 : αωξ′ 69 : χιλ. και διακ. και εξηκ. s : mille ducentis quadraginta gig : "a thousand two hundred and ninety" bo |.

7. πολεμοσ] + μεγασ gig bo | ο] ο τε A s^{2} | του πολεμησαι AC 025. 35. 432. 1957. 2019. 2023. 2040. 2041 al^{p} : > Or^{s} : του >ℵ 046. **21** (−35. 2040). 1. 69. 104. 110. 250. 314. 385. 429. 2015. 2016. 2017. 2037. 2038. 2067 al^{mu} s^{2} : ut pugnarent Pr fl : pugnabant Tyc (gig vg) arm$^{1.2.3.a}$: πολεμουντεσ s^{1} arm^{4} | μετα] κατα 1. 201. 386 al^{p} | και ο δρακων . . . αυτου] και ο δρακων και οι αγγελοι αυτου επολεμησαν 205 s$^{(1).2}$ | και ο δρακων] του δευτερου s^{1} |.

8. και] sed fl arm$^{1.a}$: >arm^{4} | ισχυσεν A **21** (−35. 205. 337. 1849 (2020). 2040). 250 al^{mu} (bo) eth : ισχυσαν (+ προσ αυτον ℵ) ℵC 025. 1. 35. 205. 337. 1849. 2015. 2019. (2020). 2036. 2037. 2038. 2040. 2067 al^{mu} Or^{s} Tyc Pr gig fl vg s (arm) : ισχυον 046. 69 : + πολεμων μετ αυτων bo | ουδε AℵC 046. **21** (−35. 205). 250. 2067 al^{mu} : ουτε 025. 1. 35. 205. 2019. 2037. 2038 al^{p} Or^{s} | τοποσ ευρεθη αυτων] τοτε ευρεθη ℵ* : τοποσ > 69 | ευρεθη αυτων AC 025. 046. 1. 69. 2020. (2040) al^{mu} Or^{s} gig vg : ~ 2015. 2036. 2037. 2067 Tyc (Pr) fl s^{2} : ευρεθη αυτοισ ℵ$^{c.c.}$ 35. 1849*.

9. καὶ ἐβλήθη ὁ δράκων ὁ μέγας, ὁ ὄφις ὁ ἀρχαῖος,
ὁ καλούμενος Διάβολος καὶ ὁ Σατανᾶς,
ὁ πλανῶν τὴν οἰκουμένην ὅλην—
ἐβλήθη εἰς τὴν γῆν,
καὶ οἱ ἄγγελοι αὐτοῦ μετ' αὐτοῦ ἐβλήθησαν.
10. καὶ ἤκουσα φωνὴν μεγάλην ἐν τῷ οὐρανῷ λέγουσαν
Ἄρτι ἐγένετο ἡ σωτηρία καὶ ἡ δύναμις
καὶ ἡ βασιλεία τοῦ θεοῦ ἡμῶν καὶ ἡ ἐξουσία τοῦ Χριστοῦ αὐτοῦ,
ὅτι ἐβλήθη ὁ κατήγωρ τῶν ἀδελφῶν ἡμῶν,
ὁ κατηγορῶν αὐτοὺς ἐνώπιον τοῦ θεοῦ ἡμῶν ἡμέρας καὶ νυκτός.
11. καὶ αὐτοὶ ἐνίκησαν αὐτὸν διὰ τὸ αἷμα τοῦ ἀρνίου,
καὶ διὰ τὸν λόγον τῆς μαρτυρίας αὐτῶν,
καὶ οὐκ ἠγάπησαν τὴν ψυχὴν αὐτῶν ἄχρι θανάτου.

2019 s^1 arm : *ευρεθη αυτω* **21** (−35. 1849*. 2020. 2040). 104. 110. 250. 314. (∼385) al^{mu} | *τοποσ αυτων ετι εν τω ουρανω ευρεθη* Pr | *ετι* > $ℵ^{c.\,c}$ 104. 2015. 2036 s arm |.

9. **ο μεγασ ο οφισ**] *ο μεγασ οφισ* ℵ 1. 2067 : *ο οφισ ο μεγασ* 617. 920. 2040 Pr bo : *μεγασ οφισ* 2038 | *ο οφισ*] pr *και* arm^2 | *ο Διαβ. και* >eth | *και ο Σατανασ* AC 025. 1. 35*. 2038. 2040. 2067 al^p Or^s s : *και* > ℵ bo : *ο* > 046. **21** (−35*. 2040). 250. 2037 al^{pm} | *ο πλανων . . . γην* >Tyc | *ο πλανων*] qui seducebat Pr (bo) eth : qui seducet fl | *εβληθη*] pr *και* gig fl $s^{1.\,(2)}$: *και επεσεν* arm^4 : "the lion fell" $arm^{1.\,2}$ | *μετ αυτου εβληθησαν*] > 506. 2015. 2036. 2037 : *μετ αυτου* > 051. 1. 35*. 2038 : *εβληθησαν* >Tyc arm^1 | *εβληθησαν*] *επεσαν* $arm^{3.\,a}$: *επεσεν* arm^2 |.

10. *ηκουσα*] *ηκουσαν* 2037. 2040 | *φωνην μεγαλην . . . λεγουσαν*] *φωνησ μεγαλησ . . . λεγουσησ* 2067 | *μεγαλην* >arm^4 | *εν τω ουρανω*] *εκ του ουρανου* 205. 2040 Tyc Pr gig s^1 $arm^{1.\,4.\,a}$: after *λεγουσαν* 1. 2037 al^p : > 452. 2021 | *αρτι* > Pr : *ιδου* s^1 | *και η βασιλεια* >fl | *και η εξουσια του Χριστου αυτου* > Tyc s^1 | *Χριστου*] *κυριου* C | *εβληθη*] *κατεβληθη* 1. 35. 2023. 2038. 2067 al^p : exclusus est Tyc : "hath fallen" arm | *κατηγωρ* A : *κατηγοροσ* ℵC 025. 046. **21**. 250. 2037. 2038. 2067 al^{pl} Or^s : "the betrayer" arm^4 | *των αδελφων ημων* > s^1 | *ο κατηγορων*] qui accusabat Pr vg s^2 : "who was betraying" arm^4 | *αυτουσ* A 025. 1. 205. 2015. 2019. 2036. 2037. 2038. 2067 : *αυτων* ℵC 046. **21** (−205). 250. al^{pl} Or^s : > bo | *θεου*] + *και του κυριου* (*Ιησου Χριστου*) $arm^{1.\,(2)}$ | *ημων*^{3} > 1. 61. 69. 522. 2015. 2036. 2037. 2039. 2067 $arm^{1.\,2.\,a}$ bo eth |.

11. *και*^{1}] *οτι* bo : >arm^2 | *αυτοι*] *ουτοι* ℵ : >Pr | *ενικησαν*] superatus est Pr | *αυτον*] ab ipsis Pr : >s^1 | *δια το αιμα*] *δια του αιματοσ* 69. 2019 $arm^{1.\,2.\,3.\,a}$: *εν τω αιματι* s^1 : *δια το ονομα* 2015. 2036. 2037 | *του αρνιου*] + *του θεου* $arm^{1.\,2}$ | *τον λογον*] >C arm^4 :

12. διὰ τοῦτο εὐφραίνεσθε οἱ οὐρανοὶ καὶ οἱ ἐν αὐτοῖς σκηνοῦντες·
οὐαὶ τὴν γῆν καὶ τὴν θάλασσαν,
ὅτι κατέβη ὁ διάβολος πρὸς ὑμᾶς, ἔχων θυμὸν μεγάν,
εἰδὼς ὅτι ὀλίγον καιρὸν ἔχει.
13. Καὶ ὅτε εἶδεν ὁ δράκων ὅτι ἐβλήθη εἰς τὴν γῆν, ἐδίωξεν τὴν
γυναῖκα ἥτις ἔτεκεν τὸν ἄρσενα. 14. καὶ ἐδόθησαν τῇ γυναικὶ αἱ
δύο πτέρυγες τοῦ ἀετοῦ τοῦ μεγάλου, ἵνα πέτηται εἰς τὴν ἔρημον
εἰς τὸν τόπον αὐτῆς, ὅπου τρέφεται ἐκεῖ καιρὸν καὶ καιροὺς καὶ

του λογου arm$^{1.2.3.a}$: το αιμα bo | τησ μαρτυριασ] την μαρτυριαν C : των μαρτυριων arm^{4} | αυτων] αυτου 172. 205. 241. 632. 2022 arm | και^{3}] οτι bo | ουκ] ουχ A | την ψυχην] τασ ψυχασ 172. 250. 424. 2018 vg$^{c.d.f.v}$ arm^{4} | αυτων] εαυτων ℵ^{c} | αχρι] μεχρι 468. 620. 632*. 866 |.

12. δια] pr και 205 eth | οι ουρανοι A 051. 1. 35. 241. 429**. 632. 1957. 2015. 2019. 2023. 2036. 2037. 2038. 2040. 2067 al^{p} Or^{s} arm$^{1.a}$ bo eth : οι >ℵC 025. 046. **21** (– 35. 632. 2040). 250 al^{mu} s : ο ουρανοσ arm$^{2.3}$: ουρανοσ arm^{4} | εν αυτοισ σκηνουντεσ A 025. 046. **21** (– 920) Or^{s} s : εν αυτοισ κατασκηνουντεσ C : κατοικουντεσ εν αυτοισ ℵ (Pr fl vg bo sa eth) : "all (>arm^{3} : 'ye' arm^{1}) who are dwelling ('the dwellers' arm^{3}) in them ('it' arm$^{3.4.a}$)" arm : εν αυτοισ κατοικουντεσ 385. 429. 506. 522. 920. 2016. 2037 (gig) | την γην και την θαλασσαν C 025. 35*. 2015. 2036. 2038. 2040 : pr εισ ℵ : pr τοισ κατοικουσι 1. 2037 : την αγαπην και την θαλασσαν A : τη γη και τη θαλασση 046. **21** (– 35*. 2040). 250. 2067 al^{pm} Or^{s} : vae terrae et mari gig fl vg s arm bo eth : vae vobis (tibi Tyc) terra et mare Tyc Pr | κατεβη] καταβαινει s$^{1.(2)}$: "is fallen" arm$^{1.2.3.a}$ | διαβολοσ] "dragon" arm$^{1.2.3*.4}$: "adversary" arm$^{3**.a}$ | υμασ] αυτουσ s^{1} | εχων] pr ο 1. 2037 arm^{3a} | εχων θυμον μεγαν] μεγαν>ℵ arm^{1} : μεγαν εχων θυμον 2067 : εχων θυμον μεγα 2020 : cum ira ingenti Pr |.

13. ο δρακων οτι εβληθη] ℵ* : οτι εβληθη ο δρακων ℵ^{c} | εβληθη] "fell" arm$^{1.2.3.a}$ eth but both = εβληθη | εδιωξεν] εδωκεν ℵ* : εξεδιωξεν ℵ^{c} : εδιωκεν gig | αρσενα ℵC 025. 35. 61. 69. 2040 Or^{s} : αρσεναν A : αρρενα **21** (– 35. 2040). 250. 2037. 2038. 2067 al^{pl} αρενα 046. 2015 : υιον s^{2} : "child" arm^{1} : "male" arm^{4} : "male child" arm$^{2.3.a}$: τον υιον (τον) αρρενα 506. 680 bo sa eth |.

14. εδοθησαν] εδοθη ℵ^{c} 205 s^{1} arm | τη γυναικι] αυτη bo | αι δυο πτερυγεσ] πτερυγεσ δυο 468* | αι δυο AC 025. 35*. 104. 181. 517*. 2015. 2019. 2036. 2038. 2040. 2067 (s^{2}) : >arm$^{1.2.3}$: αι> ℵ 046. **21** (– 35*. 2040). 2037 al^{pl} Or^{s} s^{1} arm$^{4.a}$ bo eth | πτερυγεσ] + (αι) μεγαλαι bo | του αετου] του >ℵ arm bo : pr ωσ Pr bo | του μεγαλου >arm^{1} bo | πετηται] πετεται 046*. 1. 919. 2015. 2020. 2036 : πεσηται 386 : + η γυνη bo | εισ την ερημον >1. 181. 2037 | εισ^{2} >Tyc arm$^{1.2.3}$ | αυτησ >bo eth | οπου τρεφεται AℵC 025. 1. 35*. 201. 314. 386. 2015. 2019. 2036. 2037. 2038. 2040 al^{p}

ἥμισυ καιροῦ ἀπὸ προσώπου τοῦ ὄφεως. 15. καὶ ἔβαλεν ὁ ὄφις ἐκ
τοῦ στόματος αὐτοῦ ὀπίσω τῆς γυναικὸς ὕδωρ ὡς ποταμόν, ἵνα αὐτὴν
ποταμοφόρητον ποιήσῃ. 16. καὶ ἐβοήθησεν ἡ γῆ τῇ γυναικί, καὶ
ἤνοιξεν ἡ γῆ τὸ στόμα αὐτῆς καὶ κατέπιεν τὸν ποταμὸν ὃν ἔβαλεν
ὁ δράκων ἐκ τοῦ στόματος αὐτοῦ. 17. καὶ ὠργίσθη ὁ δράκων ἐπὶ
τῇ γυναικί, καὶ ἀπῆλθεν ποιῆσαι πόλεμον μετὰ τῶν λοιπῶν τοῦ
σπέρματος αὐτῆς, τῶν τηρούντων τὰς ἐντολὰς τοῦ θεοῦ καὶ ἐχόντων
τὴν μαρτυρίαν Ἰησοῦ.
18. καὶ ἐστάθη ἐπὶ τὴν ἄμμον τῆς θαλάσσης.

Tyc Pr gig fl vg s^{2} : pr ινα Or^{s} : οπου τρεφηται 506. 517. 2017 : οπωσ τρεφηται 046. **21** (– 35*. 386. 2040). 250. 2067 al^{mu} s^{1} | εκει] >Tyc Pr fl vg bo eth : before οπου gig | καιρον και καιρουσ] καιρουσ και καιρον arm^{1} : καιρον και καιρον arm^{3} : καιρον arm^{2} | καιρον] > ℵ* : και καιρον ℵ^{c} | και καιρουσ] και > 456 s^{1} | και ημισυ καιρου >C | ημισυ] ℵ^{c} : ημισου ℵ* |.

15. εβαλεν] ελαβεν A* : υπερεβαλεν 104 | εκ του στοματοσ αυτου] tr. after τησ γυναικοσ 1 | οπισω τ. γυναικοσ after ποταμον bo sa | υδωρ] >385. 429. 522 : "venom" arm^{2} | ωσ ποταμον] εισ ποταμον 18 : >arm^{a} | ινα . . . ποιηση >bo | αυτην ποταμοφορητον ποιηση] ποιηση αυτην ποταμοφορητον C | αυτην AℵC 046. **21** (– 35. 205). 250. 2037 al^{pm} Or^{s} Pr gig vg s : ταυτην 025. 1. 35. 104. 205. 2038. 2067 al^{p} | ποταμοφορητον ποιηση] ποταμοφορητον ποιησει 104. 2019. 2038 : perderet Pr : faceret trahi a flumine vg : faceret ictu fluminis trahi ad se gig.

16. και εβοηθησεν . . . γυναικι >bo | και^{1}] sed Pr | τη γυναικι . . . η γη >337 | η γη^{2} >141. 250. 424. 452. 2018. 2019. 2021 Pr gig arm$^{1.4}$ | το στομα] του στοματοσ 18 | και κατεπιεν . . . στοματοσ αυτου > s$^{2\,(codd.)}$ | και^{3} >bo | τον ποταμον ον] το υδωρ ο A arm$^{1.a}$: τον ποταμον ο 456 : τον ποταμον υδατοσ bo | εβαλεν] ενεβαλεν 046 Or^{s} : ανελαβεν 61. 69 (69 after γυναικι ver. 17 repeats και ηνοιξεν . . . ανελαβεν) : "poured out" arm$^{1.2.3.a}$ | εκ του στομα τοσ αυτου] "upon the woman" arm^{4} : οπισω τησ γυναικοσ bo : >arm^{a} |.

17. και ωργισθη . . . γυναικι >arm$^{1.4}$ | ωργισθη] οργισθη 046. 104. 2019. 2038 : iratus Pr | ο δρακων > Pr | επι > C Pr | ποιησαι πολεμον] ~ℵ | μετα] pr και 2040 | των λοιπων] των επιλοιπων ℵ : τησ γυναικοσ και arm^{1} : > arm$^{2.3}$ | του σπερματοσ] de semine Tyc Pr vg | αυτησ] τησ γυναικοσ bo | τασ εντολασ] την εντολην Pr arm^{1} | Ιησου Aℵ^{c}C 025. 046*. **21**. 250. 2037. 2038. 2067 al^{p} Or^{s} gig vg s arm$^{3.4.a}$ bo : pr του 046**. 1. 104. 110 : του θεου ℵ* : θεου 522 : Jesu Christi Pr vg^{c} arm$^{1.2}$ eth |.

18. ver. 18 >Pr arm^{2} | εσταθη AℵC 61. 172. (205) al^{p} Or^{s} Tyc. gig vg$^{1.d.f.v}$ s^{2} arm$^{1.3}$ eth : εσταθην 025. 046. **21** (– 205). 250. 2037. 2038. 2067 al^{pl} vg$^{c.g}$ s^{1} arm$^{4.a}$ bo |.

Chapter XIII.

1. Καὶ εἶδον ἐκ τῆς θαλάσσης θηρίον ἀναβαῖνον,
ἔχον κέρατα δέκα καὶ κεφαλὰς ἑπτά, (a)
καὶ ἐπὶ τὰς κεφαλὰς αὐτοῦ ⸢ὀνόματα⸣ βλασφημίας. ὄνομα

2. καὶ τὸ θηρίον ὃ εἶδον ἦν ὅμοιον παρδάλει,
καὶ οἱ πόδες αὐτοῦ ὡς ἄρκου,
καὶ τὸ στόμα αὐτοῦ ὡς στόμα λέοντος.

καὶ ἔδωκεν αὐτῷ ὁ δράκων τὴν δύναμιν αὐτοῦ
καὶ τὸν θρόνον αὐτοῦ καὶ ἐξουσίαν μεγάλην.
3. καὶ μίαν ἐκ τῶν κεφαλῶν αὐτοῦ ὡς ἐσφαγμένην εἰς θάνατον,
καὶ ἡ πληγὴ τοῦ θανάτου αὐτοῦ ἐθεραπεύθη.

καὶ ἐθαυμάσθη ὅλη ἡ γῆ † ὀπίσω τοῦ θηρίου †,

(*a*) MSS add a gloss to prepare the way for xvii. 12: *καὶ ἐπὶ τῶν κεράτων αὐτοῦ δέκα διαδήματα.* See vol. ii. English transl., footnote *in loc.*

1. και ειδον εκ τησ θαλασσησ >205 | *εκ τησ θαλασσησ . . . αναβαινον*] *εκ τησ θαλασσησ* after *αναβαινον* (Tyc) Pr s^{2} arm eth | *θηριον αναβαινον*] ~ Tyc : + *μεγα* arm^{1} | *εχον*] *εχων* 1. 104. 110. 429. 522. 2016. 2017 | *κερατα δεκα και κεφαλασ επτα*] *κερατα δεκα και* > 1 : *κερατα δεκα . . . κεφαλασ επτα* ~ vg arm$^{1.\,2.\,a}$: *κερατα δεκα* ~ 468 | *τασ κεφαλασ*] *την κεφαλην* arm | **αυτου**] *αυτων* (025) | *ονοματα* A 046. **21** (– 2040) al^{pm} Or^{8} vg s^{2} : *ονομα* ℵC 025. 1. 2015. 2036. 2037. 2038. 2067 Pr gig s^{1} arm bo eth | *βλασφημιασ*] *γεγραμμενον* bo |.

2. το θηριον] bestiam Pr gig : bestia vg | *ην ομοιον*] ~ 172. 2015. 2018 Tyc Pr vg | *ην* > 1. 181. 209. 2038. 2067^{com} gig arm$^{1.\,a}$ | *αυτου*^{1} > Tyc | *ωσ*^{1}] similes gig | *αρκου* AℵC 025. 046. **21** (– 35. 632. 2040). 1. 250. 2037*. 2038 al^{mu} Or^{8} : *αρκτου* 35. 61. 172*. 201**. 241. 385. 429**. 522. 632. 1957. 2037**. 2039. 2040. 2041. 2067 al^{p} | *στομα*^{2} > 2020 s^{1} arm$^{1.\,2.\,a}$ | *λεοντοσ* AC 025. 046. 250. 2037. 2038. 2067 al^{pl} Tyc Pr gig vg arm bo sa eth : *λεοντων* ℵ 61. 69 Or^{8} s | *αυτω*] *αυτον* 866 | *ο* > ℵ* | *την δυναμιν αυτου και τον θρονον αυτου και* > arm^{1} | *και τον θρονον αυτου* > 2037 | *και εξουσιαν μεγαλην*] > 385. 429. 522. 919. 1849. 1955. 2004. 2024 : *και* > 104. 2038 : + *εδωκεν αυτω* A** |.

3. και^{1}] + *ειδον* 2040. 2067 Tyc vg$^{d.\,f.\,v}$ | *μιαν*] *μια* arm$^{1.\,a}$: unum caput Pr : *πληγην* (?) bo | *εκ*] > 046. 1. 205. 2019. 2037. 2038. 2067 : *επι* bo | *αυτου*] *επτα* Pr | *ωσ* AℵC 025. 1. 35*. 205. 385. 2015. 2019. 2020. 2036. 2037. 2038 al^{p} Or^{8} : *ωσει* 046. **21** (– 35*. 205. 2020). 250. 2067 al^{mu} : *ην* arm$^{1.\,a}$: > arm$^{2.\,3}$ |

4\. *καὶ προσεκύνησαν τῷ δράκοντι*
ὅτι ἔδωκεν τὴν ἐξουσίαν τῷ θηρίῳ,

τῷ θηρίῳ *καὶ προσεκύνησαν ⌜τὸ θηρίον⌝ λέγοντες*
Τίς ὅμοιος τῷ θηρίῳ,
καὶ τίς δύναται πολεμῆσαι μετ' αὐτοῦ;

5^{a}. *καὶ ἐδόθη αὐτῷ στόμα λαλοῦν μεγάλα καὶ βλασφημίας,* (*a*)

(*a*) On the restoration of 5^{b} to its original place before 7, see vol. ii., English transl., footnote *in loc.*

εσφαγμενην] *εσφραγισμενην* 386. 1957. 2037. 2067 : *εσφαγμενη* (?) arm^{1} : *σφαγησ* bo : occisum fuerit Pr | *αυτου*^{2}] > 046. 205 : *του θανατου* ℵ* (corr. first hand) | *εθαυμασθη* A 051. 1. 181. 2015. 2019. 2036. 2037. 2067 gig (s) : *εθαυμαστωθη* C : *εθαυμασεν* ℵ 025. 046. **21**. 250 al^{pl} Or^{s} bo : admiratae sunt Pr | *ολη η γη*] *εν ολη τη γη* 051. 1. 181. 2015. 2019. 2036. 2067 : in terra gig : gentes inhabitantes terram Pr : + *και ηκολουθησεν* eth | *οπισω του θηριου*] *οπισθε του θηριου* 2020 : post bestiam illam gig : ad bestiam Pr | *οπισω του θηριου* = מאחרי החיה, corrupt for בראתה החיה. See vol. i. 337, 351 |.

4. τω δρακοντι . . . προσεκυνησαν^{2} > 1. 385. arm^{2} bo | *δρακοντι*] *θηριω* arm^{1} | *οτι εδωκε . . . θηριω*^{1} > bo | *οτι εδωκεν* AℵC 025. 172. 181. 205. 209. 250. 424. 2015 (*οτε*). 2018. 2019. 2036. 2037. 2038. 2040. 2067 Or^{s} Tyc Pr vg s arm^{4} : + *ο δρακων* arm^{1} : *τω δεδωκοτι* 046. **21** (– 205. 2040) al^{pm} : *τω δοντι* 61. 69 : qui dedit gig arm$^{3. a}$ | *την εξουσιαν*] *την* > Or^{s} : + *αυτου* arm$^{1. 3. 4}$: omnem potestatem suam Pr | *τω θηριω*^{1}] *τω θηριον* 920 : *αυτω* arm^{1} | *λεγοντεσ . . . θηριω* > s^{2} | *και προσεκυνησαν το θηριον* > 051. 181. 205. 2038. 2067 arm$^{2. 4. a}$ | *το θηριον* A 2036. 2037 al^{p} : *τω θηριω* ℵC 025. 046. **21** (– 920). 250 al^{pm} Or^{s} : *τω θηριον* 920 | *τισ*^{1}] *ουδεισ* arm^{1} | *τω θηριω*] + *τουτω* s$^{1. 2}$ bo eth : illae bestiae Pr | *και*^{3} AℵC 025. 046. 1. 35. 60. 61. 69. 172. 181. 205. 241. 250. 432. 452*. 632**. 1957. 2015. 2018. 2019. 2020. 2023. 2036. 2037. 2038. 2040. 2041. 2067 Or^{s} Pr gig vg s bo eth : *η* Tyc arm : > **21** (– 35. 205. 632**. 2020. 2040). 104. 110. 314. 385. 2016 al^{p} | *δυναται* AℵC 025. 1. 35*. 172. 205. 250. 498. 920. 2015. 2018. 2019. 2020. 2023. 2036. 2037. 2038. 2040. 2067 : *δυνατοσ* 046. **21** (– 35*. 205. 920. 2020. 2040) al^{pm} Or^{s} |.

5^{a}. και εδοθη . . . βλασφημιασ > 1. 2016. 2017. 2038 Pr | *στομα* > arm^{1} | *λαλουν*] *λαλουντοσ* 205 : *λαλειν* arm$^{1. 2. 3. a}$ bo eth : loquendi gig | *βλασφημιασ* ℵC 201. 386. 2020. 2040 al^{p} vg$^{(a). d}$ s$^{(2)}$ bo arm$^{1. 2}$: *βλασφημιαι* 620. 866 vg$^{c. f. g. v}$: *βλασφημα* A 172. 181. 241. 250. 424. 632**. 2015. 2018. 2036. 2037. 2067 : *βλασφημιαν* 025. 046. **21** (– 386. 620. 632**. 866 (920). 2020. 2040) al^{mu} Or^{s} s^{1} arm$^{3. (4). a}$: blasphemare gig : + *γενεσθαι* arm^{4} |.

6. καὶ ἤνοιξεν τὸ στόμα αὐτοῦ εἰς βλασφημίας πρὸς τὸν θεόν,
βλασφημῆσαι τὸ ὄνομα αὐτοῦ καὶ τὴν σκηνὴν αὐτοῦ,
⸀καὶ τοὺς⸃ ἐν τῷ οὐρανῷ σκηνοῦντας. τοὺς

5^{b}. καὶ ἐδόθη αὐτῷ ἐξουσία ποιῆσαι μῆνας τεσσεράκοντα καὶ δύο,
7. καὶ ἐδόθη αὐτῷ ποιῆσαι πόλεμον μετὰ τῶν ἁγίων καὶ νικῆσαι αὐτούς,
καὶ ἐδόθη αὐτῷ ἐξουσία ἐπὶ πᾶσαν φυλὴν καὶ λαὸν καὶ γλῶσσαν καὶ ἔθνος.

8. καὶ προσκυνήσουσιν αὐτὸν πάντες οἱ κατοικοῦντες ἐπὶ τῆς γῆς,
⸀οὗ⸃ οὐ γέγραπται τὸ ὄνομα ⸀αὐτοῦ⸃ ἐν τῷ βιβλίῳ τῆς ζωῆς ὧν . .
τοῦ ἀρνίου τοῦ ἐσφαγμένου ἀπὸ καταβολῆς κόσμου. αὐτῶν

6. και^{1}] deinde Tyc | *το^{1}* > 175. 337. 617. 1849 | *εισ βλασφημιασ* AℵC 1. 94. 172. 250. 424. 2018. 2019. 2040 vg : *εισ βλασφημιαν* 025. 046. **21** (–2040). 2037. 2038. 2067 al^{pl} Or^{s} Tyc gig s^{2} : in blasphemia Pr arm$^{1.2.4.a}$: *βλασφημειν* s^{1} arm^{3} bo eth | *βλασφημησαι*] pr *και* bo eth : *και εβλασφημησεν* arm$^{1.2.a}$: *ινα βλασφημηση* s^{1} | *αυτου^{2}*] ℵ^{c} : *αυτον* ℵ* | *και την σκηνην αυτου* >C | *και τουσ εν τ. ουρ. σκηνουντασ* ℵ^{c} 025. 046*. 1. 205. 632**. 2020. 2037. 2038. 2067 al^{m} vg bo arm^{4} : *τουσ εν τ. ουρ. σκην.* Aℵ*C 046**. **21** (–205. 632**. 2020). 250 al^{m} Or^{s} Tyc s^{2} : *του εν τ. ουρ. σκηνουντοσ* (>eth) Pr gig eth : *των εν τ. ουρ. σκηνουντων* s^{1} : *την εν τ. ουρ.* arm$^{1.2}$ | *σκηνουντασ*] *σκηνουντεσ* ℵ : *οικουντασ* 386. 2019 : *κατοικουντασ* 149. 201 : *σκηνην* arm$^{3**.a}$: *εκλεκτουσ* arm^{3*} : >aım$^{1.2}$ |.

5^{b}. και εδοθη . . . ποιησαι >arm$^{4.a}$ | *εξουσια*> ℵ* | *ποιησαι* AC 025. 1. 94. 181. 632**. 2015. 2019. 2036. 2037. 2038. 2040. 2067 Tyc Pr gig vg s eth : +*ο θελει* ℵ : pr *πολεμον* 046 **21** (–632**. 2040). 250 al^{pl} : +*τα τερατα α εθελησε* eth : *πολεμησαι* 61. 69 Oɪ^{s} bo sa : *ποιησαι πολεμησαι* (*πολεμον* arm^{2}) *κατα των αγιων και νικησαι αυτουσ και εδοθη* (+*αυτων* arm^{1} : +*εξουσια* arm^{2}) *νικη* (*νικησαι* arm^{2}) arm$^{1.2}$: >arm^{4a} | *μηıασ* >arm^{2} | *τεσσερακοντα* AℵC : *τεσσαρακοντα* 025. **21** (–35). 250. 2037. 2067 al^{pl} Or^{s} | *τεσσ. και δυο* A 336. 620. 866 2040 Tyc gig s : *και* > ℵC 025. **21** (–35). 250. 2037. 2067 al^{pl} Or^{s} Pr vg : *μβʹ* 046. 35. 2015. 2019. 2036. 2038 al^{p} : (*και*) *δυο* >arm^{2} |.

7. αυτω^{1}]+*εξουσια* 386. 920. 2020 | *ποιησαι . . . αυτω^{2}* >AC 025. 1*. 61. 69. 181. 2038. 2067 arm^{a} sa | tr 7^{a} after 7^{b} s^{2} : after 5^{a} arm$^{1.2.3}$ | arm$^{1.2.3}$ | *ποιησαι πολεμον* ℵ 046. **21.** 2037 al^{m} Pr gig s$^{1.2}$: $\sim$1$^{**.mg}$ 172. 250. 2018 al^{p} Or^{s} Tyc vg | *μετα των αγιων* >Tyc | *νικησαι*] vicit Pr | *εξουσια*] ℵ^{c} : *εξουσιαν* ℵ* | *πασαν φυλην*] *πασασ τασ φυλασ* bo eth | *και λαον*] *και λαουσ* C arm^{4} : > 051. 1. 35. 1957. 2019. 2023. 2038. 2067 Tyc arm$^{1.2}$ bo |.

8. προσκυνησουσιν] *προσεκυνησαν* Pr vg^{v} arm$^{2.3}$ eth | *αυτον* AC 046. **21** (–35. 205. 468. 2020. 2040). 250. 2037 al^{mu} Or^{s} :

9. Εἴ τις ἔχει οὖς ἀκουσάτω.
10. εἴ τις εἰς αἰχμαλωσίαν,
εἰς αἰχμαλωσίαν ὑπάγει·
εἴ τις ἐν μαχαίρῃ ἀποκτανθῆναι,
<αὐτὸς> † αὐτὸν † ἐν μαχαίρῃ ἀποκτανθῆναι.
Ὧδέ ἐστιν ἡ ὑπομονὴ καὶ ἡ πίστις τῶν ἁγίων.

αυτω א 025. 051. 1. 35. 104. 172. 205. 468. 1957. 2020. 2023. 2038. 2040. 2067 al^{p} : > Tyc | παντεσ . . . γησ] πασα η γη arm^{I} | επι >920. 2040 | τ. γησ] την γην 920 | ου ου C Pr : ουαι A : οι ου s^{1} : ων ου $א^{c}$ (but א* om. ου) 025. 35. 175. 205. 250. 386. 617. 632**. 919. 1934. 2020. 2037. 2038. 2040. 2067 al^{pl} Or^{s} Tyc gig vg s^{2} arm bo eth : ων ουτε 046. **21** (– 35. 175. 205. 386. 617. 632**. 919. 1934. 2020. 2040). 385 al^{p} : ω ουτε 110 | γεγραπται] γεγραμμενοι s^{1} | το ονομα AC 046. **21** (– 35*. 2040). 250. 2038. 2067 al^{pl} Or^{s} Tyc Pr s^{2} bo : τα ονοματα א 025. 1. 35*. 2015. 2036. 2037. 2040 gig vg arm eth : > s^{1} | αυτου AC : αυτων א* 2040 s^{2} arm : >$א^{c}$ 025. 046. **21** (– 2040). 250. 2037. 2038. 2067 al^{pl} Or^{s} Tyc Pr gig vg s^{1} | εν] επι 046 bo | τω βιβλιω] τω >C : βιβλω א* : τω βιβλω $א^{c}$: τη βιβλω 1 al^{p} | ζωησ] + τω s^{1} | εσφαγμενου] εσφραγισμενου 1. 242. 336. 2020 Tyc | απο] προ s^{1} : pr του Pr eth |.

9. **ει τισ εχει**] οστισ εχει arm^{2} : ο εχων $arm^{3.4}$: οι εχοντεσ $arm^{1.a}$ | ουσ] ωτα s Pr arm : + audiendi arm bo eth |.

10. **εισ αιχμαλωσιαν**^{1} AאC 025. 046. 35*. 205. 2015. 2020. 2036. 2038. 2040 $vg^{a.c.f.g}$ arm : + απαγει 250 Or^{s} gig $vg^{d.v}$ s : + επαγει 2018 : + υπαγει bo : αιχμαλωσιαν απαγει 424 : αιχμαλωσιαν 1. 61. 69. 241. 632**. 2017. 2037 : εχει αιχμαλωσιαν 051. **21** (– 35*. 205. 632**. 2020. 2040). 110. 201. 314. 385. 498. 522. 1955. 1957. 2016. 2041. 2067 al : αιχμαλωτιζει (-τησει 2019). 104. 2019 : captivum duxerit Pr | εισ αιχμαλωσιαν^{2} A 218. 2018 Or^{s} gig vg s : >אC 025. 046. **21.** 1. 61. 69. 104. 110. 201. 241. 314. 385. 498. 522. 1955. 1957. 2015. 2016. 2017. 2019. 2036. 2037. 2038. 2041. 2067 arm bo | υπαγει] συναγει 1. 2037 : vadet vg^{c} : et ipse capietur Pr | μαχαιρη$^{1.2}$ AC Or^{s} : μαχαιρα א 025. 046. **21.** 250. 2037. 2038. 2067 al^{pl} | αποκτανθηναι^{1} A : On this Hebrew idiom see vol. i. 355 sq. : αποκτεινει א 632**. 2015. 2036 (gig $s^{1.2}$) : αποκταινει 051 : αποκτεννει 250. 2018. 2040 Or^{s} : αποκτενει C 025. 046. 1. 35. 104. 172. 205. 506. 620. 866. 1957. 2019. 2020. 2023. 2037. 2041. 2067 al^{p} arm^{4} bo eth : occiderit Pr vg : >**21** (– 35. 205. 620. 632**. 866. 2020. 2040). 69. 82. 110. 314. 385. 429. 2016. 2017. 2038 al^{p} arm^{3} | αυτον] pr δει אC 025. 046 al^{mu} Pr vg s^{2} | εν μαχαιρη^{2} AC 025. 046 Or^{s} : εν μαχαιρα א 35. 205. 620. 866. 2040 s arm^{4} bo : > **21** (– 35. 205. 620. 866. 2040). 69. 82. 110. 241. 314. 385. 429. 2016. 2017 al^{p} | αποκτανθηναι^{2}] αποκτανθησεται gig s^{1} sa eth : αποκτενουσιν αυτον

11. Καὶ εἶδον ἄλλο θηρίον ἀναβαῖνον ἐκ τῆς γῆς,
καὶ εἶχεν κέρατα δύο ὅμοια ἀρνίῳ,
καὶ † ἐλάλει † ὡς δράκων.

12. καὶ τὴν ἐξουσίαν τοῦ πρώτου θηρίου πᾶσαν ποιεῖ ἐνώπιον αὐτοῦ,
καὶ ποιεῖ τὴν γῆν καὶ τοὺς ἐν αὐτῇ κατοικοῦντας ἵνα προσκυνήσουσιν τὸ θηρίον τὸ πρῶτον,
οὗ ἐθεραπεύθη ἡ πληγὴ τοῦ θανάτου αὐτοῦ.

13. καὶ ποιεῖ σημεῖα μεγάλα, ἵνα καὶ πῦρ ποιῇ ἐκ τοῦ οὐρανοῦ

bo sa | *υπομονη . . . πιστισ*] ~ s¹ | *υπομονη*] sapientia gig | *πιστισ*] *θλιψισ* 498. 2020 | *αγιων*] + *μακαριος εστι* bo : + *μακαρισμος και ου θαυμασει Σαταν* eth |.

11. **ειδον**] *ιδου* 617 | *θηριον* > Tyc | *αναβαινον*] *αναβαιννον* C : *αναβαινων* 104 | *δυο*] tr after *αρνιω* 2020 : *δεκα δυο* 181 : > **21** (− 18. 35. 468. 620. 866. 2020. 2040). 42. 82. 110. 314. 385. 2016. 2017 al^p arm³ | *ομοια*] *ονομα* C : *ομοιον* bo : *και ομοιον ην* s¹ | *αρνιω*] pr *τω* 620. 866 arm^{3. 4. a} : *αρνιου* Pr vg s² | **ελαλει**] On the corruption of the Hebrew source here, see vol. i. 358 sq. : **λαλει** gig : *λαλουν* bo | *δρακων*] pr *ο* arm |.

12. **του πρωτου θηριου**] *του θηριου του πρωτου* 69 | *πασαν* > Pr arm⁴ | *ποιει*¹] *εποιει* 2020 Or^s Pr vg s² arm bo : *ποιησει* 172. 250. 424. 2018 : *ινα ποιησει* s^{(1)} : *ποιειται* 051. 35* | *ενωπιον αυτου και* > Pr arm¹ | *ποιει*² Aℵ C 025. 1. 205. 620. 632**. 2015. 2019. 2036. 2037. 2038. 2040 al^{mu} Tyc gig : *ποιησει* 172. 250. 424. 2018 s¹ : *εποιει* 046. **20** (− 205. 620. 632**. 2040). 69. 104. 110. 314. 385. 2016. 2023. 2067 al Or^s s² : fecit vg arm bo : *επι* Pr arm^{3*} | *την γην και*] *ενωπιον* 025 | *και*³ > Pr | *τουσ εν αυτη κατοικουντασ*] tr *εν αυτη* after *κατοικουντασ* C 61. 69 gig vg eth : inhabitantes terram Pr : eos qui in ea sunt Tyc | *ινα προσκυνησουσιν* AC 69. 104. 429*. 522. 2019. 2038 : *και προσκυνησουσιν* s¹ : *ινα προσκυνησωσιν* 025. 046. **20**. 250. 2037. 2067 al^{pl} Or^s : ut adorent Tyc gig arm : ut adorarent Pr : *προσκυνιν* ℵ : adorare vg | *το θηριον το πρωτον*] *τω θηριω τω πρωτω* 172. 314*. 452. 468. 2018. 2021. 2040 : bestiam priorem Tyc (Pr) | *του θανατου* > A | *αυτου*² > 025. 61. 69. 632* Pr vg .

13. **ποιει**] *ποιησει* 172. 250. 2018 Tyc s¹ arm⁴ bo : *εποιει* 2016 : fecit Pr gig vg arm^{1. 2. 3. a} | *σημεια μεγαλα*] ~ 172. 250. 2018 | *ινα και πυρ* Aℵ C 025. 1. 172. 250. 632**. 2018. 2020. 2038. 2040. 2067 al^p gig vg s² : ita ut ignem Pr : *και* > 205 Tyc s¹ arm⁴ bo eth : *ινα εν πλανη ποιη* (*ποιει* 2015) *πυρ* 2015. 2036. 2037 : *και πυρ ινα* 046. **20** (− 205. 632**. 2020. 2040) al^{mu} Or^s : *πυρ ινα* 61. 69 | *ποιη* (*ποιει* 2015 : *ποιηση* 250. 2018 Pr gig vg) *εκ του ουρανου καταβαινειν* (*καταβαιννιν* C : *καταβηναι* 172. 250.

καταβαίνειν εἰς τὴν γῆν ἐνώπιον τῶν ἀνθρώπων. 14. *καὶ πλανᾷ τοὺς*
κατοικοῦντας ἐπὶ τῆς γῆς διὰ τὰ σημεῖα ἃ ἐδόθη αὐτῷ ποιῆσαι
ἐνώπιον τοῦ θηρίου, λέγων τοῖς κατοικοῦσιν ἐπὶ τῆς γῆς ποιῆσαι
εἰκόνα τῷ θηρίῳ, ὃς ἔχει τὴν πληγὴν τῆς μαχαίρης καὶ ἔζησεν. 15.
αὐτῷ *καὶ ἐδόθη † αὐτῇ † δοῦναι πνεῦμα τῇ εἰκόνι τοῦ θηρίου, ἵνα καὶ*
λαλήσῃ ἡ εἰκὼν τοῦ θηρίου, καὶ ποιήσῃ ἵνα ὅσοι ἐὰν μὴ προσκυν-
ήσωσιν τὴν εἰκόνα τοῦ θηρίου ἀποκτανθῶσιν.

2018 : discendentem Pr) AC 172. 250. 424. 2015. 2018. 2020. 2036. 2037. 2067 Tyc Pr vg arm$^{1.2.3.a}$: de celo faceret descendere gig : *ποιη* (*ποιει* 025. 2040) *καταβαινειν εκ του ουρανου* ℵ 025. 1. 2038. 2040 al^{p} s arm^{4} bo eth : *εκ του ουρανου καταβαινη* (-*νει* 104. 314. 429. 522. 2019) 046. **20** (– 205. 2020. 2040). 104. 314. 429. 522. 2019 al^{mu} Or^{s} : *καταβαινη εκ του ουρανου* 205 | *εισ την γην* AℵC 025. 1. 205. 250. 2037. 2038 al^{mu} Or^{s} gig vg : *επι την γην* 046. **20** (– 35. 205. 2040). 61. 82. 104. 110. 314. 385. 1957. 2016. 2067 s arm$^{1.2.3.a}$ bo : *επι τησ γησ* 69 : > 35. 2040 Pr arm^{4} |.

14. πλανα] *πλανησει* s bo : seduxit Pr : *πλαναν* arm^{1} | *τουσ κατοικουντασ* AℵC 025. 046. 205. 468**. 620. 632**. 920. 2020. 2040 Or^{s} Pr gig vg s arm bo eth : pr *τουσ εμουσ* 051. **20** (– 205. 468**. 620. 632**. 920. (1849). 2020. 2040). 82. 110. 314. 385. 429. 2016. 2017. 2023 al | *επι τησ γησ*] terram Pr vg : *τησ γησ* arm$^{1.2}$ | *δια τα σημεια . . . επι τησ γησ*^{2} > 046* s^{2} | *τα σημεια*] *το σημειον* arm^{4} | *λεγων*] *λεγον* 046**. 1. 61. 69. 201. 386. 620. 2040 : *λεγοντοσ* 046.^{mg} : et dicit Pr | *ποιησαι*] pr *και* ℵ | *εικονα*] *εικοναν* A 2038 | *οσ* AC 025. 046. 61. 172. 218. 250. 424. 2015. 2018. 2019. 2036. 2038 Pr gig : *ο* ℵ **20**. 1. 2037. 2067 al^{pl} vg s^{1} : *ωσ* Or^{s} | *εχει* AℵC 025. 1. 250. 2020. 2038 al^{mu} Pr gig vg s^{1} arm^{4} bo : *ειχε* 046. **20** (– 2020). 2037. 2067 al^{mu} Or^{s} s^{2} | *την πληγην* AC 025. 35. 205. 250. 620. 632**. 2020. 2037. 2038. 2040. 2067 al^{pl} Or^{s} : *πληγησ* ℵ : *την* > 046. **20** (– 35. 205. 620. 632**. 2020. 2040). 42. 61. 69. 82. 110. 141. 201. 314. 385. 429. 452. 498. 506. 517. 522. 1955. 2016. 2017. 2021 bo | *τησ μαχαιρησ* (pr *απο* 61. 69 Pr) *και εζησεν* (*ζησεται* arm$^{1.2.3}$) AℵC 025. 35. 61. 69. 250. 632**. 2020. 2037. 2038. 2040. 2067 al^{mu} Pr gig vg s arm bo : *και εζησεν απο* (+ *τησ πληγησ* 336. 620. 1918) *τησ μαχαιρασ* 046. **20** (– 35. 205. 632**. 2020. 2040) al^{mu} Or^{s} : *τησ μαχ. κ. εζησεν απο τ. πληγ. τ. μαχ.* 205 | *μαχαιρησ* AℵC Or^{s} : *μαχαιρασ* 025. 046. **20** al^{pl} |.

15. αυτη AC 025*. (The feminine may be due to the gender of the Hebrew word חיה; but the late emendation in ℵ 025**. 046 must be adopted) : *αυτω* ℵ 025**. 046. **20.** 250. 2037. 2038. 2067 al^{pl} | *δουναι* > C arm^{3} | *δουναι πνευμα* Aℵ 025. 1. (35). 205. 2037. 2038. 2040. 2067 al^{mu} Pr gig vg s : ~ 046. **20** (– (35).

16. καὶ ποιεῖ πάντας, τοὺς μικροὺς καὶ τοὺς μεγάλους, καὶ τοὺς πλουσίους καὶ τοὺς πτωχούς, καὶ τοὺς ἐλευθέρους καὶ τοὺς δούλους, ἵνα δῶσιν αὐτοῖς χάραγμα ἐπὶ τῆς χειρὸς αὐτῶν τῆς δεξιᾶς ἢ ἐπὶ τὸ

205. 2040). 250 al^{mu} Or^{s} | *ινα και λαλησῃ η εικων του θηριου* >C 69. 336. 468*. 617. 620*. 2015. 2036 s$^{1.(2)}$ arm^{4} bo (but not sa eth) | *ινα και*] ~ Pr arm$^{2.a}$: *και* > 104. 205. 2020. 2037. 2040 gig arm^{1} : *οτι* arm^{3} | *λαλησῃ*] *λαλησει* 104. 522. 620**. 2040 : *ελαλει* arm^{3} | *και ποιησῃ . . . θηριου*^{3} >C 2015 | *και ποιησῃ . . . αποκτανθωσιν*] *και αποκτειναι οσοι εαν μη προσκυνησουσιν τ. θηριον και τ. εικονα αυτου* bo | *ποιησῃ* (on this Hebraism (= *ποιῆσαι*) see vol. i. Introd.; *Gram.* § 10. i. (*b*)) A 025. 046. **20** (− 468. 617. 620. 2004. 2040). 1. 2037. 2067 al^{pl} Or^{s} Pr gig vg : *ποιησει* ℵ 61. 69. 250. 468. 522. 617. 620. 2004. 2019. 2036. 2038. 2040 s : *εποιει* arm^{3} eth | *ινα* A 025. 104. 506. 2019. 2037. 2040 Pr gig vg s arm : > ℵ 046. **20** (− 2040). 61. 69. 172. 201. 250. 314. 385. 498. 522. 1955. 2015. 2016. 2018. 2036. 2038. 2067 al^{p} Or^{s} vg$^{il.g}$ | *εαν*] *αν* ℵ 1. 205. 2037. 2038 al^{mu} : >2016. 2040 | *προσκυνησωσιν* A 025. 046. **20.** 250. 2037. 2067 al^{pl} Or^{s} : *προσκυνησουσιν* ℵ 051. 69. 104*. 452. 2016. 2019. 2038 arm$^{1.2.a}$: adoraverunt Tyc : adoraret Pr : adoraverit gig vg : adorabant arm^{3} | *την εικονα* A 1. 2037. 2067 al^{p} : *τῃ εικονι* ℵ 025. 046. **20.** 250. 2038 al^{pm} Or^{s} | *την εικονα του θηριου*] *το θηριον και την εικονα αυτου* Tyc bo | *του θηριου*^{3}] + *ινα* 051. 1. 35. 632**. 1957. 2023 al^{p} : + neque acceperunt inscriptionem in fronte aut in manu sua Tyc | *αποκτανθωσιν*] *αποκτανθηναι* 61. 69 Or^{s} : *αποκτειναι* bo : occidatur vg$^{c.d.f.v}$ |.

16. ποιει] *ποιησει* ℵ^{c} vg s arm$^{1.2.3.a}$ bo : fecit Pr | *μικρουσ . . . μεγαλουσ*] ~ Pr arm^{4} | *τουσ*^{2} >ℵ | *και*^{3} >s^{1} | *πλουσιουσ . . . πτωχουσ*] ~ ℵ 2036 | *και τουσ πτωχουσ και τουσ ελευθερουσ*] >Pr : *πτωχουσ . . . ελευθερουσ* ~ arm^{a} | *ελευθερουσ . . . δουλουσ*] ~ 620. 1918. 2019 eth | *και τουσ ελευθερουσ*] >205. 2038 : *και τουσ δεσποτασ* s^{1} | *ινα* >bo | *δωσιν* (*δωσι* ℵ^{c}) AℵC 025. 046. 35. 42. 60. 61. 69. 172. 181. 250. 314. 432. 468. 1957. 2018. 2019. 2020. 2023. 2037. 2038. 2041 al Or^{s} : *δωσει* 1 bo : *δωσῃ* 051 arm : *δωσωσιν* 82. 104. 175. 205. 336. 429. 498. 522. 617. 620. 919. 920. 1849. 1955. 2004. 2015. 2017. 2036 al^{pl} : *δωσουσιν* 18. 91. 94. 141. 201. 209. 325**. 337. 385. 386. 456. 632. 1934. 2016. 2067 al : *δοθῃ* s : *λαβωσι* 506. 2040 : habere Pr vg | *αυτοισ*] ℵ^{c} *αυτω* ℵ* : *αλληλοισ* gig : >506. 2040 Pr vg | *χαραγμα* AℵC 025. 1. 172. 205. 241. 250. 498. 522. 632**. 2015. 2018. 2019. 2020. 2036. 2037. 2038. 2067 al^{p} Tyc Pr gig vg s arm$^{2.3.4.a}$: *χαραγματα* 046. **20** (− 205. 632**. 2020. 2040) al^{pm} Or^{s} : *το χαραγμα αυτου* 506. 2040 arm^{1} | *τησ χειροσ . . . τησ δεξιασ*] *των χειρων . . . των δεξιων* s | *τησ*^{1} >**20** (− 35. 205. 2040). 42. 82. 110. 201. 314. 385. 429. 498. 517. 522. 1955. 2015. 2016. 2017 al | *η*] *και* 181. 2020.

μέτωπον αὐτῶν, 17. *καὶ ἵνα μή τις δύνηται ἀγοράσαι ἢ πωλῆσαι εἰ μὴ ὁ ἔχων τὸ χάραγμα, τὸ ὄνομα τοῦ θηρίου ἢ τὸν ἀριθμὸν τοῦ ὀνόματος αὐτοῦ.* 18. *῞Ωδε ἡ σοφία ἐστίν· ὁ ἔχων νοῦν ψηφισάτω τὸν ἀριθμὸν τοῦ θηρίου, ἀριθμὸς γαρ ἀνθρώπου ἐστίν· καὶ ὁ ἀριθμὸς αὐτοῦ ἑξακόσιοι ἑξήκοντα ἕξ.*

2038 arm[2. 3. 4.] bo | το μετωπον Aℵ 025. **20** (– 35. 205. 468**. 920. 2020). 250 al[mu] Or[s] Tyc arm[a] (bo) eth : pr αυτο 2020 : του μετωπου C : των μετωπων 046. 051. 1. 35. 205. 468**. 920. 2015. 2037. 2038. 2067 Pr gig vg arm[1. 2. 3. 4] | αυτων² > 2015 Pr |.

17. **και**[I] Aℵ[c] 025. 046. **20.** 250. 2038. 2067 al[pl] Or[s] gig vg arm[1. 2. 3. a] : >ℵ*C 314. 2015. 2017. 2036. 2037. 2041. Pr s arm[4] bo : sic ergo facient Tyc | μη τισ] μηδεισ 172. 250. 2018 | δυνηται AℵC 18. 35. 110. 141. 172. 205. 241. 250. 385. 429. 432. 468. 632. 1849. 1955. 1957. 2004. 2018. 2019. 2020. 2023. 2040 al[mu] Or[s] Tyc Pr gig vg s² : δυναται 025. 046. 051. **20** (– 18. 35. 205. 468. 632. 1849. 2004. 2020. 2040). 1. 61. 69. 104. 201. 314. 2015. 2016. 2017. 2024. 2036. 2037. 2038. 2067 al[p] arm[1. 2] : δυνησεται arm[3. 4. a] bo : >s¹ | αγορασαι . . . πωλησαι] ~ 172. 250. 2018 | η πωλησαι] >Tyc : και πωλησαι arm[3. a] : + ετι 172. 250. 2018 s¹ | μη] μητ C | ο εχων] ο>C : η εχων 1 : εχη arm[1. 2. a] : οι εχοντεσ Tyc | το ονομα του θηριου A 025. 046. **20** (– 2020). 1. 61. 69. 104. 172. 201. 250. 314. 385. 498. 522. 1955. 1957. 2015. 2016. 2018. 2023. 2036. 2041. 2067 al Or[s] vg[g] : του ονοματοσ του θηριου C 2037. 2038 Pr vg[c. d. f. v] s[1. 2] arm³ eth : του θηριου η (και 2019) το ονομα αυτου ℵ 2019. 2020 bo : pr η Tyc gig arm⁴ : + η τον αριθμον του θηριου 046 | η] και Pr arm[1. 2. 3. a] | τον αριθμον] του αριθμου eth |.

18. **η σοφια**] sapientiae Tyc | εστιν] εχει Or[s] : tr before η σοφια gig : + και s¹ | νουν] pr τον 1. 172 : ουσ ℵ* 325*. 620 : ουν 69 : νουσ 1918 : σοφιαν arm[1. 3] | τον αριθμον] το ονομα 61. 69. 2019 | ανθρωπου εστιν] ~ 205 | και ο αριθμοσ αυτου >ℵ s¹ | και AC 025. 046. 1. 35. 60. 94. 205. 432. 632**. 1957. 2015. 2020. 2023. 2036. 2037. 2038. 2040. 2041. 2067 al[mu] Pr gig vg s² arm[1. 2. 4. a] bo eth : >**20** (– 35. 205. 632**. 2020. 2040). 61. 69. 104. 110. 172. 250. 314. 385. 498. 522. 2016. 2018 al[p] Or[s] Tyc | αυτου] + εστιν C 025. 1. 35. 60. 94. 205. 432. 1957. 2015. 2020. 2036. 2037. 2038. 2040 2041. 2067 Tyc gig vg[(-c)] s² arm[1. 2. a] bo | εξακοσιοι (-αι ℵ : -α 025. 104. 336. 385. 620. 1934 2037. 2038. 2040. 2067). εξηκοντα (+ και 2037 s) εξ Aℵ 025. 104. 149. 336. 385. 620. 1934. 2037. 2038 2040. 2067 Pr gig vg s bo : χξσ′ 046. **20** (– 149. 620. 1934. 2040). 1. 69. 250. 314. 429. 498. 1957. 2017. 2018. 2019. 2023. 2036. 2041 al[mu] : χξσ′ 2015 : εξακοσια δεκα εξ C : arm⁴ Iren. v. 30. 1 : DCXC Tyc |.

xiv. 12. Ὧδε ἡ ὑπομονὴ τῶν ἁγίων ἐστίν, οἱ τηροῦντες τὰς ἐντολὰς τοῦ θεοῦ καὶ τὴν πίστιν Ἰησοῦ. 13. καὶ ἤκουσα φωνῆς ἐκ τοῦ οὐρανοῦ λεγούσης Γράψον Μακάριοι οἱ νεκροὶ οἱ ἐν κυρίῳ ἀποθνήσκοντες ἀπ' ἄρτι. ναί, λέγει τὸ πνεῦμα, ἵνα ἀναπαήσονται ἐκ τῶν κόπων αὐτῶν, τὰ γὰρ ἔργα αὐτῶν ἀκολουθεῖ μετ' αὐτῶν.

xiv. 12-13. On the restoration of these verses to their original context, see vol. i. 368-369.

xiv. 12. ωδε η υπομονη] ο δε υπομενων μετα bo : ηδε δε η υπομονη eth | ωδε > 69 | η > 1934 | εστιν] + ωδε 1. 35. 69. 104. 205. 620. 1957. 2023. 2036. 2037. 2038. 2067 al : tr before η υπομονη Pr gig | οι τηρουντεσ] των τηρουντων ℵ 2004**. 2019. 2020. 2040 | του θεου > 1. 2067 | πιστιν] + του 35. 432. 1957. 2023. 2041 | Ιησου] + Χριστου 582. 1948. 2014. 2015. 2034. 2036. 2037. 2042 arm$^{1.2}$ bo : + χαρησονται 35* |.

13. φωνησ . . . λεγουσησ] φωνην . . . λεγουσαν 386 | φωνησ] + αλλησ μεγαλησ bo | εκ του ουρανου λεγουσησ] λεγουσησ (+ μοι 2020) εκ του ουρανου ℵ 2020. 2037 | λεγουσησ] + μοι 051. 1. 35. 205. 468. 632**. 1957. 2015. 2019. (2020). 2023. 2036. 2037. 2038. 2041. 2067 Pr gig vg^{d} arm$^{1.2.3.a}$ | γραψον > bo | οι νεκροι > eth | εν κυριω Aℵ 046. **20.** al^{pl} Pr gig vg arm bo : + ημων s^{1} : χριστω C 025 : (τω) θεω s^{2} | αποθνησκοντεσ] "should they rise" bo | απ αρτι joined with what precedes P 35. 205. (337). 468**. 498. (632**). 1957. 2004**. 2040. 2041 al s arm bo : joined with what follows 046. **20** (- 35. 175. 205. (337). 468**. (632**). 2004**. 2040) al^{mu} Pr gig vg : without punctuation AℵC 051. 175 | ναι, λεγει Aℵ^{c}C 025. 632**. 2004**. 2020. 2040 al Pr gig vg s arm$^{1.3.4.a}$: και λεγει 205. 2018. 2019. 2041 arm^{2} : ~ 046. **20** (- 632**. 2004**. 2020. 2040). 69. 104. 110. 314. 2023 al^{mu} : ναι > ℵ* 620 bo | πνευμα] + το αγιον 2004**. 2040 arm$^{1.2.3}$ eth | αναπαησονται AℵC : αναπαυσονται 046. 1. 620. 2038 al^{p} arm$^{2.3.4}$: αναπαυσωνται 025. **20** (- 620). 250. 2037. 2067 al^{pm} : αναπαυωνται 051 : αναπαυονται arm$^{1.a}$: requiescant Pr gig vg : + απ αρτι bo | εκ] απο 61. 69 | κοπων] εργων 61. 69 | των κοπων αυτων τα γαρ εργα αυτων ακολουθει] των κοπων των εργων αυτων <α> ακολουθησει bo | τα γαρ εργα . . . μετ αυτων > s^{1} | τα γαρ AℵC 025. 336. 506. 2004**. 2020. 2040 Pr gig vg s^{2} arm^{4} : τα δε 046. **20** (- 2004**. 2020. 2040). 250. 2037. 2038. 2067 al^{pl} arm$^{1.2.3.a}$ eth | αυτων] + και οδηγησει αυτουσ εισ ζωησ πηγην υδατων bo$^{(vid)}$ |.

CHAPTER XIV.

1. Καὶ εἶδον καὶ ἰδοὺ τὸ ἀρνίον ἑστὸς ἐπὶ τὸ ὄρος Σιών,
καὶ μετ' αὐτοῦ ἑκατὸν τεσσεράκοντα τέσσαρες χιλιάδες,
ἔχουσαι τὸ ὄνομα αὐτοῦ καὶ τὸ ὄνομα τοῦ πατρὸς αὐτοῦ γεγραμμένον ἐπὶ τῶν μετώπων αὐτῶν.

2. καὶ ἤκουσα φωνὴν ἐκ τοῦ οὐρανοῦ
ὡς φωνὴν ὑδάτων πολλῶν
καὶ ὡς φωνὴν βροντῆς μεγάλης.

καὶ ἡ φωνὴ ἣν ἤκουσα ὡς κιθαρῳδῶν
κιθαριζόντων ἐν ταῖς κιθάραις αὐτῶν, 3. καὶ ᾄδουσιν ὡς ᾠδὴν καινὴν
ἐνώπιον τοῦ θρόνου καὶ ἐνώπιον τῶν τεσσάρων ζῴων καὶ τῶν πρεσβυτέρων·

1. και ειδον και ιδου] et ecce vidi Pr : *και μετα ταυτα* eth | *και*^{1} > gig | *και ιδου* > gig Cyp bo (cf. eth) | *το αρνιον . . . Σιων*] supra montem Syon agnum stantem gig | *το αρνιον* A**א**C 046. **20** (– 35. 205. 468**) s arm$^{3. a}$ bo eth : *το* > 025. 1. 35. 205. 250. 468**. 1957. 2015. 2018. 2019. 2023. 2037. 2038. 2041. 2067 al^{p} arm$^{1. 2. 4}$ | *εστοσ* A**א**C 025. 2036 : *εστωσ* 046. 1. 205. 250. 2020. 2037. 2038. 2040 al^{p} : *εστηκοσ* **20** (– 205. 2004. 2020. 2040) 2067 al^{mu} : *εστηκωσ* 104. 172. 2004 : stans Tyc : stantem Pr gig Cyp : stabat vg | *επι το οροσ Σιων*] *επι οροσ* C | *μετ αυτου* A**א**C 025. 35. 205. 2020. 2037. 2038. 2040. 2067 al Tyc Pr gig vg Cyp s^{1} arm bo eth : + *αριθμοσ* 046. **20** (– 35. 205. 2020. 2040). 250 al^{mu} s^{2} | *εκατον τεσσερακοντα τεσσαρεσ* A**א**C : *εκατον τεσσαρακοντα τεσσαρεσ* 025. 250. 386. (620). 1934. 2020. 2037. 2040. 2067 al^{pm} : *εκατον τεσσαρακοντεσσαρεσ* 149 : *ρμδ'* 046. **20** (– 149. 386. (620). 1934. 2020. 2040). 1. 2038 al^{pm} | *εχουσαι*] pr *αι* 69 : *εχοντεσ* gig vg : habebant Pr Cyp | *αυτου και το ονομα* > 025. 1 | *το ονομα*^{2} > 104. 336. 522. 620 | *αυτου*^{3} > 385 | *γεγραμμενον*] pr *το* A s^{2} : *εγγεγραμμενον* 385 : *καιομενον* 1 |.

2. φωνην$^{1. 2. 3}$] *φωνησ* 2067 | *φωνην*^{1} > 920 | *εκ του ουρανου ωσ φωνην* > 620* | *φωνην υδατων πολλων και ως φωνην* > bo | *φωνην*^{2} > Tyc | *και ωσ φωνην βροντησ μεγαλησ* > 2015. 2036 | *ωσ*^{2}] aut Pr : > arm$^{2. a}$ | *φωνην*^{3} > Tyc Pr | *βροντησ μεγαλησ*] **א**^{c} : *μεγαλησ* > **א*** : ~ Pr : *βροντην μεγαλην* Tyc bo | *και η φωνη ην ηκουσα* A**א**C 046. **20**. 250 al^{pl} Pr s^{2} bo : *και* > s^{1} : *και φωνην* (-*ησ* 2067) *ηκουσα* 025. 1. 1957. 2015. 2036. 2037. 2038. 2067 arm^{3} : et vocem quam audivi Tyc gig vg : *και ηκουσα ωσ φωνην* arm$^{1. a}$ | *ωσ*^{3}] > 1. 1957. 2038. 2067 : + *φωνην* arm^{4} | *κιθαρωδων κιθαριζοντων*] *κιθαρωδον κιθαριζοντα* s^{1} : *κιθαρωδουσ* bo | *εν ταισ κιθαραισ αυτων*] *αυτων* > C : *εν τ. κ. αυτου* s^{1} : > Pr bo |.

3. και αδουσιν] *και* (> bo) *αδοντεσ* 743. 1075 s$^{1. 2}$ bo eth : et

3$^{b.\ c.}$ καὶ οὐδεὶς ἐδύνατο μαθεῖν τὴν ᾠδήν,
εἰ μὴ αἱ ἑκατὸν τεσσεράκοντα τέσσαρες χιλιάδες (*a*)·
4$^{c.}$ οὗτοι οἱ ἀκολουθοῦντες τῷ ἀρνίῳ ὅπου ἂν ὑπάγει.

4$^{d.}$ οὗτοι ἠγοράσθησαν ἀπὸ τῶν ἀνθρώπων ἀπαρχὴ τῷ θεῷ (*b*),

(*a*) Text adds following interpolation: 3^{d}. οἱ ἠγορασμένοι ἀπὸ τῆς γῆς· 4^{ab}. οὗτοί εἰσιν οἳ μετὰ γυναικῶν οὐκ ἐμολύνθησαν· παρθένοι γάρ εἰσιν.
(*b*) Text adds gloss: καὶ τῷ ἀρνίῳ.

cantabant Pr gig vg arm | ωσ ωδην AC 1. 35*. 2015. 2019. 2036. 2037. 2038. 2040 al^{p} vg s^{1} sa : ωσ > ℵ 025. 046. **20** (– 35*. 2040). 250. 2067 al^{pm} Pr gig s^{2} arm bo eth : εν ωδη (καινη) bo | ωδην καινην] ~ 1934 | καινην] + και ην ℵ (ην above the line) : pr και arm^{3} | ενωπιον του θρονου] > 42. 498. 1918. 2020 : + του θεου gig arm$^{1.\ 3}$ | και^{2} > 42. 498. 1918. 2020 | τεσσαρων > 205 | και των πρεσβυτερων > C arm$^{1.\ 3}$ | και^{3}] + ενωπιον ℵ gig s^{1} arm$^{2.\ 4.\ a}$ | ουδεισ] ουδε εισ 046. **20** (– 35. 205. 620. 1934. 2020. 2040). 110. 201. 385. 429. 1955. 2016. 2017 : ουκ arm^{4} | εδυνατο AℵC **20** (– 386. 617. 2040) al : ηδυνατο 025. 046. 250. 386. 617. 2037. 2040. 2067 al^{pl} : ου δυναται 2038 (arm$^{3.\ a}$) : ηδυναμην arm^{4} | μαθειν] dicere Pr gig vg $^{(\text{-g** discere})}$: "to know" arm^{a} bo eth | ει μη] και s^{1} | αι > ℵ^{c} 104. 620. 1849. 1955. 2004. 2015. 2017* | εκατον τεσσερακοντα τεσσαρεσ Aℵ^{c}(C) : εκατον τεσσερακοντα μιαν ℵ* : τεσσαρεσ > C : εκατον τεσσαρακοντα τεσσαρεσ 025. 386. (620). 1934. 2040 : εκατον μδ′ 1 : ρμδ′ 046. **20** (– 386. 620. 1934. 2040) al^{mu} | χιλιαδεσ > Pr | οι ηγορασμενοι απο τησ γησ] quae empta erant de terris Pr |.

4. ουτοι . . . αν υπαγει] ουτοι εισιν οι ακολουθουντεσ . . . υπαγη οι μετα γυναικων . . . γαρ εισιν 205 | ουτοι εισιν > A (205) | εμολυνθησαν] εμολυναν τα ιματια αυτων bo | εισιν^{2}] permanserunt Pr Cyp | ουτοι^{2} AℵC 025. 1. 2015. 2020. 2037. 2038. 2040 gig vg$^{a.\ g}$ s^{1} (arm$^{1.\ 2.\ 3.\ a}$) : + εισιν 046. **20** (– (205). 2020. 2040). 250. 2067 Or^{s} Tyc Pr vg$^{d.\ f}$ Cyp s^{1*} arm^{4} bo | οι^{2} > ℵ | ακολουθουντεσ] ακολουθησαντεσ 920 s | οπου αν AℵC 025. 1. 35. 172. 205. 250. 314. 1957. 2015. 2018. 2019. 2020. 2023. 2036. 2037. 2038. 2040. 2067 al^{mu} : αν > 1849 : οπου εαν 046. **20** (– 35. 205. 1849. 2020. 2040). 61. 69. 104. 110. 201. 241. 242. 385. 429. 1955. 2016. 2017. 2024 al^{m} Or^{s} | υπαγει AC 104. 172. 336. 620. 2015. 2019. 2038 s^{2} : vadit Pr : υπαγη ℵ 025. 046. **21** (– 620). 250. 2037. 2067 al^{pl} Or^{s} s^{1} : ierit Tyc (gig vg) : "shall go" arm | ηγορασθησαν AℵC 025. 1. 172. 250. 2015. 2018. 2019. 2036. 2037. 2038. 2040. 2067 al^{p} Pr gig vg s^{1} (arm^{4}) bo eth : pr υπο Ιησου 046. 051. **20** (– 2040). 69. 104. 110. 314. 385. 2016 al^{mu} Or^{s} s^{2} | απο των ανθρωπων > C | απαρχη AC 025. 046. **20** (– 620). 250. 2037. 2038. 2067 al^{pl} Or^{s} gig vg s arm^{4} bo : απ αρχησ ℵ 336. 620. 1918 : ab exordio Pr (placed after **τω αρνιω**) : > eth | **τω αρνιω**] pr εν ℵ* : του αρνιου arm |.

εἰσιν 5. καὶ ἐν τῷ στόματι αὐτῶν οὐχ εὑρέθη ψεῦδος·
ἄμωμοι ⸀γάρ ἐστιν⸁.

6. Καὶ εἶδον ἄλλον ἄγγελον πετόμενον ἐν μεσουρανήματι,
καθημένους ἔχοντα εὐαγγέλιον αἰώνιον εὐαγγελίσαι ἐπὶ τοὺς ⸀κατοικοῦντας⸁
ἐπὶ τῆς γῆς καὶ ἐπὶ πᾶν ἔθνος καὶ φυλὴν καὶ γλῶσσαν καὶ
λαόν, λέγων ἐν φωνῇ μεγάλῃ

7. Φοβήθητε τὸν θεὸν καὶ δότε αὐτῷ δόξαν,
ὅτι ἦλθεν ἡ ὥρα τῆς κρίσεως αὐτοῦ,
καὶ προσκυνήσατε τῷ ποιήσαντι τὸν οὐρανὸν
καὶ τὴν γῆν καὶ θάλασσαν καὶ πηγὰς ὑδάτων.

5. και] οτι s^1 : > Pr | εν τω στοματι αυτων ουχ ευρεθη Aℵ C 025. 1. 35. 205. 1957. 2015. 2019. 2023. 2036. 2037. 2038. 2040. 2041. 2067 al Or^s Tyc gig vg s : in quorum ore non est Pr : ουχ ευρεθη εν τω στοματι αυτων 046. **20** (– 35. 205. 2040). 69. 82. 104. 110. 250. 314. 385. 429. 2016. 2017. 2018 al (bo) eth | εν τω στοματι] εν τοισ στομασι arm^a bo | ψευδοσ] δολοσ 1. 2037 al^p arm^2 | αμωμοι γαρ εισιν ℵ 046. **20** (– 35). 250. 2037. 2038. 2067 al^{pl} Or^s vg$^{a**. c. d}$ s arm$^{(1. 2. 3). 4}$ bo sa eth : οτι αμωμοι εισιν 051. 35 : γαρ > AC 025. 181 Tyc gig vg$^{f. g. h. v}$: et inventi sunt sine reprehensione Pr | αμωμοι] αμωμητοι 104 | εισιν] + ουτοι εισιν οι ακολουθουντεσ τω αρνιω 218. 242. 250. 617. 1934 : + "before God" arm^2 |.

6. αλλον αγγελον Aℵ$^{c. c}$ 025. 35. 1957. 2023. 2036. 2037. 2040 al^{mu} Pr gig vg Cyp s arm bo eth : ∼ 218. 250. 2018 : αλλον > ℵ* 046. **20** (– 35. 2040). 2038. 2067 al^{pm} sa : αγγελον > Tyc | πετομενον AC 051. **20** (– 617. 919). 69. 250. 385. 1957. 2016. 2018. 2036. 2037. 2038. 2067 al : πετωμενον 025. 046. 1. 617. 919 al : πεταμενον ℵ | εν > 35 | μεσουρανηματι] ℵ^c : μεσω ουρανηματι ℵ* : μεσουρανισματι 1 : ουρανω αιματι s^2 | εχοντα] + επ αυτω s^1 | ευαγγελισαι AC 025. 046. **20.** 2038. 2067 al^{pl} : ευαγγελισασθαι (ℵ) 60. 218. 250 2015. 2018. 2019. 2023. 2036. 2037. 2041 : pr ερχομενον 2015. 2036. 2037 : ευαγγελιζοντα bo | επι^1 Aℵ C 025. 218. 250. 2018 s^1 : > 046. **20.** 498. 2037. 2038. 2067 al^{pl} | τουσ κατοικουντασ A 051. 35*. 61. 69. 2015. 2036. 2037 al^p s^2 Tyc : τουσ καθημενουσ ℵ C 025. 046. **20** (– 35*. 2020). 250. 2067 al^{pm} s^1 Pr gig vg : τουσ καθημενουσ (+ και 2019) τουσ κατοικουντασ 1. 205. 2019. 2038 : τοισ καθημενοισ 498. 2020 : > Cyp arm$^{1. 2. 3. a}$ | επι τησ γησ > arm$^{1. 2. a}$ | και επι παν . . . λαον > Tyc | επι^2 > 1. 2015. 2019 2036. 2037. 2038 | φυλην και γλωσσαν και λαον] λαουσ κ. φυλασ κ. γλωσσαν s^1 : πασαν φυλ. κ. παντα λαον κ. πασαν γλωσσαν bo |.

7. λεγων] > ℵ : tr after μεγαλη 104. 620 : λεγοντα 051. 1. 35 Pr Cyp | εν φωνη μεγαλη] εν > A : magna voce vg : > Tyc |

8. Καὶ ἄλλος δεύτερος ἄγγελος ἠκολούθησεν λέγων
Ἔπεσεν ἔπεσεν Βαβυλὼν ἡ μεγάλη,
ἣ ἐκ τοῦ οἴνου [τοῦ θυμοῦ] τῆς πορνείας αὐτῆς πεπότικεν
πάντα τὰ ἔθνη.

9. Καὶ ἄλλος ἄγγελος τρίτος ἠκολούθησεν αὐτοῖς λέγων ἐν φωνῇ
μεγάλῃ
Εἴ τις προσκυνεῖ τὸ θηρίον καὶ τὴν εἰκόνα αὐτοῦ,
καὶ λαμβάνει ⸀τὸ χάραγμα¹ ἐπὶ † τοῦ μετώπου † αὐτοῦ ἢ ἐπὶ χάραγμα
τὴν χεῖρα αὐτοῦ,

φοβηθητε] metuite potius Pr Cyp | τον θεον Aℵ C 025. 1. 35. 205. 250. 1957. 2015. 2023. 2036. 2037. 2038. 2040. 2041. 2067 al^{p} Pr vg Cyp s arm$^{1.2.4.a}$ bo : τον κυριον 046. **20** (– 35. 205. 2040) al^{pm} Tyc gig arm^{3} | αυτω δοξαν] ~ 2015. 2020 | αυτου > 1. 104 | τω ποιησαντι Aℵ C 025. 1. 35. 205. 250. 1957. 2018. 2019. 2023. 2036. 2038. 2040. 2041. 2067 : pr αυτω 94. 104. 336. 620. 1918. 2020 : αυτον ποιησαντα 046* : αυτον τον ποιησαντα 046**. **20** (– 35. 205. 468. 620. 2020. 2040). 2037 al^{mu} : αυτω τον ποιησαντα 468 : deum qui fecit gig arm^{2} | και θαλασσαν AC 025. 314. 2040 : και θαλασσασ 1 : και την θαλασσαν ℵ 046. 051. **21** (– 2040). 250. 2037. 2038. 2067 al^{pm} bo : και > 2019 Pr vg$^{d.f}$ Cyp arm$^{1.2}$ | πηγασ υδατων] τασ πηγασ των υδατων 61. 69 : τα υδατα bo : omnia quae in eis sunt Cyp arm$^{1.3*}$ |.

8. αλλοσ δευτεροσ αγγελοσ A 046. **20** (– 18. 35. 205. 2040). 1. 250. 2037 al^{mu} Pr arm$^{1.2.3.4}$ bo : δευτεροσ > 69 Tyc vg eth : αγγελοσ > ℵ* 2040 s^{1} : αλλοσ αγγελοσ δευτερον C : αλλοσ αγγελοσ δευτεροσ ℵ^{c} 025. 18. 35. 60. 94. 104. 141. 205. 209. 314. 432. 1957. 2015. 2023. 2036. (2038). 2041. 2067 s^{2} arm^{a} : αλλοσ > 2019 gig | ηκολουθησεν] ηλθεν 205 : ηκολουθει s^{1} : + αυτοισ 468*. 620 : + αυτω Pr s arm$^{1.2.a}$ bo eth | λεγων . . . ηκολουθησεν (ver. 9) > ℵ* (suppl. ℵ^{c}) 325. 456 | λεγων] + εν φωνη μεγαλη 205. 620** | επεσεν επεσεν A 025. 1. 35. 241. 432. 632**. 1957. 2015. 2019. 2023. 2036. 2037. 2040. 2067 al^{p} Tyc Pr gig vg s arm$^{2.a}$: "is fallen, is lost" arm^{4} : επεσεν ℵ^{c} C 046. **20** (– 35. 325. 456. 632**. 2040). 250. 2038 al^{mu} arm^{3} bo eth : επεσεν επεσεν επεσεν arm^{1} | η εκ του AC 218. 250. 424. 506. 2018. 2020. 2039. 2040 Tyc vg s : η > ℵ^{c} 025. 046. **20** (– 325. 456. 2020. 2040) al^{mu} Pr gig arm^{4} bo : οτι εκ του 1. 2019. 2037. 2067 | του θυμου τησ πορνειασ] τησ πορνειασ του θυμου 920 | του θυμου > 1. 2037. 2041 | τησ πορνειασ] τησ πορνιασ ℵ^{c}C 046 : > arm^{4} | αυτησ] ταυτησ 046 82. 104. 175. 337. 385. 617. 620. 919. 920. 1849 1934 al^{p} | πεποτικεν A 025. 046 min$^{fere\ omn}$ Tyc vg eth : πεπτωκαν ℵ^{c} 181 (-κεν). Pr arm^{4} bo sa : πεποιηκεν 919 : biberunt gig |.

9. και > 386 | αλλοσ αγγελοσ τριτοσ AC 025. 046. **20** (– 325. 456. 1849). 250. 2037. 2038. 2067 al^{pm} gig vg s arm$^{3.a}$: αγγελοσ

10. *καὶ αὐτὸς πίεται ἐκ τοῦ οἴνου τοῦ θυμοῦ τοῦ θεοῦ*
τοῦ κεκερασμένου ἀκράτου ἐν τῷ ποτηρίῳ τῆς ὀργῆς αὐτοῦ,
καὶ βασανισθήσεται ἐν πυρὶ καὶ θείῳ
ἐνώπιον τῶν ἀγγέλων καὶ ἐνώπιον τοῦ ἀρνίου.

11. *Καὶ ὁ καπνὸς τοῦ βασανισμοῦ αὐτῶν εἰς αἰῶνας αἰώνων ἀναβαίνει,*
καὶ οὐκ ἔχουσιν ἀνάπαυσιν ἡμέρας καὶ νυκτός,
οἱ προσκυνοῦντες τὸ θηρίον καὶ τὴν εἰκόνα αὐτοῦ,
καὶ εἴ τις λαμβάνει τὸ χάραγμα τοῦ ὀνόματος αὐτοῦ. (a)

(a) Vers. 12–13 have been restored to their original context after xiii. 18.

αλλοσ τριτοσ 1849 : αλλοσ αγγελοσ ηκολουθησεν τριτοσ ℵ^{c} : αλλοσ τριτοσ αγγελοσ arm$^{1.2.4}$ bo : tertius angelus Pr eth : τριτοσ > 1. 61. 69 : αγγελοσ 181 | αυτοισ] αυτω A Pr arm$^{1.2.3}$ | εν φωνη μεγαλη] εν > 617 : voce magna Pr gig vg : > bo | προσκυνει] προσκυνησει 2020 arm^{2} bo : adoraverit vg : "hath worshipped" arm$^{3.a}$ | το θηριον] τω θηριω C 468. 2040 : το θυσιαστηριον A : το ποτηριον 69 : tr το θηριον before προσκυνει 1 | την εικονα] τη εικονι 104. 468. 620. 1918. 2040 | αυτου] αυτων C | και^{3} > C 69 | λαμβανει] ληψεται arm^{2} bo : "hath received" arm$^{1.3.a}$ | το χαραγμα 250. 432. 2015. 2018. 2019. 2036. 2040 arm$^{1.2.3.a}$ s$^{1.2(?)}$: χαραγμα Aℵ 025. 046 min^{pl}. το is here necessary. Its absence is due either to a slip of the author or to a primitive corruption. | χαραγμα] nomen Pr : + αυτου s$^{1.2}$ arm$^{(1.2.3.a)}$ | του μετωπου] τω μετωπω ℵ | η επι την χειρα αυτου > s^{1} arm^{1} | αυτου^{3} > 61. 69 |.

10. και^{1} > bo eth | οινου] ποτηριου arm$^{1.2.3.a}$ | του θεου] του κυριου s^{1} : αυτου 61. 69 : > arm^{1} | ακρατου > Pr Cyp | εν τω ποτηριω] εκ του ποτηριου A 104. 336. 620. 1918 | τησ οργησ] την οργην A | αυτου > Pr arm$^{1.2.a}$ | βασανισθησεται] βασανισθησονται A 61. 69. 110. 2004**. 2019. 2040 bo | των αγγελων A 506 bo : τ. αγγ. αυτου eth : αγγελων αγιων ℵ^{c} 025. 35. 61. 2004**. 2020. 2040 gig vg s sa : αγγελων και αγιων 2038 : αγιων αγγελων 69 (+ αγιων 2019) : των αγιων αγγελων 046. **20** (– 35. 2004**. 2020. 2040). 250. 2037. 2067 al^{pl} Pr Cyp arm$^{(1.2.3).4}$: "God" arm^{a} | αρνιου] θρονου s^{2} |.

11. του βασανισμου] tormentorum vg arm$^{3.4}$: de tormentis Pr Cyp : > arm$^{1.2.a}$ | αυτων] αυτου 104. 205. 336. 452. 1918. 2021. 2023 arm$^{2.a}$ | εισ αιωνασ . . . αναβαινει > 620 | εισ αιωνασ (+ των ℵ) αιωνων Aℵ 046. **20** (– 205 468*. 920. 1934. 2004**). 250. 2038 al^{pl} Pr gig vg Cyp s arm : εισ αιωνα αιωνοσ C 205. 2015 2036 : εισ αιωνα αιωνων 025. 051. 1. 61. 69. 104. 468*. 920. 1849. 1934. 2037. 2067 : εισ αιωνων 2004** : "for ever" bo | αναβαινει] ascendet gig vg$^{c.d.g.v}$ Cyp arm bo : tr before εισ αιωνασ των αιωνων Pr arm^{4} bo sa (eth) | εχουσιν] habebunt Pr Cyp | αναπαυσιν] tr after νυκτοσ 35*. 2020 | το θηριον και την εικονα]

14. Καὶ εἶδον, καὶ ἰδοὺ νεφέλη λευκή,
καὶ ἐπὶ τὴν νεφέλην † καθήμενον ὅμοιον † υἱὸν ἀνθρώπου,
ἔχων ἐπὶ τὴν κεφαλὴν αὐτοῦ στέφανον χρυσοῦν
καὶ ἐν τῇ χειρὶ αὐτοῦ δρέπανον ὀξύ. (*a*)

(*a*) Text adds here a doublet of xiv. 18–20 from another hand. See vol. ii. 3, 18 (*ad fin.*), 21 sq.: 15. Καὶ ἄλλος ἄγγελος ἐξῆλθεν ἐκ τοῦ ναοῦ, κράζων ἐν φωνῇ μεγάλῃ τῷ καθημένῳ ἐπὶ τῆς νεφέλης
Πέμψον τὸ δρέπανόν σου καὶ θέρισον,
ὅτι ἦλθεν ἡ ὥρα θερίσαι,
ὅτι ἐξηράνθη ὁ θερισμὸς τῆς γῆς.

16. καὶ ἔβαλεν ὁ καθήμενος ἐπὶ τῆς νεφέλης τὸ δρέπανον αὐτοῦ ἐπὶ τὴν γῆν,

τω θηριω και τη εικονι 468. 2019. 2040 : τη εικονη 104 | το^2 > 1. 205. 2037* |.

14. **και ειδον** > ℵ s^1 eth | και ιδου > bo eth | νεφελη λευκη] nubem albam Tyc Pr : nubem candidam vg bo | επι την νεφελην καθημενον] supersedentem Tyc | την νεφελην] τη νεφελη 2004** | καθημενον ομοιον] καθημενοσ ομοιοσ 1. 104. 205. 620. 632. 1957. 2023. 2037. 2067 al | ομοιον > Tyc eth | υιον Aℵ 046. 42. 61. 69. 82. 110. 201. 218. 325. 337. 386. 429. 452. 456. 517. 522. 919. 920. 2016. 2017. 2021. 2024. 2036 Tyc : υιων 2015 : υιοσ 1 : υιου 025. 506 : υιω C 051. **20** (– 325. 337. 386. 456. 919. 920). 104. 250. 314. 2037. 2038. 2067 al^{mu} Pr gig vg s^1 : τω υιω s^2 | ανθρωπου] pr του s^2 : ανθρωπω 620. 2020 | εχων A 025. 046. **20** (– 325. 456. 468. 2004**. 2020. 2040). 1. 314. 2037. 2038. 2067 Tyc : pr ο 2041 : εχον ℵ^{c}C : εχοντα ℵ* 42. 325. 385. 452**. 456. 468. 506. 517. 2004**. 2015. 2036. 2040 Pr vg : εχοντι 2020 gig | επι την κεφαλην A 18. 110. 141. 201. 385. 386. 429. 522. 632. 919. 1849. 1955. 2015. 2020. 2036 : επι τησ κεφαλησ ℵC 025. 046. **20** (– 18. 386. 632. 919. 1849. 2020). 250. 2037. 2038. 2067 al^{mu} : in capite Tyc gig vg : super caput Pr | εν τη χειρι] επι την χειρα s^1 | αυτου^2] + habens Tyc : + "he had" arm$^{1.2.3.a}$ | οξυ] λευκον s^1 |.

15. **αλλοσ αγγελοσ**] ~ 2016. 2020 | εκ του ναου] tr. after κραζων A : > Pr | ναου] + αυτου ℵ : ουρανου 051. 1. 35. 104. 181. 205. 336. 632**. 2015. 2023. 2036. 2037. 2038. 2067 al^p arm$^{2.4.a}$ | εν φωνη μεγαλη] + λεγων bo eth : (arm$^{1.2.a}$) : εν μεγαλη τη φωνη 1 : > Pr | πεμψον . . . τησ γησ > s$^{(2)}$ | και θερισον > arm^2 | ηλθεν] + σου 051. 1. 35*. 181. 2019. 2037. 2038 : + σοι 104*. 620 al^p | θερισαι AC 025. 046. **20** (– 18. 468**. 632. 919. 1849. 2004**. 2020. 2040). 250. 2037. 2038. 2067 al^{mu} : pr του 18. 385. 468**. 632. 919. 1849. 1955. 1957. 2004**. 2023. 2040. 2041 al^p : του θερισμου ℵ 2020 : "of (the) reaping of the earth" bo | οτι εξηρανθη . . . γησ > s$^{1.(2)}$ bo | εξηρανθη] "is arrived" arm$^{1.2.3.a}$ |.

16. ver. 16 > arm^a | ο καθημενοσ . . . νεφελησ > s^2 | επι τησ νεφ. . . . αυτου > 1 | τησ νεφελησ Aℵ 241. 336*. 498. 2019.

18. Καὶ ἄλλος ἄγγελος ἐξῆλθεν ἐκ τοῦ θυσιαστηρίου (*a*), καὶ
ἐφώνησεν φωνῇ μεγάλῃ τῷ ἔχοντι τὸ δρέπανον τὸ ὀξὺ λέγων

Πέμψον σου τὸ δρέπανον τὸ ὀξὺ
καὶ τρύγησον τοὺς βότρυας τῆς ἀμπέλου τῆς γῆς,
ὅτι ἤκμασαν αἱ σταφυλαὶ αὐτῆς.

19. καὶ ἔβαλεν (*b*) τὸ δρέπανον αὐτοῦ εἰς τὴν γῆν,
καὶ ἐτρύγησεν τὴν ἄμπελον τῆς γῆς,
καὶ ἔβαλεν εἰς τὴν ληνὸν τοῦ θυμοῦ τοῦ θεοῦ τὸν μέγαν.

καὶ ἐθερίσθη ἡ γῆ. 17. Καὶ ἄλλος ἄγγελος ἐξῆλθεν ἐκ τοῦ ναοῦ τοῦ ἐν τῷ οὐρανῷ, ἔχων καὶ αὐτὸς δρέπανον ὀξύ.

(*a*) Text adds a gloss: ὁ ἔχων ἐξουσίαν ἐπὶ τοῦ πυρός.
(*b*) ὁ ἄγγελος is here added by the interpolator of 15–17.

2020. 2037. 2038. 2067 : *την νεφελην* C 025. 35. 175. 205. 250. 468. 617. 620. 1934. 2004**. 2040 al^{pm} : *τη νεφελη* 046. **20** (– 35. 175. 205. 468. 617. 620. 1934. 2004**. 2020. 2040). 42. 61. 69. 104. 110. 201. 1955 | *και εθερισθη η γη*] *και εθερισεν την γην* vg$^{f. v}$: demessus est terram fl : >bo |.

17. ver. 17 >69. 2039 | *εξηλθεν*] *ηλθεν* 046 | *ναου . . . ουρανω*] *ουρανου* bo | *του εν τω ουρανω*] *του* >104. 141. 620. 1849 : *τω* >C : pr *του θεου* arm^{4} : *αυτου εν τω ουρανω* 205 | *και αυτοσ* > bo sa | *δρεπανον οξυ*] *ρομφαιαν οξειαν* bo (also in ver. 18) |.

18. *εξηλθεν*] >A 2038 Pr : tr after *θυσιαστηριου* 35 | *εκ του θυσιαστηριου*] > Pr : de ara dei fl | *ο εχων* AC s gig vg (arm) eth : *ο* >א 025. 046. **20** al^{omn} fl bo | *εφωνησεν*]+*εν* **20** (– 35. 205. 325. 337. 456. 468. 2004**. 2020. 2040). 69. 104. 110. 250. 314 al^{p} | *εφωνησεν*] *εκραξεν* s | *φωνη* Aא 046. 337. 920. 2004**. 2016. 2020. 2040 fl gig vg s^{1} arm$^{1. 2. 3. a}$ eth : *κραυγη* C 025. **20** (– 337. 920. 2004**. 2020. 2040). 250. 2037. 2038. 2067 al^{pl} s^{2} bo : "tongue" arm^{4} | *λεγων*] א^{c} : *λεγω* א* : >s^{1} | *πεμψον . . . οξυ και*] >arm$^{1. 2. a}$: "come thou" arm^{3} | *πεμψον*]+ *συ* s^{1} | *σου το δρεπανον*]+*σου* 385 : *το δρεπανον σου* א | *βοτρυασ*] *βοτανασ* 201. 386 : *βοτρυσ* 2015. 2036. 2038 | *τησ αμπελου*] vinearum fl : >1 arm^{1} | *οτι ηκμασαν . . . αυτησ* >bo | *ηκμασαν* (*ηχ*- A : *ηγ*- 620) *αι σταφυλαι* AאC 025. 1. 35. 104. 205. 468**. 620. 632**. 2004**. 2015. 2020. 2023. 2036. 2037. 2038. 2040. 2067 al gig vg (fl) s$^{(1). 2}$: *ηκμασεν η σταφυλη* 046. **20** (– 35. 205. 468**. 620. 632**. 2004**. 2020. 2040). 250 al^{mu} arm$^{1. 2. 4. a}$ | *αυτησ* AאC 025. 1. 35. 205. 468**. 632**. 2004**. 2015. 2020. 2023. 2036. 2037. 2038. 2040 al^{mu} gig vg fl s^{1} arm$^{1. 2. 4}$ eth : *εν αυτη* arm^{a} : *τησ γησ* 046. **20** (– 35. 205. 468**. 632**. 2004**. 2020. 2040). 104. 250 al^{mu} s^{2} |.

19. *εβαλεν* AאC 025. 046. 35. 205. 620. 632**. 2004**. 2020. 2040 : misit gig vg fl : *εξεβαλεν* **20** (– 35. 205. 620. 632**. 2004**. 2020. 2040). 82. 104. 110. 172. 250. 385 al^{p} | *εις την γην* AC

20. καὶ ἐπατήθη ἡ ληνὸς ἔξωθεν τῆς πόλεως,
καὶ ἐξῆλθεν αἷμα ἐκ τῆς ληνοῦ ἄχρι τῶν χαλινῶν τῶν ἵππων
ἀπὸ σταδίων χιλίων ἑξακοσίων.

025. 046. **20** (– 2020). 250. 2037. 2038. 2067 al[pl] gig vg fl s[2] bo : επι τησ γησ ℵ 498. 2020 s[1] arm[1. 3. 4. a] | εισ την ληνον . . . τον μεγαν A(C) 025. 046. **20** (– 205. 386. 620. 632**. 2004**. 2040). 61. 69. 110. 141. 242. 314. 385. 452. 2016. 2017. 2021. 2022. 2023*. 2024. 2039. 2041 al[p] s[2] : τον μεγαν > 181. 424 : εισ τον ληνον . . . τον μεγαν 1. 201. 386. 498. 522. 1957. 2038 al : εισ την ληνον . . . την μεγαλην ℵ 104. 205. 250. 620. 632**. 2004**. 2015. 2018. 2036. 2037. 2040. 2067 s[1] : in torculari (-ar fl) . . . magnum Tyc Pr fl : in lacum . . . magnum (-am gig) gig vg | ληνον] αλωναν C : + του οινου 2020 | του θυμου] τον θυμον 386 : > 337. 620. 2004** arm[1. 2. 3. a] |.

20. επατηθη] επατησεν (-αν eth) arm[1. 2] bo eth : ετιθη 1 | η ληνοσ] ο ληνοσ 205. 336. 498. 522. 1957. 2004**. 2019. 2020 : την ληνον bo : in torcolari Pr fl arm[1. 2. 3] | εξωθεν AC 025. 046. **20** (– 35. 205. 2020). 250 al[pm] : εξω ℵ 1. 35. 205. 2015. 2020. 2036. 2037. 2038. 2067 : extra Tyc Pr vg fl : a foris extra gig | τησ[2]] του 452. 522 | απο σταδιων] επι σταδιων s[1] : per stadia Tyc vg : per stadios Pr (fl) | χιλιων εξακοσιων Aℵ[c]C 025. 35. 386. (620). 632. 1934. 2004**. 2040 Pr fl gig vg bo sa : χιλιων διακοσιων ℵ* 506. 680 : αχ′ **20** (– 35. 386. 620. 632. 1934. 2004**. 2040). 61. 69. 110. 314. 498. 2015 al : χιλ. εξακ. εξ. 2037 : αχς′ 2036 : δεκα και εξ eth : mille quingentis gig |.

Chapter XV.

2. (*a*) Καὶ εἶδον ὡς θάλασσαν ὑαλίνην μεμιγμένην πυρί, καὶ τοὺς νικῶντας ἐκ τοῦ θηρίου καὶ ἐκ τῆς εἰκόνος αὐτοῦ καὶ ἐκ τοῦ ἀριθμοῦ τοῦ ὀνόματος αὐτοῦ ἑστῶτας ἐπὶ τὴν θάλασσαν τὴν ὑαλίνην, ἔχοντας

(*a*) xv. 1. is an interpolation: Καὶ εἶδον ἄλλο σημεῖον ἐν τῷ οὐρανῷ μέγα καὶ θαυμαστόν, ἀγγέλους ἑπτὰ ἔχοντας πληγὰς ἑπτὰ τὰς ἐσχάτας, ὅτι ἐν αὐταῖς ἐτελέσθη ὁ θυμὸς τοῦ θεοῦ. The subject of xv. 1. is not touched upon till xv. 5, where the phrase καὶ μετὰ ταῦτα εἶδον shows that a new section and *a new subject* begin. See vol. i. 106 and footnote; vol. ii. 30.

1. θαυμαστον] θαυμασιον 61. 69 | αγγελους] angelos stantes fl | πληγασ επτα] ~ 920. 2015. 2016. 2020. 2036. 2037. 2067 : επτα > 2019 | εν αυταισ] εν ταυταις 35. 205. 2015. 2036. 2037. 2038 : in his Tyc |.

2. υαλινην] vitreum perlucidum Tyc | και τουσ νικ . . . εστωτασ επι την θαλασσαν] et super mare stantes uidi eos qui . . . uictoriam ferent fl : et superstantes uidi eos qui . . . uictoriam ferent Pr |

κιθάρας τοῦ θεοῦ, 3. καὶ ᾄδουσιν (a) τὴν ᾠδὴν τοῦ ἀρνίου λέγοντες

Μεγάλα καὶ θαυμαστὰ τὰ ἔργα σου,
κύριε, ὁ θεὸς ὁ παντοκράτωρ·
αἰώνων δίκαιαι καὶ ἀληθιναὶ αἱ ὁδοί σου,
ὁ βασιλεὺς τῶν ⸀ἐθνῶν⸁.

4. τίς οὐ μὴ φοβηθῇ, κύριε,
καὶ δοξάσει τὸ ὄνομά σου,
ὅτι μόνος ὅσιος;

ὅτι πάντα τὰ ἔθνη ἥξουσιν
καὶ προσκυνήσουσιν ἐνώπιόν σου,
ὅτι τὰ δικαιώματά σου ἐφανερώθησαν.

(a) Text adds a gloss: τὴν ᾠδὴν Μωυσέως τοῦ δούλου τοῦ θεοῦ καί.

νικωντασ] νικουντασ C | εκ του θηρ. και εκ τησ εικονοσ αυτου AC 025. 18. 35. 205. 250. 2037. 2038. 2067 al s arm$^{1.2.a}$: εκ τ. θ. και τησ εικ. αυτου ℵ 104. 336. 620. 1918. 2020 Pr fl : εκ της εικ. και εκ (>522) του θηρ. αυτου (>2040) 046. **20** (– 18. 35. 205. 620. 632**. 2020). 61. 69. 522 al : εκ του θηρ. αυτου 632** : bestiam et imaginem illius gig vg bo sa eth : bestiae Tyc | και εκ του αριθμου AℵC 025. 046. **20** (– 35. 205. 468. 620) al s arm$^{1.2.(4).a}$: et numerum gig vg bo : και εκ του χαραγματοσ αυτου και (>2018. 2019. 2036) εκ του αριθμου 051. 1. 35. 205. 250. 468. 2018. 2019. 2036. 2037. 2067 | και εκ τ. αριθ. . . . αυτου >620 Tyc Pr fl | εστωτασ > Tyc arm^{1} | τ. υαλινην >fl Pr eth | κιθαρασ AℵC 025. 35. 632**. 920. 2037. 2038. 2040. 2067 al^{pl} bo sa : τασ κιθαρασ 046. **20** (– 35. 632**. 920. 2040). 82. 104. 110. 172. 201. 250. 385. 498. 2018. 2022 al arm$^{2.4.a}$ του θεου] pr κυριου ℵ : >fl .

3. και αδ. . . . του θεου >C | και^{1} >bo | αδουσιν] αδοντασ ℵ 743. 1075. 2067 Tyc Pr fl vg s$^{1.2}$ bo | την^{1} >920 | Μωυσεωσ Aℵ 046. 1 al^{pl} : Μωσεωσ 025 al^{m} | του δουλου Aℵ 025. 1. 35. 205. 250. 632**. 1957. 2015. 2020. 2037. 2038. 2041. 2067 al : δουλοι 046. **20** (– 35. 205. 632**. 2020). al^{pl} | μεγαλα και θαυμαστα τα εργα σου] magna et mirabilia operati sunt Tyc | ο θεοσ ο > 620 | δικαιαι . . . αι οδοι σου] δικαια και αληθινα τα εργα σου s^{1} arm$^{1.4}$ | ο βασιλευσ] βασιλευσ ℵ^{c} 429. 632 : βασιλευ ℵ* 18. 94. 241. 385. 522. 919. 1849. 2004. 2039 : pr tu es fl | των εθνων Aℵ^{c} 025. 046. 051. **20** (– 2040). 1. 69. 104. 110. 250. 314. 2037. 2038. 2067 al gig Cyp arm^{4} bo : omnium gentium Pr fl arm^{1} eth : των αιωνων ℵ*C 94. 2040 Tyc vg s : "of aeons and king of all Gentiles" arm$^{2.a}$ |.

4. τισ] pr και 2019 arm^{a} | ου μη] σε ου ℵ 2040 | φοβηθη AℵC 025. 046. 1. 61. 69. 181. 205. 241. 632**. 2019. 2022. 2040.

5. Καὶ μετὰ ταῦτα εἶδον, καὶ ἠνοίγη ὁ ναὸς † τῆς σκηνῆς τοῦ
μαρτυρίου † (*a*) ἐν τῷ οὐρανῷ, 6. καὶ ἐξῆλθαν † οἱ ἑπτὰ ἄγγελοι † (*b*)
[οἱ ἔχοντες τὰς ἑπτὰ πληγὰς] ἐκ τοῦ ναοῦ, ἐνδεδυμένοι † λίθον † (*c*)
καθαρὸν λαμπρὸν καὶ περιεζωσμένοι περὶ τὰ στήθη ζώνας χρυσᾶς.

(*a*) For the probable origin of this corrupt phrase, see vol. ii. 37 sq.

(*b*) Here the hand that inserted xv. 1 changed ἄγγελοι ἑπτά into οἱ ἑπτὰ ἀγγ. and added οἱ ἔχοντες τὰς ἑπτὰ πληγάς.

(*c*) See vol. ii. 38.

2036. 2037. 2038. 2067 Pr fl gig arm bo : + σε 051. **20** (– 205. 632**. 2040). 104. 110. 250. 314. 385 al^{pl} vg s eth | κυριε > 61. 69 Pr gig arm eth | δοξασει AC 025. 046. 18. 175. 325. 456. 617. 632. 920. 1934 al : τις ου δοξασει 2040 : δοξαση ℵ 1. 35. 104. 110. 250. 337. 385. 386. 468. 919. 1849. 2004. 2020. 2037. 2038. 2067 al^{pl} : δοξασοι 205. 620 | μονοσ] pr ο 35 : pr συ ει 468 s^{1} : tu solus Pr gig arm | οσιοσ AℵC 025. 1. 205. 2015. 2036. 2037. 2038 al s^{1} : pius Pr. vg$^{a*. c. g}$: ει οσιοσ 632**. 2020 : οσιοσ ει 2019 al : pius es vg$^{a**. d. f. v}$: αγιοσ 046. **20** (– 205. 632**. 2020. 2040). 104. 110. 250. 314 al^{pl} : αγιοσ ει 2040. 2067 al : sanctus es gig arm^{4} : sanctus et pius es (es et dignus arm$^{1. 2. a}$) fl arm$^{1. 2. a}$: οσιοσ ει και δικαιοσ s^{2} | παντα τα εθνη AℵC 025. 1. 35. 205. 386. 2020. 2037. 2038. 2067 al Pr fl gig vg s arm bo : παντα 2040 : παντεσ 046. **20** (– 35. 205. 386. 2020. 2040). 69. 104. 250. 314. 385. 2022 al^{pl} | ενωπιον σου] + κυριε A 205. 2040 arm^{a} : το ονομα σου bo | τα δικ. σου εφανερωθησαν] δικ. ενωπιον σου εφαν. ℵ : (δικαιοσ) ει s^{1} | εφανερωθησαν] magnificata sunt vg$^{c. g*}$ |.

5. και^{1} > Pr fl | μετα ταυτα] μετ αυτα C | και^{2}] + ιδου Tyc Pr vg arm^{4} : ιδου bo | ηνοιγη > arm^{4} | ο ναοσ] + του θεου 620 : > Tyc | της σκηνησ] + τησ αγιασ gig : η σκηνη Tyc | εν τω ουρ.] pr ο s^{2} arm^{a} eth |.

6. εξηλθον A** ℵ 025. 046 al omn^{vi} : εξηλθαν C : εξηλθεν A*^{vi} | οι επτα αγγελοι] οι αγγελοι οι επτα 325. 456. 468 | οι εχοντεσ AC **20**. 250. 2037 al s (arm) bo : οι > ℵ 025. 046. 1. 242. 2036. 2038. 2067 al : habentes gig fl vg : cum (vii plagis) Pr | εκ του ναου AℵC 025. 1. 35. 104. 205. 241. 385. 620. 632**. 2015. 2019. 2022. 2036. 2037. 2038. 2040. 2067 al gig fl vg s : tr before οι^{2} 201. 386 s^{1} (bo) : εκ του ουρανου 60. 1957. 2023. 2041 : > 046. **20** (– 35. 205. 386. 620. 632**. 2040). 250 al Pr arm$^{1. 2}$ | ενδεδυμενοι AℵC 025. 1. 35*. 2040 al Tyc Pr gig fl vg s^{1} arm^{4} bo : pr οι ησαν 046. **20** (– 35*. 2040). 250 al^{pl} (s^{2}) arm$^{1. a}$ | λιθον καθαρον AC 242. 2020^{mg}. 2039 : lapide mundo vg$^{(-d)}$: λινον καθαρον 025. 051. **20** (– 2020^{mg}). 104. 250. 2037. 2038. 2067 al^{pl} s arm : λινουν καθαρον 046. 61. 69. 94. 498. 2019 : linteamine mundo vg^{d} : lintheamen mundum gig : lino mundo Tyc : linea munda Pr : linteamina candida fl : καθαρους λινους ℵ : "with garments of linen" bo | λαμπρον] λαμπρουσ ℵ (bo) : και λαμ-

7. καὶ ἓν ἐκ τῶν τεσσάρων ζῴων ἔδωκεν τοῖς ἑπτὰ ἀγγέλοις ἑπτὰ φιάλας χρυσᾶς γεμούσας τοῦ θυμοῦ τοῦ θεοῦ τοῦ ζῶντος εἰς τοὺς αἰῶνας τῶν αἰώνων. 8. καὶ ἐγεμίσθη ὁ ναὸς καπνοῦ ἐκ τῆς δόξης τοῦ θεοῦ καὶ ἐκ τῆς δυνάμεως αὐτοῦ, καὶ οὐδεὶς ἐδύνατο εἰσελθεῖν εἰς τὸν ναὸν ἄχρι τελεσθῶσιν αἱ ἑπτὰ πληγαὶ τῶν ἑπτὰ ἀγγέλων.

προν 2017** Tyc gig s^1 arm$^{1.2.a}$: et candida Pr (arm^4) : candido vg : >386 fl | και^2 > 1. 205 bo | περι] > 1. 181. 2016. 2037. 2067 : επι 2015. 2036 Tyc s^1 bo sa eth |.

7. εν > ℵ* 1. 104. 181. 336. 620. 2036. 2037. 2038. 2039. 2067 arm^a : unus gig fl vg | εκ > 205 | επτα^2 > ℵ | χρυσασ > Pr s^1 arm$^{2.a}$ | γεμουσασ > 325. 456 | τουσ αιωνασ των αιωνων] τον αιωνα του αιωνοσ 367. 468 : + αμην ℵ 181. 205. 209. 2015 s^1 bo |.

8. ο ναοσ] ο >1934 : + του θεου gig arm^4 | καπνου ℵAC 025. 1. 35. 205. 620. 632**. 2020. 2037. 2038. 2040. 2067 al : pr του 386 : fumo Pr fl gig vg arm : pr εκ του 046. **20** (– 35. 205. 386. 620. 632**. 2020. 2040) 250 al s bo | εκ^1 > 468* s^1 arm$^{2.3**.a}$ bo | εκ^2 >Pr arm$^{2.a}$ | εδυν. AC **20** (– 2040) al^{pl} : ηδυν. ℵ 1. 250. 2037. 2040. 2067 al^{mu} | εισελθειν] tr after ναον ℵ : ελθειν 620 | αχρι] αχρισ ου C | αι επτα πληγαι] septem (>bo) plagae illae Pr bo : septae illae plagae fl | επτα^2 > 025. 051. 1. 35. 60. 94. 181. 1957. 2015. 2023. 2036. 2037. 2038. 2041. 2067 gig |.

Chapter XVI.

1. Καὶ ἤκουσα μεγάλης φωνῆς ἐκ τοῦ ναοῦ λεγούσης τοῖς ἑπτὰ ἀγγέλοις Ὑπάγετε καὶ ἐκχέετε τὰς ἑπτὰ φιάλας τοῦ θυμοῦ τοῦ θεοῦ εἰς

1. μεγαλησ φωνησ AC 046. 42. 61. 69. 110. 175. 325. 337. 386. 456. 468. 920. 1934. 2016. 2022. 2040 al bo sa : ~ ℵ 025. 1. 18. 35. 205. 250. 617. 620. 632. 919. 1849. 2004. 2020. 2037. 2038. 2067 al^{pl} Pr gig vg | φωνησ] + εκ τ. ουρανου eth | εκ του ναου AℵC 025. 1. 35. 205. 250. 632**. 2020. 2040. 2067 al s arm^a : tr after λεγουσησ 2037. 2038 : εκ του ουρανου 42. 367. 468 arm^4 bo sa eth : >046. **20** (– 35. 205. 468. 632*. 2020. 2040) al^{pl} arm^3 | και^2 > 1. 104. 181. 205. 337. 620. 2015. 2019. 2023. 2036. 2037 al gig arm^1 bo | εκχεετε AℵC 025. 1. 181 : εκχεατε 046. 051. **20**. 250. 2037. 2038. 2067 al^{pl} : εκκεχετε (εξ- 61) 61 69 | επτα^2 >025. 1. 35. 1957. 2015. 2023. 2036. 2037. 2038. 2041 fl bo eth | φιαλασ] + quas accepistis Pr | εις την γην] επι την γην s^1 : κατω bo : εισ τ. πασαν γην eth : > fl arm^4 |.

τὴν γῆν. 2. Καὶ ἀπῆλθεν ὁ πρῶτος καὶ ἐξέχεεν τὴν φιάλην αὐτοῦ εἰς τὴν γῆν· καὶ ἐγένετο ἕλκος κακὸν καὶ πονηρὸν ἐπὶ τοὺς ἀνθρώπους.(*a*) 3. Καὶ ὁ δεύτερος ἐξέχεεν τὴν φιάλην αὐτοῦ εἰς τὴν θάλασσαν· καὶ ἐγένετο αἷμα ὡς νεκροῦ, καὶ πᾶσα ψυχὴ ζωῆς ἀπέθανεν, τὰ ἐν τῇ θαλάσσῃ. 4. Καὶ ὁ τρίτος ἐξέχεεν τὴν φιάλην αὐτοῦ εἰς τοὺς ποταμοὺς καὶ τὰς πηγὰς τῶν ὑδάτων καὶ ἐγένοντο αἷμα.(*b*)

(*a*) Text adds the gloss: *τοὺς ἔχοντας τὸ χάραγμα τοῦ θηρίου καὶ τοὺς προσκυνοῦντας τῇ εἰκόνι αὐτοῦ.* See vol. ii. 43.

(*b*) Text adds an interpolation 5^{a} : *καὶ ἤκουσα τοῦ ἀγγέλου τῶν ὑδάτων λέγοντος*, in order to introduce 5^{b}–7. These clauses 5^{b}–7 originally followed after xix. 4, to which context they are restored in this edition. See vol. ii. 122 sq., 116 sq.

2. και απηλθ. . . . εισ την γην > ℵ* | πρωτοσ] + αγγελοσ 172. 181. 218. 250. 2015. 2018. 2019. 2036. 2037 arm$^{1. 2. a}$ bo eth εισ] επι 1. 35. 205. 1957. 2015. 2023. 2036. 2037. 2038. 2041. 2067 s^{1} | την γην] τησ γησ 2038 | ελκοσ κακον και πονηρον] ελκον (-κοσ ℵ^{c}) πονηρον και κακον ℵ* : κακον > A 1849 : κακον και > 2067 bo eth : vulnus pessimum magnum Pr : ulcus saevum et malum fl : vulnus magnum (saevum vg) et pessimum gig vg | επι] εισ 1. 35. 205. 1957. 2015. 2023. 2036. 2037. 2038. 2041. 2067 al : in gig vg bo | το χαραγμα] tr after θηριου 620 : + nominis Pr | και^{5} > fl | τουσ^{3} > 104. 385. 620. 1918. 2015. 2036. 2037 | προσκυν.] tr after εικονα 1. 2037 | τη εικονι] την εικονα ℵ 1. 35. 2036. 2037. 2067 : > arm^{2} |

3. και ο δευτ. εξεχεεν > ℵ* | δευτεροσ Aℵ^{c}C 025. 94. 2040 Pr fl gig vg arm^{4} eth : + αγγελοσ 046. **20** (– 2040). 250. 2037. 2038. 2067 al^{pl} s arm$^{1. 2. 3. a}$ bo | εγενετο] + η θαλασσα fl gig s^{1} eth | αιμα ωσ νεκρου] ωσ αιμα νεκρου 104. 181. 205. 620. 1918. 2038 : velut mortuis sanguis fl | ωσ νεκρου > Pr | ωσ] ωσι ℵ : > 1. 209. 468** | ψυχη] ψυχησ A | ζωησ AC 2040 eth : ζωσα ℵ 025. 046. 051. 1. 35. 104. 205. 620. 1957. 2015. 2020. 2037. 2038. 2041. 2067 Tyc gig vg s$^{1. 2}$ arm^{a} bo sa : quae erant viventes fl : > **20** (– 35. 205. 620. 2020. 2040). 69. 110. 250. 314 al Pr arm$^{1. 3}$ | τα AC 2038 s^{2} : των 2040 : > ℵ 025. 046. **20** (– 2040). 250. 2037. 2067 al Tyc Pr fl gig vg s^{1} bo | απεθανεν] tr after θαλασση 1948. 2014. 2015. 2034. 2042 arm$^{1. 2. 3. a}$ | εν τη θαλ.] επι τησ θαλασσησ ℵ |.

4. τριτοσ] + αγγελοσ 051. 1. 35. 172. 205. 250. 1957. 2018. 2019. 2020. 2023. 2036. 2037. 2038. 2041. 2067 s arm$^{1. 2. a}$ bo | εισ] επι ℵ 051. 94. 2016 Pr vg bo sa | τασ AℵC 025. 35. 60. 1957. 2022. 2023. 2036. 2038. 2040. 2041 Pr fl gig arm bo : pr εις 046. **20** (– 35. 2040). 1. 250. 2037. 2067 al s : pr επι 94. 2016 vg | εγενοντο A 2019. 2040 Pr fl gig s arm^{2} bo sa eth : εγενετο ℵC 025. 046. **20** (– 2040). 1. 250. 2037. 2038. 2067 al^{pl} vg arm$^{1. 3. 4. a}$ |.

8. Καὶ ὁ τέταρτος ἐξέχεεν τὴν φιάλην αὐτοῦ ἐπὶ τὸν ἥλιον· καὶ
ἐδόθη αὐτῷ καυματίσαι τοὺς ἀνθρώπους ἐν πυρί· 9. καὶ ἐκαυματίσ-
θησαν οἱ ἄνθρωποι καῦμα μέγα, καὶ ἐβλασφήμησαν τὸ ὄνομα τοῦ θεοῦ
τοῦ ἔχοντος τὴν ἐξουσίαν ἐπὶ τὰς πληγὰς ταύτας, καὶ οὐ μετενόησαν
δοῦναι αὐτῷ δόξαν.
10. Καὶ ὁ πέμπτος ἐξέχεεν τὴν φιάλην αὐτοῦ ἐπὶ τὸν θρόνον τοῦ
θηρίου· καὶ ἐγένετο ἡ βασιλεία αὐτοῦ ἐσκοτωμένη (*a*) . . . καὶ ἐμα-
σῶντο τὰς γλώσσας αὐτῶν ἐκ τοῦ πόνου. 11. καὶ ἐβλασφήμησαν
τὸν θεὸν τοῦ οὐρανοῦ ἐκ τῶν πόνων αὐτῶν καὶ ἐκ τῶν ἑλκῶν αὐτῶν,
καὶ οὐ μετενόησαν ἐκ τῶν ἔργων αὐτῶν. 12. Καὶ ὁ ἕκτος ἐξέχεεν

(*a*) Several clauses lost here : see vol. ii. 45 sq.

5^{a}. του αγγελου] angelos Pr | *των υδατων*] pr *του επι* 2040 : tr after *λεγοντοσ* 205 : quartum gig |.

8. τεταρτοσ AC 025. 046. 175. 325. 337. 468. 617. 620. 632*. 920. 1849. 1934. 2004. 2040 al gig vg$^{(-d)}$ s^{2} arm$^{3.4}$: + *αγγελοσ* ℵ 051. 1. 18. 35. 205. 250. 314. 386. 456. 632**. 919. 1957. 2015. 2018. 2019. 2020. 2023. 2036. 2037. 2038. 2041. 2067 al^{m} Tyc Pr vg^{d} s^{1} arm$^{1.2.a}$ bo sa eth | *επι*] in gig vg | *καυματισαι τουσ ανθρ. εν* (> ℵ 2038) *πυρι* Aℵ 025. 35. 205. 2020. 2038. 2040 gig s$^{(1).2}$: aestu afficere hom. et igni vg : *καυμ. εν πυρι τ. ανθρ.* 046. **20** (– 35. 205. 2020. 2040). 250 al^{pl} : ignem et aestum inicere hominibus Pr | *εν πυρι*] *καυματι μεγαλω* bo |.

9. καυμα μεγα] *καυματι μεγαλω* 94. 2015. 2036. 2037 : > bo | *εβλασφημησαν* AℵC 025. 1. 205. 2019. 2020. 2036. 2037. 2038. 2040. 2067 al Tyc Pr gig vg s^{1} arm$^{1.2.4.a}$ bo : + *οι ανθρωποι* 046. **20** (– 205. 2020. 2040). 250 al^{pl} s^{2} arm^{3} | *το ονομα*] *ενωπιον* A : *κατα του ονοματοσ* 2040 : *εισ το ονομα* 2015 : > arm^{a} | *την* Aℵ 025. 35. 60. 181. 205. 432. 1957. 2019. 2023. 2038. 2041. 2067 : > C 046. **20** (– 35. 205). 1. 250. 2037 al^{pl} arm bo | *ου*] *ουχι* C |.

10. πεμπτοσ AℵC 025. 046. **20** (– 35. 205) gig vg$^{(-d)}$ s^{2} arm$^{3.4}$ sa eth al : + *αγγελοσ* 051. 35. 172. 205. 250. 1957. 2018. 2019. 2023. 2036. 2037. 2038. 2041. 2067 al Tyc Pr vg^{d} s^{1} arm$^{1.2.a}$ bo : *αγγελοσ* 1 | *τον θρονον*] *του θρονου* 2020 | *εσκοτωμενη* Aℵ*C 025. **20** (–456) : *εσκοτισμενη* ℵ$^{c.c}$ 046. 456. 385. 2015. 2037. 2067 | *εμασωντο* AℵC 025 al^{mu} : *εμασσ.* 046 al^{mu} | *εκ*] *απο* ℵ 051. 35 Tyc bo sa | *του πονου*] doloribus suis Tyc |.

11. ver. 11 > Pr | *τον θεον τ. ουρ.*] *το ονομα του θεου* (+ *του ουρ.* s^{1}) 1957 s^{1} | *και εκ των ελκων αυτ.*] > ℵ 172. 2022. 2031 arm^{4} : *και εκ. τ. εργων αυτων* bo | *εκ*^{2} > 025. 205. 2020. 2038. 2067 | *ελκων*] *ελκουσων* 2020 | *μετενοησεν*] tr after *αυτων*^{3} 468 | *εκ των. εργ. αυτων* > ℵ gig arm$^{1.2}$ |.

12. εκτοσ] + *αγγελοσ* 051. 35. 172. 205. 250. 620. 632**. 1957. 2015. 2018. 2019. 2023. 2036. 2037. 2038. 2041. 2067 Tyc Pr

τὴν φιάλην αὐτοῦ ἐπὶ τὸν ποταμὸν τὸν μέγαν τὸν ⌜Εὐφράτην⌝· Εὐφράτ
καὶ ἐξηράνθη τὸ ὕδωρ αὐτοῦ, ἵνα ἑτοιμασθῇ ἡ ὁδὸς τῶν βασιλέων
τῶν ἀπὸ ⌜ἀνατολῆς⌝ ἡλίου.
13. καὶ εἶδον ἐκ τοῦ στόματος τοῦ ἀνατολι
δράκοντος καὶ ἐκ τοῦ στόματος τοῦ θηρίου καὶ ἐκ τοῦ στόματος
τοῦ ψευδοπροφήτου πνεύματα τρία ἀκάθαρτα.(*a*)
14. † ἃ ἐκπορεύ-
εται † (*b*) ἐπὶ τοὺς βασιλεῖς τῆς οἰκουμένης ὅλης, συναγαγεῖν αὐτοὺς εἰς
τὸν πόλεμον τῆς ⌜ἡμέρας τῆς μεγάλης⌝ τοῦ θεοῦ τοῦ παντοκράτορος.(*c*) μεγάλη ἡμέρας

(*a*) Text adds gloss: *ὡς βάτραχοι· 14. εἰσὶν γὰρ πνεύματα δαιμονίων ποιοῦντα σημεῖα.*

(*b*) ℵ 051 change ἃ ἐκπορεύεται into ἐκπορεύεσθαι. Corrupt for ἐκπορευόμενα—the change being made by the interpolator of the preceding words. See vol. ii. 48. Pr (see below), recognising the need of this participle, inserts it after τρία, and some Gk. MSS insert ἐκπορευθέντα after βάτραχοι.

(*c*) MSS insert here as xvi. 15 a verse which originally stood after iii. 3^{a} and where it is restored in this edition.

gig vg^{d} s^{1} arm$^{1.2.4.a}$ bo | αυτου placed after φιαλην AℵC 046 al^{mu} : tr before τ. φιαλ. **20** (– 18. 35. 205. 632. 919. 920. 1849. 2004. 2040). 42. 61. 69. 104. 201. 314. 452. 498. 517. 2017 : > 920 | επι] in gig vg : per Tyc | τ. ποτ. τ. μεγ.] τον μεγαν ποταμον 051 | τον^{3} AC 1. 69. 172. 250. 2015. 2018. 2036. 2037. 2040. 2067 bo sa : > ℵ 025. 046. **20** (– 2040). 42. 82. 104. 201. 314. 385. 429. 432. 498. 522. 1955. 1957. 2016. 2017. 2019. 2022. 2023. 2038. 2041 al^{pl} | ευφρ.] εφρ. 046 | εξηρανθη] siccavit gig vg | αυτου^{2} > 1. 181. 205. 2019. 2038 bo | των βασιλεων] venienti regi Pr : regi venienti gig : regis arm : > Tyc | των^{2} > s^{1} | ανατολων A 051. 1. 35. 314. 468. 1957. 2015. 2020. 2023. 2036. 2037. 2041 s^{1} bo : ανατολησ ℵC 046. **20** (– 35. 205. 468. 2020). 250. 2038. 2067 al s^{2} |.

13. ειδον] εδοθη ℵ | εκ του στομ. τ. δ. . . . τ. θηρ. κ. > ℵ* | εκ τ. στομ. τ. δρακ. κ. > C 325. 337. 517. 1918 | εκ του στομ. τ. θηρ. και > 2019 arm^{1} | τρια ακαθαρ. AℵC 1. 35. 104. 205. 620. 1957. 2015. 2019. 2020. 2036. 2037. 2038. 2040. 2041. 2067 al^{mu} Tyc vg s^{1} arm$^{1.2.4.a}$: ~ 046. **20** (– 35. 205. 620. 2020. 2040). 250 al^{pl} arm^{3} : ακαθ. > 920 : τρια > gig : tres exeuntes inmundos Pr | ωσ βατραχοι] ωσ (ωσει ℵ*) βατραχουσ ℵ* 94. 498. 2019. 2020. 2023 : ωσει βατραχοι ℵ^{c} 2067 : + εκπορευθεντα 241. 2015. 2036. 2037 : > 1* |.

14. δαιμονιων] + ακαθαρτων 2040 : δαιμονων 051. 1. 35. 205. 2015. 2019. 2020. 2023. 2036. 2037. 2038. 2067 al | α (+ και 2015) εκπορευεται A **20** (– 205. 620. 2040). 69. 110. 250. 314. 385. 429. 498. 1957. 2015. 2016. 2017. 2018. 2023. 2039 al^{pl} Tyc : α εκπορευονται 046. 104. 336. 620. 1918. 2019 : εκπορευεσθαι ℵ* 051. 1*. 2022. 2036. 2037. 2038. 2040 : α εκπορευεσθαι 1** : εκπορευονται ℵ^{c} : εκπορευεται 205 : et exeunt (procedunt gig vg) Pr gig vg arm^{4} eth : > bo | επι] εισ ℵ | τησ οικ.] τ. γησ και (> 2037) τ. οικ. 1**. 2037 : τ. γησ bo | ολησ > 1* s^{1} arm^{3} bo | τον > 051. 1.

16. καὶ συνήγαγεν αὐτοὺς εἰς τὸν τόπον τὸν καλούμενον Ἑβραϊστί
Ἅρ Μαγεδών.
17. Καὶ ὁ ἕβδομος ἐξέχεεν τὴν φιάλην αὐτοῦ ἐπὶ τὸν ἀέρα καὶ
ἐξῆλθεν φωνὴ μεγάλη ἐκ τοῦ ναοῦ ἀπὸ τοῦ θρόνου λέγουσα Γέγονεν·
18. καὶ ἐγένοντο ἀστραπαὶ καὶ φωναὶ καὶ βρονταί, καὶ σεισμὸς
ἐγένετο μέγας, οἷος οὐκ ἐγένετο ἀφ' οὗ ⸀ἄνθρωπος ἐγένετο⸁ ἐπὶ τῆς γῆς — ἄνθρωποι ἐγένοντο

205. 2019. 2022. 2038. 2067 al | τησ ημ. τ. μεγ. ℵ 61. 69. 2020 : ad diem magnum vg : diei magni Tyc gig : τησ μεγ. ημ. A 2040 bo : τησ ημ. εκεινησ τ. μεγ. 046. 051. **20** (– 205. 2020. 2040). 1. 250. 2037. 2038. 2067 al Pr s : τησ ημ. εκεινησ 205 | του θεου] domini Tyc arm^{1} |.

16. συνηγαγεν] συνηγαγον ℵ s^{2} : συναξει vg$^{d. g}$ s^{1} arm$^{1. 3}$ | αυτουσ >s^{1} | τον^{1} >ℵ 61. 69 arm bo | τοπον] ποταμον A | τον^{2} >61. 69 bo | τον καλ. εβρα. >Tyc | αρ μαγεδων Aℵ 051. 1. 35. 104. 172. 205. 241. 250. 468. 620. 632. 1957. 2018. 2019. 2020. 2023. 2036. 2037. 2038. 2040. 2067 s^{2} arm$^{4. a}$: hermagedon vg : ermagedo gig : ermagedon Tyc : armageddon Pr : ermakedon bo : μαγεδων **20** (– 35. 205. 468. 620. 632. 2020. 2040) al s^{1} arm^{3} : μαγεδδων 046 : μακεδδων 61. 69 |.

17. και ο εβδ.] και οτε ℵ* (και ο ζ' ℵ^{c}) : +αγγελοσ ℵ$^{c. c}$ 051. 1. 35. 172. 205. 250. 468. 1957. 2015. 2018. 2019. 2023. 2036. 2037. 2038. 2041. 2067 al Pr gig vg^{d} s^{1} arm$^{1. 2. 4. a}$ bo | επι τ. αερα] εισ τ. αερα 051. 1. 35. 61. 69. 205. 1957. 2015. 2016. 2023. 2036. 2037. 2038. 2041. 2067 al s^{1} : in aere (-a gig : -em vg) Pr gig vg | μεγαλη > A 1. 181. 205. 209. 2038 | εκ Aℵ 1. 94. 181. 205. 209. 617. 2019. 2020. 2037. 2038. 2040. 2067 : απο 046. **20** (– 205. 617. 2020. 2040). 250 al^{pl} | ναου Aℵ 60. 61. 69. 2040 Pr vg s arm^{2} bo sa : +του ουρανου 046. **20** (– 468. 2040). 250. 2067 al^{pl} : ουρανου 1. 94. 181. 241. 2015. 2019. 2036. 2037. 2038 gig arm$^{3. 4. a}$: (+ουρ. του 468) ναου και 468 eth | απο του θρονου] του θεου ℵ : και (>201) απο τ. θρον. του θεου 201. 386 : >051* gig |.

18. και]+ευθεωσ 386 | αστράπ. κ. φων. κ. βροντ. A 42. 82. 141. 2015. 2019. 2036. 2040 al Pr gig vg arm^{2} bo sa eth : βροντ. κ. αστρ. κ. φων. κ. βροντ. ℵ* : αστρ. κ. φων. 046 : βροντ. κ. αστρ. κ. φων. ℵ^{c} 920 : αστρ. κ. βροντ. 205. 181. 2038. 2067 Tyc s^{1} arm^{4} : φων. κ. β. και αστρ. 1. 2037 al : αστρ. κ. βροντ. κ. φων. 051. **20** (– 205. 920. 2040). 61. 69. 104. 110. 141. 172. 201. 250. 314. 385. 432. 1918. 1955. 1957. 2016. 2018. 2022. 2023 al s^{2} | εγενετο^{1} Aℵ 1. 35. 61. 69. 205. 1957. 2015. 2019. 2023. 2036. 2037. 2038. 2040. 2041 al Tyc gig vg s arm$^{(2. 3). 4. (a)}$ bo : >046. **20** (– 35. 205. 2040). 250. 2067 al^{pl} Pr sa | οιοσ ουκ εγεν. . . . ουτω μεγασ] et signa magna Pr | οιοσ ουκ εγενετο] οισ ουκ εγενοντο ℵ* : οιοσ ου γεγονεν 920 | αφ ου] ex qua die gig | ανθρωποσ εγενετο A bo : ~ 2020 arm$^{3. a}$: ανθρωποι εγενοντο ℵ 046.

τηλικοῦτος σεισμὸς οὕτω μέγας. 19. καὶ (a) αἱ πόλεις τῶν ἐθνῶν
ἔπεσαν· καὶ Βαβυλὼν ἡ μεγάλη ἐμνήσθη ἐνώπιον τοῦ θεοῦ δοῦναι
αὐτῇ τὸ ποτήριον τοῦ οἴνου τοῦ θυμοῦ τῆς ὀργῆς αὐτοῦ· 20. καὶ
πᾶσα νῆσος ἔφυγεν, καὶ ὄρη οὐχ εὑρέθησαν. 21. καὶ χάλαζα
μεγάλη ὡς ταλαντιαία καταβαίνει ἐκ τοῦ οὐρανοῦ ἐπὶ τοὺς ἀνθρώπους· καὶ ἐβλασφήμησαν οἱ ἄνθρωποι τὸν θεὸν ἐκ τῆς πληγῆς τῆς χαλάζης, ὅτι μεγάλη ἐστὶν ἡ πληγὴ αὐτῆς σφόδρα.

(a) MSS insert before *καί* the words: *καὶ ἐγένετο ἡ πόλις ἡ μεγάλη εἰς τρία μέρη*. See vol. ii. 52.

35. 61. 69. 181. 2019. 2036. 2038. 2040 : *οι ανθρωποι* (*ουρανοι* 506) *εγενοντο* (> 1957 : *γεγονασιν* 337 : *εγενοντο οι ανθρ.* 205) 051. **20** (– 35. 2020. 2040). 1. 104. 110. 250. 2037. 2067 al^{pl} Tyc gig vg s arm$^{2.4}$ sa | *επι τησ γησ* > 69. 104 | *τηλικουτοσ σεισμοσ ουτω μεγασ*] > bo : tr after *εγενετο*^{2} arm^{2} | *ουτω*] *ουτως* 1. 498. 2015. 2018. 2020. 2037. 2038. 2040 al |.

19. *αι πολεισ*] *η πολισ* ℵ* s^{2} | *αι* > 2015. 2036. 2038 | *επεσαν* Aℵ^{c} 046. 051. 35. 104. 110. 337. 452. 468. 498. 620. 2015. 2020. 2023. 2038. 2041** : *επεσον* **20** (– 35. 337. 468. 620. 919. 2020). 1. 69. 250. 314. 2037. 2067 al^{pl} : *επεσεν* ℵ* s^{2} | *δουναι*] pr *του* ℵ 632**. 2015. 2036. 2037 | *το ποτ.*] *εκ* Pr | *το* > ℵ 2040 | *του*^{2} > ℵ bo | *τ. θυμ.*] tr before *τ. οινου* 468 eth : tr after *οργησ* Pr : + *και* s^{1} : > Tyc | *τ. οργ.* > 61. 69 gig arm^{4} | *αυτου*] > ℵ bo : *του θεου* 2019 eth |.

20. *και*^{1} > 1 | *πασα νησοσ εφυγεν*] omnes insulae fugierunt Pr arm bo eth | *ορη*] pr omnes Pr : + *και* 2015. 2036. 2037 | *ευρεθησαν*] + *τοτε οι απο ανατολων φευξονται επι δυσμασ και οι απο δυσμων εισ ανατολασ εσται γαρ θλιψισ μεγαλη οια ου γεγονεν απο καταβολησ κοσμου ουδ ου μη γενηται* 468.

21. *μεγαλη*] *βιαια* 920 | *ωσ ταλαντ.*] tr after *καταβαινει* 920 | *ωσ* > 2022 Pr | *καταβαινει*] *κατεβη* s^{1} arm bo | *τον θεον* > 386 | *εκ*] *επι* 205 | *πληγησ . . . χαλαζησ*] ~ 920 | *εστιν*] *εγενετο* Pr vg *η πλ. αυτ.* > vg | *αυτησ*] > 046 arm$^{2.3.a}$: tr before *η πληγη* 205 : *αυτη* 18. 69. 104. 175. 250. 325. 386. 456. 617. 620. 920. 2015. 2016. 2020. 2037 al : *αυτου* 181. 385 : a grandine Pr |.

Chapter XVII.

1. Καὶ ἦλθεν εἷς ἐκ τῶν ἑπτὰ ἀγγέλων τῶν ἐχόντων τὰς ἑπτὰ
φιάλας, καὶ ἐλάλησεν μετ' ἐμοῦ λέγων Δεῦρο, δείξω σοι
τὸ κρίμα τῆς πόρνης τῆς μεγάλης
τῆς καθημένης ἐπὶ ὑδάτων πολλῶν,
2. μεθ' ἧς ἐπόρνευσαν οἱ βασιλεῖς τῆς γῆς,
καὶ ἐμεθύσθησαν οἱ κατοικοῦντες τὴν γῆν ἐκ τοῦ οἴνου
τῆς πορνείας αὐτῆς.
3. Καὶ ἀπήνεγκέν με εἰς ἔρημον ἐν πνεύματι. καὶ εἶδον γυναῖκα
ἔχον καθημένην ἐπὶ θηρίον κόκκινον γέμοντα ὀνόματα βλασφημίας, ⸀ἔχων⸁

1. ηλθεν] εξηλθεν A | εισ] τισ 104 arm$^{3.4}$ | εκ > ℵ 2015. 2040 | αγγελ. . . . φιαλασ >Tyc | τ. εχοντων] qui habebat gig | ελαλησεν] dixit Tyc | μετ εμ. λεγ. >Tyc | λεγων] +μοι 1. 205. 2015. 2036. 2037. 2038. 2067 | τ. μεγ. > s^{1} | υδατ. πολλ. Aℵ 025. 1. 172. 181. 205. 218. 250. 2015. 2018. 2019 2036. 2037. 2038. 2040. 2067 bo : των υδατ. των πολλ. 046. **20** (−205. 2040) al^{pl} arm |.

2. μεθ ησ] +"sinned and" bo | επορνευσαν] εποιησεν πορνιαν ℵ bo sa | και . . . αυτησ >Tyc Pr | εμεθυσθησαν] εμεθυσαν 205 | οι κατ. τ. γ] tr after αυτησ 1 | εκ] απο 920 | οινου] οικου ℵ* ? | πορνειασ] πορνησ 205 |.

3. απηνεγκεν] ανηνεγκεν 920 : duxit Pr : tulit Tyc gig | με] μοι 386 | ερημον] +τοπον 2040 | εν Aℵ 025. 046. 35. 175. 205. 325**. 468. 617. 620. 632**. 1934. 2020. 2040 Tyc Pr gig Cyp vg bo (arm) : >18. 82. 93. 141. 201. 218. 325*. 337. 385. 386. 429. 456. 498. 506. 522. 632*. 919. 920. 1849. 1955. 2004. 2024*. 2039 al | ειδον] ιδα A | επι] +το 920 | θηριον Aℵ 35. 175. 205. 617. 620. 632**. 1934. 2020. 2040 : +το 18. 325. 337. 386. 456. 468. 632*. 919. 920. 1849. 2004 | κοκκ.] κογκ. 046 | γεμ. . . . (ver. 4) και^{3} >468* | γεμοντα Aℵ* 025 (s^{2}) : γεμον ℵ^{c} 046. 051. **20** (−468*). 1. 61. 69^{mg}. 110. 172. 201. 241. 250. 314. 385. 498. 522. 1955. 1957. 2015. 2016. 2018. 2019. 2022. 2023. 2024. 2036. 2037. 2038. 2039. 2041. 2067 (s^{1}) : γεμων 104. 429. 2017 | ονοματα Aℵ 025. 046. **20** (−35. 175. 205. 617. 1934). 61. 69. 104. 110. 201. 241. 385. 429. 498. 522. 1955. 1957. 2017. 2022. 2024. 2039 : ονοματων 1. 35. 61^{mg}. 172. 175. 205. 250. 314. 617. 1934. 2015. 2016. 2018. 2019. 2023. 2036. 2037. 2038. 2041. 2067 | εχων A 104. 201. 429. 919. 2017 : εχοντα ℵ 025 : εχον 046. 051. **20** (−468*. 919). 1. 250. 2037. 2038. 2067 al^{pl} | κεφ. επτ. και > 1 | δεκα] και η γυνη . . . τησ γησ (ver. 18) 025. 2020. (On this addition see Tischendorf, crit. note *in loc.*) |.

κεφαλὰς ἑπτὰ καὶ κέρατα δέκα. 4. καὶ ἡ γυνὴ ἦν περιβεβλημένη
πορφυροῦν καὶ κόκκινον, καὶ κεχρυσωμένη ⸢χρυσίῳ⸣ καὶ λίθῳ τιμίῳ χρυσῷ
καὶ μαργαρίταις, ἔχουσα ποτήριον χρυσοῦν ἐν τῇ χειρὶ αὐτῆς ⸢γέμον⸣ γέμων
βδελυγμάτων καὶ τὰ ἀκάθαρτα τῆς πορνείας αὐτῆς. 5. καὶ ἐπὶ τὸ
μέτωπον αὐτῆς ὄνομα γεγραμμένον, μυστήριον,

ΒΑΒΥΛΩΝ Η ΜΕΓΑΛΗ,
Η ΜΗΤΗΡ ΤΩΝ † ΠΟΡΝΩΝ †(*a*)
ΚΑΙ ΤΩΝ ΒΔΕΛΥΓΜΑΤΩΝ ΤΗΣ ΓΗΣ.

6. καὶ εἶδα τὴν γυναῖκα μεθύουσαν ἐκ τοῦ αἵματος τῶν ἁγίων καὶ
ἐκ τοῦ αἵματος τῶν μαρτύρων Ἰησοῦ.

(*a*) Tyc Pr vg arm^2 = πορνιῶν, which the parallelism in the next line requires. See vol. ii. 65.

4. ην] η 1 | πορφυρουν] πορφυραν 051. 1. 35. 175. 181. 205. 250. 314. 617. 1934. 1957. 2015. 2019. 2023. 2036. 2037. 2038. 2041. 2067 al^p : πορφυρᾶ s^1 | $και^2$ > 1957 | $και^3$ Aℵ 1. 104. 250. 424. (620). 2018. 2019. 2020. 2022. 2037 al Tyc Pr gig vg s^2 $arm^{3.4.a}$ bo : > 025. 046. **20** (– 620. 2020). 2038. 2067 al^{mu} s^1 arm^2 | κεχρυσωμενη] περικεχρυσωμενη 250 424. 2018 : κεχρυσωμενα s^1 : "gildings embroidered" arm^2 | χρυσιω A 046. **20** (– 35. 205. 2020. 2040). 250. 2067 al^{mu} : χρυσω ℵ 025. 1. 35. 205. 1957. 2015. 2019. 2020. 2023. 2036. 2037. 2038. 2040. 2041 | λιθ. τιμ. . . . μαργ.] ~ $arm^{4.a}$ | λιθ. τιμ.] λιθουσ τιμιουσ s^1 : λιθοισ τιμιοισ s^2 arm | μαργ.] μαργοριτασ s^1 : "pearl" arm | εχουσα . . . τ. πορν. αυτησ > 025 | εχουσα] pr και Tyc s^1 : et habebat Pr | ποτ. χρυσ.] ~ 1. 205. 1957. 2015. 2019. 2023. 2036. 2037. 2038. 2041. 2067 al : tr χρυσ. after $αυτησ^1$ 920 | εν] επι s^1 | γεμον $Aℵ^c$ 046. **20**. 250. 2037. 2038. 2067 al^{pl} : γεμων ℵ* 104. 201. 429. 2017 : pr και s^1 $arm^{3.4.a}$ | βδελ. . . . τα ακαθ.] ~ s^1 | βδελ.] βδελυγματοσ s^1 arm^4 (bo) : abominatione vg^{f**} (-nem*) | $και^6$ > bo | τα ακαθ.] τ. ακαθαρματα 2039 : immunditia $vg^{a*.c.f.g.h.v}$: -tiae Pr vg^{a**} (s^1) : -tiarum Tyc vg^d (bo) | τ. πορν. > gig | $αυτησ^2$ A 1. 35. 104. 172. 205. 241. 250. 468*. 632**. 1957. 2015. 2016*. 2018. 2019. 2020. 2023. 2036. 2037. 2038. 2040. 2041. 2067 al Tyc vg s^1 arm^2 eth : τησ γησ 046. **20** (– 35. 205. 468*. 632**. 2020. 2040) al^{mu} gig arm^3 : totius terrae Pr Cyp : αυτησ και τησ γησ ℵ s^2 : αυτησ μετα τησ γησ ολησ bo : > $arm^{4.a}$ |.

5. ονομα] ονοματα 18. 919. 2004 : > s^1 arm^2 eth | μυστηριον] sacramenti Pr : εν μυστηριω $arm^{3.a}$ | τ. πορν. κ. > gig | πορνων] fornicationum Tyc Pr vg (arm^2) | τ. γησ] totius terrae Pr |.

6. ειδα (ιδα A) Aℵ : ειδον (ιδον) 025. 046. 051 min^{pl} | $εκ^1$ A 1. 35. 104. 172. 205. 241. 429. 468**. 632**. 2015. 2016. 2017**. 2019. 2023. 2036. 2037. 2038. 2040. 2067 al^{mu} Pr gig vg s : > ℵ 025. 046. **20** (– 35. 205. 468**. 632**. 2020. 2040). 69. 82. 110. 250. 314. 385 al^{mu} | τ. αιμ.] τω αιματι ℵ* 2020 :

Καὶ ἐθαύμασα ἰδὼν αὐτὴν θαῦμα μέγα. 7. καὶ εἶπέν μοι ὁ
ἐγώ σοι ἐρῶ — ἄγγελος Διὰ τί ἐθαύμασας; ⸀ἐγὼ ἐρῶ σοι⸀ τὸ μυστήριον τῆς γυναικὸς
καὶ τοῦ θηρίου τοῦ βαστάζοντος αὐτήν, τοῦ ἔχοντος τὰς ἑπτὰ κεφαλὰς
καὶ τὰ δέκα κέρατα. 8. τὸ θηρίον ὃ εἶδες ἦν καὶ οὐκ ἔστιν, καὶ
ὑπάγειν — μέλλει ἀναβαίνειν ἐκ τῆς ἀβύσσου, καὶ εἰς ἀπώλειαν ⸀ὑπάγει⸀· καὶ
θαυμασθήσονται οἱ κατοικοῦντες ἐπὶ τῆς γῆς, ὧν οὐ γέγραπται τὸ
ὄνομα ἐπὶ τὸ βιβλίον τῆς ζωῆς ἀπὸ καταβολῆς κόσμου, βλεπόντων τὸ
θηρίον ὅ τι ἦν καὶ οὐκ ἔστιν καὶ πάρεσται.

sanguine Tyc arm | και^{2} Aא 025. 35. 205. 468. 632**. 2020. 2040 al^{mu} Tyc Pr gig vg s arm bo : > 046. **20** (− 35. 205. 468. 632**. 2020. 2040). 82. 110. 250. 385 al | εκ τ. αιμ.^{2}] εκ > 314. 2016. 2041 al : sanguine Tyc arm | μαρτ.] μαρτυριων A : pr αγιων 325. 468. 620 | Ιησου] pr του 2040 : + Christi Pr : > 1. 2019. 2067 arm^{a} | ιδ. αυτ. θαυμ. μεγ. > bo | tr ιδων αυτ. after μεγα א 2020 s^{1} | αυτην > 61. 69 |.

7. ερω σοι A 046. **20** (− 35. 205). 250 al^{mu} gig s eth : ∼ א 025. 1. 35. 61. 69. 1957. 2019. 2022. 2023. 2036. 2037. 2038. 2041. 2067 al^{p} vg : tibi ostendam Pr bo | το > arm | τ. γυν.] huius mulieris Pr | του^{3}] και 2020 : pr και 1. 2036. 2037 | τασ > 205 arm$^{2.\,4}$ | επτ. κεφ.] ∼ Pr vg | δεκ. κερ.] ∼ Pr vg |.

8. το θηριον] pr και Tyc arm^{a} eth | ο ειδεσ > Tyc | ην] η A : pr ο arm | και^{2}] sed Pr : > s^{1} bo | απωλειαν] + irae Tyc | υπαγει A 181. 468*. 2037 : vadit Pr s^{1} (eth) : υπαγειν א 025. 046. **20** (− 468*). 250. 2037. 2038 al^{pl} s^{2} arm (bo) : ibit Tyc gig vg | θαυμασθησονται A 025 s : θαυμασονται א 046. **20**. 250. 2037. 2038. 2067 min^{omn} : mirabantur vg$^{a.\,f.\,g**}$ arm^{a} | οι κατοικ.] pr παντεσ Pr arm$^{3.\,4.\,a}$ bo | επι τησ γησ Aא 025. 1. 35. 175. 205. 250. 617. 1934. 2037. 2038. 2040. 2067 al^{p} gig s arm$^{3.\,4.\,a}$ bo : την γην 046. **20** (− 35. 175. 205. 617. 1934. 2040) al^{pm} Pr vg : τησ γησ arm^{2} | ου γεγραπτ.] ουκ εγεγραπται A | το ονομα A 046. **20** (− 35. 175. 205. 468. 617. 1934). 69. 110. 385 al^{mu} s^{2} arm^{4} bo : τα ονοματα א 025. 1. 35. 175. 205. 250. 468. 617. 1934. 2037. 2038. 2067 al^{p} Pr gig vg s^{1} arm$^{2.\,a}$ eth : + αυτων arm^{a} | επι^{2}] εν 2036. 2040 Pr gig vg s^{1} arm | το βιβλιον Aא 025. 051. 1. 35. 175. 205. 250. 314. 617. 1934. 1957. 2016. 2019. 2023. 2037. 2038 al : του βιβλιου 046. **20** (− 35. 175. 205. 337. 617. 1934. 2040). 69. 82. 104 al^{mu} : τω βιβλιω 337. 2040 Pr gig vg s^{1} : βιβλω 2036 (arm) | βλεποντων] βλεποντεσ 1. 35. 1957. 2019. 2022. 2023. 2041 Pr gig vg | τ. θηρ. (οτι) ην Aא 025. 1. 35. 205. 2020. 2037. 2038. 2040. 2067 al^{p} Pr gig s arm bo : οτι ην τ. θηρ. 046. **20** (− 35. 205. 2020. 2040). 250 al | ο τι so apparently Pr vg$^{d.\,v}$ arm^{2} : οτι 046 min^{omn} gig vg$^{a.\,c.\,f.\,g.\,h}$ bo arm$^{3.\,4.\,a}$: Aא 025. s would support either reading | εστιν] εσται 386. 920 | και^{6}] + παλιν א* | παρεσται Aא* 025. 046. 051. **20** (− 632**). 69. 104. 250. 314. 2067 al^{pm} Pr arm^{4} : παρεστιν א^{c} 1. 181.

9. Ὧδε ὁ νοῦς ὁ ἔχων σοφίαν· αἱ ἑπτὰ κεφαλαὶ ἑπτὰ (a) 10. βασιλεῖς (b) εἰσίν· οἱ πέντε ἔπεσαν, ὁ εἷς ἔστιν, ὁ ἄλλος οὔπω ἦλθεν, καὶ ὅταν ἔλθῃ ὀλίγον αὐτὸν δεῖ μεῖναι. 11. καὶ τὸ θηρίον, ὃ ἦν καὶ οὐκ ἔστιν, καὶ αὐτὸς ὄγδοός ἐστιν, καὶ ἐκ τῶν ἑπτά ἐστιν, καὶ εἰς ἀπώλειαν ὑπάγει. 12. καὶ τὰ δέκα κέρατα ἃ εἶδες δέκα βασιλεῖς εἰσίν, οἵτινες βασιλείαν οὔπω ἔλαβον, ἀλλὰ ἐξουσίαν ὡς βασιλεῖς μίαν ὥραν λαμβάνουσιν μετὰ τοῦ θηρίου. 13. οὗτοι μίαν

(a) Here follows a gloss giving a second explanation: ὄρη εἰσίν, ὅπου ἡ γυνὴ κάθηται ἐπ' αὐτῶν. καί.
(b) The same gloss adds ἑπτά.

241. 336. 632**. 2019. 2036. 2037. 2038 gig s arm^{a} : επεσεν bo : > vg |.

9. ωδε ο νουσ ο εχ. σοφ.] joined with what precedes 046. 18. 69. 201. 337. 385. 386. 456. 498. 522. 919. 920. 1849. 1955 al : "he who hath heart with (and eth) wisdom let him understand" bo eth^{2} | ωδε] pr et Pr : > 046 | ο εχων] τω εχοντι s | αι] και 2040 : > 051 | επτα] > 61. 69 : tr after εισιν 1 | επ] επανω 61. 69 | οπου . . . επ αυτων] ubi . . . supra illos gig s : super quos Pr vg bo eth |.

10. και^{1} > 620 | βασ. επτ. εισιν A 025. 1. 35. 205. 241. 632**. 1957. 2019. 2020. 2036. 2037. 2038. 2040. 2041. 2067 al Pr gig vg s (arm$^{3.\ 4.\ a}$) : επτ. βασ. εισιν ℵ bo sa eth : βασ. εισιν επτ. 046. **20** (−35. 205. 632**. 2020. 2040). 250 al^{mu} (arm^{2}) | επεσαν] επεσον **20** (−35. 337. 468. 920). 42. 69. 82. 104. 250. 2067 al | ο^{1}] pr και 1 s^{1} arm bo : +δε 2041 Pr eth^{2} | εστιν] pr ουκ bo : superest Pr | ο^{2}] pr και vg arm bo eth | αυτ. δει μειναι A 025. 1. 35. 69. 2037. 2038. 2040. 2067 al : αυτ. μινε ζει (δει ℵ^{c}) ℵ* : δει αυτ. μειναι 046. **20** (−35. 2040). 250 al^{mu} (Pr) gig (vg) |.

11. και^{2} > 468*. 2040 | και^{3} > ℵ | αυτοσ A 025. 1. 35. 175. 205. 250. 617. 632. 1934. 2037. 2038. 2067 al Pr gig vg (s^{1}) bo : ουτοσ ℵ 046. **20** (−35. 175. 205. 617. 632. 1934) al (s^{2}) | ογδοοσ] pr ο ℵ 452. 2017. 2021 : octavo loco Pr | κ. εκ. τ. επτ. εστιν] cum sit ex vii Pr | υπαγει] vadet vg : ibit Pr (arm$^{2.\ 3.\ a}$) |.

12. οιτινεσ] hii Pr | βασιλειαν > bo | ουπω] ουκ A : ουτω ℵ* | αλλα Aℵ 69. 2040 : αλλ 025. 046 min^{pl} : > bo arm^{4} | ωσ βασιλεισ] regni Pr | μιαν ωραν] una hora Pr gig vg | λαμβ. . . . θηριον] "having followed the wild beast" bo | λαμβανουσιν] pr ου 620 : accipient gig vg$^{c.\ d.\ v}$: tr after θηριον 920 | μετα του θηριου] post bestiam vg |.

13. ουτοι] + omnes Pr | γνωμην εχουσιν Aℵ 025. 1. 35. 205. 2037. 2038. 2040 al^{p} Tyc (Pr) gig vg (arm) : ∼ 046. **20** (−35. 205. 2040). 250 al^{mu} sa | εχουσιν] habebunt Pr | την > 61. 69. 2038 arm$^{2.\ 3.\ a}$ | εξουσιαν A 046. **20** (−35. 205. 386. 468. 920). 250 al^{mu} arm$^{2.\ 3.\ a}$: pr την ℵ 025. 1. 35. 172. 201. 205. 385. 386. 468. 498. 920. 1957. 2018. 2019. 2023. 2036. 2037. 2038. 2041. 2067 al |

γνώμην ἔχουσιν, καὶ τὴν δύναμιν καὶ ἐξουσίαν αὐτῶν τῷ θηρίῳ
διδόασιν (*a*). 17. ὁ γὰρ θεὸς ἔδωκεν εἰς τὰς καρδίας αὐτῶν ποιῆσαι
τὴν γνώμην αὐτοῦ,(*b*) καὶ δοῦναι τὴν βασιλείαν αὐτῶν τῷ θηρίῳ,
ἄχρι τελεσθήσονται οἱ λόγοι τοῦ θεοῦ.

16. καὶ τὰ δέκα κέρατα ἃ εἶδες καὶ τὸ θηρίον,
οὗτοι μισήσουσιν τὴν πόρνην,
καὶ ἠρημωμένην ποιήσουσιν αὐτὴν καὶ γυμνήν,
καὶ τὰς σάρκας αὐτῆς φάγονται,
πυρί καὶ αὐτὴν κατακαύσουσιν ⸂ἐν πυρί⸃.

14. οὗτοι μετὰ τοῦ ἀρνίου πολεμήσουσιν,
καὶ τὸ ἀρνίον νικήσει αὐτούς,
ὅτι κύριος κυρίων ἐστὶν καὶ βασιλεὺς βασιλέων,
καὶ οἱ μετ' αὐτοῦ κλητοὶ καὶ ἐκλεκτοὶ καὶ πιστοί. (*c*)

(*a*) Text of xvii. 14–17 dislocated and glossed. On the restoration of the original order, see vol. ii. 61, 71 sq.

(*b*) A doublet here follows *καὶ ποιῆσαι μίαν γνώμην*: see crit. notes below, and cf. xvii. 13.

(*c*) What was originally a marginal gloss on xvii. 1 text adds here: 15. *καὶ εἶπέν μοι Τὰ ὕδατα ἃ εἶδες, οὗ ἡ πόρνη κάθηται, λαοὶ καὶ ὄχλοι εἰσὶν καὶ ἔθνη καὶ γλῶσσαι.*

αυτων] *εαυτων* 1 (s) : > arm$^{2.3.a}$ | *τω θηρ.*] diabolo Tyc | *διδοασιν*] *δωσουσιν* 94. 2036. 2037 Tyc bo : *διαδωσουσι* 218 : tradent Pr vg |.

17. θεοσ] *κυριοσ* 61. 69 | *εδωκεν* > Tyc | *αυτων*^{1}] *αυτου* ℵ* | *τ. γν. αυτ. κ. ποιησαι* > 94. 620. 1918 arm$^{2.3.a}$ eth | *αυτου*] *αυτων* ℵ^{c} | *κ. ποιησαι μιαν γνωμην*] > A 2036. 2037 Tyc gig vg : et esse illos in (+uno arm$^{2.3.a}$ bo sa eth) consensu (+et metu Pr) Pr arm$^{2.3.a}$ bo sa eth | *και ποιησαι* > ℵ^{c} | *μιαν γνωμην* ℵ 025. 1. 35. 2019. 2022. 2037. (2040). 2067 al : ~ 046. **20** (−35. 2040). 250 al^{mu} : *μιαν* > 172. 2018 : +*αυτων* 2040 s^{1} | *και* > gig vg bo | *δουναι*] dabunt Tyc : ut dent gig vg | *την*^{2} > bo sa | *αυτων*^{2}] *αυτω* A : *αυτου* 046. 61. 69 : > 2036 Pr arm$^{2.3.a}$ bo sa | *τελεσθησονται* Aℵ 025. 051. 1. 35. 181. 205. 209. 432. 1957. 2023. 2036. 2037. 2038. 2041. 2067 : *τελεσθωσιν* 046. **20** (−35. 205). 69. 104. 110. 250. 385. 2016 al^{pl} |.

16. α ειδεσ] tr after *θηριον* 205 eth | *κ. το θηριον*] *τω θηριω* s^{1} arm^{2} : *του θηριου* arm$^{3.a}$: + *ο ειδεσ* (Pr) : > Tyc arm^{4} | *μισησουσιν*] odio habent Tyc | *ποιησουσιν* (*ποιουσιν* Tyc) *αυτην κ. γυμνην* Aℵ 025. 1. 205. 632**. 2020. 2036. 2037. 2040 al Tyc gig vg s^{2} arm^{2} sa : *ποιησουσιν αυτην και* (> bo) *γυμνην ποιησουσιν* (-*σωσιν* 617) *αυτην* 046$^{mg(**)}$. **20** (−205. 632**. 919*. 920. 2020. 2040). 250 al bo eth : *και γυμνην ποιησουσιν αυτην* 424. Pr s^{1} arm^{4} : *κ. γυμνην* > 046*. 1. 82. 141. 218. 498. 919*. 920. 2016. 2019 | *αυτ. φαγ.*] ~ 632 | *φαγονται*] *φαγωνται* 18. 632 : edunt Tyc | *κατακαυσουσιν*] *καυσουσιν* 1. 181. 205. 2019. 2020 | *εν* A **20** (−920). 2037. 2038. 2067 al^{pl} bo sa : > ℵ 025. 046. 172. 250. 920. 2018 Pr gig vg |.

14. πολεμησουσιν] *πολεμουσιν* Tyc arm$^{2.3.a}$ | *οι μετ αυτου*]

18. καὶ ἡ γυνὴ ἣν εἶδες ἔστιν ἡ πόλις ἡ μεγάλη ἡ ἔχουσα βασιλείαν ἐπὶ τῶν βασιλέων τῆς γῆς.

quicumque cum eo erunt Pr | κλητ. . . . εκλ. . . . πιστ.] εκλ. . . . πιστ. . . . κλητ. Pr | κλητοι και >gig | και[4]] >vg[a. c. f. h. v] : οτι 1. 2037 | εκλεκτοι και > 110. 2020 | εκλ. . . . πιστ.] ~ 172. 2018. 2036. 2037 : οι εκλεκτοι . . . οι πιστοι bo | και[5] > 205. 2067 [!].

15. ειπεν A Tyc Pr vg s arm[4] bo sa : λεγει ℵ 025. 046 min[omn] gig arm[2. a] : > eth | μοι] + angelus Tyc | τα υδατα] ταυτα ℵ* : ταυτα τα υδατα ℵ[c] | ειδεσ] οιδασ 104 : vides Tyc : + και η γυνη 175. 617. 1934 | ου] super quas Pr Cyp s[1] | η > ℵ[c] | πορνη] mulier Tyc bo | λαοι] pr και ℵ | και οχλοι > vg | οχλοι . . . γλωσσαι] ~ 920 | οχλ. εισιν κ. εθνη κ. γλωσσ.] turbae (+ et gentes Cyp) ethnicorum et linguae sunt (sunt et linguae Cyp) Pr Cyp : "multitudes of nations" bo |.

18. εστιν > Pr s[1] | η μεγ.] του θεου 920 | η[4] > ℵ 18. 201. 386. 2039. 2040 | τ. βασιλεων] τ. βασιλειων ℵ arm[2. 3. a] bo eth : > arm[4] : + των 336. 620. 1918 | τησ γησ Aℵ 025. 18. 35. 175. 205. 468. 617. 632**. 1934. 2020. 2040 Tyc gig vg s arm bo eth : terrarum Pr : pr επι (046). 325. (336). 337. 386. 456. (620). 632*. 919. 920. 1849. (1918). 2004 al[mu] |.

Chapter XVIII.

1. Μετὰ ταῦτα εἶδον ἄλλον ἄγγελον καταβαίνοντα ἐκ τοῦ οὐρανοῦ, ἔχοντα ἐξουσίαν μεγάλην, καὶ ἡ γῆ ἐφωτίσθη ἐκ τῆς δόξης αὐτοῦ.
2. καὶ ἔκραξεν ἐν ἰσχυρᾷ φωνῇ λέγων
  Ἔπεσεν, ἔπεσεν Βαβυλὼν ἡ μεγάλη,
  καὶ ἐγένετο κατοικητήριον δαιμονίων,
  καὶ φυλακὴ παντὸς πνεύματος ⸢ἀκαθάρτου καὶ μεμισημένου⸣, ἀκαθάρτου
  καὶ φυλακὴ παντὸς ὀρνέου ἀκαθάρτου καὶ μεμισημένου (a).

(a) Text of these last two lines is uncertain Possibly we should read θηρίου for πνεύματος (cf. Jer. l. 39), cf. A 250. 424 Pr gig s[2] below : or else, with 250. 424 Pr gig s[2], read an additional line : καὶ φυλακὴ πάντος θηρίου ἀκαθάρτου.

1. μετα ταυτα] pr και 051. 1. 35. 104. 205. 250. 468. 2020. 2037. 2038 al gig vg eth : et Pr | αλλ. αγγ] ~ 35. 175. 242. 250. 617. 920. 1934. (1957). 2016. 2017. 2023 | αλλον] ετερον 1957 : > 1. 61. 69 arm[4] | εχοντα] pr και 205 eth | μεγ. > gig arm[2] | εκ[2]] απο 386 : + του προσωπου αυτου και bo eth |.

2. εκραξεν] εκεκραξεν A | εν A 025. 35. 432. 452. 1957.

πέπωκαν

3. ὅτι ἐκ τοῦ οἴνου [τοῦ θυμοῦ] τῆς πορνείας αὐτῆς ⸀πεπότικεν⸁
πάντα τὰ ἔθνη,
καὶ οἱ βασιλεῖς τῆς γῆς μετ' αὐτῆς ἐπόρνευσαν,
καὶ οἱ ἔμποροι τῆς γῆς ἐκ τῆς δυνάμεως τοῦ στρήνους αὐτῆς
ἐπλούτησαν.

2019. 2023. 2036. 2038. 2040. 2041 Tyc vg (bo) : >ℵ 046. **20** (−35. 2040). 1. 141. 181. 241. 250. 336. 385. 429. 522. 1918. 1955. 2037. 2067 Pr gig | *ισχυρα φωνη* (+*μεγαλη* 1. 181. 2067 : +*και μεγαλη* 205. 2019) Aℵ 025. 046. **20** (−18. 620. 632. 919. 1849. 2004). 1. 181. 250. 432. 452. 1957. 2019. 2023. 2036. 2037. 2038. 2041. 2067 vg s² (arm⁴ eth) : *ισχυραν φωνην* 18. 141. 241. 336. 385. 429. 522. 620. 632. 919. 1849. 1918. 1955. 2004 : *φωνη μεγαλη* (+*και ισχυρα* Pr) Pr gig s¹ arm²·ᵃ (bo) : fortitudine Tyc | *λεγων* > 025 bo | *επεσεν*² A 1. 35. 104. 172. 205. 468**. 632**. 1957. 2019. 2023. 2036. 2037. 2040. 2041. 2067 Tyc Pr gig vg s arm²·⁴ : > ℵ 046. **20** (−35. 205. 468**. 632**. 2040). 250. 2038 al^mu arm³·ᵃ bo sa eth : +*επεσεν* 025 | Βαβ.] pr *η* 046. 61. 69. 2067 : +*η πολισ* bo sa eth | *κατοικ.*] habitatio et refugium Pr | *δαιμονιων* Aℵ 046. 2040 Tyc Pr gig vg : *δαιμονων* 025. **20** (−2040). 250. 2037. 2038. 2067 al | *φυλακη*¹·² >Pr | *παντοσ*¹ . . . *μεμισημενου*²] omnis immunditiae et iniquitatis Tyc | *παντοσ*¹ . . . *φυλακη*² > 18. 205 | *πνευματοσ*] + *δαιμονιου* 620 | *ακαθ.*¹ . . . *ορνεου* >025. 1. 61. 69. 104. 181. 242. 617. 919*. 1934. 2016. 2019. 2020. 2036. 2037. 2038. 2067 s¹ arm² | *κ. μεμισημενου*¹ A 336. 620 gig arm⁴ : > ℵ 025. 046 min^fere omn (Pr) vg s² bo sa eth : + et omnis bestiae immundae Pr | *φυλ. παντ.*² >456. 632** | *ορνεου*] *θηριου* A | *ακαθ.*² >920 | *κ. μεμισημενου*²] *κ. μεμιασμενου* 18 : >61. 69. vg (−vg^c) : pr *και φυλακη παντοσ θηριου ακαθαρτου* 250. 424 : + et carcer omnis bestiae immundae et odibilis gig s² |.

3. *τ. οιν. τ. θυμ.* ℵ 046. **20** (−35. 205). 250 al^pl Tyc s² : *τ. θυμ. τ. οιν.* 025. 051. 1. 35. 172. 205. 241. 432. 1957. 2018. 2019. 2023. 2036. 2037. 2038. 2041. 2067 gig arm³·⁴·⁽ᵃ⁾ eth : *τ. οιν.* >AC vg : *τ. θυμ.* >Pr s¹ | *τ. θυμ. τ. πορν.*] *τ. πορν. τ. θυμ.* C | *τ. πορν.* >218 s² | *πεπ. παντ. τ. εθ.* >Pr | *πεποτικεν* 94. 432. 2019 2036 (s¹) : *πεποκεν* (*πεπω-* 35. 2037). 025. 1. 35. 2023. 2037. 2038. 2041 : *πεπωκασι* (*πεπο-* 242. 498. 617. 2020). 051. 110. 175. (241). 250. 337. 468**. 522. 617. 632. (1918). 1934. 1957. 2016. 2017. 2020. 2024. 2039. 2067 al^p Tyc gig vg s² arm²·³·ᵃ : *πεπτωκαν* AC : *πεπτωκασι(ν)* ℵ 046. **20** (−35. 175. 337. 468**. 617. 632. 2020). 61. 69. 104 al^p arm⁴ bo eth | *μετ αυτ. επορν.*] *οι μετ αυτ. πορνευσαντεσ* 256. 336. (620). 628 Tyc arm²·³·ᵃ : *μετ αυτησ* > Pr | *τ. γησ*²] *αυτησ* 1. 920 | *τ. δυν.* > bo | *στρηνουσ*] *στρηνου* C 149. 201. 241. 2037. 2067 |.

4. Καὶ ἤκουσα ἄλλην φωνὴν ἐκ τοῦ οὐρανοῦ λέγουσαν
Ἐξέλθατε ⸂ἐξ αὐτῆς ὁ λαός μου⸃, ὁ λαός μο ἐξ αὐτῆς
ἵνα μὴ συνκοινωνήσητε ταῖς ἁμαρτίαις αὐτῆς,
καὶ ἐκ τῶν πληγῶν αὐτῆς ἵνα μὴ λάβητε·

5. ὅτι ἐκολλήθησαν αὐτῆς αἱ ἁμαρτίαι ἄχρι τοῦ οὐρανοῦ,
καὶ ἐμνημόνευσεν ὁ θεὸς τὰ ἀδικήματα αὐτῆς.

6. ἀπόδοτε αὐτῇ ὡς καὶ αὐτὴ ἀπέδωκεν,
καὶ διπλώσατε διπλᾶ κατὰ τὰ ἔργα αὐτῆς·
ἐν τῷ ποτηρίῳ ᾧ ἐκέρασεν κεράσατε αὐτῇ διπλοῦν·

4. αλλην φωνην] αλλησ φωνησ C 2067 : ~ 2020 : αλλ. > arm$^{3.4.a}$ bo | λεγουσαν] -σησ 2067 | εξελθατε Aℵ 2036. 2038 : εξελθετε 025. 051. 1. 35. 205. 1957. 2017. 2023. 2037. 2040. 2041. 2067 Tyc gig vg s arm bo : εξελθε C 046. **20** (– 35. 205. 2040). 250 al^{pl} Pr | εξ αυτησ] tr after μου ℵC 025. 2020. (2067) eth : > 1. 110. 181. 2038 | εξ] απ 2067 | ο > 205. 2038. 2067 | ινα > 386 | συνκοιν. AℵC : συγκοιν. 025. 046 min^{omn} | και^2 > s^1 | κ. εκ τ. πλ. αυτ. > 025. 051. 35*. 2038 | τ. πληγων] τησ πληγης gig s^1 | λαβητε] λαθητε 386 : βλαβητε 051. 2036. 2037 (Tyc Pr) |.

5. αυτησ^1] αυτη s^1 (bo) : αυτων arm^2 : > 920 | αχρι] εωσ 025 : μεχρι 2037 | εμνημον.] + αυτησ 18. 35. 82. 110. 172. 337. 385. 456. 632. 919. 920. 1849. 1955. 2004. 2018. 2022. 2023 al^p : + αυτοισ 386 eth | θεοσ] dominus vg : dominus deus Pr | αυτησ^2] αυτων Tyc arm^2 |.

6. αποδοτε . . . αυτησ] et (> Cyp) ideo reddidit ei duplicia (dupla Cyp) Pr Cyp | αποδοτε] αποδιδωσιν arm$^{2.3.a}$ | και^1 > vg (– vg^a) | απεδωκεν] + υμιν 051. 1. 35. 175. 205. 468. 617. 632**. 1934. 1957. 2016. 2037. 2038. 2041 gig vg^v arm$^{(2).4}$: + ημιν 2067 arm$^{3.a}$ | και^2 > ℵ eth | διπλωσατε (διπλασατε 18. 2004) AℵC 046. **20** (– 35. 175. 205. 617. 620. 632**. 1934. 2020). 61. 69. 82. 93. 110. 385. 2022. 2024. 2039 al^{mu} Tyc gig vg : + αυτη 025. 051. 1. 35. 104. 175. 250. 617. 620. 632**. 1934. 1957. 2016. 2037. 2038. 2067 al s arm^4 bo : + αυτην 205 : + αυτα 2020 | διπλα A 025. 046. 051. 1. 35. 104. 175. 205. 250. 617. 620. 632**. 1934. 2016. 2020. 2037. 2038. 2040. 2067 : pr τα ℵC 18. 61. 69. 110. 325. 337. 385. 386. 456. 468. (632*). 919. 920. 1849. 2004. 2022 | (τα) διπλα AℵC 025. 35. 175. 617. 620. 632**. 1934. 2020. 2040 Tyc Pr gig vg s arm bo eth : + ωσ και αυτη (αυτοι 69) και (> 61. 69) 046. **20** (– 35. 175. 617. 620. 632**. 1934. 2020. 2040). 61. 69. 82. 110 al^{mu} | τα > 149 | εν τω ποτηριω] in calicem gig | ποτηριω AC 025. 1. 35. 175. 250. 325. 617. 1934. 2037. 2038. 2040. 2067 Tyc Pr (gig) vg s arm eth : > 620 : + αυτησ ℵ 046. **20** (– 35. 175. 325. 617. 1934. 2040). 69. 104. 110. 385 bo | ω] ωσ 172. 2020 bo | εκερασεν] + υμιν

7. ὅσα ἐδόξασεν αὐτὴν καὶ ἐστρηνίασεν,
τοσοῦτον δότε αὐτῇ βασανισμὸν καὶ πένθος.

ὅτι ἐν τῇ καρδίᾳ αὐτῆς λέγει ὅτι
Κάθημαι βασίλισσα
καὶ χήρα οὐκ εἰμί,
καὶ πένθος οὐ μὴ ἴδω·

8. διὰ τοῦτο ἐν μιᾷ ἡμέρᾳ ἥξουσιν αἱ πληγαὶ αὐτῆς,
† θάνατος καὶ πένθος καὶ λιμός,†(a)
καὶ ἐν πυρὶ κατακαυθήσεται,
ὅτι ἰσχυρὸς ὁ θεὸς ὁ κρίνας αὐτήν.

κλαύσουσιν αὐτήν. 9. Καὶ ⌜κλαύσονται⌝ καὶ κόψονται ἐπ' ⌜αὐτῇ⌝ οἱ βασιλεῖς τῆς γῆς,
οἱ μετ' αὐτῆς πορνεύσαντες καὶ στρηνιάσαντες, ὅταν βλέπωσιν τὸν

(a) On this line see vol. ii. 100.

632** | κερασατε] remixtum est Cyp Pr : "shall be mingled" arm² | αυτη²] αυτην 046. 620 |.

7. οσα] pr και Pr arm^{2. 3. a} | αυτην Aℵ*C 025. 046. **20** (−35**. 175. 205. 632**. 1934. 2020. 2040) al : εαυτην ℵ^c 1. 35**. 69. 110. 175. 205. 250. 632**. 2020. 2037. 2038. 2040. 2067 al^{pl} | τοσουτ. δοτε] κερασατε 1 | δοτε] δωτε 025 : datur Pr Cyp (arm²) | δοτε αυτ. >s¹ | αυτη >gig | κ. πενθ.] >051. 1. 35. 60. 181. 432. 1957. 2023. 2041. 2067 : +populo suo Tyc | οτι¹] και 1 : διοτι 2036. 2037 : +και 205 : >051. 2038 | λεγει] + Babylonia Tyc | οτι²] + εγω 172. 250. 2018 : >1. 620. 2067 | καθημαι AℵC 025. 35. 175. 617. 620. 632**. 1934. 2020. 2040 gig vg s arm^{3. 4. a} : καθιω 046. 61. 69 arm² bo : καθωσ 18. 82. 110. 325. 337. 385. 429. 456. 522. (632*). 919. 920. 1849. 1955. 2004. 2022. 2024. 2039 al^p : + καθωσ 468 : + ωσ 205 : ειμι καθωσ 201. 386 : sum Pr Cyp | βασιλισσα] βασιλευουσα C | ουκ ειμι] non possum esse (esse non possum Cyp) Pr Cyp |.

8. ημερα] ωρα 61. 69 Pr eth | αυτησ] pr επ s¹ (arm^{2. 3. a}) | θανατοσ] θανατου 046 arm² | και¹ Aℵ 025. 35. 205. 620. 920. 2040 Tyc Pr gig vg s^{(1). 2} arm^{3. 4. a} bo : > 046. **20** (−35. 205. 620. 920. 2040) 82. 110. 172. 201. 250. 314. 385. 429*. 498. 522. 1955. 2018 al arm² | και³ >18 | εν πυρι] tr after κατακαυθ. (arm²) bo eth | κατακαυθησεται] κατακαυθησονται Tyc : καυθησεται 337 | ο θεοσ A 2040 vg eth : ο θεοσ ο κυριοσ ℵ* : κυριοσ ο θεοσ ℵ^cC 025. 046. **20** (−175. 617. 920. 1934. 2020. 2040). 250. 2037. 2067 al Tyc Cyp gig s² arm^{3. 4. a} bo : κυριοσ 141. 175. 242. 314. 617. 1934. 2016. 2020. 2041 Pr s¹ arm² : κυρ. ο θεοσ ο παντοκρατωρ 2036 : κυριοσ ο παντοκρατωρ 2037 | κρινασ] κρινων ℵ^c 1. 175. 250. 314. 617. 1934. 2016. 2036. 2037 : (qui) iudicabit Tyc vg |.

9. κλαυσονται Aℵ 1. 18. 205. 2019. 2004. 2038. 2067 al^p :

καπνὸν τῆς πυρώσεως αὐτῆς, 10. *ἀπὸ μακρόθεν ἑστηκότες διὰ τὸν*
φόβον τοῦ βασανισμοῦ αὐτῆς, λέγοντες

> *Οὐαί, οὐαὶ ἡ πόλις ἡ μεγάλη,*
> *Βαβυλὼν ἡ πόλις ἡ ἰσχυρά,*
> *ὅτι μιᾷ ὥρᾳ ἦλθεν ἡ κρίσις σου.*

11^{a}. *καὶ οἱ ἔμποροι τῆς γῆς κλαίουσιν καὶ πενθοῦσιν ἐπ' αὐτήν,*
23^{e}. [*ὅτι οἱ ἔμποροί † σου † ἦσαν οἱ μεγιστᾶνες τῆς γῆς*] (*a*)
11^{b}. *ὅτι τὸν γόμον αὐτῶν οὐδεὶς ἀγοράζει οὐκέτι,*

(*a*) This line is provisionally restored here: see vol. ii. 102, 112. But it is best to take it as a gloss on 11^{a}.

κλαυσουσιν C 025. 046. **20** (−18. 205. 2004). 250. 2037 al^{pl} | κλαυσονται (-σουσιν)] +αυτην 025. 1. 35. 205. 2036. 2037. 2067 s^{1} : +ταυτην 2019. 2038 | και κοψ. >920 | και^{2} >bo | επ αυτη >61. 69 Pr | αυτη A 1. 205. 498. 2019. 2020. 2036. 2037. 2038. 2040 : αυτην ℵC 025. 046. **20** (−205. 2020. 2040). 250 al : αυτησ 2067 : αυτων 620 | οι^{1} >18 | κ. στρην.] >ℵ* 456 : + και στεναξωσιν ℵ$^{c. c}$ | βλεπωσιν] ιδωσιν ℵ : βλεπουσιν 051. 522. 2017. 2038 | πυρωσεωσ] πτωσεωσ ℵ* |.

10. απο] pr και Pr arm^{2} | εστηκοτεσ] εστωτεσ 2040 : στηκοντεσ 2036. 2037 : στησονται arm$^{3. a}$ bo | τ. φοβ. >1849 | του βασανισμου] τον βασανισμον 1849 (arm^{4}) : tormentorum gig : >arm$^{3. a}$ | λεγοντεσ] και λεξουσιν s^{1} arm$^{2. 3. a}$: >arm^{4} | ουαι^{2}] +ουαι 172. 250. 2018 s^{1} : >141. 2019. 2038 | η^{1} > 1934 | η μεγ. >Pr | βαβυλων] pr η 172. 250. 2018. 2023 | ισχυρα] οχυρα 2036. 2037 | μια ωρα] μιαν ωραν A 2040 : pr εν 1. 2020. 2037. 2067 | ηλθεν > A | σου] eius gig .

11^{a}. τησ γησ] σου 456 : +σου ℵ : terrarum Pr | κλαιουσιν κ. πενθουσιν AℵC 025. 1. 35. 205. 1957. 2023. 2037. 2038. 2040. 2067 (Pr) gig : κλαυσουσι (-σονται 2036) κ. πενθησουσι (-θουσιν 314) 046. **20** (−35. 205. 2040). 250. (314). (336). (1918). (2036) vg s$^{1. (2)}$ arm$^{3. 4. a}$ (bo) : κλ. και > s^{2} : και πενθ. >336. 620. 1918. 2036 : και^{2} >bo : flent plangentes Pr | επ αυτ.] tr after κλαιουσιν 2020 | επ] εν A 1. 2036 : εφ 051. 181. 2019. 2037. 2038. 2067 : pr εφ εαυτουσ 468 : >Pr | αυτην ℵC 025. 94. 336**. 620. 1918. 2017 gig vg (Pr) : αυτη A **20** (−620). 104. 250. 314. 1957. 2022. 2023 al^{mu} : αυτησ 61. 172. 2018 : αυτουσ 046 : εαυτουσ 051. 181. 2038 : εαυτοισ 1. 2019. 2036. 2037. 2067 |.

23^{e}. οτι AℵC 025. 046. 1. 35. 175. 250. 617. 620. 1934. 2037. 2038. 2040. 2067 Tyc Pr gig vg s arm$^{2. 4}$ eth : >**19** (−35. 175. 617. 620. 632. 1934. 2040). 82. 201. 385. 429. 498. 522. 1955 bo | οι^{1} >A 2040 | σου > 325. 2019. 2036 | ησαν > 386 |.

11^{b}. αυτων] αυτησ 172. 2016. 2020 | ουκετι (και ουκετι 620. 1918 : ουκ εστιν 456 : iam Pr : > arm bo eth) joined with what

12. *γόμον χρυσοῦ καὶ ἀργύρου καὶ λίθου τιμίου καὶ μαργαριτῶν,*
καὶ βυσσίνου καὶ πορφύρας καὶ σιρικοῦ καὶ κοκκινοῦ,
καὶ πᾶν ξύλον θύινον καὶ πᾶν σκεῦος ἐλεφάντινον καὶ πᾶν
λίθου *σκεῦος ἐκ ⌜ξύλου⌝ τιμιωτάτου,*
καὶ χαλκοῦ καὶ σιδήρου καὶ μαρμάρου,

13 *καὶ κιννάμωμον καὶ ἄμωμον καὶ θυμιάματα,*
καὶ μύρον καὶ λίβανον καὶ οἶνον,

precedes 025. 1957. 2023. 2036. 2037 Pr gig vg s^1 : joined with what follows AC 046. **19** al^{pl} s^2 : without punctuation ℵ |.

12. **χρυσου**] *χρυσουν* C 025. 620. 1918 : *χρυσιον* 94. 2019 | *αργυρου*] *αργυρουν* C 025 : *αργυριου* 94. 181. 201. 386 | *λιθ. τιμ.*] *λιθουσ τιμιουσ* C 025 (bo) : *λιθων τιμιων* Pr s arm^2 | *μαργαριτων* ℵ 172. 2018. 2040 Pr gig s arm$^{2.\,3.\,a}$: *μαργαριτασ* (*-ταισ* A) AC 025 bo : *μαργαριτου* 046. **20.** 250. 2037. 2038. 2067 al^{pl} vg | *βυσσ. . . . κοκκινου*] sirici et purporae et coccineae vestis Pr | *βυσσινου* AC 025. 046. **20** (– 35. 205) al^{pl} gig : *βυσσινων* ℵ : *βυσσου* 051. 1. 35. 205. 1957. 2019. 2023. 2036. 2037. 2038. 2041 vg | *κ. πορφ.* > A | *πορφυρασ* ℵC 025. 104. 205. 620. 632**. 2018. 2037**. 2040 : *πορφυρου* 046. 051. **20** (– 205. 620. 632**. 2040). 1. 69. 110. 314. 385. 2037*. 2067 | *κ. σιρικ.* > 1. 920 | *σιρικου* AℵC 025. 046. 051. 104. 620. 1849. 2017 al : *σηρικου* **20** (– 386. 620. 1849) al^{pl} : *συρικου* 172. 386. 2016. 2018. 2019 | *παν ξυλον . . . τιμιωτατου*] omne lignum incensi et omne vas ligneum et omne vas eburneum preciosum gig | *κ. παν ξυλ. θυιν.*] et omnis ligni citrei Pr : tr after *τιμ.* bo | *ξυλον*] *σκευοσ* A : *ξυλινον* 025 | *ελεφ. κ. π. σκευοσ* > arm^2 | *κ. παν σκ. εκ ξυλ.* > gig | *παν σκευοσ*^{2} > Pr | *εκ* > C 94 | *ξυλου* ℵC 025. 046. **20** (– 2040) al$^{fere\ omn}$ Pr s (arm) (bo) : *λιθου* A 2040 vg eth | *τιμιωτατον*] *τιμιον* s^1 | *χαλκου . . . σιδηρου . . . μαρμαρου*] *χαλκον . . . σιδηρον . . . μαρμαρον* s^1 bo | *χαλκου*] *καλκου* C* | *κ. σιδ.* > arm^2 | *κ. μαρμ.* > ℵ 1 |.

13. **κινναμ-** AℵC 025. 046**. **19** (– 35**. 205. 620. 919. 1934. 2020). 104. 250. 2038 al^p (Pr) vg : *κιναμ-* 046*. 1. 35**. 69. 172. 205. 314. 620. 1934. 2020. 2022. 2023. 2036. 2037. 2067 al^{mu} gig bo | *κινναμωμον* (*κιναμωμον*) AC 025. 1. 250. 2037. 2038. 2040. 2067 al^{mu} vg gig s arm (bo) : *κινναμωμου* (*κιναμωμου*) ℵ 046. **19** (– 35. 2040) al^{mu} : cinnamum Pr | *κ. αμωμον* Aℵ*C 025. 35*. 93. 172. 181. 218. 250. 314. 2016. 2018. 2019. gig vg s^2 : > ℵ^c 046. **20** (– 35*). 1. 2037. 2038. 2067 al^{pl} Pr s^1 arm bo | *θυμιαματα*] *θυμιαμα* 1. 2037. 2040. 2067 Pr gig arm^2 bo : *-ματοσ* 046. 61. 69 : *-ματων* 201. 386. 620 vg | *κ. μυρον* > C | *μυρον*] *μυρων* 386 (arm^2) : *μυρου* vg s^2 : *σμυρναν* 2036. 2037 | *λιβανον*] *λιβανου* vg | *οινον . . . ελαιον*] ~ 175. 218. 242. 250. 314. 617. 1934. 2016. 2017 | *κ. οινον* AℵC 025. 35. (175). 205.

καὶ ἔλαιον καὶ σεμίδαλιν καὶ σῖτον,
καὶ κτήνη καὶ πρόβατα (a) καὶ ψυχὰς ἀνθρώπων. (b)

15. οἱ ἔμποροι τούτων, οἱ πλουτήσαντες ἀπ' αὐτῆς, ἀπὸ μακρόθεν στήσονται διὰ τὸν φόβον τοῦ βασανισμοῦ αὐτῆς κλαίοντες καὶ πενθοῦντες, 16. λέγοντες

Οὐαί, οὐαὶ ἡ πόλις ἡ μεγάλη,
ἡ περιβεβλημένη βύσσινον καὶ πορφυροῦν καὶ κόκκινον,
καὶ κεχρυσωμένη χρυσίῳ καὶ λίθῳ τιμίῳ καὶ μαργαρίτῃ,
ὅτι μιᾷ ὥρᾳ ἠρημώθη ὁ τοσοῦτος πλοῦτος.

(*a*) Here follows an interpolation : *καὶ ἵππων καὶ ῥεδῶν καὶ σωμάτων.* See vol. ii. 102.
(*b*) Verse 14 is restored after 21 : see vol. ii. 105. 108.

(617). 632**. (1934). 2020. 2040 al Pr gig s arm bo sa eth : >046. **20** (−35. 175. 632**. 205. 617. 1934. 2020. 2040) al^mu : *κ. οινου* vg | *ελαιον*] *ελαιου* vg | *κ. σεμ.* > Pr | *σεμιδ. . . . ψυχασ*] *σεμιδαλεωσ . . . σιτου . . . κτηνων . . . προβατων . . . ψυχων* vg | *κ. σιτ. κ. κτ.* > s¹ | *και⁹* > bo | *σιτον*] *σιτου* 620 bo | *κτηνη κ. προβατα* A‮א‬C 025. 35. 205. 2037. 2038. 2040. 2067 al Pr gig (vg) s² arm^{3. 4. a} bo sa : ~ 046. **20** (−35. 205. 2040). 250 al^mu arm² : *κ. προβ.* >42. 1957 | *ιππων*] *ιππουσ* 2040 s arm² : equi Pr | *ρεδων* AאC 025. 046. 1. 18. 205. 632. 919. 1849. 2004. 2037. 2038. 2067 al^mu : *ραιδων* 051. **20** (−18. 205. 632. 919. 1849. 2004). 82. 104. 250. 314. 2016 al^mu : *ρεδιων* 61. 69. 2022 : *ρεδασ* Pr s arm^{3. 4. a} | *ρεδων και* >arm² bo | *σωμ. και* >337. 386 arm² | *σωματων*] *σωματα* s : *σωμα* bo : *ψυχων* 61. 69 : mancipia (-orum vg) Pr vg : porcorum Tyc : mulorum et camelorum sa | *κ. ψυχ. ανθρ.*] et diversi generis animalia Pr : *κ. ψυχην ανθρωπου* bo eth : >Tyc |.

15. **τουτων**] *αυτησ* Pr : *σου* bo | *αυτησ¹*] *σου* bo | *στησονται*] stabant Tyc | *δ. τ. φοβ. τ. β. αυτ.* >Tyc | *κλαιοντεσ* (*κλαυσουσιν* s² arm² bo eth) AאC 025. 1. 18. 35. 175. 250. 617. 632**. 1849. 1934. 2004. 2037. 2038. 2040 Tyc Pr gig vg s¹ arm^{3. 4. a} (bo) sa : pr *και* 046. 325. 337. 386. 456. 468. 620. 632. 919. 920 al s² arm² eth | *και* >bo | *πενθουντεσ*] *πενθησουσιν* s² arm² bo eth |.

16. **λεγοντεσ** (*λεγουσιν* 046. 522 : *ερουσιν* arm^{3. a} eth) AאC (046). 175. 325. 337. 386. 456. (522). 617 al^mu Tyc gig s² (arm^{3. a}) bo sa (eth) : pr *και* 025. 051. **19** (−175. 325. 337. 456. 617. 620). 250. 2037. 2067 Pr vg s¹ arm⁴ (eth) | *ουαι¹*] + *σοι* bo | *ουαι²* AאC 025. 35. 175. 250. 617. 1934. 2020. 2037. 2038. 2040 al Tyc Pr gig vg s arm (bo) sa eth : + *ουαι* 172. 2018 : + *σοι* bo : >046. **19** (−35. 175. 617. 1934. 2020. 2040) al^mu | *η πολ. η μεγ.*] *η μεγαλη πολισ* 2020 bo | *η μεγ. η περιβεβλ.* >א* | *η³* >A | *η περιβεβλ.*] quae vastata est gig | *βυσσ. . . . κεχρυσωμενη* > 325 | *βυσσ. . . . κοκκ.*] ~ A | *βυσσ. . . . πορφ.*] ~ Pr | *βυσσινον* (*βυσινον* 025. *βυσσυνον* 1)

17. καὶ πᾶς κυβερνήτης καὶ πᾶς ὁ ἐπὶ τόπον πλέων, καὶ ναῦται
καὶ ὅσοι τὴν θάλασσαν ἐργάζονται, ἀπὸ μακρόθεν ἔστησαν 18. καὶ
ἔκραξαν βλέποντες τὸν καπνὸν τῆς πυρώσεως αὐτῆς, λέγοντες Τίς
ἐπέβαλον ὁμοία τῇ πόλει τῇ μεγάλῃ; 19. καὶ ⌜ἔβαλον⌝ χοῦν ἐπὶ τὰς κεφαλὰς
αὐτῶν, καὶ ἔκραξαν κλαίοντες καὶ πενθοῦντες, λέγοντες

Οὐαί, οὐαὶ ἡ πόλις ἡ μεγάλη,

A‭ℵC 1. 35. 175. 250. 617. 620. 2037. 2038 al Tyc (Pr) gig vg$^{a. c. f. g. h}$: *βυσσον* 046. 18. 337. 386. 456. 468. 632. 919. 920. 1849. 2004. 2067 al vg$^{d. v}$ | *πορφυρουν* AℵC 046. **19** (−325. 386). 2037. 2038 al^{pl} : *πορφυραν* 025. 94. 141. 172. 201. 241. 250. 2018. 2019. 2067 | *και*^{2} >025. 175. 242. 617. 1934 | *κοκκινον*] *κοκκινα* s^1 | *και*^{3}] > 051. 1. 2036. 2038 arm^4 : *η* eth | *κεχρυσ.*] *κεχρυσωμενον* ℵ : *κεχρυσωμενα* s^1 (bo) : >arm^4 | *χρυσιω* AC 025. 046. **19** (−35). 250 al^{pl} : *χρυσω* ℵ 051. 1. 35. 61. 69. 1957. 2019. 2023. 2036. 2037. 2038. 2067 al : auro Pr gig vg : pr *εν* ℵC 1. 35. 1957. 2019. 2023. 2036. 2037. 2038. 2067 | *λιθ. τιμ.*] *λιθοισ τιμιοισ* s$^{(1). 2}$ arm$^{2. 3. a}$ | *τιμιω* > 046 sa | *μαργαριτη* AℵC 025. 2040 Pr arm^4 bo (sa) : *μαργαριταισ* (*-τασ* s) 046. **19** (−2040). 250. 2037. 2038. 2067 al$^{fere\ omn}$ Tyc gig vg s arm$^{2. 3. a}$ | *μια*] in hac gig | *ηρημωθη*] *ερημωθη* 051. 1. 2036. 2038 | *ο* >025. 2040 |.

17. *ο* >025. 1. 314. 1957. 2016. 2017. 2036. 2037. 2038 al | *επι τοπον πλεων*] pr *επι των πλοιων* s^1 : *επι των πλοιων* (+*ο* 1) *ομιλοσ* 1. 2037 : *πλεων επι των πλοιων* 2016 : super mare navigans Pr (bo sa) : (qui) manibus navigat Tyc | *τοπον* (pr *τον* ℵ 046. 468 : pr illum gig) AℵC 046. **19** (−35. 175. 617. 1934) al^{mu} gig vg s^2 arm : *των πλοιων* 025. 35. 181. 250. 314. 617. 1934. 1957. 2017. 2019. 2023. 2036. 2038. 2067 | *πλεων*] navigabat (-avit vg^c) gig vg^c | *κ. ναυτ. . . . εργαζονται* > bo | *οσοι τ. θαλ. εργαζονται*] quotquot mare operatur Tyc | *τ. θαλ.*] *εν τη θαλασση* Pr gig vg^v arm^3 : maria (mari vg$^{d. f}$) vg$^{a. c. d. f. g}$ | *εργαζονται*] morantur Pr | *εστησαν*] stabunt Pr arm |.

18. *και εκραξαν* > 2020 Pr | *και* > 2067 arm^4 | *εκραξαν* AC 025. 172. 2018. 2038. 2040 Tyc gig vg s^2 : *εκραζον* ℵ 046. 051. **19** (−325. 468*. 920. 2040). 1. 250. 2037. 2067 : *εκλαιον* 920 : *εκλαυσαν αυτην* s^1 : *εκραυγαζον* 42. 325. 468*. 517 : *κραξουσιν* arm | *βλεποντεσ*] *ορωντεσ* 1 | *καπνον* ℵC 025. 046. **19** al$^{fere\ omn}$ Pr Tyc gig s arm bo sa : *τοπον* A 60 vg | *τισ* >C | *πολει*]+ *ταυτη* C gig vg arm bo |.

19. *εβαλον* (*-αν* C) ℵC 046. **19** (−325. 617. 2040) al$^{fere\ omn}$ vg s (bo) : *εβαλλον* 025. 051. 325. 385. 617 gig : *επεβαλον* (*επεβαλλον* 2040) A 2040 : mittentes Pr | *χουν* >620 | *τ. κεφ.*] *τησ κεφαλησ* ℵ 2026 bo | *αυτων*] *εαυτων* C | *και*^{2} > arm$^{2. 4}$ bo | *εκραξαν* (+*φωνη μεγαλη* arm^4) AC 2018 vg s arm^4 : *εκραζον* ℵ 025. 046. **19**. 250. 2037. 2067 al^{pl} gig : clamabunt Pr : *πειθουντεσ* arm$^{3. a}$: > arm^2 | *κλαιοντεσ κ. πενθουντεσ*] > A 1 : pr *και* 325.

ἐν ᾗ ἐπλούτησαν πάντες οἱ ἔχοντες τὰ πλοῖα ἐν τῇ θαλάσσῃ,
† ἐκ τῆς τιμιότητος αὐτῆς ὅτι μιᾷ ὥρᾳ ἠρημώθη. † (*a*)

21. Καὶ ἦρεν εἷς ἄγγελος ἰσχυρὸς λίθον ὡς μύλινον μέγαν, καὶ ἔβαλεν εἰς τὴν θάλασσαν λέγων

Οὕτως ὁρμήματι βληθήσεται
  Βαβυλὼν ἡ μεγάλη πόλις,
καὶ οὐ μὴ εὑρεθῇ ἔτι.

14. καὶ ἡ ὀπώρα σου τῆς ἐπιθυμίας τῆς ψυχῆς (*b*)
  ἀπῆλθεν ἀπὸ σοῦ,
καὶ πάντα τὰ λιπαρὰ καὶ τὰ λαμπρὰ
  ἀπώλετο ἀπὸ σοῦ. (*c*)

(*a*) Text corrupt. We should read: ὅτι μιᾷ ὥρᾳ ἠρημώθη ἡ τιμιότης αὐτῆς: cf. vers. 10, 16, and see vol. ii. 106 sq. Ver. 20 is restored to its original context after 23$^{a.b}$. See vol. ii. 92 sq.
(*b*) On the restoration of the order of the text, see vol. ii. 92, 105, 108.
(*c*) Here follows a gloss: καὶ οὐκέτι οὐ μὴ αὐτὰ εὑρήσουσιν. On a possible explanation of it in connexion with the loss of 22^{b} which I have restored, see vol. ii. 92, 109, and footnote *in loc.* of English transl.

468* arm$^{3.a}$: ~ 325. 468* : tr after λεγοντεσ 325. 468*. 517 | λεγοντεσ (+voce magna Pr) Aℵ C 1. 172. 2018. 2040 Pr vg$^{f.g}$ (arm$^{2.3.a}$) bo : pr και 025. 046. **19** (–325. 468. 2040). 250. 2038. 2067 al^{pl} gig vg$^{a.c.v}$ s arm^{4} : >468** vg^{d} | ουαι^{2} AC 025. 046. **19** (–337. 468*. 2040) Tyc Pr gig vg s arm sa eth : +ουαι 172. 250. 2019 : >ℵ 141. 337. 432. 452. 468*. 506. 2019. 2021. 2040 bo | η πολ. η μεγ.] η μεγαλη πολισ 1849 | τα >1. 35. 172. 175. 617. 1934. 2018. 2036. 2037. 2038. 2067 al | εν τ. θαλ. . . . αυτησ] de mari et de pretiis eius gig | εκ τ. τιμ. αυτ. > Tyc | ηρημωθη] ερημωθη 1. 2036. 2038 |.

21. και^{1}] pr και εκραξεν φωνην bo | κ. ηρεν] tr after ισχυροσ bo | εισ αγγελοσ ισχυροσ λιθ.] εισ α . . . λιθ. A. The letters between α and λ are not visible, but the space is only enough for five or six. | εισ]+εξ αυτων 337 | αγγ. ισχ.] εκ των αγγελων των ισχυρων s^{1} | ισχυροσ] ισχυρον (tr after λιθον ℵ*) ℵ* 141. 149 : >(A) Tyc s^{2} | λιθον ωσ] >bo : λιθον >2019 : ωσ >arm^{2} | ωσ] ωσει 2036. 2037 : ad magnitudinem Pr | μυλινον (μυλικον C) AC : molarem vg (bo) : μυλον 025. 046. **19**. 205. 2037. 2038. (2067) : molam (-ae Pr) Tyc Pr gig s$^{(1).2}$ arm : λιθον ℵ (2019) | μεγαν] μεγα 2019. 2020 : tr before ωσ 2067 | ουτωσ] pr οτι ℵ 620 : hoc Pr vg arm^{2} | βαβυλων] pr illa Tyc | μεγαλη πολισ] μεγαλοπολισ 2067 | πολισ >Pr | ετι]+εν αυτη ℵ 046. 61. 69 |.

14. η οπωρα] pomorum (-a vg) Pr vg : hora gig (arm^{4}) : > arm$^{2.3.a}$ | η >C | σου^{1} placed after οπωρα Aℵ C 025. 2040 (Pr) vg$^{a.c.f.g.h.v}$: tr after ψυχησ 046. **19**. 250. 2037. 2038. 2067 gig vg^{d} s^{2} arm : in both places 172. 2018 s^{1} : >bo | τησ επιθυμιασ]

22^{a-d}. καὶ φωνὴ κιθαρῳδῶν καὶ † μουσικῶν †
< οὐ μὴ ἀκουσθῇ ἐν σοὶ ἔτι· >(*a*)
καὶ < φωνὴ >(*a*) αὐλητῶν καὶ σαλπιστῶν
οὐ μὴ ἀκουσθῇ ἐν σοὶ ἔτι.

23$^{c. d}$. καὶ φωνὴ νυμφίου καὶ νύμφης
οὐ μὴ ἀκουσθῇ ἐν σοὶ ἔτι·
22^{e-h}. καὶ πᾶς τεχνίτης πάσης τέχνης
οὐ μὴ εὑρεθῇ ἐν σοὶ ἔτι.

καὶ φωνὴ μύλου
οὐ μὴ ἀκουσθῇ ἐν σοὶ ἔτι·

(*a*) Necessarily restored, yet found in eth : see below.

η επιθυμια Pr s^{1} | *απηλθεν*] discendent vg^{d} arm^{2} | *τα*^{1} >61. 69 | *λιπαρα*] *ριπαρα* ℵ* : + *σου* 2040 | *τα*^{2} A 025. 046. **19** al$^{fere\ omn}$: >ℵC 2036. 2067 | *απωλετο* AC 025. 046. **19** (– 35. 620). 250 al^{pl} arm$^{2.4}$ eth : *απωλοντο* ℵ 35. 104. 110. 172. 336. 432. 620. 1918. 1957. 2018. 2023. 2041 gig vg bo sa : perient Pr : *απωχετο* 2067 : *απηλθεν* 051. 1. 2036. 2037 s^{1} arm$^{3.a}$ | *ουκετι*] + *αυτα βλεψεισ και* s^{1} | *ου μη αυτα* Aℵ 2018. 2020. 2040 : *αυτα ου μη* C 025. 046. **19** (– 35. 175. 617. 1934. 2020. 2040) al gig vg : tr *αυτα* after *ευρ.* 1. 35. 175. 250. 617. 1934. 2037. 2038 (arm) | *ευρησουσιν* AℵC 025. 18. 172. 250. 424. 2018. 2019. 2039 vg s (arm^{2}) bo : *ευρησ* (-*εισ* 104. 620). 046. **19** (– 18. 35). 2037. 2067 : *ευρησεισ* (-*ησ* 051). 051. 1. 35. 432. 1957. 2023. 2038. 2041 Pr gig arm$^{3.4.a}$: + *ουτε ψυχασ ανθρωπων του λοιπου εμπορευση* 241. 314. 2016 | *κ. ουκετι . . . ευρησουσιν*] joined with ver. 15 by 172. 2018. 2019 s bo eth |.

22^{a-d}. και φωνη . . . σαλπιστων] *και ου μη ακουσθη εν αυτη φωνη μουσικου και κιθαρασ και αυλου και φωνη σαλπιγγοσ ου μη ακουσθη εν αυτη* eth. Here observe that the Ethiopic has already restored the missing words in 22$^{b.c}$. | *και*^{1}] >ℵ 1 Tyc : *ουδε* bo eth | *κιθαρωδων*] *κιθαρασ* s^{1} arm^{2} bo eth | *μουσικ. . . . σαλπ.*] ~ s^{1} | *αυλητων*] *αυλιστων* 620 : sinfoniacorum Pr | *αυλ. και* > bo | *σαλπιστων* AC 025. 046. **19** al$^{fere\ omn}$ gig : *σαλπιγγων* (-*οσ* s^{1} arm^{2}) ℵ 172. 2018 s arm$^{2.4}$: *σαλπιγξ* vg bo : fistularum Tyc : tibicinum Pr : + *και* 2020 | *σοι*] *αυτη* gig vg$^{c.f}$ eth |.

23$^{c.d}$. φωνη] *φωνην* ℵ* bo | *νυμφησ*] pr *φωνη* C 920 s^{1} eth |.

22^{e-h}. κ. πασ τεχν. . . . ετι] >61. 69 s^{1} arm : tr. after *εν σοι ετι*^{2} 104. 620 | *πασ τεχνιτησ* >1918 | *πασησ τεχνησ* C 025. 046. **19.** 250. 2038. 2067 Pr gig vg s^{2} : > Aℵ bo : + *επινοια* 1918 | *σοι*^{1}] *αυτη* vg$^{c.v}$ eth | *κ. φωνη μυλου . . . ετι*^{2} AC 025. 046. **19** (– 18. 919. 920. 1849. 2004. 2020). 250. 2037. 2038. 2067 Pr gig vg arm^{2} bo : >ℵ 18. 141. 172. 385. 522. 919. 920. 1849. 1955. 2004. 2020 s arm$^{3.4.a}$ eth | *μυλου*] *μυθου* C | *ακουσθη*]

23$^{a. b}$. καὶ φῶς λύχνου
οὐ μὴ φάνῃ ἐν σοὶ ἔτι.

20. Εὐφραίνου ἐπ' αὐτῇ, οὐρανέ,
καὶ οἱ ἅγιοι καὶ οἱ ἀπόστολοι καὶ οἱ προφῆται,
ὅτι ἔκρινεν ὁ θεὸς τὸ κρίμα ὑμῶν ἐξ αὐτῆς

23^{f}. ὅτι ἐν τῇ φαρμακίᾳ † σου †(*a*) ἐπλανήθησαν πάντα τὰ ἔθνη,
24. καὶ ἐν αὐτῇ αἷμα προφητῶν καὶ ἁγίων εὑρέθη
καὶ πάντων τῶν ἐσφαγμένων ἐπὶ τῆς γῆς.

(*a*) Read αὐτῆς.

ευρεθη 046 : φανη 91. 175. 250. 314. 617. 1934. 2016 | σοι] αυτη vg$^{c. f. v}$ |.

23$^{a. b}$. και φωσ . . . ετι ℵC 025. 046. **19** al$^{fere\ omn}$ Pr gig vg s arm$^{3. 4. a}$ bo : >A 506 arm^{2} | και >046 | λυχνου] +και φωνη μυλου arm$^{3. a}$ | φανη] ακουσθη 620 | εν > C Pr gig vg s^{1} | ετι >s^{2} |.

20. ευφραινου] exultate Pr s arm$^{3. a}$: ευφραινετω (-ετωσαν arm^{2}) arm^{2} eth | επ αυτη ουρανε] ~Tyc bo | επ] εν A 522 | αυτη AℵC 046. **19** (−18. 35. 617. 2004). 250. 522 gig : αυτην 025. 051. 1. 18. 35. 617. 2004. 2018. 2019. 2036. 2037. 2038. 2067 al Tyc Pr vg | και οι^{2} Aℵ 025. 046. **19** (−35). 250. 2037. 2067 al^{pl} Tyc Pr vg$^{a. f. g. h. v}$ s arm^{3} bo : >C 051. 1. 35. 2038 al^{p} gig vg$^{c. d}$ arm$^{2. 4. a}$ (eth) | αποστολοι . . . προφηται] ~eth |.

23^{f}. φαρμακια AℵC 025. 104. 172. 2019. 2038. 2067 : φαρμακεια 046. **19** al^{pl} : (ταισ) φαρμακιαισ Tyc gig vg s^{1} bo : maleficiis Pr | σου] αυτησ arm^{2} : αυτων eth | επλανηθησαν] επλανησασ 172 s^{1} eth |.

24. εν αυτη] >Tyc : in te Pr eth | αιμα AℵC 025. 1. 2020. 2036. 2037 al^{p} : αιματα 046. 051. **19** (−2020). 250. 2038. 2067 al^{pl} | ευρεθη] ευρεθησαν 69. 104. 620. 1918 | κ. παντ. >s^{1} | και^{3} >Tyc | εσφαγμενων] εσφραγισμενων 2020 (arm$^{2. 3. a}$) : pr a te Tyc : +αγιων 468 |.

Chapter XIX.

1. Μετὰ ταῦτα ἤκουσα ὡς φωνὴν μεγάλην ὄχλου πολλοῦ ἐν τῷ οὐρανῷ λεγόντων
Ἁλληλουιά·
ἡ σωτηρία καὶ ἡ δόξα καὶ ἡ δύναμις τοῦ θεοῦ ἡμῶν,

1. μετα ταυτα . . . (ver. 6^{a}) **και ηκουσα ωσ** > 632* | μετα AℵC 025. 046. **19** (−35. 468. 2020). 250 al^{pl} Pr gig vg s^{2} bo : pr και 051. 1. 35. 468. 1957. 2019. 2020. 2023. 2036. 2037. 2038. 2041. 2067 s^{1} arm eth | ωσ AℵC 025. 046. **19** (−620.

2. ὅτι ἀληθιναὶ καὶ δίκαιαι αἱ κρίσεις αὐτοῦ·

ὅτι ἔκρινεν τὴν πόρνην τὴν μεγάλην,
ἥτις ἔφθειρεν τὴν γῆν ἐν τῇ πορνείᾳ αὐτῆς,
καὶ ἐξεδίκησεν τὸ αἷμα τῶν δούλων αὐτοῦ ἐκ χειρὸς αὐτῆς.

3. καὶ δεύτερον εἴρηκαν
'Αλληλουιά·
καὶ ὁ καπνὸς αὐτῆς ἀναβαίνει εἰς τοὺς αἰῶνας τῶν αἰώνων.

4. Καὶ ἔπεσαν οἱ εἴκοσι τέσσαρεσ πρεσβύτεροι καὶ τὰ τέσσερα
ζῷα, καὶ προσεκύνησαν τῷ θεῷ τῷ καθημένῳ ἐπὶ τῷ θρόνῳ λέγοντες
'Αμήν, 'Αλληλουιά·

632**. 2020). 250. 2037** al vg bo : tr after μεγαλην 2019 eth : >1. 104. 181. 241. 336. 620. 632**. 2020. 2038. 2067 Tyc Pr gig s arm | μεγαλην] μεγαλου 337. 632** : tr after πολλου 1957. 2023. 2041 al : > 1. 141. 2036. 2038. 2067 Pr arm^{4} | οχλου πολλου] οχλων πολλων Pr vg$^{f. g}$ s^{1} : tubarum multarum vg$^{a. c. v}$ arm^{2} : aquarum multarum vg^{d} | πολλου] >arm$^{3. a}$: + clamantium voce magna Pr | λεγοντων] dicentis gig : λεγουσαν 110 : +το 1 2037 | σωτ. . . . δοξα] ~ eth | σωτηρια] laus vg$^{a. g. v}$ | η δοξα (+ και η τιμη 632** arm$^{2. a}$ bo sa) κ. η δυν. Aℵ^{c}C 025. 35. (632**). 2019. 2020. 2036. 2037. 2038. 2040 Tyc vg s^{1} arm$^{2. a}$ bo sa eth : η δυν. κ. η δοξα (+ κ. η τιμη s^{2}) 046. **19** (– 35. 632**. 2020. 2040). 250 al^{pl} gig s^{2} arm^{3} : κ. η δυν. >ℵ* Pr arm^{4} | τ. θεου ημων > 2067 | του θεου AℵC 025. 046. **19** (– 632**). 250. 2038 al^{pl} gig bo sa : τω θεω 241. 632**. 2019 Tyc Pr vg s arm : κυριω τω θεω 1. 2037 | ημων] + est vg |.

2. αληθιναι] εκρινεν αληθη 468 | οτι^{2}] qui vg : + sic Pr | πορνην] πολιν 69. 94. 209. 241. 632**. 2023 | ητισ . . . πορνεια αυτησ >bo | ητισ . . . γην >2026. 2031. 2037 arm$^{3. a}$ | εφθειρεν ℵC 025. 1. 172. 632**. 2019. 2036. 2037. 2040 al : διεφθειρεν 046. **19** (– 632**. 2040). 250. 2067 al : εκρινεν A | πορνεια C 025. 046. **19** al^{pl} : πορνια Aℵ | και] + κσ̄ 2040 | αυτου^{2}] αυτησ ℵ* | εκ χειροσ AℵC 025. 046. **19** (– 35*. 620. 632**. 920). 250 al : εκ τησ χειροσ 1. 35*. 620. 632**. 920. 2018. 2019. 2036. 2037. 2038. 2067 al : de manu Tyc gig s^{2} sa eth : εκ (των) χειρων Pr vg s^{1} arm$^{3. 4. a}$: χειροσ >arm^{2} bo |.

3. και^{1} > s^{1} | ειρηκαν Aℵ 025. 1. 35. 172. 2018. 2036. 2037. 2038 : ειρηκασιν 61. 69. 201. 250. 386. 2040 2067 al : ειπαν (-ον 2020) C 2020 : dixerunt (= ειρηκαν or ειπον) Tyc Pr gig vg s arm$^{(2. 3). 4}$ sa eth : ειρηκεν 046. **19** (– 35. 386 2020. 2040) al bo ο >386 | αυτησ] αυτων Tyc : de illa Pr : > 1. 241. 632**. 2067 | αναβαινει] ανεβαινεν 172. 2018. 2020 s^{2} : ανεβη 2036. 2037 s^{1} arm : αναβησεται bo |.

4. επεσαν AℵC 025. 046*. 1. 325. 337. 498 620. 2023. 2036.

xvi. 5^{b}. Δίκαιος εἶ, ὁ ὢν καὶ ὁ ἦν,(*a*)
"Οσιος, ὅτι ταῦτα ἔκρινας·

6. ὅτι αἷμα ἁγίων καὶ προφητῶν ἐξέχεαν,
καὶ αἷμα αὐτοῖς ⸀δέδωκας⸁ πεῖν· ἔδωκας
ἄξιοί εἰσιν.

7. Καὶ ἤκουσα τοῦ θυσιαστηρίου λέγοντος
Ναί, κύριε, ὁ θεὸς ὁ παντοκράτωρ,
ἀληθιναὶ καὶ δίκαιαι αἱ κρίσεις σου.

(*a*) On the restoration of xvi. 5^{b}–7 to their original context, see vol. ii. 116, 120–124.

2038. 2041 : επεσον 046**. **19** (– 325. 337. 620). 250. 2037. 2067 : tr after πρεσβ. 620 | οι (>69) εικοσι τεσσ. πρεσβ. A 046. 18. 61. 69. 201. 337. 386. 920. 1957. 2004. 2019. 2036. 2037. 2039. 2067 Pr gig (s^{1}) arm : οι πρεσβ. οι εικοσι τεσσ. ℵC 025. **19** (– 18. 337. 386. 620. 920. 2004). 1. 250. 2038 al^{pl} vg s^{2} | εικ. τεσσ.] κδ' 046. 1. 35. 337. 468. 919. 920. 1849. 2004 2038. 2040 al | τεσσερα AℵC : τεσσαρα (δ' 35. 456. 2040 al^{mu}) 025. 046. min^{pl} | ζωα >ℵ* | τω (>919) θρονω AℵC 046. **19** (– 35. 386. 468. 620. 632**. 920. 2020). 250 al^{pl} : των θρονων 025 : του (>2037) θρονου 1. 35. 386. 468. 498. 620. 632**. 920. 1957. 2019. 2020. 2023. 2036. (2037). 2038. 2041. 2067 al | αμην αλληλ.] ~ 35 : >arm ^{4} | αμην >337 | αλληλ. >Pr |.

xvi. 5^{b}. δικαιοσ] + domine vg^{d} eth | ει > 104 arm$^{1.2.3.a}$ | ο^{2} AℵC 025. **20** (– 337. 617. 632*. 919. 920. 1849. 1934) al : οσ 046. 61. 69. 82. 110. 141. 337. 385. 429. 452. 522. 617. 919. 920. 1849. 1934 al^{pl} : > arm$^{3.a}$ | ην] "is" arm$^{2.3.a}$ | οσιοσ AC 046. 175. 250. 325. 337. 456. 468. 617. 620. 919. 1849. 1934. 2004. 2020 al^{mu} arm^{2} : ο οσιοσ ℵ 025. 051. 35. 94. 181. 201. 205. 314. 386. 517. 632. 920. 1957. 2015. 2016. 2018. 2023. 2036. 2038. 2041. 2067 al (arm^{4}) : sanctus vg : και οσιοσ 2040 S : et sanctus gig arm$^{1.3.a}$ sa eth : και ο οσιοσ 1. 18. 424. 2019. 2037 : et qui es pius Pr : >bo |.

6. αιμα^{1}] αιματα ℵ 620. 1918. 2019 | αγιων . . . προφητων] ~ 206. 2017 s^{1} arm^{3} | αγιων] μαρτυρων bo | και^{2}] ideoque Pr arm$^{1.2.a}$: >bo | αιμα αυτοισ δεδωκασ (εδωκασ) AC 025. 046. **20** al$^{fere\ omn}$ vg s^{2} : αιμα εδωκασ αυτοισ ℵ gig s^{1} : εδωκασ αυτοισ αιμα 61. 69 Pr (arm^{4}) sa (eth ?) : εδωκασ αιμα αυτοισ bo : αυτοισ >arm^{2} | δεδωκασ AC arm$^{2.4}$: εδωκασ ℵ 025. 046. **20** al^{omn} | πειν (πῖν C) A(C) : πιειν ℵ 025. 046. **20** al$^{fere\ omn}$ | αξιοι] pr οπερ ℵ : pr οτι 336. 620. 628. 1918 Pr (gig) s^{2} bo (sa) eth : pr ut vg$^{a.g.v}$ |.

7. του θυσ. λεγοντοσ AℵC 025. **20.** 250. 2038 al^{pl} vg$^{f.g}$ s arm^{4} bo : pr εκ 046. 1. 2037. 2067 vg$^{c.d.(v)}$ arm$^{1.2.3}$: φωνην εκ

xix. 5. Καὶ φωνὴ ἀπὸ τοῦ θρόνου ἐξῆλθεν λέγουσα
Αἰνεῖτε τῷ θεῷ ἡμῶν, πάντες οἱ δοῦλοι αὐτοῦ
καὶ οἱ φοβούμενοι αὐτόν, οἱ μικροὶ καὶ οἱ μεγάλοι.
6. καὶ ἤκουσα ὡς φωνὴν ὄχλου πολλοῦ καὶ ὡς φωνὴν ὑδάτων
πολλῶν καὶ ὡς φωνὴν βροντῶν ἰσχυρῶν, λεγόντων
Ἀλληλουιά·
ὅτι ἐβασίλευσεν κύριος, ὁ θεὸς ὁ παντοκράτωρ.
7. χαίρωμεν καὶ ἀγαλλιῶμεν,
καὶ δώσομεν τὴν δόξαν αὐτῷ,
ὅτι ἦλθεν ὁ γάμος τοῦ ἀρνίου,
καὶ ἡ γυνὴ αὐτοῦ ἡτοίμασεν ἑαυτήν,

(>arm^{a}) τ. θυσ. λεγουσαν 2019 arm^{a} : alterum (aliam vocem Pr) dicentem (-ens vg^{a}) Pr gig vg^{a} : ab altari dicens vg^{v} | αληθιναι . . . δικαιαι] ~ arm$^{1. (3). a}$ (bo) eth | δικαιαι] ο δικαιοσ bo | και^{2} >bo |.

xix. 5. φωνη . . . εξηλθεν . . . λεγουσα] A ℵ^{c} 025. 046 : φωναι . . . εξηλθον . . . λεγουσαι ℵ* : > arm$^{2. 4}$ | απο AC 046. **19** (– 35. 175. 617. 632**. 1934). 250 al^{mu} : εκ ℵ 025. 1. 35. 175. 241. 242. 617. 632**. 1934. 1955. 1957. 2016. 2017. 2019. 2023. 2036. 2037. 2038. 2041. 2067 al^{mu} | θρονου Aℵ C 025. **19** gig vg s arm$^{3. a}$ bo : ουρανου 046 61. 69 Pr | εξηλθεν] tr before απο τ. θρον. ℵ : > s^{1} | τω θεω AℵC 025. 046. 325 al^{p} : τον θεον **19** (– 325). 250. 2037. 2038. 2067 al^{pl} | ημων] υμων Pr : + αινειτε 2040 : >18 arm^{4} | και^{2} A 046. **19** al^{omn} Pr gig vg s arm$^{3. 4. a}$ bo eth : >ℵC 025 | αυτον] dominum Pr : το ονομα αυτου s^{1} | μικροι . . . μεγαλοι] ~ Pr | οι μικροι] pr και 1. 2023. 2037 al arm^{4} : pr παντεσ s^{1} | οι^{3} >175 | κ. οι μεγ.] μετα των μεγαλων s^{1} bo | οι^{4} > 18 |.

6. ωσ^{1} Aℵ 025. 046. **19** vg s^{2} bo : tr after φωνην 2019 s^{1} arm^{4} eth : >1*. 110. 172. 181. 2016. 2018. 2037. 2038. 2067 Tyc Pr gig arm$^{3. a}$ | οχλ. πολλ.] οχλων πολλων s^{1} : tubarum (-ae vg) magnarum (-ae vg) Pr vg$^{a. c. d. f. v}$ | ωσ^{2} ℵ 025. 046. **19** (– 386) Pr gig vg s arm$^{3. 4. a}$ bo eth : >A 181. 201. 314. 386 Tyc | υδατ. πολλ. . . . βροντ. ισχ.] ~ Pr | βροντ.] + πολλων και 468 | ισχυρων] magnorum vg | λεγοντων (-ουσων ℵ : -ουσησ 2067) A(ℵ) 025. 172. 314. 2018. 2019. 2020. 2036. 2037. 2040. (2067) al Pr gig vg : λεγοντεσ (-τοσ 620). 046. **18** (– 35. 2020. 2040) al^{mu} : λεγοντασ 051. 1. 35 al : dicentes Tyc | κυριοσ ο θεοσ Aℵ^{c} 025. 046. **18** Tyc gig vg s^{2} arm bo sa : ο θεοσ ο κυριοσ ℵ* : ο θεοσ ο θεοσ 2038 : ο θεοσ 051. 1. 110. 181. 2019. 2067 : κυριοσ Pr s^{1} | ο θεοσ A 1. 2023. 2040 Cyp s^{1} arm$^{2. 4}$ bo sa eth : + ημων ℵ 025. 046. **18** (– 2040). 250. 2037. 2038 2067 al^{pl} Tyc Pr gig vg s^{2} arm$^{3. a}$ | ο παντοκρ. >gig |.

7. χαιρωμεν] χαιρομεν (και χαιρομεν arm^{4}) s^{1} arm | αγαλλιωμεν Aℵ 025. 1. 94. 172. 181. 2018. 2019. 2036. 2037. 2038. 2040. 2067 : -ωμεθα 046. **18** (– 2040). 250 al^{pl} | και^{2} >s^{1} | δωσ. τ. δ.

8. *καὶ ἐδόθη αὐτῇ ἵνα περιβάληται*
βύσσινον λαμπρὸν καθαρόν. (*a*)
9. Καὶ λέγει μοι Γράψον Μακάριοι οἱ εἰς τὸ δεῖπνον τοῦ γάμου
τοῦ ἀρνίου κεκλημένοι.(*b*)

(*a*) An incorrect gloss follows in the text: *τὸ γὰρ βύσσινον τὰ δικαιώματα τῶν ἁγίων ἐστίν.* See vol. ii. 127 sq.

(*b*) Text adds a doublet of xxii. 6^{a}. 8-9: *καὶ λέγει μοι Οὗτοι οἱ λόγοι οἱ ἀληθινοὶ τοῦ θεοῦ εἰσίν. 10. καὶ ἔπεσα ἔμπροσθεν τῶν ποδῶν αὐτοῦ προσκυνῆσαι αὐτῷ. Καὶ λέγει μοι Ὅρα μή· σύνδουλός σού εἰμι καὶ τῶν ἀδελφῶν σου τῶν ἐχόντων τὴν μαρτυρίαν Ἰησοῦ· τῷ θεῷ προσκύνησον· ἡ γὰρ μαρτυρία Ἰησοῦ ἐστιν τὸ πνεῦμα τῆς προφητείας.* See vol. ii. 128-129.

αυτ.] glorificemus nomen eius Tyc arm^{2} | *δωσομεν* Aℵ^{c} Pr gig vg arm^{4} : *δωσωμεν* (*δοσωμεν* 2019) 025. 2019. 2036 : *δωμεν* ℵ* 046. 051. **18**. 1. 61. 69. 104. 241. 242. 250. 314. 1957. 2018. 2023. 2024. 2037. 2039 al^{mu} : "we give" arm$^{2.3.a}$: *δοξασωμεν* 2067 cf. Tyc arm^{2} | *τ. δοξ. αυτ.* Aℵ^{c} 025. 046 min^{pl} gig s eth : *αυτω τ. δοξ.* Pr Cyp vg | *αυτω*] *αυτων* ℵ* : *αυτου* 1. 175. 181. 250. 617. 1934. 2017. 2038 | *γυνη*] *νυμφη* ℵ$^{c.c}$: sponsa gig : + *η νυμφη* arm$^{3.4.a}$ | *αυτου*] *αυτω* arm^{2} bo : > 1. 104. 181. 336. 620. 1918 | *εαυτην*] *αυτην* 18. 2037 |.

8. *και*] + *και* 1934 | *περιβαληται*] *περιβαλητε* A : *περιβαλληται* 69. 110. 172. 522. 2023**. 2037 : *περιβεβληται* 175 | *λαμπ. καθ.* Aℵ 025. 104. 620. 1957. 2040 Tyc Pr gig vg$^{a.c.f.g.h.v}$ arm^{2} bo eth : ~ 051. 35. 2036. 2038 : *λαμπ. και καθ.* 046. **18** (– 35. 620. 2040). 250 al^{pl} vg^{d} s^{2} : *καθ. και λαμπ.* 1. 2019. 2037. 2067 s^{1} : *λευκον λαμπ.* (*αγαθον* sa) *καθ.* (*καθ. και λαμπ.* arm$^{3.a}$) arm$^{3.4.a}$ sa | *βυσσινον*^{2}] + mundum Pr : + *λευκον* arm^{2} | *τ. αγιων*] tr after *εστιν* 1 al gig vg s^{1} |.

9. *λεγει μοι* > arm^{2} | *λεγει*] *ειπεν* s^{2} bo : *ειπον* s^{1} : + *εισ* (*εκ*) *των πρεσβυτερων* arm$^{3.a}$ | *γραψον*] *παλιν* s^{1} : > 1. 2037. 2038 | *εισ* > 149 | *το* Aℵ 025. **18** (– 386. 468. 620. 2020) al^{pl} : *τον* 046. 172. 336. 386. 468. 498. 522. 620. 2020 | *του γαμου* Aℵ^{c} 046. **18** (– 620). 250. 2067 al^{pl} Pr vg s$^{(1).2}$ arm$^{2.3.a}$ sa eth : > ℵ* 025. 1. 336. 620. 1918. 2019. 2036. 2037. 2038 gig arm^{4} bo | *αρνιου*] + *εισι* s^{1} | *κεκλημενοι*] + *και δηγε και απιοι τεσ ωσ δει* (from the comm. of Aretas) 314. 2016 | *κ. λεγει*^{2} . . . *εισιν* > arm$^{3.a}$ | *κ. λεγ. μοι*^{2} Aℵ^{c} 025. 046. **18** (– 2020). 250. 2037. 2038. 2067 al^{pl} (Pr) gig vg (s) arm$^{2.4}$ (bo) sa : > ℵ* 314. 522. 2019. 2020 eth | *και*^{2}] + iterum Pr | *λεγει*^{2}] *ειπεν* s bo | *λογοι*] + *μου* ℵ* s^{2} | *οι*^{3} A 91. 242. 1934 (s^{1}) : > ℵ 025. 046. **18** (– 1934). 250. 2037. 2038. 2067 al^{pl} arm^{4} sa | *αληθινοι*] vera et iusta Pr arm^{2} | *αληθ. του θεου εισιν* A 025. 046. **18** (– 35. 2020. 2040). 250 al^{pl} gig vg$^{a.c.d.f.h.v}$ s : *αληθ. εισιν τ. θεου* ℵ* 051. 1. 35. 1957. 2020. 2023. 2036. 2037. 2038. 2067 (Pr) arm$^{(2).4}$: *του θεου αληθ. εισιν* ℵ^{c} 522. 2040 vg^{g} |.

10. *επεσα* Aℵ 025. 35. 325. 337. 386. 456. 620 al^{mu} : *επεσον*

11. Καὶ εἶδον τὸν οὐρανὸν ἠνεῳγμένον,
καὶ ἰδοὺ ἵππος λευκός,
καὶ ὁ καθήμενος ἐπ' αὐτὸν [καλούμενος] πιστὸς καὶ ἀληθινός,
καὶ ἐν δικαιοσύνῃ κρίνει καὶ πολεμεῖ.

12. οἱ δὲ ὀφθαλμοὶ αὐτοῦ ὡς φλὸξ πυρός,
καὶ ἐπὶ τὴν κεφαλὴν αὐτοῦ διαδήματα πολλά· (a)

(a) Here follows an interpolation : ἔχων ὄνομα γεγραμμένον ὃ οὐδεὶς οἶδεν εἰ μὴ αὐτός.

046. 18. 175. 468. 617. 632. 920. 1849. 1934. 2004. 2040 al^{mu} | εμπροσθεν] ενωπιον 046 | τ. ποδ. > 620 | αυτου] του αγγελου 620. 1918. 2040 | προσκυνησαι αυτω (αυτον 046) Aℵ 046. **18** Pr gig vg s^{2} arm^{2} : και (> bo sa) προσεκυνησα αυτω 025. 2036. 2037. 2038 s^{1} arm$^{3.4.a}$ bo sa eth | λεγει] ειπεν s bo | μοι > arm^{4} | ορα μη] + ποιησησ 2017. 2040 : vide ne feceris Pr gig vg : pr μη προσκυνει 468^{mg} eth : "obey (see thou art evil, and he said to me arm^{2}). Fall thou (> arm^{2}) not down before me" arm$^{2.3.a}$ | ορα > s^{1} bo | συνδουλοσ] pr οτι Pr bo eth : + γαρ gig arm$^{2.3.a}$ | σου^{2}] > ℵ 314 : + και 1. 181. 2038 | Ιησου^{1}] pr του 241. 429** : + χριστου Pr arm^{a} : (τω) κυριω arm^{2} | προσκυνησον] + μαλλον s^{1} | η γαρ μαρτ. ιησου] sanctificatio enim testificationis Pr | το πν. τησ προφ.] spiritus est et prophetiae gig : "the spirit holy which is in the prophets" arm^{2} | Ιησου^{2} Aℵ 025. 046. 1. 35. 61. 69. 181. 336. 2019. 2023. 2036. 2037. 2038. 2040. 2067 : pr του **18** (– 35. 1934. 2040). 250. 314. 2018 al^{pl} : του υιου 242. 1934 | προφητειασ] αληθειασ 2037* bo |.

11. και^{1}] και (> bo) μετα ταυτα bo eth : > Pr | ηνεωγμενον Aℵ 025. 432**. 2067 : ανεωγμενον 046. **18**. 250. 2037. 2038 al^{pl} | κ. ιδου ιππ. λευκ. > 632* | καλ. πιστ. κ. αληθ. 046. **18** (– 175. 617. 1934). 250 al^{pl} s bo sa eth : vocatur (vocabatur Pr Cyp vg arm^{2}) fidelis et verus (verax gig : + vocatur vg$^{a.c.d.f.g.h}$) Tyc Pr Cyp gig vg arm$^{(2).4}$: πιστ. καλ. κ. αληθ. ℵ : καλουμενοσ > A 025. 051. 1. (35* ?). 91. 175. 181. 242. 314. 617. 1934. 2016. 2017. 2036. 2037. 2038. 2067 arm$^{3.a}$ | κ. εν δικ. κρινει] > Tyc : aequum iustumque iudicat Pr | κ. πολ. > Tyc bo |.

12. οι δε] + οι ℵ : και οι Tyc bo | ωσ A 172. 250. 1957. 2018. 2019. 2040 al Tyc Pr gig vg s arm$^{2.4}$ bo sa eth : > ℵ 025. 046. **18** (– 2040). 1. 2037. 2038. 2067 al arm$^{3.a}$ | επι. τ. κεφ.] εν τη κεφαλη 61. 69 : in capite gig vg | εχων] et habebat (habens Pr : portabat Cyp) Pr Cyp arm^{a} | ονομα (+ μεγα Pr) γεγραμμενον A 025. 1. 35*. 104. 175. 241. 242 617. 632**. 1934. 2016. 2019. 2036. 2037. 2038 al Tyc (Pr) Cyp gig vg s^{1} arm^{a} bo sa : ονοματα (+ πολλα arm^{2}) γεγραμμενα ℵ^{c} 42. 325. 336. 468**. 517. 620. 1918 arm$^{(2).4}$: ονοματα γεγραμμενα (~ 920) και ονομα γεγραμμενον (τα ονοματα γεγραμμενα arm^{3}) 046. **18** (– 35*. 175.

13. καὶ περιβεβλημένος ἱμάτιον ⸀βεβαμμένον⸃ αἵματι, ῥεραντισ-
καὶ κέκληται τὸ ὄνομα αὐτοῦ Ὁ Λόγος τοῦ θεοῦ. μένον

14. καὶ τὰ στρατεύματα τὰ ἐν τῷ οὐρανῷ ἠκολούθει αὐτῷ ἐφ' ἵπποις λευκοῖς,
ἐνδεδυμένοι ⸀βύσσινον λευκὸν⸃ καθαρόν. λευκοβύσ-σινον

15. καὶ ἐκ τοῦ στόματος αὐτοῦ ἐκπορεύεται ῥομφαία ὀξεῖα,
ἵνα ἐν αὐτῇ πατάξῃ τὰ ἔθνη,
καὶ αὐτὸς ποιμανεῖ αὐτοὺς ἐν ῥάβδῳ σιδηρᾷ,
καὶ αὐτὸς πατεῖ τὴν ληνὸν τοῦ οἴνου τοῦ θυμοῦ τῆς ὀργῆς τοῦ θεοῦ τοῦ παντοκράτορος.

325. 468**. 617. 632**. 1934). 250. 2067 al^{mu} s^2 arm^3 | *γεγρ. ο ουδ.* > ℵ* | *ο* > arm^3 | *αυτοσ*] qui accipit gig : + *μονοσ* 2026 bo eth |.

13. περιβεβλημενοσ] circumdatus est Tyc arm$^{2.3}$: vestitus erat vg : erat coopertus Pr | *βεβαμμενον* A 046. 051. **18** (– 2040). 1. 2037. 2038. 2067 (s^1) arm sa : *περιρεραμμενον* ℵ* : *περιρεραντισμενον* ℵ$^{c.c}$: *ρεραντισμενον* 025. 2019 : *ερραντισμενον* 172. 250. 2017. 2018. 2040. Similarly Tyc Pr gig Cyp vg s^2 arm^3 bo eth | *αιματι*] pr *εν* 175. 218. 242. 250. 314. 617. 1934. 2016. 2017 | *κεκληται* Aℵ^c 025. 046. **18** (– 35. 175. 617. 620. 1934) al^{pl} vg$^{f.v}$ arm$^{2.3.a}$ (sa) : *κεκλη (το ονομα)* ℵ* : *καλειται* 1. 35. 175. 242. 250. 617. 620. 1934. 1957. 2016. 2019. 2023. 2036. 2037. 2038. 2067 al Tyc Pr gig vg$^{a.c.d.g.h}$ s^1 arm^4 : *καλουμενοσ* (s^2) bo | *το ον. αυτ.*] *αυτ. το ον.* 69 : > bo |.

14. και^1 > Tyc | *τα στρατ.*] *το στρατευμα* gig bo | *τα^1* > 61. 69. 2038 | *τα^2* 025. 051. **18** (– 325. 468. 617. 620. 920. 2020). 241. 242. 250. 429. 1957. 2023. 2024 al Tyc Pr vg s^2 sa : *αυτου* 2017 : > Aℵ 046. 1. 61. 69. 94. 104. 172. 181. 314. 325. 336. 468*. 498. 517. 617. 620. 920. 2016. 2018. 2020. 2036. 2037. 2038 gig s^1 (arm) bo eth | *εν τ. ουρ.*] *του ουρανου* (*των ουρανων* 468** s^1) 468**. 920 s^1 (arm) eth : *τω* > 2040 : > bo : tr after *αυτω* gig | *ηκολουθει*] *ηκολουθουν* 051. 1. 2020. 2037. 2038. 2039 | *εφ ιπποισ* (*ενφιπποισ* 620) *λευκοισ* Aℵ 025. 1. 104. 620. 2019. 2020. 2037. 2040. 2067 al^p : *επι ιπποισ λευκοισ* 046. **18** (– 35*. 620. 2020. 2040). 250 al^{pl} : *εφιπποι πολλοι* 051. 35*. 181. 2036. 2038 | *ενδεδυμενοι*] *ενδεδυμενοισ* ℵ* : *ενδεδυμενα* 632 : *ενδεδυμενον* 920 : pr *και* s^1 | *βυσσινον λευκον* (*λαμπρον* 94. 2037 bo) ℵ 025. 046. **18** (– 2040). (1). (94). 250. (2037). 2038 al^{pl} Pr Tyc (gig) (s^1) arm^4 (bo) (sa) : *λευκον βυσσινον* (*λευκοβυσσινον* 2040) A 2040 : + *και* ℵ 1. 456. gig s^1 sa : *λευκον* > arm$^{2.3}$ | *λευκ. καθ*] ~ 104 s^2 : *καθ. και λευκ.* arm^a : *φωτοσ λευκου* (corrupt) eth | *καθαρον*] purpureum gig : > bo |.

15. αυτου] *αυτων* s^1 arm^2 bo | *εκπορευεται*] exiebat Pr arm | *οξεια* Aℵ 025. 1. 35*. 2019. 2020. 2036. 2037. 2038 al gig vg s^1

16. *καὶ ἔχει (a) ἐπὶ τὸν μηρὸν αὐτοῦ ὄνομα γεγραμμένον,*
ΒΑCΙΛΕΥC ΒΑCΙΛΕΩΝ ΚΑΙ ΚΥΡΙΟC ΚΥΡΙΩΝ.
17. Καὶ εἶδον ἕνα ἄγγελον ἑστῶτα ἐν τῷ ἡλίῳ, καὶ ἔκραξεν
φωνῇ μεγάλῃ λέγων πᾶσι τοῖς ὀρνέοις τοῖς πετομένοις ἐν μεσου-
ρανήματι Δεῦτε συνάχθητε εἰς τὸ δεῖπνον τὸ μέγα τοῦ θεοῦ, 18. ἵνα
φάγητε σάρκας βασιλέων καὶ σάρκας χιλιάρχων καὶ σάρκας ἰσχυρῶν
καὶ σάρκας ἵππων καὶ τῶν καθημένων ἐπ' αὐτῶν, καὶ σάρκας πάντων

(a) Text adds : *ἐπὶ τὸ ἱμάτιον καί.* See vol. ii. 137.

arm bo sa eth : pr *διστομοσ* 046. **18** (– 35*. 2020). 250. 2067 al[pl] Tyc Pr s[2] | *εν αυτη*] *εν αυτω* 2020 s[1] : ex eo Pr | *παταξη*] *παταξει* ℵ 104. 385. 620 : *παταξωσιν* s[1] : *παραταξη* 325. 517 | *τα εθνη*] pr *παντα* 498. 2020 gig sa | *και*[3] >Tyc | *πατει*] *πατησει* Pr | *τ. οιν. τ. θυμ.* >s[1] | *τ. θυμου* (+*και* 1. 2019. 2036. 2037. 2038. 2067 al[p] arm[3]) placed after *οινου* A 025. 046. **18** (– 2040) al[pl] Tyc vg s[2] arm eth : tr after *οργησ* ℵ sa : tr before *του οινου* 2040 : >Pr gig bo | *τησ οργησ*] pr *και* 2040 : >s[2] arm[4. a] : + *αυτου* 620 | *θεου*]+magni Pr |.

16. *και*[1]] *αυτοσ* Tyc | *εχει* A : +*επι* (> Tyc) *το ιματιον* (*τα ιματια αυτου* s[1] : *το μετωπον* 2040 : +*αυτου* 920 bo sa eth) *και* (>s[1]) ℵ 025. 046. **18** al[omn] Tyc Pr gig vg s[(1). 2] arm (bo sa eth) | *επι* >ℵ bo sa | *τον μηρον*] *τουσ μηρουσ* s[1] arm[(4)] | *αυτου* > 920 | *ονομα γεγραμμ.* >arm[4] | *ονομα*] pr *το* 1. 2037 : >gig vg |.

17. *ενα* A 025. 1. 35. 104. 241. 632**. 1957. 2020. 2023. 2038. 2040. 2041. 2067 al Pr gig vg eth : *αλλον* ℵ 2019 s[1] arm[4. a] bo sa : +*αλλον* 172. 250. 2018 : > 046. **18** (– 35. 632**. 2020. 2040). 2037 al[pl] Tyc s[2] arm[2] | *εκραξεν* Aℵ 025. **18** (– 18. 2040) al[pl] Tyc Pr gig vg s arm : *εκραζεν* 046. 18. 181. 2040 : *κραζων* bo | *φωνη* A 025. 35. 175. 250. 468**. 617. 620. 632**. 1934. 2020. 2037. 2038. 2040. 2067 al[pl] Pr gig vg : pr *εν* ℵ 046. 18. 61. 82. 104. 325. 336. 337. 386. 456. 468*. 632*. 920. 1849. 2004 al Tyc arm[4. a] bo sa | *λεγων* >35*. 617 | *πασι τοισ ορν.*] *παντα τα ορνεα* arm[2] bo | *πασι* > 2040 s[1] | *τ. πετ. εν μεσ.*] caeli Pr | *πετομ.* Aℵ 046. **18** (– 456) al[pl] : *πετωμ.* 025. 456 al | *συναχθητε* > 051. 1. 2037. 2038 Pr | *το* (*τον* 91. 110. 385. 452. 2021. 2041) *δειπνον το μεγα* (tr after *θεου* 920) Aℵ 025. 046. 35. (91. 110). 325. 337. (452). 456. 632. (920). 1849. 2004. (2021). 2040. (2041). 2067 al : *τον δειπν. τον μεγαν* 18. 172. 175. 201. 242. 250. 314. 336. 386. 468. 617. 620. 1918. 1934. 2016. 2017. 2018. 2020 | *το μεγα του θ.*] *του μεγαλου θεου* 051. 1. 2019. 2023. 2036. 2037. 2038 arm[2. a] eth | *το μεγα* >gig |.

18. *και σαρκ. χιλ.* > 1. 2023 arm[a] | *σαρκασ*[3] > Tyc | *κ. τ. καθ. . . . παντων* >617 | *αυτων* 025. 046. **17** (– 617). 250. 2037. 2038. 2067 al[pl] : *αυτοισ* ℵ : *αυτουσ* A 61. 69 | *σαρκασ*[5]] pr *τασ* 18. 632. 1849 | *παντων*] *απαντων* 046* : +*των* 1934 : >1. 2067 s[1] bo | *τε* >1. 314. 2067 | *και*[7] Aℵ 025. **17** (– 632**. 1849. 2020) al[pl]

ἐλευθέρων τε καὶ δούλων καὶ μικρῶν καὶ μεγάλων. 19. καὶ εἶδον τὸ
θηρίον καὶ τοὺς βασιλεῖς τῆς γῆς καὶ τὰ στρατεύματα αὐτῶν συνηγ-
μένα ποιῆσαι τὸν πόλεμον μετὰ τοῦ καθημένου ἐπὶ τοῦ ἵππου καὶ
μετὰ τοῦ στρατεύματος αὐτοῦ. 20. καὶ ἐπιάσθη τὸ θηρίον, καὶ
⸀μετ' αὐτοῦ⸣ ὁ ψευδοπροφήτης ὁ ποιήσας τὰ σημεῖα ἐνώπιον αὐτοῦ, ὁ μετ'
ἐν οἷς ἐπλάνησεν τοὺς λαβόντας τὸ χάραγμα τοῦ θηρίου καὶ τοὺς αὐτοῦ
προσκυνοῦντας ⸀τὴν εἰκόνα⸣ αὐτοῦ· ζῶντες ἐβλήθησαν οἱ δύο εἰς τὴν τῇ εἰκόνι
λίμνην τοῦ πυρὸς τῆς καιομένης ἐν θείῳ. 21. καὶ οἱ λοιποὶ ἀπεκτάν-
θησαν ἐν τῇ ῥομφαίᾳ τοῦ καθημένου ἐπὶ τοῦ ἵππου, τῇ ἐξελθούσῃ ἐκ
τοῦ στόματος αὐτοῦ, καὶ πάντα τὰ ὄρνεα ἐχορτάσθησαν ἐκ τῶν
σαρκῶν αὐτῶν.

Tyc Pr gig vg s bo : >046. 61. 69. 241. 429. 522. 632**. 1849. 2020 | *μικρων* Aℵ 025. 1. 172. 175. 242. 250. 617. 1934. 2018. 2019. 2036. 2037. 2038. 2040. 2067 al^{mu} : + *τε* 046. **17** (− 175. 617. 1934. 2040) al^{mu} | *μεγαλων*] pr *των* ℵ 2040 |.

19. *θηριον*] + *και τα στρατευματα αυτου* s^{1} | *κ. τ. βασ.*] tr after *γησ* 920 | *γησ*] *οικουμενησ* 620 | *κ. τα στρατ.*] *κατα τα τρατ.* (sic) ℵ* | *αυτων* ℵ 025. 046. **17** (−456?. 620?. 920?. 2040?). 250. 2037. 2038. 2067 al^{pl} Tyc Pr gig vg s arm$^{1.4.a}$ bo : *αυτου* A 314. 2016 arm^{2} sa | *συνηγμενα*] tr after *πολεμον* 2040 | *τον* Aℵ 046. **17** (− 35. 175. 386. 617. 2020. 2040) al^{pl} : > 025. 1. 35. 175. 250. 314. 386. 617. 2020. 2037. 2038. 2067 al^{p} | *ιππου*] + (*του*) *λευκου* Pr arm bo sa eth | *μετα*^{2} > bo sa eth | *του στρατ.*] *των στρατευματων* s arm |.

20. *και*^{2} > Pr | *μετ αυτου* (*μετα τουτου* 1. 2023*. 2037. 2038) *ο* ℵ (1). 35. 69. 432. 1957. 2020. 2023**. 2036. (2037. 2038). 2041. 2067 (Pr) vg s^{1} arm$^{2.4}$: *οι* (*ο* 025 arm^{2}) *μετ αυτου* (+ *και* bo) *ο* A (025). 2021 (arm^{2} bo) : *οι μετ αυτου οι* (>424) 424 arm^{1} : *ο μετ αυτου* 046. **17** (− 35. 2020). 250 al^{pl} gig s^{2} | *ψευδ.*] *ψευδοπροφηται* 424 arm^{1} | *εν οισ επλαν. . . . τ. εικ. αυτ.*] quibus signis seducti erant adorare imaginem bestiae et qui acceperant caragma illius Pr | *λαβοντασ*] *πλανωντασ* 177. 180. 337 | *το χαραγμα*] *τα χαραγματα* 456 | *τουσ προσκυν.*] *οι προσκυνουντεσ* gig : *των προσκυνουντων* s^{1} | *την εικονα* ℵ* 920. 1918. 2020 : *τη εικονι* Aℵ^{c} 025. **17** (− 920. 2020). 250. 2037. 2038. 2067 al^{pl} : *το χαραγμα* 046 | *ζωντεσ*] *και κατεβησαν και* s^{1} : pr *και* s^{2} : *του ζωντοσ* arm$^{1.2.4}$: *ζωντασ* bo : > Pr | *εβληθησαν*] *βληθησονται* 1. 2019. 2020. 2038. 2067 : *εβαλον* arm bo sa | *οι δυο*] tr after *θειω* 920 : *αυτουσ* arm$^{1.2.a}$: *τουσ δυο* bo sa eth : >456 gig arm^{4} | *τ. πυρ. τ. καιομ.*] *την καιομ. πυρι και* bo | *τησ καιομενησ* Aℵ 025 Pr vg : *την καιομενην* 046. **17** al^{omn} gig bo | *εν θειω*] *εν τω θειω* 1. 172. 175. 617. 2018. 2019. 2023. 2036. 2037. 2038 al : et in sulphur gig : *και θειου* s^{1} : igne et sulphore Pr (cf bo) |.

21. *ρομφαια*] + *αυτου* 2040 | *ιππου*] + (*του*) *λευκου* Pr eth | *εκ*^{1}] *απο* 920 | *ορνεα*] *ερπετα* 617 |.

RESTORED ORDER OF THE TEXT.

Chapters XX. 1–3, XXI. 9–XXII. 2, XXII. 14. 15. 17.

xx. 1. Καὶ εἶδον ἄγγελον καταβαίνοντα ἐκ τοῦ οὐρανοῦ,
ἔχοντα τὴν κλεῖν τῆς ἀβύσσου
ἐν τῇ χειρί — καὶ ἅλυσιν μεγάλην ⸢ἐπὶ τὴν χεῖρα⸣ αὐτοῦ.

2. καὶ ἐκράτησεν τὸν δράκοντα, ὁ ὄφις ὁ ἀρχαῖος,
ὅς ἐστιν διάβολος καὶ ὁ Σατανᾶς,
καὶ ἔδησεν αὐτὸν χίλια ἔτη,

3. καὶ ἔβαλεν αὐτὸν εἰς τὴν ἄβυσσον,
καὶ ἔκλεισεν καὶ ἐσφράγισεν ἐπάνω αὐτοῦ,
ἵνα μὴ πλανήσῃ ἔτι τὰ ἔθνη,
ἄχρι τελεσθῇ τὰ χίλια ἔτη·

μετὰ ταῦτα δεῖ λυθῆναι αὐτὸν μικρὸν χρόνον.

xx. 1. **αγγελον**] pr *αλλον* ℵ^{c} 2017. 2050 Tyc s^{1} arm$^{1.2.a}$ sa eth : + *αλλον* 336. 620. 1918 | *εκ τ. ουρ.* > ℵ* | *κλειν*] *κλειδα* (*-αν* 620). 1. 104. 620. 2037. 2067 al | *αλυσιν μεγ.*] *αλυσεσιν μεγ.* ℵ* : *αλυσις μεγαλη* Tyc : ~ bo sa eth | *μεγ.* > Pr | *επι τ. χειρα* A 046. **18** (– 2020). 250. 2037. 2038. 2067 al^{pl} : *εν τη χειρι* ℵ 2020 Tyc Pr gig vg s arm bo sa eth |.

2. **ο οφισ ο αρχαιοσ** A (s?) : *τον οφιν τον αρχαιον* ℵ 046. **18** al^{omn} : serpentem (pr illum Pr : anguem Tyc) antiquum Tyc Pr gig vg : *τον αρχαιον* 2036 | *οσ* A 046. **18** al^{omn} : *ο* ℵ 2050 | *εστιν*] cognominatus est Pr | *διαβολοσ* A 046. **18** (– 2020. 2050). 250. 2037. 2038. 2067 arm^{4} : pr *ο* ℵ 69. 498. 2020. 2036. 2050 arm^{a} bo sa | *κ. ο σατ.* > 2050 | *και*^{2} > bo sa eth | *ο*^{3} Aℵ 046. 35. 175. 250. 325. 337. 456. 617. 1934. 2020 al^{mu} : > 051. 1. 18. 386. 620. 632. 920. 1849. 2004. 2037. 2038. 2040. 2067 al | (*ο*) *σατανασ* Aℵ 1. 175. 617. 632**. 2016. 2036. 2037. 2038. 2040. (2050) Tyc Pr gig vg s^{1} arm bo : + *ο πλανων την οικουμενην ολην* (> 61. 385) 046. 051. **18** (– 175. 617. 632**. 2040. 2050). 250. 2067 al^{pl} s^{2} | *χιλ. ετη κ. εβαλ. αυτον* > ℵ |.

3. **και . . . αβυσσον** > arm^{4} eth | *εκλεισεν*] *εδησεν* (+ *αυτον* 1) 1. 181. 2036. 2037. 2038 : *εδησεν και εκλεισεν* arm^{4} : + *το στομα αυτησ* bo sa | *εσφραγισεν*] + *σφραγιδι* eth | *επανω αυτου*] *εμμενωσ αυτον* A | *πλανηση* (*-σει* ℵ) Aℵ 1. 2036. 2037. 2038. 2040 al : *πλανα* (*-η* 2050) 046. **18** (– 2040). 250. 2067 al^{pl} | *ετι*] tr after *εθνη* s^{1} : > 1. 69. 141 Tyc bo eth | *τα*^{1}] > 35 : pr *παντα* s^{1} | *αχρι . . . ετη* > s^{1} | *αχρι*] *αχρισ αν* 2050 | *τελεσθη*] *τελεσθωσι* 141. 241. 386. 2067 | *τα*^{2} > 051. 1. 181. 2036. 2067 | *μετα* Aℵ 046.

xxi. 9. Καὶ ἦλθεν εἷς ἐκ τῶν ἑπτὰ ἀγγέλων τῶν ἐχόντων τὰς
ἑπτὰ φιάλας, † τῶν γεμόντων † τῶν ἑπτὰ πληγῶν τῶν ἐσχάτων, καὶ
ἐλάλησεν μετ' ἐμοῦ λέγων Δεῦρο, δείξω σοι τὴν νύμφην [τὴν γυναῖκα]
τοῦ ἀρνίου. 10. καὶ ἀπήνεγκέν με ἐν πνεύματι ἐπὶ ὄρος μέγα καὶ
ὑψηλόν, καὶ ἔδειξέν μοι τὴν πόλιν τὴν ἁγίαν Ἰερουσαλὴμ κατα-
βαίνουσαν ἐκ τοῦ οὐρανοῦ ἀπὸ τοῦ θεοῦ, 11. ἔχουσαν τὴν δόξαν τοῦ
θεοῦ· ὁ φωστὴρ αὐτῆς ὅμοιος λίθῳ τιμιωτάτῳ, ὡς λίθῳ ἰάσπιδι

18 (– 35. 175. 617. 1934. 2050) al^{mu} Tyc Pr gig vg$^{(-v)}$ s^{1} : pr *και* 1. 35. 175. 617. 1934. 2050 al vg^{v} arm bo eth : + *δε* 385. 429 s^{2} | *δει λυθ. αυτ.*] *λυθησεται* s^{2} : *λυσει* (*ελυσαν* arm^{2}) *αυτ.* arm$^{1.\,2}$ | *λυθ. αυτ.* A 046. **18** (– 35. 175. 617. 2020) al^{mu} : ~ ℵ 1. 35. 175. 250. 617. 1957. 2016. 2020. 2023. 2036. 2037. 2038. 2041. 2067 Pr gig vg | *λυθηναι*] *λυσαι* Tyc s^{1} | *μικρον χρον.*] ~ 2050 : pr *ετι* bo sa |.

xxi. 9. *εισ*] *ο πρωτοσ* 172. 2018. 2020 | *εκ* > 1. 172. 205. 2018. 2020. 2036. 2037. 2038. 2067 | *επτα*^{2} > gig vg | *των γεμοντων* Aℵ* 025. 181. 2036. 2038. 2050 : *των γεμουσων* ℵ^{c} : *τασ γεμουσασ* 1. 104. 2037 (s) : *γεμουσασ* 046. **18** (– 2050). 61. 110. 385. 1957. 2016. 2023. 2037. 2067 al^{mu} : plenas Pr gig vg : *εχουσασ* 2018 | *των*^{4} Aℵ 025. 1. 35. 104. 172. 205. 632**. 2018. 2023. 2037. 2050. 2067 al s arm^{4} bo : > 046. **18** (– 35. 205. 632**. 2050). 250. 2038 al^{mu} | *και*^{2} > bo sa | *δευρο*] + *και* vg^{g} arm$^{2.\,4}$: + *ινα* bo sa | *την γυναικα* (pr *και* arm$^{1.\,2.\,a}$: + *και* 42. 2017) placed after *νυμφην* Aℵ 025. 35. 172. 218. 250. 2018. 2020 Tyc Pr gig vg s (arm$^{1.\,2.\,a}$) bo sa eth : tr after *αρνιου* 051. 1. 205. 2036. 2037. 2038. 2067 al : tr before *την νυμφ.* 046. **18** (– 35. 205. 2020). (42). 104. 110. 385. 2016. (2017). 2023 al^{pl} arm^{4} |.

10. *απηνεγκεν*] *ηνεγκεν* 2050 : duxit Pr : tulit gig : sustulit vg | *εν πνευμ.* > Pr | *επι* Aℵ 172. 2018. 2050 : *επ* 025. 046. **18** al^{pl} | *οροσ*] *ορουσ* 2020 | *και*^{2} > 205 bo | *και*^{3} > arm^{2} bo sa | *μοι*] *με* 149. 325. 620. 1934 | *πολιν* Aℵ 025. 046. **18** (– 35. 175. 205. 617) al^{pl} Tyc Pr gig vg s arm$^{1.\,2.\,4}$ bo eth : + *την μεγαλην* 051. 1. 35. 175. 205. 250. 617. 1957. 2016. 2023. 2036. 2037. 2038. 2041. 2067 al arm^{a} | *την*^{2}] *και* 051. 1. 35. 175. 205. 250. 617. 2016. 2036. 2037. 2038 arm^{a} | *εκ τ. ουρ.* Aℵ 025. 046. **18** (– 18. 175. 617. 2004) Tyc Pr gig vg s arm bo eth : *απο τ. ουρ.* 18. 175. 218. 250. 617. 2004. 2016. 2017. 2018. 2039 | *απο τ. θ.* Aℵ 025. 1. 35. 104. 205. 241. 632**. 1957. 2020. 2023. 2036. 2037. 2038. 2050. 2067 al Tyc Pr gig vg s^{1} arm bo eth : *εκ τ. θ.* 046. **18** (– 35. 205. 386. 632**. 2020. 2050). 250 al^{pl} : > 61. 201. 386 |.

11. *εχουσαν . . . θεου*] > A 522 : *την φωτιζουσαν αυτην* 2050 : *η εστιν αγια η γεμει δοξησ* bo | *τ. δοξαν*] + *απο* ℵ gig : lumen claritatis Pr | *τ. θεου*] + *και* 1. 104. 205 Pr s^{1} arm$^{1.\,a}$ (bo) : + *εν η η γυνη του αρνιου η ανω Ιερουσαλημ υπο θεου κοσμηθησεται και δοξασθησεται* 743. 1075. 2067 : > arm^{4} | *ο φωστηρ αυτ.*] *ωσ*

κρυσταλλίζοντι. 12. ἔχουσα τεῖχος μέγα καὶ ὑψηλόν, ἔχουσα
πυλῶνας δώδεκα, καὶ ἐπὶ τοῖς πυλῶσιν ἀγγέλους δώδεκα, καὶ ὀνόματα
ἐπιγεγραμμένα, ἅ ἐστιν τὰ ὀνόματα τῶν δώδεκα φυλῶν υἱῶν Ἰσραήλ·
13. ἀπὸ ἀνατολῆς πυλῶνες τρεῖς, καὶ ἀπὸ βορρᾶ πυλῶνες τρεῖς, καὶ

φωσ τησ αυγησ s^{2} : εν αυτη (ησ το arm^{4} : + ην arm^{1}) φωσ arm | ομοιοσ] + εστιν Pr : > bo arm^{1} | λιθ. τιμ.] λιθου (-ων arm^{1}) τιμιου (-ων arm^{1}) arm^{1} bo : λιθοισ τιμιοισ arm$^{2.\,a}$: > arm^{4} | τιμιωτατω] τιμιω gig vg s^{1} | ωσ λιθ.] tr after ιασπιδι arm^{4} : > 051. 1. 35*. 94. 104. 181. 205. 241. 632**. 2020. 2038. 2050. 2067 arm^{2} : ωσ φωσ bo | κρυσταλλιζοντι Aℵ **18** (− 18. 337. 617. 632*. 1934. 2020. 2050) : κρυσταλιζοντι 025. 046. 1. 18. 110. 172. 337. 385. 498. 522. 617. 632*. 1934. 2018. 2020. 2036. 2037. 2038. 2050 : sicut crystallum (cristallo gig) gig vg : refulgenti in modum cristalli Pr : "crystal seeming (-gleaming arm^{1} : > arm^{4}) and (> arm^{4}) luminous (living arm$^{2.\,a}$)" arm |.

12. εχουσα^{1}] εχοντι ℵ : εχουσαν 172. 2018 Tyc : + τε 1. 2037. 2067 : et habebat (-et Pr) Pr vg | υψηλον] latum Pr | εχουσα^{2}] εχουσαν 104. 172. 2018. 2050 al Tyc : εχοντασ ℵ* : pr και 2036. 2037 : και 2067 bo : ο εχει Pr : και ειχε arm$^{1.\,2.\,a}$ eth | δωδεκα^{1}] ιβ' 046. 35. 205. 337 | κ. επι τ. πυλ. αγγ. δωδεκα > A 2050 vg^{f} arm^{4} | επι τοισ πυλωσιν 025. 046. **18** al$^{\text{fere omn}}$: επι τουσ πυλωνασ ℵ 94 : in portas (+ habens gig) Pr gig | αγγ.] angulous Pr vg$^{a.\,c.\,v}$: pr τουσ bo | δωδεκα^{2} 175. 617. 1934. 2020 : δεκαδυο **18** (− 35. 175. 205. 617. 1934. 2020). 104. 110. 172. 201. 498. 522. 2018. 2023. 2024 : ιβ' ℵ 046. 35. 205 | ονοματα^{1}] + αυτων ℵ s^{1} | επιγεγραμμενα] γεγραμμενα ℵ gig vg$^{c.\,d.\,f.\,v}$ s^{1} : εγγεγραμμενα (ενγ- 2050) 94. 2050. cf. inscripta vg$^{a.\,g}$ | α εστιν . . . Ισραηλ > arm^{a} | α εστιν > Pr arm^{2} | τα ονοματα A s : tr after Ισραηλ 2050 : ονοματα (ονομα bo) 046. **18** (− 35. 205. 2050) al^{mu} gig vg arm^{4} bo : > ℵ 025. 1. 35. 205. 241. 432. 1918. 1957. 2023. 2036. 2037. 2038. 2041. 2067 Pr arm^{2} | δωδεκα^{3}] ιβ' ℵ 046. 35. 205 | υιων Aℵ 046. **18** (− 35. 205. 386. 920. 2050). 250. 2038 al^{mu} : pr των 025. 051. 1. 35. 104. 1957. 2023. 2041. 2050 al arm^{4} : > 181. 201. 241. 386. 517. 920. 2017. 2036. 2037. 2067 s^{1} arm$^{1.\,2.\,a}$ | Ισραηλ] pr του 201. 205. 386. 2017. 2036. 2067 |.

13. ανατολησ Aℵ 025. 1. 205. 2017. 2020. 2037. 2038. 2050. 2067 s : ανατολων 046. **18** (− 205. 2020. 2050). 250 al | και$^{1.\,2.\,3}$ > 051. 1. 205 arm$^{1.\,4.\,a}$ Tyc Pr | και$^{2.\,3}$ > 2037. 2038. 2067 βορρα (-ρασ 2050 : βορα 920) . . . νοτου . . . δυσμων ℵ^{c} 025. 046. **18** (− 386). 250. (2037). 2038. (2067) al$^{\text{fere omn}}$ Tyc Pr gig vg s arm$^{4.\,a}$: ρορρα . . . βορρα . . . νοτου ℵ* : βορρα . . . δυσμων . . . νοτου (μεσημβριασ 1) A 1 : δυσμων . . . βορρα . . . νοτου 386. 1957 arm$^{1.\,2.\,a}$: νοτου . . . βορρα . . . δυσμων 522 : νοτου . . . δυσμων . . . βορρα (bo) : + και απο μεσημβριασ πυλωνεσ τρεισ 2037. 2067 | τρεισ$^{1.\,2.\,3}$] γ' 046. 35. 337 |.

ἀπὸ νότου πυλῶνες τρεῖς, καὶ ἀπὸ δυσμῶν πυλῶνες τρεῖς. 14. καὶ τὸ
τεῖχος τῆς πόλεως ἔχων θεμελίους δώδεκα, καὶ ἐπ' αὐτῶν δώδεκα
ὀνόματα τῶν δώδεκα ἀποστόλων τοῦ ἀρνίου. 15. Καὶ ὁ λαλῶν μετ'
ἐμοῦ εἶχεν μέτρον κάλαμον χρυσοῦν, ἵνα μετρήσῃ τὴν πόλιν καὶ τοὺς
πυλῶνας αὐτῆς καὶ τὸ τεῖχος αὐτῆς. 16. καὶ ἡ πόλις τετράγωνος
κεῖται, καὶ τὸ μῆκος αὐτῆς ὅσον καὶ τὸ πλάτος. καὶ ἐμέτρησεν τὴν
πόλιν τῷ καλάμῳ ἐπὶ ⸀σταδίους⸃ δώδεκα χιλιάδων· τὸ μῆκος καὶ τὸ σταδίων
πλάτος καὶ τὸ ὕψος αὐτῆς ἴσα ἐστίν. 17. καὶ ἐμέτρησεν τὸ τεῖχος

14. **το τειχοσ**] muri Pr arm^{1} | εχων A 025. 046. 1. 104. 498. 522. 1849. 2017. 2038 : εχον ℵ^{c} 051. **18** (– 1849. 2020. 2050). 250. 2037. 2067 al^{pl} : habens gig vg : ειχε 2020 arm^{a} : habent Pr : >ℵ* 2050 arm$^{1.2.4}$ | θεμελ. δωδεκα] ~ 149. 1948 bo eth : τρειμελιουσ τρεισ 2050 | δωδεκα^{1}] ιβ' ℵ 046. 35. 205. 337 | κ. επ. αυτ > 1*. 104 | επ αυτων] in ipso gig : pr γεγραμμενα (-ον bo) bo eth | δωδεκα ονομ. . . . αρνιου >2050 | δωδεκα^{2}] ιβ' (pr των 35*) 046. 35**. 205. 337 : δεκαδυο 93. 94 : > 1*. 104 Pr bo | ονοματα] ονομα bo | δωδεκα^{3}] ιβ' ℵ 046. 35. 325. 337 : >Tyc s^{1} arm$^{1.2}$ | του αρνιου] pr και Tyc Pr : του υιου s^{1} |.

15. **και^{1}** > 2050 arm^{4} | μετρον καλαμον Aℵ* 025. 046. **18** (– 2050). 250. 2067 al^{pl} Tyc gig s^{2} arm^{4} : harundinem (auream) ad mensuram Pr : μετρον καλαμου ℵ^{c} 517. 2016. 2050 cf mensuram harundineam vg : μετρου καλαμον s^{1} : μετρον >1. 2036. 2037. 2038 arm$^{2.a}$ bo eth : καλαμον >arm^{1} | μετρηση] μετρησει 046. 104. (2050). 2067 | κ. τ. πυλ. αυτησ >s^{1} arm^{2} | κ. το τειχοσ (τα τειχη Pr arm bo eth) αυτησ (>vg) Aℵ 025. 175. 205. 617. 632. 1934. 2020. 2050 Pr gig vg s arm bo eth : >046. 051. 18. 35. 325. 337. 386. 456. 620. 920. 1849. 2004 al^{pl} |.

16. **αυτησ**] tr before τετραγωνοσ ℵ : >arm^{1} | και^{3} A 2050 Pr vg s^{2} arm$^{2.4.a}$ bo eth : >ℵ 025. 046. **18** (– 2050). 250. 2037. 2067 al^{pl} gig s^{1} arm^{1} | πλατοσ] + αυτησ s^{1} arm | τω καλαμω Aℵ 046. **18** (– 35. 175. 205. 617) : pr εν 025. 1. 35 175. 181. 205. 250. 617. 2016. 2017. 2036. 2037**. 2038. 2067 : harundine (pr de vg) Pr gig vg sa : > bo arm | επι] per gig vg : ab Pr | σταδιουσ (-ου ℵ^{c}) A (ℵ^{c}) 046. **18** (– 205). 250 al^{pl} : σταδιων ℵ* 025. 1. 205. 2018. 2036. 2037. 2038. 2067 | δωδεκα Aℵ 025. 2050 : ιβ' 046. 1. 35. 205. 632**. 2018. 2038 : δεκαδυο **18** (– 35. 205. 632**. 2050). 110. 201. 385. 498. 522. 2016 al^{mu} | χιλιαδων Aℵ 025. 35*. 632**. 2020. 2050 Pr gig vg s^{1} bo : pr και 046 : + δωδεκα (ιβ' 046. 35**). 046. **18** (– 35*. 632**. 2020. 2050). 250 al^{mu} (s^{2}) : >arm^{1} | το μηκοσ] μηκουσ bo sa : pr και 2020 s^{2} : + αυτησ s^{1} arm | πλατοσ] + αυτησ 2050 s^{1} arm$^{2.4.a}$ bo sa eth | **κ.** τ. υψοσ >arm^{2} | αυτησ^{2} >205. 2050 Pr gig arm |.

17. **εμετρησεν** (-τρισεν 620. 2050) Aℵ 025. 35. 620. 2037. 2038. 2050. 2067 al^{p} Pr vg$^{c.d.v}$ s arm : εμετρηθη gig vg$^{a.f.g}$ bo : > 046. **18** (– 35. 620. 2050). 250 al^{mu} | τειχοσ] χιλοσ ℵ : muros

αὐτῆς ἑκατὸν τεσσεράκοντα τεσσάρων πηχῶν, μέτρον ἀνθρώπου, ὅ ἐστιν ἀγγέλου.

18 καὶ ἡ ἐνδώμησις τοῦ τείχους αὐτῆς ἴασπις,
καὶ ἡ πόλις χρυσίον καθαρὸν ὅμοιον ὑάλῳ καθαρῷ·

αἱ οἱ 19. [οἱ] θεμέλιοι τοῦ τείχους τῆς πόλεως παντὶ λίθῳ τιμίῳ κεκοσμημένοι·

ὁ θεμέλιος ὁ πρῶτος ἴασπις, ὁ δεύτερος σάπφειρος, ὁ τρίτος χαλκηδών,

vg$^{c.\,d.\,v}$ | εκατον τεσσερακ. τεσσ.] δ και εκατον τεσσερακοντα A : εκατον μδ' ℵ : ρμδ' 046. 1. 18. 35. 104. 325. 337. 456. 632. 920. 2004. 2020 : nonaginto octo gig | τεσσερακ.] τεσσαρακοντα 025. 175. 205. 386. 617. 620. 1934 : σερακοντα (σαρακοντα 2050) 1849. 2050 | τεσσαρων] τεσσαρισ χιλιαδεσ 2050 | πηχων] πηχεων ℵ : σταδιων arm^{a} : > Pr bo | μετρον] μετρω s^{1} : μετρα (placed before πηχων s^{2}) s^{2} bo | ανθρωπου] ουρανου 2050 |.

18. κ. η ενδωμ. του τειχ.] in structura murus gig | η^{1} Aℵ^{c} 025 Tyc s arm$^{1.\,2.\,4}$: ην ℵ* : ην η 046. **18**. 250. 2037. 2038. 2067 al^{pl} Pr vg bo | ενδωμησισ Aℵ^{c} 498. 2020 : εν δωμασι ℵ* cf gig : ενδωσισ 2050 : ενδομησισ 025. 046. 051. **18** (− 2020. 2050) al^{pl} | αυτησ > 175. 2050 Tyc arm^{4} | ιασπισ] ex lapide iaspidi Pr vg (arm$^{2.\,4}$) : pr ωσ bo : > Tyc | χρυσ. καθ.] χρυσιω καθαρω 2014. 2034. 2036. 2042 vg : χρυσιου (pr εκ Pr) καθαρου Pr s arm$^{1.\,2.\,4}$ | ομοιον] ομοια 051. 1. 35. 205. 2036. 2038 Pr : pr και gig | υαλω Aℵ 025. 046. 18. 175. 337. 456. 617. 920. 1934 : νελω (νελλω 385. 498) 35. 205. 325. 386. 620. 632. 1849. 2004. 2020. 2050 al^{pl} | καθαρω >025 | η πολισ χρυσιον . . . καθαρω] civitas aurum mundum (purum gig) simile (+et gig) vitro mundo (puro gig) Tyc gig : ipsa vero civitas ex (>vg) auro mundo similis vitreo (simile vitro vg) mundo Pr vg : η πολισ (+ολη arm^{4}) χρυσιου καθαρου ομοιον (or ομοια) υαλω καθαρω s arm$^{1.\,2.\,4.\,a}$: "the city was wrought of gold pure like glass pure" bo : ομοια η πολισ ωσ ησ η ποιησισ εστι εν χρυσιω καθαρω eth |.

19. οι θεμελιοι Aℵ^{c} 025. 046. **18** (− 35). 250 al^{mu} Tyc vg sa : pr και ℵ* 1. 35. 104. 2018. 2023. 2036. 2037. 2038. 2067 s arm bo eth : pr ubi gig : + autem Pr | τησ πολεωσ] + ομοιω 2050 : > Pr | παντι λιθ. τιμ.] omnia ex (ex omni Pr) lapide pretioso Tyc Pr : λιθοισ τιμιοισ s^{1} : παντων λιθων τιμιων arm | τιμιω κεκοσμημενοι] ~ 205 | κεκοσμημενοι] -μενω 1849. 2004 : >61. 2050 Tyc Pr gig arm | ο θεμ. . . . ιασπισ > arm^{4} | ο θεμελιοσ] pr και s^{1} arm^{2} eth : + του τειχουσ arm$^{1.\,2.\,a}$: >gig | πρωτοσ] εισ ℵ | ο^{3}] pr και ℵ Tyc s^{1} arm^{2} eth | σαπφειροσ] σαμπφειροσ 2017 : -ηροσ 051. 2020. 2050 : -ιροσ 025. 046. 2004 Pr vg gig bo : saffyrus Tyc | ο^{4}] pr και ℵ s^{1} arm^{2} eth. (Also before ο^{5} and ver. 20 ο$^{1\text{-}9}$ ℵ arm^{2} eth add και : s^{1} except ver. 20 ο$^{8.\,9}$) | τριτοσ] γ' ℵ (also δ' ε' . . .

20. ὁ τέταρτος σμάραγδος, ὁ πέμπτος σαρδόνυξ, ὁ ἕκτος σάρδιον,
ὁ ἕβδομος χρυσόλιθος, ὁ ὄγδοος βήρυλλος, ὁ ἔνατος τοπάζιον,
ὁ δέκατος χρυσόπρασος, ὁ ἑνδέκατος ὑάκινθος, ὁ δωδέκατος
ἀμέθυστος·

21. καὶ οἱ δώδεκα πυλῶνες δώδεκα μαργαρῖται,
ἀνὰ εἷς ἕκαστος τῶν πυλώνων ἦν ἐξ ἑνὸς μαργαρίτου·
καὶ ἡ πλατεῖα τῆς πόλεως χρυσίον καθαρὸν ὡς ὕαλος διαυγής.

22. καὶ ναὸν οὐκ εἶδον ἐν αὐτῇ,
ὁ γὰρ κύριος, ὁ θεὸς ὁ παντοκράτωρ, ὁ ναὸς αὐτῆς ἐστίν,
καὶ τὸ ἀρνίον < ἡ κιβωτὸς τῆς διαθήκης αὐτῆς >.(*a*)

(*a*) Lacuna restored by means of xi. 19. See vol. ii. 170 sq.

ιβ′) | χαλκηδων] χαλκι- (χαλκε- 2020) 046 min^{mu} vg$^{a.\ c}$: καρχ- 2018. 2050 vg$^{f.\ g.\ v}$ s^1 bo : καλιδων s^2 : sardonius (-icus vg^d) Tyc vg^d |.

20. σμαραρδοσ] ασμαρ- 2050 | σαρδονυξ] σαρδωνυξ 149. 1934 al^p : σαλδονυξ 2024 : σαρδιονυξ (-δινυξ 2050) A 2050 | σαρδιον] σαρδιοσ 1. 35. 104. 205. 2020. 2037. 2038. 2067 al^p Pr vg^v : sardinus (-onium Tyc : -inon bo) Tyc vg^v bo : σαριδον (σαρδον s^1) s | βηρυλλοσ ℵ min^{pl} vg s : βηριλλοσ A 385 (Tyc) Pr gig : βηρυλλιοσ (-ιον 025 : βιρυλλ- 046 : βηριλλ- 1) 025. 046. 051. 1. 61. 104. 175. 617. 2016. 2036. 2037. 2038** : βηρυλλησ 2050 : βυρηλλοσ (βυριλλ- 2023 bo) 149. 2023 bo | ενατοσ A 046 min^{pl} : εννατοσ 025. 051. 35*. 205. 241. 242. 385. 522. 632. 2016. 2023. 2037. 2038. 2050. 2067 al^{mu} : εθ′ ℵ | τοπαζιον] τοπαδιον ℵ* (s^2) : τοπανζιον (τοπανδιον s^1) 025 s^1 : παζιον 456 : topaxinos Pr : dopation bo | χρυσοπρασοσ] -ον A : -ιοσ ℵ^c : -σσοσ 104 Pr vg$^{a.\ g}$: -ινοσ 42. 325. 517. 620. 1918 Tyc : -πασοσ (-πασσοσ 498 : παστοσ 61. 141. 2024). 61. 82. 141. 337. 385. 429*. 456. 498. 522. 1849. 2024 : chrysoliprassus vg$^{f.\ v}$ | υακινθοσ] υακινθινον Tyc (bo) : iacinctus gig | αμεθυστοσ A 025. 046. 110. 175. 325. 456. 617. 620. 2004. 2038* al^{mu} : -ινοσ ℵ* : αμεθυσοσ ℵ^c 051. 18 (– 175. 325. 456. 617. 2004). 1. 104 al^{pl} : αμυθεσοσ s^1 |.

21. οι δωδεκα πυλωνεσ] duodecim portas Pr : ideo Tyc | δωδ. μαργ. >Pr | δωδεκα² >ℵ* 2030 bo | μαργαριται] + εισιν vg | ανα] ινα A 2018 : pr και 456 : pr εισ s^1 | εισ] + και 025 Tyc vg s^1 : > 205 | των πυλ. . . . μαργαριτου > bo | τ. πυλ. ην >Pr | πυλωνων] πυλων 498. 2020 : + ων ℵ* | εξ] pr ωσ 025. 046. 61. 2036 | πλατ. τ. πολ.] plateas eius Pr | χρυσ. καθ.] ex auro limpido (puro s^1 arm$^{1.\ 2.\ a}$) Pr s^1 arm$^{1.\ 2.\ a}$ | ωσ] και 051 Tyc | υαλοσ (-ον 205) Aℵ 025. 046. 175. 205. 456. 617 : υελοσ (υελλ- 385. 498. 2020) min^{pl} | διαυγησ] διαυγεσ 205 |.

22. ναον ουκ ειδον] ουκ ειδον ναον bo sa eth | εν αυτη] εν αυτω 149 : >eth | ο γαρ] οτι ο ℵ* : ο γαρ ο ℵ^c | κυριοσ ο (>ℵ^c) θεοσ Aℵ 025. 046 min^{pl} Tyc Pr gig vg s^2 arm$^{2.\ 4.\ a}$ bo sa : θεοσ 337. 1934 eth : κυριοσ 920 s^2 arm^1 | ο⁴ A s^2 : αυτοσ s^1 : >ℵ 025. 046

23. *καὶ ἡ πόλις οὐ χρείαν ἔχει τοῦ ἡλίου οὐδὲ τῆς σελήνης ἵνα*
φαίνωσιν αὐτῇ,
ἡ γὰρ δόξα τοῦ θεοῦ ἐφώτισεν αὐτήν,
καὶ ὁ λύχνος αὐτῆς τὸ ἀρνίον.

24. *καὶ περιπατήσουσιν τὰ ἔθνη διὰ τοῦ φωτὸς αὐτῆς,*
καὶ οἱ βασιλεῖς τῆς γῆς φέρουσιν τὴν δόξαν αὐτῶν εἰς αὐτήν,
25. *καὶ οἱ πυλῶνες αὐτῆς οὐ μὴ κλεισθῶσιν ἡμέρας † νὺξ γὰρ*
οὐκ ἔσται ἐκεῖ †. (*a*)

26. *καὶ οἴσουσιν τὴν δόξαν καὶ τὴν τιμὴν τῶν ἐθνῶν εἰς αὐτήν,*

(*a*) Read *καὶ νυκτός*. See vol. ii. 173.

min^{omn} | *ο ναοσ αυτ. εστιν*] tr after *αρνιον* Pr | *εστιν* > 104 | *το* > 2050 | *αρνιον*] + "the only begotten son (> 2) of God (+ is 2) altar of holiness" arm$^{1.2}$ | *κ. το αρνιον*] joined with what follows 046 s^{1} |.

23. *πολισ*] + *αυτη* 498. 2020 | *εχει*] *ειχε* arm bo | *ουδε*] *ουτε* 2050 : *και* arm$^{1.2.a}$ | *ινα*] et Tyc | *φαινωσιν*] *φαινουσιν* 051. 2050 : *φαινη* Pr | *αυτη* Aℵ* 025. 046. **18** (– 35) al^{pl} Pr gig s eth : pr *εν* ℵ^{c} 051. 35. 1957. 2023. 2037. 2041 al^{p} vg bo sa : *αυτην* 2018. 2036. 2067 al^{p} (arm$^{1.2.a}$) | *αὐτῇ· η γαρ* Aℵ 025. 35. 175. 205. 617. 2020. 2050 al Pr gig vg s arm$^{1.a}$ bo eth : *αὐτὴ γαρ η* 046. **18** (– 35. 175. 205. 617. 2020. 2050) al^{mu} arm^{4} | *θεου*] *κυριου* Pr | *εφωτισεν*] *φωτιζει* Pr eth : *φωτισει* Tyc vg$^{d.g.v}$ arm^{4} | *αυτησ*] *αυτου και* 2037 : + *και* 2036 : + *εστιν* 2021 Tyc gig vg s^{1} : + *ην* arm$^{1.2.a}$ |.

24. *εθνη*] + *των σωζομενων* 1 | *δια τ. φωτοσ*] *εν τω φωτι* 2050 Tyc vg^{v} | *και οι* > 2050 | *φερουσιν* (afferent gig vg bo : conferent Pr) Aℵ 025. 35. 2020. 2050 Tyc Pr gig vg s arm^{4} bo : + *αυτω* (*αυτη* 205) 046. **18** (– 35. 2020. 2050) al^{pl} | *την* Aℵ 025. 35. 632**. 2020. 2050 : > 046. **18** (– 35. 632**. 2020. 2050) al^{pl} | *δοξαν* Aℵ 025. 1. 35. 60. 94. 241. 632**. 2020. 2036. 2037. 2038. 2050. 2067 Pr gig (vg) s^{1} arm^{4} bo sa : + *και* (+ *την* 250) *τιμην* 046. **18** (– 35. 632**. 2020. 2050). 42. 110. 201. 209. 242. 250. 385. 429. 498. 522. 2016. 2017. 2024. 2039 al^{mu} | *αυτων* Aℵ 025. 35. 632**. 2020. 2050 al^{mu} Pr gig (vg s^{2}) arm^{4} sa : *των εθνων* (> 205) 046. **18** (– 35. 632**. 2020. 2050). 250 al^{pl} (bo) : + *και την τιμην* (+ *των εθνων* s^{2}) vg s^{2} bo | verses 25, 26 > 337 |.

25. *οι* > 205 | *οι πυλ. αυτ.*] tr after *κλεισθωσιν* sa eth | *ημερασ*] *ημερα* ℵ* : + *και νυκτοσ* arm^{a} | *νυξ γαρ*] *και νυξ* arm $^{1.a}$ bo | *ουκ*] *ουκετι* 205 arm$^{1.2.a}$ | *εσται*] *εστιν* 617 Tyc arm$^{2.4}$: *ην* arm$^{1.a}$ | *εκει*] tr before *ουκ εστιν* Tyc |.

26. *οισουσιν*] ponet Pr : *ηξουσιν* bo^{codd} (*οισουσιν* bo^{a}) | *την*^{2} > 2050 | *δοξαν*] + *αυτων* bo eth | *τιμην*] + *αυτων* bo eth | *των εθνων*] *τα εθνη* bo eth | *εισ αυτην* (in illa gig : in ea Pr) Aℵ 025. 35. 205. 632**. 2050 Pr gig vg s arm^{4} bo : + *ινα εισελθωσιν* 046. **18** (– 35. 205. 632**. 2050) al^{pl} |.

27. καὶ οὐ μὴ εἰσέλθῃ εἰς αὐτὴν † πᾶν κοινὸν † (a) καὶ ποιῶν
βδέλυγμα καὶ ψεῦδος,
εἰ μὴ οἱ γεγραμμένοι ἐν τῷ βιβλίῳ τῆς ζωῆς τοῦ ἀρνίου.

xxii. 1. Καὶ ἔδειξέν μοι ποταμὸν ὕδατος ζωῆς λαμπρὸν ὡς κρύσ-
ταλλον,
ἐκπορευόμενον ἐκ τοῦ θρόνου τοῦ θεοῦ καὶ τοῦ ἀρνίου 2. ἐν
μέσῳ τῆς πλατείας αὐτῆς,
καὶ τοῦ ποταμοῦ ἐντεῦθεν καὶ ἐκεῖθεν ξύλον ζωῆς,

⌜ποιοῦν⌝ καρποὺς δώδεκα, ποιῶν
κατὰ μῆνα ἕκαστον ⌜ἀποδιδοῦν⌝ τὸν καρπὸν αὐτοῦ· ἀποδιδούς
καὶ τὰ φύλλα τοῦ ξύλου εἰς θεραπείαν τῶν ἐθνῶν.

(*a*) Primitive corruption for πᾶς κοινός. As the rest of the verse (cf. xxii. 15) shows, only persons are contemplated: cf. vol. ii. 173 sq. arm$^{4.(2.a)}$ definitely restore the text. s$^{1.2}$ are susceptible of either text.

27. και^{1} > vg^{d} bo | εισελθη] εισελθωσιν א : εισελθοι 2050 : εσται s^{1} | εισ αυτην] επ αυτην 2050 : in ea Pr gig vg : εκει s^{1} arm$^{1.2.a}$ | παν κοινον] "anyone corrupt (of evil will arm$^{1.2.a}$)" arm | ποιων Aא^{c} 61. 94. 2021. 2032. 2050 : ποιουν 025. 046. 051. 1. 35. 175. 250. 617. 1934. 2037. 2038. 2067 : faciens Tyc Pr vg : ο ποιων א* **18** (−35. 175. 617. 1934. 2050). 42. 82. 93. 104. 110. 141. 201. 241 336 al^{pl} s (arm^{4}) : quod facit gig : οι ποιουντεσ bo | βδελυγμα] pr ωσει א* | και ψευδοσ] vitae Pr | οι γεγραμμενοι] οι εγγεγραμ. 2016. 2050 : τα γεγραμμενα s^{1} : quorum nomina illorum (sua arm^{2}) scripta sunt arm$^{1.2}$ | εν] επι bo | τω βιβλιω] τη βιβλω 2050 | τησ ζωησ > Pr s^{1} | του αρνιου] του ουρανου א : του βιβλιου 2050 : illius agni Pr |.

xxii. 1. ποταμον Aא 025. 046. **17** (−35. 175. 205. 617. 1934. 2020) al^{mu} Tyc Pr gig vg s arm$^{(1).4}$ bo sa eth : + καθαρον 35. 104. 175. 205. 209. 218. 242. 250. 506. 617. 1934. 1957. 2016. 2017. 2020. 2023. 2036. 2037. 2038. 2041. 2067 : pr καθαρον 1 arm^{a} | υδατοσ ζωησ] υδωρ ζων arm^{4} : ζωντα υδατοσ arm^{a} : aquae vivae gig vg$^{a.c.f}$ | ζωησ > Tyc | λαμπρον] λαμπροσ 2050 : λαμπρον gig : candidum Pr eth : pr καθαρον και s^{1} : > 141. 2020. 2038 Tyc | ωσ] ωσει 175. 617 | κρυσταλλον] -οσ 2050 : -σταλον 632 : + και s^{1} | του^{1} > א | θρονου] στοματοσ 61 |.

2. εν μεσω] εμμεσω A 2050 : pr και 2050 gig s^{1} : per mediam (plateam) Pr | τησ πλατειασ] των πλατειων s^{1} arm$^{1.a}$: τησ πολεωσ 1934 | και^{1}] επι s^{1} : + επι s^{2} | του ποτ.] tr after εκειθεν Tyc Pr vg s^{1} | εντευθεν] ενθεν א* | εκειθ. ξυλ. ζωησ] > א* : ενθεν א^{c} | εκειθεν A 046. **17** (−35. 205. 632**. 2050). 250 al^{pl} gig s^{2} arm$^{1.a}$ bo sa : εντευθεν 051. 1. 35. 205. 632**. 1957. 2018. 2023. 2036. 2037. 2038. 2050. 2067 s^{1} | ξυλον] "trees" arm^{a} | ποιουν א 046. 051. **17** al$^{fere\ omn}$: ποιων A 94 | δωδεκα] ιβ′ 35. 205. 337. 617 : duodecies gig arm^{1} : + και s^{1} | κατα μηνα (μηναν A) εκαστον αποδιδουν

14. Μακάριοι οἱ πλύνοντες τὰς στολὰς αὐτῶν,
ἵνα ἔσται ἡ ἐξουσία αὐτῶν ἐπὶ τὸ ξύλον τῆς ζωῆς,
καὶ τοῖς πυλῶσιν εἰσέλθωσιν εἰς τὴν πόλιν.

15. ἔξω οἱ κύνες καὶ οἱ φαρμακοί,
καὶ οἱ πόρνοι καὶ οἱ φονεῖς καὶ οἱ εἰδωλολάτραι,
καὶ πᾶς φιλῶν καὶ ποιῶν ψεῦδος.

17. καὶ τὸ πνεῦμα καὶ ἡ νύμφη λέγουσιν Ἔρχου·
καὶ ὁ ἀκούων εἰπάτω Ἔρχου·
καὶ ὁ διψῶν ἐρχέσθω·
ὁ θέλων λαβέτω ὕδωρ ζωῆς δωρεάν.

(-διδον 175) A 175. 250. 617. 2037. 2038. 2067 al s^{1}? : *κατα μηνα εκαστον* (*εκαστοσ* 2020) *αποδιδουσ* ℵ 35. 2020. 2050 al : *κ. μηνα* (> arm^{1}) *ενα εκαστον αποδιδουν* (*-διδοντα* 1 : *-διδουσ* 051. 2038) 051. 1. 205. 2038. 2067 (arm$^{1.\,a}$) : *κ. μ. αποδιδουσ εκαστοσ* 325. 337. 456. 620 al s^{2}? : *κ. μ. αποδιδουσ* (*-διδουν* 386. 632) *εκαστον* 18. 386. 632. 1849. 1934. 2004 al : *κ. μ. αποδιδουσ εκαστω* 046. (141. 1918) : per singulos menses et (> Pr gig) reddens (reddentes Pr) Tyc Pr gig : per menses singulos reddens vg$^{d.\,v}$: per menses singulos (singula vg$^{a*.\,f.\,g}$) reddentia vg$^{a.\,c.\,f.\,g}$ | *αποδιδ. τ. καρπ. αυτ.* > bo eth | *τ. καρπον*] *τουσ καρπουσ* ℵ s^{1} : *τον* > 1. 18. 61. 141. 385. 429. 632*. 1849. 2004 | *αυτου*] *αυτων* 2050 arm^{a} : > 205 | *τ. ξυλ.*] *των ξυλων* ℵ arm^{a} : *αυτου* s^{1} : + *καταγγελλεται* 175. 218. 617. 2016. 2017 | *των*] > ℵ : "the eyes of the" bo |.

14. **πλυνοντεσ** (**-αντεσ** 104. 2050) **τασ στολασ αυτων** (+ in sanguine agni vg^{d}) Aℵ 104. 2020. 2050 (Pr) vg sa eth : *ποιουντεσ τασ εντολασ αυτου* (*εμου* 2067) 046. **17** (– 2020. 2050). 250. 2037. 2038. 2067 al^{pl} gig Cyp s arm$^{(1).\,4.\,a}$ bo : (qui) servant mandata haec Tyc | *ινα* > s^{1} arm^{1} | *εσται*] tr after *αυτων*^{2} bo sa | *αυτων*^{2}] + *ωσ δε η εξουσια* ℵ* | *τοισ πυλ.*] *τω πυλωνι* s^{1} bo : + *ου μη* 2050 | *εισελθωσιν*] *εισελευσονται* s^{1} arm^{4} bo | *εισ την πολιν*] + *την αγιαν* Pr : *τησ πολεωσ* (+ *του θεου* arm^{1}) arm$^{1.\,a}$ |.

15. **εξω . . . φαρμακοι**] tr after *ειδωλολατραι* s^{1} | *εξω*] + *δε* (*και* s^{1}) s^{1} bo sa : foris autem remanebunt Pr arm^{1} : "and there shall go forth" arm$^{4.\,a}$ eth | *κυνεσ*] *κοινοι* s^{1} | *οι φαρμακοι*] malefici Pr | *και*^{2} > Tyc | *οι*^{5} > 175. 1934 | *ειδωλολατραι*] + venefici Pr : + "adulterers" arm^{1} | *πασ* Aℵ 046. **17** (– 175. 205. 617. 632**. 1934. 2020. 2050) al^{mu} : + *ο* 1. 104. 175. 205. 250. 429*. 617. 632**. 1934. 2016. 2017. 2020. 2032. 2036. 2037. 2038. 2050. 2067 al^{mu} : *παντεσ οι* 94 arm bo eth | *φιλων και ποιων* A 046. **17** (– 175. 617. 1934). 2037. 2038. 2067 al^{pl} Tyc Pr vg s$^{(1).\,2}$: *ποιων και* (+ *ο* 2018. 2032) *φιλων* ℵ 91. 175. 218. 242. 250. 424. 617. 664. 1934. 2016. 2017. 2018 gig : *ποιουντεσ* arm^{4} bo : *φιλουντεσ* arm^{a} : *φιλουντεσ ποιειν* eth |.

17. **και**^{1} > Tyc | *το* > ℵ bo | *πνευμα*] + *αγιον* arm^{1} eth | *η*

Chapter XX. 4–15.

4^{c} Καὶ <εἶδον> τὰς ψυχὰς τῶν πεπελεκισμένων διὰ τὴν μαρτυρίαν Ἰησοῦ (*a*)
d καὶ διὰ τὸν λόγον τοῦ θεοῦ,

e καὶ [οἵτινες] οὐ προσεκύνησαν τὸ θηρίον
f οὐδὲ τὴν εἰκόνα αὐτοῦ,

g καὶ οὐκ ἔλαβον τὸ χάραγμα ἐπὶ τὸ μέτωπον
h καὶ ἐπὶ τὴν χεῖρα αὐτῶν,

a καὶ εἶδον θρόνους καὶ ἐκάθισαν ἐπ᾽ αὐτούς,
b καὶ κρίμα ἐδόθη αὐτοῖς.

(*a*) I have restored 4$^{a.\,b}$ to their original place after 4^{h}. See vol. **ii.** 182 sq.

> ℵ | λεγουσιν] ελεγον 051. 35 | ερχου^{1} > arm^{4} | και ο ακουων . . . ερχου > arm^{1} eth | ο^{1} > 18 | ο ακουων] qui vidit gig : pr his Pr | ερχου και^{2} > Pr | και^{4} > arm^{1} | ο^{2} > 456 | ερχεσθω]+ et bibat Pr | ο θελων] pr και 209. 218. 2050 s^{2} arm^{a} sa : > gig s^{1} | λαβετω] λαβειν Tyc s^{2} arm^{a} : pr και s^{2} | ζωησ] pr τησ 2050 |.

xx. 4$^{c\text{-}h}$. και ειδον (2050) Cyp : και Aℵ 046. **18** (– 2050) al^{omn} Tyc Pr gig vg s arm : περι bo eth | τ. πεπελεκισμενων] -κιμενων 175 : -κημενων 201. 386 : τ. πεπολεμημενων A : occisorum Pr gig Cyp : decollatorum vg : τασ πεπελεκισμενασ s^{1} | κ. οιτινεσ] ει τινεσ ουν ℵ cf et si qui Pr gig : "they are those who" arm$^{1.\,2.\,a}$ | προσεκυνησαν] προσεκυνουν 386 | το (τω 920) θηριον Aℵ 046. **18** (– 18. 35. 175. 337. 617. 620. 2040) al^{pl} : τω (το 620) θηριω 1. 18. 35. 175. 250. 337. 617. 620. 1957. 2017. 2023. 2037. 2038. 2039. 2040. 2067 al | ουδε] ουτε 051. 1. 35. 175. 250. 617. 2037. 2038. 2067 al^{pm} | την εικονα Aℵ 046. **18** (– 620. 2040. 2050). 1. 250. 2037*. 2038 al^{pl} : τη εικονι 104. 620. 1957. 2023. 2037**. 2067 al | ελαβον] ελαβε 18 | χαραγμα]+του θηριου 2040 : +eius vg | το μετωπον Aℵ 046. **18** (– 386. 620. 2050) Pr gig arm bo : των μετωπων 104. 181. 201. 336. 386. 620. 1918. 2036. 2037. 2050. 2067 vg : +αυτων 1. 35. 1957. 2023. 2036. 2037. 2038 s^{1} arm bo sa eth | επι^{2} > 2040 | τ. χειρα] τασ χειρασ 386 vg s^{1} : την δεξιαν χειρα arm$^{1.\,a}$ |.

4$^{a.\,b}$. εκαθισαν] sedentes Pr arm^{1} | κ. εκαθισαν] (τοισ) καθισασι bo | επ] επανω 1934 | αυτουσ] αυτοισ 2050 | και^{3} > arm$^{1.\,2}$ bo | κριμα εδοθ.] ~ 386 |.

4^{i}. καὶ ἔζησαν καὶ ἐβασίλευσαν μετὰ τοῦ χριστοῦ χίλια ἔτη. (*a*)
5^{b}. αὕτη ἡ ἀνάστασις ἡ πρώτη.
6. Μακάριος καὶ ἅγιος ὁ ἔχων μέρος ἐν τῇ ἀναστάσει τῇ πρώτῃ.
ἐπὶ τούτων ὁ δεύτερος θάνατος οὐκ ἔχει ἐξουσίαν,
ἀλλ' ἔσονται ἱερεῖς τοῦ θεοῦ καὶ τοῦ χριστοῦ,
καὶ βασιλεύσουσιν μετ' αὐτοῦ [τὰ] χίλια ἔτη.

(*a*) Text adds 5^{a} : οἱ λοιποὶ τῶν νεκρῶν οὐκ ἔζησαν ἄχρι τελεσθῇ τὰ χίλια ἔτη —unobjectionable as far as diction is concerned but rejected as a gloss on the following grounds advanced by Mr. Marsh. (1) It is prosaic and made up of words borrowed from 4^{i} 3^{a} or 7^{a}. (2) If it were original we should expect it to be introduced either by καί used adversatively or δέ as in 21^{8}. The asyndetic construction in 19^{20} is not parallel, for there the thought of the preceding sentences is simply developed further. (3) It spoils the metre. (4) 5^{b} follows more naturally a positive than a negative statement.

4^{i}. κ. εζησαν κ. ἐβασιλ.] *ουσ ιλευσαν* (sic) 2050 | *κ. εζησαν κ.* >Pr | *και*^{1}] hi omnes Tyc : *οι* s^{1} : *ουτοι* (+*εισιν οι* arm$^{1.2}$) arm$^{1.2}$ eth : > bo sa | *εζησαν*] *εζητησαν* 920 : *ζησουσιν* arm$^{1.2.4}$ eth : +*μετ αυτου* bo | *εβασιλευσαν*] *βασιλευσουσιν* (*-ουσιν* arm^{4}) arm$^{1.4}$ eth | *του* > 1. 2017. 2038. 2067 | *τ. χριστου*] Iesu Pr | *χιλια ετη* Aℵ 1. 35. 175. 181. 250. 424. 617. 1957. 2017. 2023. 2036. 2037. 2038. 2041. 2050. 2067 s^{1} arm$^{2.4.a}$ bo : pr *τα* 046. **18** (−35. 175. 617. 2050) al^{pl} s^{2} : >arm^{1} |.

5. οι λοιποι . . . χιλ. ετη A 046. 35. 175^{mg}. 250. (617). 632. 1934. 2020. 2037. 2038. 2040. 2050. 2067 al^{p} Pr gig vg (arm) bo sa : > ℵ **18** (−35. 175**. 617. 632. 2020. 2040. 2050). 61. 69. 104. 110. 385 al^{mu} s | *οι λοιποι* A Pr gig vg : pr *και* 046. 1. 35. 175**. 181. 250. 336. 617. 632. 1934. 2016. 2020. 2023. 2037. 2038. 2040. 2050. 2067 arm^{4} bo (sa) eth : *και μετα ταυτα* arm$^{1.2.a}$ | *των νεκρων*] pr *εκ* arm$^{1.2.a}$: *αυτων* Pr | *νεκρων* A 35. 1934. 2020. 2040. 2050 al gig vg arm^{4} bo sa eth : *ανθρωπων* 046. 175. 250. 424. 617. 2017 | *εζησαν*] *ανεστησαν* 1. 250 : *ζησεται* (*-ονται* arm^{4}) arm | *τελεσθη*] *τελεσθηναι* 2020 : *τελεσθωσι* 2036. 2037 | *αυτη*] pr *οτι* 104. 336. 620. 1918 : pr *και* s^{1} eth : haec est itaque Tyc |.

6. μακαριοσ] pr *και* 18. 632*. 1849. 2004 | *κ. αγιοσ*] *κ. ο αγιοσ* 2050 : > 61. 69 | *εν τη αναστασει*] +*ταυτη* Pr : + *αυτου* 920 | *επι*] pr *οτι* 2050 arm^{4} : pr *και* s^{1} arm^{2} | *τουτων*] *τουτον* (*-τω* 69) 61. 69. 385. 2036 Tyc | *ο δευτ. θαν.*] *ο θαν. ο δευτ.* 1. 2023. 2036. 2037. 2038 | *αλλ*] *αλλα* ℵ | *του θεου κ. του χριστου*] pr *και* ℵ : *τω θεω κ. τω χριστω* 2020 s^{1} : *του Ιησου χριστου* (*θεου κ. του κυρ. ιησ. χριστ.* arm$^{1.2.a}$) arm | *βασιλευσουσιν* ℵ 046. **18** al^{omn} Tyc Pr gig vg s arm bo sa : *βασιλευουσιν* A | *μετ αυτου* Aℵ 046. 35. 175. 617. 632**. 920. 2020 2040. 2050 Tyc Pr gig vg s arm bo eth : *μετα ταυτα* **18** (−35. 175. 617. 632**. 920. 2020. 2040. 2050). 82. 110. 141. 201. 242. 336. 498. 1918 | *τ. χιλ. ετη* >arm^{1} | *τα* ℵ 046. 61. 69. 94. 241. 386. (632**). 920. 2020 : >A 051. **18** (−386. 632**. 920. 2020). 250. 2037. 2038. 2067 al^{pl} arm$^{2.4.a}$ |.

7. Καὶ ὅταν τελεσθῇ τὰ χίλια ἔτη, λυθήσεται ὁ Σατανᾶς ἐκ τῆς
φυλακῆς αὐτοῦ, 8. καὶ ἐξελεύσεται πλανῆσαι τὰ ἔθνη τὰ ἐν ταῖς
τέσσαρσι γωνίαις τῆς γῆς, τὸν Γὼγ καὶ Μαγώγ, συναγαγεῖν αὐτοὺς
εἰς τὸν πόλεμον, ὧν ὁ ἀριθμὸς αὐτῶν ὡς ἡ ἄμμος τῆς θαλάσσης.
9. καὶ ἀνέβησαν ἐπὶ τὸ πλάτος τῆς γῆς, καὶ ἐκύκλευσαν τὴν παρεμ-
βολὴν τῶν ἁγίων καὶ τὴν πόλιν τὴν ἠγαπημένην. καὶ κατέβη πῦρ ^{T} ἀπὸ τοῦ
ἐκ τοῦ οὐρανοῦ καὶ κατέφαγεν αὐτούς. 10. καὶ ὁ διάβολος ὁ θεοῦ
πλανῶν αὐτοὺς ἐβλήθη εἰς τὴν λίμνην τοῦ πυρὸς καὶ θείου, ὅπου καὶ

7. οταν τελεσθη (οτε ετελεσθησαν 1 : οτε ετελεσθη s^{1}) Aℵ 35. 175. 250. 617. 2020. 2037. 2038. 2040. 2050. 2067 al Tyc Pr gig vg s arm^{4} bo sa eth : μετα 046. **18** (– 35. 175. 617. 2020. 2040. 2050). 61. 69. 104. 385 al^{pl} arm$^{1.2.a}$ | αυτου >arm$^{1.2.a}$ bo eth |.

8. εξελευσεται >bo | πλανησαι] και πλανησει (+τουσ δουλουσ και bo) vg arm$^{2.a}$ bo | τα εθνη A 046. **18** (– 386) Tyc Pr gig vg s^{2} arm$^{2.4}$ (bo) eth : pr παντα ℵ 2036 s^{1} (arm$^{1.a}$) : τα >386 | τα^{2} A 046. **18** (– 149). 250. 2037. 2038. 2067 al^{pl} Tyc Pr gig vg s^{2} arm^{4} : >ℵ 61. 69. 149. 172. 2018 s^{1} bo sa | ταισ > 1. 69. 432 | τεσσαρσι] τετρασι ℵ : τεσσαρα 617 | τ. γησ > ℵ* | τον^{1} Aℵ^{c} 046. **18** al^{omn} : > ℵ* bo sa | τ. Γωγ κ. Μ. συναγ. αυτ.] "Gog and Magog shall be gathered" bo eth | Μαγωγ Aℵ* 1. 1934. 2036. 2037. 2050 bo sa : pr τον ℵ^{c} 046. **18** (– 1934. 2050). 250. 2067 al^{pl} | συναγαγειν A 046. **18** (– 35. 175. 617). 250. 2067 al^{pl} s^{2} arm$^{1.2.a}$ sa : pr και ℵ 051. 35. 175. 617. 2016. 2017. 2036 s^{1} arm^{4} : και συναγει 181 : et congregabit (-avit gig : trahet Pr) Pr gig vg | τον^{2} Aℵ 046. **18** (– 175. 617) al^{pl} : >051. 1. 175. 250. 617. 2023. 2036. 2037. 2038. 2067 | ων > 2050 | αυτων Aℵ 046. **18** (– 35. 175. 617. 1934. 2020) al^{pl} (s) arm$^{1.2.a}$: > 1. 35. 175. 242. 250. 617. 1934. 2020. 2023. 2036. 2037. 2038. 2067 Pr gig vg arm^{4} | ωσ η] ωσει 42. 82. 104. 201. 325. 385. 386. 456. 498. 620. 632. 920. 1918. 1934 |.

9. και ανεβησαν] >61. 69 : + diabolus et populus eius Tyc | πλατοσ] altitudinem Tyc gig | εκυκλευσαν A 046. **18** (– 35*. 175. 337. 617. 620. 1934. 2020. 2050). 82. 110. 385. 2023 al^{mu} : εκυκλωσαν ℵ 051. 1. 35*. 104. 175. 250. 337. 617. 620. 1934. 2016. 2020. 2037. 2038. 2050. 2067 | τ. παρεμβ. τ. αγ.] + και την πολιν των αγιων 046. 498 : την πολιν τησ παρεμβολησ των αγιων s^{1} | τ. ηγαπημενην] dilectorum Tyc : την καινην bo : την αγιαν eth | κατεβη] ascendit gig | πυρ . . . εισ τ. λιμνην > ℵ* | εκ] απο 051. 1. 35. 93. 205. 620. 2038 | εκ τ. ουρ. A 94. 181. 2036. 2037 Pr : pr απο (εκ 051. 1. 35. 93. 205. 2038) του (>35. 2038) θεου ℵ^{c} 025. 051. 1. 35. 93. 104. 205. 2037. 2040. 2050 al vg s^{2} arm^{4} : + απο του θεου 046. **19** (– 35. 205. 2040. 2050). 250. 2067. al^{pl} Tyc gig s arm$^{1.2.a}$ bo sa eth |.

10. και θειου A 025. 046. **19** (– 325. 620. 632**. 2040. 2050). 1 al sa : και (>620) του θειου ℵ 42. 94. 104. 172. 218. 241. 250.

τὸ θηρίον καὶ ὁ ψευδοπροφήτης, καὶ βασανισθήσονται ἡμέρας καὶ νυκτὸς εἰς τοὺς αἰῶνας τῶν αἰώνων.

11. *Καὶ εἶδον θρόνον μέγαν λευκὸν καὶ τὸν καθήμενον ἐπ'*
† αὐτοῦ,† (*a*)
οὗ ἀπὸ [τοῦ] (*b*) *προσώπου ἔφυγεν ἡ γῆ καὶ ὁ οὐρανός,*
καὶ τόπος οὐχ εὑρέθη αὐτοῖς.

12. *καὶ εἶδον τοὺς νεκροὺς τοὺς μεγάλους καὶ τοὺς μικροὺς ἑστῶτας ἐνώπιον τοῦ θρόνου,*
καὶ βιβλία ἠνοίχθησαν, καὶ ἄλλο βιβλίον ἠνοίχθη ὅ ἐστιν τῆς ζωῆς,
καὶ ἐκρίθησαν οἱ νεκροὶ ἐκ τῶν γεγραμμένων ἐν τοῖς βιβλίοις [κατὰ τὰ ἔργα αὐτῶν].

(*a*) Wrong construction due to editor.
(*b*) An interpolation by the editor (?) ; cf. vi. 16, xii. 14.

325. 336. 632**. 1918. 2017. 2018. 2023. 2036. 2037. 2040. 2067 al : *την καιομενην πυρι* (*θειω* bo) 2050 bo : >2038 | *και*^{3} A 025. 046. **19** (– 205. 2050). 250. 2037 al^{pl} Tyc Pr gig vg s^2 : > ℵ 1. 205. 1957. 2050 s^1 arm$^{1.2.a}$ bo sa eth | *και*^{4}] + *οπου* ℵ : > 620 | *ο ψευδοπροφ.*] + *εβληθησαν* 2050 : *οι ψευδοπροφηται* Tyc arm^1 | *βασανισθησονται*] + *εκει* 2050 | *εισ. τ. αιων. τ. αιων.* > 1. 181. 2038 arm^a | *των αιωνων* >241. 336**. 2067 |.

11. **θρονον μεγαν**] ~ bo sa | *μεγαν*] *μεγα* 2050 | *μεγαν* (+ *και* 2050 Pr arm$^{1.4}$ eth) *λευκον* Aℵ 025. 046. **19** (– 18. 175. 205. 337. 617. 2020) al Pr gig vg s arm$^{1.4}$ bo sa eth : ~ 1. 175. 205. 250. 617. 2020. 2037. 2038. 2067 arm^a : *μεγαν* >18. 337 | *επ*] *επανω* ℵ 2020 s bo sa | *αυτου* Aℵ 1. 2020. 2040 : *αυτον* 025. 046. **19** (– 2020. 2040). 250. 2037 al^{pl} : *αυτω* 218. 2018. 2038. 2067 | *του* Aℵ 025. 2040. 2050 : >046. **19** (– 2040. 2050) al^{pl} | *προσωπου*] + *αυτου* 2040 s arm$^{1.2}$ | *η γη και ο* (>2050) *ουρ.* Aℵ 025. 046. **19** (– 35) al^{pl} gig vg s bo sa : *ο ουρ. κ. η γη* 35. 60. 432. 1957. 2023. 2041 Pr arm eth | *αυτοισ*] eorum Pr bo : ab eis vg : in illis gig |.

12. **μεγαλ. . . . μικρουσ**] ~ 046. 91. 175. 242. 250. 506. 617. 1934. 2016. 2017 bo | *τ.* (*και* ℵ*) *μεγ. κ. τ. μικρ.* (*τ. μικρ. κ. τ. μεγ.*) placed before *εστωτασ* Aℵ 025. 046. 35. 205. 632**. 2020. 2037. 2038. 2050. 2067 al^{mu} Tyc gig vg s arm$^{4.a}$ bo sa eth : placed after *εστωτασ* 91. 175. 242. 250. 506. 617. 1934. 2016. 2017 : placed before *τουσ νεκρουσ* 104. 620 : >1. 18. 82. 93. 110. 201. 325. 337. 385. 386. 429. 452. 456. 498. 517. 522. 632*. 920. 1849. 2004. 2024. 2039 | *εστωτασ ενωπ. τ. θρ.* > Pr arm^2 | *εστωτασ* >61. 69. 82. 429 | *ενωπιον*] *επι* ℵ* : *ενωπιον επι* ℵ^c | *θρονου*] *θεου* 1. 2037. 2067 al | *βιβλια*] *βιβλοι* 2050 : *βιβλιον* 386 | *ηνοιχθησαν . . . ηνοιχθη*] *ηνεωχθη* ℵ* : *ηνεωχθη και αλλο βιβλιον ηνεωχθη* ℵ^c | *ηνοιχθησαν* A 025. 046. 1. 61. 69. 172. 175. 218. 242. 250. 1934. 2016.

13. καὶ ἔδωκεν † ἡ θάλασσα † (*a*) τοὺς νεκροὺς τοὺς ἐν † αὐτῇ, † (*a*) καὶ ὁ θάνατος καὶ ὁ ᾅδης ἔδωκαν τοὺς νεκροὺς τοὺς ἐν αὐτοῖς, καὶ ἐκρίθησαν ἕκαστος κατὰ τὰ ἔργα αὐτῶν.

14. καὶ ὁ θάνατος καὶ ὁ ᾅδης ἐβλήθησαν εἰς τὴν λίμνην τοῦ πυρός, (*b*)

(*a*) The text has been tampered with here. The abode of righteous souls should occur instead of "the sea." Probably *οἱ θησαυροί* or *αἱ μοναί* (John xiv. 2) or *ὁ παράδεισος* (Luke xxiii. 43) stood originally in the text. See vol. ii. 194–198.

(*b*) + *οὗτος ὁ θάνατος ὁ δεύτερός ἐστιν, ἡ λίμνη τοῦ πυρός*—a marginal gloss drawn from xxi. 8 f., where it is full of meaning, but nonsensical here.

2017. 2018 : ηνεωχθησαν (ανεωχθησαν 35. 432. 1957. 2020. 2023). 35. 104. 205. 432. 617. 632**. 1957. 2020. 2023. 2037. 2038. 2050 : ανοιγησαν 2067 : aperti sunt Tyc Pr gig vg s arm bo : ηνοιξαν (-εν 42. 325. 336. 517. 620. 1918) **18** (– 35. 175. 205. 617. 632**. 1934. 2020. 2050). 82. 110. 141. 201. 385. 429. 452. 498. 522. 2021. 2024 sa eth | κ. αλλο βιβλ. ηνοιχθη > 1 arm^{2} | ηνοιχθη A 025. 35. 141. 172. 385. 2018. 2036. 2037 : ηνοιγη 2067 : ηνεωχθη (ανεωχθη 432. 498. 2020. 2023 2041) ℵ 046. **19** (– 35). 250. 432. 498. 2016. 2023. 2038 | ζωησ] κρισεωσ s^{1} : + unius cuiusque Tyc Pr | εν τοισ βιβλοισ] εν ταισ βιβλοισ ℵ : librorum Pr : επι του βιβλιου bo eth : > arm^{a} |.

13. > arm^{1} | τουσ εν αυτη . . . νεκρουσ^{2} > 2020 | τ. νεκρουσ τ. εν αυτη Aℵ 025. 046. **18** (– 35. 205. 2020). 250 al^{pl} Pr gig vg s bo sa eth : τουσ εν αυτη (αυτοισ 1) νεκρουσ 051. 1. 35. 205. 2023. 2037. 2038. 2041. 2069 : mortuos suos Tyc arm^{a} | κ. ο θαν. . . . αυτων > 141. 1957 arm$^{2. 4}$ | και ο^{1} > 205 | ο^{1} > 325. 620 | εδωκαν ℵ 025. 046. **18** (– 1934. 2020) al$^{fere\ omn}$ Tyc Pr gig vg s bo sa eth : εδωκεν A 82. 242. 1934 : > arm^{a} | τ. νεκρουσ τουσ (τοισ 046) εν αυτοισ Aℵ 025. 046. **18** (– 35. 205). 250. 2037 al^{pl} vg s : τουσ εν αυτοισ νεκρουσ 051. 1. 35. 205. 2023. 2038. 2067 eth : mortuos suos Tyc arm^{a} : mortuos quos in se habebant Pr : mortuos suos qui in ipsis erant gig | εκριθησαν] κατεκριθησαν ℵ : εκριθη s^{1} | εκαστοσ] + αυτων s^{1} : > bo | αυτων Aℵ 35. 205. 325. 386. 620. 1934. 2020. 2050 vg s arm bo : αυτου 046. 18. 61. 69. 104. 175. 250. 337. 456. 632. 920. 1849. 2004. 2067 sa |.

14. ο^{1} > 149 | θαν. . . . αδησ] ~ gig vg eth | του πυροσ] > Tyc : + την καιομενην εν θειω bo : + την γεμουσαν θειου eth | ουτοσ] pr και ℵ | ουτοσ ο θαν. . . . (ver. 15) πυροσ > 2050 arm^{2} | ουτοσ . . . η λιμνη τ. πυροσ > 1. 94. 149. 201. 205. 452. 2016. 2021. 2038 Pr arm$^{1. a}$ bo | ουτοσ . . . εστιν > 498 | ο θαν. ο δευτ] ο δευτεροσ θανατοσ ℵ 2020 : ο θαν. δευτεροσ 2036. 2037 | εστιν placed after δευτεροσ A (ℵ) 025. 046. **18** (– 149. 205. 2050). 61. 69. 110. 172. 250. 2018. 2036. 2037 vg s^{2} : after ουτοσ 60. 432.

15. *καὶ εἴ τις οὐχ εὑρέθη ἐν τῇ βίβλῳ τῆς ζωῆς γεγραμμένος ἐβλήθη εἰς τὴν λίμνην τοῦ πυρός.*

1957. 2023. 2041 gig s^{1} arm^{4} : after *θανατοσ* 2067 : > 104 | *η λιμνη τ. πυροσ* > s^{1} arm^{4} |.

15. **και** > 325 | *ευρεθη*] *ευρεθησεται* ℵ* arm^{1} | *τη βιβλω* Aℵ 025. 35. 104. 205. 2020. 2023. 2036. 2038. 2067 al : **τω** *βιβλιω* 046. **18** (– 35. 205. 2020. 2050). 1. 250 al^{pl} |.

RESTORED ORDER OF THE TEXT.

Chapters XXI. 5^{a}. 4^{d}. 5^{b} [6^{a}]. 1–4$^{a.\,b.\,c}$, XXII. 3–5, XXI. 5^{c}, 6^{b}–8, XXII. 6. 7. 18^{a} [18^{b}–19]. 16. 13. 12. 10 [11]. 8. 9. 20. 21. See vol. ii. 144–154.

xxi. 5^{a}. Καὶ εἶπεν ὁ καθήμενος ἐπὶ † τῷ θρόνῳ †(*a*)
4^{d}. Τὰ πρῶτα ἀπῆλθαν·
5^{b}. *ἰδοὺ καινὰ ποιῶ πάντα* (*b*).

(*a*) Wrong construction due to editor.
(*b*) The text contains the following intrusion: 6^{a}. *καὶ εἶπέν μοι Γέγοναν.* See vol. ii. 203 sq. xxi. 5^{c} should be read immediately before xxi. 6^{b}. Hence correct note in Commentary.

5^{a}. **και** > 18. 82. 201. 325. 337. 385. 386. 456. 498. 632**. 920. 1849. 2004. 2021. 2024. 2039 | *ειπεν*] ait gig : + *μοι* s^{1} arm$^{2.\,4.\,a}$ bo | *ο καθ. επι τ. θρον.* > 2050 | *επι*] *εν* 172. 2018. 2036. 2037 | *τω θρονω*] *του θρονου* 1. 205. 920. 2023. 2038 al |.

4^{d}. **τα** A 025. 051. 2038 arm^{4} : pr *οτι* (ℵ) 046. **18** al$^{fere\ omn}$ Pr gig vg s^{2} arm$^{1.\,2.\,a}$ bo sa eth : + *γαρ* 2036 | *τα πρωτα*] *τα προβατα* ℵ* : *ταυτα* 2050 : *επι τα προσωπα αυτησ και* s^{1} : > arm$^{1.\,2}$ | *απηλθαν* A : *απηλθον* 025. 1. 18. 35. 104. 205. 920. 2037. 2038. 2067 al : *απηλθεν* ℵ 046. **18** (– 18. 35. 205. 920). 250 al^{mu} arm$^{(1.\,2).\,a}$: + *και* (> bo) *ιδου παντα ποιηθησονται καινα* (*κ. εποιηθησαν π.* eth) bo eth |.

5^{b}. **ιδου**] pr *και* A : + *ιδου* 2021 | *καινα* (*κενα* ℵ) *ποιω παντα* Aℵ 025. 172. 205. 432. 1957. 2018. 2020. 2023. 2041. 2050 Pr gig vg s^{1} : *καινοποιω παντα* 051. 35. 2036. 2038 : *παντα καινα ποιω* 046. **18** (– 205. 2020. 2050). 250 al^{pl} s^{2} : *καινα παντα ποιω* 1. 2037. 2067 : *ποιησω* (*ποιω* eth) *παντα καινα* bo sa eth |.

5^{c}. For text of this line see p. 379, line 5. *κ. λεγει* > arm^{2} **λεγει** (*ειπεν* Tyc vg^{f} s bo) A 046. 18. 325. 337. 386. 456. 620. 632*. 1849. 2004 Tyc Pr gig vg$^{a.\,c.\,g.\,h}$ arm$^{2.\,4.\,a}$: + *μοι* ℵ 025. 051. 1. 35. 175. 205. 250. 617. 632**. 920. 1934. 2020. 2037. 2038. 2050. 2067 al^{pl} vg$^{d.\,f.\,v}$ s^{1} bo eth arm$^{1.\,a}$ | *γραψον οτι*] ~ 205 : > Pr | *οτι* > 051. 386. 1849 s^{1} arm$^{2.\,4.\,a}$ | *πιστοι κ. αληθινοι*

1. Καὶ εἶδον οὐρανὸν καινὸν καὶ γῆν καινήν·
ὁ γὰρ πρῶτος οὐρανὸς καὶ ἡ πρώτη γῆ ἀπῆλθαν,
καὶ ἡ θάλασσα οὐκ ἔστιν ἔτι.

2. καὶ τὴν πόλιν τὴν ἁγίαν Ἰερουσαλὴμ καινὴν εἶδον
καταβαίνουσαν ἐκ τοῦ οὐρανοῦ ἀπὸ τοῦ θεοῦ,
ἡτοιμασμένην ὡς νύμφην κεκοσμημένην τῷ ἀνδρὶ αὐτῆς.

3. καὶ ἤκουσα φωνῆς μεγάλης ἐκ τοῦ θρόνου λεγούσης

Ἰδοὺ ἡ σκηνὴ τοῦ θεοῦ μετὰ τῶν ἀνθρώπων,
καὶ σκηνώσει μετ' αὐτῶν,
καὶ αὐτοὶ λαὸς (*a*) αὐτοῦ ἔσονται, λαοί
καὶ αὐτὸς † [ὁ θεὸς μετ' αὐτῶν] ἔσται αὐτῶν θεός †. (*b*)

(*a*) In the New Jerusalem God has only one λαός. Before the final judgment our author might have said that God had many λαοί. Hence λαοί (Aℵ and a few cursives) is a corruption. Otherwise if λαοί is the older reading, then it arose through a misunderstanding of the editor, and λαός (025. 046 and Versions) is a right emendation of the text.

(*b*) Read: *αὐτῶν θεὸς ἔσται* or *ἔσται θεὸς αὐτῶν*. See vol. ii. 207 sq. *ὁ θεὸς μετ' αὐτῶν* (=עמנואל) seems to have originated in an excellent marginal gloss on 3$^{b.c}$, but in 3^{e} it is wholly irrelevant and against the parallelism.

Aℵ 046. **18** (−35. 175. 205. 617) al^{mu} Tyc (Pr vg) gig s arm$^{1.2.4}$ bo sa eth : ∼025. 1. 35. 175. 205. 250. 617. 2037. 2038. 2067 arm^{a} | *πιστ. κ. αληθ.* (*αληθ. κ. πιστ.*)] + *του θεου* 046. **18** (−35. 205. 2020. 2050) al^{mu} s^{2} | *εισιν*] tr before *και αληθινοι* Pr vg : + *του θεου* 175. 250. 617 |.

6^{b}. **ειπεν**] *λεγει* ℵ arm | *γεγοναν* (*-ασιν* 2020) A 2020 s^{1} : *γεγονα* ℵ* 025. 046. 051. **18** (−386 2020) al$^{fere\ omn}$ s^{2} arm : *γεγονε* 386 : factum est Pr gig vg : > ℵ^{c} Tyc bo |.

1. **καινον . . . καινην**] *κενον . . . κενην* ℵ arm^{4} | *πρωτοσ*] *κενοσ* arm^{4} | *πρωτη* > 42. 385 Pr bo arm | *απηλθαν* Aℵ : *απηλθον* 046. **18** (−35. 205. 620). 42. 61. 110. 201. 250. 385. 429. 498. 2017 al Tyc Pr s bo : *απηλθεν* 025. 82. 91. 172. 241. 522. 2016. 2018 gig vg : *παρηλθεν* 051. 1. 35. 205. 620. 2023. 2036. 2037. 2038. 2067 al | *η θαλ. ουκ εστι*] *την θαλασσαν ουκ ιδον* A | *η*^{2} > 18. 2050 | *ουκ εστιν ετι*] *ουκ εσται ετη* 2050 : *ουκετι εσται* 205 |.

2. **και**^{1}] + ego Iohannes vg^{v} | *αγιαν*] *μεγαλην* Pr | *καινον*] *κενον* ℵ | *καινην ειδον*] ∼2050 arm^{4} | *ειδον*] tr before *την πολιν* gig vg^{v} | *εκ του*] *απ* 920 (arm^{a}) | *εκ τ. ουρ. απο τ. θεου* Aℵ 046. **18** (−35. 205. 920). 250. 2067 al Tyc Pr gig vg s arm$^{1.2.4}$ bo sa eth : *απο τ. θ. εκ τ. ουρ* 025. 1. 35. 205. 1957. 2023. 2036. 2037. 2038. 2041 al : *απο του θεου* > 2021 | *νυμφην*] + *και* Tyc |.

3. **και ηκουσα φωνησ μεγαλησ . . . λεγουσησ**] *και φωνη μεγαλη . . . λεγουσα* ℵ* | *μεγαλησ* > gig arm$^{1.2.a}$ | *εκ τ. θρον.* > 2050 | *θρονου* Aℵ 94 vg : *ουρανου* 025. 046. **18** (−2050) al$^{fere\ omn}$ Tyc Pr gig s arm bo sa eth | *ιδου*] *ιδε* 205 | *σκηνωσει*] *εσκηνωσεν* ℵ* 2050

ἀπό 4$^{a.b.c}$. καὶ ἐξαλείψει ⸀ὁ θεὸς πᾶν⸀ δάκρυον ⸀ἐκ⸀ τῶν ὀφθαλμῶν
αὐτῶν,
καὶ ὁ θάνατος οὐκ ἔσται ἔτι·
οὔτε πένθος οὔτε κραυγὴ οὔτε πόνος οὐκ ἔσται ἔτι,
xxii. 3. καὶ πᾶν κατάθεμα οὐκ ἔσται ἔτι.

καὶ ὁ θρόνος τοῦ θεοῦ καὶ τοῦ ἀρνίου ἐν αὐτῇ ἔσται,
καὶ οἱ δοῦλοι αὐτοῦ λατρεύσουσιν αὐτῷ,
4. καὶ ὄψονται τὸ πρόσωπον αὐτοῦ,
καὶ τὸ ὄνομα αὐτοῦ ἐπὶ τῶν μετώπων αὐτῶν.

Tyc gig eth | λαοσ αυτ.] tr after εσονται Pr Tyc gig | λαοσ 025. 046. **18** (– 2050). 250. 2067 al^{pl} Tyc Pr gig vg s arm bo sa eth : λαοι Aℵ 1. 61. 2036. 2037. 2038. 2050 al | και αυτοσ ο θεοσ μετ αυτων (+ και 2050 s^{1}) εσται αυτων (αυτοισ s) θεοσ A 2050 Tyc vg s : και αυτοσ ο θεοσ εσται μετ αυτων θεοσ αυτων 025. 051 : και (>ℵ) αυτοσ ο θεοσ εσται μετ αυτων (μετ αυτων εσται 046 gig) ℵ 046 Pr gig bo sa : και αυτοσ εσται θεοσ αυτων και εσται θεοσ μετ αυτων eth : min. thus ; μετ αυτων εσται **18** (– 35. 175. 205. 617. 632**. 2050) : εσται μετ αυτων 1. 35. 175. 205. 241. 250. 617. 632**. 2016. 2017. 2023. 2036. 2037. 2038. 2041. 2067 | θεοσ (+ων 181) αυτων 35*. 175. 181. 205. 617. 2036. 2037. 2038 al : >**18** (– 35*. 175. 205. 617. 2050). 1. 61. 104. 110. 250. 385. 2067 al |.

4$^{a.b.c}$. και^{1}] +αυτοσ s^{1} | ο θεοσ A 1. 2067 vg : απ (εξ 522) αυτων 18. 325. 337. 386. 456. 522. 632*. 920. 1849. 2004 al : > ℵ 025. 046. 35. 175. 205. 250. 617. 620. 632**. 1934. 2020. 2037. 2038. 2050 Tyc Pr gig s arm bo sa eth | δακρυον] δρακυ ℵ* | εκ τ. οφθ. αυτ.] απ αυτων 141. 2021 | εκ Aℵ 2017 : απο 025. 046. **18** al^{omn} | ο^{2} A 025. 046. **18** (–632**. 2020. 2050). 250. 2037. 2038. 2067 al^{pl} : > ℵ 241. 632**. 2020. 2050 bo sa | ουκ εσται ετι] ουκετι ου μη εσται 2050 | ουκ εσται . . . πονοσ >172. 522. 2018. 2067 | ουτε . . . ουτε . . . ουτε] ουδε . . . ουδε . . . ουδε 2050 | πενθ. . . . κραυγη] ∼ℵ | ουτε κραυγη ουτε πονοσ >Tyc | ουτε πονοσ] > ℵ : ου πονοσ 205. 620 : sed nec luctus ullus Pr | ουκ εσται ετι] ουκετι εσται 2050 : >Pr arm^{1} | ετι^{2}] ετι ℵ* : οτι corr first hand : >1 |.

xxii. 3. καταθεμα] καταγμα ℵ* : αναθεμα 2050 (s^{1} ?) | ετι] >ℵ* : εκει 051. 1. 35. 104. 175. 205. 250. 617. 632**. 1934. 2020. 2037. 2038. 2067 al s^{1} | και^{2}] sed Pr : οτι arm^{1} | ο θρον. . . . εσται] sedes . . . erunt vg | εν αυτη εσται] εσται εν αυτη 2050 bo sa | εν] επ 205 | κ. οι δουλ. αυτ. λατρ. αυτω >Pr | κ. οι δουλοι αυτου] και θυμοσ ουκ εσται οι δε δουλοι του θεου bo : και ουκ εσται θυμοσ κατα των δουλων του θεου οι eth | λατρευσουσιν] λατρευουσιν 18. 82. 110. 175. 181. 205. 337. 456. 522. 617. 1849. 2004. 2020 |.

4. επι] pr και ℵ : pr scriptum Pr arm^{a} |.

5. *καὶ νὺξ οὐκ ἔσται ἔτι,*
καὶ οὐχ ⸢*ἕξουσιν*⸣ *χρείαν φωτὸς λύχνου καὶ φῶς ἡλίου,* *ἔχουσιν*
ὅτι κύριος ὁ θεὸς φωτίσει ἐπ' αὐτούς,
καὶ βασιλεύσουσιν εἰς τοὺς αἰῶνας τῶν αἰώνων.

xxi. 5^{c}. Καὶ λέγει Γράψον ὅτι οὗτοι οἱ λόγοι πιστοὶ καὶ ἀληθινοί εἰσιν.

6^{b}. Ἐγώ εἰμι τὸ Ἄλφα καὶ τὸ Ὦ,
ἡ ἀρχὴ καὶ τὸ τέλος.
ἐγὼ τῷ διψῶντι δώσω ἐκ τῆς πηγῆς τοῦ ὕδατος τῆς ζωῆς δωρεάν.

5. εσται] *εστιν* 051. 35. 175. 617 s^{1} : *ην* arm$^{1.a}$ | *ετι* Aℵ 025. 82. 93. 2018. 2032. 2050 Tyc Pr gig vg s^{2} arm$^{1.4}$ bo sa eth : *εκει* 051. 1. 35. 104. 175. 205. 617. 620. 632**. 1934 al s^{1} arm^{a} : > 046. 18. 325. 337. 386. 632*. 1849. 2004. 2020 al^{mu} | *ουχ εξουσιν χρειαν* A 2050 Tyc gig vg s bo : *ουκ εχουσιν χρειαν* ℵ : *χρειαν ουκ εχουσιν* 025. 1. 35. 175. 205. 241. 242. 250. 617. 632**. 1934. 1957. 2016. 2017. 2018. 2023. 2036. 2037. 2038. 2041. 2067 al^{mu} arm^{4} sa : *ου χρεια* 046. 18. 104. 110. 325. 337. 386. 620. 632*. 1849. 2004. 2020 al^{mu} Pr arm$^{1.a}$ | *φωτ. λυχν. κ.* >2018 | *φωτοσ* (*φωσ* 2036. 2050 : +*και* s^{1}) *λυχνου* (~2020 : *εν αυτη* bo : >sa) Aℵ 94. 241. 632**. 2020. 2036. 2037. 2050 Tyc Pr gig vg s arm$^{1.4}$ (bo sa) : *λυχνου* (-*ον* 1) 025. 046. 051. **17** (–632**. 2020. 2050). 250. 2038. 2067 al^{pl} arm^{a} | *και*^{3} > 1849 | *φωσ ηλιου* A 025. 175. 181. 242. 617. 1934. 2017. 2036. 2038. 2050 : lucem (lumen Pr) solis Pr gig : *φωτοσ ηλιου* ℵ 1. 35. 205. 250. 632**. 1957. 2016. 2018. 2020. 2023. 2038. 2041. 2067 Tyc vg s arm bo sa : *φωτοσ* 046. 18. 61. 82. 104. 110. 201. 325. 336. 337. 386. 429. 498. 522. 620. 632*. 1849. 1918. 2004 | *φωτισει* A 025. 181. 452. 2038. 2050 : *φωτιει* ℵ 046. 051. **17** (–175. 617. 1934. 2050). 1. 2037. 2067 al^{pl} : inluminabit Tyc Pr vg^{d} arm^{4} bo sa : *φωτιζει* 175. 242. 250. 617. 1934. 2016. 2017. 2036 gig vg$^{a.c.g.h.v}$ s : inluminavit vg^{f} arm$^{1.a}$ | *επ* Aℵ 2018. 2050 Tyc Pr gig eth : > 025. 046. **17** (–2050) al$^{fere\ omn}$ vg arm$^{4.a}$ bo sa | *βασιλευσουσιν*] regnabit super eos Tyc : *βασιλευσ αυτων* s^{1} |.

xxi. 5^{c}. See p. 376 (*ad fin.*) sq. for notes on this line.

6^{b}. εγω ειμι το A 1918. 2020 Tyc Pr gig vg bo eth : *εγω το* ℵ 025. 046. 35. 42. 104. 172. 175. 181. 205. 218. 241. 242. 250. 506. 617. 632**. 1934. 1957. 2016. 2017. 2018. 2036. 2037. 2038. 2050 s sa : *το* 18. 61. 82. 91. 93. 94. 110. 141. 201. 325. 336. 337. 385. 386. 429. 432. 452. 456. 498. 517. 522. 620. 632*. 920. 1849. 2004. 2023. 2024. 2039. 2041. 2067 | *αλφα*] A 1. 205. 456. 2020. 2023. 2037. 2067 al^{mu} Pr vg | *και*^{1}] +*εγω* s^{1} eth | *ω*] +*και* 18. 82. 104. 337. 385. 386. 456. 632*. 920. 2004. 2016. 2041 al | *η αρχη κ. το τελ.* Aℵ 025. 046. **18** (–35. 175. 205. 617. 1934) : *αρχη κ. τελοσ* 35. 110. 175. 205. 385. 432. 617. 2017.

7. ὁ νικῶν κληρονομήσει ταῦτα,
καὶ ἔσομαι αὐτῷ θεός,
καὶ αὐτὸς ἔσται μοι υἱός.

8. τοῖς δὲ δειλοῖς καὶ ἀπίστοις καὶ ἐβδελυγμένοις,
καὶ φονεῦσι καὶ πόρνοις καὶ φαρμακοῖς,
καὶ εἰδωλολάτραις καὶ πᾶσι τοῖς ψευδέσιν—
τὸ μέρος αὐτῶν ἐν τῇ λίμνῃ τῇ καιομένῃ πυρὶ καὶ θείῳ,
ὅ ἐστιν ὁ θάνατος ὁ δεύτερος.

xxii. 6. Καὶ εἶπέν μοι Οὗτοι οἱ λόγοι πιστοὶ καὶ ἀληθινοί, καὶ ὁ κύριος, ὁ θεὸς τῶν πνευμάτων τῶν προφητῶν, ἀπέστειλεν τὸν ἄγγελον

2038 al^p arm^{4. a} | εγω ²] + και 205 arm^{1. (4)} | τω διψ.] sitientibus Tyc (arm^{1. 2}) | τω > 025 | δωσω Aℵ 025. 35. 205. 620. 632** 2020. 2037. 2038. 2050. 2067 al Tyc Pr gig vg s arm^{4. (a)} bo sa : + αυτω (αυτοισ arm^1) 046. **18** (– 35. 205. 620. 632**. 2020. 2050). 61. 82. 110. 172. 201. 242. 250. 385. 498. 2016. 2018 al arm^{(1. 2)} | τησ πηγησ > A | τησ ζωησ] > 386. 620 : vivae Tyc gig vg^{a. c. f. g. h. v} | δωρεαν] δωρεασ ℵ* 205 |.

7. ο νικων] και ο νικων (+ αυτοσ s^1) s^1 arm eth | κληρονομησει (-ση 104) Aℵ 025. 1. 35. 104. 205. 241. 432. 632** 1957. 2020. 2023. 2036. 2037. 2038. 2050. 2067 al Tyc Pr gig vg s arm bo sa eth : δωσω αυτω 046. **18** (– 35. 205. 632**. 2020. 2050). 250 al^{pl} | ταυτα] παντα 1. 2037 : παντα ταυτα arm^{1. 2. a} | αυτω] αυτων (αυτοισ arm^{1. 4. a}) A 1. 2036. 2037. 2038 arm^{1. 4. a} : αυτου Tyc | αυτοσ εσται] αυτοι εσονται 051. 1. 2036. 2037. 2038 arm^{1. a} | αυτοσ > A Tyc s^1 | μοι A 025. 046. 051. **18** (– 175. 325. 386. 456. 620) al^{pl} Pr gig vg s^1 arm^{1. a} bo : μου ℵ 175. 325. 386. 456. 620. 2038 al Tyc s^2 arm^4 | υιοσ] ο υιοσ 1957 : υιοι 051. 1. 2036. 2037. 2038 arm^a : λαοσ arm^1 |.

8. τοισ δε δειλοισ] δειλοισ δε 1 | δε] + ωσ ℵ* : > 025 | και^1 > eth | απιστοισ (πιστοισ eth) Aℵ 025. 1. 2023*. 2036. 2037. 2038. 2050 Tyc Pr gig vg arm bo sa eth : + και αμαρτωλοισ 046. **18** (– 2050). 250. 2067 al^{pl} s | και^2 > 1. 181. 205. 2023*. 2036. 2037. 2038 al | κ. πορν. > Tyc gig arm^2 | κ. π. τ. ψευδεσιν > arm^2 | ψευδεσιν] ψευσταισ A (bo) | αυτων] εσται Tyc Pr : + εσται (εστιν arm^2) vg bo arm^2 | εν τη] εστιν 2050 | εν > 620 | τ. καιομ. πυρι κ. θειω] του πυροσ 2050 : ardente (> bo eth) ignis et sulphuris Tyc bo eth | ο^1] η s | ο (> 617. 1934 al^p) θαν. ο. δευτ. Aℵ 046. **18** (– 35. 205). 250 al^{pl} arm : ο δευτ. θαν. 051. 1. 35. 205. 2023. 2037. 2038. 2067 al : θανατοσ 025 |.

xxii. 6. ειπεν Aℵ 025. 1. 175. 205. 250. 617. 1934. 2037. 2038. 2050. 2067 al^{mu} Pr vg s arm^4 bo : λεγει 046. **17** (– 175. 205. 617. 1934. 2050) al^{pm} gig arm^{1. a} | πιστοι] fidelissima (+ sunt vg^d) (Pr) vg : + εισιν και αγιοι εισιν bo | πιστ. . . . αληθ.] ~ 2050 al : + εισιν Pr gig vg^{a. c. f. g. h. v} bo | και^2 > bo | ο^1 Aℵ 61. 2018 s^1 bo

αὐτοῦ δεῖξαι τοῖς δούλοις αὐτοῦ ἃ δεῖ γενέσθαι ἐν τάχει. 7. καὶ
ἰδοὺ ἔρχομαι ταχύ. μακάριος ὁ τηρῶν τοὺς λόγους τῆς προφητείας
τοῦ βιβλίου τούτου. 18^{a}. μαρτυρῶ ἐγὼ παντὶ τῷ ἀκούοντι τοὺς λόγους
τῆς προφητείας τοῦ βιβλίου τούτου. (*a*)

(*a*) The following interpolation is inserted here: 18^{b}. ἐάν τις ἐπιθῇ ἐπ' αὐτά, ἐπιθήσει ὁ θεὸς ἐπ' αὐτὸν τὰς πληγὰς τὰς γεγραμμένας ἐν τῷ βιβλίῳ τουτῷ. 19. καὶ ἐάν τις ἀφέλῃ ἀπὸ τῶν λόγων τοῦ βιβλίου τῆς προφητείας ταύτης, ἀφελεῖ ὁ θεὸς τὸ μέρος αὐτοῦ ἀπὸ τοῦ ξύλου τῆς ζωῆς καὶ ἐκ τῆς πόλεως τῆς ἁγίας, τῶν γεγραμμένων ἐν τῷ βιβλίῳ τούτῳ. See vol. ii. 222–224.

sa : > 025. 046. **17** al$^{fere\ omn}$ | θεοσ] + omnipotens vg^{c} | των πνευματων Aℵ 025. 046. **17** (– 175. 205) Pr vg$^{f.\ g.\ v}$ s^{1} arm^{4} bo sa : τω πνευματι (του πνευματοσ s^{2} arm^{4} : το πνευμα eth) gig vg^{d} s^{2} arm^{4} eth : των αγιων 175. 205 (arm^{a}) : omnipotens vg^{a} : > 1. 2036. 2037. 2038 | των προφητων] προφητων 205 : τ. αγιων 1. 250. 2018. 2036. 2037. 2038. 2067 : τ. αγιων προφ. s^{1} | απεστειλεν] + με ℵ* 452. 467. 506. 680. 2021 s^{2} : αποστελλει s^{1} | αυτου^{1}] + δια μεσου του την οπτασιαν εωρακοτοσ Ιωαννου 35* | δειξαι τ. δ. αυτου] διδαξαι 1849 : > 18. 325*. 337. 386. 456. 632*. 2004^{1}.

7. και^{1} Aℵ 046. **17** (– 35. 175. 205. 617. 1934). 2037 al^{pl} gig vg s : > 1. 35. 175. 205. 250. 617. 1934. 1957. 2018. 2020. 2036. 2038. 2067 Pr arm bo sa | ερχομαι] ερχονται ℵ^{c} : ερχεται 181 arm^{1} | ταχυ] εν ταχει 181 s^{1} arm^{4} : + λεγει κυριοσ 2050 | τ. προφ.] + ταυτησ bo sa : tr after βιβλιου gig : > arm^{1} | τ. βιβλ. τουτου > arm^{a} |.

18. ver 18, 19 > 181 | μαρτυρω (pr η ℵ) Aℵ 046. **17** (– 175. 617. 1934). 2037. 2038. 2067 al^{pl} : μαρτυρομαι 175. 242. 250. 424. 617. 1934. 2016. 2018 | εγω] ergo Tyc : + Ιωαννησ 2050 Pr | τω^{1} > 35. 110. 468. 1957. 2023. 2036. 2038. 2041. 2067 | παντι τω ακουοντι] omnes qui audiunt Pr | τουσ λογουσ] τον λογον Tyc s^{1} arm$^{1.\ a}$ | τ. προφ.] + ταυτησ bo sa : > arm^{4} eth | εαν τισ] pr οτι bo sa | επιθη] επιθησει ℵ 2036. 2037 arm | επ αυτα επιθησει > ℵ* | επ αυτα] επ αυτω 522. 2037 : ad eam Tyc (arm^{a}) eth | επιθησει (-εται 1957. 2018. 2020) Aℵ^{c} 046. 175. 205. 250. 1957. 2018. 2020. 2037. 2038. 2050 al^{pl} Pr vg s arm bo sa eth : επιθησαι 051. **17** (– 175. 205. 1934. 2020. 2050). 42. 110. 336. 498. 522. 2023. 2041 al Tyc gig | επ αυτον] > A* : επ (> 2037) αυτω A** 61. 2036. 2037. 2050 : επ αυτα (αυτουσ arm^{4}) arm^{4} bo sa | ο θεοσ επ αυτον (αυτω) A** (late cursive hand) 046. **17** (– 35. 175. 205. 617. 1934) al^{pl} Pr gig vg s^{2} (bo sa) eth : επ αυτον (αυτω) ο θεοσ ℵ 35. 61. 175. 205. 218. 242. 250. 432. 617. 1934. 1957. 2017. 2023. 2036. 2038. 2041. 2050. 2067 Tyc s^{1} | πληγασ Aℵ **17** (– 35. 175. 205. 617. 1934) al^{pl} Tyc Pr gig vg s arm^{4} bo sa eth : pr επτα 046. 051. 35. 175. 205. 218. 242. 250. 432. 617. 1934. 1957. 2016. 2017. 2023. 2037. 2038. 2041. 2067 arm^{a} |.

19. και^{1} > 205 | εαν] αν ℵ | αφελη] αφελειται 046 : αφελει

16. ἐγὼ Ἰησοῦς ἔπεμψα τὸν ἄγγελόν μου μαρτυρῆσαι ὑμῖν ταῦτα
ἐπί ⸀ἐν⸀ ταῖς ἐκκλησίαις,
ἐγώ εἰμι ἡ ῥίζα καὶ τὸ γένος Δαυείδ,
ὁ ἀστὴρ ὁ λαμπρὸς καὶ ὁ πρωινός.

13. ἐγὼ τὸ Ἄλφα καὶ τὸ Ὦ,
ὁ πρῶτος καὶ ὁ ἔσχατος,
ἡ ἀρχὴ καὶ τὸ τέλος.

2050 : contempserit Tyc | *απο τ. λογ. . . . ταυτησ* > Pr arm^{a} *απο τ. λογ.*] *τον λογον* 2050 : + *τουτων* ℵ | *του βιβλ.*] + *τουτου* bo : > Tyc arm^{1} | *τ. προφ.* placed after *βιβλιου* Aℵ 046. **17** (– 386. 456) al^{pl} vg s arm^{4} bo : tr before *τ. βιβλιου* 201. 368. 456. 582. 1948. 2014. 2025. 2028. 2029. 2033. 2034. 2036. 2037. 2042 : > gig eth | *ταυτησ*] *τουτου* 201. 368. 386. 456. 582. 1948. 2014. 2025. 2028. 2029. 2033. 2034. 2036. 2037. 2042 | *αφελει* Aℵ 046. 175. 205. 250. 617. 1934. 2037. 2038. 2050 al^{mu} Tyc Pr gig vg s arm bo eth : *αφελοι* (*αφελαι* 325. 620) **17** (– 205. 175. 617. 1934. 2050). 42. 82. 110. 241. 1957. 2018. 2023. 2041. 2067 al^{p} | *ο θεοσ*] dominus Pr | *του*^{2} > 456 | *απο τ. ξυλου*] *απο τ. βιβλιου* 2067 Pr vg$^{f. v}$ bo : pr de libro vitae et vg^{d} | *εκ* > A 60. 2020 bo | *τ. πολεωσ*] *των πολεων* s^{1} | *τησ αγιασ*] *των αγιων* s^{1} arm$^{1. a}$: + *και εκ* gig vg | *των γεγραμ.*] *των εγγεγραμ.* 2018 : *τησ γεγραμμενησ* Tyc Pr | *εν*] *επι* bo : > 2050 |.

16. *υμιν*] pr *εν* s^{1} : > gig arm^{1} | *ταυτα* > 2050 Pr | *εν* A 94. 250. 469. 582. 699**. 2014. 2020. 2034. 2036. 2037 Tyc gig vg arm$^{1. 4}$ bo sa : *επι* ℵ 046. **17** (– 175. 205. 617. 632**. 1934. 2020) al^{pl} s eth : > 051. 1. 91. 175. 181. 205. 241. 242. 617. 632**. 1934. 2016. 2038. 2067 Pr (arm^{a}) | *τ. εκκλησιαισ*] ecclesia Tyc : septem ecclesiis Pr : pr *πασαισ* bo | *κ. το γενοσ*] tr after *Δαυειδ* 386 | *το γενοσ*] origo Pr | *Δαυειδ*] pr *του* 1. 104 al : + *και ο λογοσ* 2050 : + *και ο λαοσ αυτου* s^{1} : "of Adam" arm^{1} | *ο*^{1}] pr *και* 051. 35. 104. 205. 250. 2018. 2023. 2036. 2037. 2038. 2050 s^{1} arm bo sa : pr *ωσ* s^{2} | *ο λαμπροσ και* > 2018 bo arm^{1} | *ο*^{2} > 18 | *και*^{2} A 205 gig vg : > ℵ 046. **17** (– 205) al^{omn} Tyc Pr s arm eth | *ο*^{3} > 205 | *πρωινοσ*] *προινοσ* A 1957. 2038 : *πρωτοσ* arm^{4} | *λαμπροσ . . . πρωινοσ* Aℵ 046. **17** (– 175. 617. 1934. 2050) al^{pl} Tyc Pr gig vg s^{2} arm$^{4. a}$ eth : ~ 91. 141. 175. 218. 242. 250. 617. 1934. 2017. 2050 s^{1} |.

13. *εγω*] + *ειμι* gig vg$^{d. v}$ arm | *το αλφα* Aℵ **17** (– 35. 205. 2020). 250 al^{pl} gig bo arm$^{4. a}$: *το* A 046. 35. 205. 2020. 2037. 2038. 2067 Tyc Pr vg | *και*^{1}] + *εγω* s^{1} | *ο πρωτοσ κ. ο* (> 2041) *εσχατοσ* ℵ 046. **17** (– 2050) al$^{fere\ omn}$: *πρωτοσ κ. εσχατοσ* A 104. 110. 2014 arm$^{(4). a}$: tr after *τελοσ* 1. 35. 175. 205. 242. 617. 1934. 1957. 2016. 2017. 2023. 2036. 2037. 2038. 2067 al arm^{4} : > 2050 arm^{1} bo | *η αρχη κ. το τελοσ* Aℵ 046. **17** (– 35. 175.

12. ἰδοὺ ἔρχομαι ταχύ,
καὶ ὁ μισθός μου μετ' ἐμοῦ,
ἀποδοῦναι ἑκάστῳ ὡς τὸ ἔργον † ἐστὶν αὐτοῦ †. (*a*)

10. καὶ λέγει μοι Μὴ σφραγίσῃς τοὺς λόγους τῆς προφητείας τοῦ βιβλίου τούτου, ὁ καιρὸς γὰρ ἐγγύς ἐστιν. (*b*)

(*a*) This order is against our author's use and is probably due to the editor. See Gram. in Introd. to vol. i. Read αὐτοῦ ἐστιν.

(*b*) The following verse is removed from the text as an interpolation; see vol. ii. 221–222:

11. ὁ ἀδικῶν ἀδικησάτω ἔτι,
καὶ ὁ ῥυπαρὸς ῥυπανθήτω ἔτι,
καὶ ὁ δίκαιος δικαιοσύνην ποιησάτω ἔτι,
καὶ ὁ ἅγιος ἁγιασθήτω ἔτι.

205. 617. 1934). 250 al^{pl} : αρχη κ. τελοσ 1. 35. 175. 205. 617. 1934. 2037. 2038. 2067 al arm | τελοσ] + λεγει ο κυριοσ ο θεοσ ο παντοκρατωρ arm^1 |.

12. ιδου] pr και 1. 2038. 2067 Tyc eth | ταχυ] + μακαριοσ ο τηρων τουσ λογουσ του βιβλιου τουτου 104 | και^2 > bo | αποδουναι] αποδοθηναι ℵ* : και (> bo) αποδωσω s^1 bo | ωσ . . . αυτου] κατα τα εργα (το εργον s^1 sa eth) αυτου (αυτων gig) 2036 Pr Tyc gig vg s^1 arm bo sa eth | το > 325 | εστιν Aℵ 205. 2014. 2020. 2038 s^2 : εσται 046. **17** (– 205. 2020). 1. 42. 61. 201. 250. 429. 498. 522. 1957. 2018. 2023. 2037. 2038. 2041. 2050. 2067 al^{pl} | εστιν (εσται) αυτου (αυτω 2050) Aℵ 046. **17** (– 35. 175. 205. 617. 1934. 2020). 2014 al^{pl} : ~ 1. 35. 175. 205. 250. 617. 1934. 2020. 2037. 2038. 2067 al^{p} |.

10. κ. λεγει . . . τουτου > gig | λεγ. μοι > eth | λεγει] ειπεν Tyc Cyp s bo | μοι] + angelus Tyc | σφραγισησ] σφραγισεισ 205 | λογουσ] + τουτουσ ℵ* (del first hand) | προφ.] + ταυτησ bo | τ. βιβλ. > Tyc arm^1 | τουτου] eius Tyc : ταυτησ arm^1 | ο καιροσ γαρ] οτι ο καιροσ 1. 35. 205. 1957. 2023. 2038 Pr | γαρ placed after καιροσ Aℵ 046. **17** (– 35. 205. 620. 1934. 2050). 250 al^{pl} Tyc gig vg s arm bo sa : tr before καιροσ 82. 94. 141. 2036. 2037. 2050 : > 91. 242. 336. 517. 620. 1918. 1934. 2032 |.

11. ο αδικων] pr και 424. 2018. 2032 Pr s^1 eth | ο αδικ. αδικησατω ετι] hii qui perseverant nocere noceant Pr : qui perseveraverit nocere noceat adhuc Tyc^b (qui iniustus est iniusta faciat adhuc Tyc^a) | ετι$^{1. 2. 3. 4}$ > arm$^{1. a}$ | και (> bo) ο ρυπ. ρυπ. ετι (> arm bo) ℵ 046. **17** (– 2050). 2037. 2038. 2067 al^{pl} Tyc Pr gig vg s arm bo sa : > A 1. 218. 250. 498. 2014. 2018. 2032. 2050 | ο ρυπαροσ] qui in sordibus est Tyc^b Pr Cyp gig vg | ρυπανθητω ℵ 94. 2017 : ρυπαρευθητω 046. **17** (– 205. 2050). 2037. 2038. 2067 al^{pl} : ρυπαρωθητω 205 : sordescat Tyc Pr Cyp vg | ετι$^{2. 3. 4}$ > arm^4 bo eth | δικαιοσυνην ποιησατω ετι Aℵ 046. **17** (– 2020) al^{pl} gig vg s : iustiora faciat (iusta faciat adhuc Tyc^a)

8. Κἀγὼ Ἰωάννης ὁ ἀκούων καὶ βλέπων ταυτα. καὶ ὅτε ἤκουσα
ἔβλεψα καὶ ⸀ἔβλεπον⸁, ἔπεσα προσκυνῆσαι ἔμπροσθεν τῶν ποδῶν τοῦ ἀγγέλου
τοῦ δεικνύοντός μοι ταῦτα. 9. καὶ λέγει μοι Ὅρα μή· σύνδουλός
σού εἰμι καὶ τῶν ἀδελφῶν σου τῶν προφητῶν καὶ τῶν τηρούντων
τοὺς λόγους τοῦ βιβλίου τούτου· τῷ θεῷ προσκύνησον.
20. Λέγει ὁ μαρτυρῶν ταῦτα Ναί· ἔρχομαι ταχύ. Ἀμήν· ἔρχου
κύριε Ἰησοῦ.

Tyc^{b} Pr Cyp : δικαιωθητω ετι (> arm bo eth) 2020. 2036 arm$^{1.a}$ (bo) eth | κ. ο αγ. αγ. ετι] similiter et sanctus sanctiora Tyc Pr Cyp : >61. 2036. 2037 |.

8. **καγω**] και εγω 1. 35. 175. 205. 250. 617. 1934. 2037. 2038 al : οτι εγω arm^{1} : εγω s^{1} bo sa | Ιωαννησ] pr ο 205 | ο > 2020. 2024 | ακουων κ. βλεπ. ταυτα] βλεπ. ταυτα κ. ακουων 1 al | ακουων κ. βλεπων A 046. **17** (− 35. 175. 205. 617. 1934). 2067 al^{pl} gig vg s^{2} arm : ∼ ℵ 35. 175. 205. 218. 242. 250. 617. 1934. 2016. 2017. 2036. 2037. 2038 Pr s^{1} bo sa eth | βλεπων] ο βλεπ. bo sa eth | ταυτα] αυτα 18. 2004 : +μαρτυρω 2050 | και^{3} > 1934 | ηκουσα κ. εβλεπον] εβλεψα κ. ηκουσα s^{1} arm^{1} | εβλεπον A : εβλεψα ℵ 1. 35. 175. 242. 250. 617. 1934. 1957. 2016. 2017. 2023. 2036. 2037. 2038. 2041. 2050. 2067 al : ειδον 201. 336. 386. 456. 522. 2018. 2020 : οτε ειδον (ιδων 046 : ιδον 61. 104. 110). 046. 18. 205. 325. 337. 620. 632. 1849. 2004 al^{pl} : +ταυτα bo eth | επεσα Aℵ 1. 336. 429. 2018. 2020. 2032. 2038. 2050 : επεσον 046. **17** (− 2020. 2050). 250. 2037. 2067 : > eth | προσκυνησαι] και (>eth) προσεκυνησα arm eth : >bo sa | εμπροσθεν των] προ A | δεικνυοντοσ (διγν- A) A 046. **17** (− 35. 325. 456. 620. 1934. 2020). 250. 2037. 2038. 2067 al^{pl} : δεικνυντοσ (δικν- ℵ) ℵ 35. 60. 82. 91. 104. 325. 456. 498. 506. 517. 620. 1934. 2020. 2023. 2024. 2041 al |.

9. λεγει] ειπεν vg^{d} s bo | μοι > 205. 325. 2050 | ορα μη] + ποιησησ 2017 Pr gig vg | συνδουλοσ] pr οτι Pr | ειμι] + εγω 175. 617. 1934 bo sa eth | και^{3} Aℵ 046. **17** (− 35. 175. 205. 386. 617. 1934). 250. 2037 al^{pl} gig vg s arm^{4} bo sa : > 1. 35. 60. 91. 175. 181. 201. 205. 241. 242. 386. 432. 617. 1934. 1957. 2016. 2017*. 2023. 2038. 2041. 2067 Pr | τ. λογουσ] + τησ προφητειασ 2020 Pr arm^{a} : pr τουτουσ s^{1} | του βιβλ. τουτου] τουτουσ 2050 | τ. θεω προσκυνησον] magis Deum adora Pr : > gig |.

20. λεγει] + ο θεοσ 2050 | ο > s^{1} | ταυτα] + ειναι ℵ* arm^{4} | ναι > Pr gig arm^{a} | αμην > ℵ 2050 Tyc Pr gig s^{1} arm^{4} | ερχου Aℵ 046. 175. 205. 250. 617. 1934. 2038 al^{p} gig vg s arm^{4} bo sa eth : pr ναι (και 104). 051. **17** (− 175. 205. 617. 1934). 1957. 2018. 2023. 2036. 2037. 2067 al^{pl} Pr | κυριε] + ημων bo | ιησου Aℵ* 046. 18. 35. 250. 325. 620. 632. 1849. 2004 al^{pl} vg s sa : + χριστε ℵ^{c} **17** (− 18. 35. 325. 620. 632. 1849. 2004). 42. 91. 201. 242. 2016. 2017. 2036. 2037. 2038. 2067 Pr arm$^{4.(a)}$ bo : > gig |.

21. ἡ χάρις τοῦ κυρίου Ἰησοῦ μετὰ πάντων τῶν ἁγίων. Ἀμήν.

21. ver. 21 > Pr | η χαρ. τ. κ. ιησου > bo | τ. κ. Ιησου] του χριστου 175. 181. 617. 1934. 2016. 2017. 2023 | κυριου Aℵ 046. **17** (– 149. 175. 205. 468. 617. 1934). 250. 2037. 2038 al^pl arm^a sa : + ημων 149. 205. 468. 2067 al^p gig vg s arm^4 eth | ιησου Aℵ 506 sa : + χριστου 046. **17** al^pl gig vg s arm eth | μετα (επι arm^a bo) παντων των (> arm) αγιων (+ αυτου s^1) 046. 051. **17** (– 2050). 250. 2037. 2038. 2067 al s arm^4. a (bo) sa : μετα παντων A vg^a. c. d. g. h : μετα παντων υμων (ημων 2050) 2050 vg^f. v eth : μετα (επι gig) των αγιων ℵ gig : + εισ τον αιωνα των αιωνων bo | αμην ℵ 046. **17**. 250. 2067 al^pl vg s arm bo sa eth : > A 2014. 2025*. 2026. 2031. 2034. 2036. 2037. 2038 gig |.

Subscription.—αποκαλυψισ (-εισ ℵ) Ιωαννου Aℵ 1854 : αποκαλυψισ του αγιου Ιωαννου 2004 : αποκαλυψισ του αγιου ιωαννου του θεολογου (+ και ευαγγελιστου 1849) 325. 1849 : τελοσ τησ αποκαλυψεωσ του αγιου ιωαννου του ευαγγελιστου 82 : τελοσ τησ του αγιου ιωαννου του θεολογου θειασ αποκαλυψεωσ 522 : τελοσ του αποκαλυψεωσ του αγιου αποστολου και ευαγγελιστου ιωαννου 468 : >046. 18. 35. 104. 149. 175. 205. 429. 456. 617. 620. 632. 1934. 2017. 2020. 2023. 2050 al.

IV. ENGLISH TRANSLATION.

CHAPTER I.

1–3. THE REVELATION WHICH GOD GAVE TO JESUS CHRIST TO BE MADE KNOWN TO HIS SERVANT JOHN, AND THE BEATITUDE PRONOUNCED ON THOSE WHO KEEP THE THINGS WRITTEN THEREIN.

The book—its source and contents, 1–2

1. The revelation of Jesus Christ, which God gave unto him, to show unto his servants—even the things which must shortly come to pass; and (which) he sent and signified by his angel unto his servant John; **2.** Who bare witness of the word of God, and of the testimony of Jesus Christ—(even) of all things which he saw.

The first beatitude for those who keep the things written therein

3. Blessed[1] (is) he that readeth,
And they that hear the words of the prophecy,
And keep the things that are written therein:
For the time (is) at hand.

4–7. JOHN'S GREETING AND BENEDICTION TO THE SEVEN CHURCHES.

John's greeting to the Seven Churches

4. John to the Seven Churches that are in Asia—

Grace unto you and peace, from him which is, and which was, and which is to come,[2]

Grace and peace from God and from Jesus Christ

5. And from Jesus Christ, the faithful witness,
The firstborn of the dead, and the ruler of the kings of the earth.[3]

Sovereign of the dead and Ruler of the living

Unto him that loveth us and loosed us from our sins by his blood,

[1] On the seven beatitudes in this book, see vol. ii. 49.

[2] Here John's editor interpolates the following words: "And from the seven spirits which are before his throne"; see vol. i. 9, 11–12.

[3] The last two phrases = the Sovereign of the dead, the Ruler of the living. The primary meaning of πρωτότοκος, *i.e.* "firstborn," is wholly superseded by its secondary one of "chief," "foremost," "sovereign." See note on i. 5 (vol. i. 14).

Ascription of praise to Him as the Redeemer

6\. And hath made[1] us to be a kingdom, priests unto his
God and Father—
Unto him be the glory and the dominion for ever and
ever. Amen.

His Advent

7\. Behold he cometh with the clouds;
And every eye shall see him, and they that pierced him.[2]
And all the tribes of the earth shall wail because of him.[3]
Even so. Amen.[4]

9-20. JOHN'S CALL AND COMMISSION.

(His vision of the Son of Man, who is described in terms that recur in the Letters to the first six of the Seven Churches.)

[1] Not "and he hath made us"; for we have here a Hebrew idiom which often recurs in our text; see vol. i. 14-15.

[2] In this translation I generally use "*that*" to "introduce a statement that is essential to the complete meaning of the antecedent," and "*who*" to "introduce a non-essential statement," as Abbott, *Gr.* 218, footnote, recommends, this being the usage generally adopted by Shakespeare and Addison.

[3] Here ἐπ' αὐτόν requires this rendering. In Zech xii. 10, on the other hand, the same words mean, "they shall wail for him." We could also render "wail in regard to him": cf. John xiii. 28.

[4] Here all the authorities add: 8. "I am the Alpha and the Omega, saith the Lord God, which is, and which was, and which is to come, the Almighty." This verse is unquestionably interpolated, though I did not recognize this fact when writing my Commentary. This is proved by the evidence of (*a*) the context (or thought), and (*b*) that of the text (or grammar). (*a*) Contextual grounds. These words imply that John heard them in a vision; for otherwise he could not have heard them. But this would necessitate a foregoing statement, that John had fallen into a visionary condition or trance, such a statement as we find in i. 10 ("I was in the spirit") before his vision of the Son of Man, or his very frequent "I saw" or "I saw, and behold"; see vol. i. 106 sq. John does not fall into a trance till i. 10. If, then, i. 8 is original, the text is fragmentary. But the words cannot come from John's hand at all, as we see from (*b*). (*b*) Textual or grammatical grounds. John never disconnects ὁ θεός ("God") and ὁ παντοκράτωρ ("Almighty"), for the very good reason that ὁ παντοκράτωρ represents a genitive in the Hebrew dependent on θεός. That is, ὁ θεὸς ὁ παντοκράτωρ is a stock rendering of אלהי הצבאות (="God of hosts"); see vol. i. 20. Only an ignorant scribe could have separated the words. For John's use of this phrase, see iv. 8, xi. 17, xv. 3, xvi. 7, 14, xix. 6, 15, xxi. 22. The recognition of this fact is very important, seeing that not only has no scholar recognized the misuse of this phrase in i. 8, but none has recognized that the text in xix. 6, ὁ θεὸς [ἡμῶν] ὁ παντοκράτωρ (ℵ 025. 046 Pr gig vg^{g} s^{2}), is equally impossible with that in i. 8. Here such great authorities as A 2040 s^{1} arm$^{2.4}$ vg^{g} bo eth Cyp should at all events have led scholars with WH to bracket ἡμῶν as an intrusion, if not as impossible. In the LXX and in all works written by Jews in Hebrew or in Greek, nothing can intervene between ὁ θεός (or κύριος) and ὁ παντοκράτωρ in this phrase.

Hence i. 8 must be rejected. By its removal the right order of thought is restored. First in i. 4-7 comes John's greeting to the churches, and next in 9-20 his account of his call and commission by Christ. i. 8 is thus impossible in itself linguistically in our author, unintelligible in its present position, and intolerable as creating a breach between i. 4-7 and 9-20.

John bidden to write down his visions and send them to the Seven Churches, 9–11

9. I John, your brother and companion in the tribulation and kingdom and endurance (which is) in Jesus, was in the isle which is called Patmos, because of the word of God and the testimony of Jesus. 10. I was in the Spirit on the Lord's day, and I heard a great voice behind me, as of a trumpet, saying:

11. What thou seest, write in a book,
And send it to the seven churches;
Unto Ephesus, and unto Smyrna, and unto Pergamum,
And unto Thyatira, and unto Sardis, and unto Philadelphia, and unto Laodicea.

12. And I turned to see the voice that spake with me.

Vision of the Son of man amid the seven candlesticks, 13–19

And having turned, I saw seven golden candlesticks;
13. And in the midst of the candlesticks One like unto a son of man,
Clothed with a garment down to the foot,
And girt about the breasts with a golden girdle.

14. And his head and his hair were white as white wool,[1]
And his eyes were as a flame of fire,
15. And his feet like unto burnished brass, as when refined in a furnace,
And his voice as the voice of many waters.

16. And he had in his right hand seven stars:
And out of his mouth went a sharp two-edged sword:
And his countenance was as the sun shining[2] in his strength.

17. And when I saw him, I fell at his feet as dead. And he laid his right hand upon me, saying,

Fear not; I am the first and the last:
18. And he that liveth,[3] and was dead:

And, behold, I am alive for evermore;
And have the keys of death and Hades.

19. Write therefore the things which thou hast seen,
And the things which are,
And the things which shall be hereafter.

[1] The text adds what was originally a marginal gloss, "as snow"; see vol. i. 28.

[2] Not "shineth," which is neither good English nor a rendering of the text. The text here contains a Hebrew idiom; see vol. i. p. 31.

[3] This clause belongs to this line, not to the preceding; see vol. i. 15, 31.

20. As for the mystery of the seven stars which thou sawest in my right hand and the seven golden candlesticks—the seven stars are the angels of the seven churches; and the candlesticks are the seven[1] churches.

The seven candlesticks are the Seven Churches, and the stars are the ideals they are to fulfil

CHAPTERS II.–III.

LETTERS TO THE SEVEN CHURCHES.

(To the angels of the Churches, *i.e.* to the Churches in their potential and ideal character, John addresses the seven following letters, which come from Jesus Himself, through whom alone their ideals can be realized; for He holds them in His right hand. These Churches, which are very imperfect witnesses of God on earth, are menaced with world-wide tribulation. These Letters were written by John, probably in the time of Vespasian, and edited afresh for incorporation in the Apocalypse. See vol. i. 43–47.)

CHAPTER II.

II. 1–7. (Letter to the Church in Ephesus, which is praised for rejecting false teaching, but blamed for forsaking its first love.)

1. To the angel of the Church in Ephesus write:

These things saith he that holdeth the seven stars in his right hand,
That walketh in the midst of the seven golden candlesticks:

2. I know thy works, even thy toil and endurance,
And that thou canst not bear evil men;

But hast tried them which say they are apostles and are not,[2]
And hast found them false.

Church of Ephesus praised for its rejection of false teachers and its endurance, 2–3

[1] Nearly all the authorities read *αἱ λυχνίαι αἱ ἑπτὰ ἑπτὰ ἐκκλησίαι εἰσίν*. The position of the numeral without the article in the predicate here is parallel to that of *ἑπτά* and *δέκα* in xvii. 9, 12, xxi. 21. But here we require the article in the predicate, since the predicate is co-extensive with the subject, and since "*the* seven churches" (*τῶν ἑπτὰ ἐκκλησιῶν*) have just been mentioned. Two cursives Pr fl and arm[4] rightly omit the second *ἑπτά*.

[2] Not "and they are not"; for we have a Hebraism here; see note on 5–6, vol. i. 14.

3. And thou hast endurance,
And didst bear for my name's sake,
And hast not grown weary.

But blamed for forsaking its first love

4. But I have (this) against thee, that thou hast left thy first love.

5. Remember therefore from whence thou hast fallen,
And repent and do the first works;
Or else I will come unto thee,
And remove thy candlestick out of its place.[1]

6. But this thou hast, that thou hatest the works of the Nicolaitans, which I also hate.

7. He that hath an ear, let him hear
What the Spirit saith unto the Churches:

The victor will eat of the tree of life

To him that overcometh will I give to eat of the tree of life, which is in the Paradise of God.

8-11. (Letter to the Church in Smyrna, which is praised for its loyalty under tribulation and impoverishment, and forewarned against a still worse though shortlived persecution.)

Church in Smyrna praised for its loyalty under tribulation, and forewarned of coming but short-lived persecution, 8-10

8. And to the angel of the Church in Smyrna write:

These things saith the first and the last
Which was dead, and is alive (again):

9. I know thy tribulation and poverty,
But thou art rich;
And the blasphemy of certain of those[2] which say they are Jews and are not,[3]
But are a synagogue of Satan.

10. Fear not the things which thou art about to suffer:
Behold, the devil is about to cast some of you into prison,
That ye may be tempted, and have tribulation for ten days.

Be thou faithful unto death,
And I will give thee the crown of life.

[1] A gloss adds, "except thou repent"; see vol. i. p. 51.
[2] ἐκ τῶν λεγόντων is partitive. Our author does not charge with blasphemy all who claim to be Jews. The limitation is defined further in "and are not, but are a synagogue of Satan." But the ἐκ here may be only a sign of the genitive; see my Grammar in the Introd. to vol. i. under ἐκ.
[3] Not "and they are not"; see note on ver. 2.

11. He that hath an ear, let him hear
What the Spirit saith unto the Churches:
He that overcometh shall not be hurt by the second death.

The victor will be beyond the reach of death

12–17. (Letter to the Church in Pergamum.)

12. And to the angel of the Church in Pergamum write:

These things saith he that hath the two-edged the sharp sword:

13. I know where thou dwellest,
(Even) where Satan's throne is:
And thou holdest fast my name,
And didst not deny (thy) faith in me,

Church in Pergamum praised for its steadfastness and loyalty in the days of persecution, 12–13

Even in the days of Antipas, my faithful witness,[1]
Who was slain among you,
Where Satan dwelleth.

14. But I have a few things against thee,
Because thou hast there some who hold the teaching of Balaam,
Who taught Balak to cast a stumbling-block before the children of Israel,
To eat things sacrificed to idols, and to commit fornication.

15. Thus[2] thou too in like manner hast some who hold the teaching of the Nicolaitans.

But blamed for suffering men corrupt in doctrine and life to exist in their midst, 14–16

16. Repent, therefore,
Or else I will come unto thee quickly,
And I will make war against them with the sword of my mouth.

17. He that hath an ear, let him hear
What the Spirit saith unto the Churches.

To him that overcometh I will give of the hidden manna,
And I will give him a white stone,
And upon the stone a new name[3] written,
Which none knoweth but he that receiveth it.

The victor will be endowed with enriched powers and personality

[1] AC read "my witness, my faithful one"; but i. 5, iii. 14 support the text adopted above.

[2] The "thus" is justified by the statement in 14, while the words "thou too in like manner" involve a comparison with the Church in Ephesus, ii. 3.

[3] Though difficulties may attach to the various explanations of the "white stone," that of the new name is clear. The name stands for the man and all therein implied—his personality. For him that overcometh this personality is so transformed, developed and enriched that it is in effect a new personality, which none knoweth save God and the man himself.

13-29. (Letter to the Church in Thyatira.)

Church of Thyatira praised for its growth in things spiritual, 18-19

18. And to the angel of the Church in Thyatira write:

These things saith the Son of God,
Whose eyes [1] are like a flame of fire,
And whose feet [2] are like unto burnished brass:

19. I know thy works—
(Even) thy love, and faith, and ministry, and endurance;
And thy last works are more than the first.

But blamed for suffering a false prophetess in its midst, 20-25

20. But I have (this) against thee,
That thou sufferest the woman Jezebel, who calleth herself a prophetess,
And teacheth [3] and seduceth my servants,
To commit fornication, and to eat things sacrificed to idols.

21. And I have given her time that she should repent:
But she hath refused to repent of her fornication.

22. Behold, I will cast her upon a bed of suffering,[4]
And those who commit adultery with her into great tribulation;[5]
23. But her children I will slay with pestilence:

And so [6] all the churches shall know
That I am he that searcheth the reins and hearts,
And giveth [7] to each one of you according to your works.

[1] Lit. "who has his eyes."

[2] Lit. "and his feet"; but the possessive pronoun is really a part of the relative in Hebrew. Thus the stanza would run in Hebrew:

כה אמר בן־האלהים
אשר עיניו כלהב אש
ומרגלתיו כנחשת קלל

[3] Not "and she teacheth"; for we have here a Hebrew idiom; see vol. i. 14 sq.

[4] See vol. i. p. 71. *Here* as in iii. 9, *ἰδού* with the present indic. is to be rendered by the future.

[5] Text adds a gloss, "unless they repent of their works." These words are unnecessary. Moreover, *ἐὰν μή* with ind. (*μετανοήσουσιν*, Aℵ: *μετανοήσωσιν* C 025. 046), is against John's usage. The punishments in $22^{a.\,b}$ leave an opportunity for repentance but not the punishment in 23^a. The omission of 22^c restores the parallelism and makes this stanza a tristich as the two that follow.

[6] Here *καί* has this meaning still more strongly than in Matt. v. 15, xxiii. 32; 1 John iii. 19, etc.

[7] *ὁ ἐραυνῶν . . . καὶ δώσω.* We have here another instance of the same idiom as in i. 5^b–6 = ואתן . . . הבחן. Cp. Amos ix. 6 for a construction like that implied in the text. The judgments about to be executed in 22–23^a will

24. But to you I say, to the rest that are in Thyatira,
As many as have not this doctrine,
That know[1] not the deep things of Satan, as they call (them)—

25. I cast upon you none other burden:
Only hold fast what ye have till I come.

26. And he that overcometh, even he[2] that keepeth my works unto the end—
To him will I give authority over the nations:
27[c]. As I also have received from my Father,[3]

27. And he shall break[4] them with a rod of iron;
As the potter's vessels shall they be dashed to pieces:[5]
28. And I will give him the morning star.

29. He that hath an ear, let him hear
What the Spirit saith unto the Churches.

The victor shall share in Christ's dominion over the nations, and receive the morning star, 26–28

cause all the Churches to know that it is Christ that is the Judge, and that He judgeth now. In fact it is from such experience that they connect the judgments in 22 with the conclusion in 23[d]. The judgments are in accordance with the works. Both the sins and their punishments have become actually known to them. Hence there is no eschatological reference here to the final judgment, and accordingly *καὶ δώσω* must not be translated "and I will give," but according to the Hebrew idiom as rendered above. Here is another fact tending to prove that the Seven Letters were written at a much earlier date than the Book as a whole. The Letters insist more upon the present judgments of Providence, the Book as a whole on the final judgment.

[1] *Ἔγνωσαν*. Timeless aorist to be translated as a perfect = "have recognised" = "know." See Introd. vol. i. *Gram.* § 4. iii.

[2] Or "and."

[3] This line follows 26[b] immediately, as the exactly parallel construction in iii. 21 shows.

[4] Or "shatter" or "destroy"; see note in vol. i. p. 75 sq.

[5] *συντρίβεται* is to be taken as a Hebraism and rendered by the future; see vol. i. 77. Tyc (ut vas figuli comminuentur) Pr vg (sicut (tanquam vg) vas figuli confringentur) (s[2?]) presuppose *συντριβήσονται* and the above translation. 2050 gig (s[1] emended by Gwynn) = *καὶ συντρίψει αὐτοὺς ὡς τὰ σκεύη κτλ*. In any case the verb affects the *ἔθνη*, not the *σκεύη*.

συντρίβονται (or *συντριβήσονται*) would have seemed more natural in our text, since *ἔθνη* is thrice preceded and twice followed by the plural verb in our author (xi. 18, xv. 4). But the sing. verb occasionally *follows* the neuter plural of various nouns in our author; see vol. i. *Gram.* § 8. ii. (*b*). If this seems unsatisfactory here, seeing that *ἔθνη* is referred to in the preceding clause by *αὐτούς*, then we must regard *συντρίβεται* as a slip of the writer or a primitive corruption for *συντρίβονται* or *συντριβήσονται*.

Chapter III.

III. 1-6. (Letter to the Church in Sardis.)

The Church in Sardis blamed for its spiritual declension, and admonished to be watchful and repent, 1–3, xvi. 15

1. To the angel of the Church in Sardis write:

These things saith he that hath the seven Spirits of God,
And the seven stars:

I know thy works
That thou hast a name to live, but art dead.

2. Be watchful, and strengthen the things that remain, (but) which are ready to die:[1]
For I have found no works of thine fulfilled before my God.[2]

3. Remember therefore how thou hast received and didst hear,
And keep (them), and repent.

Second Beatitude for those who keep their garments clean

XVI. 15. Behold, I come as a thief:
Blessed is he that watcheth, and keepeth his garments,
So that he may not walk naked,
And his shame be seen.[3]

III. 3c. If therefore thou dost not watch,
I will come as a thief,
And thou shalt not know
At what hour I shall come to thee.

Yet a few in Sardis are worthy

4. But thou hast a few names in Sardis
Which have not defiled their garments,
And they shall walk with me in white;
For they are worthy.

The victor shall obtain a spiritual body, and have his name in the Book of life

5. He that overcometh shall thus be arrayed in white garments;
And I will in no wise blot his name out of the book of life,
But I will confess his name before my Father,
And before his angels.

He that hath an ear let him hear
What the Spirit saith unto the Churches.

[1] The epistolary imperfect here rendered as a present.

[2] "Works of thine" (AC). This judgment is more sweeping than the reading of ℵ 025. 046—"thy works." Sardis has failed as a centre of spiritual power.

[3] Lit. "they see his shame."

III. 7-13. (Letter to the Church in Philadelphia in which it is given unqualified approval for its fidelity and steadfastness, and promised the honour and privileges of the true Israel (9), and deliverance from the final demonic woes in the approaching worldwide tribulation (10-11). He that overcometh shall have an everlasting place in the spiritual Kingdom of God—even God's city, the New Jerusalem—and bear on his forehead God's name and Christ's own new name, 12.)

Church in Philadelphia praised for its steadfastness despite its weakness, 7-8

7. And to the angel of the Church in Philadelphia write:
These things saith he that is holy, he that is true,
He that hath the key of David,
That openeth and none closeth,[1]
And closeth and none openeth:
8b. Behold I have set before thee an open door,
8c. Which none can shut.[2]

8a. I know thy works,
That thou hast a little power,
And yet thou hast kept my word
And hast not denied my name.

Promised the powers and privileges of the true Israel

9. Behold, I will cause[3] them of the synagogue of Satan
Who say that they are Jews and are not,
But do lie:
Behold, I will make them to come
And worship before thy feet,
And know that I have loved thee.

And deliverance from the woes that are to try the faithless

10. Because thou hast kept the word of my endurance,
I also will keep thee from the hour of tribulation,
Which is about to come upon the whole world,
To tempt them that dwell upon the earth.[4]

[1] See vol. i. 86.

[2] 8b. c form a parenthesis, if the MSS order is followed. But the MSS order of the text cannot be right. Hence 8b. c are restored before 8a. Thus in 7-10 there are four stanzas: the first and third of six lines each, and the second and fourth of four lines each.

[3] Here ἰδοὺ διδῶ = הִנְנִי נֹתֵן, and indubitably refers to the future, and should be so translated (so rightly in AV.). This common Hebraism (see Gesenius, *Heb. Gram.*, transl. by Cowley, § 116*p*), where the participle = a future, is called *futurum instans*. Our author sometimes puts the present (indicative) (cf. ii. 22a) after ἰδοὺ, where it is to be rendered as a future: also xvi. 15, xxii. 7, 12. In the last three cases the ἔρχομαι may be rendered as a present owing to the idea of futurity associated with the technical use of the verb. The same variation in the renderings of this idiom appears in the LXX.

[4] The demonic temptations here referred to can only affect the unbelievers (*i.e.* "those that dwell upon the earth"; see note on xi. 10 in vol. i. 289).

The victor shall dwell for ever in God's city and bear His name and Christ's new name

11. I come quickly: hold fast what thou hast;
Let none take thy crown.

12. He that overcometh—I will make him a pillar in the temple of my God,
And he shall go out no more:
And I will write upon him the name of my God,
And the name of the city of my God,
The new Jerusalem which cometh down out of heaven from my God,
And mine own new name.

13. He that hath an ear, let him hear
What the Spirit saith unto the Churches.

III. 14-22. (Letter to the Church in Laodicea.)

Church in Laodicea denounced for its self-complacency and for its spiritual destitution despite its material wealth and intellectual culture, 14-17

14. And to the angel of the Church in Laodicea write:

These things saith the Amen,
The faithful and true witness,
The beginning of the creation of God:

15. I know thy works
That thou art neither cold nor hot:
I would thou wert cold or hot.

16. So because thou art lukewarm,
And neither cold nor hot,
I will spew thee out of my mouth.

17. Because thou sayest, I am rich,
And have gotten riches, and have need of nothing;
And knowest not that thou art (of all creatures) the (most) wretched and miserable
And poor and blind and naked:

Bidden to seek the true riches and to repent, 18-19

18. I counsel thee to buy of me gold refined by fire, that thou mayest be rich;
And white garments, that thou mayest clothe thyself,
And that the shame of thy nakedness be not made manifest;
And eyesalve to anoint thine eyes, that thou mayest see.

19. As many as I love, I reprove and chasten: be zealous therefore, and repent.

20. Behold, I stand at the door and knock:
If any man hear my voice and open the door,
I will come in to him, and will sup with him,
And he with me.

Appeal to the individual Laodicean

21. To him that overcometh, I will grant to sit with me on my throne,
As I also have overcome, and sat down with my Father on his throne.

The victor shall share in Christ's glory, as He in His Father's

22. He that hath an ear, let him hear
What the Spirit saith unto the Churches.

CHAPTER IV.

THE VISION OF GOD THE CREATOR, FROM WHOM ARE ALL THINGS.

(With iv. comes an entire change of scene. The dramatic contrast could not be greater. In ii.–iii. we had a vivid description of the Churches, with the ideals they cherished, their faulty achievements, their not infrequent disloyalties, and their outlook darkened with the fear of universal martyrdom. But the moment we leave behind the restlessness and turmoil of earth, the moral shortcomings and apprehensions of the Churches in ii.–iii., we enter in iv. into an atmosphere of perfect assurance and peace, where neither the threatenings of the powers of evil nor the alarms of the faithful on earth can awake even a momentary misgiving in the heavenly hosts that serve and worship. And yet that the manifold needs and claims of the faithful on earth were the object of God's gracious purposes becomes clear and ever clearer as we advance.)

1. After these things I saw, and behold, a door was opened [1]
in heaven, and the former voice,[2] which I had heard as of a trumpet
speaking with me, said, Come up hither, and I will show thee
the things which must come to pass hereafter. 2. Straightway
I was in the spirit:[3]

Vision of a throne and of Him that sat thereon, 2–3

And behold a throne was set in heaven,
And on the throne (was) one seated;

[1] I have taken these participles as finite verbs, a construction occasionally occurring in our author and in Hebrew, and very frequently in Aramaic. If rendered as participles the sense is not so good: "Behold, a door opened in heaven, and the former voice, as of a trumpet speaking with me, saying."

[2] *i.e.* that in i. 10.

[3] On the high probability that part of this chapter was written at an earlier date by our author and subsequently incorporated by him when he edited the complete work, see vol. i. 104 sq., § 3.

3. And he that sat was to look upon like a jasper stone and a sardius,
And there (was) a rainbow round about the throne, like an emerald to look upon.

The four and twenty Elders

4. And round about the throne (were) four and twenty thrones:
And on the thrones four and twenty elders sitting,
Clothed in white garments;
And on their heads (were) crowns of gold.

5. And out of the throne proceeded lightnings and voices and thunders,
And seven lamps of fire were burning before the throne,[1]

The four Cherubim, 6^b–8^b

6. And before the throne there was as it were a sea of glass like unto crystal;
And [2] round about the throne (were) four living creatures,[3] full of eyes before and behind.

7. And the first creature (was) like a lion,
And the second creature like a calf,
And the third creature had a face as of a man,
And the fourth creature (was) like a flying eagle.

The Cherubim praise God as Holy, Almighty, and Ever-lasting

8 And the four living creatures had each of them six wings,[4]
And they rest [5] not day and night, saying:
Holy, holy, holy (is) the Lord God Almighty,[6]
Which was, and which is, and which is to come.

[1] A gloss is added here: "which are the seven spirits of God." On the whole line see vol. i. 117.

[2] A disturbing gloss is added here: "in the midst of the throne and"; see vol. i. 118.

[3] *i.e.* Cherubim; see vol. i. 119–123.

[4] The following clause is here interpolated: "Around and within they are full of eyes"; see vol. i. 125.

[5] Pr gig and $\mathrm{vg}^{a, d}$ give "rested." See next note.

[6] The rendering "Almighty" is probably right, but by no means certain. The Hebrew behind *παντοκράτωρ* is in our author צבאות; see Isa. vi. 3. See footnote on i. 7 above. The specific word in Greek for "Almighty" is *παντοδύναμος*, which is found in Wisd. vii. 23, xi. 17, xviii. 15. It is significant that, although *κρατεῖν* has in some instances approximately the meaning of "to be powerful," in the LXX (see Esth. i. 1; 1 Esdr. iv. 38, etc.), it never has this meaning in our author nor in the NT. The two words *παντοκράτωρ*, *παντοδύναμος* are found side by side in the Liturgy of St. James; see Lightfoot. *Apostolic Fathers*, II. i. 7. In the Apostles' Creed and generally in later times omnipotens is the equivalent of *παντοκράτωρ*. The rendering "Lord God of Hosts" would be safe in any case.

9. And when the living creatures give[1] glory and honour
and thanks
To him that sitteth on the throne,
Who liveth for ever and ever,

The Elders praise God as the Creator of all things, 10–11

10. The four and twenty elders fall[1] down before him that
sitteth on the throne,
And worship[1] him that liveth for ever and ever,
And cast their crowns before the throne, saying,

11. Worthy art thou our Lord and God,
To receive the honour and the glory and the power:
For thou didst create all things,
And because of thy will they were, and were created.[2]

CHAPTER V.

THE VISION OF CHRIST THE REDEEMER, THROUGH WHOM ARE ALL THINGS.

(As in iv. we have the vision of God from whom are all things, in v. we have the vision of the Lamb, into whose hands the destinies of the world are committed, inasmuch as through His redeeming death He had won the right to carry God's purposes into effect. As in iv. the Elders and Cherubim worship God as the Creator, in v. the Cherubim, Elders, and angels worship Christ as the Redeemer, while the chapter closes in the adoration of God and Christ by all.)

Vision of the sealed book which none could open, 1–4

1. And I saw upon the right hand of him that sat on the
throne a book written within and on the back, sealed

[1] These verbs are futures and not pasts in the Greek. But the context cannot admit of futures. We have here *no prediction of what shall be under certain circumstances*, but (*a*) either *an account of what the Seer saw in a vision in the past*—in such a case we should have pasts, and so Pr vg$^{a.\,d.\,v}$ arm^{1} render—(*b*) or *a statement of the regular order of divine worship in heaven*. Since the praise of the Elders follows immediately on that of the Cherubim, the context seems to favour (*b*). Hence the futures are to be rendered as presents. The Greek futures represent Hebrew imperfects in the mind of our author *used in a frequentative sense*—a common usage in Hebrew; see vol. i. *Gram.* § 10. ii. (*h*). But (*a*) may be right, and the context refer simply to what the Seer saw in his vision. Then the futures would have to be rendered as pasts, as in the Latin and Armenian Versions mentioned above. The Hebrew imperfects in the mind of our author would explain this anomaly also. In careful translations like the LXX the uncertainty of the translators as to whether the Hebrew imperfect should be rendered by the Greek present, future, or past imperfect is constantly manifest, each of these renderings being possible.

[2] Lit. "were" (ἦσαν—so A omitting rest of line). Other MSS and Versions: "were and were created."

2. with seven seals. And I saw a strong angel proclaiming
with a loud voice, Who is worthy to open the book, and
3. to loose the seals thereof? And no one in heaven, or on
earth, or under the earth was able to open the book, or to
4. look thereon. And I wept much, because no one was
5. found worthy to open the book, or to look thereon. And

save the Lamb, whom the Seer now beholds

one of the Elders saith unto me, Weep not: Behold the
Lion that is of the tribe of Judah, the Root of David, hath
6. prevailed to open the book and its seven seals. And I
saw between the throne and the four living creatures and
the elders[1] a Lamb standing as though it had been slain,
having seven horns and seven eyes, which are the seven
7. spirits of God sent out into all the earth. And he came
and took[2] (it) out of the right hand of him that sat on

Adoration of the Lamb by the Cherubim, Elders, and countless hosts of angels, 8–12

8. the throne. And when he had taken the book, the
four living creatures and the four and twenty elders fell
9. down before the Lamb, having each of them a harp and
golden bowls full of incense.[3] And they sang[4] a new
song, saying,

Worthy art thou to take the book,
And to open the seals thereof;
For thou wast slain,

And hast redeemed unto God with thy blood
Men of every tribe, and tongue, and people, and nation,
10. And hast made them unto our God a kingdom and priests,
And they reign[5] upon the earth.

11. And I saw, and heard the voice of many angels round
about the throne;[6] and the number of them was ten
thousand times ten thousand and thousands of thousands,
12. saying, with a loud voice:

Worthy is the Lamb that hath been slain
To receive the power, and riches, and wisdom,
And might, and honour, and glory, and blessing.

[1] Here the Lamb stands between the inner circle of the Cherubim and the outer circle of the Elders. This implies a Hebraism in the text. See vol. i. 140. Otherwise render: "in the midst of the throne and the four living creatures and in the midst of the elders."

[2] The perfect is here an aorist perfect: the RV. renders "taketh"; cf. viii. 5. See Introd. vol. i. *Gram.* § 4. v.

[3] The MSS add a gloss here: "which are the prayers of the saints." The prayers and the incense were not identical; see vol. i. 145.

[4] The text has "sing"; but this can represent the Hebrew imperfect in our author's mind.

[5] In the vision the Seer sees the saints already reigning in the Millennial Kingdom. Otherwise the verb is to be given a future sense as a Hebraism.

[6] The MSS add a gloss here: "And the living creatures and the elders." See vol. i. 148.

13–14. (These two verses form the proper close to iv.–v., for they give the grand finale pronounced by all creation in praise of both God and the Lamb—the themes of iv. and v. 1–12.)

13. And every created thing which is in heaven, and on the earth, and under the earth, and on the sea, and all things that are therein, heard I, saying,

All creation unites in praising God and the Lamb, 13–14

Unto him that sitteth upon the throne, and unto the Lamb,
Be the blessing, and the honour, and the glory,
And the power, for ever and ever.
14. And the four living creatures said
Amen.
And the elders fell down and worshipped.

CHAPTER VI.

THE JUDGMENT OF THE WORLD BEGINS WITH THE OPENING OF THE SEALS BY CHRIST.

(Christ opens seal after seal of the Seven-sealed Book, and as they are successively opened a series of destructive agencies are let loose—war, international strife, famine, pestilence, the prayers of the martyrs which have become instruments of divine wrath (see footnote 2, p. 403), a mighty earthquake, cataclysms affecting heaven and earth. Through these God's judgments on evil are brought to pass. But the cosmic troubles are still future, and even when fulfilled are partial and not the immediate heralds of the end, as the dwellers on the earth apprehended (see vol. i. 183, 153 sqq.).

1. And I saw when the Lamb opened one of the seven seals, and I heard one of the four living creatures saying as with a voice of thunder, Come.

Vision of War

2 And I saw, and behold a white horse,
And he that sat thereon had a bow;
And there was given unto him a crown:
And he went forth conquering and to conquer.

3. And when he opened the second seal, I heard the second living creature saying, Come.

Vision of international and civil strife

4. And another horse, a red one, went forth:
And to him that sat thereon was given to take away the peace of the earth,[1]
And that they should slay one another,
And there was given to him a great sword.[2]

5. And when he opened the third seal, I heard the third living creature saying, Come.

Vision of famine

And I saw, and behold, a black horse;
And he that sat thereon had a balance in his hand.

6. And I heard as it were a voice in the midst of the four living creatures saying,

A measure of wheat for a penny,
And three measures of barley for a penny;
But to the oil and the wine do no hurt.[3]

7. And when he opened the fourth seal, I heard the voice of the fourth living creature saying, Come.

Vision of pestilence

8. And I saw, and behold, a pale horse:[4]
And he that sat thereon was named Pestilence,[5]

[1] So A, which omits ἐκ. But even if we retain ἐκ, with the great majority of the authorities, the sense could be the same; cf. ii. 9, "the blasphemy of (ἐκ) them." This peace is the wrong peace. Christ came to destroy it to make room for the true peace. The text recalls a saying of Christ in Matt. x. 34: "Think not that I came to send peace on the earth: I come not to send peace but a sword." Otherwise with א, etc., render: "to take peace from the earth."

[2] The sword bears here the eschatological meaning of civil and international strife. It is given by God to the faithless nations that they may destroy each other with it. See vol. i. 165.

[3] Ramsay (*Cities of St. Paul*, 430 sq.) traces these commands to ancient custom. "The annual crops may be destroyed, but that means only scarcity and high prices; a new year will bring new crops. On the other hand, the vines and the olive must not be destroyed, because that means lasting ruin. New olive trees take about seventeen years to mature. Vines also need a number of years. . . . This old principle of West Asiatic international religious law was taken up into the Mosaic Law." This is no doubt true, but our author is first of all and mainly dependent on the Little Apocalypse (Mark xiii. and parallels) and Zech. i. 8, vi. 2-7. See vol. i. 158 sqq.

[4] The MSS add a gloss: "And Hades followed with him." See vol. i. 169 sq.

[5] So θάνατος must be rendered. It bears this meaning in ii. 23, xviii. 8, and frequently in the LXX. It=דבר. See vol. i. 170. In Aquila and Symmachus דבר is rendered by λοιμός ("pestilence"), which is unmistakable in meaning, but in the LXX by θάνατος and not λοιμός. (Hence correct footnote in vol. i. 170.) Aquila so renders it in Deut. xxviii. 21; Amos iv. 10; Hab. iii. 5: Sym. in Ps. lxxvii. (lxxviii.) 48, xc. (xci.) 6; Jer. xlv. (xxxviii.) 2, and both translators in Ex. v. 3, ix. 3, 15; Ezk vi. 12, xii. 16. In Ps. lxxvii. (lxxviii.) 50 the LXX renders both מות and דבר by θάνατος.

And authority was given unto him over the fourth part of
the earth.[1]

9. And when he had opened the fifth seal, I saw underneath the altar the souls of them that had been slain for the word of God, and for the testimony which they held: *Vision of the martyrs praying for retribution on their persecutors, 9–10*

10. And they cried[2] with a loud voice, saying,

How long, O Master, holy and true,
Dost thou not judge and avenge our blood
On them that dwell on the earth?

11. And there was given to each one of them a white robe; *The martyrs given spiritual bodies*
And they were bidden to rest yet for a little season,
Until their fellow-servants also and their brethren should be fulfilled,
That should be killed even as they.

12. And I saw when he opened the sixth seal:

And there was a great earthquake; *Vision of an earthquake with other cosmic evils, 12–14*
And the sun became black as sackcloth of hair,
And the whole moon became as blood;

13. And the stars of heaven fell[3] to the earth,
As a fig tree casteth her unripe figs,
When shaken by a mighty wind.

[1] MSS add a gloss: "to kill with sword and with famine and with pestilence (or 'death'), and with the wild beasts of the earth." See vol. i. 171.

[2] Though the subject of the seal is described as "persecutions" (see vol. i. 158, 171 sqq.), in keeping with the original eschatological tradition in Mark xiii. 7–9, 24–25 (and parallels), the reader should observe that its character has been changed by our author. Here the first thought is not of the persecutors or of their victims, but of the prayers of the latter. The prayers of the martyrs, vi. 9–10, are conceived as an instrument of divine wrath. The prayers of the martyrs offered on the altar, vi. 9–10, as those of all the saints, viii. 3–4, become spiritual forces. Hence a voice from this altar, ix. 13, orders the four angels of punishment to be let loose for the second Woe, and in xiv. 18 an angel from this altar delivers to the Son of Man the divine command to undertake the judgment of the earth, while in xvi. 7 (which rightly belongs to xix., see vol. ii. 122) the altar declares, as the angels, Elders and Cherubim have already done, that God's righteousness and truth have at last been vindicated in the destruction of Rome. Thus the prayers of the martyrs and saints are conceived as bringing about divine judgment, like the other seals.

[3] ἔπεσαν should perhaps be rendered "were cast," seeing that πίπτειν is here used as the passive of βάλλειν = "casteth," in the next line. In Isa. xxxiv. 4 the same verb is presupposed in both clauses of the LXX and Sym.: πεσεῖται . . . ὡς πίπτει. See vol. i. 180.

14. And the heaven was parted,
Being rolled up as a scroll;[1]
And every mountain and island were moved out of their
places.

Men's hearts fail them for fear, 15-17

15. And the kings of the earth, and the princes, and the
chief captains, and the rich, and the strong, and every
bondman and freeman, hid themselves in the caves and
16 in the rocks of the mountains; and said to the mountains
and to the rocks,

Fall on us, and hide us from the presence of him that
sitteth on the throne,
And from the wrath of the Lamb:

17. For the great day of his[2] wrath is come;
And who is able to stand?

CHAPTER VII.

VISION OF THE SEALING OF THE SPIRITUAL ISRAEL: AND OF THEIR BLESSEDNESS IN HEAVEN AFTER MARTYRDOM.

(In the preceding five chapters there is a progressive drama, advancing in a series of visions dealing first with its chief agents: (*a*) with the Christian Church on earth, ii.–iii.; (*b*) with God from whom are all things, iv.; (*c*) with Christ, who takes upon Himself the fulfilment of God's purposes, v.; and then with the opening of the first six Seals, which are to be followed by a series of social and cosmic judgments, vi. But with vii. 1–3 a pause is made in order that the spiritual Israel may be sealed, to secure them against the coming three Woes of a demonic character, 4–8. Thus in vii. 1–8 a pause is made in the movement of the divine drama, but in vii. 9–17 there is more: there is a breach in the unity of time, a unity which has been observed in ii.–vii. 8. But this breach is full of purpose. The sealing in vii. 1–4, though it secures the faithful from demonic powers, does not secure them from suffering martyrdom. Hence to encourage them to face these impending evils the Seer recounts the vision in vii. 9–17, in which, looking to the close of the great tribula-

[1] So ℵ ἑλισσόμενος and some Cursives. So also Isa. xxxiv. 4: ἑλιγήσεται ὡς βιβλίον ὁ οὐρανός. But the best attested reading, ἑλισσόμενον, is perhaps at once original and a primitive slip for the emended form in ℵ. If ἑλισσόμενον be taken as the original and correct text, then it is to be rendered: "as a scroll being rolled up."

[2] Less weighty authorities read "their"

tion, he beholds those who had been sealed and died as martyrs, already triumphant in heaven before the establishment of the Millennial Kingdom. This vision is proleptic. It constitutes a breach in the unity of time. At its close the chronological order of events is resumed. Such proleptic visions recur with the same purpose later on.)

Destructive agencies restrained till God's servants are sealed, 1–3

1. After this I saw four angels standing at the four corners
of the earth, holding the four winds of the earth, that no
wind should blow on the earth, or on the sea, or upon any
2. tree. And I saw another angel ascend from the sun-
rising, having a seal[1] of the living God: and he cried
with a loud voice to the four angels, to whom it was
3. given to hurt the earth and the sea, saying, Hurt not
the earth, neither the sea, nor the trees, till we have sealed
4. the servants of our God in their foreheads. And I heard
the number of them that were sealed: a hundred and
forty and four thousand were sealed[2] out of every tribe of
the children of Israel.

The spiritual Israel sealed, 4–8

5. Of the tribe of Judah were sealed[2] twelve thousand:
Of the tribe of Reuben twelve thousand:
7. Of the tribe of Simeon twelve thousand:
Of the tribe of Levi twelve thousand:
Of the tribe of Issachar twelve thousand:
8. Of the tribe of Zebulun twelve thousand:
Of the tribe of Joseph twelve thousand:
Of the tribe of Benjamin were sealed[2] twelve thousand:
5.[c] Of the tribe of Gad twelve thousand:
6. Of the tribe of Asher twelve thousand:
Of the tribe of Naphtali twelve thousand:
Of the tribe of Manasseh twelve thousand.[3]

Vision of the future blessedness of those that had been sealed and suffered martyrdom

9. After these things I saw,
And behold, a great multitude, which no man could number,
Out of every nation, and (all) tribes and peoples and tongues,
Standing before the throne and before the Lamb,
Clothed in white robes, and with palms in their hands;

[1] The text here is without the article. In ix. 4, where it recurs, it has the art.

[2] The participle here is to be rendered as a finite verb. See Introd. *Gram.* § 4. ii. (*b*).

[3] 5[c]–6 have been restored to their original order, in which the sons of Leah are followed by those of Rachel, and these in turn first by the sons of Leah's handmaid and then by Rachel's. See vol. i. p. 207.

Their praise before the throne

10. And they were crying[1] with a loud voice, saying,
Salvation to our God
That sitteth on the throne,
And to the Lamb.

In which the angels join, 11–12

11. And all the angels stood round about the throne and the elders and the four living creatures; and they fell before the throne on their faces, and worshipped God, saying,

12. Amen:
Blessing, and glory, and wisdom,
And thanksgiving, and honour, and power,
And might, be unto our God for ever and ever.[2]

13. And one of the elders answered, saying unto me, These who are clothed in the white robes, who are they, and
14. whence came they? And I said unto him, My Lord, thou knowest. And he said unto me,

These are they that have come out of the great tribulation,
And have washed[3] their robes,
And made them white in the blood of the Lamb.

The blessedness of the martyrs, 15–17

15. Therefore they are before the throne of God;
And they serve him day and night in his temple:
And he that sitteth on the throne shall abide upon them.[4]

16. They shall hunger no more, neither thirst any more;
Neither shall the sun **smite**[5] them any more, nor any heat:

17. For the Lamb that is in the midst of the throne shall be their shepherd,
And shall guide them unto the fountains of the waters of life:
And God shall wipe away all tears from their eyes.

[1] Here *κράζουσι* represents the imperfect in Hebrew in the Seer's mind, and should be rendered by a past imperfect.

[2] Nearly all authorities but C Pr add "Amen"; but it seems to be here a liturgical addition, as Swete remarks: it is bracketed by WH. See note in vol. i. pp. 19, 151 sq. The MSS read: "The blessing and the glory," etc.

[3] We have here a Hebraism frequent in our author; see note in vol. i. 14 sqq. The RV. here, as always in the case of this idiom, is wrong—"Come . . . and they washed."

[4] Or: "shall cause his Shekinah to dwell upon them." See vol. i. p. 215. The construction *σκηνοῦν ἐπ' αὐτούς* is not found in any OT. version (so far as I know) except in Aquila's (Ex. xxiv. 16). In xxi. 3 of our text we have *σκηνοῦν μετ' αὐτῶν*. Now, since *σκηνοῦν* = שׁכן and על frequently follows שׁכן, *σκηνοῦν ἐπί* seems here modelled on the Hebrew, as *σκηνοῦν μετά* on עם שׁכן. Cf. the presupposed interchange of על and עם in the LXX and Theod. of Dan. vii. 13, while Matt. xxiv. 30, xxvi. 64 (*ἐρχόμενον ἐπὶ τ. νεφελῶν*) and the LXX of Dan. vii. 13, presuppose על, and Mark xiii. 26, Luke xxi. 27 (*ἐρχόμενον ἐν*), and Mark xiv. 62 (*ἐρχόμενον μετά*), presuppose עם.

[5] An emendation of Gwynn and Swete. See vol. i. 216.

CHAPTER VIII.

HEAVEN'S PRAISES STILLED THAT THE PRAYERS OF ALL THE FAITHFUL MAY BE PRESENTED TO GOD AGAINST THE IMPENDING THREE WOES.

(1, 3-5, 2 (restored), 6 (restored), 13. Amid the silence of heaven for the space of half an hour, when all praises and thanksgivings were hushed, the prayers of all the saints are presented before God, 1, 3-5, to shield them in the coming tribulation. Then three Trumpets are given to three angels, wherewith they prepared to sound, 6, whereupon the Seer beheld another vision, even an angel flying in mid heaven and proclaiming, "Woe, woe, woe to the inhabiters of the earth," *i.e.* the non-Christians and faithless, because of the three Woes that were about to come upon them, 13. On the interpolated passage, viii. 7-12, and the changes introduced by the interpolator in viii. 1, 2, 6, 13, see notes below, and vol. i. 219 sqq.)

Silence made in heaven that the prayers of all the saints might be presented before God, 3-5

1. And when he opened the seventh seal, there followed a
3. silence in heaven for about the space of half an hour.[1] And
another angel came and stood by the altar, having a golden
censer; and there was given to him much incense, that he
should offer it upon[2] the prayers of all the saints upon the
4. golden altar which was before the throne. And the smoke
of the incense went up from the angel's hand before God
5. on behalf of the prayers of the saints. And the angel took
the censer and filled it with the fire of the altar, and cast
it upon the earth. And there followed lightnings, and
voices, and thunders,[3] and an earthquake.

Three angels bidden to sound the three trumpets announcing the three Woes, 2, 6, 13

2. And I saw **three** angels; and unto them were given **three** trumpets.[4]

[1] viii. 2 is an intrusion in its present context and not original in its present form. It is restored in what appears to have been its original form after viii. 5. These changes are due to the interpolation of viii. 7-12. See vol. i. 218-222, 224.

[2] Or "on behalf of."

[3] This is the original order as in iv. 5, xi. 19, xvi. 18. See Introd. Chap. IV. where it deals with this phrase. Corrupt order in MSS, due to interpolator of viii. 7-12.

[4] The text reads: "And I saw the seven angels which stand (ἑστήκασιν. This termination -ασιν not found elsewhere in our author, who uses -αν. Cf. xix. 3, εἴρηκαν; xxi. 6, γέγοναν. See vol. i. Introd. *Gram.* § 1. iii. (*c*)) before God, and there were given unto them seven trumpets."

6. And the **three**[1] angels who had the **three**[1] trumpets prepared to sound.[2]

13. And I saw, and I heard an eagle flying in the midst of heaven, saying with a loud voice, Woe, woe, woe, to them that dwell on the earth, because of the voices[3] of the trumpets of the three angels, which are about to sound.

INTERPOLATED PASSAGE.

[7. And the first (angel) sounded,
And there followed hail and fire, mingled with blood, and they were cast upon the earth:
And the third part of the earth was burnt up,
And the third part of the trees was burnt up,
And all[4] green grass was burnt up.

8. And the second angel sounded:
And as it were a great mountain burning with fire was cast into the sea:
And the third part of the sea became blood;
9. And there died the third part of the creatures which were in the sea—that had life;
And the third part of the ships were destroyed.

10. And the third angel sounded:
And there fell from heaven a great star, burning as a torch,
And it fell on a third part of the waters, and on the fountains of waters,[5]
11.[b] And the third part of the waters became like[6] wormwood;
And † many men †[7] died of the waters, because they had become bitter.

[1] Text has "seven."

[2] Here the editor of John's Apocalypse interpolated a small Apocalypse, viii. 7–12; see vol. i. 218–222. This consisted of four stanzas of four lines each. These four plagues are modelled on the first four Bowls.

[3] Text reads: "the remaining voices." The addition comes from the hand of the interpolator of viii. 7–12.

[4] Instead of "all green grass" the rest of viii. 7–12 suggests that in the original document there stood originally: "the third of all green grass." But why the change was made is not apparent; for as it stands it is in direct conflict with ix. 4.

[5] The context requires "of the fountains," etc. See vol. i. 234. The MSS add: "and the name of the star is called Wormwood." But this clause breaks the development of thought and makes the stanza consist of five lines instead of four.

[6] So 2038 Or[s] Pr fl gig vg s[1] bo sa eth. Other authorities = "became wormwood." But the waters did not "become wormwood," but bitter in taste like wormwood.

[7] We should expect: "the third part of mankind." See vol. i. 236.

12. And the fourth angel sounded:
And the third part of the sun was smitten,
And the third part of the moon, and the third part of the stars;
So that the third part of them was darkened,
And † the day did not shine for the third part of it, nor likewise the night. †[1]]

CHAPTERS IX.–XIII.

THE THREE WOES.

(The three Woes, *i.e.* (1) the demonic locusts, (2) the demonic horsemen, (3) Satan and the two Beasts. These affect only those that dwell on the earth, *i.e.* the non-Christians, viii. 13, who had not the seal of God on their foreheads, ix. 4. The third Woe, it is true, results in the universal martyrdom of the faithful, xiii. 15; but its power to deceive and destroy spiritually is limited to the non-faithful, xiii. 14. Thus these Woes affect in the deepest sense only those who had not the seal of God on their foreheads. Yet evil at this stage appears to have triumphed, and the cause of God on earth to be brought to an end for evermore.)

THE FIRST AND SECOND WOES.

IX. (The first Woe consists of a plague of demonic locusts, which had no power to hurt those who had God's seal on their foreheads, but only those who had not, 1–11. The second Woe consists of a plague of demonic horsemen, which were let loose from the Euphrates and destroyed one-third of the heathen world, 13–21.)

CHAPTER IX.

1. And the **first** [2] angel sounded:
And I saw a star fallen from heaven to the earth,
And there was given unto him the key of the pit of the abyss.

[1] The text is hopelessly corrupt. There is no connection between the destruction of one-third part of the sun and the reduction of the *length* of the day by one-third. The corruption may have arisen in the Hebrew The Bohairic gives what was apparently the original sense: "the third part of them did not shine by day, nor likewise by night." Cf. eth. I here withdraw the note in vol. i. 237 unless so far as it traces the error to the Semitic original.

[2] "Fifth," owing to the interpolation of the four plagues in viii. 7–12.

First Woe —plague of demonic locusts, 2-3

2. And he opened the pit of the abyss ;
And there went up a smoke from the pit,
As the smoke of a great furnace ;
And the sun and the air were darkened by the smoke of the pit.

3. And out of the smoke came forth locusts upon the earth ;
And power was given them, as the scorpions of the earth have power.

No power to injure any save such as had not God's seal on their foreheads, 4-5

4. And it was said unto them that they should not hurt the grass of the earth,
Nor any green thing, nor any tree, but only the men
That had not the seal of God on their foreheads.

5. And it was given them that they should not kill them,
But that they should be tormented five months :
And their torment was as the torment of a scorpion, when it striketh a man.[1]

6. And in those days men shall seek death,
And shall not find it ;
And they shall desire to die,
But death shall flee[2] from them.

The appearance of the locusts, 7-10

7. And the forms of the locusts were like unto horses prepared for war ;
And on their heads as it were crowns like gold,
And their faces were as the faces of men.

8. And they had hair as the hair of women,
And their teeth were as those of lions ;

9. And they had breastplates, as it were breastplates of iron.
And the sound of their wings was as the sound of chariots,
(Yea) of many horses rushing to war.

10. And they have tails like unto scorpions, and stings ;
And in their tails is their power
To hurt men five months.

Their king

11. They have over them as king the angel of the abyss :
His name in Hebrew is Abaddon.[3]

[1] In my Commentary (vol. i. 222, 243) and Text I have treated this line as a gloss for the reason given in vol. i. 222 ; but it may be original.

[2] The text reads "fleeth," which seems to be a Hebraism : *i.e.* = Hebrew imperfect in the mind of the writer. See vol. i. Introd. *Gram.* § 4. i. (*a*).

[3] Text adds a gloss : "And in the Greek (tongue) he hath the name Apollyon." See vol. i. 245 sq.

12. The first Woe is past: behold, there come yet two Woes
hereafter.

13. And the **second**[1] angel sounded:
And I heard a voice from the horns of the golden altar
which is before God,
14. Saying to the second[1] angel who had the trumpet,
Loose the four angels who are bound at the great river
Euphrates.

The second Woe—the demonic horsemen from the Euphrates

15. And the four angels were loosed,
Which had been prepared for the hour and day and
month and year,
In order to kill the third part of mankind.

16. And the numbers of the armies of the horsemen were
twice ten thousand times ten thousand:
17. I heard the number of them: and so I saw the horses in
the vision,[2]
And them that sat < on them.

And they that sat > on them[3] had breastplates of fire and
brimstone:
And the heads of the horses were as the heads of lions;
And from their mouths issued fire and smoke and brim-
stone.

18. By these three plagues was the third part of mankind
killed,
By the fire and the smoke and the brimstone, which
issued from their mouths;
19. For the power of the horses is in their mouths;[4] and with
them they do hurt.

The third part of mankind slain, 18-19

[1] Text reads "sixth," owing to the interpolation of the four plagues in viii. 7-12.

[2] Text seems corrupt, but I cannot emend it satisfactorily. The fact that we have here the construction *τ. καθημένους ἐπ' † αὐτῶν †*—a construction against our author's usage—may point to the evil activities of John's editor. Cf. xiv. 15, 16, where in an interpolation the same wrong construction occurs twice. I have supposed a loss of *ἐπ' αὐτοὺς καὶ οἱ καθήμενοι* through hmt. and corrected *ἔχοντας* into *ἔχοντες*. *οὕτως*, according to our author's usage, refers to what precedes, cf. ii. 15, iii. 5, 16, xvi. 18; but it cannot do so here, for the description of the horses comes later.

[3] *i.e.* "on the horses." The text reads: *καθημένους ἐπ' † αὐτῶν †* (="sat on them"). This incorrect phrase seems due to the interpolator who tampered with the text. I here withdraw the suggestions in vol. i. 252 sq.

[4] The text adds a gloss here: "and in their tails; for their tails are like unto serpents, having heads." But the destructive powers of the horses lie in the fire, smoke, and brimstone which issue from their mouths, and not in their tails. The gloss is due to ix. 10. See vol. i. 253 sq.

The rest repented not, 20–21

20. And the rest of mankind, which had not been killed by these plagues,
Did not even repent of the works of their hands,
So as not to worship demons, and the idols
Of gold, and of silver, and of brass, and of stone, and of wood;
Which can neither see, nor hear, nor walk:

21. And they repented not of their murders, nor of their sorceries,
Nor of their fornication, nor of their thefts.

CHAPTER X.

THE SEER'S NEW COMMISSION.

(This chapter serves several purposes. It was written mainly as an introduction to xi. 1–13 (the Little Book), but partly also to prepare the way for xii. sqq. (see x. 11) and partly to declare that the time prayed for by the martyrs, vi. 9 sqq., when God's purposes, x. 7, should be accomplished, would no longer be delayed. Thus x. links together the earlier chapters with the later. A strong angel presents the seer with the Little Book (*i.e.* xi. 1–13—a transmitted source), and swears that God's purpose with regard to the world would be forthwith fulfilled, 1–7. The Seer is then bidden to eat this Book and to issue other prophecies, 8–11.)

The angel with the Little Book

1. And I saw another strong angel coming down from[1]
heaven clothed with a cloud, and the rainbow was upon
his head, and his face was as the sun, and his legs[2] were
2. as pillars of fire. And he had in his hand a little book
open: and he set his right foot upon the sea, and his
3. left foot upon the earth; And he cried with a loud voice, as
a lion roareth: and when he cried, the seven thunders
4 uttered their voices. And when the seven thunders
uttered (their voices), I was about to write: and I heard
a voice from heaven saying, Seal up the things which the
5. seven thunders have uttered, and write them not. And
the angel that I saw standing upon the sea and upon the
6. earth lifted up his right hand to heaven, And sware by
him that liveth for ever and ever, who created the heaven
and the things that are therein, and the earth and the

The seven thunders, but their message not to be written down, 3–4

God's purposes to be fulfilled without delay, 6–7

[1] The word is here ἐκ.

[2] That οἱ πόδες αὐτοῦ has this meaning here is shown in vol. i. 259.

things that are therein, and the sea and the things
that are therein, that there shall be time no longer.
7. But in the days of the voice of the third[1] angel, when
he shall sound,[2] then is the mystery of God finished,
according to the good tidings which he declared to his
8. servants the prophets. And the voice which I heard from
heaven spake unto me again and said,[3] Go, take the book
which is open in the hand of the angel that standeth upon
9. the sea and upon the earth. And I went unto the angel
and bade[4] him give me the little book. And he saith
unto me, Take it and eat it up, and it shall make thy belly
10. bitter, but in thy mouth it shall be sweet as honey. And The Seer eats the Book
I took the little book out of the hand of the angel and ate
it up; and it was in my mouth sweet as honey, and when I
11. had eaten it my belly was made bitter. And they said The Seer will afterwards issue other prophecies
unto me, Thou must prophesy again concerning many
peoples and nations and tongues and kings.

CHAPTER XI.

THE ANTICHRIST IN JERUSALEM.

(**XI. 1–13** is a proleptic digression on the Antichrist in Jerusalem. It is a digression, because the Seer turns aside from his main theme of the Antichrist as identical with Rome and its empire: it is proleptic, because in point of time it belongs to the third Woe, when Satan has been cast down from heaven, and the kingdom of the Antichrist established, xii.–xiii. This task once fulfilled in xi. 1–13, he returns to his main theme in xi. 14–xviii. The seer here uses a source which originally had in several respects a different meaning. Its present meaning is given in the short summary in vol. i. 269.)

1. And he gave[5] me a reed like unto a rod, saying, Rise The measuring of the faithful to secure them against demonic powers, 1–2
and measure the temple of God, and the altar, and them
2. that worship therein. But the court that is without the

[1] Text reads "seventh." For this and other changes introduced by an early editor, see vol. i. 219 sqq.

[2] See vol. i. 264 sq.

[3] The Greek is solecistic, and the solecism appears to go back to the Seer.

[4] "And bade" is here a rendering of λέγων, followed by an inf., as in xiii. 14.

[5] The Greek is ἐδόθη μοι λέγων, which must be rendered as if it were ἔδωκεν μοι . . . λέγων. For like abnormal constructions, see note, vol. i. 274.

temple leave out, and measure it not; for it hath been
given unto the nations: and the holy city they shall
3. tread under foot forty and two months.[1] And I will
appoint my two witnesses, and they shall prophesy a
thousand two hundred and threescore days, clothed in

The preaching of the two witnesses, 3-6

4. sackcloth. These are the two olive trees and the two
candlesticks, which stand before the Lord of the earth.
5. And if any man will hurt them, fire proceedeth out of
6. their mouth, and devoureth their enemies.[2] These
have the power to shut the heaven, that it rain not
during the days of their prophecy: and they have power
over the waters to turn them into blood, and to smite

The Beast from the abyss puts them to death in Jerusalem, and the people of the land rejoice, 7-10

7. the earth with every plague, as often as they will. And
when they have finished their testimony, the beast that
cometh up out of the abyss shall make war with them, and
8. shall overcome them, and kill them. And their dead
bodies (shall lie) in the street of the great city, that
spiritually is called Sodom and Egypt, where also their
9. Lord was crucified. And some of the peoples and tribes
and tongues and nations look upon their dead bodies
three days and a half, and suffer not their dead bodies
to be laid in a tomb.
10. And they that dwell in the land[3] rejoice over them, and
make merry; and they shall send gifts one to another;
because these two prophets had tormented them that

Resurrection and ascension of the two witnesses, 11-12

11. dwell in the land.[3] And after the three days and a half
the breath of life from God entered into them, and they
stood upon their feet, and great fear fell upon them that
12. beheld them. And they heard a great voice from heaven
saying unto them, Come up hither. And they went up
into heaven in the cloud; and their enemies beheld them.

Judgment on Jerusalem and conversion of the rest of the Jews

13. And in that hour there was a great earthquake, and
the tenth part of the city fell; and there were killed
in the earthquake seven thousand persons: and the
rest were affrighted, and gave glory to the God of
heaven.
14. The second Woe is past: behold the third Woe
cometh quickly.

[1] Vers. 3-13 are a prophecy rather than a vision. The presents in 4-6, 9-10, are equivalent to futures. The past verbs in 11-13 represent Hebrew perfects (or in some cases probably the imperfects with vav conversive); but these perfects vividly represent the prophetic future.

[2] The text adds a gloss here which is based on 5^a and xiii. 10: "and if any will hurt them, in this manner must he be killed"; see vol. i. 284.

[3] *i.e.* Palestine; see vol. i. 289.

INTRODUCTION TO THE THIRD WOE.

XI. 15–19. The proleptic digression in xi. 1–13, to which x. is an introduction, has come to an end, and our author here returns to the progressive development of the divine drama in the third Woe, xii.–xiii. Though x. in certain respects links up the chapters that precede with those that follow it, yet in the order of action xi. 14 follows immediately on ix. and the main theme is resumed in the third Woe, which is heralded by the third Trumpet. This Woe apparently results in the absolute triumph of Satan and his agents on earth and the annihilation of the Church; but the two songs in heaven, which introduce it in xi. 15–18, disclose in advance the actual issues of events: their burden is that the Kingdom of the world has in the reality of things become the Kingdom of God and of His Christ, that the time has come for the judgment of the nations and of Satan and the Beast, for the judgment of the dead and the due recompense of God's servants.

15. And the **third**[1] angel sounded; and there followed great voices in heaven, saying,

> The kingdom of the world has become (the kingdom) of our Lord and of his Christ,
> And he shall reign for ever and ever.

Song (of the Cherubim?) over the impending advent of the Lord and of His Christ

16. And the four and twenty elders, which sit before God on their thrones, fell on their faces and worshipped God, saying,

17.
> We give thee thanks, O Lord God Almighty,
> Which art and which wast;
> Because thou hast taken thy great power,
> And hast become King.

18.
> *a.* And the nations have waxed wroth,
> *b.* And thy wrath hath come,
> *h.* And <the time> to destroy them that destroy the earth,[2]
> *c.* And the time for the dead to be judged—

Song of the Elders on the impending advent of the Millennial Kingdom, the last judgment, and the final recompense of God's servants, 16–18

[1] Text reads "seventh"; see vol. i. 218 sqq. Each Woe is heralded by a trumpet blast. Before the interpolation of viii. 7–12 there were only three trumpets.

[2] In the text this clause is certainly out of place. By its restoration after 18^{b} we recover the development of events in their true order; see vol. i. 295 sqq. "The destroyers" are the first Beast, the False Prophet, and Satan as well as their adherents.

g. The small and the great.[1]
d. And for giving their reward to thy servants,
e. The prophets and the saints,
f. And them that fear thy name.

Ark of God's covenant manifested—a pledge of the fulfilment of the songs just sung

19. And there was opened the temple of God that is in heaven; and there was seen in his temple the ark of his covenant; and there followed lightnings, and voices, and thunders, and an earthquake, and great hail.

CHAPTER XII.

A RETROSPECT.

(**XII.** This chapter is retrospective. Its object is to give the reader insight into the past in order to prepare him for the crowning evil—the climax of Satan's power upon earth. But this crowning evil is not really a sign of his growing power, but the closing stage of a war in heaven, which had already terminated in the vindication of God's sovereignty, and the hurling down of Satan to earth. Hence, however, Satan and his minions, the Roman and heathen powers, may rage, but it is but the last struggle of a beaten foe, whose malignity is all the greater, since he knows that his time is short. The vision goes back before the birth of Christ, and tells with mythological colouring how Satan sought to destroy Christ, and, after His ascension, the Church itself. In setting forth his theme the Seer has borrowed the main part of this chapter from Jewish sources, which had in turn been derived from international sources, and has adapted them—though not wholly—to their new and Christian setting. The closing verses, 14–16, were written before 70 A.D., and cannot be interpreted in detail of the crises of 95 A.D., when our author wrote See vol. i. 299, 331 sq. For a summary of the chapter, see vol. i. 298 sq.)

A woman, goddess-like in appearance (=the Jewish Church), bears a child

1. And a great sign was seen in heaven; a woman
clothed with the sun, and the moon under her feet, and
2. upon her head a crown of twelve stars. And she was
with child, and cried out in her travail and pain to be
3. delivered. And there was seen another sign in heaven;
and behold, a great red dragon, having seven heads and

[1] I have restored this line immediately after 18c; cf. xx. 12. Otherwise read line *g* immediately after line *h* (And the time) to destroy them that destroy the earth, The small and the great. "The great" would be Satan and the two Beasts: "the small" would be their adherents.

4. ten horns, and upon his heads seven[1] diadems. And
his tail drew[2] the third part of the stars of heaven, and
did cast them to the earth: and the dragon stood[3] before
the woman that was about to be delivered, that he might
5. devour her child when she was delivered. And she
was delivered of a son, a man child, who shall break[4]
all the nations with a rod of iron: and her child was
6. caught up to God and to his throne. And the woman
fled into the wilderness, where she hath a place prepared
of God, that there they should nourish her a thousand
two hundred and threescore days.

Satan on his fall from heaven, which involved one-third of the angels, sought to destroy this child, 1–5ᵃ

But the child is rapt to heaven and his mother escaped for three and a half years into the wilderness, 5ᵇ–6

7. And war burst forth[5] in heaven:
Michael and his angels had to war[6] with the dragon;
And the dragon warred and his angels; and he prevailed not,
8. Neither was their place found any more in heaven.
9. And the great dragon was cast down, the old serpent,
—He that is called the Devil and Satan,
That deceiveth the whole world—
He was cast down to the earth,
And his angels were cast down with him.

Satan and his angels storm after the child to heaven, but are over-thrown and cast down to earth, 7–9

10. And I heard a great voice in heaven, saying,
Now is come the salvation and the power
And the kingdom of our God, and the authority of his Christ:
For the accuser of our brethren is cast down,
Which accuseth them before our God day and night.
11. And they overcame him because of the blood of the Lamb,
And because of the word of their testimony,
Seeing that they loved not their lives even unto death.[7]

Triumph song of the glorified martyrs in heaven in honour of their brethren still on earth

Who in the reality of things

[1] The position of the numeral before the noun is against our author's usage. But this seems due to the source.

[2] *σύρει.* Here = Hebrew imperfect.

[3] Here *ἔστηκε*, from *στήκω*, as WH. In vii. 11 our author uses *εἱστήκει* in the same sense.

[4] See note on chap. ii. 27 (translation), and vol. i. 75.

[5] The Greek is *ἐγένετο*.

[6] *ὁ Μιχαὴλ καὶ οἱ ἄγγελοι αὐτοῦ τοῦ πολεμῆσαι.* These words cannot be explained as Greek on any hypothesis save on that of their being a slavishly literal rendering of a vigorous Hebrew idiom. See vol. i. 321 sq.

[7] A pregnant expression, meaning that they esteemed life as nothing in comparison with loyalty to their faith, even unto martyrdom. I have rendered the *καί* before *οὐκ ἠγάπησαν* by "seeing that" (cf. xviii. 3, xix. 3ᶜ), as = ו in Hebrew: cf. Gen. viii. 18, xxvi. 27. This line introduces a statement of the condition under which the action denoted by the principal verb, *ἐνίκησαν*, took place. See *Oxford Hebrew Lexicon*, p. 253; Gesenius, *Heb. Gr.* p. 456 (Oxford ed.).

have already overcome Satan by their coming martyrdom

12. Therefore rejoice, ye heavens, and ye that dwell in them:
Woe unto the earth and the sea;
For the devil is gone down to you with great wrath,
Knowing that he hath but a short time.

Satan persecutes the Christian Church, but the Jewish Christian Church escapes, 13-16

13. And when the dragon saw that he was cast down to the
earth, he persecuted the woman that had brought forth
14. the man child. And there were given to the woman the
two wings of the great eagle that she might fly into the
wilderness to her place, where she is nourished for a
time, and times, and half a time, because of[1] the serpent.
15. And the serpent cast out of his mouth after the woman
water as a river, that he might cause her to be swept away
16. by the flood. But the earth helped the woman, and the
earth opened her mouth, and swallowed up the river which
17. the dragon cast out of his mouth.[2] And the dragon waxed
wroth with the woman, and went away to make war with
the rest of her seed, which keep the commandments of
God, and hold the testimony of Jesus.

Persecution of the Gentile Christian Church

SATAN APPARENTLY TRIUMPHANT: THE CHURCH ON EARTH DESTROYED.

XII. 18-XIII., XIV. 12-13. (The climax of Satan's power on earth achieved in the personal reign of the Antichrist—the Roman Empire incarnated in the demonic Nero—for three and a half years: the universal martyrdom of the faithful, and the beatitude pronounced upon them from heaven. For a summary of this section (to which xiv. 12-13 belongs—see vol. i. 368) see vol. i. 332 sq. The third Woe, which began in xi. 15-19, is resumed here, though in xii. the way is prepared for this Woe by the casting down of Satan from heaven.)

Satan stands by the sea-shore and summons to his aid

XII. 18. And he stood upon the sand of the Sea.

[1] See note in vol. i. 330 *ad fin.*

[2] xii. 14-16, which was written originally of the Church before 70 A.D., do not admit of any intelligible reinterpretation in their present context, which relates to 95 A.D. This passage, like many others, would have undergone revision had John had his opportunity; see vol. i. 299, § 1 *ad fin.*, 332.

CHAPTER XIII.

The first Beast with seven heads and ten horns—the Roman empire incarnated in the Neronic Antichrist, ii. 18–xiii. 2

1. And from the sea I saw a beast coming up
With ten horns and seven heads,[1]
And on his heads names of blasphemy.

2. And the beast which I saw was like unto a leopard,
And his feet were as the feet of a bear,
And his mouth as the mouth of a lion:

And the dragon gave him his power,
And his throne, and great authority.

The Beast's wound healed

3. And (I saw) one of his heads slain as it were unto death;
And his deadly wound was healed:

And the whole earth wondered † after the beast †;[2]

Those that dwell upon the earth worship Satan and the first Beast

4. And they worshipped the dragon,
Because he had given his power to the beast;

And they worshipped the beast, saying,
Who is like unto the beast?
And who can war with him?

Blasphemies of the first Beast, 5^a, 6

5^a. And there was given unto him a mouth speaking great things and blasphemies;[3]
6. And he opened his mouth for blasphemies against God,
To blaspheme his name, and his tabernacle,[4] and those that dwell in the heaven.

He rules for three and a half years and overcomes the saints, 5^b 7

5^b. And there was given unto him authority to act with effect forty and two months.
7. And there was given unto him to make war with the saints, and to overcome them;
And there was given unto him authority over every tribe and people and language and nation.

[1] MSS add a gloss: "And on his horns ten diadems." The position of the numeral is against our author's usage. Further, the gloss conflicts with xii. 3^c. Again, though the use of "diadems" is befitting in relation to the Emperors of Rome [cf. xix. 12 where Christ has "many diadems"], it is quite inapt in regard to the ten vassal kings of Parthia (xvii. 12).

[2] Read: "when it saw the beast." The Greek *ὀπίσω τοῦ θηρίου* implies a corruption in the Hebrew source. מאחרי (= *ὀπίσω*) is corrupt for בראתה = *ἰδοῦσα* or *βλέπουσα*. See vol. i. 337. xiii 3^c, 8 are a doublet of xvii. 8.

[3] The three verses relating to the blasphemies of the Beast, *i.e.* 5^a, 6, clearly form a tristich; and the three lines in 5^b, 7, each beginning with *καὶ ἐδόθη αὐτῷ*, just as clearly form another tristich. Hence I have restored 5^b to its original place.

[4] Possibly "his shekinah." See vol. i. 352, ii. 205 sqq.

Those whose names were not in the Book of Life worship him

8. And all that dwelt on the earth worshipped[1] him,
Whose names were not written in the book of life
Of the Lamb that hath been slain from the foundation of the world.

Seer's admonition to be faithful in the coming persecution, 9–10

9. If any man hath an ear, let him hear.

10. If any man is for captivity,
Into captivity he goeth:
If any man is to be slain with the sword,
With the sword must he be slain.[2]

Here is the patience
And the faith of the saints.

Second Beast or False Prophet from the land—the imperial priesthood, officials, and cultured classes

11. And I saw another beast coming up out of the earth;
And he had two horns like a lamb,
But † he spake as a dragon †.[3]

12. And he exerciseth all the authority of the first beast in his sight.
And he maketh the earth and them that dwell in it to worship the first beast,
Whose deadly wound had been healed.

He makes the dwellers on the earth to worship the first Beast

His signs and deceits, 13–14

Universal martyrdom of the faithful, 15

The faithless receive the mark of the Beast on their right hand and forehead, 16–17

13. And he doeth great signs, so that he maketh even fire to
come down from heaven on the earth in the sight of
14. men. And he deceiveth them that dwell on the earth
by reason of the signs that it was given him to do in
the sight of the beast; saying to them that dwell on the
earth, that they should set up an image[4] to the beast,
15. who had the wound of the sword, and yet lived. And
it was given unto him to give breath to the image
of the beast, that the image of the beast should also
speak, and to cause[5] that as many as should not worship
16. the image of the beast should be killed. And he causeth

[1] Text reads προσκυνήσουσιν. But this is a rendering of the Hebrew imperfect in the source. Cf. 4, where the past "worshipped" is rightly given. See vol. i. 353.

[2] A alone preserves the true text here. See vol. i. 355 sq.

[3] Read: "he was a destroyer like the dragon." The Hebrew of the source was here corrupt; see vol. i. 358 sq.

[4] Lit. "make an image."

[5] The Greek = "And it was given unto him to give breath to the image of the beast, that *the image of the beast should* both speak and *cause that as many as should not worship the beast*," etc. This does not represent the historical facts. It is also hopelessly clumsy. I have assumed, therefore, that there is a Hebraism in the text akin to another we have found frequently. The second beast was empowered to do two things: the first to give life to the image of the first beast, and the second—to cause all that did not worship the image to be put to death. Thus καὶ ποιήσῃ would naturally be καὶ

all, the small and the great, and the rich and the poor,
and the free and the bond, to receive[1] a mark on their
17. right hand or upon their forehead: and that no man
should be able to buy or sell, save he that hath the mark,
the name of the beast or the number of his name.
18. Here is wisdom. Let him that hath understanding
count the number of the beast; for it is the number of
a man: and his number is Six hundred and sixty-six.[2]

Seer's admonition to the faithful who are to be martyred

XIV. 12. Here is the patience of the saints, who keep the
commandments of God, and the faith of Jesus.

13. And I heard a voice from heaven saying, Write, Blessed
are the dead which die in the Lord from henceforth:
yea, saith the Spirit, that they may rest from their
labours;[3] for their works go with them.[4]

Third Beatitude pronounced by a voice from heaven over the martyred Church, xiv. 12–13

CHAPTER XIV.

PROLEPTIC VISIONS—OF THE GLORIFIED MARTYRS IN THE MILLENNIAL KINGDOM, OF THE DOOM OF ROME AND OF THE HEATHEN NATIONS.

(This entire chapter is proleptic: that is, the orderly development of future events, as set forth in the successive visions, is here abandoned (as in vii. 9–17, xi. 1–13), and the visions of coming judgments in xvi. 17–xix., xx. 7–10, are summarised in xiv. 8–11, 14, 18–20. To this summary is prefixed a description of the blessed (*i.e.* the 144,000 in vii. 4–8) on Mount Zion during the Millennial reign. This is a later stage in their blessedness than that in vii. 9–17. The object of the entire chapter is to encourage the faithful to endurance in the face of the universal martyrdom just foreseen by the Seer in xiii. 15.

ποιῆσαι, and be parallel to *δοῦναι* that precedes. But here by a common Hebrew idiom the infinitive passes into a finite verb. Thus *καὶ ἐδόθη αὐτῇ δοῦναι . . . καὶ ποιήσῃ* is a literal rendering of ויתן לה לתת . . . ותעש. In this case the imperial priesthood produce a speaking image, and cause all that do not worship it to be put to death. If we do not accept the Hebraism, then it is the image that causes the death of the faithful. But the context seems to be against this interpretation, and certainly the verse that follows is. It is the second beast in xiii. 16 that causes all to receive the mark of the beast, and historically, as we know from Pliny, etc., it was the priesthood or official classes that did so—not the images.

[1] Lit. "that they should give them."

[2] It is possible that ver. 18 is a later addition.

[3] *i.e.* the hardships, laborious toils incident to the life of faith.

[4] *i.e.* not "follow after them"; see vol. i. 370. The works are the Christlike character they have achieved; see vol. i. 372 sq.

This is done by the vision of the blessedness of the martyrs in the Millennial Kingdom, 1–5, and the vision of the doom of Rome and the heathen nations—Thus Christ's Kingdom which seemed overthrown is seen in the vision to be established on earth, and Satan's Kingdom, which appeared triumphant, to be destroyed.)

Proleptic vision of Christ's Kingdom with the glorified martyrs (= 144,000 that were sealed in vii. 4–7) on Mt. Zion in the Millennial period (= vision which comes in its due order in xx. 4–6)

1. And I saw, and behold the Lamb standing on Mount Zion,
And with him a hundred and forty and four thousand,
Having his name and the name of his Father written on their foreheads.

2. And I heard a voice from heaven,
As the voice of many waters,
And as the voice of a great thunder.

And the voice which I heard (was) as (the voice) of harpers
3. Harping with their harps, and singing as it were a new song
Before the throne, and before the four living creatures and the elders.

And no one could learn the song
Save the hundred and forty and four thousand:
4^{c}. These are they which follow the Lamb whithersoever he goeth.

The new song sung in heaven and learnt by the 144,000, 2–5

4^{d}. These have been redeemed[1] from among men (to be) a sacrifice to God,[2]
5. And in their mouth hath no falsehood been found;
For they are blameless.

Proleptic vision of the Evangelisation of the world during the Millennial period, 6–7

6. And I saw another angel flying in mid heaven, having an eternal gospel to proclaim unto them that dwell on the
7. earth, and unto every nation and tribe and tongue and people, saying with a great voice,
Fear God, and give him glory;
For the hour of his judgment is come:
And worship him that made the heaven
And the earth and sea and fountains of waters.

[1] Here it was most probably John's editor who, wrongly taking ἀπαρχή to mean "first fruits," added the following gloss: "3^{e}. who were redeemed from the earth. $4^{a.\,b}$. These are they who were not defiled with women; for they are virgins." These clauses exclude from the 144,000 all women; for the clause "who were not defiled with women" cannot be interpreted of women even metaphorically. See vol. ii. 8 sqq.

[2] The redeemed are a sacrifice (ἀπαρχή) to God, but not to the Lamb. ἀπαρχή does not mean "first fruits" here. The same interpolator who added the clauses given in note (1) has added here "and to the Lamb."

Proleptic vision of the doom of Rome and of them that worship the Beast and receive his mark (= vision coming in its due order, xvi. 17–xviii.), 8–11

8. And another, a second angel, followed, saying,
Fallen, fallen is Babylon the great,
Which had made all the nations to drink the wine [of the wrath] of her fornication.

9. And another angel, a third, followed them, saying with a great voice,
If any man worshippeth the beast and his image,
And receiveth the[1] mark on his forehead, or upon his hand,

10. He[2] shall drink of the wine of the wrath of God,
Which is mingled sheer[3] in the cup of his anger,
And he shall be tormented with fire and brimstone
In the presence of the angels and of the Lamb.

11. And the smoke of their torment goeth up for ever and ever;
And they have no rest day nor night,
That worship the beast and his image,
And whoso receiveth the mark of his name.[4]

Proleptic vision of the judgment executed by the Son of Man on the heathen nations (= vision coming in its due order in xix. 11–20, xx. 7–10), 14, 18–20

14. And I saw, and behold, a white cloud;
And on the cloud one seated like unto a son of man,
Having on his head a golden crown,
And in his hand a sharp sickle.[5]

[1] This article is necessary; see vol. ii. 15, and text *in loc.* for the cursives and versions which support it.

[2] We have here καὶ αὐτός. Three explanations are possible. (*a*) The καί is a Hebraism introducing the apodosis, and so is not to be translated; see vol. ii. p. 16. (*b*) It may be taken with the καί that follows in the third line as καὶ . . . καί, "both . . . and." But this usage is not found elsewhere in our author, though it is in J. (*c*) It may be rendered "too." καὶ αὐτός would then = "he too." But the context is against this rendering; for it presupposes that some one else just mentioned shall drink of the wine of God's wrath. But there is no such statement in xiv. 8. Besides, the phrase καὶ αὐτός (in the meaning of "he too") does not occur in our author, save in an interpolation xiv. 17, and in a Greek source xvii. 11.

[3] ἀκράτου. Can our author have taken this word to be a rendering of חמר, as the LXX in Ps. lxxiv. 9? See vol. ii. 17.

[4] Vers. 12–13, which pronounces the great beatitude on the martyred Church, has been restored to its original context after xiii. 18.

[5] Here apparently John's editor has added 15–17, which is really a doublet of xiv. 18–20. This doublet represents the judgment as a reaping of the harvest of the wrath of God. But this figure does not belong to our author, who speaks of it as a vintage; cf. xix. 15. Besides, several constructions are against his use, and the interpolator has failed to recognise the "one like a son of man" as Christ; see vol. ii. 3, 18 (*ad fin.*), 21 sq. John could never have divided the Judgment between Christ and an angel or have put any angel on an equality with Christ. It is a very stupid interpolation; for it assigns to an angel the very judgment that is to be exercised by the Word

18. And another angel[1] went forth from the altar,[2] and cried with a great voice to him that had the sharp sickle saying,

> Thrust in thy sharp sickle,
> And gather the clusters of the vine of the earth;
> For her grapes are fully ripe.

19. And he[3] thrust his sickle into the earth,
And gathered the vintage of the earth,
And cast it into the great winepress of the wrath of God.

The Son of Man treads the winepress of the wrath of God

20. And the winepress was trodden without the city,
And blood came out of the winepress even unto the horses' bridles—
To a distance of one thousand six hundred furlongs.

CHAPTER XV.

XV. 2-8. (The chronological order of events in the Seer's visions of the future is here resumed. In other words, xv. 2–8 follows immediately on xiii., for xiv. broke away from this order and was wholly proleptic. xv. 2 opens with a vision of the entire martyr host, that had fallen in xiii. and are now in heaven (as in vii. 9–17) praising God for His righteousness and proclaiming the coming conversion of the nations (that had not been deceived by Rome), who would become His servants because of His righteous acts, 2–4. Thereupon follows a vision of the dooms inflicted on Rome and the nations seduced by her in the judgments of the Bowls, 5–8.)

of God in xix. 11–21. The interpolated verses (15–17) are: 15. "And another angel went forth from the temple, crying with a great voice to him that sat on the cloud,

> Thrust in thy sickle and reap:
> For the hour to reap hath come;
> For the harvest of the earth † is dried up †.

16. And he that sat on the cloud thrust in his sickle on the earth; and the earth was reaped. 17. And another angel went forth from the temple which is in heaven, he also having a sharp sickle."

[1] Another, as distinct from the angels in vers. 6, 8, 9; otherwise render: "another, an angel."

[2] The MSS add: "who had power over fire."

[3] *i.e.* the Son of Man. The text reads "an angel"—an interpolation due to the hand that inserted 15–17. The Son of Man is never described as an angel. It is He, and not an angel, that thrusts in the sickle and gathers the vintage of the earth. Therein xiv. 14, 18–20 is a proleptic vision of the event described in the vision in xix. 11–21 where the Word of God treads the winepress of the wrath of God.

2.[1] And I saw as it were a sea of glass mingled with fire;
and them that had been victorious over the beast, and
over his image, and over the number of his name,
standing by the sea of glass, having the harps of God,
3. and singing[2] the song of the Lamb, saying,

> Great and marvellous are thy works,
> Lord God Almighty:
> Righteous and true are thy ways,
> Thou King of the nations.

4. Who shall not fear, O Lord,
> And glorify thy name?
> For thou alone art holy;
>
> For all the nations shall come
> And worship before thee:
> For thy righteous acts shall have been made manifest.

The glorified martyrs, whose roll is now complete, sing, praising God for His power and righteousness and kingship of the nations, 2–3

Who shall come and worship before Him (during the Millennial Kingdom)

5. And after these things I saw, and † the temple of the
6. tabernacle of the testimony in heaven †[3] was opened: and
seven angels[4] came forth from the temple, clothed in fine
linen,[5] pure, bright, and girt about the breasts with golden
7. girdles. And one of the four living creatures gave unto
the seven angels seven golden bowls full of the wrath of
God who liveth for ever and ever.

8. And the temple was filled with smoke from the glory of
God, and from his power; and none could enter the temple
till the seven plagues of the seven angels were finished.

Vision of seven angels who receive seven bowls of wrath, 5–8

[1] xv. 1 is an interpolation; see vol. ii. 30 sq.: "And I saw another sign in the heaven, great and marvellous, seven angels having seven plagues, (which are) the last; for in them is finished the wrath of God." This subject is not touched upon till xv. 5, as the phrase καὶ μετὰ ταῦτα εἶδον proves. This phrase is not used unless at the *beginning* of a new and important section. See vol. i. 106 and footnote.

[2] The text reads καὶ ᾄδουσιν, "and they sing" as in xiv. 3. This is the Hebrew idiom, which has already occurred frequently; see vol. i. 14 sq. That this was so understood very early we see from the Versions, which render as I do in the text: *i.e.* Pr fl arm[4. a]. We should observe the correction in א, which reads καὶ ᾄδοντας. The text here adds: "the song of Moses the servant of God and"; see, however, vol. ii. 34 sqq.

[3] A meaningless expression. Either we must excise the words: "of the tabernacle of the testimony," or, for this introduction to the Bowls go back to a Hebrew source and assume a slight corruption in the original. See vol. ii. 37 sq., where it is shown that if this introduction is from a Hebrew source we should probably read: "the temple of God which is in heaven," as in xi. 19. The corruption could quite easily arise.

[4] Text reads: "the seven angels that had the seven plagues"—a change due to the interpolator of xv. 1.

[5] See vol. ii. 38. The best MSS read λίθον. This impossible reading appears to presuppose a misrendering of the Hebrew.

CHAPTER XVI.

THE SEVEN BOWLS.

(These plagues are not in any sense a repetition of the seven Seals or the three Woes. Under the Seals (save in the fifth, where the prayers of the martyrs as spiritual judgments affect only the heathen), Christian and heathen alike suffer physically. The three Woes do *spiritual* hurt only to those who had not the Seal of God; the first two doing *physical* hurt as well: to those who had the Seal of God the three Woes could do no *spiritual* hurt, though the third could do them *physical* hurt. Since those who had been sealed have already been martyred in xiii., the Bowls affect only the heathen world.)

First Bowl poured upon the earth, 1-2

1. And I heard a great voice from the temple saying
to the seven angels, Go and pour out the seven bowls of
2. the wrath of God upon[1] the earth. And the first went
and poured out his bowl upon[1] the earth; and it became

The second in the sea, 3

3. a noisome and grievous sore upon men.[2] And the
second poured out his bowl upon[1] the sea; and it became
blood as of a dead man; and every living soul died, (even)

The third on the rivers and fountains, 4

4. the things that were in the sea. And the third poured
out his bowl upon[1] the rivers and the fountains of waters,

The fourth on the sun, 8-9

8. and they became blood.[3] And the fourth poured out
his bowl upon the sun; and it was given unto him to
9. scorch men with fire. And men were scorched with
great heat, and they blasphemed the name of God which
hath the power over these plagues, and they repented not

The fifth on the throne of the Beast, 10-11

10. to give him glory. And the fifth poured his bowl upon
the throne of the beast; and his kingdom was darkened;[4]
11. . . . and they gnawed their tongues for pain, And they
blasphemed the God of heaven because of their pains
and of their sores; and they repented not of their works.

[1] εἰς, but ἐπί in 8, 10, 12, 17 without any real difference in meaning.

[2] The MSS add the following gloss: "that had the mark of the beast and that worshipped his image"; see vol. ii. 43.

[3] Here follows an interpolation: "and I heard the angel of the waters saying," which is used to introduce 5^b–7. These clauses originally followed after xix. 4, to which context they are restored in this edition; see vol. ii. 122, also 116 sq.

[4] After "darkened" several clauses have been lost, in which the causes of the darkness and the sufferings of mankind were given. The plague of darkness could not explain the agony of the worshippers of the Beast. This plague is closely connected with the first Woe: see vol. ii. 45 sq. The phrase "because of the sores" proves that the sufferings of the subjects of the Beast cannot be explained from the text as it stands.

12. And the sixth poured out his bowl upon the great river,
the Euphrates, and its waters were dried up, that the way
might be prepared for the kings that (come) from the sun-
13. rising. And I saw from the mouth of the dragon, and
from the mouth of the beast, and from the mouth of the
14. false prophet, three unclean spirits[1] going forth[2] unto
the kings of the whole world to gather them together
16. unto the war of the great day of God Almighty.[3] And
they gathered them together to the place which is called
17. in Hebrew Har-Magedon. And the seventh poured out
his bowl upon the air; and there came forth a great
voice out of the temple, from the throne, saying, It
18. is done. And there followed lightnings, and voices and
thunders, and there followed a great earthquake, such as
there has not been since men were upon the earth, so
19. mighty an earthquake, so great.[4] And the cities of the
nations fell, and Babylon the great was remembered
before God, to give her the cup of the wine of the
20. fierceness of his wrath. And every island fled away, and
21. the mountains were not found. And great hail, (every
stone) about the weight of a talent, came[5] down from
heaven upon men: and men blasphemed God because
of the plague of hail; for the plague thereof was[6]
exceeding great.

The sixth on the Euphrates, that the Parthians might march against Rome, 12 (described more fully in xvii. 12–13, 17, 16)

Evil spirits from Satan and the Beasts mustering the nations to Har-Magedon, 13–14, 16

An earthquake follows, overthrowing the cities of the nations. Babylon reserved for special judgment, 18–20.

[1] While our text represents God as putting it into the heart of the Parthian kings, xvii. 17, 16, to destroy Rome, it is three unclean spirits from Satan and the two Beasts which muster the nations against Christ in xvi. 13–16; cf. xix. 17, 19, xx. 8.

MSS add a gloss: "As it were frogs; for they are spirits of demons working signs"; see vol. ii. 47 sq.

[2] The text here reads corruptly ἃ ἐκπορεύεται instead of ἐκπορευόμενα, which our author's usage and the context require; see vol. ii. 48.

[3] Here the MSS insert as xvi. 15—a verse which originally stood after iii. 3ᵃ, and where it is restored in this edition. It forms the second of the seven beatitudes in our author.

[4] The MSS add here: "And the great city was divided into three parts"—the contents of which are against the context, while the order of the numeral is against our author's usage; see vol. ii. 52.

[5] Lit. "cometh" = Hebrew imperfect.

[6] Lit. "is."

CHAPTER XVII.

XVII.-XVIII. THE VISION AND DOOM OF ROME, XVII. 1-6, XVIII.; THE INTERPRETATION OF THE BEAST AND OF HIS SEVEN HEADS AND TEN HORNS, XVII. 8-17.

(These two chapters are to be taken closely together. xvii. begins with a promise on the part of the angel to show the Seer the judgment of the Great Harlot; but instead he turns aside to deal with the Beast, and the promised judgment is not witnessed till xviii. Our author is here using two sources: one embraces xvii. 1ᶜ–2, 3ᵇ–6ᵃ, 7, 18, and part of 8–10, xviii. (see vol. ii. 55, 59 sqq., 94), which was originally written when Vespasian, the sixth king, was still reigning (xvii. 10). The second is fragmentary, xvii. 11–13, 17, 16, and dealt with the Neronic Antichrist, the ten kings, and the destruction of Rome.)

Vision of the woman (*i.e.* Rome) on the Scarlet Beast, 1-6

XVII. 1. And there came one of the seven angels which had the seven bowls, and he spake with me, saying, Come hither, I will show thee

The judgment of the great harlot
That sitteth upon many waters:

2. With whom the kings of the earth have committed fornication,
And with the wine of whose fornication they that dwell upon the earth have become drunken.

3. And he carried me away in the spirit into a wilderness:
and I saw a woman sitting upon a scarlet-coloured beast,
full of names of blasphemy, having seven heads and ten
4. horns. And the woman was clothed in purple and
scarlet, and adorned[1] with gold and precious stones and
pearls, having in her hand a golden cup full of abomina-
5. tions and the unclean things[2] of her fornication. And
upon her forehead (was) a name written, a mystery—

Babylon the great,
The mother of harlotries[3]
And of the abominations of the earth.

[1] Or "covered"; see note on meaning of κεχρυσωμένη here, vol. ii. 64.

[2] To be taken as an acc. after γέμον, cf. 3, and not as in RV.: nor as dependent on ἔχουσα, as suggested in my note, vol. ii. 65.

[3] So Tyc Pr vg arm². This forms a perfect parallel to "abominations." This reading of Tyc Pr vg arm may be the result of conjecture. If so, the corruption could have arisen in the Hebrew source; see vol. ii. 65.

6. And I saw the woman drunken with the blood of the
saints and with the blood of the martyrs[1] of Jesus. And
7. when I saw her I wondered with a great wonder. And
the angel said unto me, Wherefore didst thou wonder?
I will tell thee the mystery of the woman, and of the
beast that carrieth her, which hath the seven heads and
the ten horns.
8. The beast that thou sawest was, and is not, and is about
to come up out of the abyss, and he goeth his way[2] into
perdition. And they that dwell on the earth will wonder
—(all) whose names have not been written in the book of
life since the foundation of the world, when they behold
the beast, that[3] was, and is not, and yet is to come.[4]
9. Here (is needed) the mind which hath wisdom. The
10. seven heads[5] are seven kings: five of them have fallen,
the one is, the other is not yet come, and when he
11. cometh, he must continue a short time. And the beast,
that was, and is not, is himself also an eighth, and is of
the seven; and he goeth his way into perdition.
12. And the ten horns, which thou sawest, are ten kings, that
have received no kingdom as yet; but they will receive[6]
authority as kings for one hour along with the beast.
13. These have one purpose, and they give their power and
17. authority unto the beast.[7] For God hath put it into their
hearts to do his purpose,[8] and to give their kingdom unto
16. the beast, until the words of God should be fulfilled. And
the ten horns which thou sawest, and the beast,

These shall hate the harlot,
And make her desolate and naked,

The meaning of the Beast, 7

All but Christians will marvel at the Beast's return after his death, 8

The seven heads are seven kings: the sixth reigns: the seventh will reign but a short space and be succeeded by the Beast, who is one of the seven, 9-11

The ten horns are ten kings who will serve the Beast and destroy the Great Harlot, 12-13, 17, 16

[1] So rightly AV. and RV. and not "witnesses"; see vol. i. 62.

[2] It is better to follow A ὑπάγει, "he goeth his way," here than ℵ 025. 046 ὑπάγειν, "to go his way." All the time, despite his apparent recovery and triumphs, he is on the way to perdition; cf. on xvii. 11.

[3] Better so rendered than by "how that" (ὅτι). I here read ὅ τι, not ὅτι; cf. οἵτινες in xvii. 11 exactly in the same sense. We have here a parody of the divine name: "Which is, and which was, and which is to come" (i. 4, iv. 8).

[4] πάρεσται is here = ἐλεύσεται (a form our author does not use, though he uses other tenses of ἔρχομαι and ἐξελεύσεται (xx. 8)).

[5] A gloss here follows: "are seven mountains on which the woman sitteth and they." This is a second explanation thrust in from the margin.

[6] Text = "receive."

[7] The text is dislocated and glossed. 17 is to be read immediately after 13 and next 16. 14 follows on 16, because 14 records the destruction of the forces which according to 17, 16 are to destroy Rome. 15 is a gloss on xvii. 1. "And he said unto me, The waters which thou sawest, where the harlot sitteth, are peoples, and multitudes, and nations, and tongues"; see vol. ii. 61, 71 sq., 74.

[8] Text adds here an early gloss or doublet: "and to do one purpose"; see vol. ii. 73.

And be themselves destroyed by the Lamb and the Saints, 14 (a judgment implied in xix. 13^a)

And they shall eat her flesh
And burn her with fire.

14. These shall war against the Lamb,
And the Lamb shall overcome them,
For he is Lord of lords, and King of kings;
And they that are with him, called and elect and faithful, (shall overcome).[1]

The woman Rome

18. And the woman, whom thou sawest, is the great city, which reigneth over the kings of the earth.

CHAPTER XVIII.

THE DOOM OF ROME.

(This chapter deals with the doom of Rome, a vision of which had been promised by the angel to the Seer in xvii. 1. With the exception of a few clauses, it comes from a source which our author has already laid under contribution in xvii. 1–10, 18; see vol. ii. 94. It was written in the time of Vespasian, and several clauses survive attesting that period; see vol. ii. 93.)

Rome has fallen, for she hath corrupted all the earth, 1–3

1. After these things I saw another angel coming down
from heaven, having great authority; and the earth was
2. lighted up by his glory. And he cried with a mighty
voice, saying,

Fallen, fallen is Babylon the great,
And has become a habitation for demons,
And a hold of every unclean and hateful[2] spirit,
And a hold of every unclean and hateful bird.[3]

3. For of the wine[4] of her fornication hath she caused all the nations to drink;[5]

[1] Understand *νικήσουσιν*, rather than what I have proposed in vol. ii. 75. After 14 the text inserts what was originally a gloss on xvii. 1, *i.e.* 15. See note 7, p. 429.

[2] Text of this and the next line doubtful. I have followed A $min^{pauc.}$ gig arm^4.

[3] This line conflicts with the statement in xix. 3^c, according to which the smoke of Rome's burning is to go up for ever and ever. But this is due to the fact that xviii. is an early source used by our author, whereas xix. comes from his own hand.

[4] ℵ 046 Tyc s^2 read: "wine of the wrath of her fornication." I have followed 325* (?) Pr and s^1.

[5] So a few cursives and s^1 (*πεπότικεν*). This reading explains the impossible readings of the Uncials. This clause expresses the very same idea that is expressed passively in xvii. 2^b: *ἐμεθύσθησαν . . . ἐκ τοῦ οἴνου τῆς πορνείας*; cf. xiv. 8.

For [1] the kings of the earth committed fornication with her,
And the merchants of the earth waxed rich through the wealth of her wantonness.

4. And I heard another voice from heaven, saying,

Come forth from her, my people,[2]
That ye may have no fellowship with her sins,
And that ye receive not of her plagues.

5. For her sins have reached unto heaven,
And God hath remembered her iniquities.

Her sins in which the faithful are not to share called into remembrance

6. Render unto her even as she hath rendered,
And double (unto her) double according to her works:
In the cup which she hath mingled, mingle unto her double.

7. In the measure in which she hath glorified herself and played the wanton,
In that measure give her torment and † mourning †.[3]

Because she saith in her heart,
I sit as a queen,
And am no widow,
And I shall not see † mourning †.[4]

The measure of her punishment and her destruction by fire, 6–8

8. Therefore in one day shall her plagues come,
† Pestilence and mourning and famine † [5]

[1] See note *in loc.* $3^{b, c}$ are circumstantial clauses introduced by *καί* (= Hebrew ו), which state the conditions under which the action described in 3^{a} takes place. See notes on xii. 11^{c}, xix. 3, and see Oxford *Heb. Lexicon*, p. 253. Hence *καί* = "seeing that," "for." The Greek aorists are rendered by English aorists (*ἐπόρνευσαν* . . . . *ἐπλούτησαν*), as Babylon is regarded as a thing of the past in these verses. In 3^{a} the perfect is rightly used, since the results of "the wine of fornication" are enduring in the present. But in 4 sqq. the standpoint of the Seer changes. Babylon is still conceived as in being. The Greek aorists that follow have therefore frequently to be construed by the English perfect.

[2] This statement points to a source. The faithful have all suffered martyrdom. See vol. ii. 96 *ad fin.*

[3] *πένθος* ("mourning") is an idea foreign to the context here and in 8^{b}. It is not "mourning," but destruction that awaits Rome. Since *πένθος* = אֵבֶל, the latter may be corrupt for אֲבֵדָה or אֵבוּד = *ἀπώλεια* = "destruction." The same corruption is implied by the LXX in Jer. xii. 11. Hence for "mourning" read "destruction." This explanation is better than that suggested in vol. ii. 100.

[4] Read "destruction," as in 7^{b}.

[5] First of all the order seems wrong. Almost invariably in the OT. we have "famine and pestilence." Here again "mourning" cannot be right. As in $7^{b, f}$ we should read "destruction." Thus we should have "famine, and pestilence, and destruction."

And she shall be burnt with fire;
For strong is the God who hath judged her.

Dirge of the kings over Rome, 9-10

9. And the kings of the earth who committed fornication and lived wantonly with her shall weep and wail over her, when they look upon the smoke of her burning,
10. Standing afar off for the fear of her torment, saying,

Woe, woe to the great city,
Babylon the strong city,
For in one hour is thy judgment come.

Dirge of the merchants, 11-16

11. And the merchants of the earth shall weep and mourn over her,[1]
For no man buyeth their merchandise any more—

12. Merchandise of gold and silver, and precious stone and pearls,
And fine linen and purple, and silk and scarlet,
And all thyine wood, and every vessel of ivory, and every vessel of most precious wood,[2]
And brass, and iron, and marble,

13. And cinnamon, and spice, and incense,
And ointment, and frankincense, and wine,
And oil, and fine flour, and wheat,
And beasts, and sheep,[3] and souls of men.[4]

15. The merchants of these things, who were made rich by her, shall stand afar off for the fear of her torment,
16. weeping and mourning, Saying,
Woe, woe to the great city,
That was clothed in fine linen and purple and scarlet,
And adorned with gold, and precious stone, and pearl;
For in one hour are so great riches laid waste.

Dirge of the sea-folk, 17-19

17. And every ship master, and every one that saileth any whither,[5] and mariners, and as many as gain their
18. living by the sea, stood afar off, And cried, as they looked upon the smoke of her burning, saying, What (city) is like

[1] 23^e, which is quite impossible in 23 and cannot be satisfactorily restored elsewhere in this chapter, is best explained as a gloss on 11^a. It runs: "For the princes of the earth were thy merchants." In my text and commentary I have inserted it after 11^a.

[2] A 2040 vg eth read "stone."

[3] The MSS add here: "and horses and chariots and slaves." See vol. ii. 102 for the grounds for the excision of these words.

[4] Ver. 14 is transposed after 21 in this edition. See vol. ii. 105, 108.

[5] The text seems corrupt here. Pr bo sa presuppose ἐπὶ πόντου instead of ἐπὶ τόπου. Hence render "that saileth on the sea," see vol. ii. 105 sq.

19. the great city? And they cast dust on their heads, and they cried, weeping and mourning, saying,

> Woe, woe to the great city,
> Wherein were made rich all that had their ships at sea;
> For in one hour are her precious things laid waste.[1]

21. And a strong angel took up a stone, as it were a great millstone, and cast it into the sea, saying, Sudden destruction of Rome, 21

> Thus with violence[2] shall be cast down
> Babylon, the great city,
> And shall no more be found.[3]

14. And the fruits which thy soul lusted after Dirge of the Seer over Rome, 14, 22, 23^{a-d}
> Are gone from thee:
> And all the dainties and the splendours
> Are perished from thee.[4]

$22^{a, b, c, d}$. And the voice of the harpers and **singers**[5]
> <Shall be heard no more in thee>;[6]
> And <the voice>[6] of the flute players and trumpeters
> Shall be heard no more in thee.

$23^{c, d}$. And the voice of the bridegroom and the bride
> Shall be heard no more in thee;

$22^{e, f}$. And no craftsmen of whatever craft
> Shall be found any more in thee.

$22^{g, h}$. And the voice of the millstone
> Shall be heard no more in thee:

$23^{a, b}$. And the light of the lamp
> Shall shine no more in thee.

[1] On the restoration of this verse see vol ii. 106. Ver. 20 is restored at the close of $23^{a, b}$. On the restored order see vol. ii. 92 sq.

[2] Or "with indignation." But the meaning is doubtful.

[3] The beginning of the next dirge appears to be lost. On the reconstructed order of this dirge, see vol. ii. 92 sq., 108 sqq.

[4] The text adds: "And they shall no more find them" (= ולא ימצאום עוד); but this is possibly a corrupt form of the line, which is lacking in 22^{b} and which I have restored (*i.e.* לא יִשָּׁמַע בך עוד). But probably it is an interpolation; for elsewhere in this source 18^{2-27} *οὐ μή* is always followed by the subjunctive, whereas here it is the indicative; cf. xviii. 21, 22 (ter), 23 (bis).

[5] *μουσικῶν* = שִׁירִים (see LXX Ezek. xxvi. 13, Sir. xxxv. 3, 5), corrupt for שָׁרִים = "singers."

[6] Restored as the context requires. See vol. ii. 109. It is noteworthy that the Ethiopic Version has made the same restoration, see vol. ii. 352.

Seer's appeal to the inhabitants of heaven to rejoice over the doom of Rome, 20, 23[f.], 24

20. Rejoice over her, thou heaven,
And ye saints, and ye apostles, and ye prophets;
For God hath given judgment in your cause against her.

23[f]. For with **her**[1] sorcery were all the nations deceived.

24. And in her was found the blood of the prophets and saints,
And of all that had been slain upon the earth.

CHAPTER XIX.

(Response of the heavenly host to the appeal of the Seer just made—first of a mighty multitude praising God for His judgment of the Harlot City, and His avenging His servants' blood at her hands, 1-3; next of the Elders and Cherubim and of the Altar, which in like manner praise Him for that, having poured out the blood of the saints, they were made to drink each other's blood, 4, xvi. 5^{b}-7; and, finally, of the martyrs themselves, who offer their thanksgivings, for that now the Lord God Almighty has become King and that the Bride is now ready, xix. 5-7. The Bride will appear clothed in keeping with her character, 8. Thereupon the fourth Beatitude is pronounced, 9. At this stage a vision of the destruction of the Parthian kings is to be expected (see vol. ii. 114 *ad init.*, 117 *ad init.*, and note 1 on ii. 436). Now that Rome and the Parthians have been destroyed, there remains only the judgment of the kings of the earth who had shared in the abominations of Rome. These are slain by Christ, and the Beast and False Prophet are cast into the lake of fire, 11-20.)

Response of heaven to the Seer's appeal. Song of the angels on God's judgment of Rome, 1-3

1. After these things I heard as it were a great voice of a mighty[2] multitude in heaven, saying,

Hallelujah;
Salvation, and glory, and power, belong to our God:
2. For true and righteous are his judgments;
For he hath judged the great harlot,
That corrupted the earth with her fornication,
And he hath avenged the blood of his servants at her hand.

3. And again they said:[3]

Hallelujah;
For[4] her smoke goeth up for ever and ever.

[1] Text reads corruptly "thy."

[2] *i.e.* πολλοῦ.

[3] A perfect with an aorist meaning.

[4] *καί* to be taken as a Hebraism; see vol. ii. 120.

Song of the Elders and Cherubim praising God in that He hath made them, that slew the saints, to slay each other, xix. 4, xvi. $5^{b.\,c}$, 6

4. And the four and twenty elders and the four living creatures fell down and worshipped God that sitteth on the throne, saying,

Amen, Hallelujah;
XVI. $5^{b.\,c}$. Righteous art thou, which art and which wast.[1]
Holy, in that thou hast thus judged:

6. Because they poured out the blood of saints and prophets,
Thou hast given them blood also to drink:[2]
They are worthy.

The martyrs at last vindicated by God, and bidden to offer their praise, xvi. 7, xix. 5

7. And I heard the altar saying,
Yea, O Lord God Almighty,
True and righteous are thy judgments.

XIX. 5. And a voice came forth from the throne, saying,
Praise our God, all ye his servants,
And ye who fear him, small and great.

Response of the martyr host, singing, Hallelujah in that God has become king, the marriage of the Lamb come, and the Bride made herself ready, 6-8

6. And I heard as it were the voice of a great multitude, and as the voice of many waters, and as the voice of mighty thunders, saying,

Hallelujah:
For the Lord God Almighty hath become King.
7. Let us be glad and rejoice,
And give unto him the glory:
For the marriage of the Lamb hath come,
And his bride[3] hath made herself ready.

8. Yea, it hath been given unto her to clothe herself
In fine linen bright, pure.[4]

Fourth Beatitude on those invited to the Marriage Supper of the Lamb

9. And he saith unto me, Blessed are they which are called to the marriage supper of the Lamb.[5]

. . . .

. . . .

Lost vision of the

[1] On the restoration of xvi. $5^{b.\,c}$–7 to its original context, see vol. ii. 116, 120–124.

[2] On the technical meaning of this phrase, see vol. ii. 123.

[3] ἡ γυνὴ αὐτοῦ; see vol. ii. 127.

[4] Text adds an incorrect gloss: "for the fine linen is the righteous acts of the saints"; see vol. ii. 127 sq. Rather "the fine linen" is the result of such righteous acts, that is, the spiritual bodies in which the saints are clothed.

[5] Text adds here a doublet of xxii. 6^a, 8–9. 9^b. "And he saith to me, these are true words of God. 10. And I fell down before his feet to worship him. And he saith to me, See thou do it not. I am a fellow-servant with thee and with thy brethren that have the testimony of Christ: worship God: for the testimony of Jesus is the spirit of prophecy." See vol. ii. 128 sqq.

destruction of the Parthian kings[1] (proleptically referred to in xvii. 14)

11. And I saw the heaven opened;
And behold, a white horse,

And he that sat thereon—Faithful and True;[2]
And in righteousness he doth judge and make war.

12. And his eyes are as a flame of fire,
And on his head are many diadems;[3]

A Divine Warrior followed by the armies of heaven, 11-14 (a judgment proleptically described in xiv. 14, 18-20)

13. And he is clothed in a garment dipped in blood:
And his name is called The Word of God.

14. And the armies which are in heaven follow him on white horses,
Being clothed in fine linen, white, pure.

15. And from his mouth proceedeth a sharp sword,
That with it he should smite the nations:

Smites with a sharp sword the nations and treads the winepress of the wrath of God—bearing the name of King of kings and Lord of lords, 15-16

And he shall break[4] them with an iron rod:
And he treadeth the winepress of the fierce wrath of God Almighty.

16. And he hath on[5] his thigh a name written,
KING OF KINGS AND LORD OF LORDS.

17. And I saw an angel standing in the sun; and he cried
with a great voice, saying to all the birds that fly in
mid heaven, Come, gather yourselves together to the
18. great supper of God; That ye may eat the flesh of kings,
and the flesh of captains, and the flesh of mighty men,
and the flesh of horses and of them that sit thereon, and
the flesh of all men, both free and bond, and small
and great.
19. And I saw the beast, and the kings of the earth, and
their armies, gathered together to make war against him

Birds of prey summoned to feast on the slain

Beast and False Prophet overthrown and cast into the lake of fire, 17-18

[1] I have indicated a lacuna here. Where xix. 9^b–10 stands we should expect a vision relating to the destruction of the Parthian kings—a destruction prophesied in xvii. 14 (see vol. ii. 116 *ad fin.*) and implied by the epithet βεβαμμένον in xix. 13 (see vol. ii. 133). This vision appears to have been displaced by the interpolation, 9^b–10. The subjects of all other proleptic visions are rehandled in other visions in their due order. Hence we expect a vision on the destruction of the Parthian kings here in its chronological order.

[2] א 046 al^{pl} and many versions read "called Faithful and True."

[3] Here the MSS add an interpolation: "Having a name written which no man knoweth save he himself" It is an anacolouthon: it forms a break in the thought and is contradicted by what follows; see vol. ii. 132.

[4] See note on xii. 5 (translation); also vol. i. 75 sq.

[5] Text adds: "his raiment and on," see vol. ii. 137.

20. that sat upon the horse, and against his army. And the Their allies
beast was taken, and with him the false prophet that slain and
wrought the signs before him, wherewith he deceived their
them that had received the mark of the beast, and them bodies
that worshipped his image: they twain were cast alive eaten by
21. into the lake of fire that burneth with brimstone. And birds of
the rest were slain with the sword of him that sat upon prey,
the horse, (even the sword) which came forth out of his 19-21
mouth: and all the birds were filled with their flesh.

CHAPTERS XX.-XXII.

(The traditional order of the text in these three chapters is intolerably disordered and hopelessly unintelligible. The present editor has restored, so far as he can, the order of the text as it left the hand of the Seer. See vol. ii. 144-154. The restored order is given on pp. 153-154. On line 12 (p. 154) delete 6^{a}, and on line 17 insert 5^{c} before 6^{b}-8.)

CHAPTER XX. 1-3.

1-3. (Satan chained for a thousand years, and the nations set free from his deceivings.)

Chaining of Satan in the abyss

1. And I saw an angel coming down from heaven,
Having the key of the abyss
And a great chain in his hand.

2. And he laid hold on the dragon, the old serpent,
Which is the Devil and Satan,
And bound him for a thousand years:

3. And he cast him into the abyss,
And shut and sealed (it) over him,
That he should no more deceive the nations
Till the thousand years should be fulfilled.

After this he must be loosed for a little time.

Chapter XXI. 9–27.

XXI. 9-XXII. 2, 14-15, 17. (Vision of the Heavenly Jerusalem, which descends from heaven and settles on the ruined site of the earthly Jerusalem. This Heavenly City is at once the seat of the Messianic Kingdom, the abode of the glorified martyrs, and the centre of the evangelising agencies of the surviving nations on the earth, during the millennial period. Though it is not stated, we must conclude that alike the glorified martyrs and the Heavenly Jerusalem are withdrawn from the earth before the final judgment.

The tree of life (xxii. 2, 14) appears to be for the new converts (xxii. 2; cf. xi. 15, xiv. 6, 7, xv. 3, 4) and not for the martyrs, since the martyrs are already clothed with their heavenly bodies and are not subject to the second death. They had already eaten of it in the Paradise of God (ii. 7).

As one of the seven angels of the Bowls showed Rome—the capital of the kingdom of the Antichrist—to the Seer (xvii. 1), so he now shows him the heavenly Jerusalem.)

Vision of the Heavenly Jerusalem—the seat of Christ's Kingdom on earth for 1000 years

9. And there came one of the seven angels who had
the seven bowls, which were full of the seven last
plagues; and he spake with me, saying, Come hither,
I will show thee the bride[, the wife] of the Lamb.
10. And he carried me away in the Spirit to a mountain
great and high, and showed me the holy city Jerusalem,
11. coming down out of heaven from God, Having the
glory of God: her light was like unto a stone most
precious, as it were a jasper stone, clear as crystal.
12. She had a wall great and high; she had twelve gates,
and at the gates twelve angels; and names written
thereon, which are the names of the twelve tribes of
13. the children of Israel. On the east were three gates;
and on the north three gates; and on the south three
14. gates; and on the west three gates. And the wall of
the city had twelve foundations, and on them the

Its measurements

15. twelve names of the twelve apostles of the Lamb. And
he that spake with me had for a measure a golden reed
to measure the city, and the gates thereof, and the
16. wall thereof. And the city lieth foursquare, and the
length thereof is as great also as the breadth; and he
measured the city with the reed, twelve thousand
furlongs: the length and the breadth and the height
17. thereof are equal. And he measured the wall thereof,

a hundred and forty and four cubits, according to the measure of a man, that is, of an angel.

Its glorious structure and appearance

18. And the building of the wall thereof was jasper:
And the city was pure gold, like unto pure glass:
19. And[1] the foundations of the wall of the city were adorned with all manner of precious stones.

The first foundation was jasper; the second, sapphire; the third, chalcedony;
20. The fourth, emerald; the fifth, sardonyx; the sixth, sardius;
The seventh, chrysolite; the eighth, beryl; the ninth, topaz;
The tenth, chrysoprase; the eleventh, jacinth; the twelfth, amethyst.

21. And the twelve gates were twelve pearls;
Each one of the gates was of one pearl,
And the street of the city was pure gold, transparent as glass.[2]

No temple nor ark therein, nor sun nor moon to give light, but God Himself and the Lamb

22. And I saw no temple therein:
For the Lord God Almighty is the temple thereof,
And the Lamb < is the ark of the covenant thereof[3] >.

23. And the city hath no need of the sun, nor yet of the moon, to shine upon it:
For the glory of the Lord doth lighten[4] it,
And the lamp thereof is the Lamb.

Its gates always open to the nations of the earth

24. And the nations shall walk by the light thereof:
And the kings of the earth do bring their glory into it.
25. And the gates thereof shall not be shut day **or night.**[5]

[1] Though A 025. 046 omit, it seems best, with ℵ Pr (gig) arm $s^{1.2}$ bo eth to read the copula.

[2] Or. "as it were transparent glass."

[3] A probable restoration; the original is lost. The English versions conceal this loss by transposing the words "And the Lamb" into the preceding sentence. Cf. xi. 19, where the temple and the ark of the covenant are spoken of as the headcentres of the manifestations of God. In the Heavenly Jerusalem God takes the place of the first, and the Lamb that of the second; see vol. ii. 170 sq.

[4] ἐφώτισεν is either the Greek timeless aorist, Moulton, *Gr.* 135 sq.; Robertson, *Gr.* 836 sq., or it is in our author's mind a rendering of the timeless Hebrew perfect—a very common usage.

[5] The text reads: "for there shall be no night there"—a corruption due in part to xxii. 5. As in Isa. lx. 11, the text clearly ran as I have emended: "Thy gates . . . shall not be shut day or night." The alternations of day and night still prevail on the earth. It is otherwise in xxii. 5. where the New Jerusalem has come down from God to the new and glorified earth. Besides, the parallelism is against it; see vol. ii. 173.

26. And they shall bring the glory and the honour of the nations into it:

27. And there shall not enter into it † anything unclean or one †[1] that maketh an abomination or a lie:
But only they that are written in the Lamb's book of life.

Chapter XXII. 1-2, 14-15, 17.

The river and tree of life

1. And he showed me a river of water of life, bright as crystal,

2. Proceeding out of the throne of God and of the Lamb, In the midst of the street thereof:
And on this side of the river and on that was the tree[2] of life,

Bearing twelve (manner of) fruits,
Yielding its fruit every month:
And the leaves of the tree were for the healing of the nations.

Fifth Beatitude —for those who cleanse themselves and so have access to the tree of life in the City

14. Blessed are they that wash their robes,
That they may have the right to the tree of life,
And may enter in by the gates into the city.

15. Without are the dogs, and the sorcerers,
And the fornicators, and the murderers, and the idolaters,
And every one that loveth and maketh a lie.

Invitation of the Spirit and the Bride

17. And the Spirit and the bride[3] say, Come.
And let him that heareth say, Come.
And let him that is athirst come:
Whosoever willeth let him take the water of life freely.

[1] Primitive corruption for "any that is unclean or," cf xxii. 15. Only persons are contemplated as the next line shows.

[2] The term is used generically. The text implies that there are two rows of trees, one on either side of the river; see vol. ii. 176.

[3] Since the term "bride" designates the Heavenly Jerusalem in our author (cf. xxi. 2, 9), it has no doubt the same meaning here, but the idea of the Christian *community* rather than of the city is here brought forward; see vol. ii. 179.

Chapter XX. 4–15.

XX. 4-6. (Vision of the glorified martyrs who reign with Christ for a thousand years.)

Kingdom of Christ on the earth, 4–6

4^{c-h}. And <I saw> the souls of them that had been beheaded for the witness of Christ,
And for the word of God,

And[1] had not worshipped the beast,
Nor yet his image,

And had not received the mark upon their forehead
And upon their hand;

$4^{a, b, i}$. And I saw thrones, and they seated themselves thereon,
And judgment was given unto them.[2]

And they lived and reigned with Christ a thousand years.[3]
5^{b}. This is the first resurrection.

Sixth Beatitude—the blessedness of those that have part in the first resurrection

6. Blessed and holy is he that hath part in the first resurrection:
Over these the second death hath no power;

But they shall be priests of God and of Christ,
And shall reign with him a thousand years.

XX. 7-10. (Close of the Millennial Kingdom and of its evangelizing activities. Thereupon follows the loosing of Satan, the march of Gog and Magog against the beloved city, their destruction by supernatural means, and the casting of Satan into the lake of fire. The Seer does not say what became of the Heavenly Jerusalem, but its withdrawal from the earth before the final judgment is presupposed. Since "the beloved city" in xx. 9 is the Heavenly Jerusalem, the saints referred to in the same verse must include the risen martyrs.)

Satan loosed: his final efforts and overthrow, 7–10

7. And when the thousand years are fulfilled,
8. Satan shall be loosed out of his prison, And shall

[1] Text reads: "and that"; but see vol. ii. 183.

[2] This couplet occurs immediately at the beginning of ver. 4, where alike the context and the grammar are against them.

[3] Here follows an interpolation, as Mr. Marsh has suggested: 5^{a}. "The rest of the dead lived not till the thousand years were fulfilled." See Greek text *in loc.* By its removal the symmetry of the text is restored—seven successive couplets.

come forth to deceive the nations which are in the
four corners of the earth, Gog and Magog, to gather
them together to the war: the number of whom is as
9. the sand of the sea. And they went[1] up over the
breadth of the earth, and compassed the camp of the
saints about, and the beloved city: and fire came down
10. out of heaven, and devoured them. And the devil
that deceived them was cast into the lake of fire and
brimstone, where are also the beast and the false
prophet; and they shall be tormented day and night
for ever and ever.

XX. 11-15. (Vision of the great throne and of Him that sat thereon, before whose presence the former heaven and the former earth forthwith vanish. Judgment of the dead. Death and hell cast into the lake of fire.)

Resurrection of the dead and final judgment, 11-13

11. And I saw a great white throne, and him that sat thereon;
And from his face the earth and the heaven fled away,
And no place was found for them.

12. And I saw the dead, the great and the small,[2] standing before the throne,
And books were opened: and another book was opened, which is (the book) of life:
And the dead were judged out of the things written in the books.[3]

13. And the **treasuries**[4] gave up the dead which were in them;[4]

[1] The past verbs in $20^{9\text{-}10a}$ are to be explained from our author's use of Hebrew idiom, according to which Hebrew perfects (or imperfects with vav conversive) represent vividly the future events as things already accomplished.

[2] Our author elsewhere writes: "the small and the great"; see vol. ii. 194.

[3] Tautological interpolation added here: "according to their works."

[4] The text here reads "sea," but the context requires a reference to the abode of righteous souls, since Hades is the abode in our author only of wicked souls, and as such is cast into the lake of fire, xx. 14^a. The change of "treasuries"—the normal word in Judaism (50–100 A.D.) for the abode of righteous souls, or of "mansions" (John xiv. 2), or "Paradise" (?)—into "sea" was made in the interests of a bodily resurrection. But the sea has already vanished with the first heaven and earth (ver. 11, xxi. 1). According to the transmitted text only wicked souls have part in the General Resurrection and Final Judgment. In 4 Ezra vii. the text dealing with the General Resurrection and Final Judgment has also been tampered with. with a view to enforcing belief in a physical resurrection. The result of the tampering with the two texts is interesting: while in the Apocalypse only the wicked rise and are judged, in 4 Ezra only the righteous rise and are judged! see vol. ii. 194–198.

And death and Hades gave up the dead which were in them:
And they were judged every man according to their works.

14. And death and Hades were cast into the lake of fire.[1] End of death and Hades
And all that were not found written in the book of life
Were cast into the lake of fire.

XXI. 5[a], 4[d], 5[b]; XXI. 1–4[a. b. c]; XXII. 3–5. (Declaration by God that the former things have passed away and that He creates all things new. Forthwith the Seer sees the new heaven and the new earth and the New[2] Jerusalem coming down, adorned as a bride for her husband. God tabernacles with men. No more grief or pain or tears or death. All the faithful are to reign with Christ for ever and ever (xxii. 5), whereas in the Millennial Kingdom only the risen martyrs were to reign for a thousand years.)

5[a]. And he that sat upon the throne said, God makes all things new
4[d]. The former things have passed away;
5[b]. Behold, I make all things new.[3]

XXI. 1. And I saw a new heaven and a new earth; New heaven and new earth
For the first heaven and the first earth had passed away;
Nor is there any more sea.

[1] Text adds here a marginal gloss: "this is the second death, the lake of fire," drawn from xxi. 8 f., where the clause is full of meaning; but it is wholly out of place here with regard to death and Hades.

[2] Even the Heavenly City of xxi. 10, which had been withdrawn from the earth before the Judgment with Christ and the saints, is *renewed* or displaced by one of a higher nature.

[3] Text contains the following intrusion: 5[c]. "And he saith, Write: for these things are faithful and true. 6[a]. And he said unto me, They have become." xxi. 5[c]—doublet of xxii. 6[a]—is in this edition restored after xxii. 5 and immediately before xxi. 6[b]. See next page. Hence correct note in vol. ii. 203 *ad fin.* 6[a] is an interpolation. The Seer does not require such an assurance in confirmation of God's own words. Nothing can intervene between the declaration of God, "Behold I make all things new," and the Seer's immediate recognition of their fulfilment: "And I saw a new heaven," cf. Gen. i. 3, "And God said, Let there be light: and there was light." This interpolation, xxi. 6[a], "And he said unto me, They have become," is an extremely idle one—even with the traditional order of the text; for the Seer needs no such assurance, since *ex hypothesi* he has in vision already seen the new heaven and the new earth and the New Jerusalem descending on the new Earth, xxi. 1–3. Further in xxi. 5[b] the words ἰδοὺ καινὰ ποιῶ πάντα do not refer to an accomplished fact, which the traditional order presupposes. If the Seer had so intended he would have said ἰδοὺ καινὰ πεποίηκα πάντα (cf. iii. 8, ἰδοὺ δέδωκα). These words refer to the present creative act. Hence the new creation, xxi. 1–3, follows after xxi. 5[b], and the Seer in the vision sees God's words at once translated into fact. Cf. 1 Enoch xiv. 22 πᾶς λόγος αὐτοῦ ἔργον.

The New Jerusalem

2. And the holy city, New Jerusalem, I saw,
Coming down out of heaven from God,
Made ready as a bride adorned for her husband.

3. And I heard a great voice from the throne saying,

Behold, the tabernacle[1] of God is with men,
And he shall dwell with them,
And they shall be his people,[2]
And he shall be their God.[3]

God dwells with men

4ᵃ. And God shall wipe away every tear from their eyes,
ᵇ. And death shall be no more:
ᶜ. Neither shall there be mourning, nor crying, nor pain any more,
XXII. 3. Neither shall there be any more curse.

Blessedness of God's people, xxi. $4^{a, b, c}$, xxii. 3-5

And the throne of God and of the Lamb shall be in it:
And his servants shall serve him,
4. And they shall see his face,
And his name shall be on their foreheads.

5. And there shall be no more night,
And they have no need of light of lamp or light of sun,
For the Lord God shall cause (his face) to shine upon them:[4]
And they shall reign for ever and ever.

EPILOGUE AT THE CLOSE OF JOHN'S VISION.

God's testimony to John's book and His message to all men: divine sonship for the faithful: for the unfaithful the second death, xxi. 5^c, 6^b–8

XXI. 5^c, 6^b-8. (God's testimony to John's book: His message to all men.)

XXI. 5^c. And He saith, Write; for these words are faithful and true.

6^b. I am the Alpha and the Omega,
The beginning and the end:
I will give to him that thirsteth of the fountain of the water of life freely.

[1] ἡ σκηνή is probably "the Shekinah." There is no real English equivalent. Perhaps we might render: "the Presence of God is with men"; or "the dwelling of God." In no case has "tabernacle" its ecclesiastical meaning or its traditional associations; see vol. ii. 205 sq.

[2] See vol. ii. 207. crit. note on this line.

[3] See vol. ii. 207 sq.: crit. note.

[4] See vol. ii. 210 sq. φωτίζειν can, of course, be used intransitively, but John uses it only actively elsewhere: xviii. 1, xxi. 23. Otherwise render: "shall shine upon them." But in this sense we find φωτίζειν with the dat.

7. He that overcometh shall inherit these things,
And I will be his God,
And he shall be my son.

8. But for the cravenhearted and unbelieving,
And abominable and murderers,
And fornicators and sorcerers,
And idolaters and all liars—
Their part shall be in the lake that burneth with fire and brimstone:
Which is the second death.

Chapter XXII.

XXII. 6–7, 18a, 16, 13, 12, 10. (Here more than anywhere else in chaps. xx.–xxii. we have the *disjecta membra* of the Poet-Seer. I have restored the order of this section tentatively as above. xxii. 11, 18b–19 are relegated to the footnotes as interpolations. See vol. ii. 211–213, 217.)

(Christ's testimony to John's book: His speedy coming.)

Christ attests John's book, xxii 6–7, 18a

Seventh Beatitude

6. And he said unto me, These words are faithful and
true: and the Lord, the God of the spirits of the
prophets, sent his angel to show unto his servants the
7. things which must shortly come to pass. And behold,
I come quickly. Blessed is he that keepeth the words
of the prophecy of this book.[1]
18a. To every one that heareth I testify the words of the prophecy of this book.[2]

[1] This sentence forms the seventh beatitude. There is a certain fitness in the order of the seven. The first (i. 3) declares the blessedness of those who read and keep the prophecy: the second (iii. 3, *i.e.*, xvi. 15) of him who watcheth and keepeth his garments: the third (xiv. 12–13) of those who die in the Lord: the fourth (xix. 9) of those who having so died are invited to the marriage supper of the Lamb: the fifth (xxii. 14) of those who had washed their garments that they might have access to the tree of life in the heavenly city: the sixth (xx. 6) of those who have actually part in the first resurrection: the seventh (xxii. 7) of those who keep the words of this Book.

[2] The following interpolation is inserted here:

18b. If any man shall add unto them, God shall add unto him the plagues which are written in this book. 19. And if any man shall take away from the words of the book of this prophecy, God shall take away his part from the tree of life, and out of the holy city, which are written in this book"; see vol. ii. 222–224.

16. I Jesus have sent mine angel to testify these things unto you in [1] the Churches:
I am the root and the offspring of David,
The bright and the morning star.

13. I am the Alpha and the Omega,
The first and the last,
The beginning and the end.

His speedy Advent

12. Behold, I come quickly;
And my reward is with me,
To render to each man according as his work is.

10. And he saith unto me, Seal not up the words of the prophecy of this book; for the time is at hand.[2]

XXII. 8-9, 20-21. (John's testimony: the closing words.)

John's testimony: angel worship forbidden, xxii. 8-9

8. And I John am he that heard and saw these things. And when I heard and saw, I fell down to worship before the feet of the angel which showed me these things. **9.** And he saith unto me, See thou do it not: I am a fellow-servant with thee and with thy brethren the prophets, and with them which keep the words of this book: worship God.

Christ's final words and John's prayer and benediction, 20-21

20. He which testifieth these things saith,
Yea: I come quickly.
Amen: come, Lord Jesus.

21. The grace of the Lord Jesus be with all the saints. Amen.[3]

[1] ἐν. So A, etc. Other authorities ἐπί = "concerning."

[2] Here the text adds:

11. He that is unrighteous, let him do unrighteousness still:
And he that is filthy, let him be made filthy still:
And he that is righteous, let him do righteousness still:
And he that is holy, let him be made holy still.

This verse refers to the Seer's contemporaries, and declares that the time for repentance is past. But, since xxi. 6-8 refer also to his contemporaries, there is still hope for them, if they repent; see vol. ii. 221 sq.

[3] The text of this verse is very uncertain. I have followed Aℵ in reading "the Lord Jesus." The fuller title, "Lord Jesus Christ," has the support of 046 and most cursives, while the form "our Lord Jesus Christ" has the support of some cursives and nearly all the versions. Again, the Apocalypse cannot have ended with the words "with all" (A vg). Such a grace would be wholly at variance with the thought of the Seer. Only the saints or those seeking to be saints can receive such grace. Hence the reading of A vg is simply defective, and the choice must lie between the reading of ℵ (gig) "with the saints" and that of 046 $s^{(1), 2}$ $arm^{4, u}$ bo "with all the saints." This last is most in keeping with our author's views: cf. viii. 3.

APPENDIX.

FOUR PAPYRUS AND VELLUM FRAGMENTS OF THE APOCALYPSE.

FRAGMENT I. (= F[1]).

P. Oxy. viii. 1079.

(Late 3rd or 4th Cent. Verso of a papyrus roll with Exodus on recto (ed. Hunt, 1911).)

i. 4. [Ιωαννης τα]ι[ς επτα] εκ[κλησ[ιαις
[ταις εν τη] Ασια χαρις ϋμειν και ειρη
[νη απο ο ων] και ο ην και ο ερχομε
[νος και απο τ]ων επτα πνευμα
[των α (?)] ει[ω]πιον του θρονου αυ
5. [τ]ου· και απο Ιη Χρ ο μαρτυς ο πι
στος ο πρωτοτοκος των νεκρω̄
και ο αρχων των βασιλεων της γης
τω αγαπωντι ημας και λυσαντι η
[μ]ας εκ των αμαρτιων ημων εν
6. [τ]ω αιματι αυτου και εποιησεν ημ[ι
[βα]σ[ιλ]ειαν ιερεις του [1] θεω [2] και π[α]τ.ρι
[αυτο]υ· αυτω το κρατος και η δοξα
7. [εις το]υς αιωνας αμην ϊδου
[ερχε]ται μετα των νεφελων
[και οψε]ται αυτον πας οφθαλ
[μος και ο]ιτινες αυτον εξε

[1] Correction in first hand.
[2] Result of correction in first hand. Sic.

FRAGMENT II. (= F²).

P. Oxy. viii. 1080.

(4th Cent. Plate 1. Leaf from vellum Codex
(ed. Hunt, 1911).)

λγ

iii. 19. ω ζηλ~~ευε~~ ωσον [1] ουν και μετα
20. νοησον ϊδου εστηκα επι
την θυραν και ↑[2] εισελευσο
μαι προς αυτον και δει
πνησω μετ αυτου και αυ
21. τος μετ᾽ εμου ο νεικων
δωσω αυτω καθεισαι
μετ εμου ε[ν] τω θρον[ω μ]ου [3]
ως καγω ~~ν~~ενεικη~~κ~~σ[1][α
και ~~κ~~εκαθι~~κ~~σα [1] μετα τ[ο]ụ
$\overline{\pi\rho\varsigma}$ μου εν τω θρονω
22. αυτου ο εχων ους ακου
[σατ]ω τι το $\overline{\pi\nu\alpha}$ λεγει

iv. 1. ταις εκκλησιαις μετα

] κρουω ε[α]ν τ[ις] ακου[ση της
[φων]ης μ[ου και ανοιξη την θυραν και [2]

[1] Correction by second hand.
[2] The two missing lines are added by first hand at bottom of column, beginning] κρουω κτλ.
[3] Added by second hand.

λδ

ταυτα ϊδον και ϊδου θυ
ρα ανεωγμενη εν [1]
τω ουρανω και η[2] φω[2]
νη η πρωτη ην ηκουσα
ως σαλπιγγος λαλουσης
μετ᾽ εμου λεγων αναβα
ωδ~~ε~~ και δειξω σοι α δει
[γε]νεσθα[ι μ]ετα ταυτα
2. κ]ạị [2] ευθεως εγ[ε]νομην εν
[τω] $\overline{\pi\nu\iota}$ κα[ι] ιδου [θ]ρο
νος εκειτο [ε]ν τω $\overline{\omicron\upsilon\nu\omega}$
και επι το[ν] θρονον κα
3. θημενον και ο καθ[η
επι τον θρον[ον [3]
μενος ομọịọς ορασẹị

[1] Second hand. First hand wrote θυραν ανεωγμενην (?).
[2] Written by second hand.
[3] This line is added by second hand (sic) between the lines.

FRAGMENT III. (= F³).

P. Oxy. x. 1230.

(Early 4th Cent. (ed. Grenfell and Hunt, 1914).)

Recto.

v. 5. ι]δọụ εν[ικησεν
Δαυ] ειδ᾽ αν[οιξαι
6. αυτ]ου κ[α]ι ειδον εν[
ζωω]ν και εν μεσω των πρ[εσβυτερων
ω]ς εσφαγμενον εχων κερ[ατα
] τα ζ $\overline{\pi\nu\alpha}$ του $\overline{\theta\upsilon}$ απεσπαλ [1] [
7. ηλ]θεν και ειληφεν εκ της δ[εξιας
8. οτ]ε ελα[βεν

[1] A slip of the scribe for απεσταλ.

Verso.

vi. 5.] καθημ[ενος
6. κ]αι ηκουσ[α
χοι]νιξ σιτου δηναριου κ[αι
δην]αριου και το ελεον και το [
7.] οτε ηνεωξεν την σφραγ[ιδα
ηκο]υσα φωνην του τεταρτ[ου
8.]ειδ[ον

FRAGMENT IV. (= F^4).

P. Oxy. vi. 848.

5th Cent. Plate 1. Fragment of papyrus Codex
(ed. Grenfell and Hunt, 1908).)

Recto.

xvi. 17. [του ναο]υ απο του
θρονου λεγουσα·
18. γεγονεν και εγε
νοντο αστραπαι
και φωναι και βρο̄
ται· κ[αι σ[εισμος εγ[ε

Verso.

xvi. 19. λη εμνη[σθη ενω
πιον του θ̄υ· δου
ναι αυτη το ποτη
ριον του οινου
του θυμου της
[ο]ργης αυτ[ο]υ και

NOTES ON THE ABOVE FRAGMENTS

F^1.

i. 4–7. This fragment agrees word for word with A where it exists. It is true that it differs in the reading supplied by Professor Hunt in i. 4: *i.e.* [των α] εν[ω]πιον. There is not room apparently for [των των] εν[ω]πιον as in Aא. The fragment agrees throughout with C save that with A 025 it omits των αιωνων in i. 6, and perhaps rightly. It agrees generally with א save in two passages where א in i. 6 reads τ. αιων. των αιωνων and in i. 7 οψονται. It disagrees with 025 five times (1^4 α εστιν, 1^5 αγαπησαντι, λουσαντι, απο (for εκ), 1^6 βασιλεις και ιερεις) and with 046 four times (1^4 απο θεου ο ων, 1^5 λουσαντι, απο, 1^6 ποιησαντι).

Thus this fragment, so far as it exists, attests the text of A(C) as already existing in its present form at the close of the 3rd cent. or early in the 4th. The transposition το κρατος και η δοξα in i. 6 is peculiar to this fragment.

F^2.

iii. 19–iv. 2. First of all A and F^2 (as well F^{2**} = second hand in F^2) stand apart. A has two peculiar readings in 4^1 *αναβηθι* and *οσα*. Next A > *και* before *εισελευσομαι* in 3^{20}. Finally, F^{2**} reads *ζηλωσον* in 3^{19}, *ανεωγμενη* in 4^1, and *και ευθεως* in 4^2—all against A. Thus F^{2**} multiplies by 75 per cent. the differences between A and F^2 (if we leave *αναβηθι* and *οσα* out of consideration). F^2 reads *ζηλευε* in 3^{19} as A.

ℵ. F^2 is more closely related to ℵ than to any other uncial. Thus ℵ reads *και* before *εισελευσομαι* in 3^{20} and adds *ιδου* after *και*² in 4^1. It reads *ζηλωσον* in 3^{19} with F^{2**}. The *και* (a Hebraism) in 3^{20} is most probably original, but the other two are wrong.

025. This uncial > *και* before *εισελευσομαι* against F^2 and reads *ζηλωσον* 3^{19} and *και ευθεως* with F^{2**}.

046. This uncial reads *ζηλευε* 3^{19} and *και εισελ.* in 3^{20} with F^2—both right, *ανεωγμενη* in 4^1 with F^{2**}, and does not insert *και* before *ευθεως* in 4^2 as F^{2**} does.

From the above it follows that F^2 and F^{2**} agree much more closely with ℵ than with any other uncial, but have affinities with 025 and 026. 046 attests a better text here than ℵ or 025.

F^3.

v. 5–8, vi. 5–8. F^3 agrees in 5^5 with Aℵ 025 in reading *ανοιξαι*, where 046 reads *ο ανοιγων*; in 5^6 with ℵ 025. 046 in reading *εν μεσω*, where A reads *εμμεσω* and always elsewhere with C; in 5^6 with Aℵ 046 in reading *εχων*, where 025 reads *εχον* (a correction), and 6^7 with Aℵ in reading *φωνην* which C 025. 046 omit. Thus F^3 agrees so far as it goes with Aℵ.

F^4.

xvi. 17–18, 19. This fragment agrees word for word with A. Since 025 is defective here, we have only to consider the relation of F^4 to ℵ and 046. While F^4 supports A in the right reading in 16^{18} *αστραπαι και φωναι και βρονται*, ℵ* reads *βρονται κ. αστρ. κ. φων. κ. βρονται*, ℵ^c *βρ. κ. αστρ. κ. φων*, and 046 *αστρ. κ. φων*.

F^4 agrees with Aℵ in 16^{17} against 046, which adds *του ουρανου* after *ναου*, and with A 046 in reading *απο του θρονου* against *του θεου* of ℵ. Again, in 16^{19} F^4 agrees with A 046 in reading *δουναι* against *του δουναι* of ℵ, *το ποτηριον* and *του οινου* against ℵ, which omits the article in both cases, and *οργης αυτου* against ℵ, which omits the *αυτου*. Thus 046 is right five times with A against ℵ.

This fragment is interesting. Like F^1, F^4 agrees word for word with A. But whereas F^1 gives considerable support to ℵ, F^4 is with one exception against it. Next, whereas F^3 gives equal support to A and ℵ, F^2 supports ℵ more often than any other uncial.

The above fragments prove, so far as they go, the absolute pre-eminence of A. They furnish evidence for the early uncial character of certain deviations of 025 and for the antiquity of one or more false readings of 046. Next as regards ℵ, we see that, whereas it has considerable support from F^1 and the full support of F^3, it is far inferior to 046 in F^2 F^4. Unfortunately 025 is defective for F^4. From this comparison 025 emerges with a bad record. Hence, if on the exiguous evidence of these fragments we arranged the uncials in the order of merit, we should have A, C, 046. 025. All the evidence given in the Introduction, which in the main is limited to the fragments of fl and the corresponding sections in the other Versions and MSS, uphold the following order: A, C, 025, ℵ, 046. An exhaustive examination of the MSS and Versions might place ℵ before 025, but could not affect the primacy of A.

ADDITIONAL NOTE ON 13^{11b}.

THE text of this line in vol. ii. 317 should be restored as follows: εἶχεν κέρατα δύο ὅμοια <τῷ> ἀρνίῳ. The translation accordingly in vol. ii. 420 should be: "And he had two horns like *the* lamb."[1] The term "lamb" is here a symbol for the Messiah as elsewhere in our author, and earlier in Judaism, as we shall see presently. There would be no sense in saying "he had two horns like a lamb"; for some lambs have horns and some have not. The whole point of 13^{11b} consists in this, that the second Beast or Antichrist is portrayed as a Satanic counterpart of Christ, just as in 13^{3} the first Beast or Antichrist is also represented as a Satanic counterpart of Christ; for he is described as ἐσφαγμένην εἰς θάνατον.

But (as I have shown in vol. i. 340–44) chapter 13 is derived from Jewish sources, and 13^{11-18} cannot be understood apart from Jewish apocalyptic. Now, whereas in our author the Lamb is described as having "*seven* horns,"[2] *i.e.* as a being of transcendent power, a Christian development of a Jewish conception, in this Jewish source the Messiah is symbolized by "a lamb with two horns," which was definitely a Jewish conception. The explanation of this latter phrase is to be found in 1 Enoch and the Test. XII Patriarchs. In 1 Enoch 90^{9} the Maccabean leaders are described as "horned lambs" as distinct from the rest of the religious Jews who are described as "lambs." In the pages referred to in the note[1] below, I have already shown how certain religious and military leaders of Israel were so symbolized in 1 Enoch 85–90. In the Test. Joseph 19^{8} Jonathan the Maccabee, who is obviously regarded by the writer of that work as the Messiah, is symbolized by the term ἀμνός. That for the corrupt "word" in 1 Enoch 90^{38} we must read "lamb," where the Messiah is referred to, I have shown in my second edition of that book. But I herewith abandon Goldschmidt's emendation of the text which takes מלה to be a corruption of טלה, and which I then accepted, and also the hypothesis that 83–90 was originally written in Hebrew. I now regard 83–90 as derived from an Aramaic original,[3] and explain the meaningless term "word" in 90^{38} as a rendering of אֵימַר which was a corruption of אִמַּר = "lamb." There the Messiah is symbolized as a lamb of which it is said that it became great and horned: that is, it had two horns, since this is the natural number.

[1] Hence כשה in the source should have been read by the translator as כִּשָׂה, not as כְּשָׂה.

[2] See vol. i. p. cxiii sq.

[3] In my second edition, p. lxix, I left the question of the original language of 83–90 open, though inclining to the view that it was Hebrew. But like 6–36 and Daniel originally it was most probably written first in Aramaic. Later in the 2nd cent. B.C. such books were written in Hebrew.

ADDITIONAL NOTE ON THE LATIN VERSIONS.

Fragments of a Latin Version of the Apocalypse preserved in the Speculum (designated m) and found in its entirety in the Codex Gigas.

These fragments were first published by Mai in his *Spicilegium Romanum*, 1843, ix. 72–74, and are reprinted here according to Weihrich's edition (*Liber de divinis scripturis sive speculum*, Vienna, 1887). They do not represent any particular manuscript, but consist of a collection of proof passages from the O. or N.T. It is assigned to the vi–vii century. That m represents the same version as gig, a few examples will make clear.

From this comparison of versions, it will be seen that gig m represent one translation from the Greek and Cyp (*i.e.* Cyprian) Pr another. Occasionally I will append the readings of Tyc and vg. Unhappily fl is defective in the passages where m is preserved.

2^{23} qui scrutor (scruto m : scrutans Tyc vg) renes et corda, gig m Tyc vg : scrutator renis et cordis, Cyp Pr.

3^{15} Neque calidus . . . aut calidus gig m vg : neque fervens . . . aut fervens Pr Tyc(?).

3^{17} miserabilis et mendicus et nudus et caecus gig m : miser et pauper et caecus et nudus Cyp Tyc vg (> Pr).

3^{18} vestimenta . . . induaris gig m : vestiaris veste (~ Pr) Cyp Pr.

confusio nuditatis gig m Tyc vg : foeditas nuditatis Cyp Pr.

14^{10} in igne gig m : igne Cyp Pr Tyc vg.

18^{4} et (> Tyc) ne (ut non gig) communicetis peccatis ejus, et de (> Tyc) plagis ejus (+ ut m) ne accipiatis (laedamini Tyc) gig m Tyc = ne particeps sis delictorum ejus et ne perstringaris plagis ejus Cyp Pr.

18^{6} calicem quem (calice quo m Tyc) miscuit . . . miscite illi (ei m) duplum gig m Tyc : in quo poculo miscuit duplum remixtum est ei Cyp Pr Arm^{2}.

From the above, out of many like instances, it may be concluded that Cyp Pr and gig m are two independent translations of one and the same MS or possibly of two Greek MSS, which were generally in the closest agreement. The example under 18^{6} exhibits a divergence, which may represent a divergence in the Greek MSS. There are a few divergences between gig and m, which may be due to the influence of some other Latin version. Thus we have ditatus in 3^{17} in gig Cyp and locupletatus in m (and Tyc vg). Here Pr is defective.

We might *provisionally* represent the relations of the Latin versions as follows:—

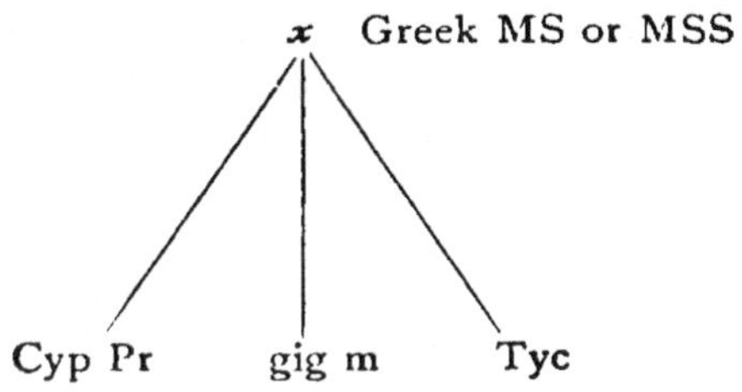

Speculum (vi–vii cent.).

2[1] Et angelo Ephesi ecclesiae scribe.
2[23] Et scient omnes ecclesiae quia ego sum qui scruto renes
et corda.
3[14] Et angelo Laodiciae ecclesiae scribe: haec dicit ille
amen, testis fidelis et verax, principium creaturae Dei.
[15] Novi opera tua, quia neque frigidus neque calidus es.
Utinam frigidus esses aut calidus! [16] Sed quoniam
tepidus, evomam te ex ore meo. [17] Quia dicis: dives
sum, et locupletatus sum, et nihil opus est mihi; et nescis
quia tu es miser et miserabilis et mendicus et nudus et
caecus. [18] Suadeo tibi a me emere aurum igne pro-
batum, ut dives sis et locupleteris; et vestimenta mea
alba, ut induaris, ut non appareat confusio nuditatis
tuae. Et collurio inungue oculos tuos, ut videas.
[19] Ego quoscumque amo, arguo et castigo. Aemulare
igitur et age paenitentiam. [20] Ecce sto ad januam et
pulso. Si quis audierit vocem meam, et aperuerit
januam, introibo ad illum, et caenabo cum illo et ille
mecum. [21] Qui vincit, dabo illi sedere mecum in sede
mea, quomodo et ego vici, et sedeo cum patre meo in
sede ipsius.
14[8] Cecidit, cecidit Babylon magna. De vino fornicationis
ejus biberunt omnes gentes. [9] Si quis adorat bestiam
et imaginem ejus, et accipit character in fronte sua aut
in manu sua dextra, [10] et hic bibet de indignatione Dei,
quae mixta est mera in calice irae ejus, et cruciabitur
in igne et sulfore in conspectu angelorum et agni.
[11] Et fumus et cruciatus eorum in saecula saeculorum
ascendit. Et non habent requiem die ac nocte qui
adorant bestiam et imaginem ejus, et qui accepit char-
acter nominis illius. [13] Et audivi vocem de caelo
dicentem mihi: scribe, beati mortui qui in Domino

moriuntur amodo. Etiam dicit spiritus, ut requiescant
a laboribus suis: opera enim eorum sequuntur eos.
17[15] Aquae quas vidisti ubi meretrix sedet, populi et turbae et
gentes et linguae sunt.
18[4] Et audivi aliam vocem de caelo dicentem: exite de ea
populus meus, et ne conmunicetis peccatis ejus, et de
plagis ejus ut ne [1] accipiatis. [5] Quia adpropinquaverunt
peccata ejus usque ad caelum, et memoratus est Deus
iniquitates ejus. [6] Reddite ei sicut et ipsa reddidit, et
duplicate duplicia secundum opera ejus. In calice quo
miscuit vobis, miscite ei duplum. [7] Et quantum
magnificavit se, et luxoriata est, tantum date ei tor-
mentum et luctum. Quia in corde suo dicit, sedeo
regina, et luctum meum non videbo. [8] Propterea una
hora veniet plaga ejus, mors et famis et luctus, et igne
cremabitur. Quoniam fortis est dominus Deus qui
judicat eam.
20[12] Et vidi mortuos pusillos et magnos stantes in conspectu
sedis. Et libri aperti sunt, et alius liber apertus est
qui est vitae. Et judicati sunt mortui secundum ea
quae scripta sunt in libris, et secundum opera sua.
[13] Et dedit mare mortuos qui fuerunt in ipso, et mors
et infernus dederunt mortuos qui fuerunt in ipsis. Et
judicati sunt singuli secundum facta sua.
21[8] Dubiis autem et infidelibus et abominandis et homicidis
et adulteris et maleficis et idolis servientibus et menda-
cibus, pars illorum in stagno ignis ardentis et sulfore,
quod est mors secunda.
22[15] Foras canes, et malifici, et adulteri, et idolis servientes.
[18] Testor ego omni audienti verba prophetiae libri
hujus. Si quis adjecerit supra haec, imponet Deus
super eum plagas quae scriptae sunt in hoc libro.
[19] Et si quis abstulerit verba prophetiae libri hujus,
auferet Deus partem ejus de ligno vitae et de civitate
sancta.

[1] Ut ne (= ἵνα μή). So Weihrich emends et [ne] in Codex Sangallensis.
MVLC om.

ADDITIONAL NOTE ON THE MILLENNIAL KINGDOM.

THE peculiar form that the Millennial Kingdom assumes in the Apocalypse is due to the results which, according to the Seer, would arise out of the conflicting claims of the Empire and the Christian Faith.

The main question at issue between them, a question which included all minor issues within it, originated in the demand that all loyal citizens of the Roman Empire should offer Divine worship to the Emperor. This claim to Divine honours was adopted by Rome with the object of unifying and consolidating all the diverse elements of the Roman Empire into a single whole. As Rome had already united all the civilized regions of the world in one universal commonwealth, so now it aimed at strengthening this bond of common citizenship by the still stronger tie of a common and universal religion, the one essential element of which was the worship of the Roman Emperor. Such a worship, of course, no Christian could render. Hence a collision of these two forces became inevitable, and in due course Rome proposed to itself definitely the task of exterminating Christianity on the ground that it was a Society guilty of high treason to the State. This came about first under Domitian. Thus there arose a conflict of two loyalties, loyalty to God and Christ on the one hand and loyalty to Caesar on the other, and our author was the first to set forth in all its seriousness the transcendent issues at stake, and to teach his brethren that to yield in any degree to such demands of the State was to be guilty of apostasy to God and the Christ who had redeemed them.

Under the conflict of his day the prophet clearly discerned the eternal issues at stake, and in this conflict he taught that no faithful follower of Christ would escape: in other words, *he foretold a universal martyrdom.* Herein our author may have found a fulfilment of the mysterious saying of our Lord: "When the Son of Man cometh, shall He find faith on the earth?"

This forecast of our author, however, was no more realized than numbers of the detailed prophecies of the O.T. But, though this element in his prophecy failed to be fulfilled, the larger spiritual truth embodied in his prophecy—that the Kingdom of this world should become the Kingdom of the Lord and of His Christ—is true for all time and all like crises in human affairs. While the human element falls away the divine remains.

But the Seer could not stop short with forecasting a universal martyrdom. For this forecast of a universal martyrdom naturally led to a recasting of the traditional expectation of the Millennial Kingdom. If the world was to be evangelized afresh, this evangelization could not be effected save through supernatural intervention, seeing that all the faithful were to be martyred before the advent of the Kingdom. Hence our Seer expected Christ to return on His Second Advent *with all the blessed martyrs* to destroy the enemies of the Kingdom (17^{14} 19^{11-20}) and to found the Millennial Kingdom in the Jerusalem that should come down from heaven, and so to evangelize the world afresh (21^{9}–$22^{2. 14-15. 17}$ 20^{4-6}).

But since John's expectation of a universal martyrdom in the immediate future was not realized, his expectation that the earth would be evangelized by Christ and the blessed martyrs from heaven, cannot be regarded as an essential element of the teaching of the N.T., seeing that the former expectation which gave it birth never itself came into being. The need for this supernatural method of Christianizing the world has not arisen. There has been no universal martyrdom of the Church. Hence since the faithful survive, Christ has committed into their hands the complete evangelization of the world.

But while the peculiar form of this expectation must be relegated to the region of unfulfilled prophecy, the truth at the base of this expectation is not thereby affected. And this truth is that ultimately the righteous shall inherit the earth. The entire Apocalypse is indeed in one respect an expansion of the two opening beatitudes of the Sermon on the Mount:[1] the first of these is, "Blessed are the poor in spirit: for theirs *is* the Kingdom of heaven" (Matt. 5^{3}). The essential element of this beatitude is conveyed in many of the Seer's words, but especially in

iii. 20. Behold I stand at the door and knock:
If any man hear my voice and open the door,
I will come in to him, and will sup with him,
And he with me."

As for the second beatitude—"Blessed are the meek: for they *shall inherit* the earth" (Matt. 5^{5})—the assurance of the truth of this beatitude shows itself in every song of the Apocalypse. whether sung by angels or saints, and this assurance gathers strength as the divine drama moves swiftly onwards, till at last in the closing millennium of the world's history the Kingdom of this world has become the Kingdom of the Lord and of His Christ.

The optimism of the man who believes in God and lives unto Him cannot be other than indomitable and unexpugnable.

[1] The so-called second beatitude, "Blessed are they that mourn: for they shall be comforted," is an intrusion in Matthew's text. V.[5] should follow immediately on v.[3].

INDEX.

I. INDEX OF GREEK WORDS,

GIVING REFERENCES TO GREEK TEXT (VOL. II. PP. 236–385), TO INTRODUCTION (VOL. I. PP. XXI–CLXXXVII), TO COMMENTARY (VOL. I. PP. 1–373 AND VOL. II. PP. 1–226), AND TO ENGLISH TRANSLATION (VOL. II. PP. 386–446), AND APPENDICES (PP. 447–457).

Order of verses in Greek Text according to which references are given in this Index: 1^{1}–3^{3ab} 16^{15} 3^{3c}–$7^{5ab. 7. 8. 5c. 6. 9}$–$8^{1. 3-5. 2. 6. 13}$ [7-12] 9^{1}–$13^{5a. 6. 5b-18}$ $14^{12-13. 1-3d [3e-4b].* 4c-11. 14. [15-17]. 18-20}$ $15^{[1]. 2}$–$16^{4 [5a]. 8-14. 16}$–$17^{13. 17. 16. 14 [15]. 18}$ $18^{1-11a [23e]. 11b-13. 15-19. 21. 14. 22a-d. 23c.d. 22e-h. 23ab. 20. 23f. 24}$ 19^{1-4} 16^{5bc-7} 19^{5-21} 20^{1-3} 21^{9-27} $22^{1-2. 14. 15. 17}$ $20^{4c-h. abi. 5b. 6-15}$ $21^{5a. 4d. 5b. [6a]. 1-4abc}$ 22^{3-5} $21^{5c. 6b-8}$ $22^{6-7. 18a [18b-19]. 16. 13. 12. 10 [11]. 8. 9. 20. 21}$.

* See restored Text, vol. ii. 422, n. 1.

II. HEBRAISMS.[1]

[1] For the following transliterations of Hebrew words, see the Greek Index : Ἀβαδδών, ἀλληλουιά, ἀμήν, Ἁρ Μαγεδών, βύσσινος, ἑβραϊστί, λίβανος, μάννα, Σατανᾶς, σάπφειρος.

III. PASSAGES IN OUR AUTHOR BASED ON THE O.T., THE PSEUDEPIGRAPHA AND THE N.T.

See vol. i. pp. lxv–lxxxvi.

IV. INDEX TO COMMENTARY,
VOLS I. AND II.

References to Introduction (Roman numerals) are given first, then references to the Commentary proper.

PRINTED BY
MORRISON AND GIBB LIMITED
EDINBURGH

CPSIA information can be obtained
at www.ICGtesting.com
Printed in the USA
BVHW081010190619
551410BV00006B/217/P

9 781314 304251